PIMLICO

317

REVOLUTIONARY EMPIRE

Staff Tutor in .... the Open University ..... cotland
and is now a freelance writer. He read English at Cambridge
and received his D.Phil from the School of Social Studies at
the University of Sussex. He was Convener of the Scottish
Poetry Library when it was founded in 1984. He is the
author of *The People's War* and *The Myth of the Blitz*, and
has co–edited *Time to Kill: The Soldier's Experience of War in
the West 1939–1945* (all available in Pimlico). He lives in
Edinburgh.

REVOLUTIONARY EMPIRE

The Rise of the English–Speaking Empires
from the Fifteenth Century to the 1780s

REVISED EDITION

———

ANGUS CALDER

PIMLICO

Published by Pimlico 1998

2 4 6 8 10 7 5 3 1

Copyright © Angus Calder 1981, 1998

Angus Calder has asserted his right under the Copyright, Designs and
Patents Act 1988 to be identified as the author of this work

First published in Great Britain by
Jonathan Cape Ltd 1981
Pimlico edition 1998

Pimlico
Random House, 20 Vauxhall Bridge Road, London SW1V 2SA

Random House Australia (Pty) Limited
20 Alfred Street, Milsons Point, Sydney,
New South Wales 2061, Australia

Random House New Zealand Limited
18 Poland Road, Glenfield
Auckland 10, New Zealand

Random House South Africa (Pty) Limited
Endulini, 5a Jubilee Road, Parktown 2193, South Africa
Random House UK Limited Reg. No. 954009

A CIP catalogue record for this book is available from the British
Library

ISBN 0-7126-6687-7

Papers used by Random House UK Limited are natural, recyclable
products made from wood grown in sustainable forests. The
manufacturing processes conform to the environmental regulations of
the country of origin

Typeset by SX Composing DTP, Rayleigh, Essex
Printed and bound in the United Kingdom by Mackays of Chatham

CONTENTS

ILLUSTRATIONS

Preface to the Pimlico Edition

For kind permission to reproduce illustrations, I wish to thank the following: American Antiquarian Society, 7; Ashmolean Museum, Oxford, 3; British Library, 5, 6; City Museum and Art Gallery, Hanley, Stoke-on-Trent, 17; Colonial Williamsburg Foundation, 36; Cyfartha Castle Museum and Art Gallery, Merthyr Tydfil, 41; Edinburgh University Library, 1, 14; Mary Evans Picture Library, 15; the Director of the India Office Library and Records, 11, 20, 28, 30, 31; Library Company of Philodelphia, 12; Mansell Collection, 27; Massachusetts Historical Society, 34; Mrs Elizabeth Murray, 23; National Gallery of Canada, Ottawa, 22; Trustees of the National Library of Scotland, 13, 18, 25; National Maritime Museum, London, 16, on loan from M.O.D. Navy: 38, 40; National Museum of Wales, 39; National Portrait Gallery, London, 4, 10, 26, 29, 37; Pilgrim Society, Plymouth, Massachusetts, 8; St Louis Art Museum, 19; Scottish National Portrait Gallery, 9, 24; Trustees of Sir John Soane's Museum, 21; Tate Gallery, London, 2; Victoria and Albert Museum, Crown Copyright, 32; Yale University Art Gallery, 33 (bequest of Edith Malvina K. Wetmore), 35 (gift of Roger Sherman White, B.A. 1859, M.A., L.L.B. 1862, Jan, 1918).

This is an abbreviated edition of a book first published by Jonathan Cape in 1981. I have changed very few words indeed, but deleted many. Sometimes I have been glad to cut out statements which now seem to me unwise or rather gassy, so modifying rather what the book says, but I have not attempted to develop any new insights. Perhaps my younger self was shrewder than I am now; in any case, he had struggled to get on top of the very large body of relevant historical writing available in the 1970s, and I have hardly explored the mountains of new work thrown up since. For this reason I have omitted the original bibliography, no longer an up-to-date guide to available reading. As for references, since the plan of the book remains exactly the same, anyone wishing to track down the source of a judgment, a statistic or a quotation can do so easily enough by consulting a library copy of the original book.

The gratitude which I expressed to many people for assistance and encouragement is as warm as ever, but I will specifically repeat only a few thanks. I marvel more than ever at the kindness of Alan Day, David Daiches, Gary Dickson and Reid Mitchell who read large chunks of my draft ms – I didn't use a word processor back in those days of ex-ed out errors and messy carbons, and the friendship of Graham Martin, who read the whole thing with typical minute conscientiousness in final draft found truly heroic expression. I now add thanks, for help with this edition, to my sister Isla.

My dedication remains the same, and represents even stronger feelings than before. David Rubadiri, a friend since 1960, in exile from Malawi for thirty years from 1964, now happily restored to his former position as his country's ambassador to the United Nations, was coincidentally on the phone from New York as I drafted this. Ngugi Wa Thiong'o endured political imprisonment in Kenya in the late seventies which drove him into exile and transformed his writing. He is now recognised everywhere in the world as a major writer of fiction and cultural critic. I salute two great Africans who have suffered enormously, in its aftermath, from the consequences of British imperial rule.

A.C.

Edinburgh, at home under the Castle, October 1997

Introduction

On September 11, 1997, as I was working on this new edition of *Revolutionary Empire*, the Scottish electorate voted in a referendum by three to one that a Parliament should be re-established in Edinburgh. The scale of this victory surprised many of us who had hoped, over many years, most strongly for such an event. The statesman Seafield had said, in 1707, as he signed the act which formally ended Scotland's independence, 'Now, there's the end of an auld sang.' A new and very different song had commenced. Yet others like myself relished the low, calm note with which it began. As the polls closed, Edinburgh streets and pubs seemed if anything less vivacious than usual. At 5 a.m., after the popular verdict had been declared, I walked through the centre of Scotland's capital and it was quieter than the mouse I detected in my living room a few days later. What had been expressed was not wild ethnic fervour – certainly not mass Anglophobia – but what the late John Smith MP had called 'the settled will of the Scottish people'.

A week later when just over 50 per cent of Welsh voters, on a much lower turnout, opted for an 'assembly' in Cardiff, the political geography displayed on televised maps matched uncannily the pattern which this book suggests for the sixteenth century, as modified by industrial revolution from the eighteenth on. The border counties, then 'marches' of England, and Normanised Pembroke, 'Little England', voted against even this modest recognition of separate Welsh identity. Support for it was strongest in the western areas where the Welsh language has maintained itself, and in the valleys which were subjected to a process akin to imperialism as alien industrialists invaded them, seeking coal and making iron. I felt, as this story unfolded, that my book had acquired new resonance.

The more so as, meanwhile, a 'peace process' was under way in Northern Ireland with the amazing effect that for the first time since 1922 a UK minister sat down in discussions with representatives of Sinn Fein, while Ulster Unionist leaders, after loud expressions of anger, came in to join them. In 1798 there were Protestants in Belfast, 'United Irishmen', who hoped, with like-minded Catholics, to create a free revolutionary polity, their ideals in effect those of Thomas Jefferson. I am reminded of Tom Paulin's poem which mentions them, 'Father of History', from *Liberty Tree* (1986):

> Folded like bark, like cinnamon things,
> I traced them to the Linen Hall stacks –
> Munro, Hope, Porter and McCracken;
> like sweet yams buried deep, these rebel minds
> endure posterity without a monument . . .

Why such men failed will perhaps be clearer from this book, along with the grounds of injustice felt by Ireland's Catholic majority which have spurred so many, so often, to violence.

I hope this book will be useful in the debates now taking place about English, Irish, Welsh and Scottish 'identities'. I hope that readers in all four quarters will be assisted to recognise the fact that we have never been 'ourselves alone' and will acknowledge, with due humility, that there have never been pure causes or chosen peoples. I remember John Prebble remarking to me in interview that when he wrote his novel *The Buffalo Soldiers*, about the US Army going into what became Oklahoma after the Civil War to force the Comanches into reservations, he did not know whether he identified most with the 'Red Indians', with the black cavalrymen sent in among them, or with the Irish, heaved from their homeland by famine and oppression, who officered these ex-slaves. The Pakistani who sells me my paper most mornings is part of the same process of history as myself, and salient in it is the disturbing figure of John Johnstone, arch-profiteer from the Rape of Bengal after Plassey: even the habitual warmth, in portraiture, of Henry Raeburn could not soften the sharp features of that cynically rapacious fellow-Scot.

I was talking just now in Film House,which provides an Edinburgh version of café society, to my erudite friend Mario Relich who has taught for many years over much of the range of courses provided by the Open University Arts Faculty. Brooding about this book, I mentioned the story of Wolfe's conquest of Quebec on the Heights of Abraham. It thrilled me when I first encountered it as a very small person in some comic-book version of British history, and the thrill was still with me when I contributed a very bad poem about Wolfe to my grammar-school magazine, back in the late fifties. In this book I have tried to 'deconstruct' the tale, but is it not the case, Mario queries, that any narrative of this dramatic kind seduces us into complicity with imperialism? We approve of heroic and successful soldiers, and forget the context of exploitation and victimisation in which their exploits occur. I think hard . . . Our evidence, I demur, is that in fact the Scots in Wolfe's army got on surprisingly well with the daring and truculent *Canadiens*, who had not cared for rule from Paris and later shared with Gaels their fur-trade routes into the vast interior. If the subsequent history of Canada is not wholly ignoble, is not unredeemed by flashes of altruism, disinterested political imagination, and comradely feeling, perhaps it does paradoxically owe something to Wolfe who hated *Canadiens*, Scots (and Yankees, and Indians) just about equally. Can 'good' come out of 'evil'? Where else would it come from? We are all capable of 'war crimes', or at least of connivance in them. The most difficult task for philosophers is not, I think, to cope with the problem of 'evil', which clearly derives from our nature as animals. It could be to explain what we mean by goodness – demonstrated as it is, sometimes, by people who have been gross delinquents and even murderers, as well as by others who might yet fall into habits of wickedness.

'Imperial history', a despised and neglected subject when *Revolutionary Empire* was first published, subsumes the histories of many peoples, and of millions upon millions of individual people, trapped in the contradictions of their own times and situations, but capable sometimes of transmitting over centuries by what they wrote, or what we read of their actions, aspirations to decency and virtue. And we cannot understand what we see around us without some sense of what empire, for the peoples of the North West European Archipelago and those living amongst us, coming to belong with us from other continents, has entailed, in losses, with perhaps some gains. After the Napoleonic Wars, distinguished Scots decided that on the Calton Hill in Edinburgh there should be a boastful replica of the Parthenon, suitable for the 'Modern Athens', to commemorate the military dead. It wasn't finished. Funds weren't forthcoming, and people have long spoken about this as 'Scotland's Shame'. But I am one of those who are glad to have all that did eventuate – merely an elegant colonnade, through which sky can always be seen, and the sun rising – a monument which is open to everything, names no one specially, excludes no one. As the great Caribbean-French poet Cesaire wrote, there is room for all at the meeting-place of victory.

Prologue:
The World is the World's World

I

In the third year of the Yungo-Lo reign period, an emperor of the Brilliant dynasty sent forth the Three-Jewel Eunuch on a mission to the Western Oceans, bearing vast amounts of gold and other treasures, with nearly forty thousand men in sixty-two ships. The exploits of this Admiral, Chêng Ho, were 'such as no eunuch before him, from the days of old, had equalled.' Beginning in 1405, on this and six later expeditions, the great junks ranged from Borneo as far as Zanzibar, from the Red Sea to the Ryukyu Islands of the Pacific. Before they left on the expedition of 1432, the last, and perhaps the most dazzling of all, sailors erected a stele in gratitude to a Taoist goddess. 'We have traversed more than one hundred thousand *li* of immense water spaces, and have beheld in the ocean huge waves like mountains rising sky-high. We have set eyes on barbarian regions far away hidden in a blue transparency of light vapours while our sails, loftily unfurled like clouds, day and night continued their course with starry speed, breasting the savage waves as if we were treading a public thoroughfare.'

Everywhere, the Chinese chronicler tells us, 'they made known the proclamations of the Son of Heaven, and spread abroad the knowledge of his majesty and virtue. They bestowed gifts upon the kings and rulers, and those who refused submission they overawed by the show of armed might. Every country became obedient to the imperial commands, and when Chêng Ho turned homewards, sent envoys in his train to offer tribute.' Yet, or so this eighteenth-century writer relates, the Eunuch's men had to fight only three times in seven expeditions. The goods they carried, we can be sure, were welcome in every port – silks, porcelains, other unmatched products of China. And they were, we are told, tolerant of the customs of others. In Mecca, where Chêng Ho's father, a Muslim, had once been on pilgrimage, 'they conversed in the tongue of the Prophet and recalled the mosques of Yunnan, in India they presented offerings to Hindu temples, and venerated the traces of the Buddha in Ceylon.'

With power like his, he could afford tolerance. Chêng Ho's 250 long-distance 'treasure ships' were drawn from a navy of 3,800, and had cannon. The largest of them would carry over 1,000 men. There was nothing anywhere to match these nine-masted products of a fertile and ancient tradition in technology which had been the first to produce the crossbow and the magnetic compass, gunpowder and cast iron, printing, stern-post rudders, paper and porcelain.

The Ming dynasty, established in the mid-fourteenth century, would endure until the mid-seventeenth, providing social stability for a population greatly exceeding Europe's. The Ming political system would survive without much change until 1912. The Emperors were seen as representatives of all mankind before heaven, rulers of the central area of the world. People from smaller nations who wished to trade with China must pay formal tribute. After Chêng Ho's tours, foreigners flocked to Peking for this purpose. But as the fifteenth century wore on, the trouble and expense of receiving tribute missions as guests of state came to seem greater than the benefits of trade. Meanwhile, the threat of the Oirats grew behind the Great Wall, on China's north-west frontier. The Brilliant Emperors sent no more expeditions. The navy was permitted to run down. By 1500 it was a capital offence against imperial regulations to build a sea-going junk with more than two masts. The ocean was left to those who might want it.

Far to the west, in the ruins of the extinct Empire of Rum there were barbarian peoples prepared to use the sea in order to reach the fabulous land of China, of Cathay, about which a travelling merchant from Venice, Marco Polo, had written at the end of the thirteenth century. The wealth of the East dazzled Europeans and humbled them. Not for four centuries would Europe's traders be able to find much market for European goods there. As late as the 1790s, when Britain's navy dominated all the world's oceans, her ambassador would be snubbed and sent away with contumely when he tried to convince the Chinese Emperor that it would be worth his while to admit the merchants of the world's first industrialised nation more freely. Yet in little more than another century after that, the Chinese Empire would be in final ruin, and European powers would govern directly 85 per cent of the world's surface while dictating terms to almost all the rest. Only Japan would retain full independence, and that at the price of imitating Europe.

Many factors involved in this have been very imperfectly studied. But it is clear that Europe could not have surged outwards without the help of borrowings from Chinese technology. And it is also clear that the lure of Cathay was a crucial incentive.

In Marco Polo's day Mongols had ruled in Peking and Mongols had controlled the whole overland trade route from there to the Black Sea. Their tolerance had permitted Polo, and other Europeans, to penetrate Cathay by land. By the fifteenth century this was impossible. To sail directly to Cathay and 'Cipango' (Japan) formed a group of motives, among others, for seafarers sent out by Prince Henry 'the Navigator' from the petty barbarian realm of Portugal. In 1434, the year after the great Ming voyages ceased, Gil Eannes, one of Henry's captains, doubled Cape Bojador, south of the Canary Islands, which, with its furious waves and currents, its shallows, its fogs, its unhelpful winds, had marked for Europeans a limit beyond which they had not dared to venture. By 1488 the Portuguese, pressing south, had discovered that Africa ended in a triangular tip, which Bartolomeu Dias rounded to enter the Indian Ocean.

In 1493, a Genoese adventurer serving the Spanish Crown, Cristóbal Colón ('Columbus'), returned from a sea voyage by which he believed he had found a direct route to Cipango and Cathay. What he had in fact found, neither Chinese, nor Europeans, had known of.

II

The inhabitants of Cipango, not in fact vastly wealthy, bothered the Brilliant Emperors with their piracies at sea. One had written to their ruler in 1380, 'You stupid Eastern barbarians! . . . You are haughty and disloyal; you permit your subjects to do evil.' Two years later the Japanese had replied: 'Heaven and Earth are vast; they are not monopolised by one ruler . . . The world is the world's world; it does not belong to a single person.'

At the time of Columbus's voyage no one – in East or West – had an inkling of all the worlds that there were in the world. It would happen that those who revealed the world to its peoples were Europeans who (like apes) had thin lips and copious body hair, rather than Africans who had little body hair, or Mongolian-type peoples, with rather more. Yet a visitor from another planet able to survey the earth in 1493 would not have discerned with ease any elements of superiority in European culture, even if China had been left out of the comparison.

The ruins of Rome would not have proved much; the largest temple in the world lay abandoned in a jungle in Indo-China. And if he had seen the stone cities built by the Incas in the Andes, the buildings of Florence, let alone Lisbon, might not have stirred him to wonder. The Koreans had been the first people to put to extensive use the method of printing from movable type. The bronze sculptures of Benin in West Africa could stand comparison with Donatello's. Were Europeans most effervescent as traders? The Javanese merchant patricians who ruled Malacca, dominating narrow straits, creamed great wealth from the growing intercourse between India and ports east. The Sultan of Gujerat, lord of ports and textile workers, rivalled in his power the grandest monarchs of India's interior.

And Christianity would have seemed less vital, even less vitalising, than Islam, which was spreading down trade routes from the Middle East, making rapid headway in Indonesia and drawing to Mecca the spectacular pilgrimage of Askya Muhammad after he usurped the rule of the powerful West African empire of Songhay in 1496. The Hausa kingdom of Kano on the fringe of his was a centre of resort for Islamic scholars from far away, and on the Swahili coast of East Africa educated Muslim ruling classes dwelt in cool stone houses and ate off Chinese porcelain in a pretty chain of trading cities. Muslims, Turks, had captured the ancient Christian capital of Constantinople in 1453, and had then swept the Balkans from coast to coast. In the 1490s they defeated Christendom's best fleet, that of Venice, and ravaged the island city's mainland territory.

Europe was smaller and poorer in the fifteenth century than it had been in the thirteenth. Then, population had expanded beyond natural resources. The climate had changed for the worse early in the fourteenth century and decades of undernourishment had assisted the work of the bubonic plague, the 'Black Death', which had swept the continent from 1348, killing a quarter or a third of its people. The plague remained a regular visitant. The expectation of life at birth and indeed into a person's teens was no more than thirty. The peasant lived with his beasts in a sooty hut. Illiteracy was still general. Pleasures and punishments were barbaric. The Church burnt witches and heretics at the stake. Even England, a country unusually centralised, had suffered a long series of civil wars. In the 1490s, invasion ravaged Italy, famine confronted Germany, outbreaks of plague in France emptied whole towns whose inhabitants fled to the forests and wastes and starved there, and Europe in general endured what was thought to be the first assault of syphilis. In an age when kings were as credulous as their crudest subjects, rumours and portents multiplied: monstrous births, rains of milk and blood, stains in the sky. Scholarly men expected the end of the world very shortly.

Confronted with these violent, demoralised idol-worshippers many Victorian explorers would have concluded rapidly that they needed to be governed in their own interests by the enlightened products of the British public school.

Yet, it was Europe which would produce such arrogant explorers. Geography is one partial explanation. Europe, V. G. Kiernan points out, 'was a big peninsula jutting out from Asia, broken up and nearly surrounded by seas. It had no huge cavernous interior like Asia's or Africa's, and always in one way or another looked outwards.' The seas, and the great river Rhine, facilitated trade in the products of areas as different in their climates and resources as Sweden was (and is) from Italy. The first countries to 'expand' overseas, Portugal and Spain, peered over a narrow strait to Africa and found themselves on an easy route to America. There was in Europe a unique balance, tension, interaction between feudal lords dominating the countryside and, on the other hand, towns, independent or largely self-governing. Both lords and townspeople cherished privileges which gave them some power of self-assertion against kings, and which ensured scope for expansionist individuals.

In medieval Europe we can see developing two interrelated prototypes of the modern version of imperialism. Land, it was understood, could be grabbed from infidels and the status of the raptors as overlords, exploiting the people as serfs or slaves, could be sanctified by the Pope and by feudal legality. In Iberia, led by the legendary Cid, Christians began in the eleventh century to wrest land from Muslims, who had left them only a small enclave. The German 'drive to the East' from the twelfth to the fourteenth centuries was a crusade against pagan Slavs. But entrepreneurs fanned the colonising fever. Forests and swamps were claimed for agriculture; the Wendish Slavs in the way were massacred, forcibly transplanted, enserfed, while around the Baltic German traders established that chain of posts which became the cities of the Hanseatic League. The landlust of noblemen married with the goldlust of merchants. By the sixteenth century, furthermore, the demand for Baltic grain from Western European towns was such that German 'junkers' ruling non-German peasants found it profitable to tie them to the land – to create, in effect, plantations with coerced serf labour. This coincided with the emergence of slave plantations beyond Europe. The rise of cities in Western Europe would very largely depend on both these developments, while the German and Polish towns in the East went into decline.

Stadtluft macht frei, said the Germans: 'Town air makes free.' Freedom attracted runaway serfs from the countryside. Yet the freedom of Florentine 'freemen' stemmed from the degradation of others. They owned many slaves. Italians had gone everywhere in Europe, as merchants, technical experts, tax farmers, entrepreneurs and moneylenders. They had developed a most significant trade in slaves. The word comes from 'Slav'; Italians went to the Black Sea where Tartars sold them captives from the Slav lands they dominated. In Venice alone 10,000 slaves were sold between 1414 and 1423. Even quite lowly people in Italy commonly used them as servants. Domestic slavery was a world-wide fact, but Italians, following ancient Roman precedents, worked up an idea which seems to be peculiar to Europeans, the island plantation tilled by slaves. In Cyprus, Italians running such plantations grew sugar cane with the labour of imported people who, by 1300, included some black Africans.

So this idea developed simultaneously with the 'commercial revolution' achieved by the Italians; along, that is, with such things as marine insurance, double entry book-keeping, bills of exchange, cheques, and banks with far-flung foreign branches. Italians opened up England, then an important, rather backward wool-producing area, exchanging the products of the Mediterranean and the East for native raw and manufactured materials. They brought new tastes, new 'needs', new perspectives and new methods. In the winter, carriers came from Westmorland, one of the lesser centres of English textile manufacture (Grasmere then had twenty fulling mills), transporting cheap but durable cloth made from the wool of hardy fell sheep, for sale direct to the great Italian galleys which called in at Southampton. They jogged back to their own rocky valleys taking casks of alum and woad for dyeing, but also luxuries – oranges, nuts and wines. The lives of Westmorland people were now involved with what happened thousands of miles away: in Cairo, for instance, where Venetian merchants haggled with the Sultan of Egypt over his imposts on the trade in 'spices', a general term for Eastern produce.

In remote Indonesian islands, the Moluccas and Bandas, and nowhere else in the world as far as was known, nutmegs and cloves grew. The tide of spices began there and flowed towards Europe gathering in silks and rhubarb, gems, cotton and dyestuffs, drugs, perfumes and unguents, all the drowsy syrups of the East, besides cloves, nutmegs and cinnamon to mask the taste of that humdrum or rotten food which even the richest in Europe ate. Pepper was the most valuable product of all, a near essential. To preserve meat for the winter with salt alone would have meant so much soaking later when the time came to eat it that it would have been tasteless. With pepper mixed in, less salt could be used. The spice trade was the richest and most risky open to Europeans. A merchant, it was said, could ship six cargoes, lose five, and still make a profit when the sixth was sold. On the spice trade Venice had risen to glory, so that in Columbus's day that small city-state seemed the mightiest power in Europe.

'Nations' in the modern sense did not exist. Nowhere in Europe did political boundaries coincide with 'racial' or even 'linguistic' ones. Maritime explorers, like artists, went where the pay was best, undeterred by any sense of disloyalty. Europe consisted of 'realms', claimed by kings, dukes and cities. These claimants were insatiably competitive. Monarchs envied, as well as feared, the despotic Ottoman sultans with their superb armies. 'Italy' and 'Germany' were divided among many small states. The realm of the king of 'France' was the most populous; that of the king of 'England' was probably the most unified, except for the smaller kingdom of 'Portugal'. While kings sought to extend their power at the expense of their own subjects, they also thought freely in terms of extending their realms beyond natural frontiers. The digestion of new territories in other continents presented no conceptual problems.

Growth in the power of kings, transforming itself later into that of 'states', would accompany the extension of European scope. But some subjects from the outset were prepared to go further and meddle with more than rulers had the imagination to propose or, sometimes, the interest to endorse. The Catholic Church, with its missionary ambitions, would keep up its own momentum overseas. Some men of the landowning strata felt short of land or had none and sought lordships over savages. Some merchants hoped for rich hauls from risky overseas enterprises. When conditions in Europe were so dismal for so many, no enterprise would lack sailors to face death in tiny ships, or soldiers to fight in little conquering armies. Power, for kings; profit, for merchants; opportunity, for all classes – these were strong enough pulls to explain the initial European impetus.

Conquistadors, merchants and kings had two advantages over all the non-European peoples at whose expense the expansion took place. One was conceptual. The discovery by fifteenth-century artists of ways of representing space in a painting through the rules of perspective was a step towards reconstructing and imagining it from a map. A second advantage owed nothing to learned argument. This was in sailing ships.

The fifteenth century had seen a marriage between the carvel-built Mediterranean ship, with its triangular lateen sail, and the tough, buoyant, clinker-built, tubby 'cog' of the North, able to fight its way up to Iceland and back on a regular run through heavy winds and seas, though its square sails gave it less manoeuvrability. Extra masts were added, and a range of hybrids came into existence, so that Spanish and Portuguese seamen, who lived at the point where the two traditions converged, were able to make immense voyages in ships which were built for the everyday trade of Western Europe.

Such ships mounted cannon. These had been used on land and sea in Europe and Asia for a long time, but in quality and quantity, Europe, thanks to its incessant warfare, was establishing a lead over other areas, and its rulers were now mounting the unreliable weapons of the day in such numbers upon their ships that the old sort of naval battle decided by boarding parties of soldiers was on its way to becoming obsolete. And Europeans had borrowed from Arabs (who had themselves borrowed from further east) enough techniques to make navigation possible in deep water under clouds and storm. They had the stern-post rudder, they had the magnetic compass, and they had 'Arabic' numerals, Hindu in origin, which made calculations of angle and distance more feasible. Accurate measurement of longitude was impossible till the eighteenth century, but using an astrolabe or simple quadrant a seaman could establish a fairly accurate latitude by taking polar altitudes.

Educated men knew about Ancient Rome and were not embarrassed by any scientific understanding of history. The exploits of Caesar, they fancied, were of a kind which they themselves could repeat. And the illiterates in the expedition could share with their betters assurance that as Christians they were, and must in the long run prove, superior. This conviction had been sharpened by the long struggle against Islam, the only other religion to match Christianity in fanaticism and missionary zeal. When Pope Pius II coined the adjective 'European' in the 1450s it was, ominously, equated with 'Christian'. Amongst the fuels which drove expansion forward, the vivid, hungry desire to put the Turks in their place and give Christian Europe its rightful position had real importance. And in those days people believed without question in the torments of hell and the raptures of paradise. Turkish power straddled the spice routes. Muslim traders flocked in eastern ports. The new-found lands to the west were full of pagans. To help to transform these depressing circumstances might assist one's fortune in that after-life which pressed so closely even on young men in days of casual slaughters and treacherous diet and inefficacious medicine.

Yet the quest for an earthly, material paradise also beckoned nobleman and commoner. Millenarian longings had frequently flamed out in the revolts of urban craftsmen, the fury of peasant insurrection. Joachim of Fiore, in the twelfth century, had prophesied a Third Age of the world in which all men would live in voluntary poverty, in joy and love and freedom, without pope or emperor or private property. His vision haunted Europe. Those who set out to sail for Cathay remembered also stories of islands of bliss to the west. By 1502, Columbus, who had started the transmutation of these islands from hopeful legend into hapless fact, was thinking of himself as the Joachite messiah, bringing in that Third Age 'of the spirit'. The belief that in new worlds life

could be just and free, would help to draw poor and wealthy alike overseas up to
our own century.

III

For the nobility of Iberia, crusading against Moors had become a traditional way
of life. In 1415, the Portuguese captured Ceuta, in North Africa, a Moorish town
where, according to a chronicler, the soldiers were astonished, 'for our poor
houses look like pigsties in comparison with these.' Ceuta was a terminal point
in the trans-Saharan gold trade from West Africa. Backward, aggressive
Portugal was one of the few European countries which did not then have a gold
coinage. The captains sent out thereafter by Prince Henry the Navigator, a
member of the Portuguese royal house, were looking for the origin of the gold
which flowed to the Moors. They found other sources of profit as they explored
down the coast. In 1441, direct shipment of slaves began. Seven years later the
prototype *feitoria* ('factory' in the old sense of the word) was set up at Arguim,
below Cape Blanco, and this was able to draw much trade in gold and ivory from
the Moors. Before Prince Henry died in 1460, his ships had probed as far south
as Sierra Leone.

Two types of imperialising activity followed. The 'factory' was a base for
trade. The overseas colony also fostered commerce, but in addition gave the
chance of a new life. Prince Henry, from the 1420s, had put colonists on the
unoccupied island of Madeira and the first boy and girl born there were named
Adam and Eve. Madeira, with its vineyards and sugar plantations, proved very
profitable, as did the Azores, also empty, which Henry peopled a little later. In
the 1470s, Spain fought Portugal over possession of the Canary Islands. Spain
got the Canaries and their stone-age inhabitants, the Guanches, were
extinguished.

A few years later the Portuguese encountered a great unknown kingdom, far
more populous than their own, south of where the river Congo discoloured the
sea for many miles with its mud-laden waters. This was the land of the
Manikongo, the 'blacksmith king'. A scenario developed which would often be
played out again. The king saw the religion of his clever visitors as a new source
of power for himself, and he was baptised. But the price of their spiritual and
technical assistance was slaves. Before long, even members of the royal family
were being kidnapped, and the nearby island of São Thomé, populated with
black slaves under white settlers, was thriving by the second quarter of the
sixteenth century on the production of that lush and sinister crop, the sugar
cane.

Meanwhile, Vasco Da Gama had opened up direct trade between Portugal
and India. When he arrived at Calicut in 1498 the zamorin, ruler of that
important town, was disgusted with the gifts which Da Gama presented to him,
and his courtiers laughed at the hoods and washbasins, hats and honey the white
men brought. The trade of the East could not be peacefully entered. The

Portuguese turned to their cannon for help. In 1510 the famous viceroy Albuquerque grabbed Goa and, so he claimed, put all Muslims in sight to the sword, or burned them alive in their mosques. By 1515 he had also seized two of the great entrepôts of the Indian Ocean trade, Malacca and, in the Persian Gulf, Ormuz.

Venice continued to thrive on spices which reached Europe by other routes than Da Gama's. Off China, the Ming coastguard fleets beat the Portuguese twice in the early 1520s. But with ships largely crewed by Asians and black Africans, a few scant parcels of white men, scattered in fortified posts from East Africa to the Moluccas, were able to domineer in Indian Ocean trade for most of the sixteenth century. And besides maintaining their bases in West Africa, the Portuguese started the permanent settlement of Brazil. Beneath all later empires, a Portuguese substratum showed, even where they had not ruled directly. They spread new crops and techniques wherever they went. Their pioneering presence brought with it a new trade language which influenced pidgins used later by all Europeans. The word 'sabby', for instance, or something like it, is found in the pidgins of Africans and of Chinese, of Caribbean and of Pacific islanders.

The Portuguese impetus, backed by Italian and German merchants, was primarily commercial. Christian fervour, and hunger for land and spoils, gave a different coloration to Spanish expansion. Hundreds of years of war against Islam had given the people of Spain's arid central plateau a characteristic noble rapacity. In between battles, soldiers accustomed to live by plunder had scorned to go back to agriculture. To conquer land, to loot it, and then to live as lord over native serfs became the ideal of a large class of men, mostly poorish *hidalgos* ('sons of someone', petty nobility), who were ready to justify their behaviour by reference to a militant Christianity and to an exalted code of chivalry. It was convenient for such people that Columbus found, not the rich trade of the East for which his own Genoese background prompted him to look, but land, occupied by apparently tractable pagans: islands, in the first instance, more Canaries.

He did not 'discover' America, whatever that means; amongst Europeans, Norsemen had certainly settled briefly in Newfoundland early in the eleventh century. But he did initiate the rape of the Caribbean. Returning to Hispaniola in 1493 with 1,200 colonists, he was soon hunting the natives with savage dogs. Indians, however, seemed to prefer death to working for Spaniards, and the conquerors, with their *hidalgo* pride, would not work themselves. The need for a third kind of person was soon very clear, and in 1510 the Spanish Crown began to license the importation of Africans. 1515 saw the first shipment of slave-grown sugar from the New World. The Indians, no more used to European diseases than they were to white concepts of slavery, were dying out with catastrophic rapidity, and loss of labour was one factor driving some Spanish colonists from the islands to the mainland, from which in 1513, at the

Isthmus of Panama, an adventurer named Balboa saw the 'South Sea', the Pacific.

Then Hernán Cortés gave Europeans a new and potent myth. Less than two and a half years after he had set out from Cuba in 1519 with six hundred companions, Cortés had made himself effective ruler of Mexico, on the ruins of the great city of Teotihuacan and of the Aztec empire which had built it. Thirteen muskets and sixteen horses had been sufficient against opponents who were still using stone-age weapons. The example which Cortés set Europe resounds through the whole subsequent history of imperialism. In the first instance his deeds inspired Francisco de Pizarro, with a still smaller force, to conquer the even more impressive Andean empire of the Incas, and Spaniards rapidly took over the more accessible parts of eastern South America.

For Spain, also, Fernao Magalhaes (Magellan) had sailed in 1519 to drive through the straits which bear his name into that sea which he called Pacific. His men went for three months and twenty days without fresh food: they ate hides from the rigging, sawdust and rats: then, after their landfall, Magellan was killed in the Philippines. But one of his captains completed, in 1522, the first circumnavigation of the globe. He brought back spices, along with fifteen survivors.

'West' had now become 'East'. This created confusion in international law. The Treaty of Tordesillas (1494) had divided the world into a Spanish half, west of an imaginary line drawn 370 leagues beyond a point in the Azores, and a Portuguese half, which included Africa and Asia as well as Brazil. The two powers now fought in the Moluccas. A new line of demarcation, east of the islands, was arranged in 1529. Spanish conquest of the Philippines followed in the 1560s, and a commerce in silk with China opened up from Manila, whither Spanish argosies sailed from Mexico. European trade routes now girdled the world.

IV

This spate of discovery and conquest brought intellectual revolution. Contrary to the cherished tale, every literate man in Europe knew in Columbus's day that the world was round. But no one had thought that there might be a continent to the west between Europe and Asia. Since Columbus died believing that he had pioneered a direct route to Cathay, it is not unfair that the continent came to be called after an Italian businessman, Amerigo Vespucci, whose travels there convinced him that this was a 'New World' for which neither Christian doctrine nor geographical theory had allowed. He publicised his views in 1504 and three years later a German, Waldseemüller, drew a map showing the new lands as separate from either Europe or Asia and giving them the name 'America'.

Most Europeans, even literate ones, were slow to react to the discovery of the

New World or to its implications. But the Englishman, Thomas More, who set his imaginary communist Utopia in the new lands in his book of 1516, exemplified the imaginative impact on advanced and speculative minds. America wasn't in the Bible. The Romans had known nothing of it. It would be absurd to suggest that the discoveries by themselves could be held to explain the large changes in European consciousness which took place in the sixteenth century. But the new theology of Luther and Calvin, with its unintentional invitations to scepticism and individualism, came after the voyages in point of time; so did the new cosmology of Copernicus, Kepler and Galileo. Amerigo Vespucci himself prefigured the spirit of Baconian science when he wrote to his patron in 1500, 'Rationally, let it be said in a whisper, experience is certainly worth more than theory.' A new audacity, and a fresh empiricism, started to march together.

The effects of invasion on America may be measurable: the population of central Mexico seems to have fallen from about 11 million when Cortés first arrived to $2\frac{1}{2}$ million by the end of the century. The material effects on Europe itself were less dramatic. New fisheries across the Atlantic were valuable, as was the new commerce with colonists. New sources of bullion were not at first very important. Then in 1545 there was a silver strike at Potosí in Peru, and from the 1560s mines were successfully exploited. They solved the longstanding problem of how Europe could pay for luxury imports from Asia. For centuries New World bullion would be essential to the far trade with India and China. Though it did not cause the startling rise of prices which had important results in sixteenth-century Europe, it certainly helped to sustain them at higher and higher levels.

But the chief 'economic' effect was surely a psychological one. European men of business were learning to scheme grandly. The long-distance trades demanded finance on a new scale. The Portuguese and Spaniards themselves lacked the required capital and experience. In 1503 the Portuguese King made Antwerp the depot for the Eastern trade. This port became the major centre of banking and finance in Europe.

Peruvian silver helped the Spanish Crown to overawe Europe, and its pikemen and arquebusiers dominated the continent's wars until well into the seventeenth century. The bullying attitudes developed towards Indians in America quickly came to bear on the Spanish people themselves. Philip II of Spain wrote in 1570 to the governor of Milan, one of his possessions, 'These Italians, although they are not Indians, have to be treated as such, so that they will understand that we are in charge of them and not they in charge of us.'

Spain was envied; Spain was feared; kings wished to imitate and to challenge Spain. When a Spaniard taxed King Francis I with his interventions in America, the French ruler drily remarked 'That the sun shone for him as for others, and he would like very much to see Adam's will to learn how he divided up the world.'

V

The French were early poachers in Brazil. It was under the French King's patronage that a Florentine, Verazzano, in 1524, first sailed the North American coastline from the Carolinas to Newfoundland, and it was Jacques Cartier from France, perhaps the most brilliant of all sixteenth-century explorers, who made three voyages to Canada without losing a ship, penetrated far up the St Lawrence, and helped to found an abortive colony there in 1540.

But the English could claim to be first discoverers of North America. From at least the 1480s, merchants of Bristol had been sending out ships to search for land in the Atlantic, and it was from this port that a citizen of Venice named by the English (after much indecision) 'John Cabot' proposed to sail west in search of spices. On 5 March 1496, King Henry VII of England granted to 'John Gabote' letters patent giving him leave and power 'to seeke out, discover, and finde, whatsoever iles, countreyes, regions or provinces of the heathen and infidelles, whatsoever they bee, and in what part of the world soever they bee, whiche before this time have beene unknowen to all Christians.' Cabot might govern these lands as the King's lieutenant, monopolise their produce, and pay the Crown 'the fifth part of the Capitall gaine so gotten'.

This was an example of the combination of private initiative with royal support which characterised the discoveries of the period, including those of Columbus. Cabot, at his own 'costes and charges', could raise only one ship, the *Matthew*, with a crew of eighteen. He sailed about May 20, 1497, and within five weeks or so arrived in Newfoundland. By August 9 he was back in London to claim his 'New Isle'. The King gave him £10 for his discovery at once, and a few months later an annuity of £20 was settled on his 'welbiloved John Calbot'. Calbot, Gabote or Cabot bought new clothes and swaggered around London in gay silken apparel. In February 1498, Henry issued him new letters patent to go back to his island, though Cabot bragged that his real intention was to reach Cipango, where he thought all the spices and jewels in the world had their origin, and to set up a 'factory' there. Of 'Kaboto's' five ships, Henry gave one, stocked by London merchants. The men of Bristol provided the others with 'coarse cloth, Caps, Laces, points and other trifles', deemed suitable for trade with pagans. One ship put into an Irish port in distress. Four sailed on and were lost. As a contemporary noted, Cabot had found 'new lands nowhere but on the very bottom of ocean'.

A Portuguese, Gaspar Corte Real, reached Newfoundland in 1500, but he too was lost on his second expedition. A disappointed rival, João Fernandes, an Azorean, formed a syndicate with other Azoreans and men of Bristol which was given letters patent by Henry in 1501. They brought the King presents of birds and wildcats from the New-found Island, and also three Indians, but no important results. Then English exploration lagged. Of the very few English New World voyages known to us from the early sixteenth century, the most memorable was Richard Hore's of 1536. A leather merchant of London, Hore chartered two ships to catch cod and to give a trip to certain sightseers, including some thirty cheerful young gentlemen of London. One ship was lost at sea. The other anchored in Newfoundland. Supplies ran out. Depressed by a diet of 'raw herbes and rootes in the fields and deserts', the passengers began to eat each other. The captain denounced this practice, whereupon the culprits agreed to do it more fairly, casting lots as to who should provide the next meal. The survivors eventually pirated a French vessel, and sailed home, past 'mighty Ilands of yce'.

BOOK ONE: 1530–1660

Cromwell the First

I

The modern imagination finds it hard to recapture the North-West European Archipelago as it was around 1530. Two kingdoms claimed all the isles between them. The monarch in England, a man of recent Welsh origins, was also titular ruler of Wales and of Ireland, and he had his eye on the realm of his weaker neighbour in Edinburgh, who called himself King of Scots. Both courts spoke versions of English, and so did most of the subjects whom the kings were actually able to control in any way. But the dialects used in different areas were still often mutually almost incomprehensible. Cornish was still spoken in the far south-west, Welsh generally in Wales, and forms of Gaelic, closely allied to each other, throughout Highland Scotland, Ireland and the Isle of Man. Man had its own 'king' until 1504, when the Earl of Derby, who held the title, agreed to become merely 'Lord of Man'. But he and his descendants effectively ruled the island until the late eighteenth century.

Nor was such virtual independence exceptional. A Campbell Earl of Argyll, or, in south-western Ireland, a Geraldine Earl of Desmond, was in most respects a hereditary king in his own right, and undercover diplomacy would recognise him as such. In Ireland, royal power stopped short a few miles outside Dublin. Even in England, in times of weak kingship, as during the Wars of the Roses, the tribalism of the periphery could spread its infection towards the centre in anarchy and rebellion.

Race-consciousness did exist among Celts, and was fostered by their poets, but there was no question that they might unite against English-speakers. Sea divided Wales and Cornwall, where Brythonic languages were spoken. Though the narrower North Channel did not prevent constant intercourse between Gaels in Scotland and Ireland who shared a Goidelic tongue and, in great part, a common culture, there were many petty chiefs divided by mutual jealousies and English-speaking rulers would always find allies among them. Institutions within the Gaelic lands reflected varying dates and durations of two great transmarine interventions. Vikings from Scandinavia had much affected the Hebrides and Man, but had made rather less impact on Ireland, while Normans had spread over most but not all of the British Isles after 1066.

The Anglo-Saxon footsoldiers of England had been the first to succumb to mounted Normans wearing mail coats and characteristic conical helmets. The Normans eventually adopted the English language, but only after making an almost clean sweep of the old Anglo-Saxon ruling class and bringing in feudal institutions previously absent. South Wales was rapidly overrun, and Pembroke became and remained a 'little England', but elsewhere the Welsh tribes rallied to regain much lost ground, and eventually a fringe of Anglo-Norman lordships to east and south girdled with moated castles a zone still basically Celtic.

In Scotland and Ireland also, Normanisation was left incomplete. By the eleventh century four distinct racial groups had come to give allegiance to the King of Scots: the Scots themselves in the west; the Picts to the north; the Welsh-speaking Strathclyde Britons in the south-west, and the Angles of the Lothians. King David I in the first half of the twelfth century brought Normans and feudalism together into his sparsely settled realm. Some Norman lords, in parts of the Highlands, adapted themselves and their feudal institutions to the role of Celtic clan chieftainship. But the north and west remained Gaelic-speaking; a deep divide was beginning within the kingdom.

The Irish, by contrast, had long shared a common culture and language, but their 'High Kings' had rarely had much authority. A chance for Norman incursion arose from the struggle of Dermot MacMurrough, King of Leinster, against his titular overlord, the High King. He did a deal with Richard Fitzgilbert de Clare, Earl of Pembroke, later nicknamed 'Strongbow' by historians. 'Strongbow' was promised Dermot's daughter in marriage and succession to rule in Leinster. In 1170, he accordingly brought over from Wales archers, and some mounted Norman knights. Dermot soon died, and as king in his own right, Strongbow submitted to Henry II of England. Though Henry had forbidden the expedition, he had in his pocket a grant of hereditary possession of Ireland which the Pope, concerned to bring the island more effectively into his own sphere of power, had made him in the 1550s. So, by the standards of the day it was not mere lawless thuggery when Henry, like so many rulers after him, legalised the results brought about by freebooting on the frontier. He came over himself in 1171, confirmed Strongbow and other Normans in the lands which Dermot had granted them, took submission from numerous native chiefs, and left a viceroy behind him. He had secured, without fighting, a claim to the island which the Irish Church conceded was just. And the flow of aliens into Ireland about this time was no crude military occupation. Land-hungry English and Welsh peasants came to outnumber the natives in many parts, but there was plenty of room for everybody. The Irish had no urban traditions, and generally left the towns to the English-speakers. As the Middle Ages wore on, the Anglo-Norman lords were gaelicised and Irish chieftains commonly borrowed some English ways. Only Ulster, never finally brought under Norman overlords, stayed more or less untouched.

Celtic Wales meanwhile part-Anglicized itself. Llewellyn the Great (1196–1240) managed to overcome the country's chronic disunity and ruled something which looked like a kingdom in North and Central Wales. Llewellyn the Last (1255–82) was recognised as *de facto* independent by the English Crown at the Treaty of Montgomery in 1267. But his dabblings in English politics brought the power of Edward I against him and by 1284, with the native upstart dead, the alien king was able to symbolise English power with four royal castles at Conway, Carnarvon, Criccieth and Harlech, under which boroughs grew up peopled by English settlers. Many prominent Welshmen had resented Llewellyn and were happy to serve the greater Crown.

The Anglo-Saxons had driven the native Celts into the hilly regions of north and west, leaving Ireland untouched (as indeed the Romans had done). The Anglo-Normans pushed further and brought with them not only the evolving English language, which gradually became a mark of boasted social and racial superiority, but also the seeds of what became capitalism. The contrast between Celt and Saxon began to crystallise as one between grain growers and people chiefly, though not solely, pastoralists. A feudal system of landholding involving inheritance by the eldest son eschewed the view that land belonged to the clan or surname or tribe as a whole and that inheritance was partible; above all the town, as it grew and its influence spread, infiltrated alien ideas, English speech, and the influence of the European trading system, into areas which became, by comparison with its own values and standards, backward. Native leaders took note and aspired. 'Without buying and selling I can in no way live', wrote the O Toole chieftain from Ireland to Richard II in 1395. '. . . I would that you send me your letters patent so that for the future I may enjoy free buying and selling in your fairs and towns.'

II

Yet England itself in the early sixteenth century was a 'backward' country, so remote from the consciousness of educated Europeans that the Portuguese poet Camoens, as late as 1572, could refer to it as a 'great northern kingdom of perpetual snow'. England's three million people were much outnumbered by the nineteen million of France Only 8 or 9 per cent of them lived in towns, as compared to 15 per cent in Spain.

England's people, like those of underdeveloped lands later, were notorious elsewhere for their 'laziness', and for the same reasons: they were underemployed. Most of them still lived in smoky, dark, stinking and cramped little dwellings made of timber and mud, dressed in skins or clothes made of leather or canvas or sackcloth, and ate black bread from wooden trenchers. Most households were still economically almost self-sufficient. Sorcery and witchcraft probably had as much influence as Christianity, and that growingly rational urban culture which had sprung up in Italy, Flanders and Germany had made as yet little impact on England. In 1500 there were seventy-three towns in Italy with printing presses while in England there were only four. Sheep outnumbered men by perhaps three to one, bearing the famous wool which had attracted Italian buyers so greatly, but which was now exported in the form of English-made cloth.

That cloth, however, was mainly distributed by German merchants from the

Hanse towns which, in the fifteenth century, had shut the English out of direct trade with their markets in the Baltic. English naval forces had failed against these competitors, and it was one signal of the ambitions of Henry VIII that he was building up a navy which reached a total of eighty-five ships; his father had found only three when he had seized power in 1485.

Where England was in advance of the rest of Europe was in its precocious achievement of something approaching 'national unity'. In the Middle Ages, England had built up traditions of strong royal authority which were to hand as Edward IV and his Tudor successors sought to repair and strengthen the powers of the Crown after a long phase of civil war. The centralisation of the economy assisted the concentration of authority. London, with its population reaching 200,000 or more by 1600, far outstripped all other towns in size and significance. It was not only the seat of the king, it was also clearly the commercial capital, and with cultural dominance added, it achieved triple hegemony unique in Europe. In some years in the 1540s nearly nine-tenths of England's exports of cloth went through it. And as a great market for food, it became a magnet by which first the South Midlands, Kent and East Anglia, then ultimately the rest of the country, were drawn into agriculture conducted for profit.

And the oligarchies which ran the smaller towns, so far from resisting centralisation, favoured the growth of royal power. In England, almost uniquely, townsmen had come to form an essential part of the machinery of royal government. They had their representatives in the House of Commons, which from 1376 had elected its own Speaker. The Tudors, driving towards absolute monarchy, relied on the support of substantial middling people. At a time when noblemen on the Continent were tending to emphasise their separate status, and had won immunity from taxation, in England the ranks of the peerage were thin, and were kept so; the broader body of knights and squires below was taxed, and merged into the shifting and amorphous class of 'gentlemen', who were themselves often hard to distinguish from merchant groups on the one hand and from substantial yeomen on the other. Whereas in France the Crown ruled in 1560 that any nobleman who engaged in trade would thereby lose his caste privileges, in England such behaviour was commonplace and accepted among 'gentlemen'. Prosperous peasant farmers by thrift and polite behaviour could win recognition as 'gentry'.

While serfdom was still the typical condition of ordinary people elsewhere in Europe, England (and Scotland) had moved away from it. Villeinage had begun to wither in England from the fourteenth century onwards; the Black Death, which made labour an item in shorter supply than land, had assisted the shift from customary tenures involving unpaid service towards leasehold and copyhold, and in effect to contractual relationships between master and man. In theory there were still some serfs in England in the late sixteenth century, but in practice a writer in 1577 was justified in the claim that 'As for slaves and bondmen we have none'.

Yet the spread over the English countryside of men pushing with a sharp eye for profit towards the gratifications of upward social mobility bore very hard, very often, on the less lucky 'free' people around them. In Henry VIII's day the encloser, the man who put up hedges and fences where there had been open fields and common lands, was generally and violently hated. While small hedged fields were traditional in some parts of the country, in much of it, above all in the Midlands, enclosure was felt as a tyrannical outrage. Villagers practising open field agriculture were used to working together, agreeing on crop rotations, sharing the common pasture. 'After enclosure, when every man could fence his own piece of territory and warn his neighbours off, the discipline of sharing things fairly with one's neighbours was relaxed, and every household became an island unto itself. This', concludes Joan Thirsk, 'was the great revolution in men's lives, greater than all the economic changes following enclosure.'

Enclosure did not go far in those early days – as late as 1700, half of England's arable land would still be under open field. But already thousands of vagabonds roamed the roads: dispossessed by enclosers; or cast away as a result of the breakup of great bands of retainers previously kept by feudal magnates but now demolished by royal policy and by the price rise; or thrown into joblessness by slumps in the textile trade.

Because of the relative weakness of English towns, clothmaking had been able to escape into the countryside, away from guild regulations which kept up the price of labour. The 'clothmakers' – the merchants who co-ordinated the numerous different processes and gave work to country people in their cottages – dominated many rural areas. The English industry had advantages over its rivals on the Continent. It commanded its own local supplies of the best wool in Europe, and, unlike its competitors in Italy and Flanders, it could exploit cheap rustic labour.

The great price rise forced by mounting population dominated European history at this time. In England the general level soared five-fold between 1530 and 1640, ferociously depressing the living standards of poor people but favouring, in such a fluid social structure, middling men – lesser landlords, farmers, yeomen – at the expense of major landlords, including the Crown. Rents, on which great men depended, lagged behind the price of foodstuffs, which lesser men, steering their agriculture towards the market, could now offer. Families claiming 'gentility' multiplied rapidly; but along with 'gentility' now commonly went a thrifty, individualistic outlook. Merchant patricians who married their daughters into the 'gentry', bought land, and took an interest in the direct exploitation of the rural poor, were increasingly meshed with 'gentlemen' who represented towns in Parliament, sent their sons into commerce, exploited mines or timber on their estates, and developed interests in shipping and foreign trade. As capitalism emerged in England, it was not simply a product of town life. The shrewd landlord, the rich plebeian grazier, the rural 'clothmaker' and the merchant-oligarch all acted in ways which helped to set England on the long road to world-wide commercial dominance.

As that expansionist, capitalist ethos developed, civilised and prosperous Englishmen were clarifying their loathing for the vagabonds of their own country, for the customs of the most backward parts of England, and for the dirty, cowkeeping Celts on its fringes.

III

The turbulence of the Celtic fringe made it a constant threat to the security of English kings, and a standing temptation until the nineteenth century for foreign enemies anxious to meddle or invade, as for pretenders seeking support. The arrival of the Tudors, and its aftermath, illustrate such factors vividly.

A Welshman from Anglesey, Owen ap Maredudd ap Tudor, had wedded, or anyway bedded, the widow of Henry V, and one of their children had married a woman who gave him a claim to the throne. Owen's grandson Henry spent twelve years in exile in the Celtic land of Brittany and became the focus of hope among the Welsh poets, who hailed him as the 'Black Bull of Anglesey'. When he landed in Pembrokeshire in 1475 to assert his claim, the greatest Welsh and Anglo-Welsh magnates threw in their lot with him. The 'Red Dragon of Cadwaladr' (emblem of the last Celtic king to rule all south Britain) flew over his army when he defeated Richard III at Bosworth. The new Henry VII named his son and heir Arthur, after the greatest of Celtic heroes.

But when pretenders rose against Henry, they too looked to the Celtic fringe. Garret More Fitzgerald, Earl of Kildare, the virtual ruler of Ireland by appointment of the Yorkist kings, gave open support to Lambert Simnel, who was crowned 'Edward VI' in Dublin in 1487. Then, after his pardon for this offence, Kildare failed to prevent the Anglo-Irish from offering a welcome to the next claimant, Perkin Warbeck. Warbeck moved on to Scotland, and King James IV agreed to help him. A Scottish army crossed the Border, and burned and looted in its favourite fashion. This in turn provoked a rebellion in Cornwall, where the inhabitants resented being taxed in respect of a fight so far away to the north of them. The 1497 rising started under the leadership of a blacksmith, Michael Joseph. It attracted the minor gentry, though more substantial landlords of Norman stock held aloof. The Cornishmen, said to be 15,000 strong, were defeated only at Blackheath, near London.

England north of the Trent, down to the eighteenth century, also presented dangers. The easier lands were commonly cultivated in the Midland-English way, but up in the hills tribalism survived. The people of Redesdale in Northumberland claimed rights of common pasture in the fells not in respect of their landholdings but in respect of their surnames, 'for that they are descended of such a surname or race of men to whom such a summering belongeth.' They still harked back to their origins in a single family, and accordingly practised partible inheritance, a custom radically opposed to the primogeniture which held sway in the south, and one which had implications for law and order.

Younger sons, instead of moving away, stayed in the valleys, overcrowding them and lending their arms to the favourite sport of cattle raiding.

In adjacent parts of Scotland English-speaking tribalism likewise prevailed, and the most notorious surnames clustered in Liddesdale – Armstrongs and Elliotts, Bells, Nixons and Crosers. The whole area north and south of the Border can be seen as a single economic and social unit, where national feeling meant little or nothing. In summer beasts were driven to high pastures; in winter the main occupation was reiving. The Liddesdale men raided deep into Durham and Yorkshire and also as far as Edinburgh in the north. The Border reiver, astride the nimble little horse which was his most precious possession, was a permanent recruit in warfare against anyone not of his own surname. A contemporary reported such men to be 'Scottishe when they will, and English at their pleasure.' But it was the existence of a frontier, creating problems of jurisdiction, and the wars of royal armies across the Border, which had fostered the lawlessness of the area. Under the weak Crown of Scotland, large Border landowners like Kerr of Cessford or Lord Maxwell wielded power outside feudal law as chiefs of their own surnames, and pursued continuous blood feuds among themselves. Lesser men who quarrelled with them were forced into outlawry with their surnames. They levied 'blackmail' (protection money), and fought each other in vicious vendettas. The minstrels devising out of ceaseless violence the richest body of folk poetry in the language 'praised their chieftains', in Walter Scott's words, 'for the very exploits, against which the laws of the country denounced a capital doom.' Such conditions affected, taking both sides of the Border together, something over 150,000 people.

In Scotland, feuding and clannishness were normal. The King of Scots' half million or so subjects were scattered in scant fertile tracts among the moorland, mountains and rough pasture which formed the vast majority of his territory. One English pound was worth four Scots pounds in 1560, twelve in 1601.

Londoners, to judge from Elizabethan plays, seem to have found it hard or impossible to distinguish between the speech of a Scot and that of an English north-countryman. Why Gaelic should have been replaced by a tongue allied to English over most of Lowland Scotland in the Middle Ages is a mysterious question about a firm fact. By the sixteenth century, the Lowlands, decisively part of Catholic, feudal Christendom, had much in common with England.

But English-speaking Scots founded a fairly strong sense of separate identity on the independence precariously established by Robert Bruce at Bannockburn in 1314. The Stewart line of kings initiated in 1371 commanded the loyalties of most Scots for over three hundred years, and of some for a half century more. But from the mid-fifteenth century, no fewer than seven successive Stewart monarchs inherited as children (or babies) through the deaths, usually violent, of their parents. With minority and regency more common than not, the great feudal magnates became virtual kings in their own areas.

Whether in Lowlands or Highlands, landlords were still war leaders whose attitude to their tenants was governed, and softened, by the belief that having plenty of men to follow you mattered much more than exacting maximum rents. Serfdom had long since disappeared, and the country had never known a peasant revolt. The humblest Scot could assuage his poverty and insecurity with fierce pride in his kinship to the great man of his name, or in the fidelity with which, freely, he followed a chosen leader in feud or war. Scots already showed a proto-democratic tendency to think that no man was worse than another. 'I am Little Jock Elliott – who dares meddle with me?' one Border reiver is said to have exclaimed as he stabbed the great nobleman who was trying to dispose of him.

The big man, chief we may as well say, leased out land to kinsmen and followers who became his feudal vassals and were legally obliged to follow him in war. Besides his own people, others would look to him in the prevailing anarchy, and these he could fasten to himself by 'bonds of manrent'. They gave armed service in return for protection. Three different kinds of tie – kinship, feudalism and manrent – therefore co-existed, sometimes reinforcing each other, sometimes cutting across each other. The Crown, in the early sixteenth century, was making only slow headway in asserting its power against barons who had come to control the sheriffdoms. Within the barony itself, a lord dealt out his own justice in his own courts and in many areas there were heritable 'regalities' where great men could legally exercise almost all the rights of a king.

Gaelic chiefs north and west of the 'Highland Line' commonly held their land by irreproachable feudal tenures, and their junior relatives were from the point of view of parchment legality simply principal tenants, while parchment bonds of manrent might legitimise the adoption into the clan of outsiders. However – and here a distinction can be seen from the Lowlands – within Gaelic culture the faith that the clan really were all one family was vital, and even such formerly Norman or Flemish lords as the Grants and Frasers of the Eastern Highlands had been able to build up a sense of clan identity based on the myth of a common parentage. Kinship, conceived in this way, could obliterate feudal loyalty. Certain chiefs were legally speaking landless, their followers all the tenants of others.

The chief's main function in the eyes of Highlanders was to lead his people into battle, and his power was both paternal and absolute. The Gaelic custom, whereby he would place his child with foster parents so that the boy grew up in a special relationship with one family of vassals, helped to bind lesser families with his own. His leading followers, *duine uasails*, were generally kinsmen of his own, who held lands from him at easy rents until he chose to replace them with closer kin.

Highlanders already liked tartan garments. Tartan plaids were used in the Lowlands as well. But a Sassenach wore his plaid over breeches. The poorer Highlanders went bare-legged, and their way of life struck Lowlanders as primitive. The hunting of red deer for food was still a common recourse. Transhumance, as in the Borders, was generally practised, with cattle taken about midsummer up to mountainside 'shielings'. Highlanders traded their beasts for Lowland corn, and the two economies were complementary. But the Church barely affected Highland life. The area had no towns, no centres of trade and 'civil' behaviour. Its people favoured instead the most uncivil custom of raiding into the Lowlands, where their wild and frequent descents were greatly feared. In the sixteenth century pressure of population was mounting on the scraps of fertile soil in the mountains and isles. The chiefs of the stronger clans had now divided most of the land between them, and no one could expand except at his neighbour's detriment. Macleods, for instance, occupied Gairloch, to which Mackenzies had legal right, and the two clans fought for a century over it.

The greatest of all Highland chiefships had been that of the Lord of the Isles, head of Clan Donald, whose Gaelic-Norse dynasty had emerged in the mid-fourteenth century, thereafter habitually claiming sovereign independence. The Scottish Crown had fought back and in 1493 the Lord was deprived of his title and his estates. Clan Donald itself fell apart as the lesser Macdonald chiefs emerged as individual powers. The Crown began deliberately to advance the scope of the Campbells at their expense. The Campbell Earl of Argyll – his Gaelic title was MacChailean Mor, 'son of great Colin' – was made Lieutenant of the Isles. His clan had before that begun the long career of expansion which made its name the mostly widely hated in Scottish lore. The Earls of Argyll used the King's favour, and their uncommonly sharp grasp of laws which other chiefs found it hard to master, to secure Campbell domination over a great swathe of territory. In Edinburgh they were civil subjects, on their own lands absolute rulers by Gaelic tradition, ready on occasion to intrigue with England or in Ulster for their own purposes.

Their position was almost like that of the Earls of Kildare in Ireland, where the area under effective control by the Crown had contracted to a small slab around Dublin, 'the Pale'. Beyond it, where 'English' settlers could still be distinguished amid the Gaels who had flowed back around them, they had to pay tribute, 'blackrent', to Irish chiefs, or were found in rebellious league with them. Such nobles of settler descent as the Geraldine Earls of Desmond in the south-west employed, like the Gaelic leaders, clans of Scots 'gallowglasses', mail-clad Hebrideans armed with ferocious axes who settled on the island permanently. Faced with the impossible cost of anything like direct rule, Yorkist kings had exalted the other great Geraldine house, that of Kildare, to the status of virtual 'High Kingship'. In so far as Ireland was ruled, which was not very far, from 1477 onwards, it was governed by the Earl of Kildare, except for a couple of years when Henry VII sent Sir Edward Poynings across to replace him. Ireland had its own parliament, though this now represented only the Leinster counties and a few towns. Poynings extracted from it his famous law. No parliament in

Ireland was from now on to pass any Bill which had not been approved by the King beforehand. Henry's wish to restore the Crown to its former powers was made clear in various other morsels of legislation, but actuality was starkly acknowledged when the parliament laid down that a double ditch should be made around the Pale to keep out marauders.

In Munster the heirs of Norman conquistadors lived by a mixture of English and Gaelic laws and customs, with the latter in practice gaining ground. In Connacht and Westmeath other 'Anglo-Normans' like the Burkes, originally 'de Burgos', were indistinguishable from their Irish neighbours. In Ulster, O Neills and O Donnells went on their purely Gaelic way. Though the Butlers of Tipperary and Kilkenny emerged in Tudor times as fairly steady friends of the English Crown, the Brehon judges of ancient tradition administered Irish law for the Earls of Ormond, and their followers went into battle with the war cry 'Butler Aboo'. The *file*, hereditary poet, whose person was sacred and whose curses were thought lethal, was as ready to flatter a Butler or a Fitzgerald (or indeed a chief in Perthshire when his travel took him there) as he was to pour praises on a pure-bred McCarthy or an O Brien of ancient Gaelic stock.

The Irish chiefs ruled what the English called 'nations', but their lands had no fixed boundaries and they measured their greatness in men, not territories. An official report by an Englishman in 1515 reckoned there were over ninety independent powers in Ireland, two-thirds of them found among 'the King's Irish enemies', the others Anglo-Norman in origin. In practice, however, most of these were loosely subject to the great chiefs whose names have been mentioned, and whose degree of power at any one time was expressed through their capacity, or lack of it, to quarter soldiers and other followers on their vassals. By contrast with Gaelic Scotland, chiefship was passed on by primogeniture only among the Anglo-Normans. Lesser chiefs were appointed by great chiefs. The latter themselves emerged by election and struggle from within the clan's ruling *derbfine*, a group composed of all those descended from one ancestor inside four generations. Anyone whose great grandfather had been a chief was theoretically eligible, and since virtual polygamy obtained, with marriage in church the exception rather than rule, while Gaelic law generously refused to distinguish bastards from legitimate children, it was commonplace for a chief to have two or three score real or putative grandsons. The succession struggles resulting were often ferocious, before the chief at last was inaugurated with rituals handed down from a distant pre-Christian past, on some primeval sacred stone, when one vassal might place a white rod in his hands and another put a shoe upon his foot.

The land was owned by the ruling clan as a whole and was freshly shared out at intervals, sometimes annually. The cultivators beneath them were mere tenants at will, wholly dependant. Irish tenants almost everywhere were the most vulnerable rural class in Western Europe. Chieftains and poets alike despised the common people – 'mere churls and labouring men, not one of

whom knows his own grandfather.' Poets, like those other guardians of
tradition, the brehons, the annalists and the physicians, formed a hereditary
caste, parasitic on the rulers. Though marriage of priests was in theory
forbidden, the Irish clergy was also hereditary; and at least two early-sixteenth-
century bishops led their clans in conflict as chiefs of their names. The Irishman
of the ruling classes, carrying his javelin overarm, riding without stirrups, was
more picturesque than useful in battle, and the hard work was done by
mercenary septs of gallowglasses and by the ordinary able-bodied freemen
fighting on foot, the 'kerns'. There was plenty of it. In the Gaelic *Annals of the
Four Masters*, the entry for 1533, a relatively moderate one in respect of
slaughters, records only two deaths by natural causes. The rest is wholly given
over to such mayhem as this:

> MacDermot of Moylurg . . . was treacherously slain by the sons of Owen, son
> of Teige MacDermot; and Owen, the son of Teige, assumed the Lordship
> after him.
> O Molloy. . . Lord of Fircall, was treacherously slain on the Green of
> Lann-Ealla by his own brother, Cucogry, and Art, his brother's son; and his
> brother, Cahir, was styled O Molloy. . .
> A great depredation was committed by O Donnell upon O Hara Boy,
> between the two rivers, because the latter had been disobedient to him.

And so on. It was as much conventional praise for the annalist to report of a dead
chief that he had made many predatory excursions through Ireland as to say that
the same man had been freehanded in hospitality. Rustling was not a crime, but
a kind of sport.

Wealth was measured in small black cattle. Chiefs had hundreds or
thousands. Transhumance was general in Ireland, and in Ulster, uniquely,
herds wandered from place to place throughout the summer. Cultivation was of
lesser concern, and such methods as ploughing with a share fastened by willow
twigs to the tails of four or so horses struck English outsiders as disgustingly
primitive. Irish culture was not static; for centuries it had been changing slowly
under influence from England. The problem would be that England had
changed far faster.

Wales, by contrast, had managed, if not to catch up, at least to follow the
richer country quite closely. Because the Welsh themselves willingly adapted,
some distinctiveness would be allowed to survive – here is a major reason for one
of the strangest facts in history, that such a small country still contains many
Welsh-language speakers and has a real sense of peculiar identity. In Ireland and
in the Scottish Highlands, only the extirpation of a whole culture would
ultimately suffice to make matters agreeable to English-speakers; and Ulster first
of all and above all would pay the full price of obstinate tribalism.

The Welsh were breaking away, far enough, from the Celtic idea that the clan owned its land in common. One factor involved in the outburst of peasant discontent which from 1400 for a few years had established Owen Glyn Dwr as an independent prince, crowned before the envoys of foreign nations, had been the disintegration of kinship and the rise of a kulak class. Then, producing a massive turnover of land, Glyn Dwr's revolt had itself helped clear the way for a Welsh gentry. By the mid-sixteenth century, a basic division between landed and landless men was established and the Welsh social structure, though not identical, was compatible with the English. And of course the Tudors themselves were sympathetic.

But their land of about a quarter-million people had no obvious centre of its own; the highland hump athwart the country prevented it. English towns, Shrewsbury and Oswestry, gave the country its economic direction by providing a market for cloth and cattle. Wales was chronically lawless and disordered. The near-independent 'Marcher lordships' which survived on its border made possible customs evasions which ate into royal revenues, and provided a haven for criminals fleeing royal jurisdiction. When magnates committed crimes, juries feared to convict them, and if such a man were fined he would extort the money as a forced 'gift' from the poor. Yet Wales was no more, if no less, vexatious, than England's northern borderlands.

The ideal for English administrators would have been two islands where men grew corn and drank beer and did these things in a settled way in seemly parishes and shires. Such people were easy to tax and easy to control. But cattle-culture as Celts and others practised it was nomadic, or semi-nomadic. What could one do with people following improper customs like those of the Scottish and Irish Gaels, who would seethe an animal's flesh in its own hide and consume blood tapped direct from living cattle? Customs in the other sense did not yield much to the Crown in such beastly areas. The revenues of all ports on the west coast, taken together with those on the east north of Aberdeen, accounted for well under 10 per cent of the King's customs in Scotland in 1542. Up to the reign of Edward I, Ireland, through feudal dues and other revenues, had brought much profit to English kings; now, if it were to be so useful again, it would have to be reconquered at great expense.

The Celtic lands and the Borders between them account for an overwelming proportion of the surviving folk traditions of Britain which children are asked to love and admire today. But sixteenth-century English-speakers associated such lore with the weakness of the Church, that cardinal instrument of centralisation, and with the tribal character of the areas which preserved it. The bagpipe which Scottish Gaels were now using to urge their forces into battle had not yet acquired pleasant associations for Sassenachs – nor had the great ballads of the Borders. Poets would be a prime and constant target for men who sought to extend the authority of English monarchy. (The Scots kings seem to have been less worried by them.) In Wales as well as in Ireland, the bard seemed an obvious enemy of the state, to be banned on principle, hanged whenever chance offered.

The English-speaking official who wanted his own royal master to have a monopoly of bullying and exaction naturally led the chorus denouncing the high-handed behaviour of Marcher magnates, Highland clan chiefs and Irish chiefs. There is no doubt that the last sort in particular, aiming to live wholly off his vassals as he travelled about, could be as oppressive in many cases as even a Tudor monarch. It is also clear enough that the periphery bristled with private armies at a time when aristocratic thuggery was receding in England. But Tudor, and Stewart, crown servants who sought royal monopoly of violence backed the use of great violence towards this end. As they succeeded, the idea gained sway that murdering Gaels, or foreigners, or Red Indians, as part of a royal army or with royal approval, was patriotic, heroic, and just, whereas to defend yourself and your way of life against the advancing forces of English-speaking empire showed human nature at its worst and most bestial. Historians tend to identify this view with moral progress; the habit of flattering power has not been confined to the Irish annalist caste.

As the middle- and upper-class English-speakers asserted themselves against the Celts around them, they developed notions of racial superiority which would easily be adapted to justify the enslavement of Africans and the conquest of the Indian subcontinent, and which many people of Celtic descent would come to share. Non-English, non-commercialised cultures were manifestly so wicked and silly that to liberate people from them must be in their best interest.

Henry VII, of course, gave the Welsh equality before the law with Englishmen. Even so their concern with livestock rather than cultivation aroused deep suspicion among English observers, one of whom wrote around 1540 that they 'did study more to pasturage then tylling, as favorers of their consuete idilness'. All pastoralists were thought 'idle'. By the early sixteenth century we find a Lowland Scots writer deploring the aversion of Highlanders to 'honest industry'. As Gaelic-speakers, they came to be sorted in Lowland minds into two sorts of inferior person – poor 'wild Irish' and prosperous 'Civil Irish'. To be 'Irish' whether in Scotland or Ireland seemed increasingly stubborn and wicked as the century wore on. Gaelic dress in Ireland seemed as uncouth and sinister as the characteristic 'glib' of hair worn over their faces by old men. Men and women had distinctive long fringed mantles, and these would excite the poet Edmund Spenser into frenzies of prurient aversion. After complaining that outlaws used the mantle as a tent and bed, that rebels used it as a shield and thieves hid their loot in it and masked themselves with it, Spenser declaimed that for a wandering loose woman it was 'half a wardrobe; for in summer you shall find her arrayed commonly but in her smock and mantle, to be more ready for her light services; in winter, and in her travail, it is her cloak and safeguard, and also a coverlet for her lewd exercise; . . . yea, and when her bastard is born it serves instead of swaddling-clouts.'

Spenser was a devout Protestant. His contempt for the Irish was reinforced by esteem for his own religion and loathing of theirs. The one thing needful to crown the sense of superiority enjoyed by English-speakers within the British Isles was the possession of two national reformed Churches.

IV

Sir Walter Ralegh would write of the 'bluff' King Henry VIII who ruled England from 1509 to 1547: '. . . If all the pictures and patterns of a merciless prince were lost in the world, they might all again be painted to the life, out of the story of this King.' Yet the continuing infatuation of English people with the disagreeable Tudor dynasty has some real basis; they consolidated the English nation-state and English patriotism, making religion one of their main means of doing so. Aiming (it can be argued) at complete despotism, Henry VIII unwittingly forwarded the creation of the English middle classes and their world-changing self-confidence.

The 'Tudor revolution in government' meant that great landed noblemen lost power both to the Crown and to the gentry and merchants represented in the House of Commons. Its presiding proponent was Thomas Cromwell, son of a tradesman, trained in business and law, who was Henry's chief minister in the 1530s, and became Earl of Essex before his royal master lopped off his head. He had learnt in Italy, land of Machiavelli, to break out of medieval ways of thinking. His great work was the 'Reformation' which ended the Pope's authority in England. The events of 1529–33 promoted patriotic self-awareness, which Henry could share with his middling subjects. Protestant doctrines as yet interested few people. What was approved of was Henry VIII's attack on the opulence and corruption of a Church which represented an intrusion of alien authority.

Cromwell wrote the preamble to an Act of 1533 which provided that appeals in spiritual causes should no longer go to Rome but be finally settled in England: 'This realm of England is an Empire . . . governed by one Supreme Head and King . . .' The word 'empire', till the nineteenth century, did not imply expansion or colonies, it simply suggested that England was self-governing, equal in independence to the Holy Roman Empire on the Continent. No foreign ruler could claim any authority. England was, in modern parlance, a sovereign national state. A corollary was that the king should rule effectively everywhere, overriding local magnates. Certain of Henry VIII's subjects could still legally claim special rights and immunities, within 'palatinates' like Durham and Lancaster, 'liberties' like Ripon and Richmond (all these four, it will be observed, in the North), and more widely wherever a lord had the right to hold his own courts. In an Act of 1536, Cromwell ended this, extending the operation of royal justice and the system of 'shires' over all England. Cromwell shared with his royal master a still more radical vision, of the whole British Isles united under one king.

Church revenues were diverted to the Crown. The monasteries and convents were dissolved and their far flung lands became Crown property. In a generation or two, these were mostly disposed of for the sake of ready money and the middling class of gentry acquired with them a vital stake in the Reformation. Over the next hundred years, knights and lesser gentry trebled in numbers while overall population scarcely doubled. In other ways also the Reformation launched tendencies ultimately fatal to royal power. Cromwell encouraged translations of the Bible and ordered the book to be placed, in English, in all churches. By 1545 Henry himself was complaining that 'the most precious jewel, the Word of God, is disputed, rhymed, sung and jangled in every ale-house and tavern.' In the Bible, men read stories of bad kings and bold, just prophets and of the military exploits of a chosen people.

Literacy became for the godly a matter of elementary self-respect. Disputing Old Testament texts helped to develop intellectual self-reliance. Craftsmen and seamen learnt to read, and could pick up new skills and new vision. Protestant religious ideas fostered individualism. The existence in England of a faith distinct from that still held in Spain, the great imperial, colonising power, would foster a spirit of crusade, aligned with envy and emulation, and would help to fuel struggle through trade and with arms on the high seas and in the New World.

Surviving Catholicism in England became identified with old-fashioned sections of society. This was true as early as 1536–7 when an idealist, Robert Aske, led the revolt in the North known as the Pilgrimage of Grace. Peasant rebels who called for the return of papal power feared that new landlords replacing the former monks would interfere with customary tenures generous by southern standards. The series of outbreaks was swiftly beaten down, a spate of summary executions followed, and Cromwell had a pretext to reduce the influence of the great northern magnates. The process was not completed till exiles and confiscations followed a later northern rising in 1569, but Cromwell's strong new Council of the North, a permanent body dominated by royal officials, would survive to preside over that consummation.

It was the counterpart of a Council in the Marches of Wales which had been set up at the start of the century. Cromwell made president of this body, in 1533, Rowland Lee, Bishop of Coventry and Lichfield, 'stowte of nature, readie witted, roughe in speeche, not affable to anye of the walshrie, an extreme severe ponisher of offences.' A contemporary claimed that Lee hanged 5,000 men in nine years of office; he was especially glad to string up those of high birth. But the Reformation meant that more was needed. The legal changes which it involved could only be carried through in Wales constitutionally if the country was unified with England.

Hence the 'Act of Union' passed through the English Parliament in 1536. It argued that Henry VIII was rightful King of Wales, yet in that country 'dyvers rightes usages laws and customes be farre discrepant frome the lawes and customes of this Realme.' Furthermore, 'by cause that the people of the same dominion have and do daily use a speche nothing like ne consonaunt to the naturall mother tonge used within this Realme' – that is, they wilfully spoke 'unnatural' Welsh – 'some rude and ignorant people' had 'made distinccion and diversitie betwene the Kinges Subiectes of this Realme and hys subiectes of the said dominion and Principalitie of Wales'. Hence Wales must now be 'for ever' incorporated, united and annexed to England. English law would now obtain in Wales, specifically in matters of inheritance – 'division or particion' of an estate, that Celtic aberration, was forbidden. The Marcher lordships were digested into five new Welsh shires – Brecon, Monmouth, Radnor, Denbigh and Montgomery – and certain English counties. However, the bards were silent. There was no outcry in Wales against the Act.

A further Act of 1542 fixed boundaries for Wales, a unit of twelve counties, from which Monmouth, despite its Welshness, was detached for legal purposes. The division was rough and ready – Welsh was spoken in parts of Herefordshire until the nineteenth century and the Council for Wales had authority over wide, not exactly defined, tracts of the English borderland. But by the 1550s the Council had established its permanent bureaucratic presence, and the fact that it was not abolished till 1688 gave Wales a token of distinct existence over a long and formative period.

Rowland Lee had doubted whether the Welsh could govern themselves under English law – where, he asked Cromwell, were the men of substance needed to make J.P.s? And because the country was so poor, the property qualification for J.P.s was waived. But the Welsh gentry were men with rising self-confidence, very happy to exploit the uncertainty about land tenures arising with the enforcement of primogeniture and other English laws. Welsh squires looked out for English wives and English squires married Welsh heiresses. It became common for Welsh gentry to send sons to England for schooling.

English laws against retainers had little effect yet. Herberts still feuded with Vaughans, though each clan would produce a great English poet in the next century. But gradually litigation began to supplant riot, with hereditary enemies taking each other to law rather than staging fights through the town or even in churches. While Wales still depended heavily on the cattle trade with England for what little cash the country could muster, other fields were now explored. Some gentry developed mines. The ports of South Wales began to thrive a little.

The Welsh, with few exceptions, remained indifferent to the Reformation, tolerating what changes it brought but not yet (not for two hundred years) displaying much vivid interest in Protestantism. However, the Reformation was crucial for the preservation of the Welsh tongue. Fearing popish contamination, Parliament in 1562 enacted that the Bible should be translated into the language which most Welsh people still spoke. Though the job was not properly done till 1588, this meant that a force which helped to destroy Cornish and which would greatly limit the literary uses of Lowland Scots – the influence of God's word in English – did not have scope in Wales. And the gentry, besides retaining a famous infatuation with their family pedigrees, still patronised bards, and wrote poems in Welsh themselves. Many gave attention to Welsh antiquities, and this was encouraged at the highest level. The Tudors were not ashamed to be Welsh. Certain patriotic themes, the alleged purity of the Celtic Church, for instance, were very useful for propaganda purposes. David Powel, compiler of a history of Wales (1584) concluded 'there was never anie thing so beneficiall to the common people of Wales, as the uniting of that countrie to the crowne and kingdome of England. . . '

The notion that 'Britain' owed its name to one 'Brutus' or 'Brut', great grandson of that legendary Trojan Aeneas who had founded Rome, seat of Empire, was one to which Welsh intellectuals clung fondly. They liked the concept of Britain itself, and while they saw themselves as the true 'Britons', they were ready in charity to style the English 'Britons' also, 'usurpers and mere possessors' though they might be. The expression 'Brytish Impire' seems to have been first used by a Welsh scientist, John Dee, in 1577. Dee was an early proponent of overseas expansion. Of that, Ireland would be the prime laboratory.

V

From the purely legal point of view, Ireland was a fief where some vassals had become unruly, and where chieftains without feudal status had usurped land from other vassals. But to English-speakers settled within the Pale, Ireland was a colonial country, with a native problem, confronted with which men were, in modern parlance, doves or hawks. In the early sixteenth century a dove-like view preponderated. The gentry of the Pale and the merchants of the isolated towns beyond it were men of property who wanted a strong administration to protect their position. Ideally, they would like to see the Gaelic chieftainships destroyed, the feudal powers of gaelicised Anglo-Norman magnates curbed, and the whole country brought under the system of law and order which now existed only within the Pale. A smallish garrison from England would be needed – but not more settlers, or even officials; the Palesmen themselves, so they thought, could enforce English custom and law. This view of matters appealed to English chief governors and statesmen because 'reformacion' seemed cheaper than thorough-going conquest and colonisation.

In 1515, bitter complaints came from the Palesmen to King Henry. The 9th Earl of Kildare, Garret Oge, had succeeded his father smoothly as ruler in 1513, but now his subjects denounced this barbaric potentate, moving about with a great troop of kerns and gallowglasses and extorting entertainment from the people, while the Palesmen themselves were having to pay blackrent to the Irish. Henry summoned Kildare to England and detained him, and sent out the Earl of Surrey as lieutenant, with a sizeable army but with plans to bring Ireland peacefully under royal control by 'politique driftes, and amiable persuasions . . .'

Surrey became the first Tudor Englishman to be transmogrified into a hawk by the Irish Heart of Darkness. At first he did pretty well, conducting vigorous campaigns on the borders of the Pale, striking agreements with great Ulster chieftains and taking a force of nearly 2,000 with him on progress through the south-east. But then the Irish damp, the insects, the diarrhoea, the uncouth language, began to invade his doings and his mind. He could hardly find healthy quarters for his soldiers; three of his servants died; no place in the country was safe; he feared for his wife and children. He was short of money and supplies. As he came to a standstill, he was asked to cut down on his English troops and to maintain himself out of the barely-existent Irish revenue. The King told him he could not afford to send reinforcements, and pay £16,000 or £17,000 a year, just to defend the Pale's four shires. But Surrey was soon asking for far more than that – 6,000 men for an unspecified number of years. These would need to be financed and fed from England. English settlers would be required to set the Irish to work on the land, and castles and towns would have to be built as the armies went along. 'After my poor opinion,' Surrey announced, 'this land shall never be brought to good order and due subjection, but only by conquest. . . '

Henry, deciding that he could not afford to maintain a viceroyalty on Surrey's scale, now turned to Kildare's rival, Sir Piers Butler, virtual Earl of Ormond, and made him ruler. But Kildare was the only available magnate who could maintain a retinue large enough to produce respect. Henry soon had to restore him. Meanwhile, the danger that Ireland might be the back door for foreign invasion increased as Henry's divorce and Reformation went ahead. Kildare turned a blind eye while the Earl of Desmond intrigued with the King of France and with the Emperor Charles V, and in 1534 he himself was summoned to England under suspicion of treason and imprisoned in the Tower. Enraged by a rumour that he was dead, his son, 'Silken Thomas', refused to act in his place and led his people against the Crown. There was no way round it; another army had to be sent from England. Sir Thomas Skeffyngton, a tough new English viceroy, led the force which captured the Kildare seat at Maynooth in 1535. Kildare had died. His son and several leading kinsmen were shortly executed. The great noble house was temporarily smashed.

Ireland from now on was to be governed by a bureaucracy in Dublin. A permanent Council was set up resembling those in Wales and in the North. By Henry VIII's death, direct Dublin rule was fairly effective over half the island. Ireland had its own 'Reformation Parliament' in 1536-7, which seems to have recognised the authority of King over Church willingly enough. The religious houses were dissolved, and over the years their property gradually came under lay owners who included some Gaelic chieftains as well as many intruding Englishmen. But the Catholic religion maintained, strengthened, and reformed itself among the people.

Henry was advised by the Dublin Council to call himself 'King' (rather than 'Lord') of Ireland to dissipate the 'foolish opinions' of the Irish that the Pope was their real overlord, and in 1541 a new Irish Parliament thrust this title upon him, so committing the English Crown to extending its authority all over the island. Through confiscations of estates held by traitors and by religious houses, the King, on paper, owned vastly increased territories, but, except in the south-east, he could not get rents from them, and where his lands were subject to raids by the natives, he could not find Anglo-Irish or English tenants to live on them. Hence it was a great object to persuade the Irish to recognise Henry as their landlord and to pay him rent. The new policy of 'surrender and regrant' for the first time embraced the Gaels within the protection of English law; they could now hold their lands in a precise legal manner and have access to the King's courts. The Palesmen, who hotly favoured this policy, believed that with the Gaels so pacified, they themselves need no longer pay for or quarter the Viceroy's unpopular standing army. Throughout 1541 the Viceroy, now St Leger, took submissions.

The parliament of 1541 actually included some four or five Gaelic chiefs. Ulick Burke became Earl of Clanrickard, Murrough O Brien was named Earl of Thomond and Con Bacach O Neill accepted the fateful title of Earl of Tyrone. Lesser chiefs became barons. St Leger seems to have been a creditable colonial administrator, able to get on with Irish lords while actively strengthening the Crown. For generations, O Tooles had harried the Pale from their base in the Wicklow Mountains. They were a small clan of virtually landless men, at odds with the great house of Kildare and with no recourse save raiding and levying blackmail. Turlough O Toole proposed a deal to St Leger. He would forego his plundering and wear English dress in return for the grant of the district of Fercullen. St Leger thought this fair enough and lent him £20 to travel to England. O Toole became the King's tenant by knight's service.

The petty Border surnames had much in common with the O Tooles. James V of Scotland had begun to imitate Henry VIII as strong new-style king. The Borders soon attracted his interest. The English had ravaged the land in a brief war in 1523 – making robbery once again seem a far safer occupation than cultivation. In the summer of 1530, James with a strong force invaded Liddesdale to confront Johnnie Armstrong, most famous of all reivers, and chief of his surname. A great ballad tells, with much dubious picturesque detail, how the two men met:

> When Johnnie cam before the King,
> Wi' a' his men sae brave to see,
> The King he movit his bonnet to him;
> He ween'd he was a King as weel as he.

Johnnie was strung up, and numerous others with him, but the Armstrongs, and the Border, remained unsubdued.

In 1540, James made a voyage round the Hebrides, taking several chiefs as hostages and gaoling them when the trip was over. That year, the whole group of Isles was formally re-annexed to the Scottish Crown. But the old Macdonald power had one last kick left in it, delivered when Henry VIII in his last years made a prolonged and notably ruthless attempt to subjugate Scotland itself. James's mother had been Henry's sister, through a marriage designed to pave a way for eventual union of the two Crowns. But the threat of Scottish-French alliance, and Henry's own ambitions, made him impatient. James died, tradition says of a broken heart, after his army was routed by smaller English forces at Solway Moss in 1542. In July 1543, Henry forced a treaty upon the Scots. Peace was to be cemented by the marriage of James's infant daughter, Mary, now Queen, to Henry's son the Prince of Wales. The Scots, with a pro-French party in control, would not accept this. The 'Rough Wooing' which followed was terrible. In 1544 English forces sacked and burned Edinburgh and ravaged the whole of southern Scotland. The French helped the Scots rally; the Wooing was repeated. Meanwhile the chiefs of the Hebrides had rallied to Donald Dubh, Black Donald, grandson of the last Lord of the Isles, on his escape after forty years in prison. Henry VIII offered Donald money for his allegiance, and Scottish and Irish Gaels combined in an unsuccessful invasion, starting from Ulster. When Donald, the last generally recognised Lord of the Isles, died in Ireland, Henry VIII paid for his funeral.

Still the Scots would not submit. The results were momentous for England. Combined with Henry's futile war against France, they permanently weakened the English Crown. By the time the expensive fighting was over, most of the monastery lands had been sold, and the mercenary army which any king needed to enforce absolute rule had been disbanded for lack of funds. Hereafter, at the first hint of war, the English state would have to ask Parliament for money. The Commons had purse-power. Protestant squires supported the Crown against magnates and foreign enemies; in return they were left to rule their own roosts.

Henry's death in 1547 left his young son and successor Edward VI under the Protection of the Duke of Somerset, who went north with the largest army yet and routed the Scots again at Pinkie. Fighting went on till the English withdrew in 1549. Queen Mary was shipped to France, where she married the King's son, while her French mother, Mary of Guise, became Regent in Scotland.

Meanwhile, Somerset took the Reformation further. A new Prayer Book, in English, not Latin, combined with a proclamation from London which ordered removal of images from churches, provoked the final risings of Cornwall, an area proud of its Celtic saints. '. . . We Cornish men (whereof certain of us understand no English) utterly refuse this new English.' After they had besieged Exeter for a month, the rebels were savagely suppressed. Devon families whose names would figure famously in subsequent overseas exploration and expansion were amongst the rebels' opponents; the episode may have helped fan the blazing anti-Catholicism of Grenvilles, Raleghs and Drakes.

The death of young King Edward brought in his sad sister Mary, determined to restore the old Catholic Church. She was too late. The gentry, grasping their former Church lands, were not going to give them up. Mary could only proceed with outside help, and her marriage to Philip II of Spain involved the virtual absorption of England into the Habsburg Empire, provoking bitter patriotic resentment. The heresy trials which the Queen opened in 1555 brought nearly three hundred people to the stake. The stench of burnt flesh gave many of her subjects a loathing of popery, and of 'Spanish cruelty', which they transmitted in published writings and popular lore down to the nineteenth century. Even when Philip drew England into war with her traditional enemy, France, in 1557, this was unpopular. Spain, on the sea, not France, on the land, was coming to seem the true national foe.

And events were in train which would help diminish the old enmity between England and Scotland. Amongst the distinguished body of hundreds of leading English Protestants driven into exile by Mary's persecution mingled the looming Scot, John Knox. They flocked back when Mary died at the end of 1558. While Queen Elizabeth, succeeding her sister, made a new, non-Catholic religious settlement with a parliament dominated by Puritans and by the influence of the returned exiles, Knox went on north to inflame the struggle against the French regency which dissident lords had already launched under the banner of Protestantism. In the spring of 1559, he broached popular revolution, unleashing a mob in Perth which sacked the town's religious houses. Elizabeth sent ships and troops north. (The French were claiming her own throne for the young Scottish Queen, Mary.) With this help, the 'Faithful Congregation of Christ Jesus in Scotland' were able to win. The Treaty of Edinburgh in July replaced the traditional Scottish alliance with France by a cordial new understanding with England.

The red-haired young woman who was to rule England till 1603 needs less introduction to readers of that country's language than any other figure in history. She was, we all know, clever and vain, personally tolerant in matters of religion, brave and yet extremely cautious and often dilatory, proudly imperious and absurdly fickle . . . What is less commonly grasped is that she was a dedicated conservative in an epoch of racing social change. The image – one is tempted to call it the 'icon' – of the Virgin Queen, as painters and poets designed it for her, was soundly calculated to create a focus of national faith, a bond of English unity, glittering, pure, untouchable, far beyond criticism, so as to hold together a society cracking and creaking under intense and novel economic and intellectual strains. We find it all, if we care to look for it, in the amazing plays of her greatest subject, Shakespeare. War and lechery, treachery and corruption are staples of public life in an age of dissolving feudalism and mounting cynicism. The medieval world order is tumbling. 'Say to the court', writes a great courtier, Ralegh, 'say to the court it glows and shines like rotten wood.' No one typifies better than Ralegh the spate of energies, idealistic and predatory, military and commercial, intellectual and solidly material which pushed England towards overseas expansion while its own backlands were still incompletely conquered.

The Age of Ralegh

I

Elizabeth's England was peaceful, compared to most of Europe, and many of its middling people prospered. Their affluence and confidence promoted a wave of new building; comfortable houses for all social groups, in town and country, except the poorest and largest class. The first distinctively English style emerged, mixing elements borrowed from the European Renaissance with Perpendicular Gothic notions. The most fecund age of English music had a domestic base in the brick mansions of the mighty, while domesticity, with a desire for privacy, informed the planning of the black and white timbered houses of lesser people, yeomen, even in some cases husbandmen. The Englishman's home was coming to be his castle – but a castle which thanks to a novel plenty of cheap glass was graced with those most unwarlike features, glass windows.

England had perhaps 3 million people in 1530, over 4 million in 1600. Mouths to feed increased faster than food. Those who had surplus produce to sell prospered. As the line of human settlement surged forward into moorlands and heathlands and woodlands, capitalistic attitudes came with it, helping to tame the backlands. Cornwall, favoured by nature with many harbours from which exports could be made to London and the Continent, was civilised swiftly away from Celtdom by a mania for agricultural advance.

Through mines in Cornwall, England was Europe's largest producer of tin, a most important export. And in other remote and hilly areas, coal-mining helped to bring wild men into the economic mainstream. The island was running short of timber, and landlords exploiting mines on their estates so responded to the demand for fuel that England was far and away the biggest producer of coal. By the end of the century, Tyneside was shipping out about 165,000 tons per year, and exports had more than quadrupled within five decades. The manufacture of window glass was one of the industries now beginning to base themselves on coal. Meanwhile, prices of goods in England, though soaring, lagged behind those in Europe, and this fostered the export trade in cloth.

Yet the Queen died £400,000 in debt. Administration was getting more expensive. Muskets and cannon were dearer than bows and arrows. Ships for the navy cost more. Royal revenue increased far more slowly than prices. England was lightly taxed, and getting used to the idea it should be. The Queen's stinginess became part of her legend, but though she doubled or trebled the Crown's income, she could not raise the money needed to take full control of England. In fact, her peddling of licences and offices for cash helped in itself to weaken her position. Half the ordinary state revenue came from customs. But customs officials who bought their jobs and were then paid next to nothing were of course willing to connive, for a consideration, at massive evasions. The Crown's attempts to increase its revenues with new duties and tariffs merely fostered the first great age of English smuggling, and the addiction of coastal gentry to piracy. In the south-west and Wales, landlords financed pirates to hijack Spanish wines or Newfoundland fish. The town fathers of tiny Welsh ports acquired luxuries like ginger and ivory which they could otherwise hardly have afforded. Officials themselves dealt most amicably with pirates. All these people were by their own lights perfectly loyal (as, no doubt, was the Suffolk landlord who sold English captives as slaves in Algiers) but defrauding the Queen was a part of their way of life. As the State captured the backlands, the gentry and merchants captured the State.

But the Queen did have patronage, and it helped her power. Noblemen clustered at court, looking for pickings. Elizabeth could balance their factions against each other, buy the loyalty of all factions, and exploit in the interests of her own influence the vines of clientage which went with them. Each landowning family struggled for its own ends, along with the other families with which it intermarried, and kinship mattered immensely, not least to the Devon network of Gilberts, Raleghs and Grenvilles. The difference from Scotland was that such groupings were horizontal; landowners commanded less and less personal, let alone 'family' loyalty from their social inferiors. A sense of kinship did not spill across classes and feudal attitudes were weakening.

Landlords had less and less scruple about evicting their tenants. While the growth of population was depriving labour of its scarcity value, the price rise relentlessly inflated the cost of necessaries for the poor. A vicious spiral was in motion. Low wages stimulated the growth of the cloth industry. The clothing boom encouraged enclosure for pasture, and so encouraged eviction which in turn replenished the pool of workless which kept wages down – until one of the main arguments for colonisation would be that it permitted the export of desperate, unemployed poor, who could be seen dying of starvation in the streets of London.

Meanwhile, to stave off revolt, the 'poor law' was developed until at the end of the sixteenth century it assumed much the form it would hold until the nineteenth. It had no counterpart in Europe. It reflected the localisation of power in England. It was the duty of the parish, under control of the J.P.s, to provide for the helpless, the aged and the sick out of a compulsory rate levied upon householders, and to provide work for those who were genuinely unemployed. The poor law had the side-effect of permitting the payment of low wages, since the parish had to subsidise families of wage-earners who would otherwise starve.

Yet the spirit of the Elizabethan Poor Law was never really like that of the cruel legislation brought in to succeed it in the 1830s. Nineteenth-century men were conscious of being capitalists, economists, individualists. Elizabethans were not; the coal-mines they worked, still small and scattered, served mostly local markets; cloth was made in workers' homes; the idea of subsistence still dominated agriculture; men still saw themselves and the world in religious terms. A very great part of what was most vital and forward-pointing in Elizabeth's England – whether in poetry, commerce or even privateering – was informed by a deeply-felt 'puritanism'. The word is elusive, but one might argue that in Elizabeth's day virtually all Protestant spirituality was more or less 'Puritan'. Though Archbishop Whitgift persecuted the more extreme 'Puritans' who wanted to do without bishops and strove for a Presbyterian or Congregational system, he was himself a strict Calvinist.

Despite – or because of – their terrifying belief that each man's fate was predestined, Calvinists devoted intense spiritual energy to the everyday tasks of the world. The Middle Ages had locked both learning and spirituality up in a celibate clergy; now both must be released into lay lives. Acting well meant hard work, constant self-scrutiny, and fierce zeal against papists. Along with such effort came a proud independence of thought and spirit.

Puritanism in its anti-Establishment form failed to capture the Anglican Church, but it won a large section of the gentry. Calvinism was a difficult doctrine, radically hostile to superstitions which still mattered to most people, and it flourished where literacy was found – in the ports, the market towns, the centres of the cloth industry in East Anglia and the south-west; in fact, in the areas and among the classes most concerned with overseas trade and expansion. Some important courtiers, led by Sir Francis Walsingham, sought an anti-Catholic foreign policy. Conservatives, led by Burghley and the Earl of Sussex, favoured the traditional understanding with Spain. The tide was set against them.

II

Calvinism was winning in Lowland Scotland. Simply as a way of organising spiritual care for the people, when the whole Catholic Church structure had degenerated, a semi-democratic congregationalism now emerged as the practical solution. Elected kirk sessions supervised ministers chosen by congregations, and since Mary Queen of Scots was not Protestant, a General Assembly of the Church was needed to act as supreme authority in her stead. After 1572 bishops were appointed, with Knox's approval, but the extremist Calvinist party led by Andrew Melville launched later in that decade a long struggle against the Crown over their existence. Meanwhile, under Knox's lead, the reformed Church had aimed at nothing less than the disciplining of the whole people. It was not until the seventeenth century that much of the way was travelled towards realising Knox's noble project of a school in every parish, but the reformation was already helping to form a dour, hard-driving, self-disciplined, self-punishing, disputatious, pedantic Lowland Scottish character. The rift between Lowlands and

Highlands was greatly widened. The Reformation made little impact in Gaelic-speaking areas, which remained part Catholic, largely, in effect, pagan.

In France, perhaps half the aristocracy went over to Protestantism, and psalm-singing Huguenot troops fought against forces rallied by a reviving Roman Catholicism, which clarified itself at the Council of Trent in the early 1560s. With France in turmoil, its power in eclipse, Spain dominated the battlefields and diplomacy of Europe. In 1580 Philip II successfully enforced a claim to the crown of the other Iberian power, and the Portuguese empire joined Spain's under his rule. Philip's vast forces were paid for by taxation which growingly crippled the Spanish economy and, above all, by annual remittance of silver from the New World. The flow turned into a flood in the 1580s. By 1600, Spain was drawing an average of 40 million ducats of silver a year from America, of which the Crown alone received 13 million. Such wealth and power were at the Pope's service. Spaniards were wonderfully brave fighters, and their pride in their faith helped them to be so.

But Protestant Europe, confronting Spain's arrogant might, developed that myth of 'Spanish cruelty' which was to fire its own soldiers, sailors and privateers for two centuries. William of Orange, leader of Dutch revolt against Spain, crystallised it in his *Apology* of 1580. William used Spain's destruction of '20 million Indians' as proof of innate Castilian cruelty, alongside Philip's murder of his son and heir and his expulsion of some 150,000 Christianised Moors from Spain.

The supposed viciousness of the Spaniards made ruthless and cynical procedures against them seem justifiable. And since the Indians of America were enduring a hellish rule, to forestall the Spaniards in New World lands which they had not yet occupied, even to oust them from territories which they possessed, could be projected as acts of Christian kindness and justice. Of course, to strike at the sources of that silver which paid Philip's armies was to aid Protestant resistance everywhere.

Yet there were important English commercial interests involved in trade with Spain. Antwerp, focus of England's overseas trade, was in Philip II's territory. And England was a weak little country when Elizabeth came to the throne; in the early years of her reign she badly needed support, which Philip, for his part, was prepared to give her. Her heir, if she went, was Mary Queen of Scots, who returned to her throne from France in 1560 and made an uneasy peace with her Protestant subjects. While Parliament in England clamoured that Elizabeth must marry, to have offspring and to avert a Franco-Scottish, Catholic succession, Philip also had no wish to see England controlled by his rival France.

Elizabeth did not marry. Mary's son James, born in 1566, would not in the end miss his English heritage, despite the fatuous conduct of his mother. She connived in the murder of her husband, married one of his assassins and was duly driven out of her kingdom in 1568. Within five years, her supporters in Scotland were mopped up, and a succession of Protestant, Anglophile regents ruled on behalf of her son. They had Elizabeth's friendship, and she did not embarrass them by returning her rival across the Border. She kept Mary in prison in England, where she became a focus of plotting and Catholic subversion.

The English alliance with Spain was crumbling from the mid-1560s. An outbreak of Calvinist rioting in the Netherlands provoked unwise repression from Philip's viceroy there, the Duke of Alba, and these troubles hastened the weakening of England's trading link with Antwerp. Elizabeth had no sympathy for rebels, but she did not stop her own subjects from helping their co-religionists, nor did she bar the swarms of refugees who fled from Alba's terror and brought great gifts to England – Flemish clothworkers took their skills to East Anglia, refugee merchants settled in London. And when in 1568 a fine shipment of bullion, despatched by Philip's Genoese bankers for the payment of Alba's troops, was driven into English waters, Elizabeth confiscated it and borrowed the money from the Italians herself. Alba embargoed all trade with England and seized English goods, and commerce with Flanders was interrupted for five years.

The Spanish ambassador was involved in the plot in Mary's favour which produced the 'Northern Rising' of 1569. The Earls of Northumberland and Westmorland said mass in Durham Cathedral, tore up the English Prayer Book and set off south with feudal hosts. The defeat of their army ended feudalism in the North. Pius V had prepared the bull *Regnans in Excelsis*, intending it to coincide with the rising. It was published in February 1570, too late to help the northern Earls. But its call to all faithful sons of the Church to help oust the heretic Queen from her throne, and its absolving of all her subjects from allegiance to Elizabeth came as a great encouragement to a fresh wave of rebels in Gaelic Ireland.

III

The English were getting uncomfortably active there, and a new kind of Englishman had begun to arrive; a Puritanical sort, commercially minded. Though Edmund Spenser came as a colonist only in the 1580s, his attitude may be taken as representative. 'And sure,' he would write, 'it is yet a most beautiful and sweet country as any is under heaven, being stored throughout with many goodly rivers, replenished with all sorts of fish most abundantly, sprinkled with many very sweet islands and goodly lakes, like little inland seas, that will carry even ships upon their waters; adorned with goodly woods, even fit for building of houses and ships. . .'

England was running out of wood. The timbers of Ireland could carry Englishmen further west. The lords of the seas might be lords of the whole world. Humphrey Gilbert, Grenville and Ralegh, with numerous less-known pioneers, had their first experience of expansion and colonisation in Ireland. Such men hated Catholic Spain, yet, by that paradox of attraction of opposites

which is so familiar to historians, they were ready to treat Gaels much as
Spaniards had treated Indians, and produce very passable replicas of the
'Spanish cruelty' which they denounced.

The 1540s had seen the first extension of the narrow Pale for centuries. Laois
and Offaly lay to the west of it, under control of the O Connor and the O More.
In 1546 they were goaded into revolt. Their lands were confiscated, and, after
sufficient slaughter, two forts were built there. Under the Earl of Sussex, Lord
Deputy from 1556, resettlement of the area began. It was 'shired' as Queen's
County and King's County and divided into townships, manors and baronies
which were dealt out to some eighty or more grantees: Palesmen, officials,
soldiers and natives. The O Connor chief and the O More were both assigned
land, on condition that they adopt the English style of dress and teach their
children English. The wild men who followed them were not appeased and
constantly harried the new counties and the rest of the Pale from the wastelands
where they found a home. 'The spoilers of the Pale', wrote the Lord Deputy in
1572, 'are named Rory Oge with the O'Mores . . . Fiach MacHugh . . . with the
O'Connors . . . the manner of their coming is by daylight with bagpipes, by night
with torchlight.'

Not that the Palesmen themselves were model subjects. Even within the Pale
illegal celebrations of mass continued. Outside it, of course, there was no
question of enforcing Anglican conformity. This does not mean that the Gaels
were good Catholics. Their behaviour would have shocked Pius V as much as
John Knox, as can be judged from the story of Shane O Neill.

In Ulster Gaelic custom survived almost untouched. The area's politics,
intricate in themselves, were tangled with those of the Hebrides and of Gaelic
Scotland in general. When Con O Neill accepted the earldom of Tyrone from
Henry VIII, his son Matthew had become his 'legal heir'. But this intrusion of
primogeniture struck helplessly against the traditional concept of elected
chiefship. While English officials saw Matthew as heir-apparent, to Con's second
son Shane he was simply a poorly qualified rival. Tough, clever and arrogant,
Shane was able at Con's death in 1559 to seize full power. The people recognised
him as O Neill, and the earldom of Tyrone became a meaningless title. Matthew
was killed by Shane's men and his eldest son Brian was murdered by Turlough
Luineach, another rival claimant. Matthew's second son, Hugh, a nine-year-old
boy, was rescued by the English and crossed the water to spend eight years as the
ward of Sir Henry Sidney, which meant that the most dedicated of Tudor
colonial governors helped to bring up a prototype of all nationalist rebels.

Shane asserted authority over a circle of satellite chiefs – MacMahon,
Magennis, Maguire, O Hanlon, O Cahan. From 1561, furthermore, he was
effective overlord also of Tyrconnell, the land to the west of his occupied by the
O Donnell, traditional rival of the O Neill power. He seized Calvagh O Donnell
and poached his wife from him. This lady was a Maclean of Hebridean family,
and widow of a Campbell Earl of Argyll.

There were plenty of other 'Scottish' Gaels in Ulster. The Mull of Kintyre, south-western tip of Scotland, could always be seen from Antrim on a clear day, only twenty miles across the water, and the annual incursion of 'Redshanks' into Ireland was a perpetual problem for the Dublin government. Hebridean chiefs brought their men across in galleys in summer to fight as mercenaries in Irish wars. Furthermore, the Macdonalds had a hereditary claim to an area known as the Glens, and a sizeable number of them were now based there and were challenging for possession of another tract, the Rout. The name of Somhairle Buidhe ('Sorley Boy') Macdonald figures constantly in the intrigues of Elizabeth's day – a most resilient and most lucky chieflet whose descendants became Earls of Antrim.

Viceroy Sussex wanted to smash Shane's power and flush out the Macdonalds. Elizabeth favoured a cheaper policy. Let Shane be recognised as legitimate heir. To Sussex's outrage, she invited the dread O Neill to visit her in England. With their long curled hair, saffron-coloured shirts, long sleeves, short coats and heavy mantles, Shane's bodyguards created a stir among the sophisticates of the city rather as if a Red Indian *cacique* had arrived. Shane, in that fawning Irish fashion which would always disgust the English, confessed to rebellion with howls and sobs, did homage on his knees, and signed a submission. But thereafter he proved a smooth enough diplomat, and made a deal with the Queen whereby he would have the rule of O Cahan's country and the greater part of Antrim, as well as Tyrone, in return for his loyalty and for driving out the Macdonalds.

But Shane thought that Elizabeth had given him authority to rule all Ulster. He was soon raiding O Donnell's country again, and when a new foray by Sussex against him failed in 1563, all the government could do was accept the position and give him a free pardon. Sussex had regular forces of under a thousand men, and Shane had five times that number of horse and foot. In October 1565 when Sir Henry Sidney came out as the new Deputy, Shane was deep in intrigues – dealing with Archibald, Earl of Argyll, the greatest power in Highland Scotland, and going so far as to ask Mary Queen of Scots to recognise him as her subject.

Sidney, aged 36, was a cultured man, father of one poet, patron of others. He was also a most experienced frontier official, who from 1565 to 1571 and again from 1575 to 1580 combined the Deputyship in Ireland with his longer-standing post as Lord President in Wales. In sharp contrast with Sussex, he belonged to the aggressive anti-papist faction led at court by the Earl of Leicester. He filled senior civil and military posts in Ireland with supporters of this faction and he favoured 'forward' policies – further forward, in fact, than the Queen was always prepared to go. Sussex had aimed at 'reformation', not conquest. Sidney had less patience. He adopted tactics which his successors would take to the point of near-genocide. He set off in September with his own horses well fed after the summer, but in time to burn the crops of the Gaels before they were harvested. Meanwhile a force he had sent round by sea penetrated Lough Foyle. Sidney met it and garrisoned there a place called Derry, with 600 foot and 50 horse. Then he marched into Tyrconnell, setting up Calvagh O Donnell as ruler again, then he proceeded southward through Sligo into Munster. His whole great march round the Gaelic periphery cost him only three men, he boasted, and those through sickness.

The Derry garrison lost heart and sailed away next spring when an accidental fire rased their camp. However, the O Donnells now beat down Shane. When he came at them with his thousands, their new chief, Hugh, rallied his few hundred and butchered Shane's army in a surprise attack as it lay, fuddled with drink, by the banks of the aptly named Swilly. While Shane's supporters submitted to Sidney, he himself – this was June, 1567 – fled to the Macdonald camp in Antrim. The Macdonalds received him pleasantly. Much wine and whiskey were swallowed. Then they paid an old score and hacked Shane to pieces.

Traditional clan violence disposed of Shane and when shortly before his death he replied defiantly to Elizabeth's overtures, his language was that of traditional chieftainship: 'My ancestors were kings of Ulster, Ulster was theirs and shall be mine.' Yet the same Shane had opened negotiations with the King of France and had employed the new dialect of militant Catholicism. The English were heretics. Let Ireland be joined to the French Crown. Such an appeal emphasised how urgent it was for the English Crown to tame Ireland. After Shane's death the drunken but shrewd Turlough Luineach succeeded him as O Neill and, while he mixed petty insubordination with ever-ready submission, Ulster remained deceptively quiet for three decades. But Sidney pushed ahead with his sharp new ideas.

He developed the concept of establishing new colonies of Englishmen through the private enterprise of individuals or syndicates of grantees. Sidney had visited Spain as a diplomat, and the charters now given to speculators in Irish lands were reminiscent of grants awarded by Spanish kings to conquistadors. They introduced a new idea into English settlement in Ireland, expressing the conscious aim of turning the native Irish into a permanently inferior and exploited labour force. Here was an attractive outlet for restless scions of landowning families. A younger son like Humphrey Gilbert could hope to become a great landed magnate, on this green and fertile frontier which teemed with cattle and fish, and where even the people, cowed, might be made useful. English gentry, especially Devonshire gentry, pressed forward to realise projects for colonies in Munster and in Ulster.

The strongest Norman prop of English rule, 'Black Tom' Butler, tenth Earl of Ormond (1532–1614) was aligned with the anti-expansionist faction in Elizabeth's court and had an especially good understanding with the Queen herself, so that when Sidney at first sided against him in his private war with the Earl of Desmond, Elizabeth called her viceroy sharply to heel and it was a triumph for Black Tom when his enemy was arrested and put in the Tower. Yet Sidney's policies still did not spare Black Tom's people. The Deputy and his council in Dublin upheld the claim of an English adventurer, Sir Peter Carew, whose ancestors had included certain Norman invaders of Ireland, to lands held by Ormond's brother Edmund. Then Carew announced his claim to part of the old kingdom of Cork, rousing the fears of Desmond's people and of the MacCarthies. When, in mid-1568, James Fitzmaurice, Desmond's cousin and rival, usurped the Earl's lands and power and launched open revolt in the south-west, the MacCarthy More joined him and so for a time did Ormond's brothers.

New English settlements had recently sprung up round Cork. Fitzmaurice ravaged them. Humphrey Gilbert commanded the English force which did much more than retort in kind, rejoicing, like others of his adventurous sort, heartily in the coming of a rebellion which gave a chance to seize lands and destroy Gaels. He slaughtered Irish women because he thought, without women to feed them, the menfolk must perish from famine. 'His manner', an observer reported, 'was that the heads of all those . . . which were killed in the day should be cut off from their bodies and brought to the place where he encamped at night, and should there be laid on the ground by each side of the way leading into his own tent, so that none should come into his tent for any cause but commonly he must pass through a lane of heads, which he used *ad terrorem* . . .' For such zeal, Gilbert was knighted by the Lord Deputy.

Meanwhile Fitton, the President of Connacht, had offended powerful local magnates. O Brien, Earl of Thomond, came out in revolt and other chiefs followed, and though they were soon quelled, by the spring of 1571 Fitzmaurice had recovered and taken the offensive again. But the mercenaries he relied on left as their contracts expired, and early in 1573, learning that he would be given mercy, Fitzmaurice submitted. The Queen was anxious for reconciliation, and gave Desmond back his freedom. Privately, both men were unforgiving. Fitzmaurice in particular was a new kind of Irish leader. His personal ambitions, insistent though they were, were legitimated by a menacing new combination of Catholic idealism and pan-Irish patriotism.

After a tour of Connacht in 1576 Sidney boasted to the Privy Council at home of the number of Irish 'varlets' he had killed there, in time of peace, with scant respect for the laws which the English were claiming to introduce. Hundreds of 'masterless men' who might have enlisted in private armies were hanged in an appalling reign of terror. Sidney did not care to acquire the least understanding of what Irish law and custom amounted to. 'Surely,' he wrote on another occasion, 'there was never people that lived in more misery than they do, nor as it should seem of worse minds, for matrimony amongst them is no more regarded in effect than conjunction between unreasonable beasts, perjury, robbery and murder counted allowable, finally, I cannot find that they make any conscience of sin, and doubtless I doubt whether they christen their children or no, for neither find I place where it should be done, nor any person able to instruct them in the rules of a Christian, or if they were taught I see no grace in them to follow it, and when they die I cannot see they make any account of the world to come.'

An English Jesuit priest posted to Limerick a few years earlier had written in a remarkably similar vein, severe as missionaries usually are amongst a 'backward' people. Yet the movement of Counter-Reformation which he represented would in the end succeed in making the Irish only too Christian. The Norman-descended aristocrats who had risen were now mostly thoroughly cowed. But Fitzmaurice formed a new conspiracy called 'The Catholic League' and set off in 1575 to enlist help in Catholic Europe.

IV

One man who would distinguish himself in war as a virtually insane anti-Catholic was Richard Grenville, a Cornish landowner, whose household was massacred and whose colony near Cork was swept away by Fitzmaurice's rebels in the late 1560s. Another man whose defiance of Spain would make him a legend was associated with the other large Irish colonising scheme: Captain Francis Drake.

In 1571 Sir Thomas Smith, one of Elizabeth's leading councillors, launched, with much publicity, a programme for colonising part of Ulster, the Ards. Smith was an enthusiast for the ancient Romans, but found a model closer to him in time for the colonial aristocracy which he intended to set up: the Spanish conquest of Mexico and Peru. He proposed that the Irish would have no legal rights and would be permitted to learn no skilled trades and to buy no land. They would become a servile labour force. To younger sons of the gentry – our law, which giveth all to the elder brother, furthereth much my purpose', Smith wrote – were offered holdings of which the smallest would be three hundred acres. 'To inhabit and reform so barbarous a nation . . . were both a godly and commendable deed, and a sufficient work for our age . . .' But Smith's bastard son, also Thomas, arrived in the Ards in 1572 with only a hundred men, ran into fierce opposition and then was killed by his own servants.

Meanwhile Walter Devereux, Earl of Essex, had come up with a still more ambitious plan. In May 1573 he proposed to the Queen that he should be given the whole of Antrim in fee, including the areas where the Scottish Macdonalds had intruded. The Queen agreed and in 1573 a great expedition set forth, half paid for by Essex himself, half by the Queen. Every 'gentleman adventurer' was to be given 400 acres for each horseman he maintained and 200 for each footman, at the rent of 2d. per acre.

Fiasco followed. The local Gaels would not be brought to decisive battle; Essex was short of stores; his 'adventurers' mostly forsook him and went home. It was the act of a desperate man when he sent three frigates under Captain Drake to Rathlin Island, a Macdonald stronghold where his men treacherously slaughtered everyone there, several hundred Scottish Gaels – old people, women and children included. Next month Essex resigned his grant. He soon died in Dublin of that miserable dysentery which plagued the English in Ireland, a Sassenach's Grave. 'Sorley Boy' Macdonald went in and destroyed his fort at Carrickfergus.

Yet this disaster did not deter further hopes of colonies, soon given scope by the forfeiture in the south-west which followed a fresh round of rebellions. Fitzmaurice, after two fruitless years in France, had been warmly welcomed in Rome by the Pope. Gregory XIII gave him troops. Though the main body were diverted on the way to fight for the King of Portugal in Morocco, Fitzmaurice had a few score with him when he landed at Dingle Bay in July 1579, and a distinguished English priest, Dr Sanders, landed with him as papal commissary. This was a crusade, but the Irish in Connacht saw Fitzmaurice as merely a raiding clan enemy. In the words of the annalist, ' . . . They proceeded to plunder the country as they passed along. The country began to assemble to oppose them; and, first of all, the sons of William Burke, son of Edmond, namely, Theobald and Ulick; and Theobald dispatched messengers to Tuath-Aesa-Greine, summoning Mac-I-Brien Ara, to come and banish the traitor from the country. Mac-I-Brien sent a body of gallowglasses and soldiers to Theobald . . . A battle was fought between both forces, in which James was shot with a ball in the hollow of the chest, which caused his death.'

Desmond's south-west remained rebellious. Relations with Spain were worsening, and the acting viceroy, Pelham, marched into Munster in 1580 determined to make it, in his own words, 'as bare a country as ever Spaniard set foot in'. To systematic devastation was added great slaughter. The rebels were forced back into the woods. But when they seemed beaten, revolt suddenly flamed out in Leinster, where Viscount Baltinglass, an ardent Catholic, and Fiach McHugh O Byrne rose in August. A new and inexperienced Deputy, Lord Grey of Wilton, came, and over 2,000 fresh troops from England with him. In the deep, boggy, heavily-wooded gorge of Glenmalure, the Leinster rebels defeated Grey's raw men and this encouraged new risings elsewhere. Then, in September, a papal fleet debouched some seven hundred soldiers, mostly Italians, in the south-western harbour of Smerwick. The officers were Spanish. Their banner was that of the Counter-Reformation. They were checked and encircled at once by zealous Protestant Englishmen.

Besieged in Smerwick, the papists craved a parley. Grey refused to offer them any conditions of surrender. They yielded nevertheless; there was nothing else they could do. Grey had no hesitation. 'Then put I in certain bands, who straight fell to execution. There were six hundred slain.' The cold-blooded massacre was neatly conducted, according to Grey's orders, by Captain Mackworth, and Captain Walter Ralegh.

Desmond had done nothing to help the papal forces. Other rebels had moved too late. Next year, Baltinglass fled the country. Yet the agonies were drawn out. Elizabeth, making one of her false economies, insisted on the discharge of more than three thousand troops. Desmond regained some ground and Grey, now almost universally disliked by English as well as by Gaels, was recalled in July 1582. Black Tom Ormond was given the chance to subdue his own hereditary foe, and he cut down Desmond's clansmen and supporters until he was sick of bloodshed. In November 1583, the last Earl of Desmond, now a half-crippled fugitive in the woods, was captured and killed by some Gaels, O Moriarties, whose beasts he had stolen.

The greater part of the old Norman-Irish aristocracy of Munster had been destroyed or had destroyed itself in the fifteen years between 1568 and 1583. Over 500,000 acres were forfeited to the Crown. Under the plans which emerged in 1585 twenty-four 'seignories' of 4,000 to 12,000 acres of arable land were to be given to 'undertakers' who would have the trouble of gathering gentlemen, freeholders and tenant farmers, along with craftsmen, shopkeepers, servants and labourers. No Irish must be allowed in the 'plantation'. The undertakers would pay no rent for a while, and thereafter only a modest one. This attractive scheme was publicised widely in England, with circulars sent to J.P.s and with leading officials packed off on tours to extol the project. Success was urgently needed.

Relations between Spain and England withered. In 1572, perhaps to conciliate Philip, Elizabeth had expelled the corsairs from the Low Countries who had been using English ports as bases. Ironically, the outcome had been the first strides towards Dutch independence. The 'sea-beggars', alighting at Brill, had found they could sweep over the northern Netherlands with the help of Calvinists in the towns there. In July the Estates of the Province of Holland had recognised the rebel William of Orange as their Stadtholder. Then, in August, Protestant Europe had been horrified by the news that the Catholic Guise faction had butchered two or three thousand Huguenots treacherously in Paris, in the 'Massacre of St Bartholomew'.

English priests were now slipping back to their homeland from the Continent, to minister to the small minority which was all that remained of English Catholicism. Such men were sent by a Pope who denied her queenship and when they were caught Elizabeth had them executed as traitors. Meanwhile, the great general Parma began to swing the balance in the Low Countries back in Spain's favour and Elizabeth was ineluctably drawn into support for his Protestant adversaries, rebels though they might be.

Events in Scotland were ominous, too. The Earl of Lennox, who won control there in 1575–80, was in touch with the Duc de Guise and his militant Catholic League. An attack on England was discussed. But Protestant nobles abducted the boy-king James in the 'Ruthven raid' of 1582. Lennox was driven into exile and in 1586 the 'Treaty of Berwick' cemented an alliance between England and Scotland. While Elizabeth would not explicitly concede that James was her heir, she agreed to respect his rights, without defining what they were, and he was given a small annual subsidy, which turned out to be the price of his mother's head; there was one plot too many in Mary's favour and she was executed in 1587.

V

England was catching up technically with her more advanced rivals. Cast-iron gun manufacture came to England only around the beginning of the sixteenth century. Henry VIII's war needs had energised production in the Weald, and by 1585 English cannon were in great demand elsewhere in Europe.

But woollen cloth remained far and away the most important English export. Historians tell us about little else when they discuss trade. English exports had grown rapidly in the late fifteenth century, then progress had slackened. London had continued rapid expansion, but this had been at the expense of such ports as Bristol and Southampton. Foreigners commonly took two-fifths or half of the cloth from London to Antwerp; the English share of the trade was monopolised by the misnamed company of 'Merchant Adventurers' established under Henry VII. In the short run, this concentration of trade in the hands of a small, very un-'adventurous', group which did no more than shovel cloth across from the mouth of the Thames to that of the Rhine (while Bristol, facing America, dropped in importance) inhibited English involvement in overseas expansion. In the long run, however, the sheaving of merchant capital in London would be to England's advantage in the distant trades where great capital was a necessity.

The trade in cloth to Antwerp reached its apogee in the late 1540s, after a debasement of the English currency. Then the government stepped in to restore the value of sterling and the Merchant Adventurers' exports slumped. This shock jolted the City of London so hard that it began at last to look for alternative markets. Quite a spate of far voyages was the result.

The most dramatic sign of the new outlook was the floating in 1552–3 of a company to pioneer a North-East Passage to Cathay. There was, of course, no feasible passage, but an important trade with Muscovite Russia resulted from the search. English cloth and metal wares could be exchanged there for fish-oil, potash, hemp and flax and ropes, and for almost a century England eclipsed all other European countries in commerce with that backward and semi-Asiatic land. The first recorded commercial voyage to Morocco dates from 1551. The trade with the Moors (cloth for sugar and, later, saltpetre) was swiftly established as a recognised and important line of business.

Meanwhile, English merchants gradually came to control more and more of their own island's trade. The Venetians ceased to pay regular visits to London after 1533 and were last seen at Southampton in 1587. The Hanseatic merchants, who had held a privileged position in London, exempt from English law, lost it temporarily in 1552 and never regained it in full. Their London headquarters, the 'Steelyard', finally closed in 1598. In the late sixteenth century, England ceased to be a semi-'colonial' country on the periphery of European trade. London was no longer a satellite of Antwerp.

The risks of the Russian trade through icy seas were enormous. The Muscovy Company (1555) was organised on the novel 'joint stock' basis. This major new device in the capitalist development of England was also employed from now on in some industrial enterprises. Merchants and others pooled their capital under a single management, and the pickings of courtiers and savings of landowners could be mobilised for trades and industries in which such people might play little or no direct part. The Guinea Company, also founded in 1555, likewise began with joint stock. But individuals and small partnerships still dominated the scene, and as soon as their distant trades were well established, both the Muscovy and Levant Companies reverted to a 'Regulated' basis. The 'Regulated Company' corresponded to the guilds which still monopolised town industry. Groups of individual merchants, banded together, each paying a fee as in the 'Merchant Adventurers', had from the Crown the right to monopolise trade in a certain commodity or a certain area. While regulation made it easier for the Crown to tap merchants' profits – they paid heavily for their privileges – it also gave trading interests access to the ears of government.

Elizabeth and her ministers invested from time to time in overseas voyages. The English government had much more to do with merchants than the French or the Spanish. It would be wrong to suppose that Elizabeth and her chief ministers had any consistent, positive commercial policy. Far from it; Burghley in 1564 actually argued in favour of reducing exports. Fear of social disorder made many high-placed Elizabethans deeply suspicious of trade and industry. But the government was short of money. The Crown was always open to bribery by pressure groups, and it was growingly forced into dependence on the goodwill of the chief cloth exporters, who could make it loans.

Like the trade with Muscovy, the Baltic trade was coming to have the acute strategic importance for the state which both would maintain till the days of sailing ships ended. Cold northern forests provided 'naval stores' of pitch and rope and timber, and as the Antwerp entrepôt failed, English merchants strove to increase direct access to them. The Eastland Company was chartered in 1579, to regulate operations in the Baltic. Antwerp, through its control of Portugal's East Indies wares and its links with the Mediterranean, had also provided the luxuries which the wealthy in England swilled and savoured and smeared on themselves. Here was a rich bait to lure merchants further afield. Huge profits could be made on wines and sugar and 'spices' – and most English imports at this time were, in fact, luxuries.

With Venice flagging and Antwerp in decline, the Dutch moved in as carriers of Baltic corn and North Sea fish direct to the Mediterranean. The English had a far smaller share of that trade, but, thanks to Cornwall, they could meet the strategic need for tin, which was essential for casting bronze cannon. For the sake of their tin, the Turkish sultan gave privileges to English traders and on the basis of these the Levant Company was formed in 1581. Through it, English cloth found a large vent. These were the early days of the 'New Draperies' – in some manufacturing areas, notably East Anglia, the classic heavy English broadcloth gave way from the 1560s to lighter and cheaper worsted and semi-worsted products, suitable for a trade with warmer countries.

Meanwhile, unregulated interlopers surged in the Levant Company's wake. English ships muscled into the Mediterranean carrying trades, transporting goods and even, in one case, troops for the Venetians themselves, and making themselves notorious for their readiness to freight Christian slaves for the infidels of the North African coast. Philip II, in 1585, moved to exclude all English ships from his dominions and failed, abjectly. They were too useful. Their ships were too fast. The great Elizabethan voyages into Arctic seas and through the Pacific should be set against a background of regular, thriving, aggressive trade to Constantinople and Leghorn, Smyrna, Aleppo, Algiers, bringing experience to seamen and giving confidence to merchants.

VI

There could be no more captivating topic than the long sea-voyages of Elizabeth's day, which found their vast and ramshackle literary monument in Richard Hakluyt's *Principal Navigations, Voyages, Traffiques & Discoveries of the English Nation*. No astronaut will seem so brave as the mariners who steered through icebergs and spent months afloat on tropical seas in ships which were tiny by modern standards. Martin Frobisher first searched for the North West Passage in a barque of no more than 30 tons. Drake's *Golden Hind*, in which he sailed round the world, was between 100 and 150 tons.

Such ships had keels of oak, decks of pine, spars of spruce. The parts under water were covered with black tar or pitch as protection against weed and barnacles, while topsides and deck were caulked with a mixture of pitch and hemp. Hemp gave the rigging, flax gave the sails. All the materials mentioned were as vital to maritime trade as diesel oil to road haulage today. To get or to safeguard supplies, it was worthwhile to fight wars or to found colonies. And as Europe's maritime expansion continued, the agriculture of whole regions would be diverted towards the supply of food for ships. While officers slept in bunks in the steerage, seamen still dossed down on the main deck, though hammocks – first seen by Columbus in the Bahamas in 1492 – were coming into use in English ships before the end of the sixteenth century. Mariners seem to have worn the same set of clothes – coarse serge gowns, loose trousers – day in day out and year in year out. They reeked. Their ships would soon reek as ballast and bilges were fouled with urine and vomit and scraps of stale food. Ducking, keel-hauling and other savage punishments met indiscipline. Sailors, while they survived them, were formed by the conditions in which they laboured. An early-seventeenth-century writer sketched the typical seaman: 'His familiarity with death and danger, hath armed him with a kind of dissolute security against any encounter. The sea cannot roar more abroad, than hee within, fire him but with liquor . . . He cannot speake low, the Sea talks so loud.'

Little record survives of voyages made by Englishmen to far continents before the second half of the sixteenth century, but we do know that in 1530 a

Plymouth merchant, William Hawkins, sent ships to the Guinea Coast and thence to Brazil, followed by Southampton merchants, seeking the coarse malagueta pepper which gave the 'Grain Coast' of Africa its title, and the 'Brazil-wood', which was used to dye cloth.

The Africa trade was revived by London merchants in 1553. Three ships were commanded by Thomas Wyndham, a Norfolk gentleman. English merchants interviewed the King of Benin in his 'great huge hall' and he gladly offered them 'four score tunne of pepper.' But it took a month to gather this precious cargo, and meanwhile, down at the coast, the chronicler tells us, 'our men partly having no rule of themselves, but eating without measure of the fruits of the countrey, and drinking the wine of the Palme trees that droppeth in the night from the cut of the branches of the same, and in such extreme heate running continually into the water . . . were thereby brought into swellings and agues: insomuch that the later time of the yeere coming on, caused them to die sometimes three & sometimes 4 or 5 in a day.' Wyndham himself died, and those of his men who survived sailed precipitately home, leaving merchants and pepper up country at Benin. But the two ships which got back were laden with a valuable cargo.

For a few years the English outpaced the French as interlopers in West Africa. But the profits to be had from exchanging basins and beads, linen and knives, woollens, kettles, brass rings and such like nicknacks, for the ivory, pepper and gold offered by peoples along the West African coast came to seem insufficient as Englishmen saw the growing trade in slaves driven by the Portuguese between Africa and America. John Hawkins, son of the pioneering William, born in 1532, had carried on the family's thriving trade. He had voyaged often to the Canaries and learnt much from the Spaniards there about conditions across the Atlantic. About 1560 he pulled out of the family business. The £10,000 he got as his share of the capital made him a man of some wealth. He shortly moved to London, and formed a syndicate there of merchants and royal officials. Their plan was to win from the Spanish Crown a share in the West Indian slave trade.

Such a scheme was not rash or implausible at that time. The sale of African slaves to the Spanish planters was conducted under the *asiento* system where the Crown sold licences to merchants and financiers who in return for their money received monopoly rights and huge returns. Most of these contractors were non-Castilian – Portuguese, Genoese, Germans, Flemings, Italians. Why should not Hawkins win permission to trade in the Caribbean, in return for assisting the Spaniards to keep down French corsairs and contraband traders?

He sailed from Plymouth with four ships in October 1562. Between Cape Verde and Sierra Leone he procured slaves, probably four hundred or so. Some he captured on shore himself, some he bought from the Portuguese. Despite the Spanish ban on foreign traders, he was able to dispose of these very profitably in Hispaniola, taking pearls, gold, hides and sugar in return. He sent two ships to trade in Spain itself, and he was so confident that his proceedings would prove acceptable that he was surprised when these were confiscated. Despite this setback, he brought back to England three ships with enough aboard to show a remarkable profit.

The Queen herself was attracted. For the next and much grander expedition planned by the syndicate, she lent a (barely seaworthy) naval vessel, the *Jesus of Lubeck*, and Hawkins's fleet flew the Royal Standard. It sailed in October 1564, it obtained its cargo of Africans after a good deal of fighting and, helped, so one Calvinistic gentleman with it suggested, by 'the Almightie God, who never suffereth his elect to perish', arrived to sell them on the Spanish Main. Though the colonists had now been specifically forbidden to trade with him, they could not resist the human wares he brought.

But the Spaniards now showed they could deal with the French themselves. In 1565 they massacred almost all the recent French settlers in Florida. Hawkins pressed ahead with plans for a third voyage but faced with Spanish displeasure the Queen withdrew her open favour and the expedition, commanded by one Captain Lovell, was baulked from trading on the Spanish Main. Even so, Hawkins pushed on, and led the fourth voyage himself, in 1567.

Spanish views were now clear. There would be no deal, no concession. Yet Hawkins sailed with two of the Queen's ships, one of them the dilapidated *Jesus*. His fleet numbered six and he took over four hundred men; this was his most imposing venture yet. Francis Drake, a distant relation of Hawkins, sailed under him. Drake was a fierce zealous Protestant, whose farming father had fled from the south-western 'Prayer Book Rebellion' of 1549 and had later served as a chaplain in the naval dockyard at Chatham.

Hawkins had to force trade on the Spanish Main town of Rio de la Hacha. Yet elsewhere commerce still went ahead without unpleasantness, and all might have ended well as before if the *Jesus* had not started to fall apart. Hawkins, rather than let the Queen's ship sink, felt compelled to put into a Mexican port, San Juan de Ulua, where the annual treasure fleet from Seville was shortly expected, convoyed by two ships of war. When it came, Hawkins took possession of a battery on an island commanding the harbour's entrance and told the Spaniards they could come in only if they gave him strict pledges. Hostages were to be exchanged. Hawkins was to be permitted to refit and revictual, on proper payment, and meanwhile to hold the battery. The Spaniards agreed, and were let in. But they had no intention of keeping their word to a Protestant interloper.

Hawkins's guns sank one warship and burnt the other, but he had to abandon the *Jesus*. He had only two ships left. Drake escaped home in one, deserting his leader. Hawkins and those with him suffered horribly on a small vessel overcrowded and undervictualled. Half or more of the crew successfully begged Hawkins to set them ashore on the Mexican coast, and many subsequently suffered the lashes and galley service awarded by Old or New Spain's

Inquisition to heretics. Most of those who stayed with Hawkins died at sea. Out of 200 leaving San Juan only 15 survived. The story of Spanish treachery at San Juan now took its place in the Protestant Black Legend.

Though one of the Queen's ships was involved, general confrontation with Spain did not result. Hawkins's interloping was not the only cause, or the main one, of breach with Spain in 1569–72. His voyages made him a very rich man. While a few other venturers followed him into the trade in human beings, English involvement soon lapsed, along with most English commerce with West Africa. But Hawkins had shown others the way to the Caribbean, and English ships flocked there from now on, imitating French and Dutch interlopers in piracy and contraband trade. The age of the 'sea dogs' had begun.

VII

Few men could yet love the sea. Its risks were fairly depicted, after all, in the procession of wrecks and disasters through Shakespeare's plays.

Sheer curiosity counted. In a famous passage, Richard Hakluyt described how as a schoolboy he visited his elder cousin of the same name, a Gentleman of the Middle Temple, and 'found lying open upon his boord certeine bookes of Cosmographie, with an universall Mappe: he seeing me somewhat curious in the view thereof, began to instruct my ignorance . . . From the Mappe he brought me to the Bible, and turning to the 107 Psalme, directed mee to the 23 & 24 verses, where I read, that they which go downe to the sea in ships; and occupy by the great waters, they see the works of the Lord, and his woonders in the deepe . . . ' The boy vowed, in his 'high and rare delight', to follow the study of geography, and at Oxford University immersed himself in every printed or written account of voyages and discoveries he could find, in ancient or modern languages. Part scientist, part economist, part propagandist, he was the natural successor-apparent to Dr John Dee, mathematician, cosmographer, astrologer and magician, who argued that conquests made by King Arthur gave Queen Elizabeth a claim to various isles in the Atlantic and that she had a right to America on the basis of the purported colonising exploits of a twelfth-century Welsh prince named Madoc. A scientist of European reputation, Dee, with his theories regarding North East and North West Passages, had an important influence on the group at court which looked towards the New World.

As the 1570s wore on, that group grew less and less disposed to hide its interest in activities which violated Spain's claims. Hostility to Spain in itself seems to have been the prime motive for the ardently anti-papist minister, Sir Francis Walsingham, who with other 'great' men – the Earl of Leicester, the Sidneys, father and son – formed an expansionist faction. 'Mercantilist' ideas, clarified notably by Hakluyt, of how trade and colonisation might promote national grandeur, also played a significant part. But so did the craving for individual profit. Just as little fishermen down in Devon when war began smartly supplied pilchards and butter to the enemy, so the high-minded, anti-papist Sidneys, owning an iron-works, were involved in the illegal trade selling precious English cannon to Spain.

Even Ralegh combined the ideals of a poet and the vision of a statesman with, on occasion, the ethics of a pickpocket. As he rose to 'greatness' in Elizabeth's court he formed the natural link between the aggressive faction there and the gentry, merchants and seafarers of his native south-west. To adapt phrases from Hakluyt, these startling adventurers bore 'fame-thirsty and gold-thirsty mindes'. They moved on from petty piracies in the Channel and blood-spattered projects for colonies in Ireland to immense ventures which brought them all the fame they had wanted, and they hitched their self-seeking so wholly to their religion and to their sense of Englishness that generation upon dazzled generation after them would hardly notice their insatiable pecuniary avidity.

As Drake was the paragon of Devon sailors, and as that sagacious slaver Hawkins rose from the Plymouth merchant community, so Sir Humphrey Gilbert and his cousin Sir Richard Grenville stand out among the seafaring gentry. They were quarrelsome, violent people. Grenville had killed a man in a brawl by the time he was twenty, running his sword six inches into him in a London street. He owed his knighthood to his services as Sheriff of Cornwall, where he made notable headway in putting down Roman Catholicism. He enslaved a score of Spanish sailors whom he brought home on one of his prizes, making them 'carry stone on their backs all day for some building operations of his, and chaining them up all night.' He somehow combined prodigal fury in action with a very passable head for business. He owned a ship jointly with John Hawkins's brother William, one with a fine record of privateering, and he also owned, as was possible then, the town of Bideford, which he made into a prosperous port. It was dynastic ambitions, not pennilessness, which took him to Ireland; he aimed that his elder son should inherit his West Country estate and that his younger son should have patrimony in Munster.

The 'younger son' factor in English expansion is famous. Humphrey Gilbert was, precisely, a younger son whose elder brother had taken the main share of the family's extensive property. There is an ominous ring to a contemporary's verdict that 'His natuer is as good as eny gentleman in England as sone as he is owt of his stormes.' His cruelty in Ireland matched his vindictiveness in other contexts. He was vain, boastful, an overreacher. Yet, amongst all the projects he spawned aimed at his own enrichment, there was a single disinterested one, for a technological university. Like Grenville, he took musicians on his voyages, men who could play while the captain ate his dinner in state. And what was a younger son of spirit to do? The great feudal households where such men had sought advancement were broken up; the monasteries which had provided a living for prospectless gentlefolk had been swept away. Gilbert gambled his life at sea. Like Grenville, he lost it with a consummate sense of heroic style.

'... Give me leave without offence,' wrote Gilbert, 'alwayes to live and die in this mind, That he is not worthie to live at all, that for feare, or daunger of death, shunneth his countrey service, and his owne honour, seeing death is inevitable, and the fame of vertue immortall.' As the public in England responded to the remarkable show staged for them by their seafarers, a belief grew up that these were great days to live in, that the English God was showing marked favour to his beloved people, that to be 'mere English', as Elizabeth phrased it, was a fine thing indeed. Above all, Francis Drake gave his countrymen pride.

VIII

In the 1560s, the Spaniards evolved a system for gathering in New World treasure which they maintained for a century and a half. In May each year one treasure fleet, the *flota*, left Seville for Vera Cruz in Mexico. In August a second fleet, the *galeones*, sailed for Nombre de Dios on the Isthmus of Panama. After the crossing of five or six weeks, it unloaded its European wares and retreated to Cartagena on the Main for the winter. In the spring, it went back to the Isthmus to pick up the silver consignments from Peru which had been brought by ships up the Pacific coast, then painfully carried by porters or mules through the jungles. The *galeones* would sail thence to Havana in Cuba for a rendezvous with the returning Mexican *flota*, and the combined fleet would return home in a heavily guarded convoy, bearing the sinews of war for Philip II's campaigns. The main streams of this great and cumbersome movement were fed by legions of ships moving along the coast. While Protestant pirates could only rarely succeed in their attempts on the *flota,* even the minor hauls from little ships and from stragglers could make a seaman wealthy.

After his dubious part at San Juan de Ulua, Drake returned before long in the swarm which preyed on the Caribbean, and learnt of the *cimarrones* ('maroons'), black slaves who had escaped and formed guerrilla bands in the unmapped backlands of the Isthmus along with the Indian women they took to bed. In 1572, Drake arrived in the Isthmus with plans to seize the main stream of Peruvian silver on the last stage of its long journey into the holds of the *galeones*.

A surprise attack on Nombre de Dios in July captured the town (as large as Plymouth) but failed to extract treasure. Drake remained on the Isthmus, allied with some 'maroons', and, in January 1573, tried out a different plan. With twenty whites and about as many blacks he marched to ambush a Spanish mule train. He took about £40,000, which he shared with some French Huguenot corsairs who had joined him.

From a tree in the Isthmus Drake had seen the Pacific. So far as we know, no English ship had yet reached the Far East or even India. Englishmen were all the more likely to credit the idea, encouraged by a misreading of Marco Polo, that there were rich lands to the south-east of Asia. For two generations, the best maps had shown a conjectural continent in the South Pacific, trending from the southern tip of South America north-west to the tropics. The existence of this great southern continent would not be disproved finally for two hundred years, and credulity was stiffened by the news, leaking in through an English merchant resident in Mexico, that a Spaniard named Mendaña was claiming to have discovered it. (What he had found, in 1567, were only the Solomon Islands, so called because his ecstatic imagination made them the land of Ophir, linked with the king of that name in the Bible.)

In any case, lavishly laden Spanish vessels now sailed the Pacific. The spices of the Moluccas were an old prize for seafarers. The West Country gentry and merchants who joined with Richard Grenville in 1574, petitioning the Queen for permission to undertake 'The discovery, traffic and enjoying for the Queen's Majesty and her subjects, of all or any lands, islands and countries southward beyond the equinoctial or where the Pole Antarctic hath any elevation above the horizon', however misty their geographical concepts, no doubt reckoned that if discovery failed, piracy would still bring them good profit.

But their supporting arguments began to develop the ideas of 'mercantilist' imperialism. The litany of objects for the adventure would be re-echoed down to the nineteenth century. 'Enlarging the bounds of Christian religion' piously headed the list. Home industry and commerce would be advanced by 'the beneficial utterance of the commodities of England' – primarily by the sale of English cloth, since *Terra Australis* was supposed to lie chiefly in temperate latitudes. 'The increase and maintenance of seamen' in the interests of English striking power at sea was an argument which would hold immense weight so long as the Royal Navy relied in wartime on men who had sailed on merchant ships during peace. 'The relief of the people at home' was an objective which would have a still longer life: while rich new trades might increase employment in industry, emigration could bring opportunity to the unemployed.

Grenville's project was later amplified to include the notion of finding the western outlet of the North West Passage by sailing up the Pacific coast of America, a sensible-looking plan when no one, except their skin-clad inhabitants, knew of Alaska or of the Rocky Mountains. The Queen blew hot and cold. Grenville was needed for military service, first in Ireland, then in Cornwall. And when the plan was accepted in 1577, a sailor was preferred to a soldier for its execution. A powerful syndicate of courtiers and officials, including Leicester and Walsingham, hijacked the scheme and employed Drake, out of a job since the failure of Essex's project for colonisation in Ulster.

The Queen gave a ship. Though she still hoped to keep peace with Spain, she seems to have seen no harm in taking the chance of direct personal profit from an expedition which she could disavow if need be. Drake had an excellent record as a gold-grabber. In the event, the lofty aim of Southern Empire was tossed overboard. Drake made no attempt to locate *Terra Australis*, and only a perfunctory search for the North West Passage. Sixteenth-century seafaring was at the mercy of hostile weather, and of the appetites of the crew.

As it was, sailors who had enlisted, so they thought, for a voyage to the Levant (this was the screen put up to deceive the Spaniards) grew restive on the initial, Atlantic stage of Drake's expedition, which left near the end of 1577 with four ships, a pinnace and about 160 men. There was serious trouble. Drake, an ebullient little plebeian, struggled for power with Thomas Doughty, the leading gentleman present. He won, and at Port St Julian, just short of Magellan's Straits, had Doughty beheaded after a kangaroo court had found him guilty of incitement to mutiny, and of witchcraft practised against the expedition. Soon after, one Sunday, Drake deposed the chaplain and preached his men a sermon himself. There were numerous gentlemen with him. He denounced their class consciousness and aversion to toil. '. . . My masters, I must have it left, for I must have the gentleman to haul and draw with the mariner and the mariner with the gentleman.' It was a remarkable moment, displaying precociously how nationalism, imperialism and democracy would, in Britain, advance pretty steadily together.

Drake sailed through the Straits, then, in bad weather, lost his companions. In the lone vessel which he renamed the *Golden Hind*, he harried the coasts of Chile and Peru, where no one expected him, taking one prize above all which filled his own ship with silver. (Altogether the expedition seems to have pirated some twenty-five or thirty vessels, besides various robberies on land.) By June 1579, having left his pursuers far behind, he was refitting at an anchorage in California. He called the country Nova Albion, 'New Britain', and claimed it for Elizabeth. This annexation had no practical sequel, nor did the 'treaty' which Drake later made in the Moluccas, where he found the Sultan of Ternate on bad terms with the Portuguese, then sailed on with several tons of cloves. When he arrived at Plymouth again in September 1580, after nearly three years at sea, he had matched Magellan's crewmen and circled the globe.

The Queen was pleased. She took all the bullion Drake had brought home and put it safely in the Tower. The other shareholders were amply contented with a 100 per cent return on their investment. Drake was knighted. Foreigners were impressed. Englishmen passed word of the voyage round with excitement. An appetite for great deeds was whetted.

IX

Meanwhile, others were no less brave, but not so lucky. The Muscovy Company claimed a monopoly of all northern exploration, but its lack of fresh enterprise irked some ambitious spirits. In 1566, in between spells of fighting in Ireland, Humphrey Gilbert found time to write a *Discourse of a Discoverie for a New Passage to Cataia*. He had petitioned the Queen for a monopoly of trade through the putative 'Strait of Anian' which he supposed to begin in the Atlantic somewhere between 60° and 70°N. and to trend south-westwards towards 40° or 50°N. Proponents of the rival North East Passage claimed that a unicorn's horn had been found on the coast of Tartary and that it could only have come with the tides through their favoured outlet, 'there being no Unicorne in any parte of Asia, saving in India, and Cataia': nonsense, Gilbert retorted, there were 'great plentie' of beasts like unicorns in Lapland. He proposed a trading base on the Pacific and colonies along the Strait.

Nothing came of this, but in 1575 the Muscovy Company's monopoly was at last breached, on the Queen's orders. The schemers now were Michael Lok, a former Levant merchant, and his nautical ally Martin Frobisher, a tough unlettered Yorkshireman who had somehow survived his first long voyage with Wyndham to West Africa when still a boy, and a subsequent career which had mingled successful piracies with two stretches in gaol. Frobisher sailed in 1576 with three tiny ships. He found a long bay in Baffin Land. He came back with word that he had discovered the Strait, with an Inuit aboard whom he claimed was a Tartar, and with a sample of black ore, probably iron pyrites, which one expert only, the others not being so rash, was now prepared to say contained gold.

Mania set in. Besides Elizabeth, great courtiers, big merchants, rushed to subscribe to the 'Company of Cathay'. Sailing north again, Frobisher wasted no time on exploration; he loaded 200 tons of ore and dashed for home. Still no one could actually extract any gold from it, yet even so the Queen increased her stake in the next expedition which left in 1578 with no fewer than fifteen ships, by far the most expensive speculation of its kind in the whole Tudor period. Fog, which made Frobisher lose his way, did ensure a contribution this time to geographical knowledge. He followed the strait later named after Hudson for 200 miles and was sure that this was the true passage. But when he got home, with yet more worthless ore, he found that faith, so rashly sustained, had collapsed. Lok went to a debtors' prison, while Frobisher returned to his piracy.

What he and his men had seen, apart from fool's gold, was not encouraging. 'Nothing fit or profitable for the use of man', as one of them put it, grew in the bald tracts inhabited by dangerous Inuits. Yet somewhere beyond were the riches of the East; in this faith the quest was resumed in the mid-1580s, under a new company, short of funds, which was led by Humphrey Gilbert's brother Adrian. John Davis of Dartmouth, the greatest scientific navigator of his times, voyaged three times in 1585-7 and in his last attempt reached the record latitude of 72° between Baffin Land and Greenland and saw open sea ahead to the West before hard winds drove him back.

Humphrey Gilbert himself had been even less lucky. In 1577, he offered the Queen a fine plan for attacking Spain in the New World. He would seize the papist fishing fleets off Newfoundland under pretext of a patent to colonise. Then he would waylay the Spanish treasure fleet. Then he would grab Santo Domingo and Cuba.

Elizabeth liked this dashing, if cruel, adventurer. In June 1578 she 'granted him letters patent of such wide scope as to deserve the title of the first English colonial charter.' He was empowered to found a colony anywhere between Labrador and Florida, along that North American coastline which England still claimed by virtue of Cabot's 'discovery'. He was given viceregal powers over his vast domain.

Gilbert brought into the scheme his two brothers, Sir John and Adrian and also both of his Ralegh half-brothers, Carew and Walter, but his main co-adventurer was Henry Knollys, son of the treasurer of the Queen's household. Characteristically, Gilbert quarrelled with him and Knollys sailed off with three of their ten ships to be a pirate in European waters. After Gilbert left with the rest, bad weather scattered the fleet and the random robberies which followed, combined with those of Knollys, were too much even by Tudor standards. Gilbert was held back by the Privy Council when he wanted to try again the next year, and was sent to serve at sea against the Irish rebels.

However, Gilbert later resumed the struggle to make something of his patent. Might not the New World provide a haven for dissidents in religion? Gilbert, surprisingly, turned for support to the English Catholic community. An Act of 1581 put them under severer penalties than before. Elizabeth, however, insisted that recusant emigrants must pay up all fines overdue in full, and the Spanish Ambassador, on his side, mobilised the priests against the scheme, which he saw as a cunning device (perhaps it was) for counteracting the growth of Catholicism by exporting the people who would support papist missionary work.

Yet Gilbert could still appeal to the land hunger of Protestants of his own class. Land in England was now very dear. Now Gilbert offered the bait of 'vast' estates, and aristocratic lordship over them. Over nine months, in 1582–3, he assigned eight and a half million acres (and seven whole islands off the coast) to Catholics alone, while Sir Philip Sidney, the poet, acquired an individual stake of three million acres.

But there would be land for poor people, too; for anyone who brought with him seed and tools to the value of forty-three shillings. Gilbert was the first Englishman to attempt a New World Utopia. He would govern with the help of counsellors chosen by the consent of the people, and the landowners under him, maintaining armed men, would also be expected to help support scholars. Friends and relations were called on for help – Walter Ralegh had risen at court and contributed heavily. But the money which Gilbert could mobilise came to pitifully little, and he could never have planted his colony securely.

Elizabeth asked Gilbert not to sail. She knew him to be a man 'of not good happ by sea'. But he insisted and left, perilously late in the season, on 11 June 1583. He had five ships, and some 260 men. The largest ship turned back after only two days. The rest reached Newfoundland in August.

According to an account of five years before, there had then been only fifty English boats exploiting the nearby prodigious shoals of cod which, salted and dried, found such a ready market in Europe. There had been as many Portuguese, twice as many Spanish ships, and three times as many French. But on 5 August 1583, at the summer settlement of St John's, Gilbert formally took possession of the island. A fortnight's merry feasting followed.

Gilbert left again, on August 20, with three ships, of which the 120-ton *Delight* was the largest. He intended to reach the mainland and work his way southwards prospecting for a suitable spot for a colony. He himself commanded his tiny pinnace, the 10-ton *Squirrel*. Edward Haies, the gentleman-captain of the 40-ton *Golden Hind*, wrote a haunting account of what followed. The night of August 28 was 'faire and pleasant, yet not without token of storm to ensue, and most part of this Wednesday night, like the Swanne that singeth before her death, they in the Admirall, or Delight continued in sounding of Trumpets, with Drummes, and Fifes: also winding the Cornets, Haughtboyes: and in the end of their jolitie, left with the battell and ringing of doleful knells.' After this music had died away, the helmsmen heard 'strange voyces' in the air. Next day, there were rain and thick fog. The *Delight* struck shoal, and most of its hundred men drowned in sight of their comrades on the other ships. Gilbert shortly agreed with Haies that they must head for England. As they set off home they saw a 'sea-monster', which looked like a lion, roared like one, and 'passed along turning his head to and fro, yawning and gaping wide, with ougly demonstration of long teeth, and glaring eies'. The cheerful Gilbert took it for a good omen, 'rejoycing that he was to warre against such an enemie, if it were the devill.' This spirit of almost rapturous fatalism, which seems characteristic of the Elizabethan personality, gave way to the time's equally typical peevishness. A couple of days later Gilbert came aboard the *Hind* and caroused with Haies, 'lamenting greatly the losse of his great ship, more of the men, but most of all of his bookes and notes, and what els I know not ... ', and beating his cabin boy in drunken fury.

Yet he left in good spirits, insisting on going back to his own absurdly small pinnace. On Monday 9 September, in foul weather and huge seas north of the Azores, the *Squirrel* nearly sank, 'yet at that time recovered: and giving foorth signes of joy, the Generall sitting abaft with a booke in his hand, cried out unto us in the *Hind* (so oft as we did approch within hearing) We are as neere to heaven by sea as by land.' He was quoting from Thomas More's *Utopia*, with its account of an ideal society in the New World. Haies thought the man was a fool, and deduced that he sailed in the *Squirrel* to prove to the world he was not afraid of the sea. About midnight, the *Squirrel*'s lights suddenly vanished. The ship was 'devoured and swallowed up of the Sea.'

Ralegh, perhaps as unpleasant, certainly still more remarkable, now took over his dead half-brother's role.

X

In the early 1580s, Ralegh, who had long hung about Court, at last attracted the Queen's full notice. He had made his mark in Ireland, partly at the massacre at Smerwick. The Queen liked fine men about her. She was much taken, we are told, with Ralegh's 'elocution', though 'notwithstanding his so great Mastership in Style and his conversation with the learnedst and politest persons, yet he spake broad Devonshire to his dyeing day.' He was tall, with an ivory complexion, wavy black hair, a high forehead, a brooding manner. His sudden conquest of the Queen brought him jealousy and enemies. Elizabeth gave him those prime favours which all her courtiers sought, economic monopolies. A patent for granting licences to sell wines was the foundation of his fortunes, followed by other profitable concessions to do with the sale of woollen cloth. In 1585, he was made Warden of the Stannaries, controlling the tin mines of Cornwall; Lord Lieutenant of that county; and also Vice-Admiral of both Cornwall and Devon. He was not one to hide his wealth; he matched the pearls in his hatband, the jewels on his fingers, with an arrogance which made many detest him.

Yet he was popular with the Devon sailors, and with the common people wherever his offices put him over them. Contradictions dominated his personality and his position. The most intelligent man at Elizabeth's court, he was kept out of positions of crucial responsibility. A serious patriot, he nevertheless sold wood from his Irish estates to the Spaniards in wartime. His greed was remarkable even by Elizabethan standards, and we must accept his enemies' taunt that 'Raw Lie' was on occasions a great liar. Also, his self-love was prodigious. He resented dependence on others and sought wealth to make himself free.

The voice of Ralegh's poetry rises sombre and thunderous over his period's prattle of lyrical conventionalities, presenting, in accents of self-transcendent self-pity, the general yet deeply personal truth that time steals all joys, from the past only sorrow stays. While his ambition pressed him to high politics, a contrary urge drove him to the solitude of scientific experiment, and to the company of a group of daring and controversial intellectuals. He was extremely learned. The friend and coadjutor of Drake was also the intimate of leading poets. He had for mentor Thomas Hariot, greatest of Tudor scientists, one of the founders of algebra, first observer of Halley's comet and a precocious thinker in the mathematics of navigation. Ralegh himself experimented, in shipbuilding as well as in chemistry. Like other advanced thinkers, he took a Faustian interest in the possibilities of magic. Inevitably he was accused of atheism, and certainly, like Hariot, he tended towards what was later known as deism. He asked sceptical questions about the existence of the soul.

Despite his own monopolies, he argued for freer trade. Above all, he grasped the importance of sea-power. 'Whosoever commands the sea, commands the trade', he wrote; 'whosoever commands the trade of the world, commands the riches of the world, and consequently the world itself.' Through him the Elizabethan mind met America, and the future.

In March 1584 he applied for, and was granted, his dead half-brother Humphrey's rights in America, saving the power to exercise a monopoly over the Newfoundland fishery. Then he sent out two ships, under Philip Amadas and Arthur Barlow, to search for a site for a colony in the area north of the Spaniards' tenuous settlement in Florida. In July they landed on Hatteras, an island forming part of the Carolina Outer Banks. They arrived home in September, bringing two Indians with them, and reported, like so many such explorers before and after, that they had seen an earthly paradise. They ignored the fact that they had found no good harbour. They vastly overestimated the fertility of the soil.

Ralegh had already enlisted the services of Richard Hakluyt for a propaganda exercise designed to attract funds for a colony. Though Gilbert and Grenville had anticipated sketchily much of what he had to say, Hakluyt's *Discourse of Western Planting*, presented to the Queen in October, deserves its reputation as the first manifesto of English imperialism. Colonisation was extolled as the best escape from a doleful economic prospect, as a panacea for almost all ills, and as a fine way to do down Spain. With colonies in America, English traders need no more confront the Inquisition in Spain, impositions in France, Danish exactions in the Baltic or the rising competition of Holland.

Convicts who would otherwise stuff English gaols can be sent to the New World to fell timber for shipmasts and make tar and cordage, or to work in the rich mines, or to plant sugar. English vagabonds will dress vines in Virginia, hew marble to make 'noble buildinges there', sow dyes and gather honey, whale, and engage themselves in 'dryinge, sortinge and packinge of fethers whereof may be had there marvelous greate quantitie.' Paupers too infirm to brave the Atlantic can be employed at home 'makinge of a thousande triflinge thinges' to trade with the Indians, whose demand for the 'coursest and basest' English (and Welsh, and Irish) cloth will revive 'decayed townes'. A few Spaniards are engrossing a vast area by bluff. The Indians could be stirred against them. But England must strike fast, or be a day late for the fair. The French are already active.

Ralegh was ready to act. He aimed to gain such pre-eminence through America, where he could be sole lord of vast territories, as his rivals had denied him in England. He was ready to risk a great deal of his own money but he had other business concerns, notably in Ireland. He raised backing from Walsingham, Grenville, London merchants and others. The Queen would lend him a Royal Navy vessel for his expedition's flagship. But she would spare him no more government backing.

His experiment would show that a steady stream of capital was needed in the early days of a colony when there might be little or no immediate return. Ralegh, however, thought that 'Virginia' must pay its way as it went along. He and his backers saw plunder at sea as the answer. He aimed that his colony should provide a base for raids in the West Indies and on the Spanish treasure fleet. By contrast with Gilbert's scheme, there would be no grants of land, and the settlers would work together as paid servants of the investors under the commander – a soldier – appointed by Ralegh.

The Queen agreed that the land to be colonised might be named 'Virginia' in honour of herself and her singular chastity, and she knighted Ralegh in return for the compliment. The first English expedition actually to form an American colony left Plymouth on April 9, 1585, in five ships and two pinnaces, with Grenville, Ralegh's cousin, in command.

XI

On the way, Grenville picked off such prizes as offered and gathered livestock, cuttings, seeds and roots for the colonists in the Spanish West Indian islands. Late in June he was trying to bring his flagship into a harbour in what we now know as the Carolina Outer Banks when it was grounded, with great loss of needed supplies. Amadas and Barlow had opted for an area which could in fact provide no useful base for attacking Spain. The Banks, formed by a long series of narrow islands, were shoal-infested and very dangerous to shipping. Furthermore, the mainland beyond them was swampy and impossible to cultivate except along the edges of rivers and sounds.

Grenville and his men soon ran into trouble with Indians. The first quarrel was picked by the English. A village was burnt and its corn destroyed. The Indians had stone tomahawks, no metal weapons at all, their tribes were petty, their villages small. But they were many and the white men were few. The offer of violence was rash as well as arrogant.

A site for the colony was settled on, Roanoke, a large island between Pamlico Sound and Albemarle Sound, where the Indians were friendly. A fort was built, Grenville departed towards the end of August and captured a rich Spanish prize on the way home. With that help, the Queen was rewarded, and Ralegh's credit stayed high.

Ralph Lane was left in charge at Roanoke, an experienced soldier who had recently served in Ireland and whose greed for Munster land had lost him the goodwill of his superiors there. With the Indians, his one idea was force. In this respect, he fell far short of two of the men with him, John White and Thomas Hariot, who worked together to evoke the region in words and pictures. White drew and coloured wonderfully lifelike pictures of Indians and their dwellings, of birds and beasts. Hariot, sent by Ralegh as scientific expert in residence, wrote a *Briefe and True Report* which became known all over Europe as one of the most authoritative accounts of American conditions, and he took the trouble to learn the language of the Indians whom he studied so respectfully.

Altogether, there were just over a hundred colonists, including several Irishmen brought by Lane from Kerry. The bulk of the rank and file were probably ex-soldiers, who had no skill at feeding themselves. The party revealed that puzzling incapacity to capture the fish swarming around them which was characteristic of Europeans in the New World. Men landed in malarial country after an exhausting sea voyage were impressed by the fact that the Indians would at first shower gifts of food upon them, and became convinced that their lack of zest for work need not produce starvation so long as they had trinkets to trade with and arms with which to assert themselves.

Though Lane prevailed upon the Indians to sow some ground for his men and to clear more for them to plant themselves, native resentment was bound to build up as the feckless white men clamoured for food. Lane chased hither and thither in search of some great thing to make all rich. He did find Chesapeake

Sound and see what is now called Virginia. He realised that with its deep water anchorage, this would be a far better site for a colony, but was distracted by Indian tales which made copper sound like gold and suggested to him that the Pacific was close, into an exploration up the Roanoke River on the mainland. And meanwhile the Roanoke chief (*werowance*), Wingina, had turned against the intruders. Hearing of Indian plans for attack, Lane himself struck and murdered Wingina. By now it was June 1586. After only a year, the colony was close to extinction. Lane and his men were short of supplies and expecting a native counter-attack. Then into view sailed Drake as their saviour.

The colonists had left in April 1585 just as real war with Spain boiled up. In May, Philip II had seized all the English ships in Iberian ports. The valuable Iberian trade had acted as a brake on English aggression. Now the clamour of England's merchants trading with Spain abetted the noise of the war party. The merchants demanded and got from the Queen permission to strike back against Spanish shipping. In August the Queen allied with the Dutch rebels. Eighteen years of open struggle with Spain began, the golden age of the privateers, and the ruin of the English Crown, which had somehow to fight on four fronts. The realm had to be defended against invasion. Expeditionary forces had to be sent to the help of allies in the Netherlands and France. Ireland, the half-closed back door, would prove the biggest front of all, and nearly a fatal one. And there was the struggle with Spain at sea which engaged the zest of merchants and plunderers. While Spain's own economy had started to weaken, England's, like that of the amazing Dutch rebels, had been growing stronger. Two rising trading powers confronted a muscle-bound empire which barred the way to their further expansion.

Providing soldiers for Europe, and then for Ireland as well, left the Queen no cash to spare. So she had no hankering for offensive war at sea. She left that to her subjects, to avid gentry and eager merchants ready to wage a guerrilla campaign in the Atlantic on their own initiative and to bring her into their joint stock on occasion. The sea war was dominated by privateers while the Royal Navy played a lesser role, under a Lord High Admiral, Lord Howard of Effingham, who was himself a promoter of privateering (and was to boot quite spectacularly corrupt).

By the end of 1585, Elizabeth, besides subsidising Henri de Navarre in France, had sent 6,000 men to the Low Countries and had also authorised the adventure which brought Francis Drake at length to Roanoke. He had cleared for the Main with thirty ships and a force of over 2,000 sailors and soldiers – all equipped by joint stock, the Queen contributing one-third of the total. Drake damaged Spanish prestige, capturing and sacking San Domingo and Cartagena, but he missed the treasure fleet, the enterprise made no profit, and this discouraged any attempt to repeat it.

On his way homewards he crippled the small Spanish colony in Florida. Then he breezed up to Roanoke itself, laden with slaves captured from the Spaniards.

He offered Lane food, arms and clothing, a ship, boats and sailors to man them. But the colonists now had wholly lost their nerve, and eagerly scrambled away in Drake's fleet.

Ralegh tried again, on an improved basis. Shareholders in the new joint-stock company would be drawn largely from those who were prepared to go in person. Each would get 500 acres of land on the strength of his undertaking to go, and further land in proportion to his investment. All would enjoy rights of self-government, while leaving representatives behind in England to use part of their investment in keeping them supplied through the difficult early stages. For governor of 'the City of Ralegh in Virginia', John White the artist was chosen. Only three of Lane's men were willing to venture again, but scores of new colonists came forward. They must have been people with some property, as farmers, tradesmen or such-like, which they could sell in order to buy their equipment. In the event, 113 settlers arrived in America in May 1587, of whom 17 were women and 9 were children.

On 18 August, a month after their coming, John White's daughter Eleanor, who was married to an Assistant, Ananias Dare, gave birth to a daughter, the first known English offspring on North American soil, who was duly christened 'Virginia'. But the colonists were already feeling a shortage of livestock, salt and various other items, so they prevailed upon White himself to sail, most reluctantly, back to England to expedite fresh supplies. Meanwhile they would move to the mainland; the objective agreed was possibly Chesapeake Bay.

White was home by early November, and Ralegh pressed ahead with plans for relief. But when Grenville was almost ready to sail in the following March, the Privy Council ordered him not to go. A Spanish invasion was threatening. England needed his ships. White was allowed to set off, but with two little pinnaces only. He seems to have been a weakish though decent man, and he could not prevent the crews embarking on piracy, even against allied ships. A French privateer paid White's ship back, and it staggered into Bideford badly mauled. The other pinnace returned some weeks later, having been nowhere near Virginia.

And now events ruled out any chance of relief for the moment. This was 1588, year of the great Armada. Philip II had gradually realised that he must come to declare war on England. The execution of Mary Queen of Scots early in 1587 left him, as he saw it, the true Catholic claimant to England's throne, her son, James VI of Scotland, being a heretic. The new Pope, Sixtus V, was willing to subsidise Spain to attack Elizabeth. Drake's raid on Cadiz in the spring of 1587, destroying 24 ships and many stores, held up the invasion fleet, but only for one year. In late July 1588, it was at last sighted off Cornwall, 130 ships, with 22,000 seamen and soldiers aboard, bent on linking up with the Spanish forces in the Low Countries and thereafter escorting troops who would cross the Channel in barges.

Against Parma's crack troops from Europe, if landed, Elizabeth would have mustered only an inexperienced militia. On paper the overall Spanish marine, now joined with the Portuguese, outweighed that of England by six or eight times. But the Channel was a great barrier. So was the quality of the ships which England now had. Since the 1560s, Sir John Hawkins had been pressing the need for speedy manoeuvrable ships of the latest design. For ten years, he had been in charge of the Navy's dockyards and building programme. England now had, besides many armed merchant ships, 25 war galleons built and armed in the newest fashion.

Despite their advantages, the English made little impression on the Armada in nine days' running fight as it sailed up the Channel and anchored at Calais. There fireships broke it up. Mauled by the English, the papists fled in disorder before a south-west wind and reached home round the coasts of Gaelic Scotland and Ireland, where several ships were wrecked. Yet two-thirds or more of the whole fleet got back. Though Spanish sea-power was hurt, the wound healed quickly. More silver flowed in from the New World than ever, in fleets still imposing and well guarded. But the blow to Spanish prestige was great. In England itself relief was exhaled in much boasting in verse and prose. The crepuscular sequel, Elizabeth's last years, the decline of English sea-power under her successors, would only make patriots cling more fondly to the myth of the Great Armada destroyed by an epic band of seadogs, Drake and Frobisher to the fore.

Counter-Armada was attempted next year, the so-called 'Portugal Adventure', a shameful disaster. Drake commanded, and bungled, a sorry attack on Lisbon and a desultory swipe at the Azores. After 1588, in fifteen years, England would gain no big victory over Spain. The war was frustrating for both sides, nerve-racking and ruinous for the English Crown. There was never a straightforward confrontation on land, though Englishmen fought in the Netherlands and in France, where Spanish troops opposing Henri de Navarre occupied Brittany, fearsomely close to English shores. Spanish naval might, through the 1590s, would pose constant threat of invasion, and God would be kept hard at work blowing to scatter Armadas.

Meanwhile, Ralegh tried to salvage White's colony. In 1589, in his third attempt, he rallied a score of London merchants whose backing, given in return for comprehensive control of the trade of the area claimed under Ralegh's patent, might have been strong enough to nurse 'Virginia' into real life. But privateering now seemed to obsess all seamen. When poor White finally sailed again early in 1590 in quest of his grandchild and those with her, it was in a spree mounted by the great John Watts, most noted of all sponsors of privateering. Watts's captain would take White only, no planters and no supplies, and then he ranged the West Indies hunting prizes for four months of precious sailing time before he made for Virginia late in the season.

White had agreed with his fellows three years before that if they departed from Roanoke in distress or under duress, they would leave a cross as a signal.

He 'found the houses taken downe, and the place very strongly enclosed with a high palisado of great trees, . . . and one of the chiefe trees or postes at the right side of the entrance had the barke taken off, and 5 foote from the ground in fayre Capitall letters was graven CROATOAN without any crosse or signe of distresse.' Croatoan was an island in the Bank to the south where there had been friendly Indians. Why had the colonists written its name there? Why had they left White's three chests of belongings, which he found in the ditch, clearly rifled by Indians?

All questions stay unanswered. White could make no search, as his Captain would not linger. Their idea was then to return to the Caribbean and then come back to 'Virginia' in the spring, but the ship was blown off course and ran all the way home. White, after so many frustrations, gave up. Certain authorities think that the colonists merged into local Indian tribes.

After 1600, Ralegh tried again to locate them. But meanwhile he became John Watts's partner in privateering. In 1591, they netted a profit, on one voyage to the Caribbean, of more than 200 per cent.

XII

John White went to Ireland, where several of Lane's men, including Thomas Hariot, also settled in Munster, pioneers nearer home. Grenville was a great 'undertaker' in this colony, and Ralegh was the most outstanding organiser of all. The largest seignory was supposed to be 12,000 acres, but thanks to the Queen's favour Ralegh got no fewer than 42,000 acres of arable land near Cork and Waterford, at an especially low rent.

By 1589 there were over 600 male English settlers, many with families. They bought English tools and stock and built farmsteads in the English style, but the original concept of a little England was sabotaged from the outset by undertakers who, to save trouble, broke the rules and gave Irish natives their land back as tenants. Edmund Spenser, who became lord of 3,000 acres in County Cork, wrote disapprovingly of the tendency, always marked in Irish history, for the English to fall into Hibernian habits. '. . . Having been brought up at home under a strait rule of duty and obedience so soon as they come thither, where they see laws more slackly tended . . . as it is the nature of all men to love liberty, so they become flat libertines and fall to all licentiousness . . .' The colony was from the first harried by Irish outlaws and men deprived of their land, and was swept away in the torrent of rebellion which flowed over Ireland from 1594 onwards.

This trouble stemmed from Ulster, fastness of Gaeldom, where the dominating figure was Hugh O Neill, Earl of Tyrone. The son of that Baron of Dungannon done to death by Shane O Neill's men, he had spent eight years in England as a youth and on his return to Ireland had collaborated with the Dublin government – even with such a menacing enterprise as Essex's attempt to colonise Ulster itself. By the late 1580s, Ulster seemed tamed. Lord Deputy

Perrot had established three garrisons there and had confirmed a settlement between Tyrone and his wily and drunken relative Turlough Luineach, the O Neill, by which the former acknowledged Turlough's captaincy and became his *tanaiste* (successor-designate). As ships of the shattered Armada passed by the Irish coast, where many were wrecked, English fears were pacified; not a rebel stirred, though some chiefs did help survivors to escape. Two henchmen of Tyrone's, on the other hand, butchered hundreds of shipwrecked Spaniards, performing on behalf of the government the vicious job which the English elsewhere did for themselves.

Tyrone fell out with Bagenal, the Queen's Marshal in Ulster. He eloped with Bagenal's sister Mabel in 1591, made her his third wife, and then, to complete the insult, disenchanted his bride by openly flaunting his mistresses before her. She went back in tears to her brother at Newry. But most likely it was a helpless instinct for self-preservation in the face of inexorable pressures which pushed Tyrone against his will into the cul-de-sac of revolt. For behind Bagenal, that angry intruder who could use the Crown's power to thwart Tyrone locally, stood a Dublin government which was gradually pressing ahead with the eradication of Gaelic Ireland, its customs and its political institutions on which the power of Tyrone himself depended. He had aimed to become the O Neill, and in 1593 the ageing Turlough Luineach relinquished that ancient title to him, a claim to traditional kingship in its own right.

Tyrone's son-in-law Hugh Roe ('Red Hugh') O Donnell had been kidnapped by Perrot and imprisoned in Dublin Castle. After five years, in 1592, he made a remarkable escape. The O Donnells now had a handsome, heroic, fresh chief. Tyrone himself liked the young man. The old rivalry of O Neill and O Donnell was shelved, and Red Hugh allied with another hothead, young Hugh Maguire, chief in Fermanagh and also Tyrone's son-in-law. For the first time the main Ulster chiefs would face outward together. Red Hugh began to form a confederation which involved leading Catholic churchmen and was in touch with Philip of Spain.

Yet when Maguire threw off the traces in 1593 and raided in Sligo and Roscommon, Tyrone accepted the government's order to quell him and co-operated with his arch enemy Bagenal to this end. He was not, in his own opinion, sufficiently thanked. Early next year he submitted a long list of grievances to the government, and Elizabeth tried to conciliate him. Now, as Red Hugh joined Maguire in revolt, it was Tyrone whom the English, rightly, saw as the great danger. Early in 1595, when they reckoned Tyrone himself had 6,000 soldiers, the government shipped over to Ireland 1,600 veterans from the wars in France, and 1,000 fresh levies from England. A great drain of English treasure and lives was beginning.

Elsewhere, England had had little success against Spain. Disillusion was setting in. Veteran warhawks were dying – Leicester in 1588, Walsingham in 1590 and then, in the next year, Sir Richard Grenville, following the *Revenge*'s famous last fight, an episode in the not very effectual attempt, over several years, to cut off the Spanish treasure fleets by a blockade in the Azores. A huge Spanish force approached. The outnumbered English fled, all save Grenville, who could have escaped but instead fought a bloody action all night against a whole fleet, alone, until, when he was mortally wounded, his men arranged a surrender. Drake, in disfavour after the Lisbon disaster, was given the chance to make, with Sir John Hawkins, another raid on the Caribbean in 1595. The old targets were aimed at, but the old flair for assault had gone. The Spaniards were forewarned; the attack was botched. Hawkins died at sea off Puerto Rico, Drake of dysentery at Porto Bello.

There were two further big naval expeditions. A successful commando raid on Cadiz by an English Armada in 1596 was followed in the next year by the total failure of the 'Island Voyage' to the Azores. But in each of those years, Protestant winds broke up Spanish Armadas aimed at Ireland, and thereafter, though there were still English troops in the Low Countries, Ireland became the main theatre of the war.

XIII

The rebellion there confirmed Ralegh's loss of interest in his Irish lands, which he made over to a friend in 1598 and finally sold altogether in 1602 to a sharp young adventurer, Richard Boyle, who founded the greatest of Irish colonial fortunes. By 1595, Ralegh had a new love, Guiana.

He had long known something about the land between the Amazon and the Orinoco which neither Spain nor Portugal had bothered to occupy. What spurred him to act was his loss of favour at court. Already frustrated by the rise in Elizabeth's favour of a dazzling new favourite, the young Earl of Essex, Ralegh had made the mistake in 1592 of marrying one of the Queen's maids of honour and of lying to keep it secret. When she found out, the Queen imprisoned both for a while. Brooding in his mansion in Dorset, Ralegh came to see a Guiana enterprise as the stroke which might restore him to glory.

He had heard of the Spanish quest for the Empire of the Gilded One, 'El Dorado', so named from its king who was supposed on feast days to coat himself from head to foot in gold dust. It was a second Inca realm, civilised, rich beyond dreams, yet utterly vulnerable to invasion, and it was supposed to lie in the Guiana Highlands. A Spaniard, Don Antonio de Berrio, had taken up the search some years before and had now, as official 'Governor of El Dorado', established a base on Trinidad. In 1594, Ralegh sent out a ship to spy on the Spaniards in Trinidad. It lost eight men in a brush with Berrio's force but Ralegh went ahead, without royal support. In February 1595, he set off with four ships and three hundred men. His idea was to reach El Dorado and verify its opulence, come to terms with its emperor, and then persuade his delighted Queen to send him back with an official expedition.

He swiftly destroyed the Spanish town on Trinidad in a surprise attack. The local Indians seemed pleased at the rout of the Spaniards. Ralegh, supposing that he had their consent, formally annexed the island, with its remarkable pitch lake which, he averred, could load 'all the ships of the world'. Then he set off to explore up the Orinoco.

He plumed himself later with his sufferings during the fifteen days which it took him to pass, with a hundred men, through the stifling Orinoco delta, lying on hard boards under the burning sun, living mostly on fish and afflicted with the stench which rose from the wet clothes of his people. There were compensations. '. . . We sawe birds of all colours, some carnation, some crimson, orenge tawny, purple, greene, watched, and of all other sorts both simple and mixt, as it was unto us a great good passing of the time to beholde them . . .' Then came a view of a great highland escarpment ahead, and the huge rolling plains of the Orinoco valley beside their route, park-like, with short green grass, and deer who 'came downe feeding by the waters side, as if they had beene used to a keepers call'.

On the way, he was careful to treat the Indians well; his men, he would swear later, never touched one native woman, though these were very handsome and 'came among us without deceit, starke naked'. But the Englishmen stole on occasions and when he could do so Ralegh made restitution and punished offenders in full view of the villagers. There was self-interest in this. Ralegh could claim later that he had everywhere shown the Indians his Queen's portrait, so she was now very famous in that part of the world, where they venerated her as '*Ezrabeta Cassipuna Aquerewana*, which is as much as *Elizabeth*, the great princesse or greatest commaunder.' Thousands of loyal subjects would make a most handsome present. Yet he seems to have hated truly the 'cruelty' which he attributed to the Spaniards, and to have viewed the Indians with genuine respect.

Ralegh heard stories which made him believe that El Dorado was truly ahead. He pressed up the tributary river Caroni looking for a passage through the escarpment, but found the way blocked soon by huge waterfalls. He would come back and try again, he decided. He left two English residents with a chief whom he much liked, Topiawari, and took the latter's son on with him to England. Here, his reception was chilly. With the Queen still deaf, he wrote and published his tale, The *Discoverie of the Large Rich, and Beautiful Empyre of Guiana*, extolling the fine climate, the bounty of nature, the mineral wealth, of 'a Countrey that hath yet her Maydenhead, never sackt, turned, nor wrought . . .'

Early in 1596 he sent Laurence Keymis back to Guiana. Keymis found a new Spanish fort at the mouth of the Caroni, and just missed the start of a disastrous Spanish attempt to sow the Orinoco basin with European settlers. When Keymis reached home, Ralegh was out of disgrace. He distinguished himself as Vice-Admiral of the Cadiz fleet, and was soon absorbed in a multitude of new duties. However, his book sold hugely. Others would soon pursue the direction he pointed in.

And meanwhile, to Ralegh's gold-haunted coastline, the privateers continued their visits.

XIV

The term 'privateer' was not in fact used till the seventeenth century, when it came to denote a ship sailing to take plunder from the enemy in compensation for goods lost by its owner through that enemy's depredations. The privateer was distinguished from the pirate by the fact that he acted by licence under some recognised authority. Philip II's seizure of English merchant ships in 1585 gave many people a real basis for privateering, but in practice the pretext of reprisal became little more than a legal fiction.

So genuine ships of reprisal mingled, in the guerrilla host which took to the sea from the summer of 1585, with private men-of-war equipped by gentlemen and merchants, and with pirates, who would not be treated as such so long as they stuck to Spanish shipping. There were about a hundred privateering voyages a year down to the end of the war in 1603. Seamen notoriously preferred these ships, though they were overcrowded (for the sake of strong boarding parties) and, hence, sadly disease-ridden, to those of the Queen's Navy where discipline was stricter and the rewards were lower. Men gambled their lives for loot, and the proceeds were on occasion enormous. In 1592 privateers captured a huge Portuguese East India carrack off the Azores, laden with jewels, silks and spices. A cargo worth perhaps £500,000 was ransacked by the mariners – and even so about £140,000 was left for the promoters, of which the Queen, a shareholder, took about half. Such bonanzas were of course rare, but most of the many expeditions to the West Indies seem at least to have covered their expenses.

This was, then, a popular sea war, waged in a roughly democratic fashion, with crews consulted on all important matters. The cumulative results were remarkable. In the course of the war, Spain and Portugal must have lost over a thousand ships, and as they ran short of vessels they became dependent on foreign carriers – the efficient Dutch were the main beneficiaries.

Some of the privateering promoters were gentlemen-amateurs inspired by notions of derring-do and chivalry, like Thomas Cavendish, a young Suffolk squire who sold or mortgaged much of his lands to help pay for the voyage (1586–8) which made him the second English commander to circumnavigate the globe. George Clifford, 3rd Earl of Cumberland, claimed in 1600 that he had spent £100,000 on sea voyages, and he had indeed sent out several fleets comparable in strength to squadrons of the Royal Navy. A contemporary said they were 'bound for no other harbour but the port of honour, though touching at the port of profit in passage thereunto'. But he so overstrained his resources that he was drawn into co-operation with London merchants for whom the port of profit was the sole target.

Ralegh's sometime colleague John Watts was probably the most active of these. As the war dragged on, the great London merchants took a larger and larger share of the risks and proceeds of privateering. The merchants financing privateering included members of the City's élite whose fortunes, stemming in very great part from sea plunder, would be available, early in the new century, to finance colonies and long voyages on a scale hitherto impossible.

Capital was concentrated, in London, in the hands of men skilled in the problems of long-distance enterprises. The building of ships – and of large ships – was stimulated. Few English sailors before the war had much experience of transatlantic sailing; such men were abundant by its end. Captain Christopher Newport was the epitome of a new kind of professional specialising in far voyages. He lost his right arm trying to capture two Mexican treasure ships in 1589, but went back to the Caribbean year after year. He came to know its coasts and waters better even than Drake, but unlike Sir Francis he did not project great schemes on his own account. He became a prosperous and respected man, who after the war took colonists to Virginia (where the town of Newport would be named after him) and finally died in Java on his third voyage for the East India Company.

The exotic luxuries brought in by privateering stimulated new tastes in England, and also the industries which served them. Perfume became the fashion. Sugar began its long march from the tables of the few to those of the many. Before the war, sugar imports, mainly from Morocco, had run at £20,000 or £30,000 a year. In three years, 1589–91, privateers alone brought in sugar worth £100,000, and a Spanish spy could report, 'sugar is cheaper in London than it is in Lisbon or the Indies themselves.' The Portuguese in Brazil were rapidly increasing their output of sugar in the last quarter of the century, and now that their Spanish King had dragged them into war their ships became an especially popular target.

And the English captured altogether three of the vast Portuguese carracks which came home laden from Golden Goa with Eastern delights. For a while London merchants found it cheaper to bring in such goods as plunder than take the risks of direct trade in the East. But the Dutch showed that it could he done. In 1598 they sent no fewer than 22 ships to the East; 4 sent earlier came home lavishly laden next year. The bowels of men like Watts yearned.

In September 1599 over a hundred London merchants promised a total of £30,000 'to set forthe a vyage this present year to the Est Indies and other the ilandes and cuntries therabouts . . . ' They elected their own committee of fifteen and sought a charter, which they received at the end of 1600. So the East India Company began, a new initiative opening a new century. In its councils, the privateering magnates provided effective leadership.

The redoubtable James Lancaster set off with four ships for the East in February 1601. They would all come home safely and profitably three summers later, after trading in Sumatra and Java. The East India Company, infant giant, foreshadowed the end of the epoch of petty stabs towards far continents by individuals and small partnerships. The Newports, managerial skippers, were replacing the Hawkinses and Drakes. London merchant interests, and those who could best work with them, had taken over the lead from the West County gentry. Now, on the bigger ships which sailed East, discipline would be exacting, the crews would no longer have a voice. A new style of merchant capitalism stepped portentously out of the violence and muddle of war.

XV

The harvests from 1592 to 1596 were bad in England. Famine or near famine resulted. Prices rose sharply. Plague raged. Returning soldiers – sick, wounded, discharged, deserting – complicated all social problems.

Meanwhile, the war was ruinous for the Crown. Costs were rising, as long-bows gave way to muskets. Elizabeth had to call six parliaments during the war, and while subsidies were readily granted, MPs grew cocky and truculent. In 1601, the royal prerogative itself was questioned, and the monopolies held by men like Ralegh were bitterly attacked. Even £2 million voted in taxes could not pay for the war. More royal lands had to be sold. Vigorous and unpopular actions raised crown income from its normal level of £200,000 per annum to £300,000 – but the minister Robert Cecil alleged in 1599 that Ireland alone had cost £4,300,000 since the Armada year.

England could not yet afford foreign mercenaries and the strain on a population smaller than that of the Low Countries, less than half that of Spain, was severe. Of 20,000 men raised for France, barely half returned. Rather more went to the Low Countries, almost as many were levied for three great naval expeditions, but Ireland was the greatest drain, drawing perhaps 25,000 men. Trained militiamen were kept in England for home defence; it was raw pressed men who were sent abroad.

In 1559, Shane O Neill's time, little more than 1,000 regular troops had been at the Viceroy's disposal in Ireland. At the height of Desmond's rebellion, nearly 9,000 had been employed. To put down Tyrone would call, at peak, for double that number. The quotas demanded from Lord Lieutenants of English counties were largely filled with men of whom the authorities wished to be rid. A critic complained, 'We disburden the prison of thieves, we rob the taverns and ale-houses of toss-pots and ruffians; we scour both town and country for rogues and vagabonds.' The masterless men of England were sent to put down the unmastered men of Ireland. To desert was for many the first and final ambition. At least half the troops probably died in service, but this would have been true in France or the Low Countries. What made Irish service uniquely unpopular was the absence of rich towns to loot in the dysentery-ridden island, and the presence of an enemy who did not follow the rules of war which Englishmen thought fair.

Half a year sometimes elapsed between pay days. So troops leeched ferociously on the natives, seizing food, drink and money wherever they could.

Even so they went short. 'Most part of the army', one captain reported from Munster, 'seem beggarly ghosts'. Men sold their equipment, even their clothes, while corrupt captains encouraged their English troops to desert and filled their ranks with Irish who would accept still worse terms, then drew full pay for them.

Irish rebels before this had been quite easy to beat. English cannon, though cumbersome on the march in a land without roads, served well to reduce Irish strongpoints. English cavalry were at a disadvantage in bogs and woodlands, but they had been able to break up any opposing body of Irish foot. Now success was far harder. A gloomy official told Robert Cecil in 1596 that Tyrone's unprecedented forces 'could now affront the royal army in the open plain, instead of as formerly only in defiles and forests.' Tyrone had officers with him who had served the English. He had a steady flow of deserters and the expertise of a scattering of Spaniards. He got some munitions, as well as gold, from Spain, and much from the Lowland burghs of Scotland, but another important source were the Crown's supposedly loyal Irish subjects. Gentlemen sold to Tyrone munitions which they had drawn from royal stores under the pretext that they were fighting the Gaels. Kerns became musketeers. Tyrone's rebels could put together a force approaching English standards in arms and in discipline. Yet the Irish retained such advantages as their mode of life gave them. Roaming cattle readily fed swift-moving horsemen. Forests and bogs and mountain passes gave ample scope for guerrilla tactics.

Tyrone's own leadership may have counted for much, but his aims will always remain obscure. Like Fitzmaurice before him, though perhaps less sincerely, he made the cause of Catholicism one with that of preserving Irish chiefship. He must have thought of uniting the country under his own rule, but in the last resort he depended on Spanish troops for victory, and if they had come in sufficient numbers, Ireland would have exchanged the rule of England for the hegemony of Spain. The scanty known facts give one licence to make contradictory judgments of the man. Some make him seem like a tragic victim, English by culture yet captured by Gaeldom. At the height of his rebel power, an English visitor saw him with his two sons, who wore English clothes and spoke English. Tyrone assured him that he was not ambitious, 'but sought only safety for himself, and freedom of conscience'. Tyrone's massive vague figure exposes all the internal contradictions of a dying Celtic order which could only submit to its own dissolution, or seek to arrest change by taking sword in hand, so hastening its own destruction. But for all this, Tyrone was the skilful and undisputed leader of a uniquely wide confederacy when he came off the fence at last in 1595.

In October that year, he and Red Hugh O Donnell appealed to Spain for two or three thousand soldiers to help them 'restore the faith of the Church' and to secure Philip II 'a kingdom'. The weather frustrated Spanish expeditions. Without foreign help, Tyrone's aims stopped short at defence. He mixed diplomacy shrewdly with aggression, sporadic confrontations with specious negotiations. After several months of formal truce, he and his allies burst out in Ulster and Leinster during the summer of 1598, and his old foe Sir Henry Bagenal marched north rashly to relieve a strategically vital fort on the Blackwater which Tyrone was attacking. The English force, over 4,000, was a large one for Irish warfare, but on August 14, in sight of the fort, at a place called 'the Yellow Ford', it was utterly shattered. Bagenal himself was killed, only 1,500 men got back to Armagh, and this was a worse disaster than English troops had ever suffered in Ireland, or would ever suffer again.

Tyrone could have struck at Dublin and captured it. Fatally, he did not, but with his allies he now dominated most of Ireland. He himself was master of almost all Ulster. O Donnell, with Burke allies, controlled Connacht. The O Mores were up in Leinster and Owney MacRory O More and Captain Tyrrell (an Irish renegade from the royal army) broke into Munster with a large force to raise support for James Fitzthomas Fitzgerald, nephew of the last Earl of Desmond and now, as claimant to his position, nicknamed the 'Sugane' (straw-rope) Earl. Those Munster colonists who could flee did so. Those who could not were slaughtered or mutilated, 'divers sent into Youghal amongst the English, some with their throats cut, but not killed, some with their tongues cut out of their heads, others with their noses cut off . . . '

Elizabeth withdrew hundreds of troops from the Low Countries, called out new levies in England, and, as a likely-looking response to a desperate situation, sent to Ireland, as Lord Lieutenant, her prime favourite, the handsome, dashing and greatly ambitious Earl of Essex. Gentlemen adventurers flocked to his popular standard. He was to have 16,000 foot and 1,300 horse, with 2,000 reinforcements to follow every three months. No commander in Ireland had ever led such a force. Essex arrived in the spring of 1599, carrying with him exceptional hopes, which he dashed with exceptional suddenness.

He dawdled through Leinster and Munster, wasting men's lives in skirmishes, but bringing not one rebel to submission. Elizabeth insisted that Essex must move to Ulster and put an axe 'to the root of that tree which hath been the treasonable stock from which so many poisoned plants and grafts have been derived.' He duly marched north with 4,000 men, but he did not fight Tyrone. In September the two men talked for half an hour without witnesses at a ford. It is quite likely that Tyrone played on Essex's ambitions to rule in England and inveigled, or half-inveigled, his support for the Gaelic cause. Certainly six weeks' truce was arranged on terms which favoured Tyrone. Then Essex received a note from the Queen ordering that no truce should be made. He at once, breaking all commands, dashed to London, to throw himself at her feet. She imprisoned him. Essex, deprived of most of his offices, plotted treason and became a magnet for all malcontents. Early in 1601, he attempted to raise London in rebellion, failed, and was executed; Ireland had ruined him, as it had killed his father.

His successor there was a man of most different mettle. Charles Blount, Lord

Mountjoy, arrived as Lord Deputy early in 1601. Though 36, he had never commanded large bodies of troops in the field before. His personal habits hardly seemed apt for Irish conditions; he was a valetudinarian, finicky about his food, who wore three waistcoats in cold weather. (Fynes Moryson, who left a famous prose portrait of him, thought his abundant use of tobacco helped to avert the ill effects of Irish provender, bogs and climate; certainly, it must have helped ward off the insects.) A model Protestant gentleman, he prayed always morning and night and scowled fiercely when men swore at his table, but he was averse to religious persecution and saw that it merely encouraged the views which it sought to extirpate. He argued intelligently with priests and Jesuits 'as upon divers occasions with other Papists his friends.'

Yet he proved most efficient, and ruthless. He spent longer in the saddle than any previous viceroy, soldiering five days a week in the depths of winter. The aim was complete conquest; the means, force applied without qualms. He planted garrisons shrewdly so as to pin rebels down in their own localities and thus prevent them from co-operating. His winter campaigning aimed to push the Gaels into starvation. It 'brake their hearts', Fynes Moryson wrote, 'for the air being sharp and they naked, and they being driven from their lodgings, into the woods bare of leaves, they had no shelter for themselves. Besides that, their cattle (giving them no milk in the winter) were also wasted by driving to and fro, and that they being thus troubled in the seed-time, could not sow their ground. And as in harvest time, both the Deputy's forces, and the garrisons, cut down their corn, before it was ripe, so now in winter time, they carried away or burnt all the stores of victuals in secret places, whither the rebels had conveyed them.' Mountjoy had able lieutenants. Sir George Carew had almost pacified Munster within a year. Ulster itself, hitherto almost impregnable, now began to fall to attack from three sides. Sir Henry Docwra garrisoned Lough Foyle and created a base in Tyrone's rear, and both he and Sir Arthur Chichester, governor of Carrickfergus, played skilfully on rivalries among the Gaels. In the summer of 1601, Mountjoy was able to enter the township of Tyrone itself. He left strong forces in Ulster, then headed south again. A Spanish landing was imminent at last. Mountjoy had ensured that it came too late.

There were too few Spaniards anyway. Another Protestant gale had reft nine ships from their fleet. Aguila, commanding the Spanish force, had under 4,000 men. They landed at Kinsale in late September, occupied the town, and stayed there. By the end of October, Mountjoy had opposed them with nearly 7,000 foot and over 600 horse. The necessary withdrawal of troops from other parts made it easy now for Tyrone and Red Hugh to bring their men south. They moved only slowly. Red Hugh, true to his Gaelic tradition, wasted three weeks ravaging Tipperary. But by early December, some 700 further Spaniards had arrived at another Munster port, Castlehaven, and had got much support from the local Irish, while Tyrone and Red Hugh were virtually besieging the English besiegers of Kinsale.

Despite 5,000 reinforcements from England, Mountjoy was now down to little over 6,500 fit footsoldiers, no more than the encircling Gaels. Sickness and large-scale desertion had withered the English army. Tyrone's view now, as before, was sagely Fabian; no need to attack, let the Sassenachs rot away. But the ardour of Red Hugh and the pressure of the besieged Spaniards overcame his caution. A plan for simultaneous attack on the English was worked out, but wangles over precedence meant that the Gaelic attack on December 24 began late. Aguila, missing them at the expected time, stayed put in Kinsale. Mountjoy left 4,000 men to confront the Spaniards and sent only 1,100 against the Gaels. But one daring English cavalry charge was enough. The Gaels ran headlong, leaving hundreds of dead, while the Spaniards who had joined them from Castlehaven stood rock firm and fought till three-quarters of them were killed. The English lost just one man.

As his followers streamed homewards, Red Hugh took ship to Spain to seek further aid; he died there, perhaps by poison, leaving sorrowing tales of the most glamorous of young rebels. The Spaniards soon surrendered and were duly shipped home by the English; there was no massacre this time. Despite the sickness which now carried off thousands of Mountjoy's men, the war was almost over. When the Deputy came north again in the summer of 1602, Tyrone took to the fern. Mountjoy systematically ravaged his lands, destroyed all the standing corn, and smashed the 'stone of the kings' used for centuries in the inaugurations of the O Neills at Tullaghoge.

The symbolism was apt. Gaelic Ireland was beaten. The English must now decide how to rule the land they had conquered.

XVI

Ireland had left Elizabeth with very scant resources for England's northern border. Good relations with Scotland were assured after 1586 and this encouraged the Queen to cut costs, while the still more impecunious Scottish King stopped paying salaries to his frontier wardens altogether. The level of violence and rapine perhaps rose. In 1589–90 men from Liddesdale alone, Armstrongs, Elliotts and the like, were averaging a raid a week; in that winter they stole more than eight hundred and fifty beasts, captured some sixty prisoners, wounded ten men, killed one, burned five houses, and took £200 worth of household goods (children's coats and cooking utensils not excepted).

The Scottish wardens, local magnates, were commonly ringleaders in feuds, but on the English side the Carey family were specialist forerunners of the colonial service. Henry Carey, Lord Hunsdon, served his cousin the Queen on the Border for nearly thirty years.

One of Hunsdon's sons, Robert, gives in his Memoirs a most vivacious account of his life among the Border tribes. In 1601, when he was warden of the English Middle March, he resolved to have it out with the Armstrongs for good and all. They withdrew to Tarras Moss beyond Liddesdale, a forest stronghold surrounded by bogs, marshy ground and wilderness. Carey sent 150 troops to encircle the Tarras by night and lay ambushes, then he attacked openly at dawn with 300 horse and 1,000 infantry. As the outlaws fled the ambushes were sprung and five Armstrong leaders were captured, whose value as hostages Carey exploited so thoroughly that he had no more trouble with the surname afterwards.

Visiting the Queen early in 1603, Robert Carey saw she was dying and took serious thought of his own future. He wrote to James VI telling him how things were and promising that when death came, he would be the first to bring news. 'On Wednesday the twenty-third of March she grew speechless. That afternoone, by signes, she called for her Councill, and by putting her hand to her head, when the King of Scottes was named to succeed her, they all knew hee was the man she desired should reign after her.' By ten the next morning, Carey was in the saddle madly riding north. He reached Edinburgh on Saturday evening, having covered 400 miles in 60 hours. James was roused from his bed. Carey knelt and saluted him 'by his title of England, Scotland, France and Ireland.'

A few days later Tyrone came in and submitted, to Queen Elizabeth. Mountjoy had heard of her death and had no right to accept the surrender, but did so. Tyrone was promised, and got, a pardon, his earldom restored, and most of his old lands back. When he did hear that the Queen had gone, he wept.

Perhaps he wept because he thought that new political complications in England might have favoured his now-dead rebellion. But in fact the Crown changed hands smoothly. James borrowed 10,000 marks from the City of Edinburgh and his family lashed out on new clothes. Then he sped south with his followers for the fat lands of England somewhat himself like the last of the great reivers. His Proclamation of the Union of the Crowns of Scotland and England announced, '. . . The Isle within itself hath almost none but imaginary bounds of separation, without but one common limit or rather guard of the Ocean sea, making the whole a little world within itself, the nations an uniformity of constitutions both of body and mind, especially in martial processes, a community of language (the principle means of civil society), an unity of religion (the deepest bond of hearty union and the surest knot of lasting peace.)' This was, of course, over-optimistic. The Highland Gaels of Scotland still did not share in the 'community of language' and were outside 'civil society'. Religious divisions would yet be involved in new wars between Scotland and England. But the Union of the Crowns would survive, and with it the Border problem melted like snow on the Cheviots in spring.

The Marches became the 'middle shires'. Trading replaced raiding. Galloway cattle travelled south safely to England. Poor cottagers were thrust out and sheep came in. The days of Fingerless Will Nixon, Archie Fire the Braes Elliott and other reivers of their like were over. The Union was followed at once by wholesale hangings. The gentry entrusted with mopping up saw the chance of helping themselves to confiscated land. Of all riding families the English

Grahams of Esk suffered worst. They had some good land on which the privateering Earl of Cumberland's eye had fallen. Scores of Grahams were sent to serve in the Low Country garrisons, but most quickly stole back, and a clutch of the surname holed up in south-west Scotland and resumed the trade of reivers. By 1606 the Commissioners appointed to pacify the Border were gaoling even innocent Grahams. Now it was first decided that the internal colonisation of Britain would provide colonists for overseas. The Grahams were to go to Ireland, where a gentleman in Roscommon wanted settlers. The gentry of Cumberland and Westmorland subscribed £300 to the cost of transportation. Scottish Elliotts were forced out in the same way. Great men whose feuds had troubled the peace kept their land; small malefactors were hanged and drowned and transported until the Borders were, in the word of the time, 'purgit'.

Peace on the Borders; and peace with Spain. The Treaty of London in 1604 ended the long war. Spain remained a great power but her northern enemies, Dutch and English, had won, and were still winning, the battle for commerce. Now peace meant that England's Western sailors could establish the first of the classic 'triangular trades', catching cod off Newfoundland and North America, taking it direct to Portugal, Spain and the western Mediterranean, then bringing home oil and fruit and wine from sunnier climes than their own.

Ralegh was now in the Tower, and would be for ten more years. James had disliked and feared him from the start. Ralegh had pressed for continued war against Spain. The King wanted peace. A ridiculous charge of treason was trumped up. To contemporaries Ralegh's imprisonment came to symbolise all their regrets for the old Queen's reign, now superseded by the graceless cavortings and craven diplomacy of an ill-favoured northern foreigner. A poet declared in 1616,

> Time never can produce men to o'ertake
> The fames of Grenville, Davies, Gilbert, Drake . . .

Pygmies had followed giants. The papists were getting off lightly. Ralegh's patent rights in America had passed into the hands of King James himself.

But in fact he used them towards the foundation of colonies which, unlike Ralegh's, endured. He came to the throne with ideas on the subject and with some, hard, experience. While Elizabeth's men had been fighting in Ireland, some of his had been trying to colonise the Hebrides. The lure there was fish, not gold, but James was right to think that nets cast for such things would eventually haul in bullion.

Thomas Smythe's Expansion

I

James VI and I grew up in a chaos of faction and internecine violence and then, despite his physical timidity, secured a grip on Scotland in the 1580s which he held for forty years. He raised up lesser landowners, especially men who gave him loyal service, so as to balance the great feudal magnates. He brought to submission the group of Catholic lords led by the Gordon Earl of Huntly. He persuaded the Kirk to bow to his authority, despite its strong Presbyterian faction. But he could not boost the royal revenue to the point where he could pay his own way. He scrounged when in pressing need. He devalued the Scottish coinage to his own short-term advantage. He made extravagant gifts to his favourites.

In the Highlands and islands James maintained the policy of using certain great clans whose own lands fringed the Lowlands to keep raids into the English-speaking areas down to a minimum. Thus, he connived in the attempted destruction by his Campbell allies of Clan Gregor. The MacGregor had been a chief of note, extolled by bards – 'gold gleameth on their hilts, the weapons of the Lion of Loch Awe.' But his estate, in truth, had been small, and his clansmen, scattered tenants of other chiefs, had become rightly notorious for their plunderings in the Lowlands. In 1610, a campaign of extermination was mounted. Twenty-eight nobles and lairds who had MacGregors as neighbours received a commission of fire and sword to 'ruit oute and extirpat all that race'. A fat price was put on the head of every MacGregor, and their name was outlawed until the late eighteenth century.

Meanwhile, the Campbells completed the destruction of the Macdonalds of Islay, symbolised by the erection (1609) of the royal burgh of Campbeltown in the Kintyre peninsula. The Campbell empire now stretched from there through the Central Highlands to Calder (Cawdor) in the north-east. Further north, in Ross, the Mackenzies had risen by similar methods, serving the Crown in Edinburgh, and appearing to do so in the Highlands, while by judicious marriages and by business cunning they engrossed a large belt of territory. As one Gordon put it, 'Thus doe the tryb of Clankeinzie become great in these pairts, still incroaching upon ther nighbours who are unacquented with the lawes of this kingdome.' But meanwhile the Gordons themselves, led by earls of Huntly and Sutherland, built up a similar empire in the north-east.

For lesser Gaels, James had no sympathy at all. An Act of 1597 ordered landlords and clan chiefs to produce title deeds to the lands which they held and to find security for regular payments of the royal rents and for the peaceful behaviour of themselves and their men, on pain of forfeiture. Since many chiefs would be unable to meet the conditions, its clear intention was to provide the Crown with large tracts of land. The preamble complained that by their 'barbarous inhumanity' the occupants had made unprofitable, both to themselves and others, lands 'most commodious in themselves as well by the fertility of the ground as by the rich fishings by sea . . .' The view that there was great wealth to be tapped in the glens and lochs informed another Act of the same year which ordained the erection of royal burghs in Kintyre, Lochaber and Lewis. Nothing came of the Lochaber project. The struggle to realise the Lewis one makes a significant story.

The fish trade was already important to Scotland's Lowland burghs. The profits to be made from fish bulked large in the arrangement which James made in 1598 with a group of twelve men headed by his cousin, the Duke of Lennox, and mostly composed of Fife barons, hence known as the 'Fife Adventurers'. These men were granted the remote isle of Lewis and Harris, with parts of Skye. Harris and also Dunvegan on Skye were held, though in James's view illegally, by a very shrewd customer, Rory Mor Macleod, chief of the branch of his clan called Siol Tormod. But the Macleods on Lewis, the Sior Torquil, were embroiled in a characteristic Gaelic succession dispute. So thither the Fife-men sailed at the end of the year, with five or six hundred soldiers and some craftsmen.

The King's plans involved 'ruiting out the barbarous inhabitantis'. These latter, however, had their own view of affairs. 'Barbarous, bludie, and wiket Hielandmen', led by one Neil Macleod, opposed the settlers from the first. So did Mackenzie of Kintail, though he was overtly obedient. He wanted Lewis himself. When the colonists, despite hostile arrows and dysentery, had begun to erect their town at Stornoway, Mackenzie shrewdly released the young man, Tormod, whom most of the clan regarded as rightful chief and whom he had been holding captive. Inspired by the presence of their true leader, the Macleods attacked and forced the Adventurers to surrender with heavy losses. In 1602, after just three years they sailed abjectly away.

James was incensed by this indignity. A fresh expedition was sent in 1605, led by Sir James Spens and Sir George Hay. Tormod Macleod seems to have picked up too much 'civility' for his own good. He accepted the offer of these men that they would send him to London to get a pardon from James. He duly went to the court, but was sent back to Edinburgh and imprisoned for ten years without trial. However, Neil Macleod, after waging guerrilla war against the new colony, attacked decisively in April 1607, destroyed £10,000 worth of property and forced a second evacuation. When a third attempt was made in 1609, Mackenzie of Kintail was entrusted with the duty of assisting it. He tricked James neatly, sending supplies of food but tipping off Neil so that the ship which carried them would be captured. Hay and Spens hurried back to Fife for reinforcements and provisions, and Neil assailed the small garrison which they had left, killed some, and packed the rest off home.

Mackenzie, in a contemporary's words, now 'catched his long-wished and expected prey'. Hay and Spens sold their rights in Lewis to him. When he died in 1611, the inveterate Neil still held out, but he met his end on a gallows two years later and Mackenzie's son had undisputed possession of Lewis, to which he soon added the new title of Earl of Seaforth. The Earl brought Dutch merchants to Stornoway, where they traded in tallow, hides, plaiding and the like. Great fleets meanwhile came yearly from Holland to reap silver harvests in Scottish waters, and Lowland enterprise could not compete with them.

However, the attempt at colonisation had given neighbouring Gaelic chiefs a bad shock, and this assisted James's policy. In 1608 Lord Ochiltree trapped, on the King's behalf, a number of chiefs whom he had invited to dinner on his ship off Mull, and they were imprisoned, in Lowland castles. They all made abject submission. In the summer of 1609 they and others signed, on the island of Iona, the so-called 'Statutes of Icolmkill' presented to them by the government. Macleod of Dunvegan, Macdonald of Dunyveg, Macdonald of Sleat, MacLean of Duart, MacLame of Lochbuie, MacLean of Coll, MacKinnon of Strath and MacQuarrie of Ulva agreed, implausibly, that they would support kirks and Protestant ministers, establish inns, limit the number of followers they maintained, stop entertaining bards, and send their sons to school in the Lowlands until they could speak, read and write English. They were to be answerable for the doings of their followers and must report in person every year to the Privy Council.

The statute which forbade drinking of wine by common people merely encouraged the islanders in the perfectly legal distillation of whisky. While the now submissive Rory Mor Macleod was given a charter for his lands, and acquired a knighthood, he continued to keep court at Dunvegan in high traditional style, and was duly praised for it by Gaelic poets:

> We were twenty times drunk every day,
> To which we had no more objection than he had.

But the Isles did become relatively peaceful.

James could not prevail upon his new English subjects to accept his suggestion of a union of Parliaments, a union of Churches, and free trade between England and Scotland, and the Scots, rather than flocking south as English prejudice insisted that they had done, continued to maintain and extend their own links with the Continent. Scores of thousands emigrated there in the seventeenth century, as mercenary soldiers, pedlars and farmers. The poverty of their homeland spurred them. James himself was glad enough to be out of the draughty, hand-to-mouth life which he had led in Edinburgh, and did not revisit Scotland till 1617. But his very absence, which lifted him from the reach of factions, probably helped tame the country. Through a governing élite of professional officials, James had the Parliament, the General Assembly of the

Church, the Court of Session and the Convention of Burghs under effective control. Townsmen, lawyers and smaller landowners supported the royal authority. The Scots were now, by their standards, docile: the English Parliament certainly was not.

II

It didn't like James much. The new King was homely, clumsy, fearful and uncouth. He was genuinely learned and highly intelligent, but he speechified too often and too long for the patience of his subjects. He was often drunk and could not disguise his homosexual proclivities. His quirks and idiosyncrasies might have been found endearing, had most not been, very typically, Scots ones. English prejudice against a Scots dynasty soon surfaced; an MP was sent to the Tower for saying that the union of England with Scotland which James wanted was as natural as the union of a prisoner with his judge. It could not be suppressed; in 1640 a Kentish preacher declared that if a Scotsman ever went to Heaven, the devil would go too.

James was extravagant. His ordinary expenditure doubled that of Elizabeth. Such vanity weighed far more in the eyes of tax-hating landed gentlemen than James's assertion of the divine right of kings, in which Elizabeth had believed, and which his Puritan opponents in Parliament also accepted. But what counted for most of all in the eventual intensification of the struggle between Crown and Parliament was probably the arrival, around 1620, of a long phase of economic depression.

The peace with Spain in 1604 gladdened the hearts of many merchants, and rising prosperity, at first, followed. James shared in it; customs revenue more than doubled in the first eighteen years of his reign and in 1621 provided three times as much income as Crown lands. Then came a crisis in European trade which lasted for generations and which has been held responsible for a wave of revolutions over the Continent in the 1630s and 1640s. The population rise of the sixteenth century was checked, and there may even have been a general decline. The great price rise jolted to a halt by the 1640s. In 1620 the conflict now known as the Thirty Years War began to rack the centre of the Continent.

Tonnage of English-owned shipping (the figures cannot be certain) seems to have risen from 67,000 in 1582 to 115,000 in 1629 and somewhere between 150,000 and 200,000 by 1660. Let us say that it may have trebled in eighty years. Transatlantic and East India trade played some part in this growth, but carrying coal from Newcastle should not be forgotten. The coastal coal trade, above all to London, waxed importantly, engaging 1,400 large ships by 1700 where it had used only 400 smallish ones at the start of the century. And trade with Europe still far outweighed fancy traffic in far continents. Here was the heart of a crisis. The Thirty Years War provoked the sudden collapse of traditional markets for English cloth. A difficult readjustment had to be made.

The so-called 'New Draperies' now became crucial. These lighter cloths did well in the Mediterranean, where the collapse of the native textile industries in Spain and Italy was obvious by the 1620s, leaving open rich markets not only in Southern Europe itself but in the Spanish colonies and in the Levant. By 1700 only half of English cloth exports were going to the traditional markets in Northern and Central Europe.

The Dutch were both coadjutors and rivals. Eighty years of war from the 1560s to 1648 established the independence of the seven United Provinces of the Netherlands. In the fifteenth and sixteenth centuries, the ports of Holland and Zeeland had won a main share of the carrying trade between the Baltic and Western Europe. By the 1590s the Dutch had evolved a basis for world power, the *fluit*, a cargo ship which because it employed fewer hands, and carried greater bulk – of Baltic grain, of timber or of sugar – could undercut all competition. During their struggle with Spain, they continued to supply their papist enemies with grain and naval stores which the latter could simply not do without, and their cynical dedication to profits became a byword among their English competitors, on whom the lesson was not wasted. By 1648, the Netherlands were a republic effectively dominated by an oligarchy of some 10,000 rich men.

Amsterdam now had a status as an international commercial emporium never matched before or, arguably, since. Yet its ruling townsmen staggered foreigners by their very lack of ostentation, their 'parcimonious and thrifty Living'. The great seaman de Ruyter would dress like the plainest sea-captain, the great statesman Johan de Witt like the commonest burgher, and neither was ever seen attended by more than one manservant, indoors or out. To a surprising extent even the people of the rural Netherlands – those narrow lands largely hard won by reclamation from the North Sea – shared in the values of town-dwellers. So far had they travelled from ideas of self-sufficiency, that frugal Dutch farmers were said to sell their high quality cheese and butter for export and buy for themselves 'the cheapest out of Ireland or the North of England.'

This was the most densely populated part of Europe. Agriculture had responded by concentrating on crops grown for cash and on cattle breeding – those cows so respectfully painted by seventeenth-century Dutch masters were fit inhabitants of a townsman's best room; they were at as far an extreme from the black beasts of the Scottish Highlands as the Dutch burgher was from a Gaelic tribesman. For centuries the Dutch had been pioneers in agricultural technique. The crop rotations which they had developed raised yields of corn remarkably. Now in the seventeenth century their efforts at land reclamation reached a peak; and they introduced high-yielding artificial grasses which enabled them to feed more animals and, at the same time, to grow more crops with the help of the manure which their livestock gave them.

Forward-looking English landowners, most famously in Norfolk, followed the Dutch example and planted turnips to feed to their cattle. The Dutch lead was pursued in crop rotation, vegetable growing, the use of windmills. But the Dutch were hard to catch. Norfolk barley was brewed in the Netherlands. Dutch herring boats plundered British waters from the Shetlands to the Thames.

The Dutch loudly preached the freedom of the seas. They must be able to go where they wanted, papal bulls notwithstanding. When they had got there, they strove to exclude all competitors, with almost complete success in Indonesia, and totally in Japan, where they were the only Europeans allowed to trade between 1639 and 1854. Against them, the merchants and intellectuals of England and other countries began to refine 'mercantilist' ideas.

In the the 1620s the government took the novel step of calling in merchant experts to advise it about the deep and complex depression which had struck English trade and industry. How was it, men were asking, that Spain, with so much 'treasure' at its disposal, could not hold on to it and was growing poor, while its Dutch enemies had built up Europe's largest commercial fleet, 'those multitudes of Ships,' Thomas Mun wrote, 'which unto them are as our Ploughs to us, the which except they stir, the people starve . . .' His credo, *England's Treasure by Foreign Trade*, quite likely written in the 1620s, though not printed till 1664, would eventually become a kind of Old Testament for English economic thinkers.

The term 'mercantilism' was in fact unknown before Adam Smith in 1776 launched his attack on the system which he called 'mercantile', associating it with two ideas which he thought especially erroneous. One was the emphasis placed on the accumulation of gold and silver, which seemed to confuse money with wealth. A second idea, found in Mun and in his successors, was that the nation must maintain a favourable balance of trade; this promoted what Smith thought vicious state interference to discourage imports and boost exports, sacrificing, Smith would say, the interests of consumers to those of producers. But now that Smith himself is no longer uncritically cited, we can see mercantilism as an adequate, if unlovely, response to the challenges of seventeenth-century Europe.

Mun was one of the state-appointed Commissioners who put forward in 1622 a prophetic set of proposals. English raw materials should be reserved to the native cloth industry by the prohibition of exports of wool, fullers' earth and so on, especially to Holland. England should reduce her need for imports by developing manufactures of her own – linen, for instance, should be made with home-grown flax. Native fishing companies should be formed and the Dutch ousted. Goods imported from abroad should come only in English ships or in ships belonging to the country which had produced them, so eliminating the Dutch middleman.

In an age of growing national consciousness and deepening national rivalries, when the zeal generated by religious conflicts began to transfer itself to the conflicts between 'states' which were beginning to be called by that name, mercantilism emphasised, not wrongly, the link between trade and power. The power of a strong state intervening forcefully in economic affairs could promote trade which in turn would breed power. Exports, and re-exports, were seen as crucial to 'treasure by foreign trade', the acquisition of a surplus of bullion. Exports to colonies were more securely maintained than exports to alien markets. Colonies meanwhile could make England (say) self-sufficient in necessities and in certain luxuries (sugar, tobacco) which would soon come to seem necessities. A surplus for re-export could be available. And Mun and others favoured internal colonialism within the British Isles themselves. Waste grounds should be used to grow commodities which would otherwise be imported.

A novel faith was emerging, both cynical and naïve, which asserted the glory and dignity of trade. Mun talks of the 'nobleness' of the merchant's 'vocation', confusing 'degree' as his forefathers had seen it. '. . . Wee ought to esteem and cherish', he says, 'those trades which we have in remote or far Countreys.' Why? What is, after all, so estimable about wresting spices from Asian cultivators? 'As for example,' Mun goes on; 'suppose Pepper to be worth here two Shillings the pound constantly, if then it be bought from the Dutch at *Amsterdam*, the merchant may give there twenty pence the pound, and gain well by the bargain; but if he fetch this Pepper from the *East-Indies*, he must not give above three pence the pound at the most, which is a mighty advantage whereby', he concludes, with what may now seem refreshing frankness, 'it is plain, that we make a far greater stock by gain upon these *Indian* commodities, than those Nations doe where they grow, and to whom they properly appertain, being the natural wealth of their Countries.'

The merchant, as Mun eulogises him – the master of the mysteries of trade, 'The Steward of the Kingdom's Stock' – is a crusader chivalrously bearing the grave risks of trade in the interest of Great England. Devoted and penny-counting, he is, in Mun's view, entitled to scorn the mass of his fellow countrymen who still share in 'the general leprosie of our Piping, Potting, Feasting, Fashions, and mis-spending of our time in Idleness and Pleasure (contrary to the Law of God, and the use of other Nations.)' Nationalism, profit and piety mesh together. Puritan dedication to work is good not only because God likes it, but because the Dutch have shown its commercial advantages.

This ideological merging of trade with nobility was very English. It reflected, for instance, and no doubt encouraged, the coalition of merchants with landed gentry and peers which was in Mun's day pressing forward maritime expansion. The surge of prosperity up to about 1615 was accompanied by a rush of investment in overseas trade and colonies. The main engine of advance was the joint-stock company, based on London but commonly raking in money from elsewhere. The country gentleman bumping up to London in his coach – such vehicles came within reach of the middling pocket by the 1590s – so as to vent his hatred of his neighbours in the law courts or his suspicions of the King from his seat in Parliament, was often attracted there to invest in some fine-looking scheme for colonies or discoveries. Joint-stock companies (unlike the regulated companies) gave him the chance of participation without expertise or responsibility. He was rarely attracted by purely commercial aims. Nor was he likely to think of emigration himself. Mercantilist arguments might have some intellectual sway over him. Patriotism moved him. And glory beckoned; gentry were far more willing than merchants to invest in the relatively small companies which promoted wild schemes, as they seemed, for settlements in Guiana or bitter New England, or for the expansion of trade with Africa. Though Sir Edwin Sandys, a substantial landowner, was egregious in the degree of his commitment – he devoted the last twenty years of his life largely to colonial interests, and achieved positions of responsibility in three major trading companies – there is a sense in which this enthusiast, suddenly seized by visions in his mid-forties, typified the whole remarkable breed of gentlemen-investors which had no counterpart on the Continent.

The middling gentleman's contribution in gross financial terms was, however, outweighed by that of peers and great courtiers, whose interest in colonies can be related to their passion for gambling at cards, and who siphoned some of the profits of office into overseas expansion. Men about court were as much involved under James I and Charles I as under Elizabeth, and their interest was shared by the malcontent 'Puritan' faction of the nobility. Professor Rabb was able to classify 5,184 investors in overseas and similar enterprises between 1575 and 1630, out of an overall total of 6,336. Over 1,000 of these were knights and gentlemen. Also involved were 179 peers. Almost 40 per cent of the members of both the 1604 House of Commons and its 1614 successor were investors, and Commons men actually composed about a fifth of the Virginia Company, of which nearly three-quarters of the directorships were held by gentry rather than merchants.

But almost all East India Company directorships down to 1630 were held by merchants, and 85 per cent of the capital in that organisation seems to have come from trade. Most money went into fields where merchants and their quest for immediate profits were dominant – into privateering and into the East India Company. In the annals of expansion from this period even Sandys or the privateering Earl of Warwick is outweighed by the great merchant Sir Thomas Smythe, son of a notoriously successful customs farmer, who had been not implausibly accused of corruption on a huge scale in Elizabeth's day.

Without the concentration of financial resources in the hands of men like Smythe who were prepared to switch them from old to new fields of enterprise, from one quarter of Earth, indeed, to another, overseas Empire could not have existed. But while mercantilism, the cult of trade, rationalised rapacity in the Indies, it also favoured expropriations at home – in the Borders and Lewis, as we have seen; in Ireland, naturally; and in England's own Fen country.

III

A writer of 1586 described the distinctive way of life of the 'rude uncivill' people who dwelt in the peat fens of Cambridgeshire. Their region was 'overflowed' by rivers in winter, and 'sometimes most part of the yeere', but when the streams retired to their own channels they left excellent feeding for cattle. The people mowed as much of the rich hay as would serve them, then, in November, burnt the rest to fertilise the soil. 'Stalking on high upon stilts' – one man so provided could drive hundreds of cattle to pasture – they devoted themselves to grazing, fishing and fowling.

In 1600, Parliament passed a 'General Draining Act'. The Fens were the largest area involved. There were few large estates there, so capital from outside was essential, and could only be attracted by the promise that those who provided it would get a portion of the acreage to be reclaimed. The natives were not prepared to co-operate in the extinction of their way of life, since lands which seemed drowned and worthless to the mercantilist mind were a source of coarse plenty to their inhabitants. Throughout the year the Fens gave employment to multitudes of cottagers, who gathered reeds, fodder, turves and many other useful things. Fish and edible fowl were God's bounty.

Amongst the numerous undertakers who set to work was that great privateering magnate, Alderman Watts. Their syndicate did exploit reclaimed land for several years, but was then turned out by the 'uncivill' Fenmen after the waters broke their banks and 'drowned all again'. The King declared in 1621 that the 'Honour of this kingdome' would not allow the Fens to continue 'wast and unprofitable' but Dutch expertise would be needed before the trick could be done. And meanwhile his Majesty's Irish colonies were presenting him with problems enough.

IV

Ireland when James I came to the throne was a ravaged land. Algerian Muhammadan pirates preyed in the long inlets of Munster. Yet the simple Irish economy had natural resilience. Herrings and salmon knew nothing of soldiers and oppression. The herds and flocks which grew by natural increase would sustain export trades in wool and sheepskins, cattle, hides, tallow and beef. Great woods still covered perhaps an eighth of the land, waiting to be ripped down by English settlers, to fuel the making of iron or to provide pipe staves for exports to the Continent, where they would be used to make wine casks. The axe opened up new lands for settled cultivation. Seeing connection between the trees and the old chiefly families and castes of learned men, a Gaelic poet would lament,

> What shall we do henceforth without timber,
> the last of the woods is fallen . . .

While the trees fell, the Gaelic order fell too.

Conquest completed, the Pale's legal system was swiftly extended over the whole country. Gavelkind and tanistry were declared void of legality. The

Gaelic upper classes were learning English and adopting the conquerors' style of clothing, though in Ulster at least the old *braccae* or trews persisted among the common people despite the denunciations of papist clergy.

The Counter-Reformation had now come to Ireland in force, and its austerity was in sharp conflict with Irish custom. Confronted by cheerful polygamy, by funeral wakes which turned into orgies marked by what seemed obscene songs and gestures, and by general ignorance of the main tenets of Catholicism, Jesuit missionaries now tried to civilise the Irish. However, Irish Franciscans working at Louvain in Europe created a Gaelic press which printed not only religious works but also books which preserved as well as could now be done the Gaels' traditions of their own history.

Irishness and Catholicism were to become identified, and the so-called 'Old English', products of several centuries of alien settlement, but still Catholic, would be driven into 'Irishness' by religious discrimination. The Gaels themselves now distinguished these *Sean-Ghaill* from the *Nua-Ghaill*, 'New English', the fiercely Protestant, curtly supremacist men who had recently come as colonists or officials and whose main vested interest was in preventing the Catholics from taking any share in political power. The greatest New England magnate was Richard Boyle, first Earl of Cork, who had picked up Ralegh's Irish domain and who came to enjoy, by 1629, an income of £20,000 a year from rents alone.

Sean-Ghaill ('Old English') seems to refer to race but in fact defined a political attitude. Some Gaels, leading O Briens, for instance, shared it with some Hibernicised descendants of Norman settlers, with the 'lords of the Pale' whose forebears had come from England long since, and with members of recent settler families (including Spenser's, of all men's) which had slumped into papistry. All these were propertied Catholics still loyal to the Crown and fearful of the 'Gaelic Irish' who might rise and dispossess them. Some two thousand Old English families owned much of the best land in the country, and their sort controlled most of the trade of the Irish ports. Though all were excluded from high office, they had a natural majority in the Irish Parliament which the government had to counteract by creating new boroughs to return Protestants. The Old English had enough influence to ensure that religious conformity was not strictly enforced. An uncomfortable half-tolerance prevailed. Meanwhile Old English unease was accentuated by government schemes for 'plantations', which made all titles to land in Ireland seem insecure.

In Leinster, grants made by Elizabeth, even by James himself, were overturned or rendered shaky in several areas. The poorer Gaels of course bore the brunt. When details of a proposed plantation in Kavanagh country were announced in 1611, the natives who held the land were shocked and angry, and some turned brigand. In 1618, three-quarters of it was in fact set aside for native proprietors, but while the chief landowners got estates good in law, the lesser ones were robbed of everything. Even some Dublin officials were uneasy about this Wexford operation, yet further schemes proceeded in Leitrim and Longford. Sir John MacCoghlan of Delvin had served Elizabeth in her wars; O Dunne of Iregan had a grant from James; both were amongst those deprived of lands. Bitter grievances were created without real gain. Very few British families were settled outside Ulster.

Though Sir Arthur Chichester, who succeeded Mountjoy as viceroy in 1605, deported several thousand 'swordsmen' for military service on the Continent, Tyrone kept almost all of his vast estates and Rory O Donnell, successor to Red Hugh, was confirmed as lord of most of Donegal and ennobled as Earl of Tyrconnell. But while they attempted to reassert the arbitrary power of Gaelic chiefdom, English feudal land tenure marched in, with English officials ready to enforce it.

Tyrone wearied of life in a conquered Ireland. Meanwhile Tyrconnell was implicated in intrigues with Catholic powers abroad, and the government heard of it. The two Earls decided on flight. On September 3, 1607 they sailed from Lough Swilly with almost a hundred followers. They made their way to Rome, where Tyrone died, aged and blind, in 1616. The 'Flight of the Earls' seemed to complete the defeat of the Gaelic social order.

Cynical shifts increased the scope for plantation. Thus Sir John Davies, the Attorney General (a Welshman, and yet another important poet to play a part in Ireland), had, as lately as 1606, adjudged clansmen, not chiefs, to be owners of Cavan and Fermanagh. Now he said that they had never been more than tenants at will. So the Crown could claim to have at its free disposal six whole counties – Tyrone, Donegal, Coleraine (later Derry), Armagh, Cavan and Fermanagh. Three or four leading Gaels were given large grants and about 280 lesser Irish proprietors received between one-eighth and one-ninth of the rest. All the remainder went to English and Scottish settlers.

Early in 1609, Scottish and English 'undertakers' were invited for tracts of 1,000, 1,500 and 2,000 acres, rent-free for two years then costing a penny farthing an acre. The needs of defence would be costly, though. Undertakers must build stone or brick houses with 'bawns' (defensible courtyards), and keep, train and arm a sufficient force. Only English and Scottish tenants were allowable. Another class provided for were 'servitors', men, mostly soldiers, who had worked for the Crown in Ireland. They were permitted to have Gaelic tenants, but would have to pay higher rent for any land leased to natives. Gaels granted land of their own would also have to build 'castles' and bawns, and would pay twice as much rent as the British undertakers.

It was important for strategic reasons that the towns of Derry and Coleraine should be strong. Early in 1610 the City of London acquired from James the area which became County Londonderry.

The City was the largest of the 'undertakers' who in the event secured over two-fifths of the land granted in the six escheated counties. The established Church received over one-fifth. Servitors and native Gaels shared most of the rest. As in Munster years before, individuals acquired far larger estates than anyone was supposed to hold. Lord Audley (Sir John Davies's father-in-law) received 3,000 acres for himself and his wife and 4,000 for two sons. The results of such greed were predictable. It was reported in 1619 that on all the Audley lands there were no bawns or strong houses, no British freeholders had been established, discontented British tenants were leaving, and a score of Gaelic gentry rented the remainder of the land. Such delinquency was common. Wild wolves and wilder robbers discouraged settlers. The Englishmen who 'undertook' were mostly unsuitable, gentlemen with too little capital who were often ready to sell their claims and retreat. The Scots, momentously, did rather better, in spite, or because, of a penchant which much distressed James, for marrying Gaelic girls, as some of them might just have done at home.

James's keen interest in Ulster prompted repeated surveys. That of 1619 confirmed a picture of partial successes and overall failure. Nearly 2,000 British families were settled. But Gaelic graziers, craving continued hold on the land, offered better rents than could be got from English tenants, so much of Ulster was still roamed by natives with their deplorable cattle. 'Londonderry', now so called, was in sad condition with too few men to defend its (very strong) wall. The surveyor Nicholas Pynnar doubted if the plantation could last. 'My reason is, that many of the *English* Tenants do not yet plough upon the Lands . . . Neither do the Irish use Tillage, for that they are also uncertain of their Stay upon the Lands . . . and were it not for the Scottish tenants, which do plough in many places of the country, those Parts may starve . . .'

After numerous ultimata had failed to oust the Gaels, James conceded at last in 1625 that they could be admitted as tenants on a quarter of the undertakers' lands. James, having tempted the City with hopes of profit, then set about reminding it of its obligations and discouraging profitable enterprise. The Londoners seem in the end to have lost about £40,000 over the venture. Their most significant energy was seen in the slow rise of Londonderry to a population of some 500 able-bodied British men in 1630, when it was by far the largest town in Ulster.

Ulster was much easier to reach from south-west Scotland than from any part of England. The first Lowland Scottish incursions preceded the main plantation, pursuing the tracks of those Highland Gaels, Macdonalds, who had in Elizabeth's reign captured the Route and the Glynns. Sir Randal Macdonnell (the Irish form of the name) was confirmed in his possessions by James in 1603. Meanwhile two Lowlanders, Hugh Montgomery and James Hamilton, had managed by sharp practice to get their hands on most of the area held by Con O Neill. By the summer of 1606, a flow of Lowland settlers into County Down had begun. Montgomery gave estates to lairds from his own district. His wife, the prime organiser of the estates, supervised the building of watermills and, with prophetic instinct, encouraged the making of linen cloth. There was soon a thriving community. Macdonnell also brought Lowlanders into his Antrim lands, and these two eastern counties of Ulster were said in 1618 to be better planted with English and Scottish settlers than some of the six which had been escheated.

Meanwhile, within the Ulster plantation proper, over 60 Scots, mostly lairds, were granted land. They were soon exporting corn and beef back to Scotland. By the end of James I's reign there were no fewer than 8,000 Scots males capable of bearing arms settled in Ulster, mainly coming from the south-west and from the Borders – whence many reivers fled James's justice. Scots quickly captured most of the export trade of Londonderry, and came to outnumber the English inhabitants there.

Irish Protestantism, where it existed, was already strongly puritanical. The influx of Scots reinforced this. Scots became bishops in Ulster and numbers of them got livings in the Established Church. But some of these were Presbyterian enemies of the episcopal order itself, and by the 1630s they would bring a vexatious third factor into Irish religion and politics. For the moment, however, James I could be satisfied that his Scottish countrymen were finding an outlet in Ulster to match that which his English subjects were making in the New World.

V

Soon after James's succession, two Red Indians gave on the Thames an exhibition of their prowess at canoeing. In 1605 a skipper, George Weymouth, who had studied the coast of Maine, came back with five more Indians, who were taken under the wing of Sir Ferdinando Gorges, governor of Plymouth. He sent a couple of them to Sir John Popham, the aged, vast and pompous Lord Chief Justice. Popham had been an undertaker in Munster and was now involved in draining the Fens. Furthermore, he had taken a special interest in the problem of vagabondage. He saw a North American colony as an outlet for the 'infinite numbers of cashiered captains and soldiers, of poor artisans that would and cannot work, and idle vagrants that may and will not work, whose increase threatens the State . . .'

Certain London merchants, headed by Sir Thomas Smythe, were clearly attracted. But Gorges and merchants of Bristol, Plymouth and Exeter were jealous of the City men. So in April 1606, James chartered two Virginia Companies. Each would be entitled to choose a spot for a colony within the vast area between 34°N. (the Cape Fear River) and 45°N. (Passamaquoddy Bay, where the boundary between Maine and New Brunswick now runs). A Royal Council in England was to have overall government of both colonies – this made it clear to Spain that she could move against the settlements only at the risk of another ruinous war.

In May 1607 the Western Company sent out 120 men under George Popham (the old man's nephew) and Ralegh Gilbert (son of Sir Humphrey and nephew of Walter), who founded a settlement at Sagadahoc in Maine. They lacked enough food for the winter and quarrelled bitterly among themselves. The experiment was abandoned in the next year, but West Country interests in fur and fish could be served just as well by transient visits to the coasts, and the Plymouth Company went on sending out ships.

The Londoners had more capital and more luck. They wisely chose Christopher Newport to command their first expedition. He had a little fleet of three ships, the largest, the *Susan Constant*, only 100 tons, which sailed from London on December 19, 1606. A hundred and forty-four men set forth. Only 105 disembarked after five unpleasant months on the still-standard route via the Canaries and the West Indies; only 38 were alive at the end of 1607. The party included labourers and craftsmen but was top heavy with 'gentlemen'. It was drawn mainly from Suffolk and London. The phase of West Country dominance in transatlantic schemes was now ending.

Chesapeake Bay was carefully investigated and a site for a fort picked at 'Jamestown', on the most impressive river they encountered. It was low-lying, marshy and malarial, but there was deep water close inshore for an anchorage and, important for purposes of defence, it was all but an island. Chesapeake Bay itself was to prove a most apt amphitheatre for exploration, trade and further colonisation. It was over 200 miles in extent from north to south and at its widest about 40 miles across. Great navigable rivers flowed into it north, west and south – the 'James', the 'York', the Rappahannock, the Potomac and the Susquehanna.

But Newport's exploring party found in the rapids on the James, at what is now Richmond, a formidable barrier to further progress, while in the week of its absence local Indians struck and only a startling burst of fire from the ship's guns saved the settlement from extinction. Before Newport sailed home with a cargo of timber, disappointment was settling in.

These early colonists themselves tell us what very little we know of the world they found. The Algonquian Indians, who had possessed the area for perhaps three hundred years, had not interfered greatly with the fecund woodland which they inhabited. Oaks and walnuts were the most common trees. The many squirrels were grey, not red like the English ones. Beavers and bears abounded. Wild turkeys ran in the woods and the rivers teemed with sturgeon. The summers were as hot as in Spain, though the winters at times might be bitter.

The red men shaved the right sides of their heads (with shells), leaving the hair on the left to grow long. While the 'better sort' had mantles of deerskin, lesser tribesmen wore grass or leaves. The women, some heavily tattooed, always wore skins about their waists and were 'very shamefast to be seene bare'. Both men and women had 'three great holes' in each ear. Some warriors wore in them small live snakes, or dead animals. A bird's wing, a stuffed hawk, a piece of copper, or even the dried hand of an enemy might provide a head-dress. Heads and shoulders were painted red, a protection against summer heat and winter cold. Even when many such tribal peoples had been encountered in every part of the world, even when serious books had explained native customs with sympathy, such brutality would begin from the simple facts of repulsion and terror.

And at this stage, informed sympathy was almost impossible. The English spoke of Indian 'towns' – they were in fact groups of twenty or thirty wooden buildings made 'like an oven with a litell hole to cum in at', in each of which six to twenty people would sleep. There were no metal tools, land was painfully cleared by scorching growing trees at their roots, beating up weeds with a crooked stick. Holes in the earth were made, also with a stick, and beans, corn and pumpkins were planted and tended by women and children. The men fished with weirs and with boats made from burnt-out trees; they hunted; and they fought wars, not usually for land or possessions, but to take women and children captive. Their code of war was elaborate, though their swords were wooden, their very sharp arrows were tipped with stone and their axes, till trade with the white man brought them the iron tomahawk, were headed only with stone, or with horn. They took scalps. Malefactors were 'broyled' to death. A hated enemy would be quartered and flayed alive, then burnt. Horrified whites rarely asked themselves whether tortures and hangings in Europe were any more humane.

Their code of hospitality made Europeans who came in peace welcome, at least formally. Each guest was offered 'a woman fresh painted red with *Pocones* and oyle, to be his bedfellow.' They worshipped, it seemed, whatever they feared – fire, water, lightning, thunder or Newport's cannon. But their religion evaded European categories, and so did their political system. These Indians had a remarkable leader, Powhatan, born in the 1540s, who had inherited control of some half-dozen villages but had in time established suzerainty over an 'empire' of eight or nine thousand people. Spaniards had first visited the Chesapeake as early as 1560. Powhatan himself may have been involved in the eradication of a Jesuit mission later sent to the area, and of the survivors of Ralegh's lost colony. Certainly, he had long known about whites and their strange capacities and the challenge which these posed to his own people's well ordered and comfortable culture. His motives now, confronted with Jamestown, must have been almost as complex as those of his contemporary Tyrone. Could he ally with them, perhaps, against his enemies beyond the falls of the James? It seems unlikely that he wished to annihilate them, and more probable that he hoped, somehow, to make them of use to his own power.

In any case, Powhatan could not fully control all the villages under him, while, exploring to the north, Captain John Smith encountered the gigantic Susquehannock Indians. Conveniently the red men were disunited as well as few. Various languages were spoken within a few score miles of Jamestown. Smith noted down words and phrases of that used by Powhatan's people. One sentence he recorded as 'Kekaten Pokahontas patiaquagh niugh tanks manotyens neer mowchik rawrenock audowgh': 'Bid Pokahontas bring hither two little Baskets and I will give her white Beads to make her a Chaine.'

There is an irreducible ground of fact beneath the haunting story of Smith and Pocahontas, of the friendship of a little Indian princess for a short, stocky, deep-bearded Englishman, much embroidered though this has been. Smith was born in 1580, son of a fairly prosperous Lincolnshire yeoman, and apprenticed at fifteen to a merchant. He escaped to become a soldier of fortune and fought against the Turks on Europe's eastern frontier. He travelled back across Europe and through Spain to North Africa, whence he sailed for a while on a pirate cruise under a French captain. Yet plunder never seems to have been his aim. He was not mercenary. Establishing colonies interested him, not the pursuit of gold mines. He was a man with qualities rare in his own or any other period – disinterested in his zest and zeal, a quick-witted observer, a good writer. He was also, clearly enough, a boy who never wholly grew up, and our imaginations sometimes insist on the truth of his stories, against our judgment, because they embody so many staples of adventure fiction. He aims at knight-errantry, quests for glory. Time and again, he effects hair's-breadth escapes from death. Mysterious foreign ladies of high birth, of whom Pocahontas is not the first, give him succour.

Though he arrived in Virginia under arrest, on suspicion of plotting to usurp control, Smith became one of the colony's first Councillors when his name was produced with the others from a box which had remained sealed during the voyage. The President elected by the Councillors was Edward Maria Wingfield, a veteran of Irish wars, conscious of his own status as a gentleman, resentful of such a jumped-up commoner as Smith. The latter in turn sneered at gentleman-colonists who lost heart 'because they found not English Cities, nor such faire houses, nor at their owne wishes any of their accustomed dainties . . .' The first months were desperate. Sickness and famine took a fearsome toll. There was constant fear of the natives. The colonists squabbled over such things as a spoonful of beer, a plateful of pease and pork, a roasted squirrel. When Wingfield was deposed by the Councillors, they accused him of atheism, because he had no Bible with him, and also of conspiring with the Spaniards, but his defence of himself centred largely on food. 'Of chickins,' he insisted, 'I never did eat but one, and that in my sicknes. Master *Ratcliff* had before that time tasted of 4 or 5.' Be that as it may, Ratcliff succeeded him.

Smith emerged as the cardinal leader, however, a resolute explorer and clever trader of trinkets for food with the Indians. In December he was captured on one of his trips and taken to see Powhatan, the first Englishman to set eyes on that potentate. He found him flanked by more than two hundred 'grim Courtiers', a tall, well-proportioned man with a 'sower looke', old, but very hardy-looking. He feasted Smith in Indian style. Then two great stones were brought before him. Smith was seized, and his head put on the stones; he thought they would beat his brains out. But '*Pocahontas* the kings dearest daughter when no intreaty could prevaile, got his head in her armes, and laid her owne upon his to save him from death: whereat the Emperor was contented he should live . . .' Smith almost certainly misinterpreted this incident; it was very likely a rite of mock execution and salvation to signify Smith's adoption into Powhatan's tribe, with Pocahontas, aged about 12 or 13, acting the pre-arranged role of foster parent. However, since she often came down to Jamestown later with embassies sent by her father, and since food came with these embassies, Smith was able to describe her as 'next under God . . . the instrument to preserve this Colonie from death, famine and utter confusion'.

Smith got back to the fort in January 1608 on the same day as Newport arrived with the first 'supply' from England. He was under pressure to come back with real gold this time – the 'ore' shipped home the year before had proved worthless. To Smith's disgust, there was soon 'no talke, no hope, no worke, but dig gold, wash gold, refine gold . . .'

The Councillors bickered; starvation impended; Smith explored up the Bay until, in September, as the only man left eligible, he was almost automatically chosen President. Newport, that most reliable of seamen, was back again later that month. His instructions were various. The merchants in London had still not made up their minds for what, if anything, Virginia was good, and, while they were still interested in minerals, Newport was to look for Ralegh's lost colony, explore the river towards the presumed Passage, and with the help of eight Polish and German experts, try to determine the prospects for industries making glass, pitch, tar and soap ashes. Also, Powhatan was to be persuaded to accept a copper crown, whereupon, in the eyes of legalistically minded men in London, he might be understood to have become King James's vassal. Against Smith's better judgment, a farcical coronation was transacted. Powhatan was presented with a basin and ewer, with an English bed and other 'civilised' furniture.

Newport left behind him seventy new colonists, including the first two women to reach Jamestown, and also continuing grave problems. Smith had to use strong-arm methods to persuade the reluctant Indians to trade corn. He ordained that except for the sick 'he that will not worke shall not eate . . .' Thirty or forty acres were dug and planted with food crops, under the instruction of two captive natives. Then in April 1609 it was found that the casked corn on which the settlers relied for food until their own produce grew had gone rotten or had been eaten by rats. Smith copied the practice followed by Indians in the lean months. While the two captive Indians, now firm friends, brought in something by hunting, Smith reduced the food problem at the fort itself by sending parties off to live off the land and sea as best they could, by fishing, gathering shellfish or eating berries and acorns. He somehow brought the colony through its crisis with only a handful of deaths.

VI

In 1609 a new charter for the Virginia Company increased the bounds of the colony, to stretch 400 miles along the coast to north and south, and from sea to sea. The authority of a 'Treasurer' in England was to be matched in Virginia itself by that of a Lord Governor appointed for life and authorised to name all members of the local Council. While the merchant Smythe became Treasurer, the governorship went to a prominent statesman, Lord De La Warr. A craze for Virginia had begun. When the Charter received the royal seal in May, 56 City companies and over 650 individuals had subscribed, and hundreds of men, women and children had volunteered to go in person.

The 'Adventure' of one's own person was regarded as equivalent to the standard £12 10s. share taken out by those who stayed in England, and would entitle the settler to a dividend after seven years. In 1616, the land already opened up would be divided. Individual shares were promised a return of 100 acres at least, and the common herd of cattle would be partitioned among the settlers.

A fleet of nine ships sailed with 800 crewmen and colonists in June 1609. The ageing Sir George Somers was admiral, Newport went yet again as Vice-Admiral. De La Warr, coming later, sent an old soldier, Sir Thomas Gates, as his deputy.

The fleet was assaulted by a tempest. The *Sea Adventure*, which carried all the leaders, was separated from its fellows but ran safely aground on rocks close to shore, and 150 people were taken off it. Luck had brought them to those uninhabited, heavily wooded islands discovered by one Juan Bermudez in the early sixteenth century but little visited since. For the moment, the 'Bermudas' became 'Somers' Islands'. During ten months they supported the castaways beautifully. There were plenty of wild hogs and turtles, good to eat. Only five of the company died, a remarkable rate for the period, before it sailed on in pinnaces which had been built from the local cedar. They reached Jamestown towards the end of May 1610.

Here, they confronted catastrophe once more. The rest of the fleet had arrived in the summer of 1609 to find eighty survivors at Jamestown. In the absence of written orders – lost with the *Sea Adventure* – Smith refused to yield up the Presidency. A period of chaos followed in which 'no man would acknowledge a superior'. Smith in disgust arranged his own passage home and George Percy, the brother of an Earl, took over as President. Appalling hardships resumed. Four hundred new colonists had arrived too late to help grow the provisions which they would need to survive. Powhatan massacred all but one of a party of thirty men sent to bargain for food. The animals brought to breed stock were eaten, then rats and mice. According to Percy, corpses were dug from their graves and devoured. 'And amongst the rest, this was most lamentable, that one of our colony murdered his wife, ripped the child out of her womb and threw it into the river, and after chopped the mother in pieces and salted her for his food . . . ' When the sleek, hog-fed castaways arrived from Bermuda, only just over sixty out of some five hundred people had survived. Gates decided to abandon the colony, and he and the survivors were actually headed homewards down the Chesapeake when they met De La Warr, sailing in with 150 new settlers.

Mortality rates which shock us now were not enough in themselves to deter Jacobean Englishmen who were used to the visitations of plague and hunger in their own country. A fresh appeal for investment in 1610 raised £18,000 and two new consignments of settlers arrived in the following summer. In spite of all setbacks, the idea of a colony of settlement had now aroused the enthusiasm of enough people to make Virginia's future safe.

The lesson of early colonisation was that a staple product must be found and reft from the soil or the forests so as to give a heavy continuous trade to the merchants at home who could supply the settlers with the clothing and tools which they needed. Virginia, goldless, silverless, lacked bait. Lieutenant Governor Gates and his deputy, Dale, both old soldiers, meanwhile held the colony together only by a draconian discipline. A drum rolled at 6 a.m. to call all those not assigned to other duties out to labour in the common fields behind palisades designed to keep off the Indians. In the autumn of 1611, Dale moved with 300 settlers to form a second township at 'Henrico', so named after Henry, the King's eldest son. Trade up the Potomac River brought not only meat and corn but also deerskins and furs which were shipped home to reward the merchants in London. Timber, however, was still the main freight. The search for exotic staples continued and Dale began the first of countless experiments in wine-making, using the native grape.

James's royal favour kept the enterprise going. For instance, he authorised the Company to raise money by lotteries, which became an important standby. Meanwhile, the Company was able to exploit Somers's rediscovery of the Bermudas which, introduced to the English public through that captivating story of shipwreck (Shakespeare employed it in his *Tempest*), had for the moment a stronger appeal to investors than Jamestown. The 'Somers Island Company' formed as a subsidiary was not legally separated from its parent till 1615. Smythe was governor of the Company – as also of the East India Company, whose guns and anchors he lent to Bermuda – and profits from Asian trade were probably most important in helping the frail western colonies stay alive.

Even more than plain John Smith's important role in Jamestown, it was a portent of New World democracy that the first governor duly appointed should be a ship's carpenter. After a phase of squabbles and cheerful anarchy Bermuda settled down to prosper. Its main product was the new wonder-staple, tobacco.

All over the world, the taste for tobacco was growing. Indians in the Americas had, in divers regions, invented the pipe, the cigar and the cigarette. Portuguese sailors had picked up the craving and spread it along their trade routes. A Frenchman named Nicot had hailed the plant's medicinal properties in the 1560s and it would take centuries for science to recognise that tobacco was at best useless and at worst lethal. Meanwhile some three score maladies would be held, by one expert or other, to be at the mercy of this botanic avenger. It was extolled as emetic, as cure for coughs.

Ralegh's explorers had met in 'Virginia' natives smoking an acrid plant, *Nicotiana Rustica*. But it was the delicious herb, *Nicotiana Tabacum*, cultivated by Spaniards in the West Indies, which established the habit in England. Ralegh smoked. Others copied the great man. By the onset of the seventeenth century, some blamed tobacco for the London fog. In the pamphlet war which ensued, James I himself smote hard with a *Counterblaste to Tobacco* (1604) which contemporaries put down to his dislike for Ralegh. By1615, however, it was reported, 'There is not so base a groom, that comes into an alehouse to call for his pot, but he must have his pipe of tobacco . . .'

About 1611, John Rolfe, a Jamestown colonist, somehow acquired seeds of *N. Tabacum* from the West Indies. In 1612 he exported a first crop to England. It was to be several years before the implications of his initiative manifested themselves, but meanwhile he did Virginia more service. He married, in 1614, the princess Pocahontas, who had been captured, held as a hostage, and meanwhile instructed in Christianity. This singular trophy of proselytising success was excellent propaganda back home, and the Virginia Company showed its pleasure by granting Pocahontas an annual stipend; while Powhatan himself accepted the match, and several years of peace with the Indians followed. When in 1616 that hard man Dale came home, he brought the couple and their infant son Thomas, so as to give Virginia the revived public interest which it badly needed.

Rolfe, now secretary of the colony, wrote a brief account of it which was sent to eminent men. Tobacco had swiftly become Virginia's 'Principall commodytie' but the colony which Rolfe described was still military in its main character. There were three classes of people – 'officers', 'labourers' fed and clothed from the company store, and a smaller and more independent class of 'farmers'. There were now six little settlements. Altogether they numbered 351 souls – 205 officers and labourers, only 81 'farmers', and 65 women and children. Rolfe's call to the English to swell these numbers sounds the terrible peal of puritan pride. Though married to one, he valued the Indians lightly. 'There are no *greate nor strong Castles*, nor men lyke the *Sonnes of Anack* to hinder our quyete possession of that *Land*. Godes hand hath bene mighty in the preservation thereof hetherto. What need wee then to feare, but to *goe up at once* as a *peculier people* marked and chosen by the *finger* of God to *possess* it? for undoubtedly he is with us.'

Meanwhile Pocahontas was making in London the stir expected of her. She was well received at court, and took part in a spectacular masque devised by Ben Jonson for Twelfth Night. But from John Smith's account of a visit to her, it seems clear that she was unhappy and confused. She died, of what it isn't quite clear, at Gravesend, awaiting passage home. Her son by Rolfe survived to help populate Virginia.

The London Adventurers would soon be torn between three factions – that of Smythe, that of the Earl of Warwick, and that of Sir Edwin Sandys, a quarrelsome visionary who was able in 1619 to take over the Treasurership with momentary backing from Warwick's supporters. But Smythe and Sandys were at one over the so-called 'Great Charter' of 1618. The land policy which this promised was complex. Adventurers still in England and 'ancient' (pre-1616) planters got initial grants of 100 acres per share with more to follow when those were 'sufficiently peopled'. Men who had gone out as Company servants would get the same when their seven years of service expired. But post-1616 settlers would be under different rules. Those who went at the Company's expense would serve seven years as tenants keeping a half share of what they produced but without promise of land at the end. Men migrating at their own cost could claim land under what historians call the 'headright principle'. This would be a fundamental basis of English settlement in several North American colonies. A settler would get a quota of land (50 acres in the first place) for each person whom he brought to Virginia at his own cost. Since one's own head counted, anyone who could afford to cross the Atlantic could claim fifty acres, and the principle further encouraged planters to bring in the labour – at first, white indentured servants – which the colony needed.

Portentously, a 'generall Assemblie' was created, corresponding to that of the shareholders in London. All male inhabitants could, at this stage, vote to elect its members, and it would meet annually to make laws, to advise the governor (who retained a veto) and to serve as a court of justice. The first Assembly met in Jamestown in July 1619 in the choir of the church, and consisted of six councillors appointed by the governor and twenty-two 'burgesses' representing eleven districts. In six days it produced a code of laws. Everyone must grow food crops. Everyone must go to church on Sunday. In the same year, a new governor went to Bermuda with instructions to call an Assembly there, 'because every man will more willingly obey laws to which he hath yeilded his consent.' This duly met in 1620. Precedents had been set which would be followed in every English colony in the New World.

In three years 3,570 people were sent out to Virginia. Scores of pauper children were swept off the London streets and shipped out to serve as apprentices. A batch of convicts was sent. To meet the shortage of women, parties of girls were consigned; a colonist could take one to wife in return for 120 lb. of tobacco. In the summer of 1620, the Company began the traffic in indentured servants which would last for a century and a half. A colonist paid a lump sum to acquire an immigrant's labour for an agreed number of years. The servant who signed indentures wrote away his own freedom. The English had entered a new commerce in human flesh.

The death rate remained stupendous. A census in 1624 showed only 1,095 people in the colony – yet over 7,500 had come out since 1607, about 4,000 since 1618 alone. And only 347 deaths could be put down to the Indian massacre which shocked the settlers in March 1622.

As the colony grew and encroached on lands where the Indians hunted and gathered berries, fresh friction was inevitable. Powhatan's brother Opechancanough had succeeded him as 'emperor' in 1618. As Indian complaints went unheeded, he united the tribes for a major assault. The colonists had become careless and overconfident. On Good Friday, the red men who came to trade meat and furs as usual suddenly turned on the whites, slaying them in their homes or where they worked in the fields. Perhaps a fourth of the colony were wiped out. But those who survived had an ideal excuse for the seizure of more land. One exulted, 'Our hands which before were tied with gentlenesse and faire usage, are now set at liberty by the treacherous violence of the Savages . . .' The Company's council in London urged 'perpetual war' against the Indians, without mercy, sparing only 'the younger people of both sexes, whose bodies may by labour and service become profitable.' After a two-year fury of burning villages, killings, destruction of crops, only shreds of Powhatan's former 'empire' were left to regroup themselves. By then, the colony's rudimentary economy was restored. Tobacco was the mainstay, and would remain so. It was a crop which ate acres and asked for more. Bermuda, with little more than twenty square miles of land, could not satisfy that plant's appetite, nor those of the London smokers. Now Virginia's destiny lay with *N. Tabacum* rather than in the hands of the God of the Israelites. James I had not scrupled to profit from the crop which he detested. It could, and can, be grown in England itself. In 1619 James's Lord High Treasurer made a deal with the Virginia and Bermuda Companies whereby all planting in England was forbidden, in return for their agreement to pay a far higher customs duty than their charters laid down. Both companies were now controlled by the Sandys faction. In 1622, they secured from the King a monopoly of tobacco importation in return for a revenue from the sales, but the details of the agreement did not please Sandys' enemies. The Warwick and Smythe factions combined against him and demanded, and got, a Privy Council inquiry.

The Company, now bankrupt, stood no chance of surviving it. In May 1624 its charter was declared vacated. The Crown itself took over. Virginia became Britain's first royal colony. A weed, rampant, might well have served for its coat of arms.

VII

A suitable emblem further north would have been a codfish, couchant. Off the shores of the territories which became 'New England' and 'Nova Scotia', and off the ragged coastline of Newfoundland, there were 'banks', submerged plateaux where the rich growth of marine life lured immense numbers of fish into shallow waters. Plankton attracted the cod and the cod drew in mariners from Europe. The Spanish and Portuguese had fallen behind leaving the English and French to compete. The French, who had plenty of cheap solar salt in their own country, practised 'wet fishing', salting the cod as soon as they caught it and rushing it back to the metropolitan market. The English were short of salt at home. Theirs was a 'dry fishery'. Cod were exposed on American shores to sun and wind which rendered them into a product much to the taste of those Mediterranean Catholics whose religion insisted on fish on Fridays. Durable lodges and platforms and stages had to be erected on land, and favoured spots were reoccupied annually by West Country fishermen.

Newfoundland's many bays made it a fine base despite the ice which locked it in during winter and the fogs which haunted it all year round. Inland, it was rugged and uninviting. White men rarely if ever strayed more than a few miles from the coast. The interior was left to the aborigines, Beothuk Indians, who visited the bays in summer, to catch the flightless great auks which, like themselves, would become extinct long before our own day.

By 1610, about two hundred ships crossed from England each year. An early Act of the reign of James I recognised the importance of Newfoundland fisheries as a 'nursery' for the Royal Navy, for which they were said to supply most of the crews in wartime. Fishermen came when the harbours were ice free in May and were usually gone by mid-September. Besides fish, they lived on hard biscuits and salt beef from England. Scurvy was commonplace, drunkenness general, and fires were frequent. However, there was rough equality. The West Countrymen worked on shares, with merchants, ship masters and crews bearing losses or taking profits proportionately. But their hold on the industry was now challenged by the great men of London and their allies in other major ports.

In 1610, a settlement was planted in Newfoundland by a powerful London–Bristol consortium which had obtained a royal charter for colonisation. Alderman John Guy of Bristol led two score men. Their beer froze in the winter. The West Country fishers, of course, were at odds with them. Nevertheless, there were takers when the Newfoundland Company, left short of money by their struggle and unable to get the revisions to their charter which would have given them control of the fishery, set about raising new capital by selling large grants of land. A Welsh knight, Sir William Vaughan of Lllangyndeyrn, depressed by the barrenness of his native soil and moved by envy of Devonshire enterprise, decided that Newfoundland had been 'reserved by God for us Britons' (the Welsh), got land from the Company and sent out in 1617 a party of Welsh men and women who throve so badly that their first governor packed all but six of them off home. Nevertheless, 'Cambriol', as the patriot Vaughan named it, may have maintained a ghostly existence into the 1620s. It was joined by some other spectral settlements, making half a dozen in all.

Meanwhile, an English sailor named Henry Hudson, sailing for Dutch backers, had written his name bold on the map of North America. He entered what is now New York harbour and explored north up the great river which he found there. On his return, he proposed a further north-western voyage to the Dutch EIC, but the English authorities would not now let him voyage 'to the detriment of his own country'. A consortium, including the ubiquitous Sir

Thomas Smythe, rose up to back new exploration in England's interest. Hudson set off in the *Discovery* in the spring of 1610 and entered the vast Bay which now bears his name. This seemed to be the Passage at last. Hudson wintered there and next year proposed to sail further. His crew quarrelled with him and left him behind in a little boat. No more was heard of Hudson, but the mutineers were not punished after they came home with such exciting news. A fresh expedition under Captain Button found that the Bay, alas, had a western shore, but even so explorations continued yearly.

The less visionary Dutch now claimed, on the basis of Hudson's voyage for them, the whole coastline from Cape Cod to Delaware Bay. A Dutch West India Company, set up in 1621, sent out a colony three years later to 'New Netherland' on the 'Hudson' River. In 1626 Manhattan Island was bought from Indians for sixty guilders' worth of trade goods and 'New Amsterdam' was established there. But commerce, not settlement, was the Dutch proclivity. Farming was neglected while quick profits were sought from furs.

The New World fur trade had achieved much importance even before the end of the sixteenth century. The main emphasis was on beaver. Craftsmen developing techniques of making hats out of felt were able to create a vogue which lasted in Europe for generations and shaped the history of North America. When the outer layers of guard hair on the beaver's pelt were discarded the soft downy fur underneath was full of tiny barbs which helped the felt to mat securely and gave a lustrous finish. It made, like tobacco, a light cargo commanding high prices, which could well support the heavy overhead costs involved in long sea voyages. The forests of North America sheltered perhaps ten million beaver. This charming, ingenious creature was easy to find. He built his elaborate dams and lodges on lakes and streams in the deciduous forests where his diet was found. The beaver's house had resisted spears and stone arrows, but now the metal hatchet could pierce it.

Planters had no use for Indians, since native men disliked agricultural work. But where the fur trade flourished, the accumulating effect of native dependence on European trade goods was compensated for by the white man's dependence in turn on Indian hunters and on the preservation of the beaver's (and native's) woodland habitat. The vaunted French superior skill in race relations really stems in great part from this simple fact of life. The French were already, by the end of the sixteenth century, closely allied with Algonquian Indians in the fur trade, and so also with the Hurons who supplied their partners with corn. It also meant that the colonies which they established would be strictly ancillary to the fur trade and that their growth would be limited and slow.

Monopoly was another natural outcome. The Indians realised that if they waited till several competing ships showed up, they could get more goods for each beaver. Meanwhile, Henri IV of France wanted a great American colony. The monopoly of the fur trade was therefore granted to a company in return for a commitment to take out settlers. In 1604 Samuel Champlain, an ex-soldier who had become Henri's geographer-royal, went out under the Sieur de Monts, a Huguenot nobleman. Over a hundred colonists travelled with them, and Port Royal, on the Bay of Fundy, in the region which the French called 'Acadie', was founded as a factory in 1608. It proved impossible to enforce a monopoly from there. Champlain saw the possibilities of the place where the great St Lawrence River narrowed so that a cannon could block the passage. In 1608 he and de Monts began to settle the site of Quebec, one of the best natural military strong-points in the world, on the only great river system which led from the heart of North America to the Atlantic seaboard.

Despite the French presence in 'Acadie', a Scottish courtier and poet, Sir William Alexander, was granted by James I in 1621 a vast area of what is now maritime Canada, which he endowed with the name 'Nova Scotia'. But a serious start on Alexander's scheme of settlement could not be made without merchant backing.

VIII

In 1614, some merchants sent Captain John Smith out whaling. He explored the coastline from Maine down to and round Cape Cod and pronounced what became Massachusetts a 'Paradise'. On his return he laid plans for colonisation before Sir Ferdinando Gorges of the Plymouth Company which could still claim the area and which sent him off in 1615 with the nucleus of a settlement. He fell foul of French pirates off the Azores. But Smith retained all his zest and became till his death in 1631 primarily a professional writer propagandising for the New World. His *Description of New England* (1616) had much influence, notably on the so-called 'Pilgrim Fathers'.

This body of ordinary, remarkable men have a special status not because they were the first successful English colonists in North America – they were not even the first comers in New England – but because it has seemed proper that they should have been. Religion was, without question, their main driving force. They belonged to the school of thought labelled 'Brownist' and persecuted in England during the 1590s as dangerously subversive. Brownists held that each congregation should organise itself under a mutual covenant to 'forsake & dame all ungodliness and wicked felloship', and should select its own pastor and officers. Brownist congregations remained independent of each other and found no warrant in the Bible for any hierarchical church structure.

A Brownist congregation had been established at Scrooby, a village in northern Nottinghamshire, under the lead of the manor's bailiff, one William Brewster. Imprisonments and fines followed. They emigrated to tolerant Holland and settled down in Leyden. They worked in various crafts and in time many became citizens. But their lives were mostly impoverished and hard. While some grew old, children fell into Dutch ways, a grief to their very English parents. And the truce between Dutchmen and Spaniards clearly would not last – indeed, fresh war did break out in 1621.

Some made terms with a very worldly Londoner named Thomas Weston who combined an ironmonger's business with smuggling cloth to the Netherlands, and who led a group of merchants, 'John Pierce and Associates', which had acquired a patent for land in Virginia. What the merchants imagined was that the colonists would labour on their behalf in America. What the Pilgrims wanted, and quite soon would get, was a situation where every man would work his own land to feed himself and his family. Disagreement boiled up when the Leyden party arrived in England to join the other colonists whom Weston had recruited. Despite it, the *Mayflower* sailed on its famous voyage on September 6, 1620.

The chunky, sluggish ship of only 180 tons left with inadequate provisions, crowded with 102 passengers and 30 or more seamen. There was sickness, and there were storms, but in a voyage of over nine weeks, only three crewmen and one passenger died.

Less than half the passengers were in fact self-styled 'saints' from Leyden – sixteen men, nine women and sixteen children. Only five were Scrooby people: William Brewster, his wife, their boys named Wrestling and Love (daughters Patience and Fear would come later) and the redoubtable William Bradford. The most prominent of the majority of non-Brownist 'strangers' was Myles Standish, a middle-aged soldier, short in stature, fiery and red-haired – 'Captaine Shrimpe' one enemy would dub him, and he would command the colony's little army. Most of the 'strangers' came from London and the south-east and were conforming Anglicans.

Their aim to settle on the Hudson River (still within bounds of the Virginia patent which they carried with them) was thwarted by shoals and breakers as they tried to round Cape Cod. So they made landfall there on November 11. The problem of self-government had to be faced at once. Within the Virginia Company's allotted area they would have come under the Jamestown governor. As it was, they had no legal status whatever. But the Pilgrims had a model to hand, in the covenants by which separatist congregations were founded. Still on shipboard, forty-one adult men among the colonists signed the famous 'Mayflower Compact':

> We whose names are under-written, the loyall subject of our dread soveraigne Lord, King James . . . doe by these presents solemnly and mutualy in the presence of God, and one of another, covenant and combine our selves togeather into a civill body politick, for our better ordering and preservation and furtherance of the ends aforesaid; and by vertue hearof to enacte, constitute, and frame such just and equall lawes, ordinances, acts, constitutions and offices, from time to time, as shall be thought most meete and convenient for the generall good of the Colonie, unto which we promise all due submission and obedience.

There were eighteen indentured servants and five hired men aboard, and the prime object of this covenant was to show them their place, to make it clear that they would have to keep it, and to maintain hierarchy as Jacobean English people valued it. But to further this purpose, it would seem, several servants were invited to sign, and did so, and the Compact deserves more credence as a first document of American democracy than a cautious and cynical generation of historians have recently been prepared to give it. Only twelve of the *Mayflower* signatories could even claim the title of 'Mister', most being mere 'Goodmen', and none of these 'Misters' had much pretension to rank.

The compacted settlers now chose Mr John Carver to be their first governor; but their own landfall must have struck all present as far more momentous than this precocious political act. They fell on their knees and praised God who had brought them again at last to the 'firme and stable earth, their proper elemente.'

After a month of exploration, they settled upon a harbour which Smith had named 'Plymouth'. It was large, well sheltered, ringed with stately woods. They pushed up cottages of wattle and daub and thatched them, laying out a village on a field where Indians had previously grown corn, with a single street running up from the harbour. Here the privations of sea-voyaging took their toll as frost, rains and winds assailed them. By the end of March of more than a hundred people scarcely fifty still lived. At the worst moment there were only half a dozen strong enough to work and care for the others. Indians had been glimpsed, and were feared. Then a brave strode into 'new Plymouth' and, amazingly, spoke English, which he had learned, he said, from fishermen up the Maine coast. What he told them made clear why so few red men had been sighted; the local tribe had been wiped out a few years before by a plague.

Not long after this, Massasoit, the great 'sachem' of the Wampanoag Indians of the region, appeared in the colony and with Governor Carver concluded a treaty which, often renewed and never seriously jeopardised, would endure till the chief himself died more than forty years later.

In April 1621, when Carver died, William Bradford was chosen to succeed him. He remained governor, with few intermissions, till his death in 1657. The orphan from Scrooby, 'fustian maker' in Leyden, became the sagacious father of his people, respected by them and by outsiders alike. The Pilgrims soon found that what became Boston Harbour would have been a better place to settle than the sparse area which they had selected. But they cared for sufficiency rather than wealth. Harvest was celebrated with Massasoit and scores of his braves in October 1621. On this first Thanksgiving Day, there were venison, duck, goose, clams and eels, white bread and corn bread, green vegetables, wild plums and dried berries, all washed down with wine made from wild grapes. Then they went on short winter rations again. In November a small ship came with thirty-five new settlers, some of them 'saints' from Leyden, and with a chideful letter from Weston. The merchants were impatient for profits. But there was also the news that their settlement had been legalised, under a grant from the Council for New England.

Meanwhile, the Pilgrims permitted no church but their own. An Anglican minister arrived. He was admitted to their congregation and even to their pulpit, but was found to be baptising children privately with Anglican rites, under the obnoxious sign of the Cross, and like certain other malcontents, he was expelled. This scandal confirmed the disillusionment of most of the colony's merchant backers. They pulled out, and in 1627 the colonists made a new deal with a few of the Londoners who still saw promise in furs. A partnership joining Bradford with seven associates in New Plymouth and four in England took on responsibility for the colonists' debts, which they proposed to meet by monopolising the fur trade. Meanwhile, the Pilgrims divided the colony which they had, in effect, bought on mortgage. Each family got 20 acres for each of its members, plus an extra share for every £10 which it had invested in the joint stock. Each share carried with it one-sixth of a cow and one-third of a goat.

Plymouth, reinforced several times in the 1620s, grew to 300 people by 1630, 579 by 1637. Bradford and his trading associates learnt from the Dutch in New Amsterdam how avid the Indians were for *wampumpeag*, white and purple beads. With 'wampum' for currency, the Pilgrims were able for several years practically to monopolise the commerce in beaver skins from large regions. They disposed of a troublesome competitor close to home, one Thomas Morton, who had taken over a settlement at what is now Quincy, Mass. A gentleman-lawyer, with Clifford's Inn education, he gleefully shocked the Pilgrims with views of right behaviour quite the reverse of their own. He rechristened his settlement 'Merry Mount', and celebrated this with an apt festival. A gross maypole was erected. A barrel of beer was brewed and everyone round invited, including the Indians.

Morton was ready to enlist any malcontent from another plantation, 'how vile soever', and to trade guns to the Indians so they could shoot beaver for him. The peppery Standish moved in to deal with this shrewd commercial rival. The Pilgrims shipped him off to England; he was soon back and causing trouble again.

Morton was only one of the opportunists from England who tried his hand in the Massachusetts area. 'New England', defined as the vast area between the 40th and 48th parallels, was now theoretically under the sole ownership of Gorges and his Council. Though an elderly man, Gorges imagined himself as feudal overlord in America with a colonial *noblesse* beneath him. But in fact the Council could not even enforce its fishing monopoly. Yet if Gorges's antique visions were as impractical as Gilbert's had been before him, there were reasons now attracting hard-headed men to the idea of permanent settlements in New England. Colonists might feed themselves and meanwhile, all year round, catch cod, gather beaver, hew lumber, and ship cargoes back to England. Though the Pilgrims disappointed their sponsors, the pattern, with variations, was attempted elsewhere. And in every case the outcome was similar – baulked of quick profits, the merchants involved lost interest. By the late 1620s there were abandoned colonies, stray settlers left to fend for themselves in small groups, at several points on the New England coast.

In its whole career, the Virginia Company had raised only some £200,000. The Pilgrims' backing and debts were in scant hundreds and thousands. Yet by 1632 the East India Company would have found £2,887,000. The City of London's commercial élite was not ready to make the long-term, fixed-capital expenditures which were needed to sustain North American plantations. But sending big ships out for spices, despite the great risks, retained its appeal.

IX

The Dutch, sending fleet after fleet East from the mid-1590s onwards, at first had a good reception from native rulers almost everywhere in South-East Asia, who looked to them for support against the Portuguese. The Dutch East India Company (VOC) was founded in 1602 and before the end of the decade had won the upper hand in the Moluccas, that scatter of islands which gave the world its cloves, mace and nutmegs. They brought a new ruthlessness with them. The Portuguese had spread the cultivation of cloves; the Dutch, in pursuit of high monopoly prices, cut trees down.

The Portuguese had never been able to stem the stream of eastern goods which reached the Mediterranean overland through the Levant. But the English Levant traders took alarm at the Dutch threat to their supplies of spices, and their money helped make the EIC a powerful consortium. A longstanding role was foreshadowed as James I soon began to turn to the Company for loans. Royal co-operation was essential. The king provided continual exemption from laws which restricted the export of bullion and was called on for support when international complications arose. But the Company was left to organise itself. The 219 original shareholders formed its first General Court and elected a 'Court of Committees' of 24 members. Sir Thomas Smythe (who else?) was chosen first governor and held the post for most of the EIC's first twenty years of existence.

The EIC still formed an association of individuals, with no capital as a corporate body. Each voyage would reward only those members who personally backed it. Of five vessels leaving London in February 1601, four were home fully loaded by September 1603. The destination had been Indonesia. Good relations had been established with the rulers at Achin, in Sumatra, and at Bantam, in Java, where a first 'factory' had been established. The first ship home alone brought 210,000 lb. of pepper, besides other spices. The market was glutted, and some of the adventurers could not dispose of their pepper for six or seven years. But the twelve 'Separate Voyages' down to 1612 brought an average profit of 155 per cent. A fresh charter in 1609 extended the EIC monopoly indefinitely. By 1613, the disadvantages of 'separate' voyaging had become obvious – different ventures were in effect in competition with each other – and a new subscription was raised on the understanding that the capital would be used over several voyages. This 'First Joint Stock' worked its way over ten years, eventually yielding a profit of 87 per cent.

In 1624, when the EIC had exported £750,000 in bullion but only £350,000 in English commodities, its apparently unpatriotic character was producing rowdy scenes in Parliament. Thomas Mun and others had to defend the export of bullion. Spices, they said, would always be in demand and would be imported, so 'treasure' would be lost by them anyway. The crucial matter was the overall balance of English trade, not the export of bullion in one direction, which was compensated for as the EIC re-exported most of its imports, so that these earned precious metals abroad. The argument would go on for many lifetimes. Meanwhile, the EIC was mastering a complicated trade in three interrelated sections. The main part of it seemed to be the commerce between the Indies and England direct. But in fact this was made economically viable only by two less glamorous sorts of venturing – firstly, by the re-export, just mentioned, of East Indian goods to Europe, where they could be used to acquire the naval stores and silver which the EIC needed; and secondly by the so-called 'country trade' in Asian waters.

Silver was the current monetary standard in Asia and its real price was much higher than in Europe; that is, a given amount of it would buy more goods. The incentive to export it would thus have existed even if English goods had been in greater demand. Involvement in the Eastern port-to-port trade became essential as a way of reducing bullion exports. The EIC, from its Third Voyage (1607 onwards), branched out in search of Asian commodities which could be used in trade within Asia itself. The importance of India was soon clear; the Dutch showed the way there, founding four factories between 1605 and 1612 on the west coast of the subcontinent. Indian textiles were coveted in the islands of the Indonesian archipelago.

The Mughal Emperor, as it was well known, would be a harder man to impress than any Indonesian king. The dynasty had been launched in 1517 when the remarkable Babur, descendant of the great Mongol conqueror Timur, had turned from his realms in what is now Afghanistan to intervene in North India, then ruled by a confederation of Afghan chieftains. His grandson Akbar, charismatic, tolerant, witty, humane, in a reign of nearly fifty years (1556–1605) extended Mughal rule from Kashmir in the far north into much of the Deccan, where the great Hindu empire of Vijayanagar was hit hard; and from Sind across to Bengal, richest area of the north, with its rice, with its silk, with its most essential saltpetre.

Akbar married a Hindu (Rajput) princess and gave natives, both Hindu and Muslim, high office and honours in return for loyal service. Like the Ottoman Turks far to their west, the Mughals opened a career to any young adventurer of talent, who could become a *mansabdar* (holder of command) in their service. Akbar divided his empire into twelve provinces; later there were eighteen. These in turn were subdivided into *sarkars* (say 'districts') and *parganas* ('subdistricts'). While the empire took in general one-third of all produce, or its value, each local community in the intricate Indian racial and religious jigsaw was left to administer its own law. The contrast between rich and poor was already acute – the highest *mansabdar*, commander of 5,000, with a salary roughly worth £24,000 a year in Stuart sterling, could live in a style to fill James's courtiers with envy. But the average peasant probably ate more than his European counterpart while being no more subject to war's disasters, and no more steadily oppressed. Under Akbar's able successor Jahangir (1605–1627), Mughal India was overall as cultured, well-governed, and comfortable as any part of the world.

The first English vessel to reach an Indian port anchored near Surat, on the north-western coast, in August 1608. Aboard was one William Hawkins with a polite letter from King James addressed to the now-dead Akbar. He went to the Mughal court at Agra to try to secure trading concessions at Surat, which lay in a major textile-producing region. He spoke Turkish, and made a good impression. Jahangir created him *mansabdar* of 400 and married him to an Armenian girl, but kept changing his royal mind about whether he would yield the requested privileges for English trade. After more than two years, in November 1611, Hawkins finally quit. Soon after, Sir Henry Middleton arrived off Surat with ships of the EIC's Sixth Voyage. Attacked by the Portuguese, then refused permission to trade by the Mughal's official, he stormed off into the Red Sea and seized every Indian ship he could find there. Piracy paid where diplomacy had failed.

The news of Middleton's depredations arrived at Surat soon after Captain Thomas Best had appeared there with the EIC's Tenth Voyage. The Red Sea trade was important to Gujerat, and it now seemed the English could prey as they wished on almost defenceless Indian ships. Early in 1613, the imperial *farman* arrived and the first English factory in Western India was duly established under Thomas Aldworth. The seizure by some Portuguese frigates of a Surat ship belonging to the Emperor's mother greatly helped the English position in India. Jahangir ordered the arrest of all Portuguese in his realm. Early in 1615, the Viceroy of Goa sent north a strong fleet to oust the English from Surat. Captain Nicholas Downton, with only four ships, beat them off.

But the English footing was still insecure. The EIC had persuaded James I to despatch to India an ambassador-plenipotentiary of far greater standing than the mere merchants who had so far tried to deal with Jahangir. Sir Thomas Roe, a great courtier, arrived at Surat in September 1615, to attempt to negotiate a formal treaty of commerce between the 'Great Mogul' and his own royal master. For two years and nine months he followed the emperor from place to place, but found that Eastern potentates were not interested in haggling over the details of trade with a man from a faraway nation which had so little to offer. When Roe left India early in 1619 all that he had secured was a *farman* providing favourable conditions for English trade at Surat in return for English protection of Mughal commerce and Indian pilgrims bound for Mecca. The EIC had found a role as naval auxiliary to the Mughal power which would last through the seventeenth century. Besides whatever vessels from England might be to hand, the Surat factory built up a local flotilla of small sea-going warships. In the early 1620s, EIC vessels helped the Shah of Persia against the Portuguese and played a major part in the capture of Ormuz from them in 1622. So in Persia, too, the EIC gained a fairly secure footing, with local headquarters at Gombroon, on the Gulf.

But elsewhere in Asia there were disappointments. Permission to trade in Japan was gained, but after ten years, in 1623, the EIC closed down its factory at Hirado as unremunerative. Short-lived posts in Siam were abandoned in the same year. A factory which did last was founded in 1611 at Masulipatam on the Coromandel Coast of eastern India, outwith the Mughal realm, but Surat and Bantam became the main centres of trade, with 'Presidencies' established in each place by which the principal factors held authoritarian sway.

In the Moluccas, while the Dutch tried to enforce total monopoly, the English were able to trade with natives resentful of Dutch rapacity. The Banda Islands, specks lost on most maps, with a total land area of only 17 square miles, where, however, the nutmeg was indigenous, now became a centre of rivalry. Here in 1615 the natives of Wai sided with the English and drove off the Dutch. Next year a Dutch fleet of ten confronted four EIC ships there and dictated terms, by which the English must remain neutral while the Dutch fought the natives, and must abandon the island if the Dutch won. Richard Hunt, in command of the English factory, breached these terms and persuaded the people of Wai and its neighbour Run to haul up English colours; and even after the Dutch had captured Wai decisively, the English held Run ('Pularoon') till 1620 and finally dropped their claim to it only in 1667.

Jan Pieterszoon Coen arrived in Java as Governor General of the Dutch East Indies in mid-1618 with expansionist plans and instructions to expel all foreign Europeans from places where the Dutch traded. John Jourdain, from Devon, the EIC President at Bantam, was another determined man. He founded a factory at Macassar in Celebes, halfway between Java and the Moluccas, which ensured a copious leakage in the Dutch spice monopoly till it was lost half a century later. The English seizure of a Dutch ship at Bantam provoked Coen to burn the EIC factory at Batavia. Undeclared war followed. Jourdain was treacherously killed under a flag of truce, but the English were ready to resume battle, early in 1620, when word came that an agreement had been reached in Europe. By an Anglo-Dutch treaty of 1619, the rival East India Companies were to share the trade of Indonesia and to bear the costs of defence jointly. The EIC were to have half the available pepper and a third of the spice trade of the Moluccas, Amboyna and the Bandas. Coen of course disliked this deal and busily made it unworkable. Meanwhile, co-operation with the Dutch was coming to seem to the EIC factors in Indonesia only a 'kind of slavery', and they had already decided to quit the Dutch settlements when word came of the 'Amboyna Massacre'.

On Amboyna (Ambon) the English traded under protection of a Dutch fort. The EIC factory here was larger than most of the English settlements now dotted across the Far East, though it was petty enough – eighteen white men scattered between several posts. The Dutch, they reckoned, had two hundred white soldiers and three or four hundred native troops; the steward of their factory, it is worth noting, was an Aberdeen Scot named George Forbis, and they employed some thirty Japanese among their mercenaries. A Japanese soldier suspected of conspiracy incriminated the English under torture. The Dutch built up a story that the English had decided to seize the fort and had employed their drunken barber, one Abel Price, to corrupt the Japanese. Price too confessed, under torture, and early in 1623 the governor, Van Speult, executed ten EIC men as well as nine Japanese and a Portuguese captain of slaves. When the news reached England fifteen months later, in May 1624, James I was outraged and 'sundry of the greatest shed tears' at the royal council table. The EIC bayed for reprisals, but Dutch help was now needed against Spain. War with Holland was out of the question. However, for fifty years and longer, the 'Massacre' would retain its place in English consciousness as a prime aggravator of anti-Dutch feeling.

Except in certain unhappy Moluccan islands and, growingly, in Java, the total European impact in the East was still puny. Wherever fair competition existed, Arab, Persian, Indian or Chinese traders could still hold back, and even improve, their position against Europeans. The 27 vessels sent back from Surat to London in the first 15 years of the factory (1615–29) amounted to a tiny proportion of India's total seaborne trade, and EIC factors there stayed reliant on native brokers.

But in England itself the Eastern trade was gathering some importance. Pepper was in this early phase by far the most valuable import. Dividends were paid in pepper down to 1627. Indigo, that rich dye, was also significant, but it was the rapid increase, from the 1620s, of Western demand for Indian calicoes which pointed the way forward. Cotton textiles from the subcontinent ranged from arse-clouts for black slaves to super-fine products coveted by great ladies, and they would find markets, re-exported, in Africa and in the Middle East. In England itself, besides lovely garments, they made napkins and table linen, bed-furnishings and wall-hangings, raising the standards of comfort and elegance of growing numbers who found that they could afford them.

The EIC had become one of the largest employers of labour in the London area. Till 1639, its policy was to own the ships it sent East, and in the second decade of the seventeenth century each of its dockyards, at Deptford and Blackwall, turned out over 30 ships of some size. Ranging from 300 tons upwards as a rule, these were some of the largest vessels owned in England. (Ships sent out to the West Indies, by contrast, ranged from only 100 to 200 tons.) Keeping them active spawned new industries – the EIC had its own iron foundries, and cordage manufactures, and also slaughterhouses to kill its own beef for its sailors. While over half the tonnage sent out was lost in the first twenty years, almost all got home thereafter.

The round trip to Surat generally took eighteen months, that to Bantam about two years. Hence the interest of Smythe and other East India merchants in the spate of expeditions, down to 1616, which searched for a North West Passage. Attempts were resumed in 1631, when Captain Luke Foxe, a shrewd Yorkshireman, sailing for some London merchants, established that there was no westward channel in Hudson's Bay. The search was dropped for a century. East Indiamen continued to make their painful way round the long and still enigmatic coastline of Africa.

X

The trade with Africa itself begun in Tudor times by the Hawkins family came to little before 1618 when, inspired by the success of the EIC, thirty-seven 'Adventurers of London' launched a Guinea Company. It established a factory on the Gambia River which later developed into a fort and also, probably in 1631, the first important English settlement on the 'Gold Coast', at Kormantin. Between these two points, it developed a useful trade in the dye called redwood with peoples in Sierra Leone and on the Sherbro River. So far, slaves were not the bait and an English captain, Richard Jobson, who explored far up the Gambia in the early 1620s, responded starchily when a Mandingo trader offered him some. '. . . I made answer, We were a people, who did not deale in any such commodities . . .'

Such self-esteeming virtue would not long survive the successful placing of English colonies in tropical America. Following Ralegh, several attempts were soon made in the stickily hot coastlands between the Orinoco and Amazon deltas. In 1604, Charles Leigh took a party to the River Wiapoco (Oiapoque), which later became the eastern border of French Guiana. They managed to grow some flax and tobacco, but Leigh died of fever and the venture was abandoned in 1606. Sir Thomas Toe, later ambassador to the Great Mogul, pushed inconclusively three hundred miles up the Amazon in 1610–11. He was a friend of Ralegh, who backed him with £600, and his aim was El Dorado. He left, at the mouth of the river, the first of several English settlements which flickered and died there.

Ralegh himself was allowed one last attempt. He used his time well in prison, conducting chemical experiments and writing, amongst other things, a *History of the World*, which, published in 1614, became the century's most printed book after the King James Bible. But the ageing man wanted freedom, and to return to Guiana, where he was convinced that he had found a huge gold-mine. After the 1614 Parliament had failed to grant him supplies, James, desperate now for money, decided to give Ralegh his way. He was released early in 1616. He sold all his own possessions and most of his wife's, and secured generous backing from friends and admirers, so that a vast force of 14 vessels and 1,000 men was possible. The Spanish Ambassador, Gondomar, saw this as a threat to his nation in the New World. He had great influence over James, who hoped for a rich Spanish match for his son Charles, and prevailed on him to announce that Ralegh would forfeit his life if he fought the Spaniards or meddled with their property. Ralegh could still gamble that if he did secure gold, the King would forgive him everything.

However, the old man had lost the knack of command. Well received by Indians on the coast, where he was still remembered, Ralegh was too ill to set out in person to find his mine. Lawrence Keymis, commanding 400 men, disobeyed orders and captured the Spanish town of São Thomé in an affray in which Ralegh's own son was killed. After a month his men forced him to return. Chided by a heartbroken Ralegh, Keymis committed suicide. The expedition fell apart in desertion and mutiny and Ralegh reached England again to find Gondomar's influence unabated. He was duly beheaded in October 1618. When his head was held up a voice broke through the shocked silence, 'We have not such another head to be cut off.' To contemporaries it seemed that a cowardly king had sacrificed the last veteran of the Armada battle to appease an arrogant Catholic Spain.

Puritans

I

English colonising in South America was ended, for the time being, in 1631, when the Portuguese wiped out a short-lived settlement on the island of Tocujos in the Amazon delta, the second such plantation attempted by one of Ralegh's former officers, Roger North. But the many small and frequently beautiful islands of the Caribbean, still covered with sumptuous virgin forest unoccupied by the Spaniards, had started to beckon.

The Carib Indians had destroyed an English settlement on St Lucia as early as 1605, and had thwarted an attempt by English merchants to colonise Grenada with two hundred white men four years later. In 1622 Captain Thomas Warner, a Suffolk man of good family, rising towards fifty, quit North's first colony in disgust at 'the disorders that did grow in the *Amazons* for want of Government' among the English there and with some companions sought a place of their own where they could be 'quiet'. They found St Christopher, later St Kitts, shaped like a tadpole, 28 miles from end to end, 68 square, dominated by mountains which rose to a peak of 3,800 feet at 'Mount Misery'. Warner made friends with the Caribs, planted a crop of tobacco, and six months later sailed away with enough of it to get London merchant backing for his proposed settlement. He returned in January 1624 with a small party (not more than nineteen men). Their first crop was destroyed by a hurricane, but a second had grown when Warner's Suffolk neighbour, John Jeaffreson, arrived in March 1625 with provisions and reinforcements.

Pre-emptively – 'Like a wise man and a good Souldier he tooke the advantage of theire being druncke' – Warner massacred the adjacent Indian village; but there was still danger as St Kitts was easily reached by Carib canoes from other islands. When a damaged French privateer appeared, the English welcomed white allies. For the first few years, English and French settlers helped each other against the common enemy, and in 1627 a formal agreement divided the island. The French took both ends, the English retained the middle. Warner, already confirmed as 'King's Lieutenant', ruled the English section until he died in 1649, a shrewd and ruthless squire who had the advantage that he could pack dissidents off to colonise fresh Leeward islands. Nevis (50 square miles) was settled by Englishmen from St Kitts in 1628, Antigua (108 square miles) in 1632. In the latter year Montserrat (32½ square miles) was occupied; before long it filled up with Irish papists. Though two rebellions would force Warner to concede an elected assembly to the St Kitts planters in the 1640s, he contrived to weather a period which had seen the second English West Indian colony, on

Barbados, several times reduced to anarchy.

Barbados was (from one point of view) a fortunate isle, never changing hands in international wars after its initial settlement by Englishmen in 1625. It was the most easterly of the Lesser Antilles, to the windward even of the Windward Islands, so that the Caribs had never settled it and could not now attack it, and even Spaniards and Frenchmen would find it hard to reach from their Caribbean bases. In 1627 a London merchant, Sir William Courteen, sent out about eighty colonists. The settlement soon throve and by 1629 there were said to be 1,800 whites (and 50 blacks) on the island. Such rapid success contrasted with the slow progress of Virginia. The tropical soil was lavishly fecund. For nearly two hundred years English colonies in the Caribbean would matter far more to people at home than those on mainland North America. As a major source of commercial opulence, the West Indies would help mightily in the political transformation of England, of which the revolt against Charles I was an early conspicuous symptom.

II

The Crown was sustained by land in an age when rents fell behind rising prices, and though James I avoided war, he had, over his reign, to dispose of much land. Power drained from the centre. From 1614 James did not summon Parliament for seven years. His favourite, George Villiers, Duke of Buckingham, was vastly corrupt, extravagant and incompetent. When James turned to Parliament again in 1621, it recovered its power, not used since the fifteenth century, to remove those of the King's ministers whom it disliked. Then it insisted on debating foreign policy; the King dissolved it and imprisoned a number of truculent members, including a man named John Pym.

A new fight with Spain was launched in pique after the humiliating failure of Prince Charles's quest for a Spanish bride. Parliament, summoned again in 1624, voted supplies for the war, but insisted that they must be administered by a committee chosen by the House of Commons. With the accession of Charles next year, strains were intensified by the new King's theological views; he was 'Arminian', following the views of a Dutch sage who undermined the cherished Calvinist doctrine of predestination and believed that salvation depended partly on what men did. The Parliament of 1626 tried to impeach Buckingham; when Charles angrily dissolved it, this meant that he got no subsidies. Charles had to sell more crown lands; when he tried to exact a forced loan from his subjects, numerous Puritan MPs refused to pay it and several were imprisoned.

The Parliament of 1628 produced the resounding Petition of Right against arbitrary imprisonment, arbitrary taxation, billeting of troops and martial law. Faithless Charles accepted it, and got his subsidies, but the assassination in the same year of Buckingham, who had enthralled son like father, made political friction if anything worse – Charles now fell in love instead with his own wife, a papist Frenchwoman. And he took into his service Thomas Wentworth, once a leader of Parliament, soon to become the King's most abhorred secular henchman. Charles's meddlings with the Church inspired frantic fears and revulsions. High office was becoming impossible even for moderate Puritans. In 1629, Charles lost patience with the House of Commons, dissolved Parliament and essayed to rule without it. Thousands of his subjects fled, in effect, to the New World, in a movement involving all classes of pious Puritan people.

Those who opposed Charles believed that they stood for the liberties of Englishmen. It is easy for any schoolboy to sneer that 'liberty' for the property-owners who sat in early Stuart parliaments meant, precisely, the rights of property-owners. Yet the potential electorate may have embraced, by the critical year of 1640, a third or more of the adult male population. Even some quite poor men could vote, since inflation had in effect degraded the property qualification which restricted the franchise in the counties to those with a forty-shilling freehold. While taxation seems a selfish enough grievance, that does not mean that the Puritans were hypocritical when they focused attention on Church affairs. Even excluding the papist Queen, there really were Catholics now in high places. Though Charles's religious mentor, Laud, who became Archbishop of Canterbury in 1633, refused a Cardinal's hat when it was offered to him, Charles really did, in 1636, accept a resident papal agent in his court. As Laud systematically denied preferment to Puritan clergy, and as his attempt to stamp out predestinarian ideas led to a ban on the reprinting of that anti-papist classic, Foxe's *Book of Martyrs*, men could be excused if they fancied a forewarning sniff of new fires of martyrdom.

Charles was favoured in his attempt to rule without parliamentary votes of money by the dwindling out of the long inflation, and also by the expansion of trade. His attempts to increase his income showed ominous success. Old laws were disinterred and the breaking of them exploited (thus, Charles enforced fines against enclosers, but not because he opposed enclosures). What could have been Charles's masterstroke was the decision in 1635 to call for the tax of Ship Money, levied in ports to support the Royal Navy, from inland towns as well. His success in raising it over the next three years showed how he might escape altogether from parliamentary control, even perhaps finance his own wars. In 1637 a rich Puritan, John Hampden, was taken to court for refusing to pay Ship Money. Seven judges out of twelve decided for the King against Hampden. Hampden paid up. What now could check the drive towards absolute rule?

III

In 1637, a local gentleman named Oliver Cromwell took the part of poor protesting commoners in the Ely Fens, deprived of much of their grazing land and of the chance to fish and to fowl by the operations of a syndicate led by Francis, 4th Earl of Bedford. A famous Dutch expert, Vermuyden, had been called in to supervise the draining of that expanse of the southern Fens which later became known as the Bedford Level. Different syndicates were at work farther north. A Fen poet wrote angrily:

> The feather'd fowls have wings, to fly to other nations;
> But we have no such things, to help our transportations;
> We must give place (oh grievous case) to horned beasts and cattle
> Except that we can all agree to drive them out by battle.

And in fact, in more than one place, fenmen, after the adventurers had started to exploit the drained land for corn and cattle, rose up, broke sluices, and seized possession again.

Charles I himself took over the undertaking of the Bedford Level in 1638, on the pretext that the syndicate was not doing its job properly. He kept on the hated foreigner, Vermuyden, and the disorders increased. A general movement of opposition was seen now over the whole area, in Lincolnshire as well as at Ely. It was resistance, in effect, to colonialism. Charles proposed to create 'several new plantations' and to build 'an eminent town in the midst of the Level, at a little village called Manea, and to have called it Charlemont' – as 'Londonderry' had been renamed, as 'Jamestown' had been created, and vastnesses to the west christened new at the whim of kings and settlers.

'Maryland', for instance, had just been born in North America, named after Charles's French wife, Henrietta Maria. It realised the vision, much flirted with since Humphrey Gilbert's day, of a refuge in America for Catholics fined for their faith in England. George Calvert had become the King's principal Secretary of State in 1619, but had resigned when anti-Catholic measures were proposed and had announced himself a Roman convert. In 1620 he had purchased land in Newfoundland, where he had established a small colony. Then in 1623 he had acquired a royal patent, enlarging the grant and erecting it into the 'Province of Avalon', so named after the traditional birthplace of Christianity in England. This was the prototype of many other patents for 'proprietary colonies'.

Basically, the 'proprietary' patent gave its lucky recipient powers within the area concerned as great as those exercised by the Bishop of Durham in his border palatinate in the fourteenth century. The idea of handing a difficult frontier over to a single viceroy had been obsolete in England since Thomas Cromwell's day, but no other precedent existed to give legal shape to so large a grant as James made to Calvert. Charles I, after reaching the throne, usually favoured proprietary patents over the other idea of making a grant to a company. In one important instance, in 1627, he gave the 'Caribee Islands' to a spendthrift favourite, the Earl of Carlisle, over the head of Sir William Courteen who had just opened up Barbados. In 1629 Sir Robert Heath was granted 'Carolana' (*sic*) to the south of Virginia and Sir Ferdinando Gorges got Maine. The idea was that the new colonies should be established under individual owners with vast feudal power. All land was to be held directly or indirectly from the proprietor who was himself tenant-in-chief under the king.

Yet unlike the inane Carlisle, Calvert actually wished to live abroad himself. Having twice visited his 'Avalon' settlement, he concluded that he should remove where 'the winters be shorter and less vigorous'. In 1628 he left for Virginia with his family, but his refusal to take the anti-papal Oath of Supremacy made residence there impossible, and he returned to England to seek permission to found a separate colony. In 1632, just after his death, his son Cecilius, second Lord Baltimore (this was an Irish title acquired in 1625), got a charter for 'Maryland', viewed it seems as a buffer colony between Virginia and the 'New Amsterdam' Dutch.

The Privy Council insisted that all passengers to Maryland took the (Anglican) Oath of Allegiance. Many evaded this somehow. But while the leading men in the expedition were Catholics, the followers whom they took with them seem to have been mostly Protestant, and Baltimore issued orders to Leonard Calvert, his brother, who went as governor, that on shipboard and in the settlement papists should practise their own rites discreetly and give no offence to the others. From the start religious toleration, even religious harmony, were seen as essential to the colony. So might the New World begin to correct the Old.

Arriving in the Chesapeake in February 1634, the colonists pitched, as a place to settle, on 'St Mary's', a site on the broad Potomac. The local Indians were friendly, and no famine confronted the two to three hundred settlers led by sixteen gentlemen with their families. These gentlemen were at once granted land and an attempt was made to transplant English feudalism lock, stock and barrel to the New World, though it was moribund in England itself. It failed. Freeholders with plots up to 1,000 acres were much more numerous than the manor lords; and those few lords who bothered to exercise their jurisdictive prerogatives, in manorial courts and so on, soon gave it up as a waste of time. In practice, local government followed the Virginian pattern, and the 'head-right' system here also became the basis of development. The interior began to fill up with tobacco farmers who struggled against the proprietors' controls. An assembly met in 1635 and quite frequently thereafter. Frontiersmen insisted on 'English liberty'.

Virginia's problems huddled so smokily around tobacco that it would have been absurd for the governor not to consult the people who grew it. In its early days, when it was fashionable, Virginia had attracted men from noble families. But by the 1620s, almost all its 'natural' élite had gone home, and the political void had to be filled by planters of humble origins, even by some who had been servants. 'Tough, unsentimental, quick-tempered, crudely ambitious men,' as Bernard Bailyn describes them they sought the maximum freedom to pursue their own interests. These easily defined themselves. They wanted aggressive expansion at the expense of Indians and, as these came along, of other colonies also. They wanted unrestricted access to land and legal endorsement as they acquired it. All this implied their own control over the colony, and that was why they quarrelled with Governor Harvey.

Sir John Harvey arrived in 1630, a proud, stubborn and ill-tempered man who wanted to be more than mere chairman of the Council. Colourful scenes resulted. Harvey outdid even his royal master in 1635 when, without consulting his Council, he imprisoned his leading antagonists and made plans to finish them off with the help of martial law. The Council deposed him, but Charles I sent him back, so he charged his opponents with treason and shipped several of them to England in their turn to be tried by the much-feared Court of Star Chamber; then he began to seize his enemies' property. But he was replaced at last in 1639, and his antics had not checked the steady development of the colony.

A census in 1625 had shown 1,478 inhabitants, of whom 269 were women, and 23 were Negroes. Plantations had by then spread along both sides of the James River. Two factors helped to keep them close to the waterside – Indian pressure, and the advantage of nearness to deep water when shipping came. But tobacco exhausted the soil swiftly, and the crop's boundless appetite for land led to steps to spread settlement across to the York River which formed the other side of the Jamestown peninsula. This in turn called for a strongly held line of settlement between the two rivers, and by 1634 a six-mile palisade connected them excluding the Indians and any question of their rights to the land. The flow of immigrants increased. By 1635, Virginia had nearly 5,000 people: by 1640, 8,000: by 1660, 33,000. Eight counties were drawn in 1634, three new ones in 1648–51, and by 1660 settlements were approaching, in various places, the 'fall line' which interrupted river navigation and still seemed to impose a natural limit to expansion.

The 'headright' principle, which brought a man new land in return for his having paid the cost of importing a fresh labourer, gave a consistent momentum to immigration, though Virginia in the 1630s attracted proportionately far fewer people than Ulster, than the West Indies, or, indeed, New England. What emerged, here as in Maryland, was a unique society of modest or small landowners, living quite simply, growing tobacco to pay for imported goods and some corn chiefly for their own consumption. Urban life did not develop importantly. The Assembly had almost complete control of the colony's finances, since the costs of government were met by public levies for which its votes were essential. Universal (white) male suffrage was not abandoned till 1655, after which all men who held houses qualified. While Justices of the Peace, as in England, became responsible for local government, the post of sheriff began to develop a greater importance than at home. There was no bishop, and hence there were no ecclesiastical courts, so marriages, wills and probates were dealt with in ordinary secular courts from the first. Virginians were reluctant to grant tenure to their clergy, and in practice ministers came to be 'hired' annually. Naturally, they were paid in tobacco.

There was of course a self-confirming, inexorable tendency; the use of tobacco as currency virtually forced men to plant it in order to buy goods and to pay taxes. But tobacco had spontaneous appeal. It was a crop through which a poor man could prosper.

The man depending on tobacco alone was in dire case when, as periodically happened, markets were glutted and prices plummeted. In 1630, for instance, Virginia tobacco sold at less than 1*d*. a lb. But planters would not be deterred. The English government helped them, imposing an adverse duty on Spanish imports – 2*s*. a lb. in 1631, as compared with 9*d*. on Virginian tobacco became a cause of bitter dissension in rural England, where Charles I in Virginia's interests had repeated his father's ban on its planting and had set off a phase of dogged resistance among the growers in Gloucestershire and Wiltshire, during which cultivation steadily expanded to other counties. In the West Indies, too, small men had rushed to feed the new taste.

IV

The Earl of Carlisle, having secured his proprietorship of 'Barbados', in practice performed as a front man for his merchant backers. Though the 'Carlisle Patent' endured in name for more than thirty years, it was always unpopular with the colonists. But then on their lush green frontier they would certainly have resented any form of government at all.

They sent the first 'Carlisle' governor back to England in chains. The second, Henry Hawley, was less frangible; he was a prototype of one characteristic Caribbean breed of seventeenth-century colonial viceroy – tough, unprincipled, bullying, quick on the draw. The planters had set up one John Powell as their governor. When Hawley arrived, this man rashly accepted an invitation to board the newcomer's vessel. He and his fellow guests were stripped and chained to the mainmast, where they stayed for nearly a month till the ship was captured by a Spanish force off St Kitts. Hawley himself somehow made his escape and contrived also to outmanoeuvre, and then have shot, yet another 'Carlisle' governor sent out to replace him. When Carlisle, in the late 1630s, at last got a royal commission for Hawley's recall, the latter nimbly erected a 'parliament' on Barbados which, duly packed with his supporters, elected him governor (and yet this opportunistically improvised organ was to prove the most enduring of all colonial assemblies). The King sent commissioners to force Hawley out in 1640. He went quietly, managed to hang on to his lands on the island, and died there at last, in 1677, at the ripe age of 80.

No frontier ever moved faster. By mid-century, Barbados and St Kitts would be among the most densely settled places on earth. This was far friendlier country than the North American mainland. The species of palm tree had their various easy uses. Leaves made buckets and covered houses. Sap gave palm wine, and one remarkable sort rising to over 100 feet had a bushlet on top which looked and tasted like cabbage and could be eaten like it. Wild pigeons were easy to catch. Turtles provided delicious meat. Nets and rope could be made from the bark of certain trees. Except for the plaguing mosquitoes and midges, there were few things about which did not come in handy.

Ecological revolution came with the white men. Captain John Smith had described how virgin Nevis looked in 1607 – 'It is all woddy . . . in most places the wod groweth close to the water side, at high water marke, and in some places so thicke of a soft spungy wood like a wilde figge tree, you cannot get through it, but by making your way with hatchets, or fauchions.' Yet sixty years later it could be said that 'at the Barbadoes all the trees are destroyed . . .' Besides shortage of fuel, soil erosion and loss of moisture would result from the massacre of trees. The land, however, would remain rich and pleasant. The climate, while somewhat enervating, was gentle. The temperature in the Caribbean rarely exceeds 80°F, though it did provide a rationalisation for the excessive drinking which at once became a feature of island societies. Plantains and sweet potatoes, wild 'plums', oranges, and pineapples all yielded interesting alcoholic beverages, before rum became the poor man's drink.

Half an ounce of tobacco seed would produce 15,000 to 25,000 plants ready for harvesting after four or six months. Tobacco was the obvious staple to grow. But it murdered the soil; after a few years, more land was essential, so tobacco was intrinsically far more suitable for a mainland colony like Virginia than for a breast-pocket island. It also demanded skill in the tending which Barbadians did not acquire. Their first attempts at the crop were 'so earthy and worthless, as it could give them little or no return from *England*, or elsewhere.' St Kitts did better, exporting nearly half a million lb. in 1638. But by now the London market was glutted, and West India exports tailed off rapidly. The need for diversification had long struck some planters, amongst whom let James Drax be sung. Astute and fortunate, he did well from his first crop of tobacco, invested the proceeds in forty-odd servants and brought them back to Barbados, then led a switch to cotton which by 1640 had virtually succeeded tobacco as the chief commodity used instead of coins in exchange. Drax, shouldering forward, began to buy small parcels of land from little freeholders. As holdings consolidated, landless and unlucky whites formed a human residue which flowed into buccaneering or into the colonisation, sponsored or freebooting, of further islands.

Frenchmen settled the two largest among the Lesser Antilles, Guadeloupe and Martinique, in 1635. But there was as yet no rivalry with England. The nationals of north-western Europe were colleagues in the invasion of the Spanish monopoly, and the ingenious Dutchmen, of course, were their leaders, trading, financing, dominating everywhere. The humble herring explains their presence, like so much else. They needed salt to cure fish. Salt could be had at St Martin and St Kitts, and at Curaçao, which last became their chief base. They soon took over several small Leeward Islands and a Dutch presence emerged in Guiana. It is probably true that without Dutch traders the English could never have launched their colonies. Dutchmen provided roots, seeds, capital, expertise, slaves, and provisions, and ships to carry the produce away; they were the main dealers in English West Indies tobacco. Meanwhile, the Dutch were gaining a hold of Brazil, the Portuguese colony which had become Europe's main source of sugar. From this, well-known consequences would follow.

V

Spanish power was declining. Even the population of Castile was falling. The coinage was debased time and again to help finance the endless war against the Dutch. Heavy taxation bore down on merchants and manufacturers. Industry after industry wilted and Spain's overseas trade passed largely into the hands of Protestant foreigners.

War with Spain was, and would long remain, a most agreeable idea to many Englishmen. When it came in 1625–30, Puritan peers and London merchants were swift into action, and the orgy of privateering eclipsed that of Elizabeth's day in volume, if not in fame. Perhaps £2,400,000 was invested in this field before the war ended in 1630 with an agreed stalemate; a return, in effect, to the terms of 1604.

France was on the way to becoming a far tougher enemy. A remarkable minister, Cardinal Richelieu, was laying foundations for a state which before long would lead Europe. In 1627 he moved, in a mercantilist spirit, to reorganise Canada, aiming at large-scale settlement in the St Lawrence Valley. The Company of New France was set up to run the colony, under Richelieu's own patronage. But England and France were at war when a French fleet sailed with hundreds of colonists, and in 1628 some privateering brothers named Kirke captured the French expedition in the Gulf of St Lawrence and went on to seize both Quebec and Port Royal. Sir William Alexander promptly asserted his 'Nova Scotian' right to the area which the Kirkes' boldness had opened up. An Anglo-Scottish consortium was founded when he did a deal with some London merchants, and in 1629 settlers were landed at Port Royal and in 'New Galloway' (Cape Breton Island). Charles I encouraged Alexander to export whole clans of Gaelic Highlanders there – 'deburdening that our kingdome of that race of people which in former times hade bred soe many troubles ther . . .' But nothing seems to have come of this novel alternative to genocide.

The French got Quebec back by treaty in 1629, and Port Royal was surrendered in 1632 when Charles swopped it for 400,000 crowns still owed to him from his French wife's dowry. But the Kirkes had done fatal damage to Richelieu's project of settlement. With the Company almost ruined and the French Crown unable to give further help, the Society of Jesus became Quebec's most effective supporter, attracting funds which helped its members build up the colony. The fur trade and efforts to convert the Hurons marched together as the Jesuits (founders of Montreal in 1643) aimed to maintain New France as what one of them called 'a holy and sacred temple built by God'. They were quite as sincere as the body of English Puritans who, in the 1630s, created 'New England' farther south.

'Puritanism', of course, is hard to define. It can be applied to those men (and women) within and outside the Church of England who held fast by the Calvinist insistence on man's sinfulness and his impotence to draw to himself God's grace; a joyless creed, it might now seem. Yet puritanism produced marvellous writers, Milton the greatest of them; it did not preclude a taste for music, which Cromwell loved; and it certainly did not always rule out drinking and dancing. It defined itself by contrast with what it hated. Puritans were sober men, or tried to be, in an age of drunkenness and of gluttony when a certain peer, in 1621, spent £3,000 on one day's meals. They extolled holy, serious living while Cavaliers made a sport of ravishing and deemed rash swordplay essential to their honour. They hungered for long intellectual sermons at a time when Laud and his followers were shifting the emphasis back to rituals. Intolerant of any views but their own, their claim for religious liberty for themselves led some of them widdershins towards toleration.

Though the 'classic' Puritan view deplored individualistic greed and was more prone to look back towards medieval communalism than forward to a commercialised world, the famous theory, associated with Weber and Tawney, that Calvinism and capitalism, Puritan values and business success, march significantly together has much palpable truth in it, however much one must emphasise the qualification that involvement in commerce pushed saints from orthodoxy towards heresy. Values had practical use where doctrines didn't. Frugality, sobriety, hard work, keeping one's word, were qualities both of good Puritans and of good businessmen. If many Puritans believed in witches and looked to portents, the movement's inherent contempt for idolatry and mystique helped agile minds within and outwith it towards scientific understanding of nature and a new realism about purely human affairs. Most importantly – and this goes for rustic-minded Pilgrims and Scottish lairds as well as for colonisers in Ireland and London merchants – puritanism gave the devoted, with stiff-necked self-righteousness, hypermanic courage. In the midst of politics, commerce, warfare, colonisation, Puritans struggled to discern the will of the Lord, His purpose in history, and their own relation to it. Once they thought they knew these, they were ready to act as befitted the chosen instruments of divine power – as daring adventurers across the oceans, as soldiers resolved and valiant in battle, as ardent and reckless propagandists for heterodox opinions.

Deprived by Charles I of Parliament, their main outlet of opposition, Puritan leaders fostered a surge of emigration calculated at once to provide a refuge for good men outwith Laud's grasp and to advance overseas the true interests of England, which were, of course, in their eyes those of Calvinist Protestantism.

Early in the 1620s, when New England was under the nominal control of Sir Ferdinando Gorges and his Council, Puritan interest arose in the south-western town of Dorchester which was much involved in the transatlantic fisheries. With a patent to hand from the Council, a syndicate was formed of people from West Country towns and countryside. A first party of fourteen men was left at Cape Ann in 1623, and additional settlers followed, but the site chosen was too far from good fishing and the survivors migrated to Naumkeag, renamed 'Salem', where they struggled through two bitter winters while White and others organised a new company to take over the enterprise. Londoners and East Anglian Puritans were brought in, and only six of the original West Country adventurers were found among the nearly ninety members of the 'New England Company' which received a grant from Gorges's Council in March 1628, embracing a slice of what became Massachusetts. The Company represented a formidable array of mercantile and landowning interests, and prominent Puritans such as the Earl of Warwick still carried impressive weight. In March 1629, the King chopped a large section out of the Council's territory and approved the charter of the Massachusetts Bay Company.

The model was the Virginia Charter of 1612; a governing body of twenty was to be chosen by all the Company's members. The crisis at home, as Charles dissolved Parliament and the Arminians tightened their grip on the Church, moved many Puritans to think deeply and fearfully. One such was John Winthrop, a gentleman-lawyer from Suffolk, aged over 40, who was in debt and had to provide for a large family. He had already sent one son to plant in Barbados. Now poor health, financial worries and the condition of England oppressed his mind. 'My deare wife,' he wrote in May 1629, '. . . If the Lord seeth it wilbe good for us, he will provide a shelter and a hidinge place for us and ours as Zoar for Lott, Sarepthah for his prophet, etc. . . .' He threw up his job in the Court of Wards and Liveries and retreated to his Suffolk estate. His troubled vision fastened on Massachusetts.

The Charter of course did not restrict membership to Puritans. The ungodly might be able to buy control. A daring scheme was evolved. The whole Company, with its precious Charter, its legal warrant, should be transferred to the New World, out of Charles I's reach. In August 1629, at Cambridge, Winthrop and eleven other gentlemen solemnly agreed to transport themselves with their families to America, so long as they could get by legal transfer the whole governance of Massachusetts. This was soon secured at a special meeting of the Company, when only a fifth of the members were actually present. Winthrop was elected governor. Through the winter, a great fleet was prepared. The first seven ships sailed next March, and before the end of 1630 seventeen vessels had taken out a thousand passengers, pioneers of the 'Great Puritan Migration'. Their leaders were the most formidable body of Englishmen ever to arrive in the New World together – men of some wealth, well-educated, politically conscious, and with firm and on the whole canny ideas about how to run a colony. A flood of newcomers pressed steadily behind them, not less than 20,000 by 1643.

Winthrop stands in his well-known portrait like an incarnation of all the severe vitality of puritanism – dark-haired, with a wide pale forehead, long nose and pointed beard, the eyes seeming to mix hauteur with other-worldly meditation, to stare across a world of sinners towards Zion. On shipboard, he lectured his fellow passengers. Massachusetts must be a model for men everywhere. '. . . We must Consider that wee shall be as a Citty upon a Hill, the eyes of all people are upon us; soe that if wee shall deale falsely with our god in this work wee have undertaken and so cause him to withdrawe his present help from us, wee shall be made a story and a by-word through the world.' Many men would fall out with Winthrop and his ways, but his bleak integrity would remain above question. He was no would-be feudal overlord, no impatient profiteer. He had a godly mission and a strong will to accomplish it.

Could the human material, even then, have matched Winthrop's exalted vision? If 80,000 English people left the country between 1620 and 1642, nearly 60,000 of these avoided the safer outlets, Holland, say, or Ireland, and crossed the Atlantic. Why did people go? The voyage would be disgusting – perhaps 200 people crowded on board a ship of normally around 200 to 250 tons. There would be five weeks at least, and perhaps several months, on a nautical diet of bad food and stinking beer. After such torture the New World itself would probably be a sad disillusionment. What was there in New England, after all, but small villages sketched on a rocky coastline, wild sea before and dark forest behind? The soil was ungenerous, the fauna horrific.

The pull of America then, at first, was not too strong. We must look to the push of conditions in England itself. 'This lande', John Winthrop wrote in 1629, 'growes wearye of her Inhabitantes . . . so as children, neighbours, and freindes (especially if they be poore) are rated the greatest burdens, which if things were right, would be the cheifest earthly blessings.'

'Canvis boothes' on Massachusetts Bay were hardly more rebarbative than the crude cotes commonly put up, windowless, with no floor but the earth, by evicted labourers on England's own wastelands. The dogs did bark and the beggars came to town, as at Exeter in December 1625, when a reputed 4,000 destitutes roamed in, and many citizens abandoned the place. Food was short, and so was firewood. It took 2,500 trees to make one ship, and while this and other industries ravaged the groves, enclosures in some areas cut peasants off from supplies of free firewood. Winters were colder than now. A Massachusetts planter wrote pointfully in 1630, 'A poore Servante here that is to possesse but 50 Acres of Land, may afford to give more wood for Timber and Fire as good as the world yeelds, then many Noble Men in England can afford to doe.'

In the town of Cambridge, throughout the seventeenth century, plague struck every five years or so, and in overcrowded London, a bad year like 1625 would carry off one-fifth of the population. Every outbreak produced a bewildered residue of parentless children, masterless journeymen, tradesmen deprived of their customers, to whom migration beckoned. Meanwhile, the woollen industry was depressed. In 1630, the accounts of merely one Surrey parish reported 1,100 idle people who depended on the clothiers for their livelihood, and 3,000 more in surrounding villages.

Yet these facts operate best to explain migration in general, the lure of the West Indies, expansion on the Chesapeake. New England was a special case. Very few servants went there under indentures. If the very highest ranks were absent, so were the very lowest, and this was the only area in which the English family was rooted from the outset; the Massachusetts courts dealt hard with men who came over without their wives and failed to send for them soon. Only here did all ages muster, children and grandparents too. And only here was there no general shortage of clergymen. Ninety-two scholarly ministers flocked to New England, often drawing admiring parishioners with them. William Stoughton, son of a Dorset emigrant, preaching at Boston in 1668, was entitled to cry, 'God sifted a whole nation that he might bring choice Grain over into this Wilderness.'

Even Winthrop's thoughts of God did not exclude care for his debts. Puritans understood that God's favour to his elect would be revealed in earthly blessings. New England aimed at practical success. A tension was there from the start between Puritan idealism and the brusque business drive of some Puritans. But such drive built up the new colony fast. Massachusetts had 6,000 settlers by 1636, perhaps 15,000 by 1642.

About one-fifth overall seem to have parted from Essex and East Anglia, but almost as many again from the West Country, nearly one-fifth also from London. The names of new settlements harped on nostalgia. 'Boston' succeeded Salem as the chief centre. 'Weymouth' and 'Dorchester' followed, and so on. By 1642 there were twenty-one villages. Intellectual life was vigorous from the first. Harvard College was founded in 1636, and from 1639 the colony had a printing press proffering sermons, psalm books and almanacs.

Gorges did not learn till 1632 what the Massachusetts Charter provided; then he made a fuss. Demon Laud headed investigations; in 1634 the Privy Council virtually abdicated its powers over all colonies to his 'Commission for Regulating Plantations'. Winthrop, convinced that this was out to destroy his Commonwealth, was horrified when the impulsive John Endecott cut the red cross of St George out of a royal ensign flying at Salem, saying that the Pope had given the King this cross. This might be interpreted as rebellion. Endecott was debarred awhile from public office. But two years later, as the cold war proceeded, Massachusetts removed the cross from all military ensigns and for half a century flew its unique flag, a red ensign with a plain white canton. The colony actively prepared for armed struggle.

It was discovered at last that the colony's charter was not in England. In 1637 the Court of King's Bench found the Company guilty in its absence, and Charles soon announced that he was taking over the management of New England and that Gorges was to be his governor. But Gorges was seventy. Charles had no funds to provide him with soldiers. Across the Atlantic a new and distinctive society went on, most impudently, creating itself.

VI

The New England spirit was seen at its sweetest in Plymouth colony, which, after the founding of Massachusetts, became a sleepy satellite of its neighbour, squeezed out of the fur trade by the early 1640s.

Smoking was forbidden. People were fined for lying, for letting their servants drink and play shovel-board on the Lord's Day, even for 'needles walkinge on ye Sabbath'. When Goodwife Mendame of Duxbury was found guilty of seducing an Indian brave, she was sentenced to be 'whipt at a cart's tayle through the towne's streets, and to wear a badge with the capital letters AD cut in cloth upon her left sleeve . . .' But the death penalty for adultery was never exacted. No witches were ever burnt here. By comparison with England's, justice in Plymouth was mild. This good-tempered society of simple, mostly ill-educated people found it hard to attract qualified ministers. Clerical influence was small. Here was one major contrast with Boston.

Another was that Massachusetts was direly embattled. It was threatened by the government at home, by Indians, and, so its rulers felt, by the enemy within represented by non-Puritans and heretical Puritans. Strong authority was needful to preserve the commonwealth and to maintain its purity. In the early days, Winthrop and his 'assistants' (the magistrates) ruled in disregard of the Charter, levying taxes for which it did not provide and leaving the freemen no role save to re-elect them. In 1634, resentment among the freemen forced Winthrop out of the governorship for three years, though he regained it and held it, with two short interruptions, till his death in 1649. The 'General Court' of shareholders was domesticated as an assembly. Both a majority of magistrates and a majority of deputies had to vote favourably before a motion could go through. Friction resulted, and in 1644, after a wrangle over the ownership of a sow, in which most of the magistrates backed the rich merchant Robert Keayne and nearly all the deputies favoured the poorer plaintiff Mrs Sherman, the General Court was divided into two houses, which were to sit apart and communicate formally.

Civil and religious affairs were inseparable. Clergy were consulted by magistrates on difficult matters. Magistrates intervened in the life of the Church and in moral questions; they sought out heresy, and sentenced people for it. Heretics threatened Church and commonwealth equally, and if Massachusetts was the best-schooled place in the world, this was partly because of the wish to implant conformity in the minds of the young.

Common sense modified would-be theocracy. The colony, short of men to work and to defend it, found it prudential to be lenient. It was common to remit in part or in whole the sentences of those who acknowledged their guilt and said that they would reform. There were few hangings, and prisoners only served short terms.

But justice, predictably, favoured the well-to-do. Gentlemen were rarely whipped, drunken masters were rarely punished. No one in Massachusetts was a 'democrat', and John Winthrop voiced the conventional wisdom of his age when he said that democracy was 'the meanest and worste of all formes of Government.' Only church members could be freemen, though non-freemen were by the late 1640s allowed a share in local government. Women and indentured servants did not count. But the townships were run by 'selectmen' with an occasional 'town meeting' exercising veto power.

The 'covenant theology' favoured by New England leaders related in economic life to the business deal, and in politics to the idea of social compact. God makes a fair bargain with man. If man will believe in Christ the mediator, he has fulfilled the contract and God must redeem and glorify him. 'You may sue him of his own bond written and sealed', one divine had declared, 'and he cannot deny it.' Each man makes his own individual covenant with God, renouncing his liberty to do anything but what he has promised. Extended into Puritan notions of government, the 'covenant' temper of mind had portentous implications, at home as well as in Massachusetts. Men enter freely into covenant with each other, as each has done with God. Thereafter, they must show absolute obedience to godly magistrates as they should to God. But neither God nor magistrate can be arbitrary. Both rule by reasonable agreement with consenting individuals. Furthermore, the magistrate is not God. Any other 'saint' chosen by God is clearly as good a man as any magistrate. Thomas Hooker, a representative New England divine, argued: '. . . Take the meanest Saint that ever breathed on the earth, and the greatest scholar for outward part, and learning, and reach and policie, the meanest ignorant soule, that is almost a naturall foole, that soule knowes and understands more of grace and mercy in Christ, than all the wisest and learnedst in the world, than all the greatest schollers.'

The aim of the godly in Massachusetts was to establish a purified Church which would come to the rescue of the mother Church in England. Yet from the outset their congregations looked oddly like those of the Pilgrim 'separatists'. Though, after 1637, synods were held at various times, each Massachusetts church was independent of all others.

However, a common view spread. John Cotton, teacher at the Boston church from 1633, a brilliant luminous divine, argued that a church must include only those who had 'saving faith', and this was the basis of the so-called 'New England Way'. A candidate for church membership was grilled by an elder, then the whole congregation would join in the inquiry. In 1636, the General Court restricted freemanship in Massachusetts to those who had passed such examination. The 'sanctified', those whose actions seemed to confirm that they were in enjoyment of grace, 'dramatised their solidarity in Sabbath observance, sober dress, oath-keeping, sexual propriety, and so on . . .' In England these had been marks of non-conformity. Here, the 'saints' were conformists and their

manners stamped the whole society. Delinquents were first admonished, then
censured by the vote of the whole church. If they persisted, they were
excommunicated and the pastor in the name of Christ delivered them over to
Satan. But again, there was nothing arbitrary about this. Debate, painful and
thorough, surrounded each case. The whole society was alive with argument.
There were sermons morning and afternoon on Sundays, lectures on weekdays.
An earnest spirit could move from lecture to lecture, church to church,
comparing what different divines were saying. Notes taken in sermons were
discussed at home afterwards. Debate was as characteristic of those people as
discipline.

VII

Doctrinal disputes led to some breaking away. But splits were inherent also in
the economic basis of settlement. Most colonists aimed to create a self-sufficient
agriculture like that of rural England. Yet the soil was sparse, and good land
round the Bay soon filled. Meanwhile, only trade with England could bring the
clothes, tools and so forth required by an English type of society; and only furs
offered a ready item of exchange for such manufactures. Local furs were soon
exhausted and from 1633 there was a rush for the wilderness which lay between
Massachusetts and the Dutch settlements on the Hudson. Word came to the
Bay of rich meadows along the Connecticut River. John Winthrop's son, also
John (the first notable Jr in North American history), with backing from Puritan
lords and gentry in England, including the famous names of Pym and
Hampden, proposed to set up a plantation at its mouth.

It was swiftly agreed that an independent government should be established.
The Reverend Thomas Hooker led thirty-five men and their families overland
through rugged country in the summer of 1636. The white man's westward
drive in North America had begun as the settlers prodded their cattle before
them, fed on the milk which they provided, and slept in the open, 'having no
pillows to use to take their nightly rest but upon such as their father Jacob found
in the way to Padan-Aram.'

Connecticut grew slowly, to only about 3,000 people by 1654. Without much
sea-going trade, they developed a way of life based on grain-growing and the
rearing of cattle, the latter providing meat, and milk, leather, and strength for
ploughing and hauling. A man's status was measured by his herd. There were,
in effect, neither rich nor poor. Without a charter, the settlers, like the Pilgrims
before them, made their own social contracts, evolving in 1639 their famous
'Fundamental Orders', from which all reference to the authority of the King was
omitted, perhaps deliberately.

Another new colony to the westward was founded at New Haven by the
Reverend John Davenport in 1637. Several wealthy London merchants
provided the backing and the site chosen (in Long Island Sound at the mouth of
the Quinnipiac River) seemed to promise, with its spacious harbour, a busy

trade and fat profits from beaver skins. But the river was narrow and short, beavers were few. As the colony's once-hopeful merchants scattered and the remaining settlers farmed the poor land, New Haven became the most theocratic of New England colonies, under the virtual dictatorship of Theophilus Eaton.

Rhode Island, by contrast, developed as a true 'haven' for various kinds of heretic. Its pioneer was Roger Williams, a young divine from a London merchant background, who was a centre of storms from his first arrival in Massachusetts in 1631. His sincerity was respected by all his adversaries, while his charm made them sorry to censure him, but his very own way of reading the Bible equipped him with a range of horrific ideas. An orthodox Calvinist, but an extreme purist, he denied that the New England settlers could consider themselves a chosen people – '. . . In respect of the Lord's special propriety to one country more than another, what difference between Asia and Africa, between Europe and America . . .?' Massachusetts, he said, had no scriptural right to persecute dissidents. Its churches contained hypocrites; elect mingled in them with non-elect, the 'herds of the world' with the 'flock of Christ'. Church and State, he held, should be completely separate. Only Jesus had the right to judge men in spiritual matters; they should be left alone, their opinions tolerated, till He made His harvest and sinners were properly punished. But Williams's Christ was not stern. He had been 'a beggar's brat laid in a manger and gallows-bird.' God's son represented all the earth's dispossessed. He also exemplified love for all men and unconcern for worldly possessions. The Christian's task was to imitate him.

Williams's ideas regarding the Indians raised in a most embarrassing form from the niggling matter that Puritans who had proclaimed the aim of converting the red man, were doing little or nothing about it: and meantime encroaching on Indian lands. While their doctrine instilled a contempt for all people outside their own covenant with God, Williams assumed that all men were sons of Adam and Indians were no worse than white men. He liked many of them. Trading among them he journeyed, he said, hundreds of miles through their lands without danger, sharing their diet of parched or boiled maize, their dried chestnuts, their strawberry bread and currant bread, their dried smoked fish, the clams which they boiled to make broth. He sold them the Dutch and English cloth mantles which they preferred to their own furs, and noted their shrewdness in bargaining. His *Key into the Language of America*, published in London in 1643, was in effect the first objective anthropological study of Indian culture, as well as the first textbook by an Englishman on any Indian tongue. He respected even the Indian way of government. Their chiefs, he said, would do nothing 'unto which the people are averse, and by gentle perswasion cannot be brought'; and *they* persecuted no man for his religion. Williams made little attempt to convert them to his; his Calvinist logic taught him that there was no point in getting them to submit to set forms of worship.

He moved from his first post as teacher at Salem to Plymouth, where he shocked governor Bradford by telling him that the colony's patent from James I was worthless, since the country had belonged to the Indians and James had had no right to give it away. Returning to Massachusetts, he made the same point to Governor Winthrop. These and other opinions were too much to stomach; he was banished. In January 1636, with one companion, he headed south, through the hardships of bitter winter. Four others came to join him in founding, at a site bought from the Indians in Narragansett Bay, a new place called 'Providence', where land was shared on principles of equality, people governed themselves through a social compact, and liberty of conscience was an agreed principle.

Ironically, Williams's move suited Massachusetts real-politics pretty well. John Winthrop, who liked him, saw his usefulness as a mediator with the Indians. Trouble had long been brewing with the Pequot tribe which had moved into the area between the Connecticut River and Narragansett Bay. Pequot attacks on fur traders and then, in 1637, on the Connecticut settlements prompted a war of extermination, in which whites joined with Indian allies. Williams, settled amongst them, helped to keep the Narragansett Indians loyal, literally sweetening their chief with gifts of sugar. At the climax of the brisk campaign, several hundred Pequots were surrounded in their fort at Mystic, which was set on fire; those who ran away were hewn down and run through. The Puritans attributed this pleasant outcome to the general fast ordered in Massachusetts for the previous day, and their Lord wore his Old Testament face. 'It was a fearfull sight to see them thus frying in the fyer, and the streams of blood quenching the same, and horrible was the stincke and sente ther of; but the victory seemed a sweete sacrifice, and they gave the prays thereof to God . . .'

Meanwhile tensions within Massachusetts produced the 'Antinomian Controversy' of 1635–8. Its background is found in the uneasy position within the godly commonwealth of two groups: women, at large, and the merchant class.

In the Puritan farm, workshop or business, the wife worked alongside her husband as partner. And in Winthrop's Boston, women actually outnumbered men among the 'elect' who were church members, though three male colonists, it would appear, arrived in New England for every two women. Shortage of women on the frontier, which contrasted with a surplus of them in England, made for easier marriage and higher status. Puritans eschewed the idea that marriage was a sacrament as a 'Popish error', and the civil, contractual basis of union was one of the legal differences between New and Old England which helped give women a measure of security and, in effect, of independence which they could not enjoy at home. Yet the family was conceived as a sphere where the father's role was to teach and chasten servants, women and children alike. Winthrop's journal shows more than one instance suggesting that puritanism could drive wives to desperation, such as that of the woman who fell out with her husband, was expelled from the Salem congregation, was whipped at the magistrates' order, and later, 'possessed with Satan', broke the neck of her three-year-old daughter that she might save her from future misery.

The businessmen likewise suffered, though less painfully, from the ambivalence of Puritan social doctrine. The founders of Massachusetts retained a traditional belief in the 'just price' and were ready to regulate both prices and wages. This proved impossible. While scarcity of skilled workmen pushed wages up to the point where a carpenter or a mason could find himself as prosperous as his social superiors, people were willing to pay almost anything for imported, manufactured necessities. Mere tradesmen from London became merchants and dominated Boston and neighbouring towns, yet they provided only two out of the twenty-two magistrates elected over the first ten years. In 1639, Robert Keayne was fined £200 in the General Court for 'taking above sixpence in the shilling profit; in some above eight pence; and in some small things, above two for one.' He was also severely admonished by the Church. Since he was a devout man, this pained him deeply.

Anne Hutchinson was the wife of one prominent early merchant, the sister-in-law of another, the parent of a third, as well as the mother of fourteen other children. She developed her own 'antinomian' doctrine that the saint who felt the presence of God in his or her own heart was freed from the shackles of moral law, since whatever he or she did must be God's will – 'I live but not I but Jesus Christ lives in me.' In her forties, with powerful mind and attractive personality, Anne gathered women around her for regular meetings. Some men were coming too. The Holy Ghost within her, as she understood it, gave her the right to preach to both sexes alike. All authority was threatened, that of magistrate, minister, along with that of the male head of the family.

Why shouldn't the saved merchant do as he liked? Most of the Boston church came round to her way of thinking. So did Sir Harry Vane the Younger, a man of distinguished family who was elected president of the colony in 1636. But clergy and magistrates struck back, with the country people behind them. Next year, Vane was voted from office and Winthrop, re-elected governor, led a thorough campaign against Mrs Hutchinson and her followers. After a trial for sedition before the General Court, Anne was sentenced to be banished as a 'woman not fit for our society'.

One of her followers was William Coddington, a merchant and probably the richest man in Boston. He and eighteen others incorporated themselves as a 'Bodie Politick' under Christ and moved southwards. With Roger Williams's help, Coddington bought the island of Aquidneck, similar in shape to Rhodes, from which the colony would eventually get its name. Here Anne and her family settled in 1638 in the town of 'Portsmouth'. Deposed as chief magistrate in favour of Anne's husband, Coddington moved on with his faction to found 'Newport' on the same island. The two embryonic towns merged next year in a miniature state. 'Rhode Island' for Anne Hutchinson proved as quarrelsome as Massachusetts, and she ranged on after her husband's death to settle a remote spot in the Dutch territories. Her six youngest children were with her. In 1643 she was murdered, with five of them, in an Indian rising. The sole survivor, a daughter, lived several years with her captors. Restored at a truce, she was loath to leave them; she had forgotten her own language.

Another great troublemaker had entered Williams's sphere, Samuel Gorton, radical spokesman for the lower orders, who founded a settlement at 'Warwick' which fizzed with so many dangerous ideas that the Massachusetts authorities moved in to stamp it out in 1643 and took him and twenty-five fellow colonists to Boston. The sympathy of the poor there made it impossible for them to punish him, and he was back before long. So there were now four independent towns in the area where Williams had been the white pioneer. That seeker of lost Zion had been joined by some Baptists and had communed with them for a while, then had broken away (while maintaining friendly relations) to make a church of two with his own wife. Sick Indians, Indians wanting shelter, Indians asking advice constantly came to his house. The wilderness was not only a fact which he lived with at Providence, it was his image of the world, through which men of all races moved seeking the truth.

Williams was a trader. As his neighbour Coddington would have agreed, toleration was essential in trade. How could Englishmen do business in Italy or in Constantinople if they could not co-exist peacefully with papists and brown infidels? How could they trade in India save by the forbearance of Muslim rulers?

VIII

Charles I's reign was a dim time for the East India Company. Profits were disappointing. Famine stifled commerce in Gujerat in the early 1630s, making times hard for the Surat factory. Whereas 50 ships had been sent East between 1620 and 1630, only 37 went in the following decade.

The Dutch overweened more than ever. They gained an ascendancy in Siam which would last for decades and intervened in Ceylon, whence they ousted the Portuguese by 1663. Malacca fell to them after a long blockade in 1641, and in the same year they became the sole Westerners allowed to trade with Japan. From 1642 to 1661, they controlled Formosa. Their sea-explorer Tasman followed up earlier Dutch sightings of the coast of Australia (first noticed in 1616) and in 1642–3 reached Tasmania and New Zealand. These had as yet not economic significance, but the Dutch colony founded in 1652 at the Cape of Good Hope was directly useful in provisioning ships on the way East.

The EIC, true to its age, spliced business with piety. Its coat of arms bore the sanctimonious pun *Deus Indicat*, 'God Points the Way'. In 1611, it sent East for the 'better comfort and recreation' of its employees the works of the famous Puritan thinker William Perkins, as well as Foxe's *Book of Martyrs* and Hakluyt's *Voyages*. Its instructions to its servants mixed concern for economy (thus, there should be no unnecessary shooting-off of salutes when captains went ashore) with more directly puritanical maxims. Gaming and dicing were forbidden. Excessive drinking was denounced. Company servants were placed under a collegiate regime which in theory, if not in fact, made it possible to enforce temperate behaviour.

But the English vied even with the notorious Dutch in the depth and frequency of their compotations. The word 'punch' entered the English language from the Marathi *panch*, meaning five, which signified the five ingredients of an insidious brew mixing sugar, lime-juice, spice and water with arrack, the local spirit. In five years, 1630–1634, 48 out of 190 EIC factors died, and one modern authority would suggest that drink accounted for most of them.

Without drink, how bearable would life have been? Since white women were absent, EIC servants turned, like the Dutch and Portuguese, to native women. A British proverb in India one day would be, 'Necessity is the mother of invention and the father of the Eurasian.'

Controlling whole territories, Portuguese and Dutch had comported themselves with racialist arrogance, holding many slaves and living, in Goa and Bantam, with great ostentation. This the English could not do. Nor were they tempted to missionary endeavour, unlike the Portuguese and even the Dutch. The English, with no territory to speak of, acquired a habit of concentrating on trade and leaving the natives to their own religion.

Their scope was enlarged greatly in 1640, when Fort St George was established at the village which later became Madras, on the Coromandel Coast. The English centre on that coast, from 1611, had been at Masulipatam. But cotton chintzes were cheaper to southward, and the English eagerly accepted the invitation from a local ruler which gave them a new headquarters. By 1652 Madras was so important that the 'Eastern Presidency' was transferred there from Bantam. The English had meanwhile moved into Bengal. There was a factory at Hugli from 1651, and soon sub-factories in the Ganges valley.

Long afterwards, this slow and gradual expansion would seem to have been begotten by manifest destiny out of inevitability. Yet the EIC's very existence was still fragile. In the mid-1630s Charles I backed the interloping 'Courteen Association', in which he was credited with £10,000 worth of free stock. The chief actors in this enterprise were a famous courtier, Endymion Porter, and two London merchants, Sir William Courteen and Sir Paul Pinder, who had lent the King vast sums of money. Courteen will be remembered as the founder of Barbados. The Association did not thrive. All the ships of its first expedition (1636) were taken or destroyed by the Dutch. But a few short-lived factories were established in India, and meanwhile the EIC was weakened not only at home but in the East, where the piracies of Courteen's ships in the Red Sea led to the imprisonment, by way of retaliation, of its own servants in Surat.

Just as Charles I's shortage of cash prevented him from having any effective foreign policy – with no parliament to back him, he could not afford war – so, as the Courteen Association showed, it distracted him from establishing any coherent 'mercantilist' policy. There were haverings over the important Newfoundland fisheries. In 1637 Sir David Kirke, once the privateer captor of Quebec, came up with a scheme, backed by London merchants, which would give him and three great noblemen proprietary rights over practically the whole fishing area of north-eastern America. The West Countrymen, after Kirke had gone out as governor in 1638, complained not only that planters were bagging the best fishing places and destroying their property, but that Kirke was licensing taverns in despite of his charter and making their fishermen unfit for work.

Kirke was a staunch Royalist. But Charles was prepared to permit noted Puritans to essay an imaginative plan in the Caribbean. Though it failed, the 'Providence Island' scheme was second in significance only to Massachusetts among new overseas ventures of Charles's reign. Its first mover was Robert Rich, second Earl of Warwick, that jolly Puritan whose fortune matched his name. Besides being active in the Virginia, Somers Island and East India Companies, Warwick had helped finance North's Guiana expedition in 1619; in the same year one of his ships had landed the first cargo of black slaves ever sold in Virginia; he had helped to get the Pilgrim Fathers their patent; and in the late 1620s, authorised to privateer against Spain, had joined with London merchants to launch a whole fleet of predators. He now conceived that Santa Catalina, a speck off the coast of what is now Nicaragua, would be a good place for a Puritan colony. The name 'Providence' was invented for it. It looked a fine base for privateers. In 1630 a company was chartered.

The list of its investors might serve also for a roll-call of leaders of Puritan opposition in Parliament. Its treasurer was none other than John Pym, who made its affairs his main interest through the 1630s. Its base was six miles long and four miles wide, large enough for purposes not unlike those of an aircraft carrier. Ninety Englishmen landed in May 1631. Their governor, Philip Bell, had instructions to confiscate and destroy all cards and dice, and he forbade mixed dancing, which became possible next year when women and children arrived. His mace had a silver plate at one end on which was portrayed the Company's seal: '. . . viz. three islands and the words written about it *Legem ejus expectabunt*, taken out of Isaiah, 42.,4, "The islands shall wait for his law", which prophecy we hope', added the Company, 'may in some sort be fulfilled by planting the Gospel in those islands.' Tobacco, cotton, madder and indigo were planted as well. Piracy was on the agenda from the first, and the vision of a godly commonwealth rapidly broke down in practice. When the last group of distinctively Puritan immigrants arrived in July 1633, the minister who led them was so shocked by the gulf between project and reality that he shortly went home to voice the complaints of the more sincere settlers. The next batch sent out were indentured servants recruited by paid agents.

By 1635, 'New Westminster' had church and governor's house built of brick, and the island bore 500 white men, 40 white women, a few children; and 90 black slaves. One Samuel Rishworth had protested against the introduction of these last and had assisted a number to escape. The Company sneered at his 'groundless opinion that Christians may not lawfully keep such persons in a state of servitude during their strangeness from Christianity.' Religion, he should learn, consisted 'not so much in an outward conformity of actions as in truth of the inward parts.' (Respectable Puritan men could, when their profits were touched, sound as 'antinomian' as Mrs Hutchinson.) As privateers brought hijacked ships to the island, these provided cheap Africans a-plenty. The sale of slaves to other plantations became an important trade for Providence. A slave revolt at the end of 1638 was suppressed only with great difficulty.

A Spanish attack on Providence, beaten off in 1635, came most opportunely. The Company asked for, and Charles gave, permission to make reprisals. Its promoters, who had been losing heavily on the colony, now reorganised it for blatant depredation. Settlers were encouraged to privateer and to pay for their own defence out of the profits. When the Spaniards failed again in 1640, the deputy governor executed papist prisoners who had been promised their lives; then, when both the island's ministers of religion protested, shipped them home in chains, consigning them to the hands of Archbishop Laud as 'disaffected' from Anglican conformity. It was an odd outcome from all the colony's pious aims. The Spaniards compelled its surrender in 1641. They were merciful. The women and children were sent home to England, the men taken as prisoners to Spain. Vast hauls from privateering were now exposed to the eyes of its victims. The loss of Providence rankled among its promoters and their allies in England, though these Puritans were by now embroiled in climactic struggle against the King at home.

IX

Ireland saw Charles I's regime at its most vigorous, Scotland the King at his weakest and silliest. Here were the flashpoints of revolutionary civil war.

As the half-closed back door, still, to England, Ireland demanded a strong army. By 1622, the force which existed was pitiful and its pay was two and a half years in arrears. From that year, to help the Crown's quest for money, the work of the Irish Court of Wards was expanded. It bore hard on the Catholic 'Old English' landowners. Minors from Catholic families were brought up as Protestants, the greatest example being James Butler, later first Duke of Ormond, a dominating figure in seventeenth-century Irish history. Catholic heirs were forced to take the oath of supremacy or to leave themselves at the Court's mercy. Most of the land of Catholic wards was leased to Protestants. The 'Old English' were now faced with piecemeal destruction.

Yet this was the very class to whom Charles I had to turn for financial support as war, from 1625, reopened the danger of Spanish invasion of Ireland. Hence the bargain summed up in the 'Graces' of May 1628. In return for three annual subsidies of £40,000 each, the King offered fifty-one concessions, which he promised would be confirmed by a parliament. Grace 24 met the fears of landowners that their property could be snatched from them – except in King's and Queen's Counties the Crown would renounce all titles to land of more than sixty years' standing. Grace 25 covered the only area, Connacht and Clare, where this guarantee was not enough.

The Old English were so frightened of the native Gaels that they felt a desperate need for the King's army. The parliament promised to them was not summoned, yet the subsidies still came in. The faithless Charles realised he need not call one. While most of the Graces (probably) were implemented, Articles 24 and 25 were not, and as relations with Spain eased, the Dublin authorities launched severe anti-Catholic policies. For three years, 1629–32, Ireland was ruled, in the absence of a viceroy, by two 'New English' Protestants, Adam Loftus and Richard Boyle, Earl of Cork, as Lords Justice. Then Charles appointed as Deputy, Thomas, Viscount Wentworth, forty years old when he came to Ireland, a strong administrator at the peak of his powers, a man of angry, self-interested determination to enhance the power of the king whom he served, and whose full confidence he enjoyed. Writing to Laud, Charles's other prime henchman, in 1633, Wentworth called for a common policy of 'Thorough' – driving 'through' ('thorough') all interests which lay in the way of the religious and administrative unity of the realm. Ireland, it seems, was being consciously used as a testing ground for policies to be tried later in England.

Aiming to bring the King's wretched Irish army back to discipline, Wentworth, although no soldier, set an example by drilling his own troop of sixty in person. A letter writer described him at this work 'on a large green near Dublin, clad in black armour with a black horse and a black plume of feathers . . .' Saturnine, militant, burnished and autocratic, the black man's goal was a French-style absolutism. Pursuing it, he was ready to bully and lie with as strong a conviction as his untrustworthy master.

The subsidies granted in 1628 were about to run out. The Irish government was running at an annual deficit of about £20,000 and had a gross debt of £76,000. Cork and Loftus in 1632 had proposed to meet this situation by reimposing the fines levied on papists for not attending the right church on Sunday. Typical Caroline deviousness ensued. Charles, at Wentworth's instigation, sent a letter to the Lords Justices authorising this step, though only as an alternative to subsidies, but smearing responsibility for it on them and ordering that this letter be made public. The aim was to persuade the Irish Commons to vote money. Cork, never outdone in shiftiness, concealed the letter, began to levy fines and tried to fix the blame on Wentworth. Wentworth, however, made sure that Cork was held responsible, then graciously withdrew the threat of fines, which sufficed to persuade the grateful Old English to renew the subsidy for another year. This was the classic policy of divide-and-rule, which Wentworth later described as being to 'bow and govern the Native by the Planter and the Planter by the Native'.

He despised the self-interested New English clique who formed the Irish Privy Council – 'a company of men the most intent upon their own ends that ever I met with.' His struggle with them matched, in exaggerated form, his royal master's contest with English Puritan landowners, and every victory which he scored over them seemed ominous to their counterparts in England. To his unscrupulous victims, his methods appeared shockingly unscrupulous. Cork had acquired his vast fortune largely by cheating Crown and Church. Wentworth had him prosecuted and fined to the tune of £15,000. Loftus spent sixteen months under arrest.

But Wentworth, while 'violently zealous in his master's ends' was 'not negligent of his own.' He chased and very swiftly got wealth by the methods of his age – selling offices which were in his gift and taking every chance which his high position afforded for helping himself, and his friends, to what was going. He profited vastly from the Irish customs. His income from Irish sources was £13,000 a year. The vast house which he built for himself near Naas cost £22,000. Besides 14,000 acres granted him by the King he bought, for a total of £35,000, some 20,000 acres of Irish land. Sheer jealousy must gather men against him.

The parliament which he summoned in 1634 unanimously voted subsidies, to cover six years, of £120,000 – neither 'Planter' nor 'Native' daring to seem remiss and give cause for him to favour the other side. But Wentworth did not intend to fulfil the King's promise. With the subsidies safely granted, he gave out that only ten of the Graces would pass into law and the most important of these confirmed the titles of Protestant undertakers in Ulster and Leinster.

Wentworth proceeded to violate Article 25. 'Plantation' was pushed forward into Connacht. Under the Burke Earl of Clanrickarde and the O Brien Earl of Thomond, the province had been generally 'loyal' in Tyrone's war. Wentworth now proposed to confiscate lands even in Clanrickarde's county of Galway, which Boyle himself had never thought of touching. Three other counties were affected. Under the 'stern looks' of Wentworth in person, juries in Sligo, Roscommon and Mayo 'found' for the King. But in August 1635 the Galway jury stood fast and refused to find the King's title except for part of the lands, even though Wentworth himself was there, staying impertinently in Clanrickarde's house, and, it was angrily noted, 'casting himself in his riding boots upon very rich beds'. The Sheriff of Galway died in the prison where Wentworth flung him. His jurymen were tried in the Court of Castle Chamber (Ireland's equivalent of the notorious Star Chamber) and each was fined £4,000, plus imprisonment. When at last they gave in and agreed to the King's title, their fines were reduced and they were released. Instead of the quarter or third originally intended, Wentworth vindictively now proposed to plant half County Galway with new settlers.

In fact, Wentworth could not recruit settlers, and Clanrickarde sustained a successful fight at the royal court, where his family had influence. The plantation made no progress; all Wentworth's brutal deployment of arbitrary power had done was to drive the Old English towards desperation. Otherwise, certainly, his rule seemed effective. His government's debts had been cleared, the army revitalised, administration reformed. Algerine pirates in 1631 had sacked Baltimore in the south-west and carried off over a hundred people to slavery; but Wentworth could claim that he had cleared the seas. Trade throve, enriching the Crown from rising customs. Yet everything he did alienated someone. Merchants were worried by tightening royal control. The Ulster planters also were agitated. Ulster Scots were shocked by the Laudian programme which Wentworth had brought over for the Irish Church.

Except around garrisons and plantation settlements the established Church of Ireland had little life or influence. Its only real centre of relative strength was Ulster, and this was because the inflowing Scots had found no trouble in joining a Church which, by articles adopted in 1615, was strongly Calvinist in emphasis. Meanwhile, toleration had been sufficient over the years to permit the Roman Church to strengthen itself. Priests were trained by hundreds in Europe. Most dioceses now had resident Catholic bishops.

Into this froward ambience, Wentworth imported his chaplain, one John Bramhall, an ardent Laudian. Bishop of Derry from 1634, Bramhall became the effectual primate of Ireland. The nominal primate, Archbishop Ussher, was helpless, as Laudian bishops fresh from England were rushed into vacant sees, as the 39 articles and the English canons were introduced, and as fines and imprisonments enforced conformity. The Earl of Cork had raised an immense monument in black marble to his late wife, at the spot in St Patrick's Cathedral, Dublin, where the High Altar had formerly stood. In the interests of Laudian ritualism, he was compelled to take it down stone by stone and to re-erect it elsewhere.

But it was in Edinburgh that revolt against Laud took fire. Revolution in Scotland preceded, and made possible, revolution in England.

James VI and I had boasted once that he governed Scotland with his pen in London, though others had failed to do so with the sword. But he had lived in Scotland as child and man, and this largely explains the contrast between his success and his son's ruin. Charles, though he kept a Scottish accent till his head fell, understood his compatriots even less well than he understood the English.

In England, by 1637, Charles had few real friends left. He had alienated most of the peerage and gentry and could not rely even on all his bishops. But his enemies seethed in impotence. There was no rival claimant to the Crown whom they could support, there was no military force to speak of except that controlled by the King, and Puritan peers like Bedford and Warwick grudgingly played ball with Charles rather than risk their great possessions. Defiant squeaks from New England frightened no cats. But in Scotland a magnate like the Earl of Argyll would have a family tradition of thinking himself, in most respects, as good a man as the king.

Charles ruled Scotland, by the pen, through a feeble Privy Council in Edinburgh. There were few Scots now at his court (the debt-ridden Alexander, laird of Nova Scotia, being one main and fairly distinguished exception). Such Scots as sought him out there found their accents and penury mocked by the ceremonious elegance of that extravagant ambience on which the painter Van Dyck conferred so much vapid nobility. They went back to join those who grumbled that the King was dominated by Englishmen, nursing their grievance that they were absented from the rich pickings (for instance, whole empires in the New World) which fell, plop, plop, from the King's plate, while their country was denied any share in England's expanding overseas trade. When Charles visited Scotland in 1633, he loathed his own down-at-heel, uncouth people and those who met him disliked him for showing it.

He had started his reign with a blundering show of power. Approaching half of the landed income of Scotland came from former church property. By his 'Revocation' of 1625, Charles reasserted the Crown's right to all these and to the teinds (tithes) which they yielded. He intended only to take back a little, paying compensation to those who lost it, and in fact he could not afford to proceed thus in more than a few cases. But he insisted on full surrender although he had no intention of taking advantage of it. Great landowners were outraged. As in Ireland, the feeling arose that no rights to land were secure, and watching Wentworth at work, it was not absurd to suppose that the same sweeping methods might be tried in Scotland.

Presbyterian ministers were now a smallish minority, many of them abroad in Ulster. Most Scots accepted the compromise evolved under James VI and I, whereby the Kirk (after 1610) had bishops, but these acted as moderators of synods. James had offended many with his 'Five Articles of Perth' of 1618, which had prescribed kneeling at holy communion and celebration of Christmas and Easter as holidays, but thereafter had had the sense not to press too hard against Puritan prejudice. The Scottish Church was in better shape than the English, its ministers were better paid and probably better educated; Scots liked it the way it was.

Charles didn't. Dogmatically Laudian, he tried to enhance the pomp of the Scottish bishops, and he pushed them forward as agents of his own power, making them take an increasingly large political role. Realising that he could not force the English liturgy as it stood upon Scotland, he ordered the Scottish bishops to suggest alterations. The result was a new Anglicised prayer-book imposed with amazing casual recklessness; neither Parliament nor Church assembly was consulted. Meanwhile increased taxation was spreading anger. When the new prayer-book was introduced into St Giles' Cathedral, Edinburgh, in July 1637, the lower orders assuaged their own feelings by hurling stools and bibles at the Bishop. Petitions for the withdrawal of the new liturgy flooded in from other places. The Bishop of Brechin read the book to his congregation with a loaded pistol in each hand.

Malcontent nobles were willing to lead popular anti-Laudian agitation, amongst them the charming and gifted James Graham, Earl of Montrose. A revolutionary junta, 'the Tables', emerged, representing nobility, lairds, ministers, townspeople. By February 1638 a document had evolved, the 'National Covenant', which yoked both patriotism and holy fervour. It invoked the rule of law, as established through Parliament. Its aim was conservative, to defend the Church as preferred by the nation and the property rights of the Scottish subject. It pledged those who signed it to oppose innovations and all, including the King, who sought to make them. Changes would be the 'subversion and ruine of the true Reformed Religion and of our Libertie, Law and Estates.' The signatories, however, might also conceive themselves as bound, with all true Scots, in a special treaty with God. The Scots could be seen as a chosen people. Whereas to those pondering New English history the word 'covenant' would eventually come to seem rather gentle and lovely, almost the same thing as 'democracy', the results which flowed from a parallel theological view in Scotland gave the word 'covenanter' bloody and tragic significance, mixing it with intolerance and massacre.

In the Greyfriars church in Edinburgh, on February 18, leading nobles and lairds signed. Next day ministers and townsmen came forward. Copies were sent to every burgh and parish and, willingly or unwillingly, a great proportion of the whole people subscribed, or lifted up hands in church to signify assent. Ministers accepting the new liturgy were deposed. The Tables began to buy arms abroad and to drill troops.

Charles reacted as ineptly as possible. He withdrew the offending prayer-book, yet planned nevertheless to suppress the insolent Scots. He sent a Scots favourite, the Duke of Hamilton, north to lie, temporise, and pretend to negotiate. Meanwhile he had to grant the General Assembly of the Church which the Covenanters demanded – and then packed. This met in November, defied Hamilton, annulled the new liturgy and other 'popish' innovations, and deposed the bishops. The Scottish Privy Council's feckless rule had collapsed. All but one of its members walked out of the revolutionary Assembly. The one who stayed was squinting Archibald Campbell, 8th Earl of Argyll and perhaps the most notable man in all his line, who combined Presbyterian zeal with the familiar Campbell trait of dynastic ambition.

Where could Charles find an army? In the summer of 1639 he at last scraped one together, drawn largely from the English militia and financed by loans and gifts from rich papists and various office-holders and toadies. While Montrose, for the Covenanters, marched north to capture the resolutely episcopalian city of Aberdeen, the main Covenanting army sang its way south to oppose Charles. It was too strong for him. He did not fight. At Berwick, he promised the new rulers of Scotland a free Parliament and a free Assembly. Predictably, the new Assembly was still more defiant, declaring episcopacy to be contrary to the Law of God, and the new Parliament confirmed its acts. It made subscription to the

Covenant compulsory and there was nothing which Charles could do to close its proceedings. Meanwhile, he had turned to his trusted strongman, Wentworth.

Numerous Ulster settlers had subscribed to the Covenant. Wentworth had acted quickly, expanding his army and stationing a large force at Carrickfergus to prevent any alliance with Scottish rebels. In May 1639 he imposed a 'Black Oath', repudiating the Covenant, on all Scots in Ulster. Many took it, unwillingly. Many fled to the woods and hills, or to Scotland. Many were gaoled in Dublin. Wentworth thought of expelling every unpropertied Scot from Ulster. But then he was summoned back to London. He became Earl of Strafford and Charles's chief minister. With Charles he drew up a fatal plan for an army of 9,000 men, to be created in Ireland and used against Scotland. Despite the obvious dangers, Catholics were given command of companies. Many junior officers, most of the rank and file, were self-confessed papists. From this desperate scheme, the wreckage of Charles's power in all three countries would follow.

Charles had tried, absurdly, to drive a common programme 'thorough' vested interests in three very different countries. In both the major islands of the British archipelago, the motley array of enemies whom he had raised up now moved to revenge themselves. Scottish Protestant zealots and Irish priests, offended English gentry, cantankerous London traders in fur and tobacco, got their various blows in. The monarchy staggered.

X

Even now, when Strafford (as Wentworth now was) returned briefly to Ireland in March 1640, he was able to get new subsidies from the Irish Parliament. But Charles was less fortunate. His need for money compelled him to summon an English parliament, which met in April and May and was so truculent that he dissolved it without getting any money. Again, he managed to scrape an army together to face the Scots. It was routed. The Covenanting army occupied Newcastle and Charles had to agree to pay them £850 a day while they stayed there and waited for him to come up with terms that would satisfy them. Short of conceding all their demands, Charles could do nothing but call another parliament. There followed perhaps the first general election to centre on national politics. The large electorate was impassioned. Of sixty-six candidates nominated by Court agencies, all but fourteen were defeated. The best-educated House of Commons in English history met in November for what became the famous 'Long Parliament', its members in effect under Scots protection and, like the King, subject to Scots blackmail.

Presbyterians had seized their chance and had made their ideas dominant in Scotland. The Scots leaders seem to have agreed with Pym's men, the Providence Island Party, that they would delay concluding a treaty with the King until Parliament got what it wanted from him. In return they demanded not only their £850 per diem but a pay-off of £300,000 and the abolition of bishops in England. Under Pym's management, Parliament pushed through legislation removing hated grievances – Ship Money, the Star Chamber – attacking Laud and his bishops, and trimming the royal prerogative. Strafford was impeached for high treason, and in May 1641 his career ended on the executioner's block.

His enemies in Ireland had gleefully fed Pym's party with evidence useful towards his impeachment. Once his back was turned, the Irish Parliament jumped out of its characteristic subservience. Many supporters of Strafford's regime who sat in it were preoccupied with raising his famous army. Old English Catholics and New English dissidents combined in an alliance which could not last long but which was sufficient to give them a majority for a year. Strafford's deputy was forced to drop the scheme to plant Connacht. The subsidies recently granted were whittled down by nearly three-quarters. Then, with the common enemy dead, this movement promptly petered out. The Old English had got what they wanted. Charles, in desperate need of Irish support, had confirmed the Graces.

Wentworth's splendid financial policy was in ruins. By June 1641, Crown debts in Ireland stood at £140,000. The English Parliament insisted that the vast new Irish army must be abandoned, as Charles himself could not possibly afford it. Though a thousand men were shipped off to serve under the Spanish Crown, thousands more lingered in Ireland and Charles secretly schemed to keep them intact, and even expand them, as a weapon against the English Parliament. But meanwhile a conspiracy sprouted among the Gaels, promoted by Roger Moore from Kildare and involving Lord Maguire and various prominent Ulstermen. With so many papists armed by the King, tinder awaited the match. Army officers were drawn in. A two-pronged plan was devised. Dublin Castle, with its store of arms, was to be seized and at the same time Sir Phelim O Neill was to raise rebellion in Ulster.

The strike at the Castle was aborted by treachery, but Sir Phelim rose as planned and captured Charlemont and Dungannon, the two key points of central Ulster, on the night of October 22, 1641. The aim of the Gaelic leaders was not revenge with the sword for their injuries. Charles's intrigues made them think that he wanted a rising and would reward those who rose. They hoped rebellion would achieve a bloodless coup which would put them in a strong position to bargain over their grievances. Their chief object was religious liberty, though they must have nursed some confused hopes of regaining land once theirs. They intended to attack English positions but to leave alone the Ulster Scots. But their followers had no time for political sophistication. As they assailed a plantation which was already weakened, physically and morally, by Wentworth's policies, revenge tempted them irresistibly. Atrocity stories flowed into Dublin with refugees from Ulster. An eye-witness reported their coming in – 'Wives came bitterly lamenting the murders of their husbands; mothers of their children, barbarously destroyed before their faces; some over-wearied with long travel, and so surbated, as they came creeping on their knees; others frozen up with cold, ready to give up the ghost in the streets . . .'

It was said that a priest in Longford, when the rebellion spread there, had given the signal for massacre by 'ripping up the parson with his own hands'. Such stories were believed. They confirmed racist prejudice – Gaels were beast-like as well as Catholic. Hence, when the chance arose, Protestant reprisals were beast-like in turn. Yet in Cavan, O Reilly's country, the desire of Gaelic leaders to spare needless bloodshed was apparent. The Scottish vicar of Lurgan, Andrew Creichton, received a message that no Scot would be harmed, and was able to help the refugees moving south. He made friends with a leading O Reilly's mother on the grounds of common kinship with the Earl of Argyll, and this kindred, he said, 'stood me in great stead afterwards, for although it was far off and old, yet it bound the hands of the ruder sort from shedding my blood.' And when Bishop Bedell, Englishman and Protestant, died of typhus, the O Reillys overruled the Catholic Bishop of Lismore. Bedell had been well-liked in his district – he had been the first to translate the Old Testament into Gaelic – and many weeping Gaels were present when he was buried by Protestant rites.

Very few people in England or Scotland would have believed in the O Reillys' humaneness, or would have been prepared to reciprocate it. The atrocity stories reached England most opportunely for Pym and his party. Parliament had lost its Scottish protection. The King had gone to Edinburgh in August and had made his peace with the Scots leaders, conceding all their demands and confirming rebels in office, Argyll amongst them. Before his return, the Irish 'news' struck. No one in England had expected rebellion. Ireland had seemed peaceful and prosperous. Charles's most determined opponents in Parliament were, probably, shocked in all sincerity as they heard tales of Protestants roasted and eaten alive, Protestant prisoners fed on garbage and offal. But they did not follow courses designed to get swift relief to their co-religionists. They used the commotion for their own ends.

Many contemporaries would believe that within a couple of years of the insurrection, some 200,000 Protestants had been murdered, otherwise done to death, or expelled from their homes in Ireland – and a Jesuit, stupid man, would gleefully claim in 1645 that by this time 150,000 heretics had been killed. More temperate commentators would talk of the massacre of some 37,000, 40,000 or 50,000 Protestants at the start of the rebellion alone. These figures, coined in the mewling infancy of statistics, were, of course, nonsense.

But the notion of a plan to slaughter all Protestants suited the Pyms and Cromwells very well, especially as Charles I was implicated by a forged royal commission which Sir Phelim O Neill flaunted. Thousands of miserable colonists had crossed to England for refuge. Most MPs had friends if not kindred in Ireland. Could any true Christian be safe from the diabolical schemes of the King's papist controllers? How could Charles be trusted to handle the army which must be sent to repress this rebellion? Pym, in the Commons, now proposed, with success, that Parliament must make it a condition for giving financial support to this end that the King should appoint only such great officers as Parliament was willing to trust. Then, more narrowly, the Commons carried their 'Grand Remonstrance' which identified the Irish rebellion as part of a Catholic plot threatening all three kingdoms, and accused Charles of setting up arbitrary government and relying on the support of a popish and malignant party. Charles attempted to arrest five MPs for high treason, Pym among them. They fled into the City of London, now dominated by their supporters.

Thanks partly to the troubles recently facing the cloth trade with northern Europe, the merchants who traded to the Middle East and to the East Indies had ousted the Merchant Adventurers as the leaders of London. They faced in turn the challenge of a third group of traders, preoccupied with the new transatlantic colonies and resentful of the oligarchy, meshed by intermarriage, which was based on the monopoly privileges of the Levant and East India Companies. Few East India merchants had shared Sir Thomas Smythe's breadth of interest. It had been left to hundreds of pettier men to keep trade with Virginia, Massachusetts and Barbados speeding. The leaders who had swiftly emerged among them, dominating the trades in tobacco and provisions, were closely linked with Warwick and Pym. They were frustrated by the high customs duties, which Charles I could not afford to lower.

Hence, while the aldermen-oligarchs of the City establishment were mostly supporters of King Charles – despite the Company's problems with the 'Courteen Association', only two EIC directors are known to have favoured Parliament – the 'colonial-interloping group', as Robert Brenner has called them, were 'overwhelmingly' on Parliament's side. These men and their allies, in a kind of coup, broke the power of the City establishment and controlled England's commercial and financial centre.

The King found the metropolis too hot for him and retired to Windsor. The army for Ireland which Parliament now set out to organise became a pretext for preparations for conflict with the King.

The Ulster rebels had soon moved south to seize Dundalk, though with few arms and little military experience they had been unable to root out several dogged centres of Protestant resistance in their rear. Risings of Gaels in parts of Leinster followed. The whole of the standing army in Ireland remained in Dublin, except for one garrison at Drogheda. Landowners all over Ireland were thus left unprotected. The Old English gentry knew that the authorities distrusted them. They could only save their estates by some kind of bargain with the advancing rebels. Two incidents late in November completed Old English alienation. One government force, on the way to relieve Drogheda, was routed at Julianstown, while another relieved Wicklow swiftly, then fell to summary execution of the townspeople. Julianstown seemed to show that the government was too weak to defend loyal subjects, and Wicklow that it would not be too careful in its choice of papists to slaughter. Within a few days the Old English

of the Pale were up in rebellion, still protesting their loyalty to King Charles.
Wentworth's policies and Charles's intrigues had helped drive into one camp
the descendants of Tudor settlers and those of Gaels whom they had
expropriated, but the Catholics thus combined still saw themselves as the King's
allies against the English Parliament and its Puritan managers.

In August 1642, the King raised his standard at Nottingham. Civil war in
England began. It was partly a war between life-styles. Parliamentarians, called
'Roundheads' although their leaders wore long hair, distrusted the fashionable,
extravagant ways of the Royalist 'Cavaliers'. It was more importantly, of course,
a war over religious ideas. Puritans generally fought for Parliament, Laudian
Arminians and papists on the King's side.

But it was also a revolutionary war, the product of great and cumulative
changes sweeping England away from feudalism into a new phase where the
operations of the market would dominate social relationships. The numbers of
men in the landed class of gentry had multiplied three times (to about 15,000) in
the century since Henry VIII had put monastery lands up for sale, while the
population as a whole had scarcely doubled. Many were no longer prepared to
fawn on peers or to give unquestioning respect to an impoverished and
discredited Scottish dynasty. Parliament's defiance expressed the desire of some
upper-middle-class men for a reordering of the polity which would give them
greater legal and economic scope – freedom of speech, freedom from arbitrary
arrest, free consent to taxation, emancipation from monopolies granted at the
royal whim.

The rural poor and the urban wage-earners on the whole seem to have stayed
neutral in sympathy, so that both King and Parliament had to resort to
conscription. But while the rich merchant oligarchs, as in London, were likely
to favour Charles, artisans and shopkeepers, like small freeholders and yeomen,
were drawn to the other side. Parliament gathered behind it, not to the taste of
most of its members, a mass of religious and political sectaries, brandishing
every heresy known to man, drawn in great part from the lower-middle
orders.

Many thousands of sermons, speeches, pamphlets and newspapers swarmed
from the presses. The favourite heresies of the common people, long cherished
in secret in town and countryside, now erupted into public debate. Anti-
clericalism and hatred of religious images were respectable enough these days;
but men and women were also heard denying the doctrine of the Trinity,
espousing the 'mortalist' doctrine that the soul died with the body, and wedding
far-out theological notions with unmistakable 'levelling' class feeling. The Bible
could be cited in support of almost any idea, including, of course, polygamy.
The book of Revelations was favourite study among artisans as well as
university-trained intellectuals; both sorts of reader could equate Charles and
the Pope with Antichrist, and might expect the imminent reign of God's saints
on earth, the millennium. Amongst Baptists and Quakers, Ranters and

Levellers, Diggers, Fifth Monarchists, Muggletonians and a myriad other groups, much superstitious absurdity might be found.

But also ideas which even the twentieth century would find challenging or disturbing. Some women preached in public. Free love had its antinomian advocates. Fair and equal access to land was demanded. Roger Williams and Anne Hutchinson were moderate, old-fashioned persons compared with many of the new prophets. Presbyterianism, though still a revolutionary force in Scotland, became a conservative one in England. Denying man's inherent sinfulness and emphasising man's freedom of choice, 'popular' versions of Arminianism emerged, utterly different in bearing from Laud's appealing to confident men of the urban middle classes.

If Laud's or Calvin's authority should not prevail, why should Aristotle's or Galen's? Earlier in the century, Francis Bacon had argued that modern men could advance beyond ancient knowledge. By careful study of the world around him, by co-operative research, scientists could change man's earthly condition for the better. Like William Harvey's discovery of the circulation of the blood (1628), Bacon's thought gained wider hearing after 1640; by the 1660s the new scientific outlook would have official state backing, and its relationship to industrial and commercial advance would be obvious to most reflective men.

Meanwhile, as conflict spread over three kingdoms and into the colonies, many men, rich and poor, picked their sides not out of deep conviction but as opportunism or old quarrels dictated. Longstanding contests between gentry families were sanctified. Winds of decentralisation blew through the three realms. In Ireland anarchic confusion resulted. In Scotland, class conflict boiled up along with a great revival of feuding. Wales, mainly Royalist, regained strategic importance.

In England, there was stalemate at first, despite the organisational genius which Pym brought to his side. He and his friends could see only one way to break the deadlock. The Scots must be won as allies. They would be difficult yoke-fellows. The Scottish noblemen who had supported and, in effect, launched the Covenant were finding the Kirk which they had helped to refresh most uncomfortable. Puritan Presbyterian ideals now had hypnotic sway. Zealous plebian ministers presumed to dictate behaviour to the mighty. But Archibald Campbell, Earl of Argyll, was prepared to co-operate with their godly aims while exploiting the situation to further his own house's inveterate ambitions. Other noblemen, full of justified suspicion, began to shift back towards King Charles, and one of these was the able Montrose. Argyll used the Covenant as a pretext for taking fire and sword to his clan's foes. The Ogilvies, kinsmen of Montrose, suffered, and in the summer of 1641 he himself was briefly imprisoned because he had been corresponding with the King.

Extremists were jumping into the saddle. They wanted to exalt the ministers over the laity, noble and commoner alike; to create a theocracy. They had a grandiose vision of national destiny. In 1581, in 1590 and 1596, the Scots, as it seemed to these enthusiasts, had covenanted as a whole people with each other and with God to defend the best of all reformed Churches. Now the National Covenant had confirmed the status of the Presbyterian minority as prophets of divine inevitability. Archibald Johnston of Warriston, a lawyer who had helped write the Covenant, was not alone in seeing a 'verrie near paralel betuixt Izrael and this churche, the only two suorne nations to the Lord' – nor in talking as if Church and nation were one and the same thing.

The sworn nation was swift to send troops to Ireland, at the request of the English Parliament. A proclamation from Charles I denouncing the rebels arrived in February. Properly used, this might have swayed the Old English back. But the Protestant Lords Justices did not want submissions. They deliberately discouraged them by throwing the first who surrendered into prison. Swayed by the characteristic New English avarice, they wanted Catholics to stay out in rebellion so that their lands would be forfeited. The English Parliament thought on the same lines. Their idea, evolved by February 1642, was to make Ireland pay for its own suppression. There would be forfeited land in every province, and plenty of it to go round. Two and a half million acres, Parliament thought, nearly one-fifth of all the profitable land in Ireland, could be promised as security to English 'Adventurers' who were now invited to put up money to support the war. Pym and Cromwell invested £600 each. Altogether 1,533 'Adventurers' came forward to assist in this revival of Elizabeth's method of fighting the papists on a joint-stock basis. They would get their reward only if the rebels were defeated, and almost unconditionally defeated; thus, only a drastic and punitive settlement could suit them. But for the moment, the whole Adventure was the tool of an English party. The first £100,000 raised, and the forces gathered for Ireland, were cynically diverted for use against Charles at home. Meanwhile, the Old English were bound in the last resort to support Charles, since only a royal victory could secure their lands.

So the struggle was going to be long and bitter. Major General Robert Monro, who arrived in Ulster with 2,500 Scots in April, could not do enough to break the stalemate. A veteran of the Thirty Years War, like many mercenaries who had returned to Scotland at this promising juncture, he was ruthless even by the standards of his profession. He soon captured Newry. He massacred the garrison and townspeople. The rebels were not cowed by such barbarism; they retaliated in kind by murdering prisoners. And though they were too poorly armed and led to stand against regular troops, there were not enough of the latter to hold down whatever territory might temporarily be won from the rebels.

In this situation, the Catholic hierarchy moved towards the creation of an Irish state. At a meeting of bishops with leading nobles and gentry in July 1642, a provisional government was set up. The aims of the war were defined as defence of the Catholic religion, and of the King's prerogative. An oath to association was agreed on, to be administered to all and sundry by the clergy, binding the swearers to restore Catholicism as it had been established before the

Reformation. Ironically, there was evident influence from the Scottish Covenant – and in this case also, a conservative rebellion by landed men was pushed towards zealous extremism by the influence of the clergy.

Owen Roe O Neill, nephew of the great Tyrone, came back to his native land with a reputation, earned fighting for Spain, which he did little to justify. Another mercenary, Colonel Thomas Preston, of distinguished Old English family, returned about the same time and was given command in Leinster to match Owen Roe's in Ulster. The two men mistrusted each other, and this was bad for discipline, which was weak anyway.

The Supreme Council had summoned a General Assembly, elected like a parliament, to meet at Kilkenny in October. Its business was conducted in English, which shows how far Gaelic leaders had already been weaned from their native culture. The 'Confederation of Kilkenny' was to be a union of all Catholic Irish, with no distinction of race. However, the new Supreme Council, or ministry, was dominated by the Old English element, which craved an agreement with the King at all costs, and the Assembly voted an 'Old English' solution to the land question – ownership should be stabilised as it had been in October 1641. There was an inherent contradiction from the outset between Old English moderation and the aims of Gaels who had long since lost their land and who were willing to fight indefinitely in the interests of the true religion.

The Protestant side was also disunited. James Butler, 12th Earl of Ormond, commanded the government forces. Handsome, punctilious in dress and display, Ormond was not a great soldier or a brilliant politician, but he was able to get on with Catholics. He acted as Charles's agent in negotiations with the Confederation which continued over months of indecisive fighting, until in September 1643 a truce was signed. The Confederates agreed that each side would keep what it had, and they would pay Charles £30,000. The Dublin government was then free to send 2,500 troops to England, where they were swiftly routed.

Meanwhile, Parliament had bought the Scots, or some of them, at a heavy price. The cost of hiring 21,000 troops was a less grievous burden than the Solemn League and Covenant of 1643 upon which the masters of Scotland insisted. As the Scottish Covenanters saw it, this agreement meant that they and Parliament would work in harness to establish Presbyterianism not only in their own countries, but also in Ireland, and would punish all who opposed this aim, which they further implied should be extended into a European crusade. Covenanting pride supposed that the forms of the Scottish Kirk could be extended to two kingdoms each larger and more populous than Scotland. Many English intellectuals and radicals believed that the chosen nation was their own. But Parliament set up the so-called Westminster Assembly to discuss the reform of the English Church. Though the eight Scottish envoys present were disappointed by what seemed the lukewarmness of the English, who wouldn't let their Church assembly legislate in its own right as theirs did, and still thought that the idolatrous Christmas holiday should be observed, the Scottish Kirk accepted the Calvinist 'Westminster Confession of Faith', so that, ironically, its chosen creed would forever bear the name of an English place and originate from a conclave where Scots had had no vote.

The English Presbyterians adopted the Scottish model of organisation with the important difference that they favoured lay supremacy rather than clerical. Even so, their implicit tolerance put them at loggerheads with 'Independents' like Cromwell who looked to New England rather than Scotland and favoured a Congregationalist basis. But all who wanted to beat the King were, if grudgingly, glad when the Covenanters crossed the Border in January 1644 and besieged Newcastle.

XI

Charles had given Montrose the titles of Lieutenant Governor of Scotland and Captain General. While the Covenanting army was occupied in England, Montrose joined in the Highlands an army sent over from Ireland by the Royalist Earl of Antrim, and partly armed and supplied by the Catholic Confederates. Its commander was Alasdair Macdonald, a giant (seven feet high, so they said), styled 'Colkitto' by English writers, including Milton, who couldn't spell Gaelic. 'Colkitto' had had no trouble, once in the Highlands, in raising his own tribe, the Macdonalds, against their hereditary foes, Argyll and the Campbells. The clans now divided, for or against Montrose or the Covenant, on their own bases, not in response to principles. Montrose pursued the cause of the King along with his own ambitions.

Europe hailed him as a great commander, but his effectiveness derived from his understanding that with a force mostly of Highlanders the normal rules of soldiery could, and indeed must, be flouted. To their rapid mobility in their own habitat, Highland Gaels had in the sixteenth century added a new technique, the ferocious mass charge on foot with drawn claymores. But the capture of Aberdeen which he soon effected showed the limitations of his kind of campaign. The city and the area round it were stubbornly Royalist and episcopalian in their sympathies. Here was the best available reservoir of broad-based support for the King. But for three days Colkitto and his tribesmen plundered, murdered and raped.

Argyll came up in pursuit. Montrose led him a wearisome chase round the Eastern Highlands, beat him at Fyvie when he at last caught up, then vanished into the mountains. In the dead of a bitter Caledonian winter, he brought his men unexpectedly down upon the Campbell stronghold at Inverary. Argyll himself escaped in a boat, just in time, but his lands were ravaged. Soon three armies converged to trap Montrose in the Great Glen. In snow and wind he escaped by a march into the pathless mountains, from which he fell on the Campbells massed at Inverlochy. Argyll had to flee again as his clansmen were slaughtered. Even this feat was exceeded next summer when Montrose struck south, crossed the Forth and crushed a Covenanting army at Kilsyth. This was August 1645. He was master of all Scotland. The Covenanting leaders escaped the country. Edinburgh, Glasgow, the landowners, submitted.

But this time his Highlanders weren't allowed to plunder. They had joined him to beat Argyll. Now Argyll was beaten. They dribbled homewards.

As Montrose's guerrilla campaign had got under way, Parliament's Covenanted allies had marched to Long Marston Moor in Yorkshire. In the biggest battle ever fought on English soil, on July 2, Scottish reinforcements arrived at just the right moment to help Oliver Cromwell, commanding the horsemen of eastern England, recover and break the Royalist cavalry for the only time in the war. Charles's defeat at Marston Moor gave Parliament control of the North. It confirmed the stature of Cromwell as soldier, and preceded the creation of a New Model Army, the first force to wear the red uniform which the British would carry to battlefields in every continent.

Cromwell's name by modern reckoning would have been Williams. He was descended from a sister of the famous Thomas Cromwell who had married a Welshman. When heralds came to devise a crest for Oliver, they would include the arms of the last Prince of Powys. However, to look at and hear Oliver was *echt* English, a ruddy-faced man with long brown hair and a big nose, careless of clothes and appearance, devoted to horses and hawking, a pithy phrasemonger on many occasions but blurting and tortuous when it came to oratory. 'I had rather be overrun', he once declared, 'with a Cavalierish interest than a Scotch interest; I had rather be overrun with a Scotch interest, than an Irish interest . . . all the world knows their barbarism.' Yet his loathing of religious intolerance (bar papists, of course) was deep and sincere. He was his own man in religion, a searcher who once said that he would rather permit Muhammadanism in England than risk the persecution of one of God's children.

By birth and background he was an English Puritan gentleman, born in 1599 in the East Anglian heartland of puritanism. Plenty of relatives were in the House of Commons when he entered it in 1628. He shared their enthusiasm for New England; he came near to emigrating in the 1630s, pined often to live in a godly New World commonwealth, and corresponded when at the height of his fame with the pastor of Boston, Massachusetts, John Cotton. His temperament suited Calvinism well. He was a manic depressive, his life marked by bouts of wild glee and phases of deep indecision. He took the Calvinist doctrine of providence literally and made it the basis for his actions. Every event came about because God willed it to happen. Slow to decide what God's will might be, he was swift, decisive and ruthless in action once he presumed that he had discovered it.

He made men of low birth officers, so long as they were godly. 'I had rather have a plain russet-coated captain that knows what he fights for, and loves what he knows, than that which you call a gentleman and is nothing else.' The New Model Army which Parliament created so as to have a national force independent of the regional preoccupations of the gentry would be the most revolutionary item in British history. Cromwell did not create it alone, but he showed that he could lead it best.

At Naseby in June 1645, the New Model Army defeated one of the King's forces. At Langport on July 2, the other royal army was shredded. Charles's only hope now was Montrose, whom he ordered to march south to meet the Covenanting contingent led by the brilliant David Leslie. At Philiphaugh in the borders, Montrose was caught off guard. His infantry, after surrender, were massacred in cold blood on the orders of the godly ministers who dominated Leslie's army. The humiliation of God's chosen race by a band of Gaelic savages was savagely avenged. Early in 1646 Charles, preferring Scots rebels to English, surrendered himself to the Covenanting army encamped at Newark.

The Covenanters could do nothing with this king who would not be a Presbyterian and in January 1647 they sold him to the English Parliament for £200,000, half the money now due to them, and went home. The victorious English revolutionaries were now split between the factions to which the rough and misleading labels 'Presbyterian' and 'Independent' attached themselves. The army, 'independent' in bias, hijacked the King in June 1647 from the Presbyterian-dominated Parliament. In August the army occupied London. The troops had elected 'agitators', to voice their demands for pay and for religious toleration. The influence of the 'Levellers' was growing among them. These men stood for the lower-middling people, attracting, besides the rank and file of the army, yeomen, small businessmen, and craftsmen. They wanted the franchise extended to all except servants and beggars. They wanted a republic, no king. They wanted the House of Lords abolished, along with excise and tithes. They wanted free schools and hospitals, general reform of the law, the election of magistrates. They worried Cromwell deeply, and those to the right of him still more so.

Class feeling was hardening in Scotland also. To most of the nobility, it seemed that the only way to safeguard their traditional dominance of society was to save the King. But the General Assembly of the Kirk was under the control of men for whom the terms of the Solemn League and Covenant were as indestructible as the stone of their hills. The King's refusal to accept them damned him. In December 1647 three Scottish lords, amongst them the learned and pliable Earl of Lauderdale, made an agreement with Charles, who refused to swear to the Covenant but agreed to establish Presbyterianism in England for a trial period of three years, and to give Scots the same commercial privileges as his English subjects. While the Scottish Parliament supported this 'Engagement', Argyll and the standing Commission of the Kirk opposed it, and did their best to prevent the recruitment of an army.

The 'Engagers' took a force of 20,000 men into England where Cromwell cut them to pieces near Preston in August 1648. The 'Second Civil War' was brief. Royalist risings in support of the Scots in various parts of England and in South

Wales were swiftly suppressed. To Cromwell God's witness against the King seemed confirmed. The rout at Preston triggered coups in both England and Scotland.

The heartland of support for Presbyterianism and the Covenant was in south-west Scotland. Clydesdale, Ayrshire and Galloway bore their crop of opinionated small men – petty lairds, owner-occupying peasants. Recruiting for the King had sparked a rebellion here in June. The insurgents had dispersed, but now they rallied again and marched on Edinburgh. When they went to the capital to buy corn in the summer, the Westland men drove their horses with the cry 'Whiggam! Whiggam!' Hence their seizure of Edinburgh was the 'Whiggamore Raid', and the word 'whig' entered the English language. The lay government fled and the militants of the Kirk were left in power. Cromwell came up and lent them troops, and they were able to impose their minority opinions on the country. A rump of the Scottish Parliament passed, early in 1649, an 'Act of Classes' excluding from all public office and military command not only supporters of Montrose and 'Engagers' but even those who had not actively opposed them, as well as all guilty of immorality. The Church itself was purged, and there was what one contemporary called 'daylie hanging, skurging, nailling of luggis . . . and boring of tounges' for moral as well as political offences.

So 'whigs' now ruled Scotland. The word 'tory' came, in this period, from Ireland. That island, in the mid-1640s, was in extreme confusion. Monro's Scots were still in Ulster to fight for the Solemn League and Covenant and in Munster a noted Protestant Gael, Lord Inchiquin, known as 'Murrough of the Burnings', had swung his force on to Parliament's side. Neither of these subscribed to the truce which the third Protestant leader, the Royalist Ormond, maintained with the Catholic Confederacy. Within the Catholic camp, there was growing division. While the aristocratic Old English tended to favour the truce, many of the Gaels opposed it and provided recruits for a clerical faction headed by Pietro Scarampi, the Pope's envoy. Desperate for Confederate support, Charles secretly gave the Earl of Glamorgan, an English papist, a rash commission to treat with the Confederation behind the back of Ormond. In the autumn of 1645, Glamorgan made a deal whereby Catholics in Ireland would get possession of all churches and church property not actually in Protestant hands in return for supplying Charles with 10,000 troops. When word of this agreement leaked out, Charles had to repudiate it, but the suggestion – not unfair, at this time – that he was in conspiracy with the Irish papists, did him enormous harm in England. The deal which Ormond finally made with the Confederation in March 1646 said nothing about church property or a new status for Catholicism.

This compromise outraged the man who had recently arrived in Ireland as papal nuncio, Giovanni Battista Rinuccini. Elderly, unworldly, unbending, he had the treaty condemned at a synod which threatened all who accepted it with excommunication. Catholic noblemen were unimpressed, but the common Gael was easily stirred by the priests; as in Scotland, the clerisy threatened aristocratic leadership. The veteran Owen Roe O Neill had just gained the one major victory for the Catholics in the war. At Benburb his pikemen had routed Monro's over-confident Covenanters. ('The Lord of Hosts', wrote Monro characteristically, 'had controversy with us to rub shame in our faces . . .') Now, instead of pressing his victory home, O Neill piously hurried to help Rinuccini, who with his support entered Kilkenny in September, deposed and imprisoned the Supreme Council, and made himself the Confederation's new president.

The Confederate forces now prepared to attack Dublin. Ormond was saved by a quarrel between the Irish commanders, O Neill and Preston. O Neill withdrew. Preston intrigued with Ormond. The failure to take Dublin discredited Rinuccini, but the Assembly which he called early in 1647 was still obdurate against the peace treaty, and Ormond saw no chance to hold the capital. He handed the city over to the English Parliament.

The new Parliamentary commander, Michael Jones, soon routed Preston when the latter advanced again towards Dublin, and Inchiquin was so successful in Munster that, in May 1648, the Confederate Council had to make a truce with him. Rinuccini once again proclaimed excommunication against all who adhered to it. The Confederation fell into internecine strife. The baffled Rinuccini retreated to Rome, lamenting that the Irish were 'Catholic only in name'. He had done his unwitting best to wreck their cause, and the Pope made his displeasure plain on the nuncio's return.

Confusion was now compounded as the Second Civil War blew up in England. The Scots in Ulster fell out with the local Parliamentary commander and he had to seize their garrisons. Inchiquin declared for the King and begged Ormond to return. After coming to terms with Ormond, the Confederation was formally dissolved in January 1649.

This was a famous month. Other European monarchs had been killed by their subjects. But a group of Englishmen were the first to try and condemn in a court of law a man whom they recognised as king. In December 1648 the army 'purged' Parliament, which had been negotiating with Charles. Colonel Pride, a former brewer's drayman, new man of a new era, arrested 45 members and turned back 96 others. The 'Rump' which remained passed an ordinance for the King's trial. The proceedings which followed were justified in terms which would later resound through the entire Atlantic arena. Ultimate authority lay with the people. The King held office only as their trustee. And on January 30, to Europe's astonishment, the King was beheaded.

The Scots, even hard Covenanters, were shocked, and proclaimed the dead man's son Charles II. They would have to be dealt with, but England and Ireland came first. Cromwell suppressed the Levellers in his army, then crossed to Dublin in August with 3,000 Ironsides.

Ormond sent the best of what was left of the Royalist army to garrison

Drogheda, so Cromwell's first stroke was to besiege that town. It fell after eight days, on September 11, 1649. What followed made one of the reddest stains on the Irish historical memory. Cromwell himself wrote, '. . . Our men getting up to them were ordered by me to put all to the sword; and, indeed, being in the heat of action, I forbade them to spare any that there were in arms in the town.' Some townspeople and several priests were among the slain, though there is no evidence to support the legend that the whole civilian population was massacred. The killing of virtually all the garrison was, however, a savagery without precedent in the English civil wars. Altogether between two and four thousand people were slain. Cromwell was normally a humane and merciful man. It seems clear that at Drogheda he was possessed by one of his manic rages. Beyond that, he shared the view of Ireland which most Englishmen held. Irish papistry was maliciously evil. 'You, unprovoked, put the English to the most unheard-of and most barbarous massacre (without respect of sex or age) that ever the sun beheld', Cromwell would later write in a 'Declaration' addressed to the Catholics. 'And at a time when Ireland was in perfect peace, and when, through the example of the English industry, through commerce and traffic, that which was in the natives' hands was better to them than if all Ireland had been in their possession and not an Englishman in it.'

The North was soon almost wholly in English hands. Cromwell marched south and besieged Wexford from October 1 to October 11. When his troops entered the city they ran amok. He made no attempt to check them. Between 1,500 and 2,000 people were butchered. The once-thriving seaport was almost emptied of people and Cromwell was pleased by the thought that it was now open to English settlement.

Though outnumbered three or four to one by Ormond's forces, Cromwell's Ironsides overran most of the country before he himself left in May 1650. His nine months in Ireland were enough to secure what later became known as the Protestant Ascendancy. Before the end of 1650 the beaten Ormond had sailed for France. By mid-1652 the major remaining Royalist forces had been defeated or had surrendered. But many Irish soldiers turned brigand. The word 'tory' was now being applied to such men who linked their robberies with political resentment.

'Tory' Charles II would later say that Calvinism was no religion for a gentleman. But in June 1650 he had perforce to subscribe to the Scottish Covenant. An invasion on his behalf by Montrose, from the Orkneys into northern Scotland, had been quickly defeated and Montrose himself had been hanged in Edinburgh. Now the Covenanting regime had a king whom they had sworn to their cause. Cromwell, whose attitude to Protestant Scots was quite different from his view of papist Irish, pleaded with them to be more tolerant – 'I beseech you in the bowels of Christ think it possible that you may be mistaken . . . There may be a Covenant made with death and hell.' Failing, he invaded, and on September 3, 1650, was trapped at Dunbar by a Scottish army led by

David Leslie, once his able colleague. But there was a committee of godly ministers advising Leslie. Their knowledge of military affairs came from close study of the Old Testament. They advised that the Scots should desert their impregnable upland position and fall on the English, whom they outnumbered two to one. They came down, shouting, 'The Covenant!' The English cried 'The Lord of Hosts!' and slaughtered them. The Scots, one contemporary said, were 'driven like turkeys'. Three thousand were killed, ten thousand captured – more than half the Scottish army. It was the greatest victory of Cromwell's career.

The rout at Dunbar made Argyll and other relative realists inside the Covenanting party ready to co-operate again with the 'Engagers' whom they had spewed out of their mouths. By the following summer the 'Act of Classes' had been in effect rescinded and the King had been crowned; by Argyll himself, who else? But Cromwell had occupied Edinburgh. He let the new Scottish army, 'Engagers' within it again, pass him by to invade England, where, at Worcester, exactly a year after Dunbar, he defeated it utterly. English forces thereafter occupied all Scotland. In October 1651 the London regime announced that England and Scotland were henceforward one country.

In the same year was published the greatest work of English political philosophy, Thomas Hobbes's *Leviathan*. Inspired both by the new scientific learning which had been making headway through all England's troubled years, and by loathing of civil war and its insecurity, Hobbes brought a startling realism to the discussion of political power and of human society. This confident materialist described man as an automaton who could act only out of hope of advantage to himself. Religion was only valuable as a means of securing submission to secular authority: reason, not revelation, was the way to the truth: God was merely the first mover who started the universe going. All sovereignty was based, not on divine right, but on covenants made by men. Though the orthodox, of course, could not stomach such stuff, Hobbes, prophet of reason, represented the wave of the future. Let enterprising men cease to argue about free will and instead apply such wills as they might have to their own enrichment. The State had nothing to do with God or morality. Born out of fear, it existed as power. Let power be used on behalf of trade.

Under the Rump Parliament England was governed by a Council of State of forty-one men, with a quorum of nine. The royal arms came down. There was new coinage, a new Great Seal. Monarchy and House of Lords were abolished. Political sovereignty was stripped of mystique. All men could see that men unmade kings, even if men could make them again. Experimentation continued. At the army's urging, in 1653, Cromwell turned out the Rump. Now came the 'Barebones Parliament' with 144 members selected by the army. An extremist minority of millenarian 'Fifth Monarchists' pushed hard for radical reform, and the majority, propertied men, voted its dissolution to safeguard their class. So Cromwell became Lord Protector, much, in effect, like a constitutional monarch, and as such often at odds with his parliament. Though unprecedentedly high taxation gave it double the income Charles had ever commanded, Cromwell's state was still not solvent. The army and navy were costing too much.

XII

At least, after the queasy 1630s and the disrupted 1640s, there was now plenty of employment in England. There was less impetus to emigration. The great folk movement across the Atlantic was over, and would not resume in spate (except from Ulster and the Scottish Highlands) before the mid-nineteenth century. But the rulers of Republican England were enthusiasts for empire, and they took measures to ensure that planters got able bodies to labour for them.

The idea of 'transporting' felons was old. The governor of Virginia in 1611 had been willing to welcome convicts as a 'readie way to furnish us with men and not allways the worst kind of men.' But only a few score had gone to the New World before Cromwell's day. Then in 1655 a relatively straightforward procedure was introduced. Felons could be pardoned on condition that they left the country for a certain term of years. Scores were now succeeded by hundreds.

Another source of supply was prisoners, mostly Scots, taken in battle. Several hundred were despatched into servitude after the battle of Preston in 1648. Of the 1,250 Scots prisoners intended for America after Dunbar and the 1,610 or so allotted after Worcester, only a small proportion reached the colonies (where, lean, hungry, hard-working, they commonly thrived).

The Scots were not shocked by the loss of a few hundred young men; far more had gone to serve and die overseas in the Thirty Years' War. National pride was affronted by defeat, and under the Cromwellian constitution of 1653 Scotland was allowed only thirty MPs (the same number as Ireland) to sit with four hundred Englishmen at Westminster.

Zealots within the Church of Scotland abhorred the toleration of other Protestant views which the Cromwellian Union entailed. Deviant sects crept in and established themselves – for instance, a small body of Scottish Quakers emerged. But apart from an abortive Royalist rising in the Highlands in 1653–4, the years of Union were years of calm. Under the largest army Scotland had ever seen, even the Gaels were uncannily peaceful. Cromwellian rule was, for the most part, both fair and efficient. In the years of civil war, lairds, burgesses and lawyers had figured with a new prominence, while religious doctrines had come to seem more important than kinship and clannish loyalties. Feuding was obsolete. The last fortified house to be built in Scotland dates from 1661. Cromwellian rule furthered the work of transformation begun in the 1640s, when the power of aristocratic magnates had for the first time yielded, before that of ministers and the lairds supporting them. And in another respect also, the English regime carried forward the work of the Covenant. An Act of 1656 took Scottish sabbatarianism to its highest pitch. It forbade anyone to frequent taverns, dance, hear profane music, wash, brew ale or bake bread, 'profanely walk' or travel or do any worldly business on a Sunday.

The Irish were less amenable, despite and because of the horrors which they had endured. Sir William Petty, the pioneer statistician (of whom more later), estimated that when the war ended in 1653, 616,000 people had perished, leaving 850,000 survivors. He reckoned that 167,000 people had died from sword, famine, 'and other Hardships' and 450,000 from the outbreak of plague which swept Ireland in 1650. The four Parliamentary Commissioners who ruled Ireland under the Rump reported most gloomily back to London. The numbers of tories were 'daily increasing'. Cattle stocks were so run down that four-fifths of the best land in Ireland lay waste and uninhabited. The task of reconstruction lay in English hands. The Irish Parliament was done away with and the MPs who sat for Ireland in Westminster were largely English army officers.

In theory, many Englishmen were enthusiasts for Ireland, though not for the Irish. Advanced social reformers and scientific thinkers hoped, like Wentworth before them, to use Ireland as a kind of laboratory in which ideas could be tested for later application to England. Such institutions as Ireland had had in Church, law and education had been decayed or swept away by war, and whereas England bristled with powerful vested interests, in Ireland the natives could mostly be ignored. Protestant landowners had their own hopes of improving their fortunes by scientific agriculture and by the exploitation of the mineral wealth which the island was falsely supposed to contain, and several of the most prominent were drawn to the ideas of the advanced circle which centred on the Puritan sage Samuel Hartlib and directed Baconian thinking to practical ends – universal education, experimental medicine, general economic reform, the world supremacy of England. Hartlib himself hoped to establish in Ireland a clearing house for scientific and experimental ideas, and though this was not achieved, several of his associates were busy and prominent on the island in the 1650s, involved in educational schemes and above all in the surveying of lands preparatory to a resettlement. But the island was not a white paper. There were people there.

There simply was not enough money for visionary schemes. In 1649–56 over £1,500,000 had to be transmitted from England to help govern it, while under £2 million were raised in the island itself. This subsidy was progressively snipped, and the Irish came under swingeing taxation, so heavy that it was a deterrent to new immigration from England. Cromwell's son-in-law, Ireton, was dominant after he left, then in 1652 another son-in-law, Fleetwood, took over, and finally in 1655 his son Henry came out to hold charge. He conciliated the native Protestant elements and Presbyterianism in Ulster flourished under his rule. There were a good many nominal converts to the reformed religion, since Catholics were, for instance, threatened in 1656 with the loss of two-thirds of their property unless they abjured papal supremacy. But the hold of Rome was essentially stronger than ever.

The old attack on the Irish way of life was resumed. The seizure of 'vagrants' was enjoined in a stream of orders recalling Elizabethan resentment of nomadism. Now the idea was to transplant these nuisances to the 'Caribbee Islands'. In a typical case, in June 1654, Colonel Stubbers was 'authorised to transport out of Connaught for the West Indies, three score Irish women that are vagrants, idlers and wanderers . . .' Some Irish soldiers, as they surrendered, were sent to Barbados, to make their contribution to the delightful accent of speech on that island.

The simple Irish economy was resilient. By 1655 the effects of war had worn off sufficiently for the government to permit export of the traditional produce – tallow and hides, butter and meat and livestock. Customs revenue soon returned to its high level of the 1630s. Agricultural prices stayed up while rents were extremely low, depopulation meant that landlords were eagerly seeking tenants, and the arbitrary authority of old proprietors had commonly vanished. Perhaps the lesser Irish found new opportunities. Nobody knows. There is no record of their opinions.

What is indelibly written into history is the Cromwellian scheme for the mass transportation of all Catholic natives to the west of the island. The spirit was Philip II's or Stalin's. The execution fell somewhat below modern standards.

The decision taken in 1642 that the repression of Ireland should be paid for out of forfeited estates had always implied a general resettlement of Irish lands. In fact the 'Adventurers' of that year – mostly merchants, with Londoners predominant – had put up only £30,000. Their entitlement came to less than a million acres and it was now assumed that ten million – half the land of Ireland – would be escheated. How could the rest be used? The solution lay to hand in the vast army of up to 35,000 English soldiers now occupying the country. Irish acres, no longer attractive to English investors, could still be the means of paying soldiers cheaply.

An amazing Act of 1652 was the basis of the resettlement. It condemned perhaps 100,000 Irish rebels to death (which only a few hundred actually suffered) and to total forfeiture of their lands. In addition three or four more classes of Irish defined as relatively 'innocent' were to lose a third or two-thirds of their holdings and to be given lands equal to the remainder wherever Parliament chose they should go. While about 180,000 acres were confiscated from Royalist Protestants, the chief effect of the Act was to dispossess almost every Catholic landowner. Descendants of Tudor planters suffered with Gaels, Bagenals, Raleghs, even a Cromwell, were included in this almost clean sweep, and Oliver himself had to intervene on behalf of Edmund Spenser's grandson, whose family had slumped into papistry.

A further Act in September 1653 provided that all Catholic Irish, including those technically 'innocent', were to be barred from the whole country east of the Shannon. Even in the territories of Connacht and Clare which were reserved for them, the Irish were not to live within four miles of the sea or the Shannon, nor on any island. They were to be cut off from all direct contact with Europe and the wider world. All natives entitled to lands under the 1652 Act were to remove west of the Shannon by May 1654, and any who lingered thereafter would be put to death.

The scheme was impractical as well as brutal. The English planters who were to take over would need Irish labour. Even if it had been possible to find hordes of English people prepared to work in Ireland, their labour would have been much more expensive, and they would not have been prepared to pay such high rents as the natives. Irish labour was cheap labour. The 'final solution' ran counter to the best interests of the Protestant landowning classes.

It seems that while most Catholic landowners were unable to prove enough 'innocence' to entitle them to any Connacht acres at all, and so lost everything, some 2,000 were assigned, between them, about a quarter of the whole area of Connacht and Clare. But the mass of natives stayed east of the Shannon. A census of 1659 shows that even in Ulster there were only four English and Scots to every ten Irish. In Leinster the ratio was under one to six, in Munster less than one to ten. The intention had been to settle over 1,000 English Adventurers and perhaps 35,000 soldiers in Ireland, but it seems that only 500 Adventurers and 7,500 soldiers actually established themselves. This was a large influx compared with earlier plantations – but whereas those had been concentrated in compact areas, the newcomers now were scattered over three provinces. The Scots in effect had transformed Ulster; the Cromwellian English could not exert such influence. The vision of a 'civil' Protestant Ireland was still, and always would be, chimerical.

The rank-and-file soldiers who had been thought of as a resident garrison not only settled in smaller numbers than had been hoped but showed a distressing, inevitable propensity to go bush; it was reported in 1659 that many had 'married Irish Papists, contrary to sundry Declarations made in that behalf'. But of course there were important outcomes. Officers commonly bought up allotments given to rank and file and even those granted to papists in Connacht; many of these men founded great landed families. Altogether about a third of the land of Ireland, some 6½ million acres, was divided up among new Protestant owners. Meanwhile, the leading towns were subjected to Protestant takeover. Numerous Catholic merchants now decamped to the Continent. The purge went furthest in Waterford, whence all papists were expelled by an order of March 1651, and in the once-thriving port of Galway. Here and elsewhere it proved impossible to get the right kind of settlers to move in. Suitable English failing, attempts were made to attract New Englanders, Huguenots, Dutchmen, all without much success. Dublin, already a mainly Protestant town, profited from the problems of the outports to confirm its dominance of Irish trade.

Though a Catholic merchant community would grow afresh, Protestant grip of the rule of the towns was another enduring legacy of the Cromwellian period. The papist 'Old English' had now been driven down into one mass with the Gaels. Catholics had owned three-fifths of Irish land in 1641; in 1660 they had under one-tenth.

Cromwellian treatment of Wales was in extreme contrast, though no area had given more support to King Charles. Puritanism had had very few adherents in Wales before the civil war. The Welsh gentry were generally Royalist, and the commoners so responsible to Charles's call that one Cavalier called the country 'the nursery of the King's infantry'.

The conversion of Wales to a better religion was now made a high priority. In 1650 an Act for the Propagation of the Gospel in Wales was passed, and that famous Fifth Monarchist general, the millenarian Thomas Harrison, headed a commission of seventy set up to implement it. For three years Wales, under this body, had a degree of autonomy not known since 1536, or after 1653, but self-government did not come into it. The proportion of Welsh gentry among the Commissioners was very small. The aim was Anglicization. The conversion of Welsh Celts evoked far more purposeful effort than that of Irish Gaels. There were three editions of the New Testament, and one of the whole Bible, in Welsh between 1647 and 1654. But the day when Calvinism would dominate most Welsh hearts and minds was still very far distant. Nearly three hundred unsatisfactory clergymen were ejected but with so few Welsh Puritans it was impossible to replace them. The net result of the Commissioners' work was to prolong Welsh 'backwardness' by leaving many parishes without regular church services. While many of the Welsh gentry were ruined by their outlays on behalf of the King, and by fines after the war, so slumped to become mere farmers, the more fortunate families which kept their heads above water and formed for generations thereafter the country's small ruling élite remained mostly reactionary in their outlook.

Under the Protectorate centralisation of government came to an extent never felt in Britain before. In 1655 Cromwell put England and Wales under the direct rule of eleven Major Generals, plenipotentiaries who confronted the local gentry with powers of interference comparable to those of French *intendants* or of Turkish satraps. Justices of the Peace, now overborne in their own patches of rule, loathed these incomers, who were often men of humble origin (thus, Berry, who ruled Wales, had been a mere clerk in an ironworks, and the pedigree-conscious native gentry were deeply insulted). The civil war phase had given the various countries and regions of Britain much greater independence. But now old Councils in the north and in Wales were abolished. The Major Generals carried a common policy into every district, organising militia, enforcing punitive taxes on Royalists, executing the poor laws, purging the JPs and even 'promoting virtue': they were, for instance, told to suppress horse-racing. Cromwell, who had once spoken up for the fenmen, was the chief advocate after the civil war of an Act designed to complete the drainage work on the Bedford Level. Despite more riots by the common fenmen, the work was finished by 1652, after Scots prisoners captured at Dunbar had been drafted in to alleviate shortage of labour.

Central power was still too small to police rural England, as the case of the West Country tobacco-growers showed. During the civil war years, they had got on with illegal planting untroubled. Cromwell moved against them again. But soldiers sent down in 1654 to the great tobacco centre of Winchcombe in Gloucestershire found themselves faced by a local force of three hundred horse and foot. So it went on. The list of counties where the authorities were ordered to put down tobacco lengthened from year to year as cultivation spread from Wales to Essex, from Devon to Yorkshire. When the home industry died out in the 1690s this was probably due to the improved quality and lower price of the Virginian product rather than to any government action.

But while the mercantilist 'Old Colonial System', which was established by law from this time on, was not and could not be watertight – the State, as we have seen, could not yet consistently enforce laws against any body of subjects determined to evade them – the first Navigation Acts passed by the Rump in 1650 and 1651 did mark a crucial shift in policy, away from the old idea that trade was best controlled through the grant of particular privileges to particular companies, towards a new concept of general regulations. The Navigation Act belonged to the same region of mind as Hobbes's *Leviathan*. The old aim that royal power should check the private greed of enclosers, usurers and profiteers was giving way to the notion that national interests existed beyond morality.

The first Navigation Act, in 1650, forbade all foreign ships to trade in any English colony. The second, in 1651, prohibited the import of any goods from Asia, Africa or America except in ships from England, Ireland or the colonies in which a majority of the crew also came from these areas. No European commodities were to be imported except in English, Irish or colonial ships or in ships of the country in which the goods had been produced. One aim of the two Acts was to prevent the Dutch from trading into the empire as middlemen. The context which gave rise to them was one of rebellion in the New World colonies, which had dealt happily with the Hollanders in the centrifugal 1640s. When the City of London feasted Parliament, Council of State and the Army officers after Cromwell had suppressed the Levellers in 1649, its Lord Mayor was Thomas Andrews, a leading American trader and interloper in the East Indies. Such men helped directly to frame the new mercantilist-expansionist policies, and gratefully acted to organise and supply naval expeditions sent out to oust their Dutch competitors.

XIII

New England had relied on the cash brought in by new migrants to pay for its imports of English goods. The ebb of emigration in the 1640s caused a chronic shortage of specie, barter had to suffice and people hoarded commodities as a form of capital; one Plymouth lady who died in 1654 left no fewer than eighteen tablecloths and sixty-six napkins. Massachusetts responded to the crisis with ambitious attempts to establish a self-sufficient economy. In 1641 the

Massachusetts General Court began a drive to develop local resources. But what followed illustrated why Americans would not be able to flourish in manufacturing till the nineteenth century. John Winthrop Jr went to England and got backing there for a company which set up ironworks at Braintree and Saugus. There was from the outset a ruinous tension between the desire of English investors for profit – they wanted to be allowed to export the iron out of New England – and the colonists' wish to keep for their own use all the pots, pans, anvils, scale weights and so on which Saugus was soon producing. All they could offer for them were corn and chickens. In 1652 the concern was bankrupt, and by the mid-1660s the works were abandoned.

The one field in which real advance was made was shipbuilding. A 300-ton ship – large for the day – was made at Salem as early as 1641. This industry throve because it met local needs in the overseas commerce which in fact proved to be Massachusetts' salvation. Self-sufficiency was impossible, but the Boston merchants worked out for themselves a middleman role within the evolving Atlantic system of trade. Once the furs were gone, New England would have little to offer which Old England did not produce herself. So exchanges had to be made in places outside England, and profits turned into credits in England.

New Englanders began to infiltrate the commerce in dried cod which English merchants carried on with Southern Europe and with the 'Wine Islands' – Madeira, the Azores, the Canaries. They formed partnerships for this trade with merchants in London, or set up consortia of their own. Since English merchants kept their grip on the initial outward voyage of boats laden with trade goods for New England colonists, the Bostoners could never control the whole triangle of trade. But by 1660 they were masters in their own fisheries, and a fleet of locally owned and run ships were plying to Iberia and the Wine Islands. Having used fish to get their foot in the door, they learnt of demand there for foodstuffs and for timber (wine makers always needed wood for their casks) and they began to export these too. In 1644 one ship went further. After calling at the Canaries it proceeded to the Cape Verde Islands for slaves, took these on to Barbados and exchanged them there for tobacco. This was the small beginning of a trade with the Caribbean which within a few years was vital both to New England and to the Islands.

Such energetic merchant activity tugged at the seams of the godly commonwealth. It also made Massachusetts separatism unviable. In the late 1640s, Massachusetts made the spectacular claim that it was beyond the reach of English law – 'our allegiance binds us not to the laws of England any longer than while we live in England . . .' The context of this was the General Court's quarrel with seven 'Remonstrants' in the colony who had demanded toleration for Presbyterianism and had taken their case to London. In the outcome, Parliament upheld the Massachusetts position, but the remark, like the episode, spotlighted how far the Bay Colony was now out of step with English Puritans. In the 1630s, Massachusetts men had been conscious of themselves as heroes of the movement. Now puritanism at home had relaxed and diversified. The ardent proponents of national interest had small opinion of New England. Cromwell himself now looked on the area 'only with an eye of pitie, as poore, cold and useles.' He wanted to get its colonists to resettle in Ireland or in the Caribbean. Tropical islands suited the aim of national greatness far better than a truculent base for cod-fishing.

But the English government sent out in 1653 vast orders for New England tar, turpentine and timber. The reason was war with the Dutch, who had enough influence in the Baltic to shut off their enemy from the 'naval stores' which that area, crucially, provided, and who rubbed the lesson in by shooting high and destroying masts and rigging. England won that first Dutch War of 1652–4. This was really the most significant happening of the Interregnum. The navy was under Parliament's control during the first Civil War of 1642–5, and this was crucial, both in preventing foreign interference and in securing London from blockade. The new Republic of 1649 acted swiftly to build up English naval potential.

A new body of Naval Commissioners under Sir Harry Vane took over administration and organisation. Three colonels of the New Model Army were made 'Generals at Sea', and one of these, Robert Blake, born in 1598 as the son of a Somerset merchant, enjoyed for eight years an almost unequalled record of naval success. Between 1649 and 1651, the strength of the fleet was virtually doubled, with forty-one new ships added. In 1650 Blake's squadron appeared in the Mediterranean. For the first time the English state's power was strongly felt there. French ambition was checked. Diplomatic recognition from Spain and Portugal for the new English Republic was promptly secured.

Now the English could take on even the Dutch. The context of war was longstanding commercial rivalry. The pretext was a quarrel over protocol at seas between Blake and Admiral Tromp. The English captured 1,500 or so prizes, more than double their own total merchant tonnage. These ships were now used by Englishmen. In 1653, Blake's blockade of the coast of Holland thwarted Dutch trade and fishing and threatened Amsterdam with ruin. By the Treaty of Westminster the Dutch agreed to pay compensation for the Amboyna massacre, to acquiesce in the Navigation Acts, and to make an annual payment for the right to fish in English waters.

Massachusetts refused to help fight this war. Cromwell sent west an expedition designed to attack the Dutch in New Amsterdam, but also to overawe the Massachusetts magistrates. The war ended before much could be done, though the French were flushed out of Nova Scotia, which became English again for thirteen years. And the rulers of Massachusetts had seen English force on a new scale, and could recognise that their old style of defiance of English governments was no longer practical.

The same sermon had been preached to the north and the south. Sir David Kirke, the Royalist governor of Newfoundland had been arrested in 1651. The

Republic appointed Commissioners to rule the island and instituted a convoy service for the fishing fleet. Meanwhile, Barbados, Virginia and Maryland had been brought to heel by the English navy.

XIV

Whereas in New England religious dissidence was confined to Puritans who were natural supporters of Parliament, the southern colonies were split as England itself was.

In 1642 the most durable of colonial governors, Sir William Berkeley, arrived in Virginia. He was still quite young, well connected, much travelled, well educated, a courtier and believer in the Divine Right of Kings. The colony was much of his way of thinking, but even here quite a large body of 'schismatics' emerged. There was, however, no great repression of Puritans, and a fresh Indian rising emphasised the common problems of settlers of all views. Powhatan's successor, old Opechancanough, engineered it in the spring of 1644, in response to a generation of creeping encroachment upon the lands of his people. About five hundred settlers were killed. Two and a half years of slaughter and burning by whites followed before the Indians came to terms and 'ceded' the whole peninsula between the Falls and Hampton Roads. In return they were promised, faithlessly, undisputed possession of all land north of the York River. Thirty years of unstable peace followed.

In 1651, two Commissioners for the Commonwealth turned up with a strong force. Generous terms were granted in March 1652. The control of the colony by the Assembly was confirmed, and Berkeley stayed on, though a Puritan governor succeeded him. For Maryland matters did not go so well. In this colony of a few thousand souls, the actions of the Commissioners and the intrigues of Baltimore precipitated a miniature civil war.

But the revolutionary period, for all these alarms and excursions, was one of steady expansion for the tobacco colonies. The nucleus of the 'Southern Aristocracy' arrived in the 1640s and 1650s. Berkeley's switch from the life of Charles's court to colonial administration exemplifies the motives which brought out others, the first bearers of names which were to become famous, Bland and Carter, Byrd, Mason and so on. Like him they were younger sons of families long associated with Virginia. They took over family claims to large tracts which had already been brought under cultivation. They had no need to pioneer. Though middling in class, they were close enough in their origins to the top to nurse aspirations to aristocratic standards.

Both Governor Bell on Barbados and old Warner on St Kitts were too canny to declare for either side during the civil war, when the Caribbee Isles, or rather their richer men, flourished. But in 1647 their owner, the Earl of Carlisle, leased them to Lord Willoughby of Parham, who shortly broke with Parliament and fled to Holland. In 1650 he sailed to the West Indies with a commission from Charles II to govern Barbados. He arrived to find the island riven by faction.

The established planters in general seem to have had Puritan leanings, but from the mid-1640s a stream of Royalist exiles chose Barbados rather than prison, men with the means to prosper and make their presence felt. After Willoughby's arrival scores of pro-Parliament men were expelled or left. Antigua also declared for King Charles. Then, in the autumn of 1651, came the Republic's naval squadron under Sir George Ayscue. It was big enough, eight hundred men in seven ships. After several score Barbadians had been killed or captured, Colonel Thomas Modyford, one of the Cavalier newcomers, showed the opportunist flair which would give him a lucrative career in the Caribbean and went over to Ayscue with his whole militia regiment. The terms were generous and seemed to guarantee to the island free trade with all friendly nations. This was not Ayscue's intention – he seized most of the seventeen foreign ships he had discovered in Barbados harbours. But the Navigation Acts were for the moment a dead letter here. The new governor put in by Ayscue actually encouraged illegal trade and when Admiral Penn arrived in 1655 to further Oliver Cromwell's 'Western Design', he in turn found fifteen foreign vessels in port.

The 'Western Design' followed English naval muscle-flexing in the Mediterranean. In 1654 Blake had smashed a squadron of Barbary pirates and had extorted by gunboat diplomacy a satisfactory settlement from the rulers of the pirate ports of Tripoli and Algiers. Portugal in the same year conceded such rights by treaty to England that she virtually became an English protectorate. Englishmen were to have freedom to trade in Portuguese Africa and India, and also, with some restrictions, in the rich land of Brazil. Portuguese would hire English ships, but not those of any other nation. Cromwell asked for similar concessions from Spain. Spain refused. Cromwell launched war. His Design pointed backwards and forwards. The aims – conquest, plunder, trade and colonisation in the West Indies – took up those of Ralegh and of the providence Island Company. The object was permanent settlement on Spanish-owned land and an invasion of Spain's commercial monopoly. But in its bad organisation, the expedition sent to achieve this prefigured a long series of clumsy English forays into the Caribbean.

The force arrived on Barbados and came to a standstill there, 'eatinge up the island', as one of its members put it: food ships failed to arrive from home, so local supplies were commandeered. Money was seized from the island's excise revenue and of nearly 4,000 whites recruited to fight, some were indentured servants who had not completed their time, and whose owners were very displeased. Barbadians clearly feared that any new colony set up by the expedition would rival their own in production of staples, and this made them indisposed to co-operate.

The commanders, Penn and General Venables, had wide discretion as to which Spanish land they might aim at. They plumped for Hispaniola. After three useless weeks the expedition headed for Jamaica, a fairly large island which might, conquered, be enough to defend Penn and Venables against the

Protector's terrible wrath. It was easy to capture. There were about 1,500 Spanish subjects on the island, most of whom lived by keeping or hunting cattle. On 17 May 1655, after only a week, most gave in. But one native of the island, Cristobal Ysassi, held out with a small band in the hills until 1660, helped and fed by black cow-catchers who had been slaves of the Spaniards. Complete victory came only when the leader of these black 'maroons' deserted to the English, but other blacks held out and formed the nucleus of a guerrilla community which would trouble settlers for eighty more years.

Penn and Venables scurried home, each anxious to make his excuses first to Cromwell; both were clapped in the Tower for a few weeks. Epidemic flamed through the force they had left behind. Of the original 7,000 English soldiers, half died within six months and barely 1,500 survived the first two years. Eventually, after two commanders had died, the able Colonel D'Oyley was left in charge and he wore down and finally drove out Spanish resistance. Colonisation meanwhile proceeded slowly. To join the soldiers, who were intended to settle there, 1,600 to 1,800 colonists came from the Leewards in 1657, of whom, after shocking mortality, not 80, it was said, remained alive there three years later. Others arrived from Barbados, Bermuda and New England. But good planters were now hard to find. Jamaica's agricultural progress would be extremely sluggish. Its immediate future was more as a base for naval aggression and robbery. The English Navy ravaged a number of the smaller Spanish towns on the mainland. Then in 1659 one Captain Myngs swept through four such places and came back to Jamaica with loot worth £300,000. A new age of plunder was dawning for Englishmen.

XV

Blake made naval history by spending a whole winter off Spain blockading Cadiz, and then, in April 1657, with brilliant aggression, destroyed a plate fleet in the Canaries. He died at sea soon after, but his exploits had shown that England could now challenge Holland, humiliate Spain.

Such success had cost money. High taxation and military rule made English gentlemen hope for a change. When the Lord Protector himself died in September 1658, his position passed to his unforceful son, Richard Cromwell, and the monarchical Republic could not long survive. Parliament and army tussled again for control, till General Monck, commander in Scotland, marched south as the strong man bringing hope and order. A Scottish Assembly had voted him £50,000. He could pay his troops; General Lambert, sent to oppose him, couldn't. Arriving in London, Monck got on good terms with the merchants, and wisely did not seek supreme power. In May 1660 Charles II returned as King with the agreement of a new Parliament.

Monck's Scottish provenance had significance. Britain had been tightly centralised. Now the periphery triumphed over the centre. The local gentry got their way. The J.P. returned to his own. What was restored at the 'Restoration' could be seen as the constitution of 1641. In England the king was to rule with the Lords and Commons in Parliament. Scotland reverted to being a separate policy under the Crown. Conservative elements, landed men, wealthy merchants, had survived the challenges to their position made by Royalists, 'whigs', and Levellers, then by Fifth Monarchists, Quakers and Major Generals.

And yet so much had changed, over more than twenty years of crisis and revolution, debate and experiment. An institution restored is never the same as one which has merely developed. Disruption had swept through both islands. Ireland was now secured for Protestant greed. In Scotland lairds and lawyers were poised to draw power from the great feudal magnates. In England, still moving fastest, feudal moulds were at last broken for good. Land worth millions of pounds had changed owners, lost by the Crown, lost by the Church, or lost by more than seven hundred Royalist proprietors. Much of this remained in the hands of its purchasers, and all lands formerly held from the king by feudal tenure had been converted to freehold. At the same time, the effort, canalised by the Levellers, aimed at securing the tenure of copyholders, had been vanquished along with the parallel movement to protect common rights to common land. The yeoman and peasant, defeated, were on their way out. The big men who could extrude them from their holdings were now independent of all check save that of legislation which, through Parliament, they could themselves influence.

Puritanism had done revolutionary work, yet was itself shattered and, in its classic form, outmoded, by the revolution which it had made. From the loins of Calvinism heresies and worse had been born. The sons of John Winthrop epitomise much of what happened. The younger John was brilliant, restless, and pliable, greatly concerned with the things of this world. Stephen fought for Parliament, then became a loyal adherent of Cromwell and of his policy of toleration. Samuel settled in the West Indies, and, most delinquent of all, turned Quaker. Old John had views on economic affairs which were in essence still medieval. Profiteering was sin. Usury was evil. Such views now died with such men.

As Christopher Hill has put it, 'The idealists, on both sides, were sacrificed.' Many loyal Royalist gentlemen never recouped their losses. The visionary Puritans Vane and Harrison were quickly disembowelled. The free-thinking sectarians, Baptists as well as Quakers, were after 1660 harried along with the die-hard Covenanters. The men who emerged triumphant from the upheaval and joined the ruling class, setting the pace at court, dominating the administration, were those who had known how to trim and when to change sides. Now such persons would dominate Charles II's colonial policy. Viscount Saye and Sele, 'Old Subtlety', had once been a member of the Providence Island Company, but he survived to sit on Charles II's Committee of Trade and Foreign Plantations, alongside Anthony Ashley Cooper (Lord Shaftesbury) who had begun his political life in the Barebones Parliament, that assembly of zealots, yet himself did not believe in more than the cool deism of the advancing 'Age of Reason'. Then there was George Downing, more than any other one man the architect of the 'Old Colonial System' – one of the first strokes of legislation after the Restoration was a revised Navigation Act. Downing's parents had emigrated to Massachusetts. His mother was John Winthrop's sister. He himself had been Harvard's second graduate. He had served in Cromwell's army in Scotland and had 'represented' Edinburgh in the Cromwellian parliament of 1654. A jealous admirer of the Dutch, he had been sent as a diplomat to the Hague. In 1660 he made his peace with Charles, blaming his former alignment on his New England training. He sold his old associates to the King's executioners and in return received a baronetcy. In New England thereafter they said that a man who betrayed his trust was an 'arrant George Downing'.

Sir William Petty, born in 1623, son of a Hampshire weaver, went to sea at twelve as a cabin boy, picked up some education from Jesuits in France, studied medicine in Holland and when still in his twenties became in succession Professor of Anatomy at Oxford and Professor of Music at Gresham College in London. In 1652 he went out to Ireland as physician-in-chief to the army. He wormed his way into the post of surveyor of confiscated lands. He executed the task wonderfully in the famous 'Down Survey' which took little more than a year, a triumph for science and also a gold-mine for Petty: he made a profit of £10,000 in cash. Through purchase and graft he now turned himself into a major Irish landowner. By the Restoration he held perhaps 100,000 acres, having meanwhile occupied high political office in Dublin. His success caused a bitter political storm and in 1659 he had to defend himself before the House of Commons.

He had once been the great Thomas Hobbes's research assistant. He shared Hobbes's political philosophy. In the forefront of science in his day, he valued all knowledge by its practical usefulness, hence finding René Descartes lacking. His main pioneering was in social science. Marx and Engels would one day regard him as the founder of political economy. Mercantilist in his view of foreign trade, he innovated in seeing labour as the source of wealth, going on to argue that the labourer should be given 'just wherewithall to live' – if he were paid double he would do only half as much work.

This remarkable man had one characteristic which barred his way to the high office he craved. He 'did not much notice other human beings.' It coloured his interesting plan, perfected in 1687, for the treatment of Ireland. This was beautifully simple. A million Irish should be transplanted to England, leaving just enough people to manage as many cattle as the country could feed. He reckoned some 300,000 herdsmen and dairywomen would suffice. Anyone staying in Ireland must take an English name. Everyone should wear the same clothes, those 'most commodious' for their employment. The Highlands of Scotland, he added, somewhat prophetically, should get the same treatment.

These sagacious suggestions were buttressed by Petty's statistics. He was not, as some have said, the inventor of statistics, but he gave them a new name, 'political arithmetic'. One example of his methods deserves full quotation. He is deliberating upon the loss of people in the Irish rebellion of 1641–53. 'The value of people, Men, Women and Children in *England*, some have computed to be £70 *per* Head, one with another. But if you value the people who have been destroyed in *Ireland*, as Slaves and Negroes are usually rated, *viz.* at about £15 one with another: Men being sold for £25 and Children £5 each; the value of the people lost will be about £10,355,000.'

Here Petty shows his kinship of spirit with that able Roundhead, James Drax, who had pioneered cotton production in Barbados. About 1642 Drax saw a new scope for self-interest and led the movement on that island to sugar, helped by his Dutch acquaintances. In their way, such men as Drax were as revolutionary as any regicide. Slave labour was ideal for the plantation's monotonous, killing routines. As Petty wangled his wealth among the white non-men of Ireland, black non-men were starting to give a firm base to England's coming mercantile greatness.

BOOK TWO: 1660–1763

King Sugar

I

Imperialism has transformed the world. The fact which creates 'world history' is the industrial revolution launched in north-western Europe, initially in Great Britain, by the 1780s. As industrialism emerged, a new attitude to profit would also emerge. If by mass-production one could make a small profit per sale on a very large number of identical items, this gave one more in the long run than a very large profit on each of a small number of luxury goods, and the man of capital was released from dependence on the richest consumers, the old ruling class, and could begin to reshape the world after his own bent.

Into the seventeenth century an older attitude to money still ruled. The object of merchants and manufacturers was not to expand the market but to corner it. The trade in cloves and pepper for which four European nations fought in the East Indies was one where very high profits could be made on a small bulk of goods. When they won the battle, the concern of the Dutch was not to increase the output of spices in the Moluccas but, on the contrary, to restrict and monopolise it. However, a different kind of colonial trade had grown up side by side with the fort-and-factory style, the middleman role, which the Dutch had inherited from the Portuguese. The tobacco plantation, still more the sugar plantation, were harbingers of revolution. Both products, momentously, were habit-forming. The market for them was virtually limitless. This encouraged increased production, which drove down the price and so spread demand further. Concentration on one product made agrarian self-sufficiency out of the question. The plantation had to depend on a flow of tools, clothing and even food and drink from industries in Europe which thus gained a large new market for such items, sold and exported in bulk.

This new system created, and came to depend on, what we would now call a 'rising standard of living' in Europe, as demand for tropical produce grew to the point where luxuries like tobacco and tea became virtual necessities. We can only speculate vaguely about the extra energy which cane sugar must have injected into the bodies and minds of Europeans. It must have been quite an important factor in Europe's rise to world dominance, along with the stimulant effects of tea and coffee, replacing alcoholic drinks which fuddled consciousness.

Large-scale production of sugar had been pioneered in Brazil in the last quarter of the sixteenth century. The carrying trade, like so many others, had fallen into Dutch hands. The Amsterdam refineries were finding a growing market in Europe, and the Dutch were in general piling up surplus capital, shipping, and manufactured goods which needed an outlet. Hence Dutch merchants encouraged English and French settlers on the Caribbean islands to start cultivating the canes.

By 1644 James Drax had done so well that he could bear the cost of importing thirty-four new black slaves. The crop boomed on Barbados as planters found they could make four times as much from it as from tobacco, and sugar penetrated the Leewards also, though its development there would be far less dramatic. The Dutch were most happy to supply the rollers, coppers and so on needed for processing; they could provide slaves also, and they were willing to give credit before the first crop. Several planters went to Amsterdam to seek financial aid directly. London merchants also began to pour in capital, though they could not match the easy terms of the Dutch. By the late 1640s the 'sugar revolution' was under way.

From the first there had been some large plantations on Barbados. But before sugar came the landed proprietors on the island were typically small men farming five to thirty acres. Now people already rich took an interest in sugar; some of the Royalists who moved into the island in the late 1640s were men of considerable wealth. By its very nature, sugar production demanded large estates. The mill – 'ingenio', as it was called – was a quite costly assemblage of equipment, and it needed to draw cane from a wide area if it was to be kept occupied. Large units using slave labour would be more efficient and profitable. Slaves were expensive, and were needed in mass.

Richard Ligon, a Cavalier who came to Barbados in 1647 and helped the astute Colonel Modyford manage his land, reckoned that a man needed at least £14,000 to get settled in a 'sugar work'. By mid-seventeenth-century standards, a sugar plantation was big business. The one which Ligon worked on contained '500 Acres of Land, with a faire dwelling house, an Ingenio plac'd in a room of 400 foot square; a boyling house, filling room, Cisterns, and Still-house; with a Carding house, of 100 foot long and 40 foot broad; with stables, Smiths forge, and rooms to lay provisions, of Corn, and Bonavist; Houses for *Negroes* and *Indian* slaves, with 96 *Negroes* and 3 *Indian* women, with their Children; 28 Christians, 45 Cattle for work, 8 Milch Cows, a dozen Horses and Mares, 16 Assinigoes.' (These last were donkeys.) Modyford paid £7,000 for a half share in an estate which eight years before had been worth only £400 altogether.

Thanks to the war between Dutch and Portuguese in Brazil, prices of sugar were most temptingly high, and they remained so during the 1650s. James Drax, knighted by Cromwell in 1658, lived 'like a Prince', according to Ligon. Drax's Royalist rival Walrond matched his style. As men such as these consolidated holdings of several hundred acres each, yellow fever, probably brought in slave ships, raged through Barbados from 1647 to 1650 and carried off perhaps a third of the total population. Many petty men died. Rich men took over the land. In 1645 there were said to be 11,200 proprietors, holding an average of less than ten acres each and outnumbering their Negroes two to one. In 1680 there were still just over 3,000 property holders, but the 175 big planters each of whom owned more than 60 slaves had over half the total acreage and formed the richest ruling class in the English New World.

By 1661, the trade of Barbados employed 400 ships a year. From now on England's imports of sugar would always exceed its combined imports of all other colonial produce. Though prices for sugar inevitably fell, there was not the least danger that the limits of the market would be reached and Barbados, followed by other islands, drove towards monoculture. Planters neglected the fine and abundant local fish; it would mean diverting labour from sugar to get it. In the early 1670s Barbados had to import three-quarters of the food it required.

By the end of the seventeenth century King Sugar would have unchallenged reign over the island colonies. His rule meant terrible labour, fierce discipline, foul stenches. Canes were planted on ground painfully hoed – ploughs could have been employed, but that would have meant leaving servile labour unused for much of the year. The five dry months from January to May were a period of frantic harvesting. After a growing period of fourteen to eighteen months, the canes were taller than the men who slashed them down. Their sugar would spoil unless they were swiftly processed, preferably within a few hours. Unloaded from the backs of donkeys, the canes were fed between vertical hardwood rollers geared together with cogs and attached to a vertical axis which was rotated by long sweeps commonly yoked to horses or oxen. Barbadians soon saw the advantage of windmills. The juice crushed out by the rollers was borne away down a pipe to a cistern. In the boiling house, it was expertly ladled from copper to copper until, in the fourth or fifth, it was ready for crystallisation. Then it was ladled into a cooling tank. While still lukewarm it was put into large earthenware pots with holes in the bottom then passed to the curing house, a large building where the molasses slowly drained from the crystals of sugar and was collected as a valuable by-product. The pots drained for at least a month; then, in the 'knocking room', the golden cones of crystals were released.

Making sugar imposed such hard conditions on all involved that Thomas Tryon, writing about 1700, found it in him to pity even the master – his lot was 'to live in a perpetual Noise and Hurry and the only way to render a Person Angry, and Tyrannical too; since the Climate is so hot, and the labour so constant, that the Servants night and day stand in great Boyling Houses, where there are Six or Seven large Coppers or Furnaces kept perpetually Boyling; and from which with heavy Ladles and Scummers they Skim off the excrementatious parts of the Canes, till it comes to its perfection and cleanness, while others as Stoakers, Broil, as it were alive, in managing the Fires; and one part is constantly at the Mill, to supply it with Canes, night and day . . .' The sugar mill prefigured the later cotton factory. It required a large, disciplined, strictly controlled labour force, concentrated around fairly expensive fixed capital.

Various qualities of product emerged. To simplify a rather bewildering topic, we may distinguish between 'muscovado' – basic raw sugar – on the one hand and, on the other, two sorts of refined sugar. 'Clayed' white sugar could be produced on the plantation by covering with wet clay the pots where the muscovado stood draining; as water seeped down, it would remove much impurity. Fully refined white sugar could be made by melting muscovado, boiling it again, and then claying it. In the interests of sugar refiners in England itself, refining in the colonies was eventually checked by an Act of Parliament in 1685 which taxed imports of white sugar very heavily in relation to brown. Hence the staples of the English West Indies came to be muscovado and its by-products, molasses and rum.

Sugar culture also produced two different kinds of human being: masters, and slaves.

II

Though there were no natives on Barbados, Indians could be imported from other islands and from the mainland. While the men could be used as footmen and fishermen, the women were set to making cassava flour and bread and to making sailcloth, tents and hammocks out of the local cotton. But the docile Arawaks were not very numerous and the Caribs seemed to offer no medium way between armed co-existence and total extermination.

For labour, anyway, red men would not suffice; this the English deduced like the Spaniards before them. Founded as white plantations on lines like those of Virginia, the English (and French) islands progressed, if that is the word, towards a society based on slavery to an extent never seen before, through an intermediate stage where the recruitment and domination of white indentured servants established commercial and managerial precedents for the later and greater handling of black men.

At home in England, temporary indentured labour was not necessarily demeaning – it was perfectly normal for the sons and daughters of artisans and yeomen, even of parsons, in effect not unlike apprenticeship. The system did enable some people to emigrate who had reasons for wanting to go – a valid hope of self-betterment, for instance. But most servants went to the West Indies and North America because of the blandishments or pressure of entrepreneurs who had a pecuniary interest in the valuable business of shipping, and of deceiving, them. The voyage out would most likely be appalling. One ship in the 'servant trade' lost 130 out of 150 on board.

The 'indenture' was a form of legal contract by which the servant bound himself to do what his master told him well and faithfully for a given length of time. In return the master undertook to transport the servant to a colony, and to give him shelter and clothing and food, perhaps also a reward in clothes, equipment, or land at the end of his term. The time specified varied upward from four years. Servants were almost always indentured in the first instance to

a merchant, an emigration agent, a ship's captain or even a common seaman
rather than to a planter, and when they arrived were sold off to the highest
bidder. While their terms lasted they were chattels; they could be won and lost
at cards, their legal status was far lower than that of freemen, though they were
not quite slaves.

The trade flourished from early Jamestown days on towards the end of the
eighteenth century. From first to last most of the victims were young. The
proportion of women rose markedly as time went on. Most women, if they
survived disease on shipboard and after landing, stood some chance of pleasure
in life, employed as domestic servants rather than in the fields and quite likely
to marry the master or his son. But, especially where the West Indies were the
goal, the records of this large exodus generally reek of misery, pathos and waste.

It cost a merchant from £4 to £10 to ship a servant to the colonies, where he
or she would sell for from £6 to £30. Besides this tempting direct profit, there
was the point that live human bodies could replace ballast in ships sent out to
load tobacco or sugar. There could thus be a double gain, on people as well as on
produce. Hence the eager activities of the so-called 'spirits', emigration agents.
Some were commissioned officially by the promoters of colonies, others were
hired by merchants or ships' captains, others still were free-enterprisers on their
own accord – the 'crimps' who brought candidates for servitude before
magistrates for legal registration, then turned them over to a merchant or
skipper.

The 'spirits' were generally loathed. One reason was that they were the
recourse of runaway prentices, runaway wives, runaway husbands, escaped
prisoners, desperate thieves and so forth – of anyone anxious to evade justice or
responsibility. But it was the practice of kidnapping which earned them most
odium. Shipowners and captains anxious to make up a load would pay a pound
or two and ask no questions. Wandering children would be lured with sweets,
drunks picked out of the gutter. The victims were made amenable, with strong
drink or with wild tales of the little work done by servants in the New World and
of 'the pliant loving natures of the Women there'. For decades, the authorities
struggled fitfully against the practice.

In the 1680s, Chief Justice Pemberton launched a fierce campaign against
kidnappers. The result was that merchants ceased altogether to ship servants;
there had been no wholly legitimate trade in them. By the eighteenth century,
crude kidnapping seems to have abated, though there were still cases of it (most
notoriously in 1728, when the son and heir of the Earl of Anglesey was seized).

In the 'Caribbees' the Irish, who were very poor, perhaps more gullible, and
certainly less protected against kidnappers, came to provide the main source of
labour. Montserrat was virtually an Irish colony from the late 1630s. The
Dutch, opportunist as ever, competed briskly with English merchants in the
trade in servants from south-west Ireland, and it was in vain that the Barbados
Assembly tried to prohibit it in 1644. One authority estimates that Irish made

up more than half the population of the English West Indies by mid-century. Irish servants more than once (on Bermuda in 1661, on Barbados in 1692) were found to be plotting insurrection with black slaves. The servant trade from Ireland at last grew too gross for the Cromwellian Council there to stomach and in 1657 it revoked all the Orders which had been granted to various persons for carrying 'idle and vagabond' Irish to the plantations, remarking that kidnappers had been sweeping in not only Irish innocents but English residents as well.

By this time it seemed clear that white servants were likely to be, if not Irish, otherwise disreputable. 'This Illand', noted one observer on Barbados in 1655, 'is the Dunghill wharone England doth cast forth its rubidg . . . a whore if handsume makes a wife for some rich planter.' Hundreds of women, in fact, were not long after this seized in the London brothels and houses of ill repute and shipped to Barbados to make themselves useful as breeders. But the flow of white men was not adequate for a booming island – 2,331 indentured servants in the seven years from 1654 to 1660.

Richard Ligon alleged that white workers were worse treated than black. His own account of Barbados hardly bears this out – thus he notes that when cattle died by accident or disease the servants were given the meat, the blacks only the skin, head and entrails. Yet the treatment of whites which he describes was severe enough. A bell summoned them to work at six in the morning, they laboured until eleven, then were given a 'dinner' of 'Lob-lolly' (maize porridge), 'Bonavist' (beans) or potatoes, washed down with 'mobbie', made of fermented potatoes. (The blacks, however, got nothing better than water.) At one o'clock they returned to the fields, they worked till six, then they returned to have more of the same fare for their supper. They slept in crude cabins, in hammocks or on bare boards. 'I have seen an Overseer beat a Servant with a cane about the head, till the blood has followed, for a fault that is not worth the speaking of; and yet he must have patience, or worse will follow. Truly, I have seen such cruelty there done to Servants, as I did not think one Christian could have done to another.' While poor food and hard work were the common lot in England, vicious continual discipline was not.

The evidence is that most of those who survived servitude were wrecked by it. A visiting physician in the 1680s remarked on the 'yellowish sickly look' of the poorer whites. Whereas in mainland North America there was always a chance, slim but enticing, that a servant who lived would come to own land of his own, in the West Indies the acres swiftly ran out. The only compensation for years of toil offered as 'freedom dues' anywhere by the 1680s was a few hundred lb. of sugar or (on Jamaica) forty shillings in cash.

Yet the islands needed white men, not simply as labourers, but as militiamen ready to serve against the French or to put down a black uprising. Hence as the years went on their assemblies passed codes unmatched on the mainland, prescribing amounts of food and clothing which servants must be given that were, by current standards, lavish indeed. Ideally, they shouldn't be Irish or even English. 'Scotchmen and Welchmen we esteeme the best servants', a St Kitts planter, Christopher Jeaffreson, wrote in the 1680s. But he indicated, in this letter to London, that the Leewards would accept anything. '. . . If Newgate and Bridewell should spew out their spawne into these islandes, it would meete with no less incouragement; for no gaole-bird can be so incorrigible, but there is hope of his conformity here . . .'

White servants were prone to insubordination. Barbados saw an attempt at concerted rebellion in 1634, and in 1649 many of the servants on the island agreed to rise and cut their masters' throats. Like the former plot, this was betrayed, and 18 ringleaders were executed. After earning their freedom, servants would form a sediment of 'loose, idle, vagrant persons', a blot on the prestige of white men, a burden on the parish, broken in health and morals, sodden in rum, unemployable. Blacks, owned from cradle to grave, would be more efficient, and also less hard to discipline.

III

As hard and degrading tasks were more and more commonly done by black men under the overseers' lash, the idea gained force that Africans were servile drudges by nature, and that the work which they did was morally and physically impossible for white men.

Like other Europeans, the English saw the origins of slavery as lying in the capture of prisoners of war. To spare a prisoner's life was to acquire power over it, virtually absolute power. Slaves were commonly treated like beasts. They were commonly infidels or heathens. Therefore African prisoners were in every way apt as slaves. Their defeat in war was presumed. They were thought to be beastlike – by an unlucky coincidence Africans and chimpanzees were seen together by Europeans in West Africa and the assumption that there was some affinity between black men and apes became commonplace. 'Blackness', the African's salient quality, was in English culture deeply associated with evil. It was hard to explain why the Indians of Brazil were 'red' yet Africans on the same latitude were black; clearly, greater closeness to the sun did not determine pigmentation. The curse of Noah upon Ham and Canaan in Genesis (9:19–27) seemed to provide an answer. Since Ham has seen his father Noah naked, the old man curses Ham's son Canaan – 'a servant of servants shall he be unto his brethren.' Nothing is said about blackness, but the biblical text clearly implies slavery. The curses of blackness and of slavery could be conceived as working together upon all Africans, seen as descendants of Ham.

In 1636 the governor and Council in Barbados resolved that blacks and Indians brought to the island for sale should serve for life 'unless a Contract was before made to the contrary'. There had been blacks in Virginia since 1619, though their numbers reached only 300 within the next thirty years. By mid-century, both here and in Maryland, some blacks were serving for life and some black children were inheriting servile status, although other Africans worked

under indentures, and some were free and were property-owners. In 1640 a
Dutch servant, a Scots servant and an African ran away together in Virginia.
While the two whites, on recapture, were sentenced to four years' extra servile
labour, the African was to remain a slave for the rest of his life. In the same year
blacks were specifically exempted from a Virginian law which required all other
men to be armed.

The New England Puritans showed characteristic scruples over the issue. In
1641, the Massachusetts General Court laid down that there should be no
'Bond-slavery Villenage or Captivity' except in the case of 'lawful Captives
taken in just Wars'. Thus the enslavement of conquered Pequot Indians was
acceptable, and so somehow was their exchange, in 1638, for African slaves from
Providence Island.

As it was, indeed, in England. Blacks were a common sight in London after
the Restoration. To have one as a domestic was fashionable. They spread widely
over the country – twelve black slaves lived with their families in
Nottinghamshire in 1680. In the previous decade, the recognition that men
might be judged commodities had decisively entered English law. The wording
of the charter given to the Royal African Company in 1672 showed the new
readiness of Englishmen to drop the phrase 'Negro-Servants' and talk of black
slaves as chattels. Five years later the Solicitor General gave his opinion that
'negroes ought to be esteemed goods and commodities within the Acts of Trade
and Navigation'.

IV

In the seventeenth century, somewhere over 1,300,000 slaves seem to have been
imported into the New World from Africa, as sugar cultivation spread from
Brazil to the Caribbean. Between 1701 and 1810 another 6 million would make
the 'Middle Passage', then approaching 2 million more before the trade ended
in 1870. Altogether, the best estimates suggest that between 8 million and 10½
million black slaves entered the Americas – excluding those others, certainly
millions, who perished at some point in transit. The great majority of
immigrants into the New World up to the end of the eighteenth century were in
fact black. The economy of the continent, from Maryland southwards, was at its
base a mainly African creation. Though Brazil, over the whole period of the
trade, was the greatest single digester of slaves, the English colonies in North
America and the Caribbean absorbed about 2 million, more than the whole of
Spanish America and more than the French Caribbean.

The Portuguese had begun the trade and for approaching two centuries had
virtually monopolised it. Wars and raids in the region now known as Angola
destroyed, by the 1660s, their hapless client Kingdom of the Kongo. On the east
coast, the powerful Shona kingdom of the Mwenemutapa in the Zambesi valley
had been wormed by estates (*prazos*) established as private slave-worked
concessions by Portuguese adventurers. Slaves crossed the Atlantic from this

region too. But the coast of Guinea was pre-eminent. Here other Europeans picked up the jargon of slaving as the Portuguese had established it. Negotiations became 'palaver'. The headman or official who sold slaves was a 'caboceer' (*caboceiro*). To kidnap someone for slavery was to 'panyar' him, to bribe a native ruler was to give him a 'dash'.

The Dutch founded their first base in Guinea in 1611 or 1612. Twenty-five years later they seized the main Portuguese fort on the Gold Coast, Elmina. The Dutch West India Company, started in 1621, was imitated by other North Europeans. The English 'Gynney and Bynney' (African) Company had a permanent fort on the Gold Coast from 1631. The Danish West India Company (1625) and the Swedish African Company (1647) were both mainly umbrellas for Dutch capitalists who resented the Dutch West India Company's monopoly. The Baltic German Duchy of Courland developed interests on the Guinea Coast. A French West Indian Company pitched in during the 1660s, a Brandenburg Prussia company in the 1680s. The squabble between all these rivals was indecisive and fitful. European rulers esteemed the African trade highly, but it was not quite valuable enough to justify the expense of constructing and keeping up all the forts which were needed to uphold an effective monopoly. In any case, there were Africa powers far too strong to be trifled with.

In the first phase of sugar production in the Caribbean the Dutch were the main suppliers of slaves, as of most other things needful. The English Guinea Company was weak. Charles II chartered in 1660 the 'Royal Adventurers into Africa', a monopolising company, with his brother James, Duke of York, as governor. Though the Duke of Courland had helped Charles in his exile, Admiral Robert Holmes shooed his tiny settlement out of the Gambia, and James Island in that river was occupied and fortified. Other posts were established on the Gold Coast. The 'Second Dutch War' was sparked off by further aggression by Holmes, who swept down the Gold Coast capturing Dutch forts after the Dutch had obstructed English trade. Admiral De Ruyter, following quickly behind him, knocked the English in turn out of all their settlements save the just-captured Cape Coast Castle. The Dutch thereafter mixed cold war and peaceful co-existence with the English, who made Cape Coast their main base. But the war had ruined the Royal Adventurers, who found themselves unable to exploit their own monopoly. Hence the emergence in 1672 of the Royal African Company, favourite child of the Royal House of Stuart. Charles's charter granted it all the lands and trade of the West African coast between Cape Blanco and the Cape of Good Hope for a thousand years. The advertised target of £100,000 for subscriptions to the new company was swiftly passed.

But big City men were cautious, with good reason. In its first twenty years, its fattest, the RAC paid an average annual dividend of only about 7 per cent – a small return for speculation in distant trade – and it had to borrow money in order to fork out even this much. Manufacturers complained that the RAC artificially stunted their exports. They wanted free trade with Africa; so did merchants outside the RAC, above all the men of Bristol. And West Indian planters insisted, it seems rightly, that the Company simply could not meet their demand. The development of Jamaica was retarded. In its most successful phase, the 1680s, the RAC supplied over 5,000 slaves a year to the English West Indies; yet towards the end of that decade it was estimated that Jamaica alone needed 10,000 a year, the Leewards 6,000 and Barbados 4,000.

Expectation of life was generally lower then everywhere in the world, but there seems no doubt that sugar production killed men exceptionally fast, and this was especially true in the 'frontier days' when a class of *nouveau riche* planters rose up suddenly, mostly exempt from those paternalist feelings on which some of their inheritors would pride themselves, and, even outside the ferocious demands of harvest time, ready to work their slaves at a brutal rate clearing virgin land for more canes.

The average slave survived no more than ten years of plantation life. A man owning a hundred slaves would have to buy eight or ten every year to keep numbers up. Home-grown slaves were not economical. It was cheaper to import fresh men than to have women wasting their time rearing families. Traders normally brought two men from Africa for every one woman. Female slaves in the West Indies had remarkably low fertility. In the Caribbean the net natural decrease of population was commonly 20 in the 1,000 per annum, rising as high as 40 per 1,000. The low cost of African labour, Philip Curtin concludes, led the South Atlantic system of trade 'into a pattern of consuming manpower as other industries might consume raw materials.' In 1695 a slave could be bought in Jamaica for £20. He had roughly the same money value as 600 lb. of muscovado sugar sold in London, or as the cost in Europe of sixteen 'trade guns'. But at this time eight trade guns would buy a slave on the African coast, while a good labourer purchased in Jamaica could be expected to add more than 600 lb. to the plantation's production in his first year of work.

Unable to get all the slaves for which they were avid, West Indian planters turned to Madagascar for more. That area lay outside the RAC's monopoly, within that of the EIC, who made no effort to stop the trade. And interlopers moved in on the Guinea Coast itself. In 1679–82, while only about 70 Company ships arrived in the West Indies, at least 32 interlopers, probably many more, turned up carrying slaves. The RAC could seize only four of these.

The RAC's forts in Guinea cost about £20,000 a year in upkeep, and this expense helped to make it uncompetitive. Interlopers could offer more for slaves on the coast and still undersell the Company in the West Indies. From 1686, the RAC licensed private ships to voyage to Africa, and this was a tacit admission that its monopoly was unenforceable.

V

In Elizabeth's day and in those of the early Stuart kings, monopolies had been a consistent grievance. The monarch had sold to favourites the right, in effect, to tax item after item; bricks and buttons, butter and beer, paper and pepper, herring and hats – in 1621 there were said to be, all told, 700 monopolies. Three years later Parliament had invaded the royal prerogative and declared them illegal, but Charles I had continued to grant them. They interfered with the natural channels of trade and they hurt manufactures by raising the cost of industrial needs like coal and alum. The Civil War swept them away.

By 1660 overseas trade had become an obsession, even a fetish, with England's rulers. The Commonwealth had initiated a comprehensive plan for developing trade with the colonies. Now Charles II's government carried it forward. His first parliament of 1660 passed a revised Navigation Act. This was in essence a combination of the Acts of 1650 and 1651, to which a list was added specifying those goods which were to be sent from the colonies only to England and not to other countries. All the main colonial products were listed except the fish of Newfoundland which found such a lively market in Southern Europe. The Staple Act in the same year made illegal the taking of goods direct to the colonies from any foreign country, even in English ships; Dutch linens, for instance, or French brandy, must now first be landed in England and then reshipped. So, according to law, the colonies must now market nearly all their produce in or through England and must buy goods only from England. But within England their sugar, tobacco and dyestuffs were given an effectual monopoly by the imposition of duties several times higher on any of these things imported from foreign sources. The colonists were regarded as Englishmen and the Acts were supposed to be to their advantage. The Acts fostered English sea-power for everyone's benefit.

The tonnage of English shipping seems indeed to have soared in the next quarter century, by 75 or even 100 per cent. From about 115,000 in 1629, it had risen to some 150,000 or 200,000 tons by 1660. By 1688 it stood around 340,000. In the last forty years of the century, exports increased by more than half, imports by just under a third, and a deficit of £300,000 on foreign trade was transformed into a surplus of £600,000. This has been called 'the Commercial Revolution'. By 1700 shipping was one of the largest employers of labour in the country, involving perhaps 10 to 20 per cent of the total working population outside agriculture.

In the early seventeenth century, the Netherlands had been the chief source of English imports and market for exports and a main supplier to England of shipping services. By 1700, Holland was still the main market for exports, but England was drawing more imports from her own plantation colonies. Nearly two-thirds of England's re-exports now came from outside Europe. Woollen cloth down to 1640 had been the only major English export, yet by 1700 it counted for only half, and two-fifths of the export trade was composed either of re-exports of non-European goods or of exports to India and America. Imports from Asia and the New World had made no more than 7 per cent of the total in 1621. By 1700, they were accounting for 34 per cent. Even by 1640, tobacco had been the greatest single item in London's import trade; then imports quadrupled by the 1660s. In that decade English West Indian sugar, undercutting that of Brazil, captured the North European market. By the end of the century half of English imports of sugar were being re-exported to the Continent, along with most of the tobacco coming from the colonies, and with Indian calicoes brought home by the EIC which found avid customers in Europe.

Liverpool's rise from the obscure life of a small fishing village began within the seventeenth century, but at this time the revival of Bristol was still far more striking. The growth of the western ports in general is a main feature of the period, reversing the trend which had made London utterly dominant. Customs revenue at London increased well over five times between 1614 and 1676. Over the same period, that of Hull and Newcastle nearly tripled. But Exeter's quadrupled, Plymouth's multiplied eight times. The revenue of Bristol multiplied twenty times. At the end of the century, roughly half of the vessels entering its port came from the New World.

Bristol had a share in the classic triangular trade which took Newfoundland cod to Southern Europe and brought back oil, fruit and wine. By the 1630s, its trade with Ireland had been gaining a new vitality. Bristol men purchased there not only skins and coarse cloths but also foodstuffs – beef and bacon, fish, pork and barrelled butter – which found good markets among West Indian planters. Sugar was the main basis of Bristol's growth. John Knight showed the way in 1654 when he set up the town's second sugar refinery, linked with an estate on Nevis which he bought at the same time. Other refineries followed. Bristol men added a further colonial interest by interloping eagerly in the new slave trade. Bristol's carrying and re-export trade were matched now by lively processing and manufacturing industries. In the first half of the eighteenth century, the town's population doubled, to 100,000.

This left it, however, still far behind London, which even now handled between two-thirds and three-quarters of all overseas trade. In the early seventeenth century London's quarter of a million people had spilled out beyond the old City walls to east, west and south. A hundred years later, when population stood around 675,000, the central areas alone held as many people as more than one quite impressive foreign state. Its role in the origins of industrialism was one of incalculable but huge importance. There was no industry in Europe like Newcastle coal. Demand from London drove the owners to dig increasingly deep pits involving expensive drainage systems and still more expensive pumping machinery. Investment was needed in timber, in horses, in wagonways, and in wharves. Large capital became the rule, so did large labour-forces. The great burnings of coal brought by sea from Tyneside drove wealthy people in London to settle in the west of the city, whence the prevailing winds drive, and symbolised the city's significance as a centre of mass consumption unequalled anywhere in the world.

Here was a vast market to tempt rural landlords into improvements in transport and in agricultural efficiency, and to draw brewers and other industrialists into technical innovation. Meanwhile, the concentration of wealth in the hands of London merchants supported risky trading far overseas and made possible by the end of the century the developing in England of financial institutions as good as, or better than, those of the Dutch. English financiers after 1660 invented the banknote. From London, its use spread slowly outward till by the mid-eighteenth century such paper money equalled about a third of the amount of circulating silver and other coin.

Without a vigorous home market, concentrated precociously in London, England's expansion overseas could hardly have taken place at all. The English poor were still very poor indeed. But demand for what had been luxuries was spreading as the export trades fostered rising incomes which stimulated fresh investment in industry, providing in turn increased employment and opportunity. The price of sugar fell by half in the forty years after it was first planted in Barbados. Because labour in India cost so little, calicoes could be carried 10,000 miles and remain inexpensive compared to European textiles.

An important law of 1701 would forbid the EIC to bring calicoes into Britain where they would harm the native textile industry. Over the previous century an industry had grown up in Lancashire using cotton, mixed with flax, to make 'fustians'. The Middle East had once been the main source of cotton, but the West Indies were taking over. The Lancashire industry was from its early days in the seventeenth century dominated by merchant capitalists. Weavers in Europe and in London had long defied the 'Dutch looms' which quadrupled ribbon output per man but in Lancashire, hitherto rural, without well-organised crafts, the capitalists had their way and the new machines came into use soon after the Restoration. By the 1680s they were a common sight in the small town of Manchester, where the industry's organisers could act without restraint, since there was no corporation. Looms were grouped in batches of half a dozen to a dozen in what were already small-scale factories, though no power was yet used save human sinews.

The English, not hitherto notably inventive, were now initiating technical advances. In Charles II's reign they were recognised as masters in the delicate art of making watches and clocks, a prototype of all precise engineering. The foundation in 1662 of the famous Royal Society in London symbolises the new zest in England for what we now call science and technology. The impact of this on agriculture was obvious. At the same time as animal fattening took over large areas of the Midlands and East Anglia and as fruit-growing increased near London and in the west, English production of corn was pushed up by larger yields per acre.

Charles II's land settlement gave to those who had. The stronger Royalists got their lands back. The stronger among those who had bought confiscated lands in the interregnum were able to hold on to them. The consolidated class of haves set about making strong defences against any fresh invasions of the gentry's status. The fact that England, one of the first countries to break from feudalism, now seems among the most feudalistic and backward-looking lands in the world, with its monarchy and its House of Lords and its quaint old universities, reflects the strength of reaction after 1660, which froze the country's institutions at a transitional point. The dominant landowners were commercially minded. From the 1660s, corn laws protected them against foreign competition in their main cash crop. They exploited the timber and gravel and coal they found upon their estates, they allied themselves by marriage as well as an interest with merchants and with the growing professional classes. Beneath them, their leases created a middle class of tenant farmer. The poor stared at them across a social ravine. The notorious Game Laws date from this period. By a law of 1671 only a freeholder worth more than £100 a year was allowed to kill birds or beasts even on his own land. Game was reserved for the wealthy. The poor were disarmed. The parson rode to hunt along with the squire, no longer a zealous independent theologian but a parasitical spokesman for the ruling class.

Inclined to papistry, Charles was himself not a deeply religious man and probably meant it when, before his return, he promised his subjects 'liberty to tender consciences'. Nor was it wholly denied them. For the first time in English history, heresy became legal. Sephardic Jews opened the first synagogue in London in 1662 and were soon playing an important part in finance and commerce. But the squires in Parliament, from 1662, pushed through a string of Acts excluding nonconformists from any share in central or local government, barring them from the universities, and penalising more directly those who continued to worship outside Anglican forms. Persecution raged in the 1660s, when thousands of Quakers, for instance, were gaoled, and again in the early 1680s. Presbyterians, Baptists, Congregationalists clung to their faith by sheer strength of character.

The King had been summoned home by a parliament which he had not himself summoned. A conflict existed between the privileges of Parliament, now confirmed, and the royal prerogative, now reasserted. The latter could beat down the Irish and Scottish Parliaments into impotence, but it could not control the English Commons, or stop the English gentry ruling their own localities. The King could not reign, or, at least, could not pursue any active foreign policy, without money. Unable to get his way with the Commons, he turned to Louis XIV of France for cash. From 1670 till 1678, when he fell out with Louis, Charles was taking secret bribes from France. In the next phase, 1678–81, his quarrel with the Commons brought England close to revolution again. For the last four years of his reign, he did without Parliament, and became a client of France once more.

Perhaps the devotion of writers and thinkers and statesmen during his reign

to promoting England's greatness through overseas trade arose in part from the
fact that home politics were miserably unsettled; the quest for profit abroad
could seal differences and harmonise interests, enriching not only the King's
luckier subjects, but, through the customs returns, the monarch himself. The
group of efficient civil servants which emerged in this period was orientated
towards external aggression. Among its most striking figures were William
Blathwayt, secretary to the Committee for Plantations, and Samuel Pepys,
ablest man on the naval board. Both were friends of Sir William Petty, attracted
by the new science of statistics. Thanks to such men, despite all political
turbulence, England by 1714 'probably enjoyed the most efficient government
machine in Europe.' But it was a machine built for war, tested by war and
improved by war. The question was, who to fight?

The Iberian powers, excellent trading partners for England, seemed well
beaten. Good relations with Lisbon were confirmed by Charles II's marriage in
1661 to a Portuguese princess, whose dowry included the island of Bombay,
which Charles II made over a few years later to the EIC, and also Tangier, in
Morocco, which proved too costly to keep up. It needed a garrison of 3,000 men.
The attacks of the Moors were too hard to repel. In 1683 the English withdrew.

The Dutch seemed to many prominent Englishmen both the best exemplars to
follow and the most obvious target. In the second Dutch war the great aim was to
seize shipping. The war (1664–7) coincided with two immense disasters for
England. A great epidemic of plague in 1665 was followed by the burning of over
400 acres of densely populated housing in London in 1666. Dutch blockade stifled
London's trade and Dutch ships broke into the Thames and the Medway. After
so much disaster, the English modified the Navigation Act in Holland's favour,
returned Surinam to the Dutch, but kept New Amsterdam. From this point, the
natural drift of Anglo-Dutch relations seemed to be towards lasting peace. The
Dutch feared French power on land, and many English merchants and manufacturers were coming now to realise that France, the largest country in Europe,
must be England's most dangerous competitor. As he swam against the tide into
dependence on France, Charles II could carry with him the City merchants
involved in the great trading companies which depended on royal charter and
favour, but not the City as a whole, whose turbulent anti–establishment politics
would be a problem for English kings for a hundred years more.

Charles would have liked, of course, to be absolute like Louis XIV. His own
character was an impediment. He was a genial man, but lazy and profligate,
witty but short on dignity, giving the lead to a court which flaunted its idle
lewdness and lived as if it must be aware that the restored Stuarts could not last
for very long. Besides, Charles had no strong standing army, and could not
afford one. The navy was no help to him at home; the very basis of England's
rising prosperity, since it was sea-power, acted against absolutist ambitions, by
diverting money from soldiers to ships.

Charles's alliance with Louis launched England into the third Dutch War

(1672–4). Charles spent £6 million and gained nothing. Catholic France was surely the proper enemy. In 1678, Titus Oates, a disgusting liar, electrified Britain by his pretended discovery of a 'Popish Plot' to kill Charles II, massacre Protestants, and install Charles's brother James, who was avowedly papist, upon the throne. Charles lost control of the Commons and of the country. A reign of terror followed against those imagined to be in the 'Plot'. The Commons struggled to outlaw James's succession to the throne. The words 'whig' and 'tory' were snatched from the Celtic fringe and hurled as terms of abuse. 'Tories' supported the royal prerogative which was Charles's greatest weapon, 'whigs' aimed to exclude James from the heritage of his childless brother. In 1681, Charles dismissed his last parliament and, helped by Louis, proceeded to rule on his own and to lay the basis for absolutism. Magnates as well as old revolutionaries were implicated in the 'Rye House Plot' to seize the King in 1682, and its discovery prompted fresh persecution of Dissenters. The Bench of Judges was purged, and Charles set about winkling the whigs from their bases in the town corporations, calling in ancient charters and granting new ones. When Charles died in 1685, England was drawing closer to the French model.

In Charles's reign Wren devised St Paul's Cathedral as a symbol of empire. An Englishman, Newton, was at work on ideas in mathematics and physics which revolutionised all human thought, and John Locke, in opposition to Charles, shaped the theory that governments must rule with the consent of their subjects. This was not a barren age in England. Yet the tone of its life disgusted good men. John Bunyan, a Baptist field-preacher imprisoned for his beliefs, produced in 1678 a fable eschewing the world's ways which became a seminal work in English popular culture. In *Pilgrim's Progress*, Christian and his companion Faithful are put on trial in the town of Vanity Fair. Faithful is tortured and finally burnt after one Pickthank has testified that he had 'railed on our noble Prince Beelzebub' and had spoken contemptibly of that Prince's good friends, 'the Lord Old Man, the Lord Carnal Delight, the Lord Luxurious, the Lord Desire of Vain-Glory, my old Lord Lechery, Sir Having Greedy, with all the rest of our nobility . . .'

The ideals and ideas of the revolutionary 1640s were driven down into the middle and lower orders of society. Lord Hategood and Sir Having-Greedy might battle each other in paranoiac factions, yet the reign of their kind seemed secure. Dissenters, however, cherished notions which, transmuted by passage through the years, would one day challenge the rulers again, as democracy, liberty, equality, fraternity. Meanwhile, blocked from using their talents in politics or in the professions, their cleverest men turned their energies to trade and industry. Contemporaries soon saw and announced the connection between Dissent and business success. Meanwhile, similar repression of Christian radicalism in Scotland had helped towards creating a nation which would one day become signally wedded, not to a Covenant with Yahweh, but to advance through technology and trade.

VI

On the face of it, Charles II's Restoration brought a return to the system by which his father and grandfather had governed Scotland. The Earl of Argyll was executed, along with a few other figures identified with rebellion. Charles ruled through a Privy Council in Edinburgh, a parliament firmly under control, a tame convention of Royal Burghs, and a Church to which bishops were now restored, though as before they had to work with presbyters. But much had in fact changed. The fractious nobility had been chastened and tamed. The magnates, having seen how their power stood or fell with the King's, were content to make trouble only through 'loyal' opposition in Parliament. Charles II's reign saw a great systematisation of Scots law, and quarrelsome men now found in litigation satisfaction for which they could no longer risk armed feuding.

The lawyers, mostly of lairdly origins, were a powerful new element in society, and a far more modern-minded one, for the most part, than the burgesses of the old-fashioned Scottish towns. But trade now spilled out of the burghs as landowners became commercially conscious, promoting new towns of their own and in many cases turning traders themselves. The administration in Edinburgh tried very hard, though with scant success, to promote manufacturing industries and to strengthen native trade and fisheries.

As the western ports rose in England, so rose Glasgow. In 1612, Glasgow was only the fifth burgh in Scotland in wealth. By 1705 she was easily second, a bustling town with handsome new buildings, catching up with Edinburgh. The stimulus provided by commerce with the Scottish colony in Ulster was for the moment perhaps the main factor in Glasgow's elevation. The relative pacification of the Highlands helped to open up trade with that region. And Glasgow merchants were early ready to seize chances of semi-licit trade with England's New World plantations. The town had the foresight to construct down the Clyde, in 1667, Port Glasgow, a harbour able to take the large vessels which were needed to brave Atlantic storms. By the 1680s, Glasgow was getting six or seven American cargoes, of sugar and tobacco, per year.

Yet the immediate hinterland of Glasgow in south-west Scotland was a centre of political trouble throughout Charles II's reign. The vast majority of ministers in this region refused to accept the restoration of bishops, though elsewhere even in the Lowlands most conformed, and acquiescence was all but universal north of the Tay. The rebels of the 'Whiggamore' country were, of course, ejected from their livings, and because they continued to find a loyal following, the ideals of pure presbytery and of the Covenants still held menace to the Scottish authorities. Some noblemen remained Presbyterians, but none were now ready to revolt for the cause. So the lower classes of the south-west went ahead against the bent of their feudal superiors; this was a novelty in Scotland's history.

The reaction of petty landowners, who were abundant in the south-west, to the reimposition of feudal ties broken during the Cromwellian occupation may have been one basis for the emerging movement. The first crisis, however, was triggered by the Dutch War of 1664–7, which was widely unwelcome to Scots, as it deprived the country of its main Continental trading partner. The government had laid down that Nonconformists must pay fines if they absented themselves from the approved churches. Now they sent troops in to collect these fines as a way of paying for Scotland's share of the forces required for the war. The soldiers quartered in the south-west abused their position. Extortion provoked revolt. A body of about 3,000 'whigs' headed for Edinburgh in November 1666. They were easily dispersed at Rullion Green in the Pentlands, but the authorities stupidly over-reacted, hanged over 30 captured rebels, and gave this new Covenanting movement its first consignment of martyrs.

The Duke of Lauderdale now came to the fore in a political struggle among Charles's ministers in Scotland and for a dozen years, as Secretary for Scottish Affairs, he was virtually ruler of the country. He was patriotic and learned but also immensely, inventively corrupt. However, like his royal master, he preferred toleration to bullying. The 'indulgences' of 1669 and 1672, which permitted Presbyterian ministers, if they accepted certain terms, to preach legally, split the opposition between the intransigents and those who followed 'indulged' clergy. The die-hards continued to worship in open-air 'conventicles', swords at the ready, and before long repression was renewed. In 1677, landowners were told they must sign bonds for the loyal behaviour of all persons living on their lands. For many in the south-west this demand was impossible to meet; nonconformity was too general. To discipline the area, Lauderdale sent in the famous 'Highland Host' of 1678. Six thousand Gaelic-speaking clansmen, as well as three thousand Lowland militiamen, were told to take up free quarters on all who refused to sign a promise of conformity. Peers suffered along with commoners. The host plundered at will. No one was killed in a month or so of pillaging, but the 'whigs'' anger at their immense losses was inflamed further by the fact that Highland savages had been the cause of them.

A new rising could hardly be long delayed. In May 1679 the spark was provided by the murder of the unpopular Archbishop Sharpe on a moor in Fife by a band of self-righteous men who firmly believed him to be the devil's agent. They fled to the south-west, where others massed to support them, and soon captured Glasgow. Charles II sent his illegitimate son, the Duke of Monmouth, with a large force, to help suppress them. The rebels fell into furious factional dispute and were easily routed at Bothwell Bridge near Glasgow. Monmouth, a friend of English Dissent, presided over a short period of relative leniency, when most of the 1,400 or so prisoners were set free on promise of not rising again. But as white hope of the English opposition, Monmouth became suspect to Charles at the same time as the furore over the 'Popish Plot' made it necessary for James, Duke of York, to leave England. Monmouth was exiled to the Continent; James went to Edinburgh where the Privy Council organised a reign of terror which continued and even intensified after his return to England in 1682. Peaceful Presbyterians as well as extremist rebels were harried and hunted and merely to have shown friendship towards a man who had fought at Bothwell Bridge could cost a Lanarkshire or Ayrshire farmer his life. John Graham of Claverhouse was the commander chiefly identified in later popular lore with the policy of driving people back to the official Church and quelling resistance by brutal summary methods. He went down in Lowland legend as 'Bluidy Clavers', persecutor of sainted martyrs.

A potent myth was born out of persecution. Charles II himself remarked once that 'there was no natione or kingdome in the world, where the tenants had so great a dependance upon the gentlemen, as in Scotland.' Events in the 1680s helped to create a counter-tradition, of self-reliance as against subservience. Deserted by nobles and gentry but cherished by common folk, the hunted minority who followed the few remaining field-preachers injected doctrines which cut against feudal and clannish dependence. They became known as 'Cameronians' after their leader Richard Cameron who died in a skirmish in 1680. Cameron was a merchant's son and one of his hearers recalled him saying 'after these defections and judgements are over, ye may see the nettles grow out of the bed-chambers of noblemen and gentlemen and their homes, memorials, and posterity to perish from the earth.' His successor, Donald Cargill, had the gall to excommunicate Charles II and all his ministers. A moderate Presbyterian minister complained of such men as these that they extolled 'the ignorance, simplicity, indiscretion, and infirmities of the poor vulgar, a thing not to be gloried in, nor boasted of . . .' In other words, they thought the ideas of the poor might be worth more than those of the rich.

Behind the tobacco magnates of eighteenth-century Glasgow, behind an artisan class which would make two successive industrial revolutions, stood ancestors who had fled from Bothwell Bridge.

The same may be said, however, of many Protestant Ulstermen. Self-righteousness and boastful intolerance would be another inheritance from the Cameronians. The Ulster Scots grew greatly in numbers in Charles II's reign. Preachers outlawed at home sought refuge in Ireland, where Alexander Peden, one of the best-loved Covenanting ministers, prophesied 'hunger, hunger in Derry, many a black and pale face shall be in thee.' Or so it was said, after such things had come to pass.

VII

Protestant planters in Ireland had given Charles II valuable backing in the preliminaries to his Restoration, and he had to accommodate their interests. He announced late in 1660 that the Cromwellian newcomers were to keep what they had acquired, although Irish deprived of their lands on the grounds of religion or Royalism were to get back what they had lost. While, furthermore, soldiers who had served Charles abroad would also have claims to reward in Irish acres.

Ormond, now created a duke and reappointed Lord Lieutenant, commented wrily that they would need to discover a new Ireland, as the present one wasn't large enough. So it proved. Under the Act of Settlement passed in May 1662 by the Irish House of Commons, now exclusively Protestant, dominated by recent settlers, 'innocent' Protestants and papists were to be given their lands back. The Court of Claims now set up found 'innocent' a vast majority of those who came before it, and fears of dispossession made some Protestants plot an abortive coup. A squalid deal followed. The more prominent Catholics threw over the rest. Even so, large surrenders of land were required from Protestants and there were fierce words and half-drawn swords in the Irish Commons before Ormond soothed tempers and the angry newcomers realised that the proposed arrangements at least gave them security.

But most Catholics had been cheated. Petty, who was most certainly not one of the losers, observed in the 1670s that the old distinction between Gael and Catholic settler was 'asleep now, because they have a Common Enemy'. Protestants held almost all Ulster and four-fifths of Leinster and Munster.

For most of Charles II's reign, Catholics were not persecuted, and at times the Roman hierarchy 'was able to function more freely than it had done for over a century'. But Titus Oates's 'Popish Plot' led to pressure on the easy-going Ormond. Though he evaded the extremes of persecution urged on him, action was taken to expel bishops and regular clergy. Those who remained were hunted. Oliver Plunket, Roman Archbishop of Armagh, a saintly man who had co-operated with the government against the 'tories', was seized and, since no Irish jury would have convicted him, was sent for trial to London charged with treason. He was executed there in 1681 despite the wishes of the King and the disgust of Ormond at perjured witnesses who 'went out of Ireland with bad English and worse clothes and returned well-bred gentlemen, well caronated, periwigged and clothed.'

Even in good times, Catholics forced to pay tithes to Protestant clergy had little left for their own priests. Catholic education was tolerated only locally and spasmodically, though a Jesuit school which flourished awhile in Drogheda was good enough to attract many sons of Protestant gentry. Gaelic poets lamented that in the great houses now the harpstrings were untouched and the pipes unplayed, that dancing and mirth were no more and that penny-pinching oafs had usurped the places of old chiefs, yet some were prepared to write in praise of Protestant newcomers, so it must be presumed that some of the latter were ready to pay them.

Missionary clergy continued to struggle against irregular marriages, drinking at wakes and succouring of tories, though the native priests were commonly prone to indulge in whiskey in public and were mostly ill-educated men. A visitor to the south-west in 1703 would report that the poor there rarely spoke English 'unless forced', but the alien language continued its progress and most people were coming to understand it. When an Irish translation of the Bible was at last published under Protestant auspices in the 1680s, this was too late either to further the Reformation or to halt the ebb of Gaelic. But the poor retained their pre-Christian superstitions.

For the moment, only the endemic tories were in active revolt. They were popular heroes. The prime Robin Hood was Redmond O Hanlon, famed on the Continent and among the poor, an educated man who had lost his land under the Restoration Settlement. He haunted the mountains north of Dundalk, in Ulster, till he was betrayed and executed in the early 1680s. Toryism reflected not only the dying Gaelic tradition of reiving, but also the growing traffic which flowed along Ireland's roads and could be preyed upon with profit. Dublin, like London, was spreading its commerce to hitherto isolated parts of the country. With around 60,000 people by 1685, Dublin was the second city of the empire, sustained by its dominance in the trade with England and by the demand of country landowners for skilled craftsmanship and imported goods, with numerous coffee houses and bookshops, a learned Philosophical Society (1682) and a new theatre (1662). Ormond had acquired in France a taste for architectural grandeur and encouraged Dublin's transformation towards the impressive capital which it became in the eighteenth century. Cork, no less than half its size, throve on trade with the New World. And Ulster, hitherto poor and backward, was beginning to rise. A spate of new settlers from Scotland, and England, helped to build up the linen industry from the 1680s, and Belfast, by 1700, was the fourth port in Ireland, eclipsing Limerick and Galway.

Perhaps many Irish were better off than before. The potato, established from the 1650s, certainly strengthened, at this stage, the national diet. Petty raged against the chimneyless hovels in which the poor lived, full of soot and smoke, vermin and damp, and against the fact that the Irish poor still remained self-sufficient, rarely buying anything made outside their own village. But he noted one breach in the rule that they ignored foreign commodities. 'Tobacco taken in short Pipes seldom burnt, seems the pleasure of their Lives, together with Sneezing: Insomuch, that 2/7 of their Expence in Food, is Tobacco.'

War and confiscations had shaken land loose from communal control, and landlords in Ireland now found it relatively easy to direct their production towards foreign markets. Deforestation doomed the iron industry, since the island had little coal. But as land was won from the forests, it fed sheep and cattle and Ireland sent butter to the Continent, supplied wool for the English textile industry, and sold salt beef to sea captains and to West Indian slave-owners.

By the early 1660s there was a thriving trade in live cattle and sheep exported to England. The squires at Westminster would not stand for this competition, and the 'Great Cattle Act' of 1667 forbade it, as well as the import of Irish beef, butter, and pork. This left Ireland dependent on trade outside British markets, and so exceptionally vulnerable to wars. But Frenchmen and Spaniards eagerly purchased the cheap and excellent Irish salt beef. Perversely, some of the most backward parts of the British Isles became largely dependent on markets far overseas. In 1666 nearly three-quarters of all Irish exports had gone to England, but by 1683 the proportion was less than a third, though French tariffs then reduced Irish trade with France, and the rise of linen, which found a market only in England, swung the pendulum back. Ormond encouraged the industry, which was complementary to English woollens rather than competing with them.

For ten years from 1671 the direct import of various products, including sugar and tobacco, from the colonies into Ireland, was banned, and the prohibition was resumed in 1685. But the Navigation Acts bore hard only on a few importers. Direct and indirect trade with the New World flourished.

Indeed, by the mid-1680s, Irish prosperity was beginning to worry some people in England, not just because they were crudely jealous, but because of its political side-effects. Charles II in 1665 had been granted by the Dublin Parliament customs and excise in perpetuity. He did not thereafter need to summon this body, and his increasing income from Ireland helped him defy his London Parliament. The situation looked ominously like that of the late 1630s.

VIII

A powerful group of courtiers, politicians and peers gave a strong lead in expanding overseas trade. Amongst them were the King's brother James, Duke of York, whose work for the navy redeems him from the historian's general charge of ineptitude; his cousin, Prince Rupert, once the dashing leader of the Royalist cavalry and the Royalist fleet; George Monck, now rewarded for his part in the Restoration with the title of Duke of Albermarle; and Anthony Ashley Cooper, soon created Earl of Shaftesbury. Closely associated with this group were the leaders of the new bureaucratic class, including Blathwayt, Pepys and another famous diarist, John Evelyn. The City merchants were more than just in attendance; in Sir Josiah Child they threw up the most remarkable man of his age, so far as England's overseas interests went. Born in 1630, probably a London merchant's son, he made his way in the 1650s by furnishing stores for the navy. Already a rich man, he bought £12,000 worth of East India Company stock in the early 1670s, made himself probably the Company's largest shareholder, and came to rule it absolutely as its governor in the 1680s. When he died in 1699, his estate was well over £200,000. His brother-in-law became Duke of Chandos, one granddaughter a Duchess of Bedford, and a grandson Duke of Beaufort. Farsighted and domineering, he once remarked that all trade was 'a kind of warfare'.

'Mercantilist' views now reigned. 'Acquisitive trade' had become an ideal. Advanced economists placed a new emphasis on the value of labour. The brilliant Petty suggested, in 1662, that compulsory labour – 'slavery' – should be substituted for the death penalty in cases of theft. Child emphasised in his famous *New Discourse of Trade* that besides being a 'Duty to God and Nature', to find employment for the poor would greatly enrich the country, just as

'Lessening the Number of our Holly-Days would encrease the days of our Working, and Working more would make us Richer . . .' Since labour at home was now seen as so valuable – and the more there was of it, the lower wages would be – the desire for greater population in England might seem to conflict with any call for emigration. Some writers actually argued that colonies were an evil, on such grounds. The reply from men such as Child was that, if potentially evil, they were necessary. Child reasoned that the plantations, buying English goods and employing 'near two thirds of all our *English shipping*', had actually increased population in England. Every Englishman in Barbados or Jamaica created employment for four men at home.

Child was a strong and consistent advocate of religious toleration. In England, the force of the Dutch example was accepted. A tolerant country would attract skilled people – Jews, Huguenots – from abroad. By contrast, in France, Colbert's mercantilism was accompanied by religious persecution more thorough than any seen in England, and the great exodus of skilled Huguenots in the 1680s would be a vast gain for Britain, Ireland and North America.

English authorities press-ganged men for the navy; the French condemned criminals wholesale to labour for decades in the state galleys. England, from 1700, would prohibit the import of printed calicoes; in France even their manufacture at home was forbidden and some 16,000 people are said to have lost their lives through the enforcement of this ban between 1686 and 1759. Colbert's mercantilism, and that of his successors, was imposed on the French nation from the top, whereas in England, merchants were commonly to the fore, demanding freedom from certain controls at the same time as they urged the State to fight in the interests of mercantilist goals.

In 1657, Cromwell granted the East India Company a new exclusive charter which set its affairs on a far firmer basis. It ended the old system of terminable joint stocks. From now on stock was to be permanent and non-returnable, and this meant that the long-term interests of the Company could be advanced free of the clamour for quick profits.

The fresh charter granted by Charles II in 1661 did not break continuity, though it widened the EIC's powers, giving the Company the right to make war against any non-Christian prince within the limits assigned to it. In return for such generosity Charles II asked for, and got, a loan. The EIC was beginning its long career as an indispensable prop of government finance. Charles seems to have received over £300,000 in gifts and loans from the Company. The shareholders would not mind. Royal support was ensured. Meanwhile, subscribers to the new joint stock were richly rewarded. A £100 share was worth £245 in 1677, £360 or even £500 in 1683. In 1675 Company exports worth £430,000 brought back produce worth more than £860,000.

Charles II had returned to confront a huge deficit and exiled courtiers anxious to make up their losses had flocked home at his heels. Despite Parliament's grant of £1,200,000 annually, the King's difficulties persisted and he still had to sell manors for ready cash like his royal predecessors. He and his courtiers found overseas expansion a partial answer to their problems. Virginian trade alone came to bring Charles £100,000 a year, and this was equal to his secret subsidy from Louis XIV. Loyal followers could be rewarded with grants and offices overseas.

Merchants did not recover under Charles the dominating role in expansion which they had had under Cromwell. They were used. Their brains were picked. But except in the EIC, the City was not allowed to lead. Meanwhile, at home and abroad, Charles II's reign saw the nascence of a small sub-class of administrators specialising in colonial government. William Blathwayt, Secretary to the Lords of Trade in 1679, auditor general of the royal revenue in America in 1680, used office to enrich himself. Crown servants overseas likewise saw office as a source of personal profit. The governors of the colonies now became sole responsible agents for carrying out the Acts of Trade there. They had in their gift, furthermore, public offices making the holders responsible for collecting taxes and for allocating grants of land. They and their chosen few, creaming the system, became a focus of jealousy for those excluded, and this largely explained the character of 'politics' in all the colonies.

There were already fears that the colonies must eventually crave and assert independence. And Ireland and New England presented problems to mercantilist thinking which were, in effect, insoluble. Neither could produce much that could not be grown or made at home; each was thus a potential competitor. Both, in particular, acted as suppliers of produce to the West Indian islands so that Child amongst others argued that English landowners were suffering. Another point which weighed with Child was that neither used black slavery. The mass demand for clothing, tools and produce from slave plantations seemed to Child the major benefit of empire. On top of this, the New Englanders smuggled colonial wares into foreign markets and took foreign goods back to the colonies, undercutting English merchants in both spheres. For such reasons Child argued that New England was 'the most prejudicial Plantation to this Kingdom.'

It was mostly New England activities which explained the new Act of 1673 aimed at tighter control of colonial trade. It provided for the appointment of customs officers in the plantations who would act under the jurisdiction of the Commissioners of the Customs in London.

This was part of a general trend, from the late 1660s, towards greater central control of the colonies. A new body, the 'Lords of Trade' (Lords Committee of Trade) was set up early in 1675, comprising nine Privy Councillors. Its aim from the outset was to make the colonies wholly obedient to the Crown. The colonies at this time were seen alternatively as 'possessions of the nation' or as 'dominions of the king'. Charles II favoured the latter view, of course. Overseas his absolutist proclivities could find expression. An attack on colonial charters was launched. The Bermuda Company lost its charter in 1684, and in the same year

Massachusetts at last was deprived of its quasi-independence.

The new policy swaggered fiercely. The conquest of New Amsterdam in 1664 had been effected by methods essentially like those of Queen Elizabeth. Charles II had provided the ships, but the soldiers, somewhere over 300 of them, had been recruited for the service of an individual, James, Duke of York. By 1676, by contrast, rebellion in Virginia was swiftly met with a royal force of 11 ships and over 1,100 soldiers. At about the same time, Edward Randolph was making himself deeply unpopular as royal superintendent of customs in Boston, and in 1677 an attempt was made to apply 'Poynings' Law', that veteran device for shackling the Irish Parliament, to the assembly of the island of Jamaica.

But royal power wasn't sufficient. Parliament wouldn't give positive help to the King in such huffing and puffing. The Jamaican planters successfully called the bluff of the Lords of Trade. Virginia, garrisoned for five years by royal soldiers, eventually sent them away when the Assembly simply refused to pay for them. The new royal customs collectors could not, of course, stamp out smuggling, and they ran into clobbering opposition from local ruling cliques. Colonies were expected to raise the costs of their own administration. In return, they would demand, and it proved that they must be given, substantial self-government. Rhode Island could thus be as tolerant as it wished; neither here nor elsewhere were English religious policies imposed.

The effectual unifying bond of the empire was the growing English navy. In the fifty years after the Restoration an average of about a quarter of State expenditure was directed to naval needs, with more beyond this spent on naval ordnance. Increasing drill marched with a hardening class structure. In the days of Blake and Cromwell, 'tarpaulins' (lower-class sailors) had risen to become captains and admirals. But along with the formal creation, in 1677, of a professional corps of officers – no one could become a lieutenant unless he passed an examination in seamanship and navigation – there came an almost complete blockage of this kind of upward mobility. The better-off classes made the navy a source of secure careers for their sons.

Only a small proportion of common seamen spent all their lives in royal service. Since Elizabeth's time, 'impressment' had been used to gather in hands in times of war. The procedure now became standardised. The Privy Council would issue an order to the Admiralty for a general impress. The naval authorities then sent down warrants to local authorities. These in turn appointed 'presters' to recruit men either on sea or on land. Sailors were taken off colliers in the North Sea and returning merchant ships in the Channel. Kidnapping was commonplace. Once in the service, seamen found discipline savage. By Act of Parliament captains would give the death sentence not only for murder but for striking an officer, even for sleeping habitually on watch. Men preferred the merchant service, where pay was not always better, but where it was less likely to be delayed.

The fact that the Newfoundland fisheries were seen as prime 'nursery of seamen' largely dictated the attitudes of the home government towards the sketchy colony on the island. Settlers could live, it seemed, only by fishing. But their little boats gave them no experience of deepwater sailing, and in any case they were too far away to be easily pressed as need arose, whereas the ships which voyaged from English West Country ports came back regularly every year. The colonists were a lamentable nuisance. In the mid-1670s there were, in any case, merely 523 of them, scattered in 30 or 40 settlements, which were linked only by steep pathways through thick woods. Around this permanent nucleus of families, there was a shifting population, generally well over 1,000, left behind by the West Country vessels so as to save freight and food on the return voyage. All told there were only 167 houses and the inhabitants outnumbered their own livestock.

But the London and Bristol merchants who supported them against the West Country interests which retained a monopoly in the fisheries set up a cry at home for strong civil government. The home authorities came down on the side of the West Countrymen, whose charter was confirmed, and strengthened. New regulations in the 1670s denied the colonists right to settle within six miles of the coast. The effective 'governor' was the commodore of the naval convoy which came each year to help the fishing ships get home safely. The commodore of 1675, Sir John Berry, told the inhabitants for the second time that they must either leave the island or settle inland. But this was wholly impracticable, and Berry sensibly became a spokesman for the settlers. The home government let them stay there.

Meanwhile, the New England merchants had moved in, along with some Scots and Irishmen. This incursion alarmed the government more than French competition. A provision of the 1663 Navigation Act was that salt could be freely imported to Newfoundland for the sake of the fishery. This made smuggling easy, since Southern Europe was the prime source of salt. By 1680 the commodore was reporting 100 vessels engaged in illegal trade. Newfoundland had become in effect an entrepôt for smugglers and interlopers. Here Scottish merchants could acquire tobacco, and from here Virginian planters could draw supplies of French liquor; one master of a brigantine seized in 1688 with brandy aboard innocently explained that 'he took it up floating in the Sea and might have taken up a great deal more.'

New Englanders even tried to enter the fur trade of Hudson's Bay, the vast icy area which Charles II made over to the most long-lived of all chartered companies. English interest was attracted by two French trader-explorers. In the 1650s the Sieur des Groseilliers, and Pierre Esprit Radisson found that superb furs could be had far to the north of the French settlement at Quebec, and proposed a direct trade by sea into Hudson's Bay. The French authorities were not attracted; characteristically, they insisted on funnelling all trade through the St Lawrence, where it could be taxed; and the governor of Quebec alienated the two explorers by despoiling them of most of their profits. They turned to the English. In London, they were given an audience and pensions by the King, and a consortium was formed to take advantage of their knowledge and experience.

The fur trade, valuable in its own right, had a certain strategic significance. Russia, once an exporter of furs, now showed a strong demand for beaver. The Dutch were supplying Muscovy with the French surplus. If England broke into this trade, it would reduce dependence on Dutch intermediaries for vital supplies of 'naval stores' from the Baltic. Nevertheless, the capital raised in ten years – £10,500 – was less than was needed to buy one sugar plantation. Two ships were sent in 1668. Only the *Nonsuch* reached Hudson's Bay, with Groseilliers aboard, but that proved enough. 'Fort Charles', a pallisaded house, was erected at the southern extremity of James Bay.

In 1670 Charles granted the 'Governor and Company of Adventurers of England trading into Hudson's Bay' a charter which, despite many attacks, survived for two hundred years. Its affairs were to be managed by a governor – Prince Rupert for the first dozen years, then James, Duke of York – with a deputy and a committee of seven. These men were to control the 'sole Trade' of an area, 'Rupert's Land', which proved to comprise nearly 1,500,000 square miles. The aims were diffuse at first. Groseilliers and Radisson had talked of an easy route, part overland, to the Pacific. Colonisation was on the agenda. But the fur trade swiftly proved to be the only practical way of exploiting the grant, and the company, uniquely, kept a charter for a colony which was used in effect purely for trade.

Profits were slow to come. The Company survived because of its growing mastery of a very difficult trade, which was always useful but never opulent. Hudson's Strait provided the only route in and out of the Bay, and currents, tide and ice restricted navigation to a few weeks in mid-summer. By August, ice was drifting in the Bay again. Of the three or four ships a year which came from England, one or more would commonly be lost. The stubbornness of such conditions deterred illegal traders.

The French were very worried by English rivalry. The rivers draining into the Bay were natural arteries for the fur trade. The English had cheaper trade goods and the advantage of low ocean freights. The French responded to competition by direct aggression – thus, Fort Charles was seized in 1671 – and by a more subtle and dangerous method; their 'wood-runners', *coureurs de bois*, wooed Indian tribes back by taking trade goods direct to them rather than leaving them to find their own way to the English.

Some of the goods which the latter were offering can be seen from a list of supplies sent out in 1684: '. . . 300 guns for Bottom of the Bay, 100 guns for Pt. Nelson etc., to be made by 3 different gunsmiths . . . 1000 hatchets from 10d to 14d each, 1800 long knives at 2/9 per doz., 900 long small knives, 1000 Rochbury large knives, 500 Rochbury small knives, 1000 Jacknives.' By this time there were several posts on the Bay, though their combined population in

1687 would be only 89 men in the Company's employ. The first governor at Charles Fort had been Charles Bayly, a Quaker released from imprisonment in the Tower of London on the surety of its governor, who was one of the initial investors. The committee in London was insistent that Indians must be mildly treated, and long-term interests thus prevailed over two-fisted swift exploitation. Bayly was liked and trusted by Indians, and built up a good trade with them. His successor (1679), John Nixon, was perhaps a Scot, and certainly advocated the use of Scots in the Bay rather than the 'London childring' whom the committee were recruiting.

Such men developed specialised skills which made them indispensable, and gave the Company its strength. It had no other commanding advantage, certainly no monopoly, since, besides the French, it had to compete, even on the English market, with the fur traders of the province now known as 'New York'.

IX

The conquest of New York was involved with fresh attempts to discipline New England. That difficult province, or rather the Boston merchants who dominated its economic life, had found a place in the evolving Atlantic economy which made links with Restoration England vital. While merchant families in Boston retained 'umbilical' links with London, New Englanders transplanted to the West Indies and became factors for Boston merchant there. The great Hutchinson network will illustrate how matters worked. Richard Hutchinson, brother-in-law of the 'antinomian' martyr Anne, exported manufactured goods from London to brothers and nephews of his in Boston who sold them in the Bay area and, through middlemen, to more distant settlers. They maintained a large trade with the Caribbean, exchanging provisions and cattle for cotton and sugar which they sold for credit in London. Their West India trade was largely handled for them by Richard's nephew Peleg Sandford of Portsmouth, Rhode Island, who exported their horses and produce to Barbados, where they were sold by two brothers of his own. The fact that in a trustless age ties of kinship and a common language made it easier to establish and to maintain commercial relations kept New England tethered to Old England despite its merchants' utter disrespect for the Navigation Acts; the colonies depended on the goodwill of a small group of Londoners for their supplies of manufactured goods.

Three towns only, all in Massachusetts Bay, were in continuous commercial contact with the metropolis, and of these Charlestown and Salem were far less important than Boston. That port within 30 years had grown to 3,000 people. Into it, foodstuffs, timber and livestock drained from the whole of New England.

The Boston merchants exploited their virtual monopoly greedily. One witness reported that if they did not make 100 per cent profit on their dealings with the settlers in Maine they would 'cry out' that they were 'losers'. The fishermen there, who bought cloth from them at three times the price it commanded in England, and who relied on them wholly for cables and cordage, anchors, lines, hooks, nets and canvas, fell into a kind of slavery. They would get ruinously drunk on a merchant's wine and, once in his debt, would be at his mercy. The farmers of Rhode Island were also resentful; the colony's General Court complained in 1658 that the Bostoners could 'make the prices, both of our commodities, and their own also, because wee have not English coyne . . .' This same shortage of currency meant that the Bostoners anxious to expand could only do so by getting increasing control over valuable natural resources. They looked for timber inland and established sawmills. They raised horses and sheep themselves instead of relying on small farmers. They built ships for themselves to save freight charges, and to earn carriage fees. Avid for real estate, they acquired properties piecemeal; they purchased land from natives, they foreclosed on debtors, and they obtained grants from colonial governments. And they speculated in land, acquiring blocks of wilderness in New Hampshire, Maine or western Massachusetts for the sake of timber or possible furs, or in the hope that it would increase in value as settlement expanded.

New England life was losing its quasi-egalitarian character. In 1658 Massachusetts introduced a property qualification for voters. In Plymouth ten years later the qualification was set at £20 rateable estate. Connecticut, by the Restoration, had introduced a higher one, £30, for full citizenship. From 1657 till his death in 1679, this colony had as its governor the ingenious John Winthrop Jr. After Charles II's return, the status of the lesser New England colonies was problematical. Connecticut had only scant legal basis, New Haven no basis at all. Boundary disputes would rankle on for decades.

Hence the need to sort out New England squabbles on the spot provided an effective cover, in 1664, for an expedition aimed at the unsuspecting New Amsterdam Dutch. Three Commissioners for New England went with the conquering force, with the aim of bringing the area for the first time effectively under royal government. They were civilly received in the lesser colonies, but when they presented their credentials in Boston the Massachusetts General Court stonily declared their commission invalid, since the authority which it conveyed conflicted with that of the Massachusetts charter which the King had renewed three years before.

The capture of New Netherland was a far easier matter than the taming of Massachusetts. The town itself housed 1,500 people in 1664, but the whole colony had a white population only one-fifth of New England's. It was a polyglot arena. Besides Dutch, French and Portuguese, and Jews, there were the remnants, digested in 1655, of an abortive Swedish colony on the Delaware which had in fact been mostly composed of Finns. From the 1630s, English people had been settling Long Island, and Peter Stuyvesant, the famous governor who arrived in 1647, had had much trouble with their characteristic demand for an elective assembly. The Dutch had settled land long claimed by England. Charles II presented his brother with the whole region from the

Connecticut to the Delaware (and also with a vast tract of Maine) before sending the expedition under Richard Nicolls. Only a handful of people were killed in the swift conquest.

For the first time Englishmen were faced with the problem of ruling alien colonists. Nicolls, now governor, followed generous policies. All who would swear allegiance to Charles were promised denizenship, religious freedom was given to Dutch Reformed and Lutheran settlers. Only a few colonists left, and even the ousted Governor Stuyvesant, after a trip to Holland to clear the record, came back in 1667 and lived in 'New York' until his death. No elective assembly was set up. The Dutch Reformed Church remained the most influential denomination in the colony for a long time after the conquest, and the upper Hudson River settlements stayed Dutch in language, custom and law for many years. In 'New Netherland', land had been granted free of quitrents. Fresh colonists from England and New England would hardly be happy to live side by side with the old settlers whose grants were now confirmed if they themselves were asked to pay quitrents. Hence the quitrent in 'New York' was no more than a formality. James, Duke of York, could extract scant pickings from his vast colony, and his interest in it must have been primarily political rather than economic. Indeed, even before Nicolls reached New Amsterdam, James had been granted away for a nominal consideration the whole area which became New Jersey.

The beneficiaries of this largess were Sir George Carteret and John, Lord Berkeley (the latter a brother of the governor of Virginia). Carteret had seized and held the Channel Island of Jersey during the civil war, and had given Charles II shelter there: hence the territory's chosen name. The two proprietors sent out a governor in 1665. By 1668 the new colony had a general assembly. Two years later, a demand for quitrent sent settlers into open rebellion. New Jersey life was largely shaped from the outset by truculent men from New England, who introduced the town meeting style of local government.

Barbadians had taken the initiative in the projecting of another proprietary colony far to the south in 'Carolina'. There was no idea in this case of any significant shipment of colonists from the mother country. Overspill from existing settlements was expected to provide planters.

By the 1650s the coastline between the Chesapeake and Florida had attracted Virginians, percolating southwards. In the early 1660s, New Englanders set up an outpost near the mouth of the Cape Fear River. But the prime mover in proposals for a new proprietorship was Sir John Colleton, a Royalist planter from Barbados who came home at the Restoration. In 1663, Charles granted the area to a powerful eight-man consortium, which included the Earls of Clarendon, Albemarle and Craven, and Sir Anthony Ashley Cooper, not yet Earl of Shaftesbury, besides Carteret, Colleton and the two Berkeley brothers.

The avarice of the proprietors was their undoing. They demanded ½d. an acre rent, and that 20,000 acres should be reserved for them in every settlement undertaken. In return, they were not prepared to spend much. Development in northern Carolina was very halting. Barbadian adventurers were more attracted by areas further south, where they set up a colony on the Cape Fear River. By 1666, 'Charles Town' was said to have 800 people, but settlers were soon restive. Because much of the land was swampy and sandy, settlements were dangerously scattered along some sixty miles of the river. The local Indians were aggressive. By the autumn of 1667 the colony was abandoned.

The future Earl of Shaftesbury now gave a lead, with the help of his assistant, later famous, John Locke. In 1669, the proprietors agreed that each would contribute £500 to a fund to found a settlement in the 'Port Royal' area south of Cape Fear. The proprietors planned to reserve a fifth of the land to provide seignories for themselves, while another fifth would give baronies to a hereditary aristocracy. Locke helped Shaftesbury draw up 'Fundamental Constitutions' which were as outlandish as they were ineffectual. The noblemen were to be called 'landgraves' and, using the Spanish word for Indian chieftains, *caciques*. The aim was to attract rich men to the colony by the promise of great acreages, honour and power.

The colonists who reached the coast in 1670 built a new 'Charles Town' at a site which they called Albemarle Point. Fresh settlers came from the West Indies. Since access to waterways was so crucial to planters, the colonists ignored the proprietors' orderly plan of settlement in squares of 12,000 acres each, 40 such to constitute a country; they followed instead the natural highways, the Ashley and Cooper Rivers, and yet a third 'Charles Town', later to be the remarkable, sinful city of Charleston, grew up where the two rivers converged. (The name was transferred to it in 1680.) Meanwhile South Carolina colonists struggled to find an economic future. The hoped-for Mediterranean staples did not flourish. The Chesapeake settlements, in times of glut, provided too much competition for a new tobacco colony.

X

In the mid-1670s 'King Philip's war' in New England and 'Bacon's Rebellion' in Virginia marked, after two generations of relative peace, a crisis in the relations between red men and white in North America.

To begin with, then, the English did not displace Indians, they moved in among them. In southern New England the Indian population, of about 20,000, was little if at all lower in 1675 than it had been at the beginning of the century. But by now there were about two Europeans for every one Indian.

So colonists lived everywhere close to Indian neighbours – and intermarriage was not uncommon. From Maine southwards to the upper part of Carolina the Indians of the coastal plain all belonged to the linguistic family of Algonquians and Siouans. Despite Winthrop's convenient notion that they were nomads, almost all tribes lived in villages. Seasonal migration was part of the way of life; in summer Indians might live near the planted fields while in winter they would find a more protected site and in spring they would camp to fish near the falls of a river. But each tribe occupied territory with clearly understood boundaries. The fields and garden plots belonged to particular families and groups, and the rest was common hunting ground. However, land was not 'owned' as the English thought of ownership. It was occupied under a temporary arrangement that might be altered whenever conditions warranted a change. Here was immense scope for interracial misunderstanding, and a basis for the myth of Indian dishonesty.

As, from the 1650s, the English settled south of Virginia, they came into contact with a variety of language families. The south-eastern Indians depended still more on agriculture than the Algonquians, and their political organisation was generally stronger. There were numerous confederacies, some under absolute rulers. The largest tribe, the Cherokees, gathered some 20,000 people in 60 towns, while to the south of them the Creek confederacy numbered some 50 towns. These peoples, with the Choctaws, Chickasaws and Seminoles, would become the 'Five Civilised Tribes' of the early nineteenth century, demonstrating that Indians could adapt in the face of the challenge of European culture. But in the early days, there was almost no contact between the world-views of Indians and of whites. Each to the other seemed unpredictable; each thought the other profoundly treacherous. To most whites, Indians seemed obviously and intrinsically 'savage'.

Just as the Irish, as wandering herdsmen, were self-evidently barbaric, so the Indians as huntsmen were wicked wasters of the land which they traversed. John Locke was the most distinguished exponent of the idea that hunters might justly be forced to alter their economy by an agricultural people. And in a most revealing way, the conversion of the Indians to Christianity was seen as somehow inseparable from their conversion to European dress and agriculture. The most famous missionaries to figure in the sparse annals of English efforts towards conversion – Father White and the Reverend John Eliot – both identified change of dress with change of heart. White referred to 'Christian apparrell'.

When in 1618 the Virginia Company set aside 10,000 acres to support a 'University and College' for training Indian children in 'true Religion moral virtue and Civility', large sums were raised from charity. But nothing came of the idea. Nor did the English Jesuits get very far in Maryland. White lived with an Indian 'Emperor', cured him of disease, and accepted his grateful conversion. 'The Emperor', as the Jesuits proudly reported, 'has exchanged the skins, with which he was heretofore clothed, for a garment made in our fashion.' White later converted the principal men of another village and by 1642, after eight years, the mission was reporting quite considerable successes. But in the religious and political confusion of the mid-seventeenth century, this effort petered out.

The Reverend John Eliot in New England was, along with certain neighbours, the only English missionary in the New World to get the steady and relatively heavy support from England which was essential to success (and which Canadian priests had from France). In the charter of the Massachusetts Bay Company, the conversion of the natives was proclaimed to be the 'principall ende of this Plantacion' and the colony's seal displayed a native with a label issuing from his mouth, 'COME OVER AND HELP US'. But New England puritanism was as ill-adapted to missionary work as any religion could be. Because of the Puritan insistence on rigorous preparation for church membership, long years of labour would be required to bring the natives up to standard. Quick conversions would be as undesirable as forced baptism. Beyond all this, Puritans shared a scorn of the Indians. Calvinism held that even those who had never seen a Bible and had no chance to hear the gospel preached were damned, just as surely as any saint was saved.

The first Indian convert seems to have been made by Thomas Mayhew Jr, son of the owner of the island of Martha's Vineyard, in 1643. By 1652 the Mayhews had nearly three hundred professed converts and had opened a school. But Eliot, rather than either Mayhew, became the hero of the hagiographers, because he was just the man whom Massachusetts colony found ready to hand at a tricky political moment when it was potentially at odds with both the Presbyterian and Independent factions in the English Parliament. The charter was vulnerable, hence the colony's rulers were sensitive to the charge that its 'principall ende' had been neglected.

Eliot, minister at Roxbury, aptly so named in its rocky neighbourhood, emerges from the accounts of those who knew him as a 'cheerfull', friendly, selfless but rather sententious man. In 1646, when he was forty-two, he began to preach to the Indians at their nearest village in their own language. He won friendship by handing apples and cake to the children, tobacco to the men. News of his work was before long published in England and the Rump Parliament, in 1649, chartered the 'Society for the Promoting and Propagating the Gospel of Jesus Christ in New England' ('New England Company'). Its members were chiefly wealthy Puritan merchants. Every parish minister in England and Wales was obliged to make a house-to-house canvas for funds. Remarkable sums flowed in; by 1660 nearly £16,000 had been contributed.

Eliot's programme was an expensive one. He wanted to get the Indians to live in settled townships, to farm in a European way with English tools, to use European clothes and to learn in European-type schools. At Natick, eighteen miles south-west of Boston, he built up a village, from 1650, where he organised his 'Praying Indians' into a little scriptural commonwealth, with a constitution based on the eighteenth chapter of Exodus, under which they elected rulers of tens and of fifties. Eliot himself preached at the meeting house there fortnightly while remaining minister at Roxbury. So rigorous were the tests applied that Indians were not allowed to form their own church until 1660. Meanwhile, however, Eliot found so few whites to join him in the work of conversion that he had to use Indian assistants. An 'Indian College' was built as part of Harvard to house Indians who would train as ministers. But students were hard to find. Only one actually graduated, Caleb Chesschanmuk, in 1665; he died of tuberculosis next year. The Indian college was pulled down in 1698. However, a handpress in the building produced Eliot's most remarkable legacy, his MAMUSSE WUNNEETUPANATAMWE UP-BIBLUM GOD, a translation of the Bible into Algonquian which he completed in 1658. This was the first Bible printed in any language on the American continent, and was followed by a stream of other devotional works and primers for Indians.

Eliot would refer to Daniel Gookin, lay superintendent of the Praying Indians from 1661, as his 'only cordial assistant'. However, by 1674 there were seven 'old' Praying Indian townships in Massachusetts, while nine more 'new' ones had recently been founded in the Nipmuc country to the west, fifty to seventy miles from Boston and far beyond the then frontier. Altogether Gookin could claim some 1,100 Praying Indians in Massachusetts, besides several hundred more in Plymouth Colony and the Christian Indians of Martha's Vineyard and Nantucket. Each soul had cost something like £10 to win; the Catholic missionaries in Canada had won far more souls far more cheaply.

The price which the Indians paid for conversion is indicated by the humiliating terms of a loyalty oath imposed on red Christians along Cape Cod at around this time. 'Forasmuch as the English and wee, the poor Indians, are of one blood, as Acts 17th, 26, for wee doe confesse wee poor Indians in our lives were as captives under Sathan and our sachems, doeing their wills whose breath perisheth, as Psalmes 146.3.4; Exodus 15,1,2 &c . . . and besides, wee were like unto woulves and lyons, to destroy one another . . . therefore wee desire to enter into covenant with the English respecting our fidelities, as Isai; 11.6.'

Indians settled under white magistrates and dependent on supplies of English goods had lost all basis for pride and independence. To convert Indians, in English eyes, must be to 'civilise' them. To 'civilise' them was in effect to destroy them. Any Indian who sincerely converted must live with a view of himself as a Christian being only on probation and by sufferance. The Indians at Natick in the mid-1680s said that they preferred their (white) preacher to use English rather than their own language, because English people then came to hear him and this made the occasion more respectable.

To be English was to want to sell woollen cloth. It had long been urged as a motive for colonies that Indians could be brought to want woollens though they produced none themselves. And as Indians lost their hunting grounds and the fur trade decimated the animal population, to wear 'Christian apparrell' would in fact become almost essential. Meanwhile, to be Indian was to be ready to trade furs. The Indian had to. If he refused, his Indian enemies would get the guns and destroy him. Guns anyway made hunting easier, which in turn made it easier to supply white men with furs in exchange for more guns.

Supplies near the coast were running out, and tribes there could only retain economic independence as middlemen in the trade with the interior or by seizing in warfare a new hunting ground. But those who did remain in the fur trade became captives rather than partners. They specialised as hunters, forsaking other aptitudes, swiftly destroying their own means of subsistence. Unused to alcohol, Indians had no social conditioning to control its use and easily became utter drunkards. 'If they are heated with Liquors they are restless till they have enough to sleep; that is their cry, "Some more, and I will go to sleep . . ."'

But the fur trade alone would not have destroyed the Algonquians. Advancing white settlement was a more dangerous enemy, leaving pathetic scraps of once confident tribes in its wake. By the late 1640s Virginia, after its second Indian rising, was clearly moving towards the invention of the 'reservation', which would remain over three centuries the white man's only answer to the 'Indian problem', save genocide. The colony passed laws to protect the Indians and to define mutual responsibilities. From 1656 it was laid down that Indians must not be treated as slaves; from 1662 the great man of each Indian township was made answerable for the misdeeds of his people, who had the right to gather seafood, berries and fruits outside the bounds allotted to them by law only if they acquired a licence from two justices.

In Virginia, the date of the 1622 massacre was annually commemorated to remind people of the need for vigilance, and emigrants at mid-century were advised that a complete suit of light armour was necessary. Every settlement in New England came to have its garrison house, or houses, with walls that could stop arrows and unusually heavy doors, where people could resort in times of danger. From the 1640s onwards there were nearly two generations of general peace on the frontier. In New England, terrible conflict at last exploded just when the region's furs were virtually exhausted. The Indians now had no economic role to play in the colonies' development. 'King Philip' preferred a desperate, doomed attempt to drive the whites into the sea, over the prospect of slow extinction.

The long peace between Plymouth Colony and the Wampanoag Indians had endured without fatal strain till the death of the ancient sachem Massasoit in 1661. Before he died, he had asked the General Court of Plymouth to give English names to his two eldest sons. They thought of the two kings of Macedonia. Wamsutta became Alexander and his younger brother Metacom was named Philip. Alexander had to struggle to exert his authority over tribesmen who were increasingly restive about white encroachment. His truculent postures made the authorities over-react. They seized him and took him to Plymouth. On his return to his own people, he died – some Indians said of bitterness, others blamed white man's poison. Philip, succeeding him, nursed a deadly grievance. For thirteen years he kept the settlers on edge with rumours of war, till conflagration broke out in 1675.

The spark was the murder of a 'Praying Indian' named Sassamon, who had attended Harvard but had later served Philip as an adviser. Three Indians were hanged for his murder. Philip's people did not see how the white men had a right to try Indians for crimes against other Indians. On June 20, a group of young Wampanoags rampaged into the township of Swansea, shooting cattle and ransacking houses, but it was an English youth who spilt the first blood three days later, provoking Wampanoag retaliation.

Plymouth called other colonies to help. Philip and his people lived in the Mount Hope Peninsula, where swift action could have bottled them up. But the colonists let him escape and he found his way to the country of the Nipmucks in western Massachusetts. Heartened by Philip's example, they joined in. The townships of the Connecticut Valley were ravaged.

This was now, on both sides, a war aimed at extermination, as in September when Indians trapped a provision train and killed 68 colonists with it. Philip's lead was followed by some – but not all – of the New England tribes. The colonists, rightly, doubted that the Narragansetts would stay neutral. The tribe had gathered on a fortified island. On a Sunday, of all days, white troops moved in to massacre them, men, women and children. The 'Great Swamp Fight', in bitter December weather, also killed perhaps a fifth of the English involved, by exposure as well as by native arrows.

The Indians responded in kind. Town after town was burnt. Of the 90 white settlements in New England, 52 were attacked and more than a dozen almost completely destroyed. Providence was burnt in March and Roger Williams, now over seventy, limping, was one of twenty-seven men who 'stay'd & not went away' and painfully rebuilt the town. His forty years of conciliation had failed.

Like the Gaels of Scotland, Indian tribes aimed in warfare at plunder and at immediate gain. They rested between raids. They could not sustain a long campaign. By the spring, braves hiding out far from their homelands were leaving the war parties to look for places where they could fish or grow corn. Philip was driven from his winter camp near Albany by hostile Mohawks, and, as through the summer his allies were wasted by slaughter and by defection, he fatalistically trekked back to his homeland at Mount Hope. Here in August he was tracked and shot.

Philip's skull stared for decades from the spike where it was stuck in Plymouth. His people were sold into slavery, mostly in the West Indies. Groups of Indians who had not joined him, and had put themselves under the protection of the colonial authorities, were packed off to be sold as slaves in Tangier. 'This useage of them is worse than death', was the horrified comment of John Eliot, who now had to begin all over again, with only four 'Praying' townships surviving.

Roger Williams, like other pioneers, had long been lamenting the way things had been going. 'Sir,' he had written to the younger John Winthrop in 1664, 'I fear that the common Trinity of the world, (Profit, Preferment, Pleasure) will here be the *Tria omnia*, as in all the world beside: . . . that God Land will be (as now it is) as great a God with us English as God Gold was with the Spaniards.'

The Wampanoag lands were now open to white settlement. Their sales helped to finance a new meeting house in Plymouth.

The colonies estimated their total war expenses at over £100,000. Thousands of whites were killed. Many others were maimed or crippled. But the God Land rewarded his devotees. Men had been encouraged to enlist in the militia with the promise of land afterwards. They had fought for land. Those who survived got land. An economic boom followed in the decade after the war.

The North American mind was permanently affected. It was all very well for ministers to explain that war was God's judgment on New England for its backsliding (Eliot ascribed divine wrath to the new fashion of wearing wigs). The lesson which people insisted on learning was that the only good Indian was a dead one.

In Virginia, godly principle had always offered less obstruction to racialism. News of 'King Philip's War', reaching the southern colonies, swiftly convinced people that there was a general conspiracy of Indians all along the frontier. Nat Bacon's Rebellion followed.

XI

After Virginia had suppressed Opechancanough's rising, in 1646, the assembly had voted to build four forts inland which became posts from which fur traders sent expeditions deep into the interior. The treaty of 1646 which had promised Indians land and hunting grounds north of the York River had soon been violated, as tobacco farmers pressed impatiently on.

Tobacco insisted on fresh land, and then on more fresh land. It quickly exhausted the soil it grew on. After the third crop, planters replaced it with maize or wheat. Then they let the land grow up again in underwood. Few men bothered to pen their cattle so as to fertilise weary soil, and the value of the vast beds of marl found in the colony was not recognised until the mid-eighteenth century. Cultivation became habitually reckless and wasteful simply because so much land was available.

Livestock had their important place in a modest way of life which centred on tobacco, cattle and work. Pork was the staple meat, and pigs rooted for themselves in the woods until hog-killing time in the autumn. The slowness with which ploughs came into use was an index to the character of the whole way of life. There was little call for them. As forest was cleared, stumps were left in the ground which would have held up a plough. By the time these had rotted, the ground had been exhausted and abandoned. Tobacco was mistress; tobacco didn't linger. Legislation demanded that each farmer must cultivate a certain acreage of maize and wheat, and Virginia did not fall like Barbados into reliance on imported food. But no substitute for tobacco as a cash crop proved acceptable.

Tobacco was the effective currency. Virtually all accounts were carried on the books till the tobacco crop had been cured. Then they all fell due at once, and payment was largely a matter of book-keeping transactions. A fresh immigrant had to plant tobacco to pay his way. A poor farmer had to sell tobacco to live.

Tobacco was first planted in sheltered beds in the woods about mid-January, then transplanted to the fields, usually early in May. It required watchful care. Cut as soon as it was ripe, it was stored in large barns, up to 60 feet long. Fire was not yet used to hasten the curing, which was left to the air itself and took five or six weeks. When the leaves had been taken down, stripped from their stalks, and assorted according to grade and quality, the tobacco was packed into casks which ran up to 1,000 lb. in weight. Most tobacco was delivered to receivers acting on behalf of merchants to whom the planter was already indebted. Some planters, the best placed, themselves acted as merchants, distributing imported goods and taking crops in payment. Special ships were built to carry as much tobacco as possible, with huge holds and tiny cabins. The largest might take 600 casks, or 300,000 lb. Grumbling planters were at the shipowners' mercy. The selfishness of English merchants would be their partial undoing: Glasgow men, willing to give better prices, were infiltrating before the close of the century.

Smuggling, largely through Scottish ships, was endemic. Virginia itself taxed tobacco, imposing an export duty of 2s. per hogshead from 1658 to supplement the colony's poll tax. The duties in England were very heavy. With the planter selling tobacco for as little as 2d. a lb., temptation, for him as well as for merchants, was irresistible.

Berkeley, chosen as governor again by the Assembly in 1659, ruled as a planter among planters. Titular aristocrats were absent, but the wealthy man, as in the West Indies, would acquire the dignified name of 'Colonel' from his command in the militia. The governor's personal clique, by the 1660s, formed the 'Council'. In the colony's bicameral legislature this corresponded to the House of Lords, as the House of Burgesses matched the House of Commons. By contrast with New England, Virginia at this time showed little or no common purpose or idealistic public spirit. It produced a political tradition which emphasised individual liberty, and an economic one characterised by prodigal, heedless waste. Neither showed the least charity for the Indians or for their way of life.

Though the Susquehannock Indians had long been allies of Maryland, guarding the colony's northern approaches, their lands were encroached on as tobacco expanded. In 1674 the Maryland English abandoned the Susquehannock and made peace with the Seneca, who were traditional enemies of both. The Susquehannock fell back to the north bank of the Potomac river. Their presence stirred up the Indians in that area; overcrowding led to shortage of food, and thence to raids on the colonists. In 1675 a planter in Northumberland County, Virginia, was murdered by a party of Doeg Indians. The county militia rode furiously into Maryland after the Doegs. A Doeg chief and ten of his people were pistolled to death, but another white party, blinded with rage and fear, fell upon some Susquehannocks and had slaughtered fourteen before an Indian ran up to the colonel and 'with both hands Shook him (friendly) by one Arm Saying *Susquehanougs Netoughs i.e.* Susquehanaugh friends, and fled. Whereupon he ran amongst his Men, Crying out, "For the Lords sake Shoot no more, these are our Friends the Susquehanoughs."'

Friends no longer. The Susquehannocks rose and fought, and the combined militias of two colonies could not contain them. They fell on Virginia's frontier plantations. Governor Berkeley ordered a punitive expedition but then, for reasons not clear, retracted the decision and persuaded the assembly to settle for a defence. His refusal to yield to popular pressure as the Indians burnt and slew as far south as the James set a spark to discontent over a complex of other grievances.

Berkeley's personal clique, over his long years in office, had grabbed much of the best land as well as the most lucrative offices. Leading fur traders were closely identified with him and he was not immune to the charge that he was holding back reprisals against the Indians in his friends' interests. Nathaniel Bacon, emerging as leader of the malcontents, exclaimed, 'these traders at the head of the rivers buy and sell our blood.'

Bacon had been less than two years in the colony. His father was a wealthy Suffolk squire who had packed him off to Virginia with the colossal nest egg of £1,800 after his shocking behaviour had caused scandal in England. As a cousin of Lady Berkeley's, he had promptly acquired a seat on the Council, but the governor had proved unamenable to his joint bid, with William Byrd, for a monopoly of trade with the Indians. Still in his twenties, Bacon was clearly unstable, if not actually mad, a man of 'ominous, pensive, melancholly Aspect . . . despising the wisest of his neighbours for their Ignorance, and very ambitious and arrogant.'

In the spring of 1676, Bacon accepted command of a vigilante group which aimed to force the governor's hand. It moved against the Pamunkey Indians, whom Berkeley rightly regarded as faithful allies. The governor denounced this as rebellion and tried to propitiate the populace. The franchise had been restricted in 1670 to freeholders only; now Berkeley issued writs for a new assembly for which all freemen would have the vote. Bacon, after indiscriminate slaughter of friendly Indians in the forest, came out, gained election to this new assembly, submitted to Berkeley, was given back his seat on the Council and, probably, was promised command in the war against the Indians.

Then, while assemblymen tried to appease their poorer constituents' grievances by a string of populist Acts, Nat Bacon flounced out of Jamestown. Back home in the upper parts of the colony, people learnt that he had not yet got his commission as leader against the red men. A party of armed men followed him back to town. The scenes which followed anticipated both Grand Opera and the Hollywood Western. The rebel confronts the governor. Old Berkeley bares his bosom, urging his men to shoot him if he ever gives a commission to such a rebel as Bacon, then offers to measure swords with his young adversary and to settle their quarrel by single combat. 'God damne my Blood,' swears Bacon, 'I came for a commission, and a commission I will have before I goe.'

Berkeley had to give way to armed force. Next day Bacon, commission in hand, was off to shoot more innocent Indians. However, just as he was ready to move, word came that Berkeley had again proclaimed him a rebel. He turned back to settle the matter. But Berkeley had failed to get support. According to one, as it were, savoury account, when the governor summoned up the militia of Gloucester and Middlesex counties, there 'arose a Murmuring before his face "Bacon Bacon Bacon" and all Walked out of the field, Muttering as they went "Bacon Bacon Bacon" . . .' The governor fled to the eastern shore of the Chesapeake. Bacon, now master of most of Virginia, bound people to follow him by oath, and unleashed them to loot his opponents' estates. Berkeley, returning, likewise offered plunder as bait for support. Bacon left off his rather indecisive operations against the hapless Pamunkeys, and marched in to capture Jamestown, which he burnt, church, statehouse and all. After this last wild gesture he died of 'a Bloody Flux'. His lieutenant soon submitted to Berkeley and the rebellion ended many weeks before troops arrived from England, in January 1677.

Confronted by over 1,000 soldiers, with Colonel Jeffreys, new governor-designate, at their head, Berkeley still displayed his inveterate tetchiness, and sailed off to die in England after insulting his replacement. The rebellion, his personal disaster, had been a cataclysm for the Virginian Indians. Some tribes were completely extinguished.

As for the planters, Bacon's episode was no more than a somewhat extreme symptom of the frontier condition of life. Everywhere, even in parts of New England, colonists in the New World were undisciplined and always hard to rule. This was, after all, the heyday of a sort of men who took to extremes the democratical tendencies of the frontier – the 'buccaneers' of the Caribbean.

XII

'Privateering', 'buccaneering' and 'piracy' are three shades in a continuous spectrum. 'Privateering' was legal. 'Buccaneering' became so for a while in the Caribbean. The 'buccaneers' were a cosmopolitan, rootless body of men. It is characteristic that the classic account of their doings should have been written by one Exquemelin, who sailed with them, of whose nationality no one is certain. Was he French, Flemish, Dutch, a Breton? Like those English who settled on French islands, those Dutch who traded with all comers, in their pursuit of fortune they did not mind whom they served or pillaged. Their shifting communities absorbed shipwrecked sailors, runaway servants, deserting soldiers, escaped criminals. Though the bulk seem to have been 'English' or 'French', two of Exquemelin's minor heroes are the always-unlucky 'Bartolomeo el Portugues' and 'Rock the Brazilian', who was in fact a Dutchman born in Groningen.

The word 'buccaneer' derives from a Brazilian Indian name for the wooden gridiron on which strips of meat were broiled. On Hispaniola, towards the mid-seventeenth century, a body of men gathered who lived by hunting the great herds of pigs and cattle descended from those escaped from Spanish settlements. They sold the hides and smoked meat to planters or passing ships. As the herds declined, more and more men took to piracy. Then, as the century wore on, English and French governments sought their service. The 1660s were their heyday.

Though famous leaders arose – Henry Morgan, most celebrated Welshman of his time; a Dutchman, Scot or Englishman named Mansfield; an especially cruel Frenchman nicknamed 'L'Ollonais' – the buccaneers remained essentially anarchists recognising only their own code. They had their say in the destination of a raid and in the share which the leader was to get. They agreed in advance on rewards for those wounded; the loss of an arm to strike with would, for instance, be repaid with six hundred pieces of eight or six slaves; a mere eye earned only a hundred, or one slave. The remaining spoil would be shared equally. As Exquemelin said, they 'only cared to fight for booty', but in its pursuit they were as brave, perhaps, as any soldiers ever have been.

Many of them found a patron in Colonel Thomas Modyford, representative Englishman of this phase of frontier history, who went to Jamaica as governor in 1664, from Barbados, where his pragmatism had prospered in the sugar boom. He was, in effect, a Hobbesian, game for any device which worked. He welcomed the immigration of Jews. He would have been happy to see Dutchmen planting on his sparsely settled island. He ruled for seven years as an independent autocrat, disregarding instructions from home and summoning only one assembly. Meanwhile, the island throve as a base for buccaneers, who sacked scores of ill-defended Spanish towns and villages around the main, some of them over and over again.

The Spaniards still wanted Jamaica back. For the moment there was no strong English naval or military presence in the Caribbean. In 1657, Governor d'Oyley had invited the buccaneers to transfer their base from Hispaniola to Jamaica. The freebooters, some 1,500 strong, were Jamaica's only defence. When the second Dutch War broke out in the mid-1660s, there was really no alternative to using them. A force was sent out to capture the Dutch islands of St Eustatius and Saba, and was then called to help St Kitts, where the French had attacked their English neighbours. Finding little enthusiasm among them for attacking the Dutch, Modyford concluded that he must give them letters of marque against the Spaniards. He was able to get the tacit permission of the English government. For five years or so Harry Morgan hammered the Spaniards as he pleased.

Morgan, born about 1635, came from a substantial South Wales family. One uncle had returned from mercenary service in Europe to soldier as a Cromwellian general; another, Edward, had been Charles I's commander in

South Wales and after the Restoration was made lieutenant-governor of Jamaica, where young Harry had settled as a member of the English invading force and was becoming a major planter as well as the buccaneers' favourite leader. Under Modyford, Morgan became the right arm of English rule in Jamaica. He was given a free hand, and his followers paid themselves in plunder. Modyford put up excuses and took his cut, while the King received his fifteenth and James, Duke of York, Lord High Admiral, his tenth of all the rich booty taken.

In 1668, Morgan raided Cuba, then struck at Porto Bello on the Isthmus, with a force of 460 buccaneers. Only eighteen buccaneers lost their lives. The booty worked out at £60 per man. The pickings would never be quite so rich again. An assault on Maracaibo next year gave only half as much profit per head.

Morgan's commission was against Spanish shipping; it did not license him to land and to sack Spanish towns. The outraged Spanish authorities proclaimed war in retaliation against all English south of the Tropic of Cancer. Modyford now had to commission Morgan as admiral and commander-in-chief to fight the Spaniards on land and sea. Ironically, in the same year, 1670, negotiations in Europe produced the Treaty of Madrid by which Spain at last conceded to the English a right to exist in the New World. There had long been hopes of a peaceful trade with the Spanish possessions. Now the way seemed open. Modyford was ordered to suppress privateers. But Morgan had already sailed, for his most remarkable exploit, the sack of Panama, with a force of thirty-seven ships and several smaller vessels.

He took 1,200 men on a gruelling march across the Isthmus where they routed in pitched battle a Spanish army which was picturesquely but ineffectually reinforced with two herds of wild bulls, and captured the city in a couple of hours. 'Whenever a beautiful prisoner was brought in,' Morgan 'at once sought to dishonour her.' But the Spaniards, forewarned, had shipped off most of their treasure. Profits were smaller than hoped, only £50 a head, and Morgan's career of grand larceny ended in bitter arguments over shares with his men.

The buccaneers had two uses for money: drink, and women. Their hauls poured straight into the hands of the traders of the town of Port Royal, which duly flourished like the green bay tree. Exquemelin reported of his companions on Jamaica, 'They are busy dicing, whoring and drinking so long as they have anything to spend . . .' Yet the buccaneers served cold-sober political strategies. Besides helping Spain's rivals force doors in the Caribbean still wider, they put into circulation lots of that scarce commodity, ready money. And Morgan was greatly admired in England.

However, the English government was now on friendly terms with Spain, and gestures had to be made. Modyford was recalled in 1671 and spent two years in the Tower. Morgan was soon after shipped home, though he was not imprisoned. After the new governor, Sir Thomas Lynch, had offered the buccaneers a pardon and land, Morgan, who must have had charm, was sent back by the King with a knighthood and the office of lieutenant-governor. Modyford also returned, as chief justice. In 1680 a further treaty with Spain was signed at Windsor, and thereafter even Morgan seems to have worked to repress privateering in the interests of trade with the Spanish colonies. The end of his career as public servant, if that was ever the right name for him, came in 1682 when he and his clique were pushed out of office by Lynch, returning for a second term. In his early fifties, he died six years later, sallow, pot-bellied, 'much given to drinking . . .'

Since Spain refused to recognise their rights of possession, the French authorities went on employing buccaneers long after the English had stopped. But by the end of the century, all 'official' buccaneering was over. Piracy remained, preying impartially on ships of all nations without any gloss of legality whatsoever.

The buccaneers had furthered, rather than held back, Jamaica's development. The real check was shortage of slaves. The Royal African Company could not meet Jamaican demands. On an island with many wild acres, and an established colony of fugitive maroons, to hold slaves once they were bought was more of a problem than elsewhere in the English Caribbean. Between 1673 and 1694 there were six sizeable slave revolts on the island. But Port Royal, thanks in great part to the buccaneers, was an impressive town in 1692, with perhaps 10,000 people, the largest English settlement in the New World. It had hundreds of four-storeyed brick buildings and rents were said to be as high as in central London. Then, on an almost cloudless June day, retribution struck. In a couple of minutes of earthquake, most of the town was 'swallowed into the Sea'. Port Royal never really recovered, and Kingston usurped its position. A Sodom had been chastised, though seeing what went on elsewhere in the Caribbean, the Lord was oddly selective in his vengeance.

With Spanish power curtailed and the Dutch increasingly on the defensive, rivalry between France and England was beginning in Charles II's reign to become important. But no power had at this time resources in ships and soldiers to dominate the whole area. The outbreak of war in Europe was followed by a game of general post in which various ill-defended islands changed hands. Then at a peace treaty in Europe whatever had been gained was handed back or swapped.

A typical swap at the Treaty of Breda in 1667 gave the English title to New York in return for handing over Surinam, which from 1652 had attracted thousands of English settlers. But the practical internationalism of this frontier meant that the Dutch did not scruple to call in English craftsmen to help them develop their acquisition. It also made Jews conspicuous all over the Caribbean. In 1680 there was about one Jewish household in Bridgetown for seven English. Their role in Jamaica also became important; by 1693 the council there was complaining, 'the Jews eat us and our children out of all trade.' The Sephardic network of contacts made Jews expert and invaluable in trades legal and illegal.

Thus, Jews led in trade with the Spanish colonies, which was an essential source of bullion, so much sought in that mercantilist age, and greatly needed to provide coinage in the New World. In 1685, English governors were authorised to give it all possible encouragement, so long as the Spaniards themselves inserted nothing which might compete with English manufactures. Trade between English and Dutch colonists went on even when the two countries were formally at war. The Dutch were still ahead of the English in sugar refining and could process the product more cheaply, so they could offer a good sum to the planter and still get sugar at lower prices than those they paid for re-exports from England. St Eustatius ('Statia') in the Leewards was well placed for illicit trade. A Royal Navy officer detailed to enforce the Navigation Acts noted in 1687, 'The Dutch ships generally send their long boats to St Christopher's once or twice a week on pretense of getting water, though one boat load of water would last them a month . . .'

The logwood trade which attracted buccaneers and others to the Central America mainland was another lucrative business which could not be contained within the Acts. Despite its confusing name, 'logwood' was cut in sticks a yard long and two or three inches in diameter from a certain gnarled tree. In Europe, these were ground to powder and used by dyers to give cloth a good base or foundation for other colours, which it made brighter. The wood was readily found on the stretch of shoreline running from the Gulf of Campeche around the Yucatan peninsula and down to the coast inhabited by Moskito Indians in what is now Nicaragua. The discharge of Morgan's privateers stepped up a trade which had gone on casually for decades. By the mid-1670s scores of ships went annually from Jamaica, and hundreds of non-Spaniards, mostly 'English', settled permanently on the coast and perpetuated some of the buccaneer tradition. The English authorities established a form of loose protectorate over the Moskitos.

New Englanders, of course, would not resist a valuable trade which could hardly be policed from Jamaica. They sold the logwood in Holland and France at below the English re-export price. In the 1680s nearly half the ships supplying the English West Indies came from New England, and over half the ships entering and leaving Boston were in the Caribbean trade. They brought in 'refuse fish' for slaves, grain for masters, horses to drive mills and heavy timber to build them, prefabricated frames of houses, and above all oaken shooks to be coopered into hogsheads for sugar and molasses. They made life extremely difficult for the theorists of mercantilism.

To such thinkers sugar was the perfect commodity. 'The Kingdom's Pleasure, Glory and Grandure . . . are all more advanced by that,' wrote Dalby Thomas, 'than by any other Commodity we deal in or produce, Wool not excepted . . .' As the emphasis of mercantilist theory shifted from bullion towards manufacturing industry, the islands, which bought all their manufactured needs, seemed more and more exemplary. The paradox was that they provided infinite scope for evasion of the Navigation Acts, both in letter and in spirit. The planters themselves wanted to trade with the Dutch and sell sugar direct to Europe. They were very hard to govern at all. Vessels carrying vital letters might be lost at sea, and with bad weather or enemy action, ships might take months to get from London to Barbados. And governors sent out with strict instructions to enforce royal authority would find it difficult to resist the arguments, and still more the favours, of wealthy planters.

Apart from an assured market for their sugar in England, what the evolving 'Old Colonial' system offered the planters was military and naval protection. But England, in the seventeenth century, had few or no ships to spare for colonial defence. Regular troops were hardly in better supply. Planters retained the Englishman's suspicion of standing armies and, still more to the point, were furious at the thought of having to pay for one. A hundred or so soldiers stationed on the Leewards in the mid-1670s were said to be 'naked and starving' under the eyes of their French enemies.

The cry of 'no taxation without representation' originated in the West Indies. In 1660, the island council, formerly nominated in England, was made elective in response to colonists' pressure. What was largely at issue in all this was not a precocious passion for democracy, but the fear of a return to effective proprietary rule under the old Carlisle Patent. Hardfaced men who had done well out of the sugar revolution were not unhappy when Charles II, in 1661, announced that he was taking proprietorship himself. When the first royal governor arrived in 1663, they swiftly made a deal with him whereby the proprietary dues and rents were cancelled, they were confirmed in their estates, and they gave in return a 4½ per cent duty on all exports, on the understanding that the moneys accruing to the King would be used to pay the cost of royal government. But this duty, which also applied to the Leewards, was to become a recurrent grievance during the 175 years of its charging.

In theory, the islanders might now have been at the Crown's mercy. In practice, Charles II characteristically diverted the 4½ per cent duty into other purposes than administering colonies, so the governor still had to rely on the Assembly for revenue. This thwarted a serious attempt by Charles to assert his authority in the 1670s. In 1678, the Lords of Trade began their abortive attempt to impose Poynings' Law on Jamaica. The plan was to recast the entire government of the colony, raise revenue without an assembly, and make Jamaica as tame and profitable as Ireland. But in Barbados as well as in Jamaica, the attempt to impose closer control was soon abandoned, in the face of the obstinate facts of distance and of rebellious self-interest.

One rather exceptional governor, Sir William Stapleton, who ruled the Leewards for thirteen years down to 1685, did show a vision transcending his own interests; that is, he was a proficient bully in the wider English interest, though he was, in fact, a Catholic Irishman. His ferocious temper did not impair his popularity in the islands, where rage was no uncommon thing. He bullied the Caribs, mounting two expeditions against their bases. Rather amazingly, he even contrived to persuade the four principal Leewards to send representatives to a common general assembly.

But he could not eradicate the planters' resistance to the idea that all four islands should logically share the same laws and reluctance to share in the cost of military operations which were good for the English power in general. Barbados men were perfectly happy to see their compatriots on the Leewards battered by the French or raided by Caribs, regarding them not as fellows but as competitors. And when the Nevis Assembly was asked to participate in an assault on the Caribs, who had recently ravaged Antigua and Montserrat, they objected on the grounds that their own island had not been troubled by Indians 'these twenty years'. On another, later occasion, the Nevis planters surrendered their stronghold to the French rather than see their canes burnt.

As the Royal African Company found, such men were adept at avoiding payment. Extracting debts from defaulters was often impossible. Coins were in short supply, for a start, and payment in sugar offered scope for fine little tricks as valuations fluctuated. Even where coins were in use, the chronic debtors who manned the island assemblies had a standing temptation to overvalue them, and deliberate clipping, as well as much wear created abundance of 'light' money. The courts were slow, and if their machinery worked at all it favoured debtors. Besides, planters made the laws. On some islands, there were no prisons.

Yet the 'groans' of the plantations, as one writer called them, were constantly relayed to England. When sugar duties were raised in 1685, the planters and their allies set up a shriek till the addition was repealed eight years later. The basis of their despair was merely that after the great sugar boom ended with the 1650s, men who had been getting rich very fast had to be content with getting rich slowly. For muscovado worth perhaps 35s. per hundred lb. in London in 1657, the price fell to 15s. 9d. in 1686. The planter was meanwhile paying his 4½ per cent duty, and slaves were costing more, so his profits shrank quite painfully. Furthermore, Barbados was beginning to confront problems of soil erosion and soil exhaustion which would become more widespread in the next century. Dung was used to revive the soil. '. . . We rake and scrape Dung out of every Corner,' exclaimed the 'groaning' pamphleteer of 1689, Edward Lyttelton. '. . . Hath our dear Mother no *Bowels* for her Children, that are now at the last Gasp, and ly struggling with the pangs of Death?'

This was colonial rhetoric as it would be heard many times thereafter. Men used loud words partly through fear of not being heard far away, while they inflated or even invented 'facts' secure in the knowledge that these could not easily be checked. But the clamour over the 'Impositions' of 1685 showed how absolute a master sugar now was in Barbados. Because investment in plant and in slaves had been so heavy, it was no longer possible to switch swiftly to another crop when prices fell.

There were still thousands of small English freeholders in the West Indies, farming up to a dozen acres with the help of their children, indentured servants and one or two slaves. While great planters dominated in sugar, small men could eke out a living from the minor staples. The Irish on Montserrat still grew much tobacco. Jamaica found a ready market in England for ginger and pimento, dyewoods, preserved fruits; and for cotton. Even after sugar had become the leading product on Jamaica, cotton increased its acreage there, and everywhere in the West Indies cotton now stood second to sugar. By 1690, the Lancashire fustian industry seems to have been drawing about seven-tenths of its ginned raw cotton from the West Indies. Indigo was a crop, yielding a valuable blue dye, which needed quite a lot of equipment and labour, and it was grown on middle-sized plantations; there were three or four score of these in Jamaica in the 1680s. Finally, chocolate was now becoming known and appreciated in England. When the English conquered Jamaica in 1655, they found 'cocoa walks' there, orchards, as it were, of ten or twelve acres. This was the most aesthetically pleasing of staples. The island exported quite large quantities.

But despite the opportunities given to small men by the minor staples and by the demand for provisions, white numbers in the older colonies fell in the third quarter of the seventeenth century. Barbados stabilised at around 20,000 whites, a drop of perhaps a fifth in twenty-odd years. The Leewards by the 1670s had two or three thousand apiece. Disease was not the only determining factor, though yellow fever came in with black slaves, and the islands developed a distinctive local malaise, the 'dry belly ache' or 'dry gripes', from poisoning caused by the distillation of rum in leaden pipes. Colonists were caught up into armies, lost heavily in French raids, or sold out to wealthier men and sought better luck elsewhere. A writer of 1667 claimed that at least 12,000 whites had emigrated from Barbados, 'wormed out of theire small settlements by theire more suttle and greedy neighbours'. While New England provided food and ships for new colonies, Barbados gave men.

Poor men ventured in the abortive colony on St Lucia (1664–7) or set off to seek out plunder in Jamaica. Rich men looking for land for younger sons interested themselves in Carolina and in Antigua, the latter still only one-third settled around 1690. And new black labour far outweighed the trickle of fresh indentured servants. By the end of Charles II's reign, Barbados had reached the ratio of whites to blacks – roughly one to three – which would be maintained there throughout the eighteenth century. On the Leewards, taken as a group, the ratio was still about one to one, but in Jamaica some 15,000 whites were already outnumbered by slaves. The implications deeply worried administrators, who saw the need to maintain a white militia which could overawe and defeat black rebels.

In 1672, with war in the offing, the Jamaica assembly passed a law requiring each planter to keep one white servant for every ten Negroes. Other island assemblies also imposed quotas and efforts were made by the authorities to force and even, in effect, bribe planters to accept servants. Never to much avail. The ratio of blacks to whites overall went on rising.

The stratification of classes on the islands was fixing itself in the repulsive shape it would keep as long as the 'Old Colonial System' endured. The majority were black slaves. 'Above' them, but hardly better off, was a morass of poor whites who, if they retained any energy, went in for fishing, smuggling or piracy. Otherwise they lounged, and drank crude rum till they died and the land crabs nibbled their corpses in the gutters. There was a largish, middling class of white shopkeepers, artisans and petty planters. At the peak of the pyramid were the rich sugar men.

By 1680, on Barbados 175 individuals (one in sixteen of the landholders) owned more than half of the white servants, slaves and acreage. On Jamaica the top men were probably fewer, their holdings bigger. Rich planters came from many sources. Some were ex-Roundhead soldiers, some Royalists. Some came from landed, others from merchant families. Their chief common characteristics were the constitutions which permitted them to survive the white West Indian life-style, and the mentality of the entrepreneur. They found no high culture on the islands, and had no wish to create any. Their most attractive quality might appear to be their religious tolerance, except that it seems on examination to have amounted to no more than acceptance of different styles of laxity. Priestless Catholics planted alongside lapsing Dissenters and nominal Anglicans. Clergymen were few, ill-rewarded, and mostly of poor human quality.

Law was, in effect, the planter's religion. Since there were no surveyors to run the boundaries and conveyancing was rudimentary, titles to land were always extremely uncertain. '. . . Every one is a lawyer in these partes', one St Kitts planter wrote in the 1670s, asking for law books from home. Most colonial assemblymen had no legal training. 'As far as I have observed,' one governor noted, 'the laws of England and the customs or pretended customs of the islands take place by turns, according to the fancy of the judge.' The courts were scenes of brawling disorder, with pleaders and judges often drunk – 'more like a Horse-Fair or a Billingsgate,' Governor Modiford once remarked.

The greatest English historian to have written about the West Indies of that day, Richard Pares, observes that life there 'seems to have been one long quarrel, in which business, law and politics were all mingled.' Jamaica, even in 1690, seems to have had no schools at all. If anything raised the planter's soul somewhat above the earth, it was military or civil ceremony. Great planters paraded as colonels of the militias, and uniforms were in use from the 1680s. Salutes of guns and gluttonous public dinners greeted new governors. Protocol was always a problem; men stood on what they imagined was their dignity.

The cruelty of the laws bearing on slaves has to be set in perspective. In Barbados, by legislation of 1688, a black man who stole as much as a shilling might be executed for the crime, but this was no more than standard English law of the period, when some three hundred crimes were designated felonies, punishable by death. While in England royal pardon would save half or more of the offenders from the gallows, in the West Indies planters were unlikely to execute a creature belonging to one of their fellows without what seemed to them some overwhelming reason. The death rate among slaves must likewise be set against that among the plantocracy. The Price family which became the wealthiest on Jamaica was prolific in children above the average, yet expectation of life in its first three generations in the West Indies seems to have been no more than 24 years; 35 years or so was the general run in England.

These facts allowed, the treatment of blacks must still be seen as exceptionally cruel. Slaves, if not executed, were punished sadistically. Lash wounds were rubbed with melted wax. Half a black's foot might be chopped off; he might be castrated. Most planters seem to have accepted that the best way to make use of the slave who cost them so much was to drive him hard for as long as he could stand. Huts were exiguous and almost unfurnished. Diet was minimal at the best of times. And when profits shrank, the slaves were given still less and were worked harder yet, in dangerous conditions. The groaning planter pamphleteer whose voice we have heard already waxed obtusely eloquent on the wastage of lives. A third of all freshly imported slaves, he suggested, would die before they did any work at all (demoralised, we would now add, in a strange place, and subject to novel diseases and hardships.) 'When they are season'd, and used to the Country, they stand much better. But to how many mischances are they still subject? . . . By many Accidents they are disabled, and become a burden: they will run away, and perhaps be never seen more: or they will hang themselves, no creature knows why.'

Such unaccountable beasts: in some ways it would have been convenient if they had been able to explain themselves better. But to teach them English, or, still more, to convert them to Christianity, was fraught with a fearful risk; property would be transmuted into humanity. A black man made Christian could not be made to work on Sundays. And he would have to be taught in English; the 'Gentlemen Planters' in London, approached on the subject of conversion by the Lords of Trade in 1680, insisted that 'the disproportion of blacks and whites, being great, the whites have no greater security than the diversity of the negroes' languages . . .'

The whites paid the price of their greed in constant fear. The first slave revolt on an English island had occurred on St Kitts as early as 1639, when scores of black men and women had escaped into the woods. As land was cleared, this recourse became impossible on the smaller islands. On Jamaica, flight to the wastelands remained an outlet for rebels. Elsewhere, blacks would have to conspire to seize the whole island. Such conspiracies were rare, and were always betrayed by timorous slaves. Blacks had good cause for fear. The whites had guns and would show no mercy. A conspiracy on Barbados in 1675 was savagely punished, property or no property. Six slaves were burnt alive and eleven beheaded. Eight years after, a black was burnt alive merely for using threatening language. The whites were as vigilant as brandy-soaked men could be, and as the years went on they were more and more cast in the mould made by their own oppression. Only a few stood against the prevailing mores, amongst them Morgan Goldwyn – an Anglican clergyman who, after living on Barbados, published in the 1680s tracts attacking the planters for their fear of baptising their slaves – and also quite a number of Quakers.

Like Anne Hutchinson's 'antinomianism', Quakerism, which extolled the inner light found within each individual, had strong appeal for some men whose economic activities took them beyond the boundaries of what had been acceptable to any church. Numerous prominent planters on Barbados were early converts and there were six Quaker meetings on the island in 1680. Some Quakers were rich; most Quakers owned slaves. Persecution set in almost at once. Some 237 Friends suffered between 1658 and 1695 at the hands of Barbadian authorities who fined and in many cases imprisoned them for refusing to bear arms, to swear oaths, to pay clergymen's dues. The story was similar on Antigua, and in Jamaica, where George Fox, the sect's founder, set up seven meetings. His followers most perversely stood for humane standards. Quaker midwives gave their services free to poor people and even to slaves; as if the islands wanted black babies when strong black men could be bought. In Bridgetown, Barbados, Quakers established a school where poor children were taught gratis. Though George Fox when he preached to slaves on Barbados in 1671 was careful to tell them to remain faithful to their masters, he rounded on the planters there and asked them, 'is not the Gospel to be preached to all creatures? and *are they not Men*? And are they not part of your families?' To no avail; five years later a law was passed against the Quaker practice of having slaves at their meetings. Any slave found at one would be forfeit and half his price would go to the informer. It seems the Quakers had been drawing hundreds of blacks, but they stood to lose their property if they persisted in their principles and their witness in the islands faded from prominence. They now had a large scope for activity elsewhere in the New World.

XIII

Except for the traffic in indentured servants, mostly to the tobacco colonies, emigration from England to America was slack after the Restoration. But in the 1670s a large new wave of migration began. It was aimed chiefly at the middle area of the seaboard between New York and Maryland, and its most obvious element was Quakerism.

The Society of Friends had grown under George Fox's leadership from the 1650s. In its early days it shocked Royalists and orthodox Puritans alike. Its adherents took the logic of Protestant individualism to an extreme, giving women a leading role, with virtual equality, and not hesitating to preach radical doctrines to their servants. The refusal of Quakers to take off their hats before magistrates, and their insistence on using the levelling 'thou' or 'thee' when addressing others of whatever station made them alarming deviants in a status-conscious age.

The roots of Quakerism were chiefly among the lower orders, amid yeoman farmers, husbandmen, artisans, shopkeepers and hired servants, and it had strongholds in the poorest sections of England, the remote west and hilly north. There was also a concentration in the south-east, where London alone was said to have 10,000 Quakers in 1678, but in the great city also, the sect drew from the poorest classes. There were between six and seven hundred families of Quakers in Ireland in the 1680s, largely concentrated in and around Dublin, but also dominating the trade of the great New World-facing port of Cork.

The Quakers in fact swiftly began to spawn immensely successful business communities. They were hardworking, frugal, horrified by idleness, cautious and strictly honest in their dealings; and like other dissenters they were wholly barred from lucrative careers except in trade. By the end of the seventeenth century it could be said, quite correctly, that the Gracechurch Street Quaker Meeting in London was composed of the City's richest trading men, including such pioneers of banking as the Barclays, Gurneys and Lloyds. Hence the curious paradox that the Quakers, appealing to poor men and savagely persecuted, soon developed political influence.

Their eruption in New England in the late 1650s was dramatic. One young woman Friend entered the church at Newbury, Massachusetts, stark naked, and walked down the aisle, explaining afterwards at her trial that her aim had been to show those present the nakedness of their rulers. In 1658 the New England Confederation ruled that all heretics must be banished on pain of death. Four Friends were in fact hanged in Massachusetts, but popular opposition to such savagery ensured that when a fifth was condemned the authorities dared not execute him.

Rhode Island became a Quaker base. 'They begin to loath this place', it was wrily noted there, 'for that they are not opposed by the civill authority.' They converted William Coddington, founder of Newport; by 1690 nearly half that town's population were Friends, and the whole colony was under their dominant influence. Meanwhile, in 1671, Fox, with the suitably apostolic number of twelve companions, arrived in Barbados, and, starting from there, ranged the whole of English America. In 1700, when there were perhaps 50,000 Quakers in Britain, there were at least 40,000 in the New World.

This remarkable expansion produced in West New Jersey and Pennsylvania two distinctively Quaker colonies. In 1674 John, Lord Berkeley sold his interest in New Jersey to a Quaker named Edward Byllinge. Byllinge went bankrupt and quarrelled with a Quaker associate in the enterprise. It was policy among Friends that disputes should be settled privately rather than in the courts, so trustees were appointed for West New Jersey and Byllinge's half-interest was divided into 100 shares, of £350 each, which were mostly purchased by well-to-do Quakers. The trustees drafted 'Concessions' which embodied the most advanced concepts of personal liberty, since they reflected the drastic experience which Quakers were having of the perverted operations of English law. '. . . We put the power in the people.' Byllinge violated the Concessions in the early 1680s, proclaiming himself governor and sending out a deputy, but this man proved tactful enough to gain acceptance from the colonists.

East New Jersey in 1683 came under the control of twenty-four new proprietors, including five Scots, one of whom was a very prominent Quaker, Robert Barclay of Urie. A surge of some five hundred Scottish settlers crossed to join the thousands of Englishmen already there; these newcomers were mostly not Quakers, but persecuted Presbyterians. By 1692 a Scot, Andrew Hamilton, would be governor of both the New Jerseys, now combined again.

William Penn was a proprietor both in East and West Jersey, but from 1681 his main interest was in the province which Charles II granted to him personally. Born in 1644, he was the son of the Admiral Penn sent to the West Indies by Cromwell. Having acquired an Irish estate from the Protector, the Admiral prudently switched to support Charles II in 1660. Not only did he serve the Stuarts, he also lent the royal brothers money, of which £16,000 was still unreturned in 1681, eleven years after his death. Dying, he had asked James and the King to show goodwill to his son.

Young Penn had turned Quaker in his early twenties, though not before he had made a Grand Tour of the Continent and had come back, according to Pepys's wife, 'a most modish person . . . fine gentleman', with an affected manner and Frenchified clothes. He was gaoled several times, though James, Duke of York, intervened in 1669 to get him released from the Tower. The death of the Admiral next year left him a wealthy man, and as such he naturally moved at the front of the Quaker drive to found colonies. Whereas most Quakers showed their own hair, Penn wore a wig. He was attracted to the life of a free-spending country gentleman surrounded by servants. He achieved it in England, and took it with him to America, where the city he founded, Philadelphia, would become a major centre of attempts by others, also, to replicate that lifestyle. His own writings blend, in the Quaker way, mysticism with practicality. His argument that people should act according to the rules of nature which are 'few, plain, and most reasonable' take us towards the centre of eighteenth-century secular Enlightenment, with which judicious Quakerism, as the hot sect cooled, would harmonise remarkably well.

However, there is no need to question Penn's sincere wish to provide a refuge for his own sect where Quaker ideals could be put into practice. A Quaker paper of 1680 enumerates the sufferings of Friends since the Restoration: 243 had died in prison, 276 were currently in gaol and some had been there for years. Nearly 200 had been banished. What with imprisonments and seizures of property, 10,778 Friends had suffered directly. This was the context in which Penn asked that the King's debt to his dead father should be met by the grant of a province in America.

Charles II complied but then, it would seem, enjoyed himself teasing the well-bred Dissenting bore. Penn wanted the land to be 'New Wales' or, in view of its forests, 'Sylvania'. Charles insisted upon 'Pennsylvania', out of respect for the late Admiral, and so worked a commoner's name into the title of lands half as large again as Scotland. Penn went on to invest in his new lands more heavily than any other Restoration proprietor.

This was, as he saw it, to be a 'colony of heaven', where a whole society would live in accord with the Quaker apprehension of Inner Light within all men, under a government whose fundamental law would be the Sermon on the Mount.

The project was an instant success. By July 1683 as many as 3,000 people may have entered the beach-head of the new colony on the Delaware river. At the end of the century, Pennsylvania was not far short of 20,000. Persecution alone could not explain this. Quaker meetings were schooled to accept suffering and were not readily inclined to grant the necessary credentials to members proposing to go to America merely to evade trouble. Poverty may have been a stronger push; men from the bleak northern dales were drawn in such numbers to the rich uplands of Chester County, Pennsylvania, that as late as the mid-eighteenth century a broad Yorkshire dialect prevailed there. An important group of Welsh Quakers, probably fairly prosperous, were pulled by the vision of a New Wales where, as they said at the time, they could try to decide disputes among themselves 'in a Gospel order', and not 'entangle' themselves with 'laws in an unknown tongue' – the obnoxious language, of course, being English. In general the appeal of Pennsylvania seems to have been less the negative one of a refuge than the positive one of a sphere where Quaker ideals and energy could find full scope.

The offer of land was imaginatively made. A well-to-do man could buy 5,000 acres for £100, a poorer one could rent 200 acres for a penny each, and those poorer still were offered a stake of tools, stock and seed upon an agreement to develop an assigned acreage through seven years, at the end of which they might buy the land; while large blocks could be purchased by groups wishing to settle as whole communities. Penn was famous in Europe as well as at home and his very clever propaganda campaign was conducted in Dutch, German and French as well as in English.

Toleration was assured to any believer in the one God, though only Christians could vote or hold office. But the constitution was aristocratic; the elected assembly was to have no power except that of yielding or refusing consent to laws proposed by the governor and council, and while the latter was elective, Penn seems to have expected that social convention would ensure the choice of wealthy men. He believed, with other Quakers, that all men were inwardly equal, but accepted current social ideas about the natural existence of inferior and superior men; just as, in nature, cedars were higher than brambles.

He wished sincerely, however, that dealings with Indians should be peaceful and just. Like toleration, good race relations were economically shrewd; they could save his colony the costs of defence which were borne elsewhere. Penn and his agents purchased each tract in turn from native holders in such a cordial way as to convince the red men that justice was being done. The Delaware Indians were in fact docile until the 1730s; the Quakers were lucky to have them as neighbours rather than the belligerent Iroquois, who might have made pacifism less feasible.

Penn landed in his new kingdom in 1682, fully intending to reside there permanently. He supervised the building of a gracious mansion for himself and the laying out of 'Philadelphia', so named from two Greek words meaning 'brother' and 'love', on a spacious rectangular plan; with straight streets running parallel, two wide avenues bisecting each other. Merchants flocked in, chiefly Quakers not from England but from other colonies where they had grown wealthy. The richest man, Samuel Carpenter, came from Barbados; Isaac Norris, noted in politics, from Jamaica; the very wealthy Edward Shippen from Boston; and the new town's first mayor from New York.

From his friend James, Duke of York, Penn in 1682 acquired a title to the area which became the state of Delaware, but which for many years to come was known as the 'Lower Counties'. This tract west of Delaware Bay already had a few hundred settlers, and besides some English, there were relics of earlier settlements made by Swedes, Finns and Dutch. 'German-town', founded near Philadelphia in 1683, was actually first settled by Dutchmen, though Quaker settlers from the Rhineland were shortly attracted by Penn's propaganda and acquired, in Francis Daniel Pastorius, a remarkable intellectual to lead them. But the great influx of Germans would come only in the next century; up to 1700, it is reckoned, settlers in Pennsylvania were roughly two-thirds English, one-tenth Welsh and one-tenth Irish.

The Colony of Heaven and the City of Brotherly Love soon fell into factions. The Welsh, led by John Ap John, were given a tract of 50,000 acres variously known as 'New Wales', 'Cambria' and 'the Welsh Tract', but before long Penn's governor ran a county line through the middle, which had the political convenience of splitting the solid Welsh bloc of voters. A controversy with Lord Baltimore over his border with Maryland forced Penn to sail home in 1684, and he did not return for fifteen years. His hopes of wealth from the quitrents due to him were disappointed as they proved very sticky to collect. As soon as Penn left, his fellow Quakers, who were securely in a majority of the population and in control of both Assembly and Council, fell out among themselves, and in the 1690s there was even a doctrinal schism amongst them. One thing only seemed to unite everyone – hot resentment of proprietorial government.

One deputy governor put in by Penn would before long be recalled in humiliation after friction with the colonists, remarking of the Philadelphia Quakers as he departed that 'each prays for his neighbour on First Days and then preys upon him the other six.' But political quarrels, as this remark rather suggests, did not affect success in trade.

The town of New York suffered from the advent of Penn's colony, losing its trade in tobacco and peltry with the Delaware River. Philadelphia soon outstripped the older port, which depended chiefly on Boston for its supply of English goods and had no established contacts with London of its own. The revenue of New York, since settlement was still sparse, had to depend on the fur trade, and Governor Dongan, a Catholic Irishman, aimed to capture control from the Canadian French. But he lacked the resources to do so. His colony was a cartographical nonsense. Long Island, which belonged historically and geographically with New England, was its main centre of population; the governor had the expense of defending and trying to govern his royal master's territories in Maine, and Albany up-river was jealous of New York City. New York was still the only English colony which had no representative assembly. Dongan, when he arrived in 1683, had borne instructions to set one up. Eighteen representatives, mostly Dutch, now drafted an ambitious 'Charter of Libertyes' for the colony, which James confirmed next year. But he had not sent it back when his brother died. The Charter was aborted, as James developed his own extensive plans, in the New World as well as at home.

Parcels of Rogues

I

The succession in 1685 of this Catholic monarch was bound to arouse fear and rage. James, while his brother had been taming England, had been working to secure his own position in Scotland, where a parliament in 1681 passed, at his suggestion, two Acts. The first declared that no difference in religion could disqualify a rightful successor to the throne. The second was the notorious Test Act which imposed an oath on all persons engaging in politics, who must now swear that they would never try to make any alteration in the government of Church or State. The Earl of Argyll, son of Montrose's great rival, was one of those who refused to take it. He escaped to Holland. On James's succession, Argyll returned with three hundred supporters and attempted to raise rebellion, but he was swiftly caught and, like his father before him, executed. Meanwhile, the Duke of Monmouth, with even fewer followers, sailed from Holland to Devon and rallied an army of some 7,000 among the Dissenting freeholders and unemployed clothworkers of the south-west. But his inexperienced soldiers were routed by James's regular troops. Lord Chief Justice Jeffreys dealt out punishments brutally in his 'Bloody Assizes' on the western circuit. Besides perhaps 300 sentences of death, some 800 people were condemned to be transported to the West Indies, and various courtiers were granted the right to sell them. The Queen, amongst others, made a considerable profit.

The militia had proved ineffectual in operations against Monmouth's rising. This suited James well; he could argue that a strong standing army was essential. But he insisted on his right to have papist officers in it. The parliament summoned early in his reign had at first been complaisant; the elections had proved the value of his brother's purge of the boroughs, and the whigs were now broken and dispirited. But James asked too much. The Commons would not stand for Catholics in civil or military office. James prorogued Parliament in November 1685 and thereafter went his own way. The purge of officeholders which he now mounted was in effect an attack on the power of the aristocracy and the major gentry. Most Lord Lieutenants of counties were deposed. Nearly half the JPs were ousted, tories as well as whigs were alarmed as papists, even a Jesuit, found high places in government and as the commander of the Royal Navy was turned out in favour of a Catholic. A huge army, some 16,000 troops, was quartered on Hounslow Heath each summer, as if intended to overawe London, and in Ireland a great Catholic force was being created by James's subordinates. With Anglican opinion thoroughly alienated, James turned to court the Nonconformists, amongst whom William Penn was his close associate.

The tests which since the 1660s had barred Dissenters from office were suspended, and as the remodelling of corporations was pressed forward, jumped-up sectarians joined obscure Catholics in the government of proud old towns.

This was in effect an attempt at revolution from above. It offended almost every powerful vested interest. When a second Declaration of Indulgence towards Nonconformists was proclaimed in May 1688, the clergy generally refused to read it aloud in church as ordered. Now came the last straw. James had hitherto lacked a male heir. He was elderly. Men could console themselves that things must change soon. In June his wife produced a son.

The threatened ruling class was in no mood for heroics. The situation recalled that of 1640 in so far as a papist army in Ireland hung as a threat over England; but, unlike his father, James had a strong force at home and the Commons had voted him revenue for life. Besides, the 1640s had shown that great men who raised rebellion ran the risk of inflaming lesser men; levelling ideas would be at work again. But a *deus ex machina* was available. William, Prince of Orange, ruler of the Netherlands, was James's nephew and also his son-in-law. He moved carefully, making it clear to prominent men in England that if they wanted him to come, he must have a written invitation. This was duly provided, with seven names on the document from great aristocratic families.

James saw what was impending and hastily reversed all his policies. But he was too late. On November 5, 1688 William disembarked at Torbay in Devon with the largest army ever to land in England, some 15,000 men. The cowardly English ruling class gave him little military support, but James's army retreated before him, riddled with disaffection. As William moved steadily up to London, James ran away. By Christmas, he was in France, and 'Jacobitism' had been born.

England had no king, if James was held to have abdicated. A 'convention' met early in 1689, Parliament under another name, and drew up a Declaration of Rights which outlawed James's practices and with them absolutism. William and his queen, Mary, James's daughter, were jointly offered the crown. A set of transactions marked by extreme caution on all hands, and with gross personal betrayal by many of those closest to James, would be awarded the name of the 'Glorious Revolution'. John Locke had returned from exile and he could rationalise what had happened in terms which would be accepted by men all over the English-speaking lands. His *Essay of Civil Government* argues that government is based on contract. Men agree to form an ordered society. When the king whom they have entrusted with government flouts his trust, revolution is the ultimate safeguard of law. The aim of government is to preserve property.

England became a constitutional monarchy, though the constitution was not codified. Government policy was from now on restrained by specific appropriations of money made by Parliament. Most of the country's political men endorsed the war against France into which William promptly pulled England.

Such a war had never been waged from the island before, with the enemy engaged not only at sea but on frontiers in the colonies and, in association with allies, on the continent of Europe itself. The hundred-year squabble between Crown and Parliament was over. Spending on the navy had hovered in the 1680s at between £330,000 and £470,000 a year. In 1696–7 it stood at £2,821,931 – and yet the proportion of public money being used in this field was not much greater. State spending vastly increased as Parliament voted money without inhibition. To keep William's war going, Parliament had to meet every year to grant funds. This habit was never broken. The king's prerogative of summoning Parliament lapsed. And since William had to accept, in 1694, an Act by which an election must be held at least once in three years, the next two decades saw a preposterous effusion of political faction, as whigs and tories, regrouped, contended for power.

Religion remained a bitter topic. But toleration was now made law. Nonconformists, as the ruling class wished so fervently, were barred again from public affairs, but they were made free to have their own places of worship under certain conditions. Catholics in England reverted to their position under Charles II – or perhaps they were slightly less disadvantaged. In Ireland, of course, the tale was a very different one.

II

James sent over his brother-in-law, the Earl of Clarendon, to replace the aged Ormond as viceroy, but the real ruler of Ireland during his reign was his friend Richard Talbot, a prominent Irish Catholic landowner, to whom he gave the title of Earl of Tyrconnell and the command of the army. A purge and reconstruction of this force began in the summer of 1686. By the autumn there were 5,000 Catholics out of 7,500 private soldiers, and within a couple of years most of the officers were also Catholics.

Some of his fellow papists disliked Tyrconnell, who was arrogant, quick-tempered and blustering. To Protestants, of course, he was a bogeyman. In January 1687, he formally succeeded Clarendon as Lord Lieutenant.

As Catholics reappeared in the Irish Privy Council, in town corporations, as local magistrates, even as judges, a trickle of perturbed Protestants began to emigrate from Ireland.

One of James's most serious mistakes was to call over Irish troops in 1688 to support him. While their drafting weakened Tyrconnell's force in Ulster, the civilian populations of London and Portsmouth hated the papist barbarians and there were scuffles in the streets. Deep resentment within the English army helps to explain its later reluctance to fight for the King. In the north, those Protestants who stayed formed armed associations which effectively controlled large areas, and Derry went into open rebellion. Presbyterians were heartened by the news from Scotland.

The Revolution of 1688 was a purely English initiative, and it was not until

James called the Scottish army south that the south-western Covenanters rose against the hated episcopalian clergy and a mob in Edinburgh drove the Jesuits out of the Palace of Holyrood and sacked the royal chapel. A Convention of Estates met in March 1689 and heard a moderate letter from William and a threatening one from James. The majority settled for William. Amongst the minority, Graham of Claverhouse, newly ennobled as Viscount Dundee, took the lead. Though he was Protestant, he stood no chance at all of making his peace with a Williamite regime; his reputation as persecutor was too well-established. He withdrew from the Convention, which declared him a rebel and went on to offer terms to William and Mary. Tolerant William shied for a moment at a clause in the oath proposed to him which obliged him to root out heretics, but was assured that this was mere form. In July 1689 prelacy was formally abolished in Scotland and Presbyterian government was restored. The ministers ejected since the Restoration were reinstated and dominated the General Assembly of the Church, which they purged of more than half its clergy. But the heady conditions of the 1640s could not be revived. The Kirk was now subject to parliamentary statute, and civil penalties could not now be enforced for ecclesiastical excommunication. The Covenants, overtly re-affirmed, were tacitly conceded to be a dead letter. Though the newly ousted ministers formed the basis of an underground episcopalian Church, the days of religious warfare were over. The more ardent Cameronian Covenanters split, and while some stuck to their creed in a series of little sects, others joined the new Cameronian Regiment which was set up to fight for William.

Dundee had rallied an army in the Highlands. The Campbells, of course, were for William – James had executed their chief, the Earl of Argyll. Now various chiefs feared the coming revival of Campbell power. Though James, while king, had been as unsympathetic to the Highland Gaels as any of his predecessors, Macdonalds, Camerons, Stewarts, Macleans and others were now ready to fight for him. Dundee showed he could lead them well. At the pass of Killiecrankie late in July a classic Highland charge destroyed the Williamite army sent against them, though at the moment of victory Dundee himself was killed. Jacobitism had won its first battle in Scotland, and found its first hero. But Dundee's successor, Colonel Cannon, could not match his flair. In August, the Jacobites were repulsed at Dunkeld, a gate to the Lowlands, by the Cameronian Regiment, whose Colonel had fought for the Covenant in the Bothwell Bridge rising. The Presbyterians showed impressive courage. Scotland was saved for their creed, and for William. Next year, the Jacobites were beaten again, and their challenge collapsed.

In Ireland, the Williamites found success far more difficult. Tyrconnell manoeuvred skilfully for control, playing for time by suggesting that he might go over to William while actually raising 40,000 more troops for James. In March 1689 his army defeated an Ulster Protestant force in the 'break of Dromore' and soon only Derry and Enniskillen held out. Tyrconnell's success helped to persuade Louis XIV that he should support James in an attempt to regain his throne through Ireland, and just before Dromore a French fleet of 22 ships brought their king to the Irish, along with supporters from all three of his kingdoms, besides French officers, arms and ammunition. He made a triumphal progress from Kinsale to Dublin, welcomed, as one contemporary witness put it, 'as if he had been an angel from heaven'.

But James was not interested in the prospect of reigning over Ireland in Ireland. He wanted to cross to Scotland as soon as possible and thence strike into England. Meanwhile, he showed his mortification when his beloved English navy was bested by the French fleet which landed further troops for his cause at Bantry Bay. Irish Catholics were soon disillusioned with him. The foreigners who had come with him did not disguise their contempt for the Gaelic rabble who would fight on his side. A French leader wrote to Louis XIV, 'The Irish recognise that the Englishmen close to the king, even the Catholics, are their greatest enemies.'

So James could not hope that the Irish Parliament which he summoned for May 7 would produce legislation acceptable to opinion in England. But he had to call it. He was short of arms, of supplies, of money. Thanks to Tyrconnell's purges, this 'Patriot Parliament' contained only six Protestants in the Commons and five in the Lords. James was compelled to give his sad consent to a Bill, odious to his English supporters, which swept away the land settlement of the 1660s and authorised dispossessed papists to take steps to get their property back.

James's first stroke on arrival had been to proclaim freedom of religion for all, and an Act of Parliament now made this law. He hoped to pursue a conciliatory policy, leaving Church of Ireland vacancies unfilled and using the money to subsidise Catholic priests, while providing that Catholics and Protestants should each support their own clergy. Later he tried, without much success, to stop Catholics seizing Protestant churches. His moderation pleased neither side.

The Patriot Parliament set aside the restrictions imposed by the English Navigation Laws, and James had to block Bills which attempted to give special favour to France. Trade had in fact collapsed, and this bore hard on the royal revenue. The Parliament was generous with its grant, but the amounts raised fell far short of what had been granted and with expenditure on the army running at ruinous heights, James turned to minting brass and copper money, which devalued so rapidly that by the spring of 1690 it was common to give 50 shillings of brass money for a guinea. Protestant toasts later would include brass money, along with popery and with wooden shoes, among the horrors from which William III had delivered the British Isles.

And the men of Derry would become the prime heroes of Protestant mythology. When James advanced towards the town in April 1689, it was packed with refugees. About 30,000 people were crammed within its narrow walls, 500 yards long by 300 wide. There was some ill feeling between

Presbyterians and episcopalians, and the governor, Robert Lundy, a Scots Protestant, gave only hesitating allegiance to William and did not believe that the place could be defended. But Derry, reinforced from London, had proclaimed William and Mary, and its denizens were braced to resistance by fears of a repetition of 1641. Lundy was ousted and replaced by two new governors, Major Baker and a die-hard Church of Ireland minister named George Walker. A siege of fifteen weeks began. Before the end dogs and cats, rats, hides and tallow would be eaten, 'a handful of sea-wrack or chickweed fetched a penny or twopence.' The defenders had only new regiments of inexperienced soldiers. The enemy killed just eighty, but famine and sickness reduced the force from 7,500 to about 4,300, of whom more than a quarter were unserviceable. The supply of cannonballs eventually failed, and pieces of brick were covered with lead. But the besiegers had only one gun heavy enough to make any impression on the famous walls.

The Jacobites were fewer and sickness and desertion quickly eroded their ill-equipped force. Their best hope was to starve Derry into submission. Food and four regiments were on the way from England and the Jacobites built a boom across the river Foyle to block their passage. On July 28 two ships broke the boom, laden with peas, flour, beef and biscuits. The Jacobites now could do nothing but raise the siege, which is said to have cost 15,000 lives altogether, mostly from disease and starvation. The stubbornness of Derry had baulked James's plan to cross to Scotland.

Meanwhile, the Protestants of Enniskillen had harried the Jacobite communications, had carried off thousands of cattle and sheep, and, in their mounted raids, had seemed to threaten Dublin itself. Soon after the siege of Derry ended, they routed a much larger Jacobite force at Newtownbutler. Jacobite morale was low when, on August 13, 10,000 troops in William's service arrived in Ulster under the command of Marshal Schomberg, a famous French veteran. More soon followed. While all Catholics aged between 16 and 60 were ordered to arm themselves, James's own French generals advised him to retreat. But late in August he marched north.

French and Irish officers quarrelled continually. James, unimpressed with his native soldiers, shipped 5,000 off to France, where they formed the nucleus of the famous Irish Brigade, and received 6,000 troops sent by Louis XIV in exchange. Many of these were Walloons and Germans, some of them actually Protestant. This was becoming a most cosmopolitan struggle. William, to add to his Dutchmen and Germans and Huguenots, had hired 7,000 Danes, and Jacobite propaganda, recalling the Norsemen, deplored this calling in of 'the old invaders of our country'. Ireland, as never before or since, was a theatre of European war, waged by William and his allies against Louis. To mark its importance, William came in person in June 1690. Ireland had seen no king since Richard II. Now it was honoured with two at the same time, but just as James thought of Dublin as a stepping stone towards London, so William counted Ulster an outpost of Holland. Neither had real sympathy with the preoccupations of any of Ireland's inhabitants.

James fell back before William to the River Boyne. On June 30 an engagement took place which became the most famous event in Irish history. James had about 25,000 men. William's 36,000 were far better equipped, especially in artillery. The struggle was fierce for a while, Tyrconnell's cavalry charged time after time. Schomberg was killed. William kept saying, 'my poor guards, my poor guards.' He lost about 500 men, James twice as many. The Jacobites were forced into disorderly retreat. And James lost face. While his rival had shown reckless courage and had been slightly wounded, James had fled from the battlefield in haste, and took ship for France next morning.

James's supporters were left resentful and disillusioned. He himself blamed the Irish for running away, and his instructions to his infant son, written two years later, advised him to root out the Gaelic language and to tell the Os and Macs of Ireland firmly that their forfeited lands would never be restored; nor should natives be trusted with high office.

The Jacobite army retreated to Limerick. Tyrconnell was now for surrendering. But Patrick Sarsfield, idol of the army, 'a man of an amazing stature, utterly devoid of sense, very good natured and very brave', still insisted on dying hard. William wanted to offer generous terms, but the revengeful Irish Protestants would not let him. The Jacobite leaders had to fight on if they wished to retain their estates. A desperate three-week defence of Limerick, in which unarmed men threw stones and women fought in the breach with broken bottles, forced William into retreat.

But James's French troops went home, and his Irish warriors were confined behind the line of the Shannon. Sarsfield, now named Earl of Lucan, resented Tyrconnell's authority and neither got on with the new French commander, St Ruth, who arrived to lead the army in May. The Jacobites, probably due to treachery, lost the key town of Athlone and the Irish troops there were butchered. But St Ruth still had about 20,000 men, equal to the numbers commanded by a Dutchman named Ginkel for William, when the two sides met in decisive battle at Aughrim in County Galway on July 12. There seems to have been treachery on the Jacobite left wing, and after St Ruth's head was blown off by a cannonball, massacre followed. Over 7,000 Irish were dead before night stopped the slaughter. Corpses were strewn for almost four miles around. 'It isn't the loss of Aughrim' became the Irish way of saying that a misfortune was bearable. This one was not. Four hundred officers died and many of the Jacobite aristocracy were captured.

Within a month even Sarsfield was ready for surrender. His own chief interest in the negotiations which began on September 23 was to get permission for the Irish army to go to France, and Ginkel readily conceded not only this, but also transport to take them there. The hard bargaining took place over the Irish who would remain.

The military articles of the Treaty were faithfully executed. By Christmas an estimated 12,000 Irish troops had been taken in English ships to France, where they gave James II his own army till the European war ended, but thereafter were absorbed into the French forces. Sarsfield himself died in battle for the French a couple of years later, and the 'wild geese' whom he led earned a reputation for ill-rewarded bravery on the battlefields of Europe. Many Jacobite Irish, it is worth remembering, opted to serve William, who consigned a select 1,400 of them to fight for his ally the Emperor.

The civil articles, however, were never fully honoured, despite William's own wish that they should be. They did help to regain or preserve the property rights of several hundred Jacobite landowners. But Protestant opposition was so bitter that confirmation by the Irish Parliament came only in 1697, and the Bill then presented bore little resemblance to the original treaty. Articles giving Catholics back their position under Charles II were wholly overridden by the notorious penal legislation against them which began in William's reign. By an Act of 1697, which William had to approve, Catholic bishops and regular clergy were banished.

The land settlement, though the scale of transfers was small compared to those of 1652 and 1665, rounded off a century of confiscations. William struggled with his English Parliament over the forfeited estates. He was at first able to make vast grants to his personal favourites. The English Commons fought back and regained control of the forfeited lands by an Act of 1700. Matters were finally settled only in 1703. By that time, the Catholic share of profitable acreage was reduced from 22 per cent in 1688 to only 14 per cent, and as penal legislation drove many landowners into Protestantism, it fell further still, to a mere 5 per cent or so by 1776.

As in Scotland, traditions of military valour stem from this period. The Enniskillen Fusiliers would match the Cameronian Regiment in reputation. Meanwhile William's birthday, November 4, became a holy day in Ulster. Year after year the renegade Lundy would be burnt in effigy and the brave defenders of Derry would be extolled. While Ulster Protestants nurtured a potent mythology, Catholic resistance in Ireland was almost broken, though 'rapparees', ex-soldiers from the 1689–91 war, succeeded the 'tories' for a time as patriotic brigands.

Meanwhile, what was left of the old Gaelic order would die rather more peacefully than that of the Scottish clans. Some chiefs now lived in hovels, but west of Galway, about the end of the seventeenth century, an English traveller named Dunton visited the O Flaherty, chief of a famous fighting clan, who still kept something like traditional state in his 'long cabbin', a booley or summer dwelling, with 'walls of hurdles plaister'd with cow dung and clay'. He was surrounded by a 'greate company of his relations . . . a parcell of tall lusty fellows with long hair.' Nine brace of ferocious wolfhounds mingled quietly with the company. A whole sheep was devoured at supper, and afterwards all present, 'even the lady herself', enjoyed Dunton's tobacco; she said they needed something like that in such a moist country. O Flaherty apologised for their 'barbarous' way of life; he had been to Dublin and had seen how things should be done, but old habits, he confided, died hard.

The house was a single long room without partitions. The whole company lay down to sleep here, on green rushes (full of 'white snayles'), but Dunton was given sheets and soft white blankets. 'I wonder'd mightily to heare people walkeing to the fire place in the middle of the house to piss there in the ashes, but I was soon after forced to doe soe too for want of a chambrepot . . .' Next morning, O Flaherty, after a breakfast of meat and rough whiskey, invited him to 'walk a small mile to view theire deer'. Dunton was surprised that there should be a deer park in so wild a place. But indeed, there was not. After a trek over mountains and through bogs, they came to an untouched vale amid 'lovely green mountaines' and there on the hillsides were 'hundreds of stately red dear'. They returned to the cabin for a vast dinner, with a whole carcase of beef, mutton as well, and tall heaps of oatcakes, a delicious cold milk drink, whiskey and ale 'such as it was'. Then they rode back to hunt the deer with 'above thirty footemen' following them.

The new Ireland retained only hospitality from this dying, archaic way of life. The thriving city of Cork greatly impressed an English merchant in 1703. 'They drive a very great trade to the West Indies with their provisions, chiefly by Bristol men who flock hither to load about September and October for Jamaica, Barbadoes, Antegoa, and the other islands of the West Indies, with beef, pork, butter, candles, etc.'

III

The monopolies of the East India Company and of the Royal African Company were both closely identified with the royal family and hence were imperilled by the 'Glorious Revolution'. James II was the governor and largest shareholder in the RAC until his flight. It now lost confidence in the legality of its own charter, stopped seizing interlopers, and had to settle with traders whose goods it had impounded before the Revolution. So the African trade was opened up. The Company's forts, however, were seen as essential safeguards of English interests in Africa. A 10 per cent duty was imposed by Parliament on exports to Africa by non-Company ships – henceforward known as 'Ten Per-Centers'. In return these would have the same privileges at the forts as RAC vessels. The money raised by the duty would help to pay for the upkeep of the forts.

The Company made great efforts to compete. It sent out Sir Dalby Thomas, a formidable, aggressive man, who was also a well-known expert on trade, as its Agent General at Cape Coast Castle from 1703. But war with France weakened its position; about a quarter of its ships in the war years were taken by the French, and losses in this way ran up to about £300,000 by 1713. The French drove the RAC out of its posts on the Gambia for five years in the 1690s. But the 'separate traders' or 'Ten Per-Centers' still throve. An official enquiry showed that between 1698 and 1708 they had imported about 75,000 slaves into the New World colonies as compared with the RAC's 18,000. In 1712 the Act of 1698 expired and was not renewed. The men of Bristol had triumphed and in their wake followed the ships of Liverpool. The RAC now had no monopoly – and no 10 per cent. Yet it retained its forts.

It is necessary to understand that, apart from the Portuguese in Angola and Mozambique, no European power, at this stage, was able to control more than a scrap of Africa. The myth that West African societies were at this time hopelessly backward, infantile in comparison with those of Europe, must now be totally dismissed. The vast region embraced, indeed, a number of societies which were perhaps even larger than Europe's, and just as men in the Highlands of Scotland or in Lapland were very different from people in London or Bordeaux, so there were simple cultures as well as highly sophisticated ones in Guinea. Overall, there was a range of industries – cloth-making, mining, metal-work, building and so forth – comparable to that found in other pre-industrial societies. Africans, as well as Arabs, Berbers and Jews, were prominent in trans-Saharan commerce, which from the eleventh to the seventeenth centuries had been the main source of gold for the international economy.

South of the shoreline, as it might be called, between desert and savanna, Mande, Hausa and Yoruba traders had ranged widely, linking forest and plain. There were many markets in Guinea, and merchants were highly regarded men. There were cities, in the forest region as well as in the savanna, which matched those of Europe. A Dutchman who penetrated Benin in 1602 thought it comparable with Amsterdam. At this time Benin was probably larger than any English town except London. For some African rulers, trade in slaves was vital even before the European impact was fully felt. In the city-states of Hausaland, slaves were central to economic life. 'They were employed for agriculture as well as in war. They were in themselves an international currency as well as a means of earning currency.'

The key to the role of slaves in West African economies was underpopulation, the very factor which would make servitude seem essential in Virginia. Because land was plentiful, hired labour would be too expensive. Many West African cultures were based on arduous and sophisticated agriculture. Draught animals, ploughs and wheeled vehicles were not generally used, though Africans did know about them; they were unsuitable in local conditions. Their absence, however, created a great need for diggers wherever agriculture moved beyond peasant subsistence, and for carriers where trade developed. Chattel slavery was a consequence. Many slaves worked in large gangs in gruelling and perilous roles – as roadmakers, front-line soldiers and, most taxing of all, as cutters of rock salt in the Saharan mines. However, the institution was commonly far milder than in the West Indies. The slave's colour was the same as the owner's. In some contexts slaves rose to important positions in the State or engaged in skilled work, and there was a general trend towards their assimilation into society as they gained certain rights in return for their loyalty. Among the Mande up the Gambia, an English factor would note in the 1730s, 'Some People have a good many House-Slaves, which is their greatest Glory, and they live so well and easy, that it is sometimes a very hard Matter to know the Slaves from their Masters or Mistresses . . .'

Few white men got so far inland. The Senegal and Gambia rivers were exceptional in the chance they provided for contact with Africans of the interior. The great artery of the Niger was hidden from white understanding until the nineteenth century. The power and pugnacity of the African states which existed behind most parts of the coast meant that far forays on land were almost impossible. Disease also sapped European initiative. Between a quarter and three-quarters of any group of Europeans arriving fresh on the coast would die within a year; thereafter, the death rate would be about 10 per cent. Guinea was, unbelievably, four times as dangerous to whites as the West Indies or India. Its swamps harboured a species of malaria far more virulent than that still found in those days in the English fens and the Irish bogs. European medicine was at this stage no more efficacious than that practised by Africans. It failed to distinguish malaria from yellow fever, another persistent killer. Most Africans acquired immunity to these diseases in childhood; a white would become unscatheable only if he survived his first attacks. Meanwhile, the value of quinine against malaria was only fitfully appreciated from the 1670s on, and the favourite white doctor's technique of bleeding sufferers would commonly help to hasten their deaths.

However, the RAC maintained its sometimes spectral footing on the coast. Besides its James Fort at the mouth of the Gambia, the RAC on occasion established factors quite far up the river. 'Senegambia', as this region is commonly called, had once provided a great proportion of the slaves shipped to the New World, but its importance in that respect had, relatively, much declined. Ivory, beeswax and hides were valuable items of trade, along with a substance named 'gum Senegal' which came from acacia trees and was prized in textile manufacture. The James Island fort led an especially vexed existence. Deserted after French attack in 1695, it was resettled in 1699, abandoned again ten years later, resumed in 1713. (Then in 1719 it was vacated once more, for a couple of years, after a raid by a Welsh pirate named Howel Davis.)

Further south, the RAC had posts in Sierra Leone – at Bence Island and at York Island on the Sherbro River. Around here the main attraction was redwood, a coveted dye. From the Sherbro to the Gold Coast stretched the 'Windward Coast' where no European settled and trade was conducted solely from ships; yet in the 1680s more goods were consigned from England by the RAC to this region than to any other section of Guinea, and the Company's agents in the Gold Coast were very jealous of the 'Windward' trade.

However, the Gold Coast remained far and away the chief centre of European competition. By 1700 there were about thirty-five white posts there, several meriting the name of 'castles'. The RAC, besides Cape Coast Castle, had several smaller factories. Slaves from this region had a remarkable reputation in the West Indies, where they were known as 'Coromantees'. They often led revolts there, and some planters eschewed them, but experts valued them highly. Christopher Codrington, governor of the Leewards, wrote of them in 1701 with the affection which men normally reserve for good horses or motor cars. 'All born heroes,' he called them.

So the RAC aimed to get as many slaves as possible from the Gold Coast. But its vessels commonly had to fall back on other sections to make weight. They would press on towards the despised human wares of the 'Slave Coast' and Angola. East of the River Volta, slaves were virtually the only item brought to trade. The RAC were established at Whydah (Ouidah) from 1683. It became a free port where factors from several nations competed. Captain Thomas Phillips, who sailed for the RAC in 1694, bought 1,300 slaves in nine weeks there in 1694. Though the 'King' of the place walked barefoot through the mud and water of his palace yard 'with as little concern as any of his poor subjects', Phillips was told that he could raise 40,000 of the latter within a day, and when he gave audience he was surrounded by 'nobility upon their knees'. This disagreeable man was amply strong enough to dictate terms to Europeans. He and his kind, the quite petty rulers of towns on the Gold and Slave Coasts and in the Niger Delta, were certainly not helpless victims of white rapacity. They were as shrewd in their dealings as the city fathers of London or Bristol.

In other places, individual African merchants became virtually 'kings' in their own right. Dutch and English competed for the good will of John Kabes of Komenda, a merchant prince whose profits came not only from the slaves and ivory which he bought from inland traders and resold to Europeans, but also from the flotilla of canoes which he hired out to the whites to enable them to move their goods from fort to fort, from the salt-making industry in which he engaged, and from his maize farms, worked by slave labour, which supplied both factories and ships with their daily bread.

In many respects, such African middlemen had the whip hand. Slaving was no crude exchange of human beings for rum; Africans were selective, demanding customers. When the English tried to sell them bad trade guns, they insisted on better. Nor were they easily fobbed off with rum adulterated by sea water. They were, after all, up to tricks of their own, filling the middle of cast ingots with lead, mixing brass filings with gold dust and treating the skins of sick slaves with palm oil and lime juice so as to give them the gloss of health. Their demands for goods were extremely various; an experienced trader reckoned that 150 different commodities were required for trade on the Gold Coast alone.

Even on the Gold Coast, where it was relatively thickest, European population at the end of the seventeenth century was minuscule. Captain Phillips was contemptuous of the 'small white square house' at Succandy, which was supposed to be a fort, though its eight or ten little guns were 'good for nothing but to waste powder, being all honeycomb'd within, and the carriages rotten and out of order', while the Agent was raving mad in his bed on account of a quarrel with a Dutch merchant over a mulatto girl. But Cape Coast Castle was quite impressive, with brick walls 14 feet thick, plenty of great guns, rum vaults, workshops, repositories for up to 1,000 slaves. The Agent General, based here, commanded RAC employees elsewhere on the Gold Coast, and normally at Whydah as well – some fourteen or fifteen settlements.

The forts had some power over the African settlements which grew round them. But Sir Dalby Thomas, Agent General early in the eighteenth century, was a would-be Cortés or Clive in the wrong place at the wrong time. He told his employers in 1706 that if he had a hundred and fifty good soldiers he could destroy the Kingdom of Fetu which ruled around Cape Coast and 'foarse an inland trade'. But even when he succeeded in installing a supposedly pro-English Queen of Fetu, against the Dutch candidate, he shortly had to report that the lady in question was 'very villainous in turning the trade from us underhand.' Even the sizeable mulatto population which had arisen from natural incontinence could not be relied on to be subservient. Sir Dalby had to drive away a remarkable mulatto named Edward Barter whom the RAC had educated in London and sent back as an agent; he had made himself an independent trader, controlling all the commerce of Cape Coast, and flaunted his own miniature fort and personal army.

Cohabitation with black or mulatto 'wives' – very cheap to keep, Phillips noted, and docile because they could be turned away at pleasure – was almost the only solace available in the notorious climate, which, in their different seasons, provided scorching heat, torrential rain, thick fogs and piercing cold Harmattan winds. Men drank from fear of death, and so hastened their deaths. Phillips noted that the place where dead whites were buried by the factory of Whydah was 'call'd, very improperly, the hog-yard'.

Left short of English employees, the RAC had to turn to foreigners. In the 1690s, about three-quarters of the men at Cape Coast seem to have been non-English, and Phillips found that of the three chief merchants in charge there one was a Roman Catholic Irishman and another was a Scot – 'a very sober quiet honest man, and understood accounts to perfection.' The chaplain was Irish (presumably Protestant), the surgeon was another Scot.

The nature of the main business, slaving, was itself a deterrent, of course, even then. Captain Phillips returned from his slaving voyage in 1694 so ill that he gave up the sea and retired to his native Wales, where he wrote that blacks 'excepting their want of christianity and true religion, (their misfortune more than fault) are as much the works of God's hands, and no doubt as dear to him as ourselves . . .' Others, like him, would have found the trade physically disgusting.

He haggled at Whydah every day for nine weeks at the 'trunk' where the

African middlemen collected their slaves, and he often fainted with the stench, 'it being an old house where all the slaves are kept together, and evacuate nature where they lie, so that no jakes can stink worse . . .' To meet growing European insistence on speedy delivery, African traders took to storing slaves in such warehouses, 'barracoons', and in some cases whites themselves established floating barracoons in hulks off shore. The slave had to survive conditions in these places after a journey from his point of capture which seems often to have been very long indeed. Once purchased, each slave was carefully scrutinised, with the aim of discarding the elderly and the diseased, especially those who suffered from VD. 'Our surgeon,' Phillips wrote, 'is forc'd to examine the privities of both men and women, with the nicest scrutiny, which is a great slavery, but what can't be omitted.' The Captain's problems did not end there. 'The negroes are so wilful and loth to leave their own country, that they have often leap'd out of the canoos, boat and ship, into the sea, and kept under water till they were drowned . . . they having a more dreadful apprehension of *Barbadoes* than we can have of hell . . .' Sharks swarmed round the slave ships and, according to Phillips's information, followed them to the West Indies in expectation of dead blacks thrown overboard.

On the voyage, white men had to supervise blacks who vastly outnumbered them. Big ships were used. They had to be heavily manned – thirty or forty seamen at least, and sixty or seventy in the largest vessels which could carry four or five hundred slaves. Proportionately, it seems, more white seamen than slaves would lose their lives, commonly to the killer mosquito. 'Beware and take care, Of the Bight of Benin,' sang the sailors, 'For one that comes out, There are forty go in.' On shipboard, slave revolts were frequent, and savage measures were taken by frightened whites. 'I have been inform'd', wrote Phillips, 'that some commanders have cut off the legs and arms of the most wilful, to terrify the rest . . .'

Phillips was overloaded. The 'white flux' killed 320 out of the 700 slaves aboard his *Hannibal*. But the purely physical horrors of the Middle Passage should not be exaggerated. White indentured servants, even free immigrants, suffered appalling conditions on shipboard in the Atlantic, and often their mortality rates were as high. Seamen were brutally treated as a matter of course, and sadistic captains were certainly not confined to this one trade. Transmitting slaves became an expert craft as time wore on. The captain's job was to get his cargo to port; he would be rewarded accordingly. A sensible slaving skipper made sure that his valuable freight received plenty of food and exercise and kept his ship as clean as he could. The worst horrors of the trade were psychological. Africans suffered extreme shocks, while the Europeans who stayed in the trade were inured to the treatment of other people as items of merchandise. One slaver noted laconically that, when slaves had tried to starve themselves to death, he had been 'necessitated sometimes to cause the teeth of these wretches to be broken . . . and thus have forced some sustenance into their throats.' The same man observed (and other evidence bears him out) that the Africans thought that the white men were cannibals and that they were being carried like livestock to the slaughter.

Phillips remarked of his fellow slaving captains that 'they would deceive their fathers in their trade if they could.' Yet their profession carried little or no stigma, at this time. There seemed to be no way of doing without the trade. The RAC, noting that its monopoly of African products imported direct to England was far more profitable than its trade in slaves, would have preferred, from the mid-1690s, to give the latter up altogether. Sierra Leone dyewood could be bought for goods worth about £3 a ton and sold in London for £40 or more; the direct voyage there and back was shorter than the 'triangular' passage via the West Indies, and there was no need to give credit to cheating planters. Why could not plantations be established in Africa itself? The answer was that cheap African labour was more valuable in the New World; the temptation to export any worker was too high. The RAC, under pressure from the West India lobby, asked its factors not to cultivate any more cotton or sugar cane.

While the English share in the slave trade would grow, English dominance in sugar production would be lost to the French in the second quarter of the eighteenth century. But for the moment it was assured. Production in the English islands doubled or trebled between 1660 and 1700, and at the latter date, they seem to have been providing nearly half the sugar consumed in Europe, while the Caribbean trade accounted for 7 per cent of all English merchant tonnage and 11 per cent of the value of the country's overseas commerce. The islands exported to England commodities worth over £700,000 per year (1698–1700); by comparison, goods from Virginia and Maryland were worth only £230,000.

The stimulus which the triangular trade gave to English manufactures can be inferred from the pattern of RAC exports. Besides re-exporting East India textiles to Guinea, the Company depended in early days on goods acquired in Europe – iron and copper from Sweden or Germany and trade guns from Holland rather than the inferior English ones which the Africans would not take. But this dependence was outgrown very rapidly. English rum replaced French brandy. Knives and the like, once bought in Amsterdam, were made in the English Midlands, where between 1690 and 1701 Samuel Banner of Birmingham supplied the RAC with over 400,000 knives and 7,000 swords. Demand for long runs of identical, cheap items harbingered industrial revolution. By the beginning of the eighteenth century, guns of the Dutch type were mass-produced and the cheap fabrics once obtained from Dutch suppliers gave way to Devonshire serges.

The importance of Africa to England was symbolised by the making of a new coin, the 'guinea', from the fine gold which the RAC imported; half a million were issued between 1673 and 1713. Large numbers of people in and around London and Bristol profited directly from the slave trade; this was a time when great men and little liked to invest in a one-eighth, or one-sixteenth, or smaller share in a ship. Liverpool men were now moving in, led by the Norris family, lords of the manor of Speke Hall yet also most active merchants, who dominated life in and around the port. Thomas Norris was Sheriff of Lancashire and MP for Liverpool. Sir William Norris was ambassador to the Great Mogul. Richard Norris was Lord Mayor of Liverpool in 1700.

The African trade was essential to the rise of the growing Lancashire textile industry. A third of Manchester's textile exports went there up to 1770, while half went to the West Indies and the American colonies. The industry might have been strangled in infancy by the competition of Indian textiles. But there was a vast demand for these latter in Guinea. Hence both the Lancashire clothiers and the EIC could thrive.

IV

The East India Company had acquired its first territory in 1659, the uninhabited island of St Helena in the South Atlantic. The excellent climate had made this a place of refreshment for Company ships since the earliest days. The aim now was to countervail Dutch occupation of the Cape of Good Hope and to secure a base from which homeward-bound ships could be convoyed. The EIC put in a resident governor, though at first it was hard to find settlers. The spot was excruciatingly lonely. By 1670 there were no more than forty-eight whites and eighteen blacks on the island.

Bombay, a second island, was acquired from Charles II in 1668. It lay well south of the factory of Surat, which within twenty years it had supplanted as the centre of EIC operations in Western India. It offered a superb harbour. It also gave independence; on this small patch the EIC was supreme and the Mughal emperor or his governor could not seize its possessions as he pleased. Merchants of all races were attracted to such a promising site, and within a few years the population, so it was said, rose from 10,000 to 60,000, which would have made it, after London, the second city of the empire. Yet its early days under EIC rule were fraught with problems. The spot was extremely unhealthy for Europeans. The English there soon acquired a proverb, 'Two Monsoons are the Age of a Man.' Of twenty-four passengers who arrived in one ship at the start of the rainy season, twenty had been buried before it ended.

The pirates of the Malabar Coast were a menace to shipping. The mainland, which itself produced little of commercial value, was held by pugnacious Marathas who were at war with the Mughal. Beyond this, the Dutch remained a danger. Gerald Aungier, President at Surat from 1669 to 1677, lined the shore at Bombay with Martello towers, completed a main fortress with heavy ordnance and sixty light fieldpieces, and drummed up a militia among the residents, which he stiffened with over 400 regular soldiers, mostly European or Eurasian. Then, in 1672, he moved to Bombay himself. The show of force which the place made deterred a Dutch fleet from pressing its attack the next year.

A Fellow of the new Royal Society, John Fryer, who travelled to India in the early 1670s, looked wryly upon Bombay. Aungier, when he dined, had 'Trumpets usher in his Courses, and Soft Musick at the Table'; he went out in a coach drawn by large milk-white oxen, or was carried in a palanquin. Yet, Fryer observed, 'for all this Gallantry, I reckon they walk but in Charnel houses . . .' The EIC had sent out Englishwomen, but their children were 'sickly', more so than those of mixed race. Fryer noted that the natives and seasoned Portuguese lived to 'a good Old Age' and plausibly attributed this to their temperance. The English, here and at Surat, as he portrayed them, were almost at the mercy of the native trading class, the *Vani*, whom they called 'Banyans', and who, Fryer said, hung on them 'like Horse-leeches' sucking both '*Sanguinem & Succum* (I mean Money) . . .' The EIC maintained a master to teach its young servants to read and write the native language, and there was some financial incentive to learn. Yet few tried, and fewer succeeded.

The position at Madras was similar, the EIC's Chief Merchants at Fort St George were Indians. But the English chief spared no expense to impress orientals with his dignity. He hanged natives when he pleased, and Englishmen for 'piracy' – an offence which could be broadened to include crossing a strip of water (the fort had a river behind it) with property which might be presumed stolen. Yet such pomp and powers were accorded to a man whose salary stood at no more than £300 a year. Middle-class Englishmen were already picking up strange habits in India.

Madras itself had perhaps 40,000 people around 1670. Many Portuguese had taken up residence there. The Agent was chief over all the scattered English factories on the East Coast.

The Bengal factories were reputed the laxest in India. The main EIC settlement, dating from the mid-century, was at Hugli, long the chief mart of Western Bengal and a renowned centre of weaving. Later there were two other main factories at Cassimbazar and Balasore, three outlying ones, and one small agency. The chief of all was an unscrupulous person named Matthias Vincent. The EIC accused him of 'Diabolical arts with Braminees', of exercising charms and of using poisons, but what worried them most was his bold trading in his own interest, his ready palm for a bribe, and the countenance which he gave to interlopers. The trade pursued here grew and grew in importance. Bengal, besides its abundance of wheat and rice, sugar and hemp, flax and opium, teemed with weavers producing desirable textiles – silk 'taffaties', the striped or checked cotton cloth known as 'gingham' and a variety of other cotton wares plain and patterned. The EIC's servants organised, and exploited, native weavers, advancing them money, thus getting them under their control; it was now becoming easier, Vincent wrote in 1676, to persuade them to comply with the written contracts which specified quality, colour and so forth best suited to meet demand in England. Beyond all this, the Company, in the 1670s, actually sent out skilled English silkworkers to Bengal – throwsters, dyers, and weavers

– to orientate, as it were, the production of goods for the European market.

Bengal also provided saltpetre, a commodity vital to English interests, both in India and in Europe, during an age of almost continuous warfare. By 1680 the area was a magnet for interlopers. Technically, any Englishman sailing the eastern seas without EIC permission was an 'interloper', including the pirates who preyed on all comers from bases in Madagascar and elsewhere. But serious traders could drive a lucrative commerce, selling their ships in the East and remitting the proceeds covertly through the Dutch East India Company, or taking the risk of bringing their rewards home in the form of diamonds and pearls. And EIC servants and agents were commonly friendly; interlopers could provide them with freight for their own private commerce.

EIC servants were barred from trade in the most valuable Indian commodities. But this did not stop them from amassing large fortunes, if they lived and were lucky. They could buy goods which they then sold at a profit to the EIC, and could throw on to the Company bad debts advanced in their private trade. The worst goods might be sent home in the EIC shipments, the best reserved for their own use in the 'country trade'. This commerce along the Asian coasts was engaged in by the EIC on its own account – Sir Josiah Child reported in 1681 that twenty-five EIC vessels were trading from port to port in the East. In any one of these, it was noted, there might be no more than half a dozen English sailors, the rest of the crew being made up of thirty or forty 'INDIANS called LASCARS'; the latter word would remain in use down to our own day. The profits from 'country trade' remained essential to the Company because they reduced the quantity of bullion which it had to export.

Apart from precious metals, the chief EIC exports into the East remained lead, iron and cloth. But even now English cloth could not command markets to match those found in Britain and Europe by the products which the EIC fleets brought back.

Tea was first imported in the mid-seventeenth century. Trade with China provided it. EIC servants in Surat had used it since the 1630s at least, though strictly as an auxiliary to harder liquors. It was first purchased or drunk in England in the 'coffee houses' which opened in London from the early 1650s. After Catharine of Braganza brought the tea-drinking habit with her from Portugal, it acquired high fashion. The EIC drew in regular shipments from about 1670. At this time, tea was thought a fine medicine and had 'the Repute of prevailing against the Headach, Gravel, Griping in the Guts . . .' It was heavily taxed in England, and this restricted its popularity, but by the late 1690s, imports were running at between 70,000 and 100,000 lb. a year. Then, from the early years of the eighteenth century, the spread of tea-drinking made the leaf (still generally Chinese in origin) prime among all the smuggler's choice wares.

Pepper, indigo, and cotton yarn also found buyers but textiles, in Charles II's day, were the EIC's chief, and most controversial import, rising from an average of 160,000 pieces a year in the 1660s to 750,000 by the 1680s, with a peak total of no less than 1,700,000 in 1684. As well as taffetas and ginghams, there flooded in chintzes and quilts and 'Bastards', 'Cassaes . . . Mulmulls . . . Silk Romalls . . . Nillaes . . . Fine Humhums'. English woollen interests inveighed against 'Heathens, who work for a penny a day and destroy Christians', as one of their spokesmen in the House of Commons put it in 1677. The class-conscious complaint was heard that even kitchenmaids could afford to wear Indian scarves.

The English silk industry seemed imperilled. The EIC in the early 1680s was, from one side of its mouth, ordering raw silk from Bengal with the unctuous explanation that it would 'set the poor on work' at manufactures at home, and with the other, clamouring for wrought silk. The merchants in London who traded with Turkey were as aghast as the English silk manufacturers. With the woollen interests, both joined the powerful coalition which was assembling against the EIC, along with whigs suspicious of the Company's close relations with the Stuart Court, economists who deplored its bullion exports, and interlopers and others who wanted a free, or freer, trade with the East.

There were thus two bizarrely conjoined trends of attack. One suggested that all trade in textiles with the East was injurious. The other, taken by those who wanted to enter that very trade, denounced the EIC, its monopoly and all its works, with the aim of securing a new and less exclusive organisation. The EIC had, in Sir Josiah Child, a pamphleteer as fertile, sage, and inventive as any who might be found to enter the field against it.

Child was a director of the Company from 1673, its governor in 1681–3 and again in 1686–8, its deputy governor during the rest of the 1680s, and then as a grey eminence, dominant figure in its councils until he died in 1699. His power was based on his vast individual shareholding and he justified his virtual dictatorship on the grounds that 'a small interest will never awaken a man so often in the night.' He was, justly, accused of defending his policies with the help of lavish bribes, and also of manipulating the market in EIC shares by putting about rumours of losses at sea. He would send one set of brokers out shaking their heads and implying bad news, with shares of his own to sell, then, as people rushed to unload, another set of his brokers would begin to buy.

This was, it should now be clear, one of the deeper minds of that era. Child met the general arguments against East Indian trade by conceding, as he had to, that his Company imported more than it exported, and carried out of the land much gold and silver. But he had the point on his side that EIC re-exports to Europe, running at £500,000 or so per year, brought home considerable profit. Anyway, no English goods would be sold in the East at all if the EIC did not export them. He had the strong points to put that England must have a powerful company in the field to match those of Holland and France; that joint stock was the only safe way to carry on the trade; that the EIC's factories and forts had cost it over £300,000; that it had to deal in the East with over 100 kings and rajahs and that if it were abolished at least forty ambassadors, each carrying large presents, would be required to support the English position. He professed himself a foe to monopoly in general, but this, he insisted, was a special case. He was quite right.

The areas where the EIC traded had once more become violent and competitive. In India itself, the Mughal Emperor Aurangzeb, who ruled for forty-eight years, fought campaign after campaign in the south from 1681. In 1686–7 he crushed two independent powers, Bijapur and Golconda, which had survived in the Deccan, but then he spent the rest of his life struggling with the Marathas. He smashed their unified kingdom, and before his death in 1707 ruled, between Kabul and Madras, a larger political unit than the subcontinent has seen since; but bands of tough, ruthless Maratha horsemen continued to raid over vast areas. Meanwhile, the French were increasing their ambition in the East. Their East India Company, founded in 1664, settled in Pondicherry, south of Madras.

The Dutch were expanding their power in Indonesia. The English had long been established at Macassar, in Celebes, but in 1667 the Dutch prevailed on the local ruler there to expel all other Europeans except themselves. In Java, they took the first, portentous, involuntary steps towards conquest. In the early 1680s the English were forced to leave their Bantam factory.

However, the EIC found a new base on Sumatra. The Dutch had just broken the control over the pepper trade there which had been exercised by the city-state of Atjeh. In 1685 the local rulers at Bengkulu – a place which the English would call 'Bencoolen' – anxious that the Dutch should have competition, signed a treaty giving the EIC a large tract of ground and a great measure of control over local supplies of pepper in return for a guaranteed price. The site was, to say the least, unhealthy. After a little over three months, in constant rain, the English chief was reporting: 'The Sick Lye Neglected, some cry for remedies but none to bee had: those that could eate have none to Cooke them victualls, soe that I may say the ones dies for hunger & the other for want of Remidies, soe that wee now have not liveing to bury the dead . . .' Yet the settlement survived, and others in West Sumatra followed. The English soon found enough heart to begin bullying the natives, enforcing compulsory planting of pepper and putting local rulers in the stocks when they failed to produce enough at the low price which was offered.

Child wrote to Madras late in 1687 that the EIC's aim was 'to establish such a politie of civill and military power, and create and secure such a large revenue to maintaine both . . . as may bee the foundation of a large, well-grounded, sure English dominion in India for all time to come.' But dominion 'in' India meant no more than the rule of certain safe places, Bombay, Madras, as centres of trade. The real thrust of the new policy was towards 'a large revenue' to support 'civil and military power'. The Company's rule over its servants and others must be asserted. The factories must be fortified and garrisoned till they were strong enough to repel Dutch, French, Marathas, Mughals, all-comers. The new policy provoked resistance. In Bombay, the garrison revolted and its commandant, Keigwin, for a time ruled the settlement. In Madras, the inhabitants, now asked to pay the full cost of repairs and fortifications, went on strike against the house tax and were only brought to submission by the threat of expulsion.

Sir John Child, Sir Josiah's namesake but not his close relative, was a heavy-handed president in western India. When he was appointed, in 1686, to the new title of Captain General and Admiral and Commander-in-Chief of all the EIC's forces throughout its possessions, including Madras and Bengal, his powers matched those of Tyrconnell in Ireland. Sir Josiah's new policy for Madras was shrewdly Machiavellian. He recognised that the people there would more willingly pay 'five shillings towards the public good, being taxed by themselves, than sixpence imposed by our despotical power . . .' The EIC used its own authority, in 1687, to grant Madras a charter, erecting a corporation of a mayor, twelve Aldermen and sixty or more burgesses. The first aldermen appointed were an even stranger crew than the mixtures of papists and Quakers which James II was foisting on English towns. Only three were EIC servants. There were two Portuguese merchants, one French, three Jews, and three Hindus. This might look like a remarkable recognition of the right of coloured peoples to share in their own government, but the Agent Elihu Yale, in fact, overruled them as he pleased, and by 1690 the number of English aldermen had risen to eight.

In 1686 James II confirmed the EIC in possession of all the jurisdiction, civil and military, which it could possibly want. Royal admirals and officers of justice were commanded to help the expression of its powers on land and at sea. Child boasted that the King had turned his Company from 'mere trading merchants' into 'the condition of a Sovereign State in India'.

But it still couldn't repress Thomas Pitt, the most flamboyant of all interlopers. He was born in 1653, the son of a Dorset rector of gentle origins. He first went East in the EIC service as a seaman, but settled at Balasore in Bengal in 1674 and drove a lucrative trade there for seven years despite repeated commands from the EIC directors that he should be arrested and deported. Pitt sensibly married the niece of Vincent, the EIC chief at Hugli. In 1681 he boldly came home with his wife and their infant son, whose own son would one day be Earl of Chatham. The Company had already sent off William Hedges as Agent in Bengal, with orders to arrest Vincent. But Pitt caught him up on the way, entered Balasore eleven days before Hedges's arrival, and spread the report that there was a new Company and that he, Thomas Pitt, was its Agent.

Vincent took himself off into the Dutch factory with all his papers, under the protection of a guard of soldiers in his own pay. The EIC raged in vain against Pitt, this 'fellow of a haughty, huffing, daring temper', who paraded into Hugli with four or five files of well armed troops in red coats and 'great attendance of Native Soldiers with Trumpeters'.

It was no use appealing to the Mughal's Bengal viceroy; Pitt could out-bribe the EIC. He and Vincent went home rich men in 1683. When they were arrested at the EIC's suit, each was able to give £40,000 security. Wealth, however gotten, must have its way. Vincent was knighted by James II, and Pitt, after four years' litigation, paid only a trifling fine. He became an MP in 1690 and bought control of two Commons seats. He was the first of the great 'nabobs', using the wealth of the East to make himself powerful at home.

Meanwhile grand troubles, long maturing, came to the EIC in Bengal. Mughal officials demanded constant presents and bribes. Shaista Khan, Aurangzeb's veteran viceroy, troubled the EIC with what they and imperialist English historians after them would choose to call 'exactions'. There was persistent friction over way dues and customs. Hedges had come to agree with the leading EIC men in the province that 'the trade of this place could never be carryed on, and managed to the Company's advantage', till they 'fell out', quarrelled, with the Bengal government, and forced it 'to grant us better termes'. Early in 1686, the directors decided to fight. An expedition was equipped, six companies of infantry with ten warships. On the west coast of India, it was to cut off native shipping and declare war on the Mughal Emperor. On the east coast, it was to pick up, if possible, 400 more soldiers at Madras, bring away the EIC servants from Bengal, capture and fortify Chittagong (meanwhile seizing all Mughal ships at sea), then advance up the Ganges and extort a treaty from the viceroy of Bengal. In the autumn of that year, just two ships with a few lightly armed tenders entered the Hugli with some 300 soldiers, intended to make war on an empire where the viceroy of Bengal alone could lead 40,000 men into action.

The EIC chief in Bengal was now a resourceful man named Job Charnock. His birth had been obscure; his life was invested with romance. The English told after his death the story, perhaps even true, of how he had rescued a Hindu widow from the flames to which the custom of *sati* consigned her, had lived with her happily for many years, had set up a magnificent tomb for her, and sacrificed a cock there every year to her memory. Local Indians would fable how 'Chanak', facing great Mughal forces with only a few men and a single ship, caught the sun's rays with a burning glass and burnt the river face of the city of Hugli as far as Chandernagore. He had arrived in India in the mid-1650s, had been chief at the Patna factory for many years, and was an old hand thoroughly seasoned, to the point of adopting native customs and losing most traces of his own religion. Hedges, whose coming temporarily blocked his way to the overall headship in Bengal, was deeply suspicious of him, believing that he embezzled saltpetre, practised extortions upon the weavers and was in league with interlopers. All this seems likely, nor do the scandals related to Hedges about his dealings with native women seem implausible. Charnock certainly kept as his servant a white man, named Harding, whom the Company had dismissed for 'Blasphemy and Athisticall Tenetts'. Charnock certainly bragged that 'never no chief was yett

able to contend with him.' But he was also noted for his truculence towards the
Mughal authorities, and he was uniquely esteemed by the directors at home,
who lavished praise in their letters on 'our old and good servant Mr Charnock'
and his 'integrity'.

The Mughal governor of Hugli moved against the English factory there in
October 1686. Charnock commanded a strange assortment of soldiers – Hindu
Rajput warriors who retained their own dress and customs, under their own
officers, together with some native Christians who were known as 'Portuguese',
and with a handful of English troops united with these in one company, which
wore red uniforms trimmed with blue. Altogether, there were less than 400.
They were now locked in by a Mughal force of 3,000 foot and 300 horse,
virtually under siege, and forbidden to resort to the market. After a skirmish, a
truce followed. Charnock led his forces down river to a place called Sutanuti,
some seventy miles from the sea, with a good anchorage for ocean-going ships
which had long made it a centre of trade. The settlement stood on swampy banks
with brackish malarial lagoons inland which stretched for over 100 square miles
and made assault from the east impossible. It was an obvious place to go. It
became the site of one of the greatest cities in the world. But not immediately.
The viceroy would not come to terms and Charnock retreated to Hijili, on the
coast, an island swamp full of wild beasts where a local landowner had
previously agreed that the English might set up a fort and factories. From here,
Charnock's men sacked the important town of Balasore.

Aurangzeb heard about this several weeks later. He was in the south, busy
capturing Hyderabad. We may infer how little the news hurt him from the fact
that he had to call for a map in order to find out where Hugli and Balasore were.
Meanwhile, as the heat intensified through March and April, the English at
Hijili began to run out of provisions and die. Mughal troops beset the island
closely, and fired on it from a powerful battery. In mid-May, thousands of
Shaista Khan's soldiers came up. The town of Hijili was seized, and only
desperate fighting saved the English fort. By September, Charnock was installed
at Sutanuti once more.

Captain Heath arrived with a fresh naval force and ordered that Charnock's
surviving troops must sail with him to Chittagong. Around the time that James
II was deposed at home, but all unwitting of that event, Heath and Charnock
abandoned Sutanuti again and set off down river. Early next year, the English
arrived at Chittagong. Bathos supervened. The place was far too strong to
attack. The Mughal Emperor was neither much amused nor much displeased.
The English were no more to him than moles in his garden; and like moles, they
had their uses. Aurangzeb first punished them; having conquered Golconda, he
turned his local officers loose. The remaining Englishmen in Bengal were driven
out. The factories at Masulipatam and Vizagapatam on the east coast were
seized, as was Surat on the west. Bombay was attacked. But the English were
still a danger to Indian seaborne commerce and to the routes which took Indian

pilgrims to Mecca. When Sir John Child, from Bombay, sued for peace at the end of 1689, Aurangzeb was not long in granting it. His conditions were that Child should be expelled (in fact he had just died), that the English made humble submission, that they paid a fine of 150,000 rupees, that they restored all the goods they had plundered, and that they promised to behave better in future.

In August 1690 Charnock was back at Sutanuti, where, by contrast with Hugli, the English could always bring up sea-going ships and use the guns of these to defend themselves. Within a decade, there was a busy new town with '1200 English inhabitants, of whom 460 were buried between the months of August and January in one year'. Indian and Armenian merchants congregated in 'Calcutta', as the place came to be called, and doomed Englishmen kept coming to try to profit from its commerce. Charnock died early in 1693. His last years had been no more edifying than his earlier ones. His temper, never good, had grown worse. His successor as chief in Bengal accused him of having enforced no discipline and of having no regard for Christianity, so that 'severall of English men's black wives turned Papist that were not soe before.'

The war against the Mughals confirmed the EIC in a new, and wiser, outlook. Land war against the emperor was now conceived to be impossible, though it was realised afresh that sea-power could in the end secure terms. But the war had cost the Company £400,000, over and above huge losses by shareholders, and by the King, through the interruption of trade. The EIC was weakened at a critical moment in its struggle with its enemies in London.

The Glorious Revolution was in itself a dangerous blow. The new parliament was clearly hostile. The chorus of complaint from English textile interests mounted. A mob of 3,000 weavers assembled to attack Child's mansion, and the EIC itself nearly lost its treasures when East India House was assailed. The woollen interests would seem to win their point in 1701, when a famous Act was passed which forbade the use or wear in England of Indian and Chinese silks and of Indian prints, printed calicoes, striped or checked cottons, though this would be a Pyrrhic victory, since the Lancashire cotton industry would thrive on the production of local imitations. A powerful association of merchants outside the EIC was formed by 1691, in effect as a rival organisation. In October that year the House of Commons resolved that a joint-stock company with exclusive privileges was the best means of trading with the East, but the question remained, which company? Child put his trust in bribes, and spent £80,000 on corrupting the King's ministers and his court. He was able thus to secure a new charter in 1693 – but one which doubled the Company's capital and restricted individual members to no more than £10,000 in stock. Any merchant could now join on payment of £5, and the Company must export £100,000 worth of woollens annually.

Thomas Pitt had suffered losses as a patron of privateers in the French war, and so returned to the East to shake the money-tree once more, this time with the tacit knowledge and consent of William III. He was soon flourishing at Hugli again. The EIC had no stomach for a fresh fight. Word of Child's bribes had reached the public, and its then governor had been committed to the Tower. The House of Commons had in effect endorsed interloping. The Company now came to terms with Pitt's co-partners in England and sent orders to Bengal that he should be given all assistance in getting home. According to the Bengal Council, Pitt 'to the last made a great bounceing' and 'carried himself very haughtily'. He would be back before long, a poacher turned gamekeeper, as the EIC's governor in Madras. Child was strongly opposed to the choice of that 'roughling, immoral man', but had to accept strange allies in the struggle against the rival 'Dowgate Association'.

V

A dozen general elections between 1689 and 1715 rubbed home the new importance of Parliament as the main road to power, to office, and to the profits of office.

In the 1680s it might still cost only a few pounds to contest the election for a small borough; by the 1720s to fight there would demand hundreds. Direct bribery was not widespread, but the candidate would be expected to give his supporters food and drink, and to promise fine things to the electors – a town hall, a school, a water supply, plate for the corporation. Votes were traded, also, for patronage. Sir Henry Johnson, a rich East India merchant whose daughter married an earl, became MP for Aldeburgh after the Glorious Revolution. To consolidate his position there, he plied the local gentry with exotic presents from India. He also entertained applications for the East India Company clerkships.

Since votes were now so valuable, borough after borough acted to cut down its own number of electors. As party conflict bruised on, the swollen electorate was trimmed. It was now the tories who were commonly elected in the seats with the widest franchises, and who tried to defend the broad spread of votes among the people, whigs who acted time and again in Parliament to restrict the franchises. The tories spoke for the 'Country' against the 'Court', for small squires, yeomen, the cheated and the unlucky against the great and fortunate. Yet when in office they used their opponents' methods, lavishing lucrative posts on their supporters and so undermining their own position; the whigs floated on the wave of the future. The new whig party was in a minority in the country, but had a majority among the peers. Titled whig families were leagued with financial interests in the City of London. They sought, in the end successfully, for control of the vast new scope for patronage which the expansion of government opened up.

By the first years of the eighteenth century the Navy, with over 200 ships and about 50,000 seamen, was a grand reservoir of lucrative employment. In 1711 England had at least 70,000 soldiers in the field. Both these organisations, quite monstrous by prevailing standards, had to be clerked, had to be kept posted, had to be victualled. To support them, governments had to raise unheard-of sums in taxation. A Land Tax (1694) was one device which lasted; its inequitable collection bore hard on minor tory squires. Customs collection grew with trade; by 1718, there would be 561 full-time customs officers in the Port of London, besides over 1,000 part-timers. Plymouth and Liverpool would have over fifty full-time officers each; even the tiny port of Fowey in Cornwall would have twelve. There was a growing number of customs officials in the colonies, which also required postal clerks, army officers, judges, and formed quite an important field of patronage. The new administrative system was corrupt from top to bottom. While the numbers of people employed to collect taxes rose, the yield of each tax steadily fell. Commissions in the army were bought and sold while promotion of men without riches or influence became increasingly rare, and the soldiers went short of food, clothing and arms as their officers reimbursed themselves. Yet the system worked. England did not lose her wars.

'King William's War' did not, on the face of it, go very well. The English army was locked in a war of entrenchments and sieges in Flanders. Louis XIV's fleet was trounced at La Hogue in 1691, but this was small gain, as the French diverted their seamen into privateering, and England tasted the same punishment which its mariners had once meted out to Spain. Thousands of ships were lost, and an elaborate system of convoys was required to protect English trade.

But even the check to commerce was a gain for English industry. Strengthened by Huguenot expertise and capital which had migrated from France in the 1680s, it began to produce local substitutes for goods imported formerly from the Continent; paper and silk, cutlery and glass. There was an astonishing surge of speculation in new projects. The number of joint-stock companies in England and Scotland rose from 22 in 1688 to nearly 150 by the end of 1695. Besides prompting the rapid development of marine insurance, in which England would lead the world for so long, the war led to the creation in 1694 of the Bank of England. The government was in dire need of money. There were plenty of Englishmen so avid to invest that they were putting their money into hare-brained projects. Now approaching 1,300 shareholders came together in one grand finance company. In return for raising £1,200,000 to be lent to the government at 8 per cent, the company was incorporated as the first English joint-stock bank and empowered to issue notes, to discount bills and so forth. A stronghold of whiggery from the first, it brought a new flexibility and security to the nation's monetary system. The war, which cost about £40 million, left a debt of over £14 million, and a vital role not only for the Bank, but also for the East India Company.

Though few men-of-war could at the moment be spared to enforce the existing Navigation Acts, a new one was passed in 1696. Its aim was to tighten up the entire system. Colonial governors were made liable to a fine of £1,000 and dismissal for allowing breaches of the Act. Vice-Admiralty Courts were shortly set up in the New World to try infringements.

The Lords of Trade who had kept watch over the colonies from the mid-1670s had faltered in the commotions since 1685. Parliament wanted a Council of Trade controlled by itself. The Crown fought back to protect its prerogative. The new Board of Trade which emerged, though its name survives to this day, and though it was a precursor of the far later Colonial Office, was merely an awkward compromise. It included two peers and five experts, amongst whom the relatively idealistic John Locke balanced the thoroughly self-interested Blathwayt. Its role was advisory, not executive. At first its members showed energy – in 1697 they met more than four days a week – but in the early years of the new century, this fell away, and the Board became increasingly insignificant. New men who came on it were chiefly concerned with the £1,000 a year it paid them.

Meanwhile, the committee of the House of Commons which conducted a full-scale inquiry into trade in 1696 turned, in effect, into a court before which the EIC was tried. Its opponents raked up grievances old and new. The virtues of the 'joint stock' and of the 'regulated' sorts of company were proclaimed by their respective adherents. Yet what emerged was not decision upon the form of English trade with the East, but the impeachment of Lord Belhaven, William Paterson and others for 'high crimes and misdemeanours'. Their offence had been to organise the 'Company of Scotland for Trade with Africa and the Indies'.

VI

Scotland was not for the moment a military danger. After Dundee's Jacobite followers had gone home or had been beaten, garrisons had been put into the Highlands. At Inverlochy, where the Great Glen of Loch Ness, cutting the Highlands in two, debouched to the south-west, Fort William was erected, for rather different purposes than the strong building of the same name which would shortly arise at Calcutta. The aim was not to repel civilised might but to restrict the disorders which might be caused by those clans of Gaelic barbarians who had still not sworn allegiance to the Dutch King and whose mistrust of the now-triumphant Campbells still made them dangerous to the state which the Campbells supported.

In this context came about the most notorious of Highland massacres – most famous not because it was the worst but because it was ordered from London rather than from Edinburgh. William's chief agent in Scottish affairs was a clever lawyer, the Master of Stair. Dissident chiefs refused to take an oath of allegiance to William without the consent of the exiled James II. William offered pardon for all offences if they came in to swear by January 1, 1692. James's letter authorising his followers to do so was not received in the Highlands till just before Christmas. Even so, some chiefs came in by the stated time, and a minor Macdonald chieflet, MacIain of Glencoe, was able to give good excuse when he had his oath taken only six days late. But Stair, long before this, had decided to make an example of some Highlanders. The Macdonalds, as the 'only popish clan', seemed to him suitable victims – 'it will be popular to take a severe course with them.' Whether the Glencoe men were in fact Catholics is doubtful. But their sept was small, and relatively easy to get at. They were notorious raiders and rustlers, 'the worst', Stair alleged, 'in all the Highlands'. He decided that no one must escape. The passes out of their glen must be sealed. All must die.

A regiment of Campbells was now in existence. Soldiers from it, under Campbell of Glenlyon, were ordered into the bleak glen to do the job. For nearly a fortnight they enjoyed Macdonald hospitality. Then, one snowy morning in February, the trustful MacIain was shot down from behind as he called for a dram for his guests. But the massacre was botched. The passes were not sealed. Though thirty-eight Macdonalds were killed, ten times as many escaped to skulk on the bare hills. Colonel Hill, an old Cromwellian soldier who commanded at Fort William, an Englishman, was ordered to kill the remainder but pleaded for them instead, and after six months the sept occupied Glencoe once more. On the face of it, the massacre worked. The remaining chiefs were quick to submit. But the atrocity, which shocked Scotland, was a gift to Jacobite propagandists. Stair's political enemies used it to oust him from the office.

Most important Scots were trying to move away from the nation's violent past. The last wolf in the country seems to have perished about this time, though the last witch would not be executed until 1727 (fifteen years after England's last witchcraft case). The modern dining-room was taking the place of the baronial hall. Even on Skye, Macleod of Dunvegan now ate in private, to the dismay of his bards. The wealthier classes cherished Dutch linen and, though there were few roads fit to drive them on, imported English coaches to show that they could afford them. As in Ireland, even the poor now chewed, smoked and sneezed tobacco.

The English were noticing that some tobacco now slipped in through Glasgow. But well-to-do Scots themselves were perturbed by the country's lack of success in overseas trade. The native shipbuilding industry was minimal, and merchants relied on vessels bought in Holland or Norway. Yet imports were, or seemed, essential. Scottish coopers bought staves from Ireland and ready-made iron hoops from Flanders. The Dundee linen weavers used Polish flax. French claret was virtually a national drink.

England was, and growingly so, the most important area for Scottish foreign trade – the only place where Scots cattle would wend on the hoof for sale, and the only place where Scots could find an outlet for their poor-quality linen. But the English put up, then increased, tariffs against Scottish linen. They protected the Tyneside coal-mines against competition from the Forth. Scottish governments did their best to retort in kind. A Scottish Navigation Act in 1661 had matched the English one. In the 1670s, amid hopes and fanfares, a Royal Fishery Company was established with a monopoly, but it collapsed within eleven years. The government tried to stimulate the manufacture of better woollen cloth, but the products could not compete with the English for price and quality even on the home market. Of new industries founded, only sugar refining had much success.

An independent Scottish foreign policy would have ruled out war with France, an important trading partner. But the Union of the Crowns, and William III's war against Louis XIV, exposed Scots merchants to privateers against whom they had no fleet to protect them, while the relatively small body of Scottish seamen was depleted to fill the English navy. The 1690s were years of dire crisis. Bad harvests in 1695, 1696 and 1698 produced such horrors that it was said that in some rural areas a third or even a half of the population died or left the country. On top of this, all the main export commodities, except cattle to England, were now affected by tariff barriers and prohibitions abroad. The French forbade the import of Scottish woollens and fish. Tariffs since 1670 had blocked the export of Scottish corn to England; now they were raised against it in Norway, too, a vital source of ships and timber. Competition from Belgian mines, a reduction of export duties by the English, and prohibitive rates imposed in the Spanish Netherlands themselves, stemmed the traditional trade in coal to the Low Countries. The English in 1698 increased the duties on Scots linen, while the new Navigation Act passed two years before had been largely aimed at Scottish interlopers, and raised questions about the legality of Scots holding office in English colonies.

The promise of the New World was growingly obvious. A settler in East New Jersey reported home in 1685 that he had met a man 'who was sent away by Cromwell to New England, a slave from Dunbar. Living now in Woodbridge like a Scots Laird, wishes his countrymen and his Native Soyle very well, tho' he never intends to see it.' Andrew Hamilton, governor of New Jersey from 1692, a Scot, was accused of being a 'great favourer of the Scotch traders his countrymen', and was temporarily robbed of his office on the grounds that he was not a 'natural born subject of England' as the terms of the Navigation Act of 1696 demanded.

Everywhere outside the Highlands, landlords were becoming commercially minded, aiming to sell their agricultural surplus when there was one, to make textiles, to profit from coal and lead. The country thus with remarkable solidarity pitched itself into a rash bid for effective economic independence. What would abort it before long was the fact that trade across the Border in linen and cattle was the most useful of Scotland's real assets.

Scotland already had a share in one important colony, in Ulster. There was a brisk trade exchanging Scots coal and manufactures for the produce of the settlers there. But Ulster farmers could offer nothing not grown or made already on Scottish estates, and the landowners who dominated the Scottish government did everything possible to stop imports of victuals from Ireland. A tropical colony giving Scotland its own source of sugar and of tobacco would be far more acceptable. And some Edinburgh merchants were taking an interest in the possibilities of trade with Africa. In 1693, then, the Scottish Parliament passed an Act giving permission for the formation of joint-stock companies to trade with countries not at war with the Crown. This opened the way to a further Act of 1695 establishing the 'Company of Scotland for Trade with Africa and the Indies'.

At this stage, some London interlopers saw a Scottish company as a means of attacking the RAC and EIC monopolies, and the primacy given to Africa in the name suggests that the weaker RAC was the main target. That Guinea was forgotten and the 'Indies' became paramount had much to do with the personality and ideas of a prominent London-based Scot, William Paterson. He had recently taken a leading part in the formation of the Bank of England, but he had nursed for years the dream of an entrepôt on the Isthmus of Darien, that narrow neck of land where Central and South America join. Paterson – pious Christian and pushful businessman, patriot Scot and ardent internationalist – was a man whose apparent self-contradictions would often recur among his Caledonian compatriots. He had left his homeland young and had knocked about as a trader in the Caribbean before settling in London. When he was consulted by those creating the new company, the intention was to find half its capital in England, and an equal number of London-based and Scottish-based directors were appointed. Paterson assumed leadership at the London end. From the outset his thinking was idealistic and grandiose.

To Paterson it was 'this great and noble Undertaking.' To others it seemed no more than a squalid fiddle by certain people aiming to break the EIC monopoly who, when they failed in that aim, went on to deceive the Scottish people with impossible promises. The aim was to raise £300,000 in each country. Subscription books opened in London first, in November 1695, and were closed after little more than a fortnight with that much money promised. But the House of Lords intervened and summoned the London directors for questioning. The Commons, as we have seen, resolved to impeach twenty-three people, but since an essential witness, the Company's secretary, had prudently removed himself to Edinburgh, the trial could not go forward. But the London investors took fright and withdrew their money. The few directors who remained loyal retreated to Scotland. And in that country, there was a surge of feeling recalling the Covenant of 1637. The cause of a trading company now united a people as the reformed religion had once done. When William dismissed the Scottish ministers who had, he said, 'ill served' him, this news fanned the enthusiasm.

The Company's Scottish directors, a few months before, had thought £300,000 was more than their nation could raise. Now they threw caution away and appealed for £400,000 (sterling), in effect about half the total capital which was available at that time in Scotland. They got it. Covenanter and Cavalier, whig and Jacobite subscribed together. The Earl of Argyll put up £1,500, the Viscount of Stair £1,000, the landed classes together nearly half the capital. The merchants of Glasgow and Edinburgh found another quarter, those of the lesser burghs joined in, and the rising class of lawyers added their piles. In less than six months, by early August 1696, the subscription books were filled and a first call on the subscribers had already produced £100,000. Yet this was a year of famine, the second in succession.

The directors still toyed with the ideas of the African slave trade. But the persuasive tongue and epic imagination of William Paterson convinced them that they, the Scots, must now try to realise his vision of an entrepôt on the Isthmus which could gather, he argued, the trade of the whole world. Darien was the 'door of the seas and the key of the universe'; it would enable its proprietors to 'give laws to both oceans', Atlantic and Pacific, and 'to become arbitrators of the commercial world, without being liable to the fatigues, expenses and dangers, or contracting the guilt and blood of Alexander and Caesar.' Sir Josiah Child knew better: 'All trade is a kind of warfare.'

Paterson showed his fellow directors an account of Darien written by a young pirate, who proclaimed the soil fertile, the Indians friendly, the whole country a leafy El Dorado, rich in colours and scent. Hadn't Morgan and other buccaneers quite recently shown how weak Spain was in this area? There was, furthermore, nothing that the English could do to prevent a settlement on the Isthmus.

However, when Paterson went abroad to seek capital, the Dutch East and West India Companies blocked his way in Holland, and the English consul in Hamburg baulked him there by threatening the city's rulers with King William's displeasure. The first wise impulse of the directors in Edinburgh was to wind up. Their second was to appeal to the King. William equivocated. No German money came in. The Darien venture went ahead.

Twelve hundred men, a quarter of them 'gentlemen', were gathered. Soldiers recently discharged at the end of William's war with France made up much of the party, and one of the more resourceful members, as it turned out, was Thomas Drummond, who as a grenadier captain had played a grim and notable part in the massacre at Glencoe. In November 1698 the fort and township of 'New Edinburgh' was founded in Darien, now renamed 'Caledonia'. The commonplace horrors of first settlement in the New World, and the East, at that time, were repeated. The Scots suffered as the Jamestown settlers had suffered and as Englishmen had done, more recently, at Bencoolen. Disease raged; food was short; the Council squabbled. But the first messages home were optimistic. The Indians were friendly. Ships from New England and Jamaica were willing to trade. What destroyed the colonists' spirit was the news that the governor of Jamaica, in common, as it turned out, with all the English colonial authorities, had ordered that the Scots must not be dealt with or helped in any way whatsoever. William, anxious for friendship with Spain against France, had disowned the Scots in face of Spanish protests. In June 1699 the survivors abandoned their cluster of huts and rude fort on the Isthmus. More than 300 had died already. Many more perished on a dreadful journey via Jamaica to New

York; the English authorities in both places were unable to help and were obliged to obstruct. In the end, only 300 sailed from New York home.

In Scotland, public demonstrations of joy had marked the news that the settlement had been made, followed by rage when word came of the English proclamations against 'Caledonia'. An expedition to reinforce it, with 1,300 people, including 100 women and 4 ministers of the kirk, was sent out in the summer of 1699. This new party, after a few demoralising weeks, had to meet a determined Spanish attack by land and by sea. Resistance would have been crazy. Surrender on generous terms, in April 1700, was followed by a second, and final abandonment of 'New Edinburgh'.

Meanwhile, shame and despair in Scotland had turned outwards as indignation against the King and the English. The Scottish Parliament was hastily adjourned, in May 1700, when it tried to insist that the Darien settlement was within the terms of the Act of 1696, though William now said it was not. Four great ships had carried the second party of colonists. None returned, and only a handful of the people whom they had carried.

There was little the Company could do. Africa was remembered. Four ships were sent. One came back, and its cargo of gold dust and ivory brought the Company its only trading profits, some £48,000 (Scots).

It was its own folly, not English hostility, which had led to the Company's wasting complete over £150,000 (sterling), perhaps a sixth or a quarter of Scotland's total liquid capital. It had attempted an enterprise which even the English or French could have pulled off only in favourable circumstances, yet it had come nowhere near to assembling the financial resources required. But hardly a family of substance had not lost money or kin through Darien, and rage against the English seethed.

VII

In Scotland there would always be many detractors, indeed haters, of William III, whose reign was marked by famine, by Glencoe, and by the disaster at Darien. For the New England colonists, by contrast, the Glorious Revolution of 1688 would become a sacred moment, the writings of Locke a species of holy writ. To understand why this was so, we must return to the scene in Boston in the 1670s.

The heirs of Gorges and Mason, whose stake dated back to the earliest days of New England, pressed their claims to Maine and New Hampshire respectively. The Lords of Trade decided to demand that Massachusetts sent agents to London to respond to these claims, and Edward Randolph, a young man related by marriage to the Masons, was given the job of special courier. He was hard up, ambitious and grasping.

He wanted the Crown to intervene in Massachusetts so that he could receive office under it, and he reported home accordingly. The colony's leaders, he said, were 'inconsiderable Mechanicks', merely front men for Dissenting zealots who

were 'generally inclined to Sedition'. The Crown, he reckoned, was losing over
£100,000 a year in customs.

At first Randolph did not have things all his own way. In 1677, the Lords
Chief Justices in London upheld Gorges's right to Maine but decided against
the Mason claim and found the Massachusetts Charter valid despite Randolph's
propaganda against it. But then the colony overplayed its hand. It made what
was almost a unilateral declaration of independence. The General Court
declared that the Navigation Acts were in force 'by the authority of this Court'.
It was argued that since Massachusetts was not represented in Parliament, laws
passed there could not bind its trade; however, its assembly would humour the
English by passing the Acts itself. The Lords of Trade were soon clear that only
revocation of the Charter and the appointment of a royal governor would suffice.
Meanwhile, Randolph was appointed collector of customs for New England,
and came back in December 1679 as the first salaried civil servant ever stationed
by the Crown in Boston.

He found some support. There were many wealthy merchants who looked
socially and culturally to England for models, who recognised their dependence
on the English trading system and who resented – this was an old grievance –
the fact that rich men were outvoted in the General Court by the representatives
of petty traders and country cultivators. Those who hoped for religious
toleration also sided with Randolph, as did opportunists of all sorts. In New
Hampshire, an area of vast forests and few white denizens, Randolph was able,
in 1680, to bring to birth the second royal colony in North America. But in
Massachusetts he met frustration. His salary was only £100 a year. His aim was
to augment it with the 50 per cent of confiscated goods which would be due to
him as informer against smugglers. His rapacity ran up against the stolid
defiance of Massachusetts juries.

In October 1684 the Massachusetts Charter was declared vacated in the court
of Chancery. The years during which this threat had overhung the colony had
seen the strains of its life emphasised. A synod of clergy and lay elders which met
in Boston in 1679 to discuss God's controversy with New England reported a
vast mass of iniquities. Heretics were numerous. Swearing had increased. The
disposition to slumber during sermons was growing. Mixed dancing was
rampant. While the wealthy speculated in land, workmen demanded
unreasonable wages. In fact, all such abominations were symptoms of a
prosperity based, though chiefly for town dwellers, on trade.

But rural die-hards still dominated the General Court. To such men the
willingness of the 'moderates' to negotiate over the Charter and to accept even
its disappearance was base dereliction and blasphemy. The Charter was the
safeguard of the Congregational Church system, and men whose lives centred
on the land feared that if it was voided, their holdings would revert to the
Crown. What was at stake was the character of Massachusetts village life, in
which religious intolerance consorted with the co-operative farming of land still

held in strips in open fields, and with the herding of animals communally. The 'moderates' ran into furious vituperation. Joseph Dudley, son of a founder of the colony, went to England on a mission of negotiation in 1682 and on his return was dismissed from his seat as a magistrate. But God was extremely quarrelsome. In May 1686, this same Dudley became president of a temporary Council of quislings, dominated by rich merchants.

Richard Dunn has commented on the 'overbearing executive style of the 1680s'. In each colony Charles II's agents aimed to prise out of power whichever local interests were in control and to substitute a new combination of persons prepared to work under the governor who served the King. In the West Indies, Dutton in Barbados, the Duke of Albemarle in Jamaica, Sir Nathaniel Johnson in the Leewards, all called on the grumbling small farmers to help them push the bigger landowners from their entrenched positions in council, assembly and judiciary; this was a counterpart of the attack on the corporations in England which, under James II, produced an Anabaptist Lord Mayor of London. The most striking exemplar of the drive to royal absolutism would be Edmund Andros in the novel 'Dominion of New England'.

Andros had first arrived in America in 1674 as governor of New York, and had soon outraged New Englanders by reviving James, Duke of York's claim to the western part of Connecticut. Only a show of force on their part had stopped him from making this good with his troops. Now, in December 1686, he appeared in Boston, and began a revolution from above which matched in miniature his royal master's work in England. James broke with the English Parliament; Andros did away with representative bodies in New England.

Andros was empowered to govern Plymouth Colony and to annex Rhode Island. Both were smoothly taken over. Connecticut was soon added to the list. New York and New Jersey were brought in during 1688. But Andros was moving too fast, like James at home. He alienated the well-to-do 'moderates'. He alarmed all landholders when he ordained that new grants of undeveloped land should be subject to a quitrent of 2s. 6d. per 100 acres, and that all existing titles were to be reviewed for confirmation subject to such payment as he, Andros, might decide.

New England learnt only slowly and piecemeal of the 'Glorious Revolution'. Official confirmation of the accession of William and Mary did not arrive until May 26, 1689, three months after they had accepted the crown. But already, on April 18, the townspeople of Boston, getting wind of events in Britain, had dealt with Andros and his Dominion. Dissident 'moderates' like Wait-Still Winthrop, grandson of the founder, joined with unreconciled supporters of the old Charter such as the famous minister, Cotton Mather. Under the guidance of these men, over a thousand Bostonians rose in arms, forced a bloodless capitulation, and had the satisfaction of imprisoning Andros, Randolph and Dudley. A provisional 'Council for the Safety of the People' took over while the other New England colonies went ahead and re-established their former governments.

In Virginia, the revolution was transacted peacefully. In Maryland, rebellion forced the surrender of Lord Baltimore's governor and his Catholic-dominated council. In New York, more drastic conflict happened. At the end of May, a large part of the militia, led by a malcontent merchant of German birth named Jacob Leisler, and supported by 'mob' action, seized Fort James at the lower end of Manhattan island. A representative convention gave authority to a Council of Safety and named Leisler Commander-in-Chief. The new governor, Henry Sloughter, nominated in England in September 1689, took a year and a half to reach his post, and Leisler, who had assumed the title of 'Lieutenant Governor', had to meet the shock, early in 1690, of the sack of Schenectady by a French and Indian force.

He was able to arrange a concerted attack on the French with the New England colonies. Massachusetts, in April 1690, had sponsored a successful venture against Port Royal in Acadia, where a weak French garrison had promptly surrendered and much plunder had been taken. Sir William Phips, leader of the expedition, was an archetype of the local boy made good. A native of Maine, illiterate till his teens, he had risen as seaman and trader and had become famous after he had found, on behalf of an English syndicate, a sunken Spanish treasure ship off Haiti. (Phips had cleared £16,000 himself, and James II, receiving £40,000, had knighted him.) Now the sack of Port Royal made him a popular hero in Boston, plunder in hand begot a taste for more, and the northern colonies were emboldened to mount an ambitious joint plan for the conquest of Canada. An overland strike from Albany against Montreal was to coincide with an amphibious assault on Quebec led by Phips, who took 32 ships and 1,300 soldiers with him. But his attack failed, and the other invasion aborted below Lake Champlain.

After Sloughter's arrival Leisler was hanged for treason. But New York at last got a representative assembly to match those now restored elsewhere. The delays which had undone the luckless Leisler reflected the fact that the new regime in England had at first no time to spare for the plantations. When it moved, the results were somewhat paradoxical. William had no prejudice against men with a reputation for upholding the royal prerogative, and Andros, sent home for trial, soon returned to the New World as governor of Virginia, while Dudley became president of the Council in New York and Randolph was commissioned as surveyor general of customs for the whole of North America. The Catholic Lord Baltimore was deprived of political control of Maryland, which came under royal rule for a quarter of a century until another Lord Baltimore prudently converted to Anglicanism in 1715. William Penn stood in greater danger, as one of James II's most conspicuous favourites. In 1689, there was a warrant out for his arrest under suspicion of high treason, and he was indeed involved in Jacobite intrigues towards an invasion from France before he finally submitted to William III in 1694, and won control of his colony back.

Massachusetts was given charge of the whole of Maine and digested little

Plymouth Colony. A new charter in 1691 ensured that existing titles in land held and that colonists need not pay quitrents to the Crown, but William III insisted there must still be a royal governor, who would have power to adjourn, prorogue and dissolve the House of Representatives and to veto its legislation, all of which must now be sent to England for approval. This emaciation of Massachusetts' liberty did not worry the thriving merchants, who through alliance with the governor could now make the Council their political voice.

Phips, still a local idol, was made governor and arrived in May 1692 to find the notorious Salem witch-hunt in progress. This episode coincided with deeply felt outrage among traditionalists over the new charter and reflected deep social unease in the colony. The mania began when two sick children in Salem claimed that a black servant, Tituba, was bewitching them, others cried out against her, and she 'confessed'. Children, servants and women, all underprivileged in Puritan society, fed the growing hysteria which began with informers, mainly girls, naming lowly neighbours as witches who were afflicting them and swept on till the accusations struck at Lady Phips and other prominent people. Some fifty persons who 'confessed' were spared. Those subjects who denied guilt suffered. A court, opening on June 2, had by September 22 condemned 27 people to death, of whom 20 had been executed. There were 100 people in gaol awaiting trial and double that number had been accused but not yet imprisoned. At this point Phips at last called a halt.

Larzer Ziff had seen the craze as originally a spasm amongst the weakest elements of Massachusetts society 'whose lives were no longer of public consequence as the politics of empire took hold . . .' The fact that the accusers were frail and lowly showed that even the least of the people which God had chosen mattered. Massachusetts retained an unearned notoriety (in persecution of 'witches' it had never matched Scotland, or England) and Cotton Mather justly earned the obloquy of posterity by writing to whitewash the trials for English readers.

The colony from its beginnings had been alienated from the Crown, but with the Stuarts ousted, all seemed different. Massachusetts divines poured sycophantic praise on their Calvinist new Dutch monarch; Mather hailed him as 'the Phoenix of this Age' and William became a symbol of Protestant virtue, the champion of truth against Papist France. However, Massachusetts leaders still showed a very good conceit of their colony's special status in the eyes of God. Mather boasted that his fellow colonists had 'proportionately more of God among them than any part of mankind besides'.

While Boston merchants, true to form, throve on the wartime conditions which deflected so much English shipping from the New World trades, frontier settlers fought deadly war against French and Indians. English outnumbered French in North America by about twenty to one. When the Canada colony was taken under direct royal control in 1663, New France had only about 2,500 settlers. By 1676 there were 8,500. An influx of colonists sponsored by the

French state included consignments of young pauper girls (*filles de roi*) who were expected to breed, promptly. The Canadian population doubled in each generation. Other policies were far less successful. Colbertian mercantilism aimed to create on the St Lawrence a replica of rural France, chiefly devoted to sending flour, provisions and timber to the French colonies in the West Indies. The fur trade stood in the way. Its lure took Frenchmen through the unexplored continent and established claims to enormous territories almost in Louis XIV's despite.

The Comte de Frontenac was governor in Quebec from 1672 to 1682, and from 1690 until his death in 1698. A brave old man with a violent temper, he was also extremely greedy and fostered the fur trade, from which he himself profited greatly, in spite of the orders which he received from home. Under his governorship, the Sieur de la Salle explored the Mississippi valley down to the river's mouth and claimed the whole for the Crown, committing France to struggle, eventually, for a continent. The society which Frontenac ruled was, like him, insubordinate and obsessed with furs. Even the Jesuits who dominated its religious life were tied to the fur trade by their interest in the conversion of the Indian sellers and middlemen. In theory government was royal and autocratic. The Council and the officials were all chosen by the King. But in practice the colonists were as free as they wished to be.

The land was divided among feudal *seigneurs*. These granted holdings in turn to vassals who paid very modest dues. Canadian feudalism ruled out land speculation. The *seigneurs* stood to make little, were drawn into the fur trade, and helped to swell the numbers of the *coureurs de bois* who met the competition of the Hudson's Bay English and the Albany Dutch by undertaking long voyages to trade with remote tribes, cutting out the middlemen and spending as much as two or three years at a time away from the colony. English trade goods were generally cheaper, and English woollen cloth was superior in quality. But the red men sensibly liked brandy better than rotgut rum.

The *coureur*, whether a hired *engagé*, an entrepreneur in his own right or a freebooter interbreeding with red women and trading shamelessly with the Albany men, was a counterpart, in the forests, of his contemporary, the buccaneer. But they were heroes in New France, a markedly individualistic society. Peasants resisted attempts by the Crown to gather them into villages for defence. Every Canadian became an irregular soldier.

Three times in the 1680s and 1690s the legendary D'Iberville, who almost always fought against odds and was never beaten, led parties of Canadians which swept the Hudson's Bay Company out of its forts; leaving on each occasion only one. Meanwhile Frontenac waged *la petite guerre*, sending raiding parties against English frontier townships and hostile Iroquois villages. New France overdid it. By 1695 supplies of furs were running at four times the demand of the French market, and next year clear orders were sent from Paris that the up-country trade must be stopped.

Meanwhile the English were learning, like the Canadians, methods of forest fighting from the red men. Each side provoked Indian allies to massacre. The sufferings of English men, women and children, taken on long marches through the snows and then forced to work for the Indians as slaves, confirmed the stereotype of the red man's inhuman ferocity. Scalp hunting was seen by the North-east American Indians as the way a young brave gave proof of his entry into manhood. The English were shocked by it. Yet they encouraged it, offering bounties in King Philip's war and thereafter for the heads of their own enemies, and they allied with the Iroquois, a people detested by their red neighbours for their cruelty. The Iroquois tortured captives, for instance sticking short pieces of wood all over a man's body, then setting them alight; or they might tear all his flesh off while he was still alive. On the other hand, they neither burnt witches nor employed the cat-o'-nine-tails.

The so-called 'Five Nations of Iroquois' – Mohawks, Oneidas, Onondagas, Cayugas and Senecas – lived across upper New York colony. There were other Iroquoian-speaking people. Amongst these, the Hurons and Susquehannocks were cardinal enemies of the Five Nations, but the Tuscaroras migrated north to join them in the second decade of the eighteenth century after losing a war with Carolina, and became the sixth member of the league, which controlled the Mohawk valley, the easiest route between the eastern seaboard and the fur-filled heart of the continent.

The solidarity of the Five Nations was attributed by legend to the efforts of a Mohawk chief or shaman named Hiawatha in the late sixteenth century. The constitution of their league may have influenced that of the USA. At the annual summer conventions, the fifty Council members voted by tribes, each tribe having one vote. The five nations only rarely agreed to unite against a common enemy, but blood-feuds and serious internal strife were avoided. The fifty federal Sachems or Peace Chiefs were appointed by women and could only be deposed by women; this was because the basic Iroquois social unit was the mother with her children. So the League linked five republics in which women had a crucial position at every level of decision-making.

Allied with the English in the 1690s, the Iroquois suffered heavy losses from casualties and from defection to the French, whose priests converted numerous tribesmen to Catholicism. The main body stood by the English, who asked for fewer beaver skins for their guns. But it was the far more numerous English whose greed for land threatened them in the long run.

By 1700 'English' colonists possessed the coastline from Maine to South Carolina. Most people still clung to the shorelines and navigable rivers which gave a direct link with Europe. Boston, at or near 7,000, was the largest town. Virginia and Maryland had perhaps 90,000 colonists, New England about the same number, the 'Middle Colonies' something above 50,000 and the Carolinas perhaps 16,000; altogether, about a quarter million – far fewer than the population of London. However, numbers – as in New France – had doubled, perhaps trebled, since 1660. The New World, in temperate regions, was healthier and more evenly prosperous than the old. Families seem to have been on average twice as large as in England. More children survived infancy.

Every frontiersman carried, except at his peril, a flintlock musket, rather inaccurate beyond fifty yards, but deadly enough at close quarters. However, abundance of timber was an immense advantage, and venison and wild turkey from the forests, supplementing beef and pork from domestic animals able to graze widely, meant that new colonists ate far more meat than people back home. There was plentiful maple sugar and, to southward, native exotica such as peaches. Abundance of land made tillers extremely careless. Even the thrifty New Englanders seem to have discarded the more difficult English agricultural practices, without, however, adopting the best Indian ones.

Established farmers, except in New England, soon acquired more land than they could work with their own hands. The labour of free whites was from the outset extremely expensive. The unskilled worker could command two or three shillings a day compared to a shilling in England, while artisans and craftsmen could ask as much as 8s. 6d. Free workmen could soon afford to buy land themselves and would ride away to independence. The demand for servants was so hot that numerous Turks were imported into the Chesapeake.

New England, with no headright system, and few large holdings, scorned the servant trade. After the great influx of the 1630s, its population grew by natural increase, supplemented by seamen glad to resign or desert from shipboard life. But land grants in New York were very large, and the inhabitants clamoured for all the servants merchants could bring them, and more. That they were left short reflected the greater attraction of Pennsylvania, where the Quakers, furthermore, frowned on the use of black slaves. Maryland and Virginia had a steady supply from the tobacco ships. The only North American colony which had to offer special inducements to bring in white servants was South Carolina which, with an actual majority of black slaves by 1708, was in the same predicament as Jamaica and Barbados.

Even so, no North American colony was glad to accept felons, of whom some 4,500 were destined to transportation from England in the last four decades of the seventeenth century, though far fewer would have been shipped or would have arrived. By 1696 the Board of Trade found that only Barbados would still accept them, and even there women and children were not wanted. The problem was temporarily mitigated by renewed war early in the eighteenth century, which gave felons alternative employment in the forces.

The only advantage of buying convicts was that they served seven or fourteen years. By the end of the seventeenth century, a five-year term for indentured servants over a certain age was laid down by law in Virginia and Maryland, and a similar law was made in South Carolina by 1717. It can be argued that the greater rarity of active unrest shows that even people under indentures felt better off in America than in England. But Maryland court records show that a significant number of servants committed suicide. Clearing virgin forests under duress was punishing. Most runaway servants, being white, made good their escape, but newspaper advertisements commonly described them as having collars round their necks.

On the face of it, servants once freed should have been able to prosper. In Pennsylvania and the colonies southward, the authorities, to encourage expansion, granted land on easy terms. Some servants in fact did well. Up to 1666, it would seem that a third or more of landholders in Virginia had come in under indentures. But then, three-quarters of all colonists had entered in that condition. A. E. Smith has calculated that over the whole colonial period in North America, out of ten servants eight either died during their time, returned to England afterwards, or became 'poor-whites'. Only one would become a landholder, and the last would go to work for wages. Yet there was never much hint of concerted rebellion amongst servants in any mainland colony. Running away was easy in early days. Later the influx of black slaves helped to pacify truculence, giving the hardest-ground white servant a consciousness of status.

In 1671 there were still only a couple of thousand slaves in Virginia. Tobacco did not insist on slaves like sugar. Why did slavery and North American society become inseparable? Greed for acres is one major explanation. 'The God Land' ruled in Virginia still more strongly than in New England; the headright system ensured that land could be claimed in respect of slaves imported; the supply of servants from England was never enormous; shipmasters could supply black people on the spot in return for tobacco and other produce. By 1700 slaves in Virginia were the chief basis of the acquisition of title to land, and the colony had perhaps 6,000 blacks. Within the next decade, Virginia's slave population doubled.

South Carolina had been under West Indian influence from its beginnings. In the last decade of the seventeenth century, rice became the colony's chief staple, and this crop was slave-cultivated from the outset. South Carolina borrowed from the already mature slave code of Barbados, and legislation there was the harshest on the mainland; blacks had no rights at all.

Virginia codified its slave laws in 1705. By now quite small landowners were committed to the institution. From 1691, Virginian law, which had previously borne hard on the practice, outlawed interracial sexual liaison completely as 'abominable mixture'.

There were, and had long been, free people of colour in Virginia. In 1654, 100 acres had been granted to a Negro carpenter on the basis of headrights conferred in respect of two whites. In 1697, John Nicholls left by will 500 acres to two mulattoes, presumably his own children. But when another Virginian planter in his will had not only emancipated a slave, bequeathing him a house and as much ground as he could cultivate, but had also appointed him guardian of a girl ward of his, and overseer of her property, a court had not allowed him to fulfil such offices. Free blacks could own Indian or black slaves, but no longer white servants. In 1723 black freemen, along with mulattoes and Indians, would be specifically excluded from voting. Meanwhile, emancipation was frowned on. A Virginian law of 1699 required the exportation of every African freeman within six months of his emancipation, on penalty to the planter of a levy upon his own property.

By this time, Massachusetts law also was overtly prejudiced, distinguishing mulattoes as well as Negroes in a separate category. A traveller of 1687, commenting on the scarcity of white labour there, alleged that every household in Boston, 'however small may be its Means', had one or two blacks. A patently racialist Massachusetts Act of 1705 'for the Better Preventing of a Spurious and Mixt Issue' imposed a duty of £4 a head on all blacks imported.

One of the most perfected expressions of prejudice to be found at this time comes from the wife of a Boston merchant, Sarah Kemble Knight, who travelled through Connecticut in 1704. She wrote sharply that the people there were 'too Indulgent (especially the farmers) to their slaves: suffering too great familiarity from them, permitting them to sit at Table and eat with them, (as they say to save time,) and into the dish goes the black hoof as freely as the white hand.'

Mrs Knight's worldly snobbery was symptomatic. Boston now had scores of public houses. New England and Pennsylvania were chaste places compared with Barbados or Jamaica, but the whores of Boston were famous throughout the colonies and the Philadelphia Quakers sometimes tippled quite heavily. Dress among Puritans and Quakers was decorous, but black was not general, let alone uniform. Puritans approved of athletic sports (including cricket, an early passenger to America) and had no objection to secular songs if they were not bawdy.

The Puritans were turning into the Yankee, byword the world over for commercial sharpness. Sobriety, thrift and frugality – 'credit-making virtues' – dominated in Boston and Philadelphia. But the seemingly inexhaustible acres of virgin land on which successful traders would cast lustful eyes gave American capitalism an especially marked tendency, which it has never lost, to the reckless, improvident exploitation of natural resources.

Resilient optimism was to be a more pleasant outcome of the scope for westward expansion. Toleration, if not always tolerance, was another liberating force at work. It was rare for any one denomination to have a clear majority in any single polity, and so, as Richard Hofstadter puts it, America 'stumbled into virtue'. In 1660 only Maryland and Rhode Island had been officially tolerant, and other colonies had been under theoretically tight State-Church rule. Yet by 1700 even Massachusetts, thanks to pressures from England, had made ample concessions.

Though New England Congregationalism differed markedly from Virginian Anglicanism, each was remote in practice from the Church of England. Neither colony had bishops. While in New England marriage was from the outset a civil contract, in Virginia, where the civil authority issued licences, it tended to become so. Where Anglicanism was not established, it appealed chiefly to a self-conscious élite, hopefully sycophantic before the English governor, anxious to emphasise the gap which new-made wealth had set between themselves and the ordinary colonist.

There were people in North America who saw themselves as gentlemen and were seen to be so. Deference was still given readily to a Winthrop or Carter. But in terms of English society then, they were what we would call middle class. 'No house in New England hath above 20 Rooms,' it was reported in the 1670s. 'Not 20 in Boston, which have above 10 rooms each . . . The worst cottages in New England are lofted. No beggars. Not 3 put to death for theft.'

This was at the other pole from the West Indies, where contrasts in wealth were sharp, as in the homeland. The difference has been established by Richard Dunn, comparing probated estates in Jamaica and Maryland in the late seventeenth century, as these are shown in inventories. Proportionately, there were ten times as many wealthy men in Jamaica, and the wealthiest there were very much richer. The contrast with New England was stronger still.

But whereas few planters in the Caribbean owned more than a handful of books, Massachusetts could boast many sizeable libraries, partly because New England clergymen were commonly well-to-do, whereas West Indian parsons were almost poor-whites. Largely because very few mainland colonials were rich enough to support a position in English society as prestigious as that which they could enjoy, big fish in small pools, in America, absentee landownership never became common, as it was in the West Indies and in Ireland. Cultural standards reflected this fact. By the 1670s Harvard was managed by its own graduates rather than by men trained in England. The College of William and Mary in Virginia was founded before the end of the century, and Yale just into the eighteenth, taking its name later from Elihu Yale, born near Boston in 1648, who served for five years as governor of Madras and assisted the college in Connecticut with a gift of books and pictures worth £560.

Boston had its own printing press before the Civil War, Philadelphia almost from its inception. Literacy, unusually widespread in England itself, was even more so in the northern colonies. There was not much call for light literature; Virginian planters seem to have been almost as fond of reading sermons as Massachusetts magistrates. The great Anglo-Welsh religious poet George Herbert was far more popular in North America than any writer of love lyrics.

Good books could be imported from England, along with kettles and cloth. Verbally fluent young men in North America would aspire in politics rather than literature. As in ancient Athens or Renaissance Italy, the abundance of servile labour helped to support a remarkably widespread participation in the running of affairs, both in Church and State.

Massachusetts with, after 1691, its new 40s. freehold qualification, still had almost universal male suffrage. Pennsylvania came to provide an exceptional instance of assembly-power. Penn returned in 1699, planning to live out his days in the New World; two years later he reluctantly conceded a 'Charter of Privileges' by which the Council was excluded from legislation, though the governor would still have a veto. But even Pennsylvania was not 'democratic'. In practice, its politics were dominated till 1756 by an oligarchy of wealthy Quakers, of whom Penn himself, an authentic English gentleman, wrote sarcastically, 'There is an excess of vanity that is apt to creep in upon the people in power in America, who, having got out of the crowd in which they were lost here, upon every little eminency there, think nothing taller than themselves but the trees . . .' He was bitter not only against the anti-proprietorial opposition led by a Welshman named David Lloyd, but also over the fact that his quitrents did not come in.

While Quakerism became the religion of plump merchants who still dressed plainly, but in the finest cloth, a revived and rather militant Anglicanism tried to regain lost ground in America. From 1685 James Blair, a Scottish Anglican clergyman, settled in Virginia as Commissary for the Bishop of London. This was the first appointment in the colonies to an office with general supervisory over Church and clergy. Blair married into Virginia's élite and was strong enough, with the Bishop's help, to get Governor Andros removed from office in 1698; then he engaged, with other Council members, in a furious struggle with the new governor, Francis Nicholson. The Church in Virginia had been virtually Congregational in form. Local landowners, as vestrymen, had hired and fired clergymen. The house of burgesses backed Nicholson against Blair, but the latter's connections in London finally unseated this governor also. Blair's counterpart in Maryland was Commissary Thomas Bray, founder of the Society for the Propagation of the Gospel. After a long struggle with local Quakers (and their lobby in London), Anglicanism was established by law in Maryland from 1702. Two years later the South Carolina Assembly excluded Dissenters from membership and provided for an Anglican establishment, but the Nonconformists made such a powerful fuss that revised legislation in 1706 removed Church membership as a test for office.

New England clerical families intermarried, and only a few exceptional men could penetrate their caste. Against the Congregational tradition, they began in the 1690s to organise themselves as a professional group, and to strive for control of the churches. In Connecticut, in 1708, a quasi-Presbyterian system was adopted by law, under which neighbouring churches formed 'consociations' and parcels of ministers were to examine and license candidates for their own profession. Village Hampdens thwarted a movement towards this in Massachusetts, but rustics could not prevent the formation of Boston's fourth church in 1698–9 by some of the richest merchants, who adopted a refined and ritualistic degeneration of Calvinist practice.

The merchants who went to this polite place had the farmers under their thumbs. In debt with them for imported goods, the latter could only pay with produce, and their labour was thus exploited with classic directness. Yet it must be emphasised, over and over again, that this colony and Virginia were, and would remain, far more homogenous and socially open than any European society.

The system of rule was self-contradictory. In the colonies the royal prerogative was still not trammelled, as it had been in England after 1689. If king or parliament at home chose to overbear the colonists, they had hardly a legal leg to stand upon. Yet the Board of Trade was not powerful at home. While monarch, or Commons, or Lords, or a Secretary of State, could take an initiative in colonial affairs, depending upon the matter involved it would engage the admiralty, the war office, the treasury, the customs commissioners, the law officers, the high courts, or the Bishop of London. Delays and inefficiencies were inevitable; by virtue of this the colonists were not over-governed and could successfully play one authority off against another.

The chief parcel of people who had an interest in strong and uniform rule were the small group of professionals in the colonial civil service. That experienced governor Francis Nicholson backed the Board of Trade as, after peace came in 1697, it commenced a drive to resume for the Crown all the proprietary charters. Penn went home in 1701 to fight. His parcel, the well-to-do Quaker lobby in London, was too strong for the Board. Though New Jersey's 72 proprietors finally surrendered their political rights to the King in 1702, the Board could not get its grander aims passed by a not-very-interested Parliament, at three attempts in six years. Penn's triumph was somewhat Pyrrhic. He fell disastrously into debt and spent eleven months in prison in 1708. He attempted to sell his province to the Crown, and agreement (£12,000) had actually been reached in 1712 when a partial stroke prevented him from completing negotiations. He lingered in rural England, fuddled and quiescent, until his death six years later left Pennsylvania to his heirs.

Vice-Admiralty Courts were erected between 1697 and 1701 in eleven jurisdictions in the New World. The aim was to cope with pirates and smugglers. The Board dealt quite successfully with piracy. This was a major problem, as peace demobilised seamen trained in maritime combat. The Indian Ocean was the main centre. Most of the pirates there were said to be English. Pirate ships were fitted out in the North American colonies, manned there, and supplied by colonial vessels at their bases in Madagascar. The New World colonies themselves suffered; John James, in 1699, plundered the coast at will from North Carolina to New York. But pirates were otherwise welcome for the coin they brought in. Governors often accepted bribes; so did jurymen. The Board of Trade obtained royal permission to have the rogues shipped for trial in England, and the notorious Captain Kidd, captured in New York, was brought to London in 1700 with 31 of his fellows; he and 11 others were duly hanged, as were 26 out of nearly 100 pirates whom Governor Nicholson sent from Virginia. All this was of great importance to the East India Company; or rather Companies, there were now two. The Mughals blamed them for all piracies.

VIII

In 1698, the monopoly of the East India trade was, in effect, put up for auction. The EIC, weakened by losses to the French, offered to loan the government £700,000 at 4 per cent interest, in return for confirmation of its charter. The rival 'Dowgate Association' offered £2 million at 8 per cent, and won. Parliament ordained that a 'General Society' of the subscribers to their loan would have the monopoly until at least 1714. Its members could either trade separately or unite in a fresh joint stock. Most chose the latter, and in September 1698 a new East India Company was incorporated by royal charter.

However, the old EIC bought its way into dominance in the new company, subscribing, through its treasurer, no less than £315,000 to the loan, and carried on perfectly legally. The New Company, having lent its original capital to the government, found it hard to raise more from its members. The squabbles which arose in the East did neither any good.

William Norris, MP for Liverpool, was created a baronet and sent out as Royal Ambassador to Aurangzeb. He went with a large retinue in gorgeous liveries, thinking that he could march across war-torn India and approach the Emperor in fine style. He finally obtained an audience with Aurangzeb in April 1701, nineteen months after his first landing in India. Six months later, having got nowhere, he quit without taking personal leave of the monarch. He died on the voyage home. His embassy cost vast sums and achieved only negative results; after his impolite departure from the Mughal court there were imperial proclamations that the goods and persons of Englishmen should be seized. The New Company suffered heavily in Bengal, but the Old Company held out in Calcutta, and Madras survived three months' siege by Daud Khan, the Nawab of the Carnatic.

As the King himself wished, the Old and New Companies amalgamated in 1702. After a transition period of half-and-half, the Old Company surrendered its charter in 1709 and made its possessions, Bombay and St Helena, over to a 'United Company of Merchants of England Trading to the East Indies'. By the second decade of the eighteenth century, most of the dust had settled, and monopoly in the Eastern trade was fully restored. In return for concessions by Parliament, the United Company was required, in 1708, to lend the exchequer a further sum of £1,200,000, making £3,200,000 in all, on which it would get only 5 per cent interest. The right of Parliament to control the conditions under which monopoly operated was thus established, and the EIC ranked alongside the Bank of England as one of the indispensable pillars of national finance.

As the situation stabilised for the English in the East, an essential feature was that, like the French and the Dutch, the EIC at Surat was compelled to sign a security bond for the payment of any losses from piracy by Mughal subjects. The three nations divided these losses, and policed the waterways between them, the Dutch taking the coast from Surat to the Red Sea, the French the Persian Gulf and the English the Bengal and Coromandel coasts. After Norris's rudeness and its repercussions no more ambassadors were sent. The Emperor left the English to govern themselves.

The politics of the presidencies were infinitely sordid. The governor would always be under the suspicion of the directors at home and liable to supersession when the next ship arrived. He chaired a small council whose members he could not override, and who commonly amused themselves writing spiteful letters to London behind his back. The pomp which the governors always adopted masked their practical lack of power. The tone of their remarks upon council members suggests an ambience where the finer flowers of human nature bloomed rarely if at all. 'I shall not rake into his dirty ashes', Elihu Yale once commented on a young man whom he was accused of poisoning.

Feasting remained as gross, and as suicidal, as compotation. We read of twelve or fifteen courses as a rule served for both dinner and supper. Madeira became a common English tipple in the East, but 'Shiraz wine' from Persia was also used, and so, to disastrous effect, was the local spirit, *arrack*. Immoderate habits abetted disease in its scything. Of forty-six men appointed to serve the EIC in Bengal between 1707 and 1711, twenty-nine perished in India, and this rate, around two-thirds, remained standard thereafter.

On the face of it, it seems hard to understand why people went East. The United Company settled on a series of graded ranks for their covenanted servants. After five years as a 'Writer' one became a 'Factor', then, three years further on, a 'Junior Merchant' and finally, after three more, a 'Senior Merchant'. Promotion was strictly by seniority. Pay was piffling. Only the governors received enough to subsist on.

Nevertheless, Writerships were coveted in Britain. Certainly highly respectable commercial families which often intermarried between themselves and seeded an Anglo-Indian 'caste' habitually sent their sons East. They expected that the profits of private trade there would bring them, if they survived, quite ample fortunes. The EIC let its servants ship very little to England on their own account, but since the 1660s it had given them almost complete freedom to trade in Asian waters. Some operations were humble and routine. Thus, we read of a ship sent, in 1714, from Calcutta to Junk Ceylon in Malaya for tin and dried fish. It was to sell the fish at Malacca for sugar and rattans, and these in turn were to be disposed of on the Malabar Coast of India, whence pepper could be procured for sale in Madras. But there were also valuable long-distance trades westward to Persia and Arabia.

The growing success of English shipowners over their Asian competitors in the carrying trades at this time owed nothing to technical superiority. They too employed mostly Asian crews on ships built in Asia, which were no better armed than native-owned vessels, and which asked for much higher freight charges. The chief factor seems to have been the diplomatic prowess of the EIC, under whose vast umbrella all Englishmen in the East sailed and traded. It had won striking privileges at key ports. Indians despatching merchandise on risky long voyages preferred English-owned ships, not just because of these direct benefits, but because the EIC's reputation would deter customs collectors and other officials from high-handed exactions and might even hold the ubiquitous pirates back from attack.

But it must be stressed that EIC personnel still played only a small role relative to the vastness and variety of Asian commerce. In their small communities, there was as yet little disposition to harp on racial superiority. Of 119 Englishmen on the Coromandel coast in 1699, fourteen had wives who were 'castees' (as pure Portuguese were called), four were married to 'mustees' (who mixed Portuguese and Indian parents), two had French wives and one had espoused a Georgian. The number with English wives was only twenty-six. Availability was limited. There were at this time fourteen widows to choose from, but only ten single English young women. It was arduous and risky to sail to India. It was perilous and unpleasant to live there. One young lady wrote to Governor Pitt, 'Could I have got home to England, I wod not have staid here for the best husband in India.'

The yellow malarial Englishwoman could barely compete in allure with the native dancing girls. The EIC servants and other English traders liked these *Nautch* girls, and otherwise borrowed whatever Hindu and Muslim customs they fancied. At home they ate in the English way at table, but among natives would lie on carpets in the Indian fashion. They buried their many dead in elaborate tombs designed, it would seem, to outmatch those of Muhammadans. They wore native clothes indoors, chewed pan and betel, and smoked hookahs. They ate kebabs and pulaos and mango pickles as well as dishes cooked in the English or Portuguese style.

Unlike Norris, experienced India hands comported themselves discreetly. Even the 'roughling' Thomas Pitt wrote obsequiously to Daud Khan, the Emperor's viceroy, in 1701: 'I have with great impatience waited for your arrival at Ascot which being informed of two days ago I celebrated with great joy, preparing my people to wait on you with such acknowledgements of respect as I was capable of providing.' Sheer laxity, as in the Caribbean, must have bred tolerance among them; but the overwhelming numerical mass of adherents of non-Christian religions would have compelled them anyway to be modest about their own. There was no missionary effort. 'In *Calcutta*,' remarked a Scottish merchant, Hamilton, wrily, 'all Religions are freely tolerated, but the *Presbyterian*, and that they brow-beat.'

Bencoolen in Western Sumatra remained even unhealthier than the EIC's Indian settlements. York Fort, impressive seen from the sea, was not truly formidable, and in 1714 Governor Collet abandoned it and set up headquarters at Fort Marlborough, built a couple of miles to the south. Even this stronger place was captured by natives in 1719 and returned only when the English agreed to exact less pepper. The garrison was a problem. English soldiers died quickly. Slaves from Madagascar proved unsatisfactory. Here as in India the half-caste Portuguese 'Topazes' were the mainstay, supplemented in this case by Bugis from Celebes. The surrounding country was wild. Relations with the natives were bad. Food was scarce. Labour costs were high. The whites had nothing to do but squabble. With scarcity of white females of any shape, interbreeding with natives was commonplace, and here, in contrast with India, Eurasian half-castes came to fill even senior posts in the Company's service.

Bombay, after the war with the Mughal, stood only above Bencoolen among the EIC's settlements; there seem to have been no more than twenty-six Europeans there in 1699. Madras had about twice as many. Though it was scorchingly hot from April to September, this was a healthier place than Bombay or Calcutta. Fort St George with its red laterite walls, the colour of rusty iron, its four bastions, mortar and fifty-six guns, was built on sand. The White Town within its walls had half a dozen 'strait handsome streets' of brick houses with flat roofs where the denizens might take what air was to be had. The EIC servants were supposed to keep apart from the scores of thousands of natives in the 'Black Town'. Collegiate discipline still survived; EIC men could not live outside the fort without special leave and had to attend morning and evening prayers.

But the barracks was, in 1711, described as the 'scene of many a drunken frolick'. About that time, it numbered some 250 Europeans, some 200 'black Mungrel Portuguese' and 200 natives. The white soldier could live well on his pay; meat, fish, poultry and clothing were cheaper than at home. '. . . Not a common soldier in the place but has a boy to wait on him.' Soldiers might marry papist women so long as the children were brought up as Protestants, hence there was a school in Madras intended to imbue them with the correct principles. Elihu Yale had encouraged Armenian merchants to settle, egged on by that prophet of tolerance, Sir Josiah Child. Yale's father was Welsh and he himself retired, aged just over 50, to Plas Grono in north-east Wales. It was probably for this reason that a new stronghold built by the EIC near Cuddalore, well to the south of Madras, in 1690, was given the name 'Fort St David'.

Calcutta was fortified with the Mughal's leave in 1698. The EIC became *zemindar*, tax collector, in three villages, which altogether covered only a fraction of the area later occupied by the city. For an annual rent of 1,200 rupees to the Mughal, the Company was free to tax and govern almost as it pleased. Next year, the Bengal EIC was given its own presidency, based on Fort William in Calcutta.

In 1706, Calcutta's population was reckoned at 17,000. The underpaid native collectors employed to take taxes were from the outset prone to fraud and extortion. The EIC also relied on native policemen. The regular garrison at Fort William was only 150 men of all races. But the brick fort was solid above a town of thatched hovels built among stinking pools of water, with large wastes of unreclaimed land all around it.

IX

Early in 1702, William III's horse stumbled on a molehill and threw him. He died shortly afterwards, and Jacobites then and much later cheerfully toasted the mole who had slain him. His sister-in-law and successor, Anne, had no heir, and was well on in years. But Parliament had already ruled against a Jacobite inheritance. The Act of Settlement, 1701, fixed the succession in the ruling house of the German Electorate of Hanover, who were descended from James I's daughter Elizabeth.

It was an era of explosive succession problems. In 1700, Charles II of Spain had died, leaving his crown to Philip of Anjou, Louis XIV's grandson. The prospect that France and Spain, with their overseas empires, might share the same king aroused understandable fears in England. A French company now acquired the *asiento* from the Spanish Crown, the monopoly of selling slaves to Spanish America. In 1701, Louis XIV prohibited English imports into France, and requested Philip V of Spain to do the same. When James II died in the same year, Louis recognised his young son as James III. With Dutch and Austrian allies, England now fought 'Queen Anne's war', which lasted eleven years, in Europe and in the New World.

Almost everywhere else in Europe, warfare nowadays enhanced the grip of military despotism. Monarchs personally controlled large armies. In England, by contrast, the navy was run by an independent board, the Commons had control of the army, and the Secretary to the Forces sat in their House. There was no general conscription. Foreign mercenaries were hired for use in Europe. Over such English forces as existed, parsimony reigned. While officers defrauded their soldiers, and also the government, Whitehall cheated both officers and rank and file. In Cromwell's day, the common soldier had had status. Now he was despised and rejected of men. Condemned criminals were drafted, as were debtors and unemployed. All were subject to horrifically brutal punishment; scores or hundreds of lashes with leather thongs might be given; the tongue might be bored with a hot iron for swearing. (But the army still swore, and it looted and raped without mercy.) Casualties on troop transports at sea were commonly higher than on slave ships. 'Of 5000 men shipped from the West Indies to Newfoundland in 1702–3, only just over 1000 survived the voyage.' Even on the shorter voyage to Spain, losses of over a third were suffered.

Yet, under the Duke of Marlborough, the English army was the best force in Europe. His ruffians were victorious over the French at Blenheim in 1704, at Ramillies two years later, at Oudenarde in 1708. Meanwhile, the Methuen Treaty with Portugal (1703) gave English manufacturers a virtual monopoly of trade with that ally and her empire, and the capture of Gibraltar in 1704 assured the English and Dutch command of the Mediterranean.

The main show was in Europe. Marlborough and Anne's chief minister, Godolphin, would spare few vessels to protect colonial trade, and colonists in

Virginia were required to pay themselves for the small-arms which their governor requested.

The quarter century of wars which began with the Glorious Revolution had opened badly for the English in the Caribbean. The Irish on Montserrat stood by King James; the Irish on St Kitts rose on his behalf, killing, burning and destroying 'all that belongs to the Protestant interest'. In 1706, the colony on the Bahamas, established since the mid-seventeenth century, was temporarily wiped out, and St Kitts and Nevis were devastated. Montserrat's turn came in 1712. There was little effective retaliation. The object of an expedition from England in 1702 was to destroy the French colonies in Martinique and Guadeloupe, to attack the Spaniards on Cuba and, if possible, on the mainland, and then sail north to hit the French in Canada and Newfoundland. The wrong kind of ships were sent, without enough artillery. The troops were lamentably equipped, and, as usual, the naval commander was at odds with the general.

This general was a planter, the third Christopher Codrington. His grandfather, the first Christopher, had been an early planter on Barbados. The second Christopher had moved on to the Leewards, where he and his brother acquired the entire small island of Barbuda. He fought the French ably during King William's war, but he died in 1698 under the shadow of disgrace for his involvement in illegal trade with the enemy. His son succeeded him as governor of the Leewards, and also as the wealthiest English landowner in the West Indies, with holdings on Barbados, Nevis and Antigua.

The second Christopher had been a rumbustious and self-serving planter politician of a familiar type. The third was a rarer case. Educated at Oxford, he became a Fellow of All Souls, and used his boundless resources to buy rare books from all over Europe. He wrote verse, and was a friend of Locke, of Addison, and of Matt Prior, the poet, who, later, as a member of the Board of Trade, gave him useful political support. Meanwhile, Codrington gained a high reputation as a soldier in the Low Countries.

He did not return to the Leewards till 1701. Attempting to enforce the Navigation Acts, Codrington found that he could not trust a single official under him and discovered 'so generall a Conspiracy in People of all ranks and qualitys here to elude the Acts of Trade, that I have the Mortification of Knowing a hundred things are done every day, (which I cannot possibly prevent), prejudicial to the trade and interest of England.' He claimed that to be an honest governor was costing him £1,500 a year out of his own pocket. With donnish hauteur he referred to the officials who administered justice as 'Little animales who call themselves Lawyers'.

His attempts at reform, which seem to have been sincere, ran up against intractable opposition. He went too far when Mead, the customs commissioner on Antigua, was clearly obstructing justice in his own favour. As governor, Codrington intervened directly in the business of the court. Caught later in the act of smuggling, Mead went to London to vilify Codrington. Though a House of Commons inquiry acquitted him of all imputations, Codrington was permanently embittered by the calumny of his opponents.

Meanwhile his health had broken down. The home government decided to replace him. Colonel Daniel Parke was given the governorship as a reward for bringing the news of Blenheim to Queen Anne. Parke resented his predecessor and showed it. Tired of feuding, Codrington retreated to Barbados in 1707 and applied himself to the study of Church history and metaphysics. When he died three years later, only 42, Parke wrote savagely at the news, 'They say he broke his heart, not being able to gett the better of me.'

His will epitomised Codrington's aberrancy. Two plantations on Barbados, and the greater part of Barbuda, went to endow a college to be established under the care of the recently founded Society for the Propagation of the Christian Religion in Foreign Parts. The man had been sick of the world and all its works. His college was to be monastic, its clergy under vows of poverty, obedience and chastity. The Society, while accepting the gift, and the slaves, scotched the notion of monasticism, and planters on Barbados, led by their governor, resisted the creation of the college, which did not materialise till 1745, when it became the only significant secondary school for boys in the English West Indies.

Parke's end was still more startling, though less edifying. On his day of triumph at Blenheim, Marlborough had promised Parke, one of his aides-de-camp, the governorship of Virginia, where the latter had been born. Parke was disappointed with the Leewards, which seemed to offer only slim pickings. He whined in official letters home that he was 'roasted in the sun, without the prospect of getting anything.'

Planters made more than one attempt to assassinate Parke. He made the wife of a prominent islander his mistress, then tried the man for his life after he had killed someone 'by accident'; the jury, of course, acquitted Parke's rival. In 1710 he dissolved the Antigua Assembly. Armed planters rallied to its support. Parke gathered the soldiers he could trust, mounted a field gun in Government House and refused to surrender. The place was stormed. Four of the rioters died, with eleven of Parke's supporters. The governor himself was butchered. Accounts varied as to the details. The most colourful had the maimed governor hauled naked along the road and left to die under that sun which he so detested. A more moderate version was that the rioters tore his clothes off, dragged him about the house by his testicles, beat him on the head and broke his back with the butt ends of their guns. Then one of them 'spitt in his face in the agony of death.'

Governor Douglas, his successor, took no action until he had pocketed bribes from everyone anxious to be exempted from nomination as ringleaders. Only three men were arrested and tried, and they were not executed. After a notable course of corruption, Douglas himself was recalled to England and given a five-year gaol sentence.

The violence of life on Antigua was far from unique. In the year after the rising against Parke, the always tumultuous politics of the few and impoverished

1 (*above*) An Elizabethan artist's picture (1581) of 'Wild Irish' attacking the Pale

2 (*left*) Captain Thomas Lee, dressed for soldiering in Ireland, by Gheeraerts (1594)

3 (*above*) Dr John Dee, magician and geographer

An · dñi · 1571 ·
ÆTATIS · SVÆ ·
29 ·

Sir Richard Grenville, killed
in a sea-fight near the Azores,
1591.

4 An unknown artist captures superbly the pride and violence of Sir Richard Grenville (1571)

5 'Their dances which they use at their high feasts' – John White's drawing of 'Virginian' Indians

6 'The Town of Pomeiock', in 'Virginia', drawn by White

7 John Winthrop the elder

8 Edward Winslow, a 'Pilgrim Father' (1651)

9 Archibald Campbell, eighth Earl of Argyll – the Covenanting hero

10 The first Duke of Ormond, unswerving Irish Royalist, after Lely

11 Malay slaves at Bencoolen (Sumatra) by Alexander (1794)

12 Sugar-making in the mid-seventeenth century. Slaves feed cane into the roller mill which is powered by cattle. The juice runs to a cistern (E) and is ladled into coppers (K) for boiling

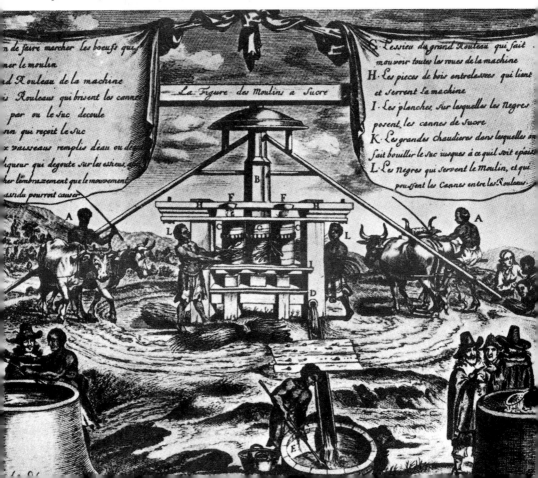

13 In this racist depiction
(published in 1803), a cowering
Cudjoe makes peace with the
British

14 Africans carrying slaves to ships
off the Gold Coast, by Johannes
Kip

15 Prince of Wales Fort, Hudson's Bay, as seen in the 1770s

16 An eighteenth-century view of Sandy Point, St Kitts, looking across to the smuggler's paradise, St Eustatius

17 (*above*) 'Success to the Africa Trade', a 'Delft' punchbowl made in Liverpool

18 (*right*) Olaudah Equiano, Ibo slave turned anti-slave trade propagandist

19 (*below*) Sea-captains carousing in Surinam in the mid-eighteenth century, by John Greenwood

ROMANS: 20 A classical Clive, by Peter Scheemakers (1764)

21 Robert Adam's design for Admiral Boscawen's tomb

22 'The Death of General Wolfe', by Benjamin West

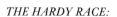

THE HARDY RACE:

23 (*right*) Lord
Dunmore, last Royal gov-
ernor of Virginia, by
Reynolds, in Highland
tartan

24 (*far right*) Corporal
Samuel Macpherson,
leader of a mutiny of
Highland soldiers, 1743

25 (*below*) Fishermen
and their wives near
Inverness in the 1720s

26 Henry Grattan, patriot orator, by Francis Wheatley

27 Cork in the mid–eighteenth century

28 Siraj-ud-daula by an Indian artist

29 Sir Eyre Coote, East India Company general
(attributed to H. Morland)

30 Fort William, Calcutta, in the early 1750s

31 The Palmer family, by Zoffany – an Englishman in India with his native wife and children

32 An Indian artist depicts a European smoking a hookah

33, 34 and 35 A well-dressed colonial lady (Mrs Mary Pickman) by John Singleton Copley contrasts with the rugged frontiersman Daniel Boone (by Chester Harding) and the revolutionary Congressman Roger Sherman (by Ralph Earl, *below right*), a severe figure in the Puritan tradition

36 A propagandist tea-pot

37 Captain James Cook – a non-idealised portrait by J. Webber, who sailed with him

38 Webber's portrait of a Tahitian 'princess'

39 The Parys Copper Mine on Anglesey, by J. C. Ibbetson

40 View from Point Venus, Tahiti, by William Hodges

41 Cyfartha Ironworks, Merthyr Tydfil, Wales, by J. C. Ibbetson

planters of North Carolina erupted into a little rebellion. This was followed by two years of war with the Tuscarora Indians, in which South Carolina was also involved. But both Carolinas profited from the bounties on the production of 'naval stores' offered by Parliament in 1705, when Sweden was unfriendly and Baltic supplies were at risk. In the previous year the importance of rice, Charles Town's staple, was recognised when that grain was 'enumerated' under the Navigation Acts. It was eaten by people in Europe who could not afford wheat. Charles Town prospered.

French wars made the West Indian islands more dangerous and less appealing. Above all, with sugar prices falling and French competition increasing, the advantages of being closer to Westminster were clear. Henry Drax, whose forebear had pioneered in the introduction of sugar, led a movement in the 1680s of big Barbadian planters back to permanent residence in the motherland. The sugar lobby had always outpointed others in imperial politics. The power of sugar interests at home was now reinforced by opulent absentees. The government was prepared to send large expeditions to die in the Caribbean. It was far slower to give military help to North American colonists. A significant contrast of attitudes was the result. English West Indians slumped ungratefully into dependence on aid from home, while North Americans were beginning to develop their own military traditions.

Luckily for them, New France during Queen Anne's war was starved of military assistance. But Albany had a most profitable clandestine trade with Montreal, so New York Colony was not very interested in fighting the French. Massachusetts was left for years to shoulder the burden almost alone. Paradoxically, Boston boomed, with the stimulus given by war-funds disbursed by Whitehall. In 1714, Massachusetts had 1,100 ships, of which 678, nearly two-thirds, had been added during the war years.

On the frontier line of defence which stretched some 200 miles from western Massachusetts into Maine, local inhabitants were reinforced by drafted militia-men and by volunteers, who were drawn by the prospect of plunder, by the liberal bounties paid for Indian scalps, and by the chance to sell young red captives into slavery. Undiscriminating sweeps were made into Indian country. Villages were burnt, crops destroyed in the fields, red men were cut off from their fisheries.

From 1709, the home government was committed to a renewed attempt to destroy the French position in Canada. Since the prime mover of the scheme was a Scot, it also marked the beginning of 'British' Empire. In 1707, Scotland and England became one country.

X

Cromwell's Union of the two countries in 1654 had been imposed by an army of occupation. But a pro-Union lobby developed in the northern kingdom. The restored Stuart monarchs no longer had the capacity to prevent their English parliaments passing laws, like the Navigation Acts, which were prejudicial to Scotland. The Scottish Convention which ratified the Glorious Revolution approved – unanimously, according to one source – overtures to England for Union. Meanwhile Scottish aristocrats more and more commonly tried to narrow the gap between their standard of living and that of English magnates by marrying English brides with lush dowries.

The Darien episode produced awkwardly matched swings of opinion. On the one hand, it made William III an enthusiast for Union; in February 1700 he urged the English House of Lords 'very earnestly' to seek this solution. On the other, it helped make the Scottish Parliament evil-tempered and difficult to manage. Even a fairly lavish outlay in bribes could not stop it passing an address to the King, early in 1701, which denounced English 'intermeddling in the affairs of this kingdom'. Anti-English feeling was inflamed by the blatancy with which Scottish ministries were now manipulated by the London government. The English Commons were huffy enough themselves. They refused to accede to William's wish for Union. As a dying man, in 1702, he renewed his plea, and Queen Anne echoed it in her first speech to Parliament. For her, both English houses passed a motion empowering the government to appoint commissioners to negotiate with the Scots. But after a few weeks negotiations broke down. The Darien Company was an impassable obstacle.

In the single-chambered Scottish Parliament the great nobles sat with 'barons' representing the shires who were in general much under their influence, and with burgh members sent up by narrow, self-elective town councils which spoke only for the merchants and master craftsmen. But organisational changes since the Revolution had given it the right to initiate legislation, and greater scope for troublemaking. In the parliament of 1703, there were three loosely defined parties. The 'Court Party' consisted of the 'ins' who held the great public offices and of others who followed these men from self-interest either gratified or hopeful. The 'Country Party' rallied the 'outs'; they wanted adjustments which would give Scotland the benefits of free trade with England and her colonies but without any loss of Parliament or separate identity. The third faction, the 'Cavaliers', were Jacobites and episcopalians. Trouble between England and Scotland suited the cause of the exiled Stuarts well, though many with Jacobite sympathies had a soft spot for Anglican, Stuart, Queen Anne. The Cavaliers stood with the Country Party and both groups looked for leadership to the Duke of Hamilton, one of the most striking, but also one of the most slippery, of a line long renowned for its shiftiness. He had a distant claim to the Scottish Crown, and was a hero of the Edinburgh 'mob', but he had heavy debts and large estates in England as well as an aversion to any development which might bar his own way towards the throne, now that Queen Anne's lack of direct heirs left both kingdoms up for grabs.

Among so many parcels of self-seeking men, Andrew Fletcher of Saltoun was able to give the last years of Scottish independence a few unexpected touches of rhetorical dignity. He had no family whose interests he must promote. Therefore, he could ignore the temptations of office and denounce those who felt compelled to scramble for them. 'He was Bless'd,' one Jacobite, Lockhart of Carnwath, wrote, 'with a Soul, that Hated and Despised whatever was Mean and Unbecoming a Gentleman, and was so Stedfast to what he thought Right, that no Hazard nor Advantage, no not the Universal Empire, nor the Gold of *America*, could tempt him to yield or desert it.' An East Lothian laird, born in 1653, Fletcher had gone into exile after opposing James, Duke of York, in Parliament, had joined in Monmouth's rebellion and had then, like so many Scots of his day, roamed Europe, roving in Spain and fighting the Turks in Hungary. He had returned with William III in 1688, but within a few months had joined the opposition to the new king, though he remained staunchly anti-Jacobite.

His fundamental ideal seems to have been a republic dominated by land-owners. (He had his counterparts among the 'Country' whigs now in opposition in England. Like him, they detested standing armies and looked back to Ancient Rome.) Confronted by the famine of the late 1690s, he had noted the vast increase of beggars – there were 200,000 in Scotland, he reckoned – and had argued that these idle people should be compelled to work as slaves. He was not a narrow nationalist. He admired the English and their love of freedom and sketched a vision of Europe divided into ten portions, each to contain ten or twelve sovereign cities under one monarch. Small governments could not bully their neighbours, so the scourge of war would be lifted. In small societies the 'corruption of manners' was less likely. Elevating the classical ideal of honourable simplicity, Fletcher anticipated some characteristic views of the late eighteenth century.

Behind his time and ahead of his times, the pedantic Fletcher was no politician. Compromise was beyond him. His hot temper involved him in ludicrous quarrels in Parliament. He had no gift of extemporary debate. But the speeches of this 'low thin man, of brown complexion, full of fire, with a stern, sour look . . .' made much impression on the house, where his arguments – in part – were useful to other persons who wished to cause trouble.

The succession question gave them a chance to create serious problems. The English government was, of course, very anxious that the Scottish Parliament, like the English, should choose the House of Hanover. The Duke of Queensberry, who, as the Queen's Commissioner, 'managed' (that is, bribed) the Scottish Parliament, tried and failed in 1703 to do a deal with the Jacobite members. Thereafter, Parliament could not be controlled. It refused to discuss the voting of money until it had dealt with the succession question, and then evolved an Act of Security which laid down that the Queen's successor should be nominated in Scotland by the Estates, should be a Protestant, and should not be the successor to the throne of England 'unless that in this Session of Parliament there be such conditions of Government settled and enacted as may secure the honour and independency of the crown of this kingdom, the freedom, frequency, and the power of Parliament, and the religion, liberty and trade of the nation from the English, or any forraigne influence.'

Unable to carry the Hanoverian succession, Queensberry fell for the moment from office. Factions shuffled themselves. A 'New Party' replaced the old 'Court Party', drawing 'in' some of the former 'outs'. But when the new Commissioner, the Marquis of Tweeddale, confronted Parliament in 1704, it still refused to vote money until the Act of Security was accepted. A French invasion of Scotland seemed at this juncture quite likely. The English ministry gave in to Scots blackmail. The Act was made with a touch of Tweeddale's sceptre. Daniel Defoe's contemporary verdict was that the Act 'effectually settled and declared the independency of Scotland, and put her into a posture fit to be treated with, either by England, or by any other nation.'

France, for instance. Unless the two British kingdoms were united, England would have an open back door again. The Act of Security called on landowners and towns to arm their people. Rumours came south that the Scots were buying arms in Holland. The English Parliament now used blackmail in turn. The 'Alien Act' of February 1705 was a well-measured ultimatum. It would make all Scots except those already settled in England, Ireland or the plantations into 'aliens'. It would prohibit the import into England of Scottish cattle, sheep, coals and linen. The Scots would thus be conclusively shut out of colonial trade and deprived of their vital market in England. But the Act would not come into operation until Christmas. Meanwhile the Scots were offered a last chance to negotiate for 'entire and compleat union', or at least to accept Hanoverian succession.

The first, predictable, result of this Act was to intensify Scottish anger. This was demonstrated in a grisly incident. One of the Darien Company's ships had recently disappeared. It had in fact been seized by a Madagascar pirate and destroyed off the Indian coast. But drunken talk by some of the crew of an English Indiaman which was unwisely docked at Leith convinced the Company's secretary that the captain of this ship, the *Worcester*, had been responsible for the loss of the Scottish vessel, and had killed its commander. This was totally false, but Captain Green and two subordinates were convicted and hanged on Leith Sands in April 1705, against Queen Anne's clear wishes; the Scottish Privy Council felt obliged to permit the lynching rather than risk the fury of the Edinburgh 'mob'.

So the 'New Party' fell from Anne's favour. Politicians manoeuvred for office again. The 'Old Party' came back, with a 25-year-old soldier, the Duke of Argyll, as Queen's Commissioner. Despite his youth, Argyll was tough and insistent. After several weeks of struggles, Parliament agreed, first that there should be negotiations with England, secondly that the Commissioners undertaking it should be nominated by Anne rather than by itself. A volte-face by Hamilton settled the matter. Even so, he was not included in the list of thirty-one Commissioners. Almost all were safe 'Old Court Party' figures.

When the two sets of Commissioners met in April 1706, the English suggested 'Incorporating Union', with one parliament serving both countries; the Scots wanted 'Federal' Union by which their nation would retain its own Parliament and institutions but mutually hostile laws would be repealed and Scots would enjoy free trade with England and her colonies. After a fortnight, matters were squared. The Scots got free trade – a principal aim – at the tolerable expense of losing their parliament. Scotland would keep its own laws and lawcourts in matters concerning 'private right'. A so-called 'Equivalent' was devised to heal the raw wound of the Darien venture and to compensate Scots for taking on the burden of helping to pay for England's fast-growing National Debt. A sum of just under £400,000 would be used to pay the public debt of Scotland, to reimburse the Darien Company's shareholders, and to make good losses incurred through the conversion of Scottish coinage to the English standard.

Representation in Parliament was settled by some clever arithmetic. Scotland was thought to have two million people to England's six million, giving a ratio of 1:3. But her people were far poorer, and Scotland's contribution to the Land Tax would be only about 1:40. This ratio would give Scotland only 13 MPs, while the first one would suggest 170. A medium was fixed at 45. Only 16 Scottish Lords, chosen by their own peers, would sit in the Upper House. The crosses of St George and St Andrew were to be joined in a new flag to represent the whole kingdom; so the Union Jack was created.

By July 23, 1706 the Commissioners were able to announce to the Queen the end of their labours. That the Treaty would be accepted by the English Parliament was a foregone conclusion. The outcome in Scotland was unpredictable.

A swarm of pamphleteers got to work to help the Scottish Parliament make up its mind. Defoe came to Edinburgh as a propagandist for the Union, and as a spy for Godolphin. William Paterson, the visionary of Darien, laboured on the same side. They had the arguments of commercial hard-headedness. Their most voluble opponent, an industrious hack named Hodge, could only appeal to sentiment or argue by dubious analogy: Portugal was richer now she had moved from union with Spain.

In taverns and market places the noes had it. Defoe observed that hatred of the proposed treaty was such that if the articles had been published before the Commissioners had reached home, few of them would have ventured into Scotland 'without a guard to protect them'. But he also remarked on the disunity of the opposition, who could agree only on the negative. While in England High Tories had opposed Union because it would mean digesting an established Presbyterian Church, in Scotland the zealots of that Kirk feared the loss of all that had been won in 1689.

The men who had to breast the wave of anti-Union feeling were

Queensberry, now reappointed Commissioner, and the Secretary of State, the Earl of Mar. They did very well. The attitude of the New Party, now nicknamed the 'Squadrone Volante', was crucial; twenty-five or so in number, they held the balance in Parliament. The court lured them with baits of office and money. Parliament met on October 3. On the 15th, Queensberry got a majority of sixty-six for the vital motion to go ahead to consider the articles of the treaty.

But a week later the Edinburgh 'mob', drums beating, ran riot, maltreating every known Unionist it saw. As voting proceeded clause by clause, there were constant threats against Queensberry's life. Over a third of the shires, and a quarter of the royal burghs, sent in addresses against the Union; not one came in for it. In Glasgow, where the magistrates had decided not to petition for continued independence (what innocents they would have been to do so, considering the legal trade in America which the Union would open up to them), rioters pillaged the provost's house and compelled the city fathers to sign an anti-Union address. The Covenanting west fizzed once more. Hundreds of farmers gathered at Dumfries and burnt the articles of Union at the market cross. There were plans for a new 'Whiggamore Raid', at which a cross-bred alliance of Cameronians and Jacobites would evict the Parliament and declare for King James III. But the Duke of Hamilton declined the leadership offered to him, pointing out that the English had massed troops on the Border. Hamilton was still the hero of the Edinburgh 'mob'. (This term, then as now, had pejorative implications. No substitute was available, but it must be understood that in the eighteenth century, quite well-to-do people commonly took part in mob action, that they, like the poor, had no other way of making their opinions felt, and that 'mobs', though destructive, were selectively so, and could be remarkably self-disciplined.) If the Duke had wanted to use physical force to thwart Union, he might have done so. But he was not a revolutionary, nor cut out to be a hero. Hamilton himself proposed an opposition walk-out from Parliament. But on the day he refused to come to the House, pleading a severe toothache. Frog-marched there all the same, he still did not make the gesture expected of him. His vacillation demoralised his followers and made the Union certain.

With various minor amendments, the whole Treaty was passed. The English Parliament swallowed all changes, together with a further Act embodied with the Treaty and guaranteeing the continuance of a Presbyterian Church 'without any alteration . . . in all succeeding generations' and laying down that all office bearers in the Scottish universities would have to be Presbyterians. 'Now, there's ane end of ane auld sang,' Seafield said, as he signed the English Act of Ratification and formally wound up Scotland's independence. In April 1707, the Scottish Parliament dissolved. On May 1 the Union was inaugurated with a service in Wren's new St Paul's Cathedral.

There is no way of knowing now whether most Scots were adamant against Union. Parliament represented the views of privileged classes, and its members gave Queensberry comfortable majorities. In the case of Article IV, which embodied freedom of trade, the voting was 156 in favour, only 19 against. There was less enthusiasm, of course, for the abolition of Parliament itself, but even here the majority was two to one. Why did the same Parliament which had seemed so anti-English in 1703–4 now vote consistently for Incorporating Union?

One traditional answer, given enduring currency by Robert Burns, was that Union was 'bought and sold for English gold'. Some politicians certainly asked a price and were given it. The Duke of Argyll received a generalship for himself and a peerage, the earldom of Islay, for his brother. As William Ferguson summarises matters, 'In an effort to win votes all sorts of inducements were held out. Payment of arrears of salaries to office holders was made conditional on their supporting the treaty. Partly for this end, a sum of £20,000 sterling sent up from the English treasury was secretly disbursed by the Scottish treasurer, the Earl of Glasgow.' But payment for votes was now part of the British system of government. The fact that it was used in this case does not prove that men voted as they did merely because they were bribed. One could argue as plausibly that politicians had passed the Act of Security so as to put up their own selling price.

There were powerful negative reasons impelling leading Scots towards Union. The alternative was to strike for independence under a non-Hanoverian king, presumably Stuart. A Stuart king would have tried to reclaim the English throne. If he had failed, the English would have enforced Incorporating Union on their own terms. As Fletcher himself put it: 'This country must be made a field of blood in order to advance a Papist to the throne of Great Britain. If we fail we shall be slaves by right of conquest; if we prevail, have the happiness to continue in our former slavish dependence.'

And the economic spurs working Scotland towards Union were decisively important. Scotland's main exports were linen and black cattle, which could be sold only in England, and wool, which went largely to France, but was in great part smuggled out of England first. If the Border were policed, the wool trade would be stunted. Worse still, landowners all over Scotland would suffer – 'unless our cattle and linen can be otherwayes disposed on, we are utterly ruined should those laws take effect,' the Earl of Roxburghe had exclaimed in a letter. Trade with England, running at about £114,000 (sterling) per year in 1698–1700, had fallen to £54,000 per year in 1704–6.

In the last Scottish Parliament, barons from the shires were only four to three in favour when the whole Treaty was passed. The burgesses from the towns were three to two in favour. But the peers, great landowners, voted more than two to one for Union. Landowners had shown their interest in colonial trade when they had subscribed half the capital of the Darien Company. Those who sold corn or coal, salt or cattle from their lands, and who had linen industries on their estates, had a vital need of the English market.

The Scots were poor, and getting poorer. The English upper and middle

classes waxed fatter every day. The disparity in wealth between the two
countries, marked in 1603, was still greater now. This partly explains how the
English could be generous. What were a few hundred thousands disbursed to
whining Scotsmen compared with the millions of the National Debt? Besides
improving the chance of a safe Hanoverian, Protestant succession, the Union
gave England certain striking rewards. Economic historians of the future would
applaud the 'creation of a British common market embracing almost 7 million
people, much the largest free trade area in contemporary Europe . . .'
Contemporaries were perhaps more impressed by the prospect sketched by
Daniel Defoe. 'Scotland is an inexhaustible treasure of men, as may be
demonstrated by the vast numbers they have in our army and navy, and in the
armies of the Swede, the Pole, the Muscovite, the Emperor, Holland and
France. What might not England now do, had she in her pay all the Scots
actually in the service of these princes, where they are daily cutting one
another's throats, and, at the expense of their country's impoverishment, gain
the empty reputation of being the best soldiers in the world. This was a treasure
beyond the Indies . . .'

This implication of Union was at once grasped in the 'Indies' themselves.
Governor Daniel Parke, that old soldier, wrote from the Leewards in January
1707 asking for 10,000 Scots whom he could throw at the throats of the French
and Spaniards, 'with otemeal enough to keep them for 3 or 4 months'. The
warm sun, he thought, might thaw out their Calvinism, and 'if I gett them all
knock'd on the head, I am off the opinion the English Nation will be no great
loosers by it.' With Union shortly impending, his joke was sternly rebuked;
Queen Anne, he was informed, thought the Scots good subjects and good
Christians.

And so Whitehall was prepared to hearken to Samuel Vetch, a Scot with a
record which would have distressed it before the Union. He was the son of a
famous Covenanting minister exiled in Holland under Charles II. He had joined
the Darien expedition and had the luck not only to survive but, landed in New
York, to marry the daughter of a Scots trader, Robert Livingston, who was also
the son of a Covenanting exile, and whose wealth and consequence were already
enormous. However, Vetch had felt it needful to better himself further by some
illicit trade with the French, for which the General Court of Massachusetts
convicted him in 1706. Partly to clear himself, he set off for England.

Here was another Scottish visionary, less idealistic than Fletcher or Paterson.
The paper, 'Canada Survey'd', which Vetch laid before the Board of Trade in
1708 made frequent and no doubt exultant use of the terms 'Great Britain',
'British trade' and 'British Empire'. It gave a persuasive picture of the fragility
of the French position in North America, where a handful of men were spread
from the Gulf of St Lawrence to the Gulf of Mexico. 'Britain' should strike now
while the enemy was still weak. The capture of Canada would 'not only afford a
booty to the captors farr exceeding all the expence of the undertaking, but

infinitely advance the commerce of the British over all America, and particularly make them sole masters of the furr, fish and navall stores trade over all the Continent . . .' Canada would become 'a noble Colony, exactly calculate for the constitutions and genius of the most Northern of the North Brittains.'

Queensberry and Hamilton used weight on behalf of their compatriot's scheme, and it gained remarkably swift acceptance. By February 1709, Anne had approved it and Vetch was commissioned as colonel and charged to raise forces in the colonies. New England greeted him with great enthusiasm. There were soon some 1,500 men in arms along the Hudson River-Lake Champlain corridor and the veteran Francis Nicholson was on hand to command a march upon Montreal. However, the promised expeditionary force from England was cancelled. Nicholson went to London to try to revive the government's commitment, but returned, in July 1710, with only 400 marines and two men-of-war. With colonial assistance these proved enough to effect with ease, and with permanence this time, the conquest of Acadia, now 'Nova Scotia' once more, which was agreeable no doubt for the new 'North Britons' of Vetch's homeland.

Nicholson's walkover at Port Royal made Vetch's final solution to the problem of Canada seem plausible. In May 1711, 64 ships, including 11 men-of-war, sailed to Boston with over 5,000 troops, mostly veterans of Marlborough's campaigns as well as 6,000 seamen.

The force outnumbered the population of Boston. New England farmers and traders had a heyday supplying it with provisions. A thousand more fighters were found in New England, and Nicholson was to command a separate force of more than 2,000 white colonists and over 800 Indians (mostly Iroquois) who were to strike overland while the great Armada attacked up the St Lawrence. But in bad weather late in August nine transports were dashed to pieces on the north bank of the St Lawrence. Nearly 800 lives were lost. Admiral Walker gave up and sailed home, and Nicholson stopped his march in disgust.

English and French came finally to terms with the Treaty of Utrecht in March 1713. The whigs claimed that this was a treacherous tory sell-out. Yet Britain, as we may now call the nation, had won great advantages. Philip V of Spain was to renounce any claim to the throne of France; the two realms must never be united. Britain was to possess the whole of Hudson's Bay and the whole island of Newfoundland, as well as Nova Scotia and, at long last, St Kitts complete. From Spain, Britain received Gibraltar and Minorca and – most coveted prize of all – the *asiento*, conceded for thirty years; a monopoly right to ship 4,800 black slaves a year to Spanish America.

Scots swarmed eagerly into the wide-open world. Too greedily, in the case of Governor Douglas, Parke's successor in the Leewards; but his successor was also a Scot, yet another Hamilton. Not surprisingly, lands in the former French part of St Kitts found their way into Scottish hands. In the Leewards, from now on, 'The contribution of the Scots was far out of proportion to their numbers.'

Their superior education helped. Scots professional men turned planters in time and founded dynasties.

Barbados retained a markedly English character, but within fifty years of the Union Scots owned around a quarter of all the taxable land on Jamaica, and throve there in general better than the English. Scots were clannish still. Family feeling overflowed into fellow feeling. Paranoid, sober, industrious and thrusting, Scots clustered together far overseas and helped each other forward, summoning recruit after recruit from the bleak homeland to lusher pastures. While Scots seized new opportunities, the English gained from the long-delayed release of Scottish intellect and commercial energy.

Ireland was not so lucky. The Navigation Act of 1696 placed it clearly 'beyond the pale of commercial privilege'. Trade had recovered swiftly from the Jacobite war. Ulster, where merchants had done well from provisioning William's armies, moved forwards especially fast; famine in Scotland brought immigrants flooding into the region, bringing their capital with them. The island had long found markets abroad for cheap woollen friezes, which did not compete directly with higher class English goods. Now, with the stimulus of an influx of Huguenot craftsmen and Huguenot money from France, Ireland began to export 'New Draperies'. This competition incensed clothing interests in south-west England, and after three years' effort, in 1699, they secured an Act from the English Parliament which forbade the export of woollen goods from Ireland to foreign countries; duty on their import into England was already prohibitive. Irish production of woollens continued to rise slowly – the home market was, after all, sizeable – but a shock had been vindictively administered.

Why did not the Irish use blackmail like the Scots? The answer was simple. The Protestant propertied men who now monopolised the Dublin Parliament represented only an insecure minority, which must depend in the last resort on English arms. An Irish counterpart of Fletcher, William Molyneux, did publish in 1698 a pamphlet which argued that the English Parliament had no right to make laws for people not represented within it. '. . . To tax me without Consent, is little better, if at all, than downright Robbing me.' The pamphlet, often reprinted, would fuel the partial patriotism of later spokesmen for Protestant Ireland against Westminster. But Molyneux was slapped down easily enough. Irish Protestants saw themselves as essentially English. Their attitude to the mass of Irish, the Catholics, was made clear enough by the laws passed in Dublin.

British governments were normally more tolerant than the parcel of colonists ruling across the water. But for the sake of getting money Bills through the Irish Parliament, Westminster was ready to let Dublin have its punitive way. The Irish Catholics, after all, were natural rebels. A great part of their aristocracy was now fighting in Europe in the armies of Britain's enemies. Until 'James III' died in 1766, his advice in Irish ecclesiastical matters was taken by the papacy. The association of Catholicism with Jacobitism and treason provided a rationale for the so-called 'Penal Code' constructed against its adherents in Ireland. The code waned only after James III's death.

A Dublin Act of 1704 'to prevent the further growth of popery' laid down that no Catholic might buy any interest in land, except in a lease of no more than thirty-one years. He could not bequeath land in a will, so his property would be split among all his sons at his death; but if the eldest conformed to the Church of Ireland he would obtain all of it, and, by a further refinement of legislative viciousness, if he did so during his father's lifetime, the latter would become merely his life tenant. Catholics were barred from all public employment. They might not send their children for education abroad and had to take an oath abjuring the Jacobite Pretender before voting in parliamentary elections. (In 1728, they were deprived of the franchise altogether.) Let the great historian Lecky take us further: 'They could not be sheriffs or solicitors or even gamekeepers or constables. They were forbidden to possess any arms . . . They could not even possess a horse of the value of more than £5, and any Protestant on tendering that sum could appropriate the hunter or the carriage horse of his Catholic neighbour.'

The aim of the code was not to destroy Roman Catholicism. It would have been most inconvenient for its framers if it had done so. The vast majority remained Catholic; hence, that majority were subordinate and open to easy exploitation. Religion, not race, was the dividing factor by which Protestant landowners sought exclusive privilege, but the drive of the Code was virtually to create two different races, identified with two different classes, the haves and the have-nots.

Many landed families deserted Catholicism so as to enjoy the rights of Anglicans. A few preserved faith and fortune together by the good luck of having no more than one son, or through the collusion of Protestant neighbours. Others, like English Dissenters, found an outlet in trade. The Irish Catholics were, at least, white. The letter of the law was more savage than its execution. However, it achieved its ostensible object. Many Catholics who might have led rebellion went abroad. Those who stayed, and retained property, shunned political activity for fear of attracting attention to themselves. Such Protestant gentry as called themselves 'tories' disliked the native papists far more than they loathed English whigs. In 1715, no one in Ireland moved on behalf of James III.

Empire of the Oligarchs

I

Defoe had prophesied that the Scots would more and more bless God for the Union which had removed them from 'the petty tyranny of their own constitution' to be 'made one with the freest nation in the world'. In the short run, it did not seem like that at all. Just after the Union, the French launched 25 ships and 12 battalions of infantry, carrying the Stuart Pretender James III with them, and designed to land in Scotland and enlist local Jacobite help. The British navy, and contrary winds, thwarted this attempt of 1708. The Scots closed their ranks in face of English inquiries, but habeas corpus was suspended and numerous noblemen and gentlemen, from the Dukes of Hamilton and Gordon down, were arrested in a sweep which bundled notorious Roman Catholics together with such Protestant anti-Jacobites as Fletcher of Saltoun. The government could not find enough evidence to convict a single prisoner, and the feeling south of the Border that Scots had been let off lightly produced a Treason Act in 1709 which extended harsher English laws to Scotland. After the tories gained a Commons majority, the vengeful feelings of Anglicans against Scots Presbyterians were released. The Toleration Act of 1712 permitted Anglican worship in Scotland. The Patronage Act restored to lay patrons the right to appoint ministers to livings which they owned, reversing the settlement of 1690, and for seventy years, the General Assembly of the Kirk would regularly protest about this. Then, in 1713, despite an article in the Treaty of Union which ruled out the extension of the English malt duty to Scotland during the present war, there was an attempt to do just that. Scots in Parliament moved the repeal of the Union, and the motion was lost merely by four proxy votes.

All this helped to give Jacobitism a persisting natural base in Scotland considerably broader than it could now find in England. James III's 'reign', for those who acknowledged him, would be the longest in British history, beginning in 1701 and ending only with his death in 1766. But piety would be his undoing. He promised English tories that, if he ruled, he would secure the Church of England, but he would not give up his own Catholicism.

Whereas the whigs were quite tightly organised, and were solid in defence of the Revolution Settlement of 1689 and in support of a Protestant succession which would secure a limited monarchy, their tory rivals were divided. Some supported the centrist Harley, Earl of Oxford, some followed the brilliant Henry St John, Viscount Bolingbroke. As Queen Anne's health failed, defection of tories to the whig side began. When she died in 1714 the whigs were able to seize control and to ensure a peaceful succession for George I, Elector of Hanover.

Having won the General Election of March 1715, they purged tories great and small from public office and its sweets, and they threatened the tory leaders with impeachment for treason. Bolingbroke's panic flight to France could be represented as an admission of guilt. The popular, brave but stupid Duke of Ormond, Marlborough's tory successor as commander, began to prepare a rising in the west then, hearing that troops were coming to seize him, he too fled to France. While the whigs had the backing of the City of London, English Jacobitism drew what strength it had from archaic or defeated classes – impoverished gentry in the north, depressed peasantry in the south-west.

According to James III's plan, a rising in the south-west, centred on Bath, would be supported by sideshows in the north and in Scotland. But in the autumn the whig government acted decisively to smash the south-western organisation, and so the Scottish insurrection went forward alone. Its leader was 'Bobbing John', the Earl of Mar, who had helped to get the Treaty of Union through and had held office in the tory administration. Having tried, but failed, to ingratiate himself with George I, he had returned to his base in north-eastern Scotland. On September 6, the standard of James III and VIII was raised at Braemar. Mar soon led a formidable force of clansmen and men from the episcopalian north-east. Meanwhile, Thomas Forster, MP for Northumberland, with the young Earl of Derwentwater, mustered in northern England what one malicious contemporary called 'an army of fox-hunters armed with light dress swords'. Scottish Lowland Jacobites crossed the Border to join them.

Between the two Jacobite armies, 'Red John of the Battles', the Duke of Argyll, had wisely concentrated at Stirling the government's few regular troops in Scotland. With ten or twelve thousand men, far outnumbering Argyll's forces, Mar fussed and fiddled at Perth while the English-Lowland combined army wandered into Scotland, failed to take Dumfries, then marched vaguely off towards Liverpool. Forster thought Lancashire would revolt. But textile industries were already reducing the backwardness of the county. Cotton and lost causes would not, in Britain, mix well together. The rebels were stuck in Preston with armies advancing against them from south and east. After losing only about seventeen men, they tamely surrendered on November 13. Seventy-five English and 143 Scottish noblemen and gentlemen were captured, along with over 1,000 Scottish troops and a few hundred English common soldiers.

On the same day, one of the oddest of all battles was fought north of Stirling. Mar had at last decided to march past his adversary and Argyll, outnumbered three to one, moved to oppose him at Sherrifmuir. Neither side showed much zest for killing. Argyll's forces drove Mar's left wing in rout, but Mar's chased the government left almost as far as Stirling, and the Jacobites should have turned to annihilate the whigs. Mar dithered. Since the Jacobites did not enter the Lowlands, Argyll could justifiably claim the victory.

As usual, the Highlanders in Mar's army now drifted home. However, James

III, with a few companions, arrived in the north-eastern bleakness at Peterhead on December 22. Before long, he had set up a chilly court at Perth. He was disappointed in his supporters, and they with him. He was pale-faced, gloomy and sanctimonious. As Argyll advanced, the retreat from Perth was ordered and on February 4 James took ship for France again. English and Dutch troops looted the north.

The whigs had had a fright and reacted vengefully. Nineteen Scottish and two English peerages were forfeited and seven lords were condemned to death, though only two were in fact executed: young Derwentwater and the Scottish Viscount Kenmure. There was the usual mass transportation of hundreds of lesser rebels to the New World. But the harshness of the English authorities was not matched in Scotland. As Duncan Forbes of Culloden wrote, there were 'not 200 Gentlemen in the whole Kingdom' who were not 'very nearly related to some one or other of the Rebels.' The rank and file were pardoned as briskly as possible. Judges connived at ensuring that forfeitures were not effective.

Under English pressure, James was expelled from France. In 1718 he took up residence in Rome, where he stayed for the rest of his life, a papist at the heart of papistry. Spain was at war with Britain and a plan was devised whereby Ormond would go with a Spanish force to raise the west of England, while a smaller expedition would rally the Scottish clans. The winds were, as usual, Protestant. Ormond's armada was broken up by a gale. The luckless Earl Marischal, reaching the isle of Lewis with only 300 Spanish soldiers, found little support among the Hebrideans. When it came to a fight, in Glenshiel on the mainland, in June 1719, his Highlanders soon ran away and the Spaniards, who stood firm, had to surrender.

Bolingbroke fell out with James and was permitted in 1723 to return to England. No politician of his stature and gifts would be found on the Stuart side again. The Septennial Act which the whigs had passed in 1716 had ushered in something like a one-party state. Extending the maximum life of a parliament from three to seven years, it reduced the frequency with which the tories might appeal to the electorate and raised the value of parliamentary seats since men were prepared to pay more for benefits which they could enjoy longer. The whigs had wealth on their side. Their rich men bought up the boroughs, while the larger county electorates commonly favoured the tories who came to form a permanent minority in the Commons. Governments for nearly fifty years would change only as a result of faction among the whigs as they quarrelled over the spoils. To ensure their own dominance they were prepared to desert old whig principles; thus they shamelessly made use of the royal prerogative and of the Crown's resources of patronage. Fearful of the Pretender, they favoured, and kept up, a long peace with France, and swallowed the Treaty of Utrecht which they had once denounced as a tory iniquity.

As we have seen, Britain had won great advantages through this Treaty, amongst them, the monopoly right to ship 4,800 black slaves a year to Spanish

America. This *asiento* was in fact worth less than men supposed. But it helped to inspire the manic excesses of speculation known as the 'South Sea Bubble'. The tories in 1711 had set up the South Sea Company as a counterpoise to the great whig moneyed corporations, the Bank and the East India Company. Its nominal orientation was towards the Pacific. In practice, it acquired the *asiento* and all its promise. The whigs now tried to use it to cope with the National Debt, which had risen five-fold between 1695 and 1713. The interest on the Debt was paid from taxation. The whigs wanted to reduce the hated Land Tax and so make it easier for them to reconcile tory squires to their supremacy. A scheme was floated by which the South Sea Company was to take over the whole National Debt, except for the stocks held by the Bank and the EIC. Holders of government stock were to be persuaded to exchange it for South Sea stock, at a lower rate of interest, but with the prospect of fabulous profits from the Company's trade. The rush of stockholders after this bait pushed up the price of South Sea stock till it reached £1,050 for a £100 in midsummer 1720. The boom enabled the Company's directors to engage in sharp practices; ministers, and the King's mistresses, were implicated. Meanwhile, the great sums realised by those who bought South Sea stock on the up and sold it as it climbed further, encouraged a wild burst of speculation. All kinds of bogus and chimerical companies were floated to take advantage of people now eager to invest but unable to afford the South Sea prices.

When the bubble burst and South Sea stock plunged, former holders of government annuities were left holding paper worth far less and confronting with rage the vast fortunes which lucky investors had milked from the boom. At this point Robert Walpole, whose hands were – or seemed – clean, emerged from the lower ranks of the government as the man who could save the situation. He was close to the directors of the Bank of England, and was able to pull off a solution which minimised the loss of South Sea investors and set the Company itself on the road to becoming a stalwart financial corporation, dealing mainly in gilt-edged securities, and only marginally concerned with trade. He preserved certain great persons from punishment by the judicious sacrifice of some lesser ones to the rage of the Commons. With the gratitude of King and Court on his side, he arrived in the spring of 1721 as Chancellor of the Exchequer and First Lord of the Treasury, to dominate politics for a generation, as one of the last of the great royal favourites and as the first 'prime minister' in anything like the modern sense.

Walpole's origins were not exalted, but typical of those of the gentry who sat in the House of Commons, except that he came from the county of Norfolk which had taken the lead in applying the new agricultural techniques introduced from Holland in the seventeenth century. The agriculture which used turnips and clover and looked to the expanding market belonged to an ambience very different from that of the tory squire.

Walpole's appetite for power was matched by his greed for wealth. His tastes were notoriously extravagant, and he built himself a palace on his ancestral estate at Houghton. Politics made him rich. By the standards of his day, Walpole was never blatantly corrupt; he operated in the gloaming between due reward and outright theft. No one could deny his real ability. He was hard-working and hard-headed. Coarse-featured, stocky and forceful, seemingly frank and open, he was in fact devoid of principle, but his sun of cordiality never set, and his powers of persuasion kept the Commons under his control. He operated with cheerful mendacity and with moderate, common-sense brutality over the most graceless phase of British political history, which spawned minor counterparts in most parts of the empire; subtle Islay in Scotland, perdurable Speaker Boyle in Ireland, opulent Charles Price in Jamaica.

The system of rule over which he presided was both strong and (in a sense) cheap. The JPs, unpaid, still ran their localities; central government was still largely oiled with fees and perquisites rather than salaries. Each politician sought to reward his family, friends and supporters by finding them places – real jobs, or sinecures – where they could sip or gulp at the public revenues.

Walpole allied himself with Thomas Pelham Holles, first Duke of Newcastle, the greatest owner of borough seats in the country (controlling perhaps a dozen or sixteen), with Newcastle's brother Henry Pelham; and with a rising lawyer, Philip Yorke, who later became Lord Hardwicke. These men helped themselves and their cronies manipulate elections with large sums of money from the government's secret service fund. Even so, and even despite the large 'Court and Treasury Party' of office-holders who sat in the Commons, the government could not reliably control more than about 150 votes in the 558-member House. There were many backbenchers, not professed tories, who prided themselves on their 'independence' and it was Walpole's capacity to persuade these gentry to vote for his policies which sustained him in power for twenty years. The 'prime minister' and his clique of some four close associates, forming a kind of inner Cabinet, were able in general to get the King to accept their advice, but the monarch retained real power. Walpole's standing at court depended on his control of Parliament; the latter in turn required continual royal favour, providing him with the bait which would draw ambitious men to his side. He came, through his use of the Crown's resources, to command a wider scope of patronage than any minister before him.

The English milord was becoming a byword for wealth. The biggest British landowners, with £40,000 or £50,000 a year, were richer than many small independent rulers in Europe. In the English social pyramid, a top group of some four hundred great families surmounted perhaps twice that number of gentry families who were distinctly wealthy, three or four thousand families below them of middling landowners and perhaps 15,000 or more petty gentlemen with only a few hundred pounds a year. Land was more and more an aristocratic-cum-gentle monopoly; the class of small owner-occupying free-holders was in decline. Very few merchants or bankers could as yet match the wealth of the territorial magnates, and these latter dominated political life. Power begat money which begat more power.

Money was taking on new and preternatural life. Money battered down that yeoman class which had formed the backbone of Cromwell's army. Money had less and less time for the crafts of the old-fashioned urban artisan. Money sneered at Jacobite squires and lairds. Money was up-to-date in its ideas, accepting the thinking of Hobbes and Newton and Locke, who in various ways helped Money to explain why it was that God (who still existed, and would punish those who defaulted on payments) had no objection at all to Money. Money was, Money opined, in accordance with the natural order of things which God had created and left, as was now understood, to its own development. The laws of Money were like those of gravitation; God had little more to do with them; He was like the king of a *laissez faire* nation; He might intervene if He wanted, but it would be bad form. The earth revolved round the sun; Britain and her colonies revolved around Money.

Money's alternative name, when it sat on the bench of justices, was Property. Property had no trouble explaining what crime was; crime was an attack on Property. The prophet Locke had proclaimed that government had 'no other end but the preservation of Property'. As David Ogg has written, if Property is seen as the foundation of civilisation then England was the most civilised state in Europe, 'because property was protected there by a penal code more brutal than any to be found elsewhere.' By the end of the eighteenth century, there would be more than two hundred felonies, punishable by death, on the statue book. 'Men were executed for stealing five shillings; a girl was hanged for stealing a handkerchief.' While the black slave was defined as a thing, as 'property', the English labourer was now 'free' of feudal ties. But what he grew or made with his hands was more and more conceived as something alien to himself. It was the property of the landlord or of his employer; he had no claim to what he produced, and could be hanged if he asserted a claim.

When Jonathan Wild, thief-taker and also gang boss, was exposed and executed in 1725, writers seized at once on the analogy with Walpole. This was, with good reason, the great age of British satire, with Swift and Pope, Gay and Hogarth striking at the perversions of life around them. The finest talents of the time were deeply alienated from Walpole's 'Court' regime and tended towards the 'Country' opposition represented in Parliament by a queasy alliance of whig 'outs' with the remnant of the tory party. Under the leadership of the returned Bolingbroke, a recension was produced of the 'Country' ideology latent or present everywhere in the English-speaking world. (Fletcher of Saltoun had been spokesman in Scotland for one variant.) The voice of the English opposition, expressing the anger and fears of the lesser gentry, the lower clergy, the threatened craftsmen and the petty merchants, was also eagerly heard across the Atlantic. It did not attack the Hanoverian settlement, and it paraded a patriotism which extolled the glories of commerce and empire.

English liberty, as these men explained, depended on a balanced constitution. Crown, Lords and Commons each had a proper role. Now Walpole was using, so the theory went, the patronage of the Crown to undermine the independence of Parliament. The true English virtues were industry, simplicity, honesty and patriotism; Walpole sapped them all with his encouragement of idle luxury and excessive wealth. North American colonists would remember the doctrines expounded in Bolingbroke's mouthpiece, *The Craftsman*.

Walpole did his best to muzzle his critics. A tax on newspapers (1725) put up their price. Editors were harried and gaoled and from 1737 the stage was censored and effectively gagged. And yet those French thinkers who were advancing the movement of ideas which we call the 'Enlightenment', against a regime and Church far more repressive, looked with admiration towards an England which seemed to them already 'enlightened'. Voltaire, twice imprisoned in the Bastille for his writings, stayed three years in England in Walpole's day and applauded the religious tolerance which he found there, the absence of press censorship and the mysterious lack of a legally closed and privileged class of noblemen. Montesquieu's great *Spirit of the Laws* (1748) would applaud the English constitution and the liberties enjoyed by Englishmen, and would approve of the separation of powers, as the author saw it, between Legislature, Executive and Judiciary. This also was noted in North America.

Nor was this the worst age in which to be poor in England. Population was still growing more slowly than trade, crops, and wealth. Corn was cheap. The countryman was commonly better off than before or later. Diet was healthier. Real wages were higher. The prosperity of English tenant farmers, and even of English labourers, was envied by visitors from Europe. In the favoured home counties, female servants were now getting tea, no less, both in mornings and in afternoons. Trade could now be seen to benefit even the lowly.

Compared to the great boom after the Restoration, and the stupendous one which commenced in the mid-eighteenth century, English trade grew languidly at this time. The special relationship with Portugal forged in the first ten years of the century gave Britain access not only to that country's home market, but to her colony of Brazil, where gold had been found in the 1690s. Both became virtually part of the English colonial system. European Portugal took Newfoundland fish and English cloth in exchange for oil, oranges and wine; it was now that 'port' wine became a standard British tipple. The gold rush to the Minas Gerais region of the Brazilian back country, which made Lisbon one of the wealthiest cities in Europe again, was of still greater advantage to the British. While export of gold from Portugal was theoretically prohibited, British warships in fact loaded it regularly, as did the packet boat from Falmouth which maintained a weekly service to Lisbon from 1706 onwards. Meanwhile, it was notorious that the British merchants who handled wine exports made far larger profits than the growers.

Between 1721 and 1742, the value of British exports probably rose by a third, imports by just over a fifth. Yet it was the relative stagnation of the British economies in the age of Walpole which impressed many contemporaries. The avid expectations of the Bubble days had come nowhere near realisation. Britain's industries lacked the stimulus provided by war conditions, and its traders could not see the Royal Navy seizing new markets and opportunities for them. Hence, by the late 1730s, a chorus baying for war.

Walpole did not want war. Peace was essential to Walpole's clever attempts to balance all interests in harmony and reconcile all possible groups to the Georges. For most of his rule, Walpole kept the Land Tax as low as 2s. in the £ – in 1731–2 it was only 1s. But the threat of war in 1728–9 sent it up to 3s., and the actual arrival of war in 1727 and 1740 brought it back to 4s. France, with a child, Louis XV, on the throne, had for the moment an equal interest in keeping things cool, and between 1717 and 1740 understanding between the two countries, steadily wearing threadbare because they were natural rivals, maintained a precarious balance of power.

And in these quiet days, Walpole brought the 'mercantilist' system to its apogee. With Scotland digested and Ireland under secure control, old frowns unwrinkled. The tropics and sub-tropics called out for linen clothing, as did increasingly fastidious taste in Britain itself. Rising demand had perforce been met, since England produced little, by fine linens acquired in France and Flanders, coarser cloths from Germany and Holland. Now the linen industries of Ireland and Scotland were deliberately encouraged. These provinces of the empire, during the first half of the eighteenth century, made Britain self-sufficient in this important commodity.

Walpole's tried policy was consistently protectionist. In 1722 he abolished export duties on nearly all manufactured articles. The import of some foreign manufactures was banned altogether, and high duties were set on others. British manufacturers were also protected against British workers. Walpole's day saw legislation to keep wages low, to make it harder for unemployed men to obtain poor relief, and to outlaw nascent trade unions ('combinations').

At Westminster well-organised lobbies jockeyed for position, using pressure in and outside Parliament. Walpole was always attentive to the wishes of the great City companies; the Bank, the East India Company, the South Sea Company and the Russia Company. Adjustments to the navigation code reflected the strengths of lesser competing lobbies. The Irish lobby showed its power in 1731 when the Navigation Acts were revised to permit direct imports of non-enumerated goods from the colonies to Ireland. The West India lobby had plenty of muscle. The North American colonies, with their diverse and divergent interests, were weaker. This was reflected in a series of measures which emphasised their auxiliary status in the empire. In 1732 the English hatters won a significant bout – colonists were forbidden to export hats or felts, a particular instance showing the general intention that colonists should import

British goods, not create their own manufacturing industries. And the Molasses Act of 1733 was a triumph for the West Indian planters over the New Englanders.

However, North Americans showed few signs of pique over Acts which in practice had little effect on them. This was the period of 'salutory neglect'. The colonies were the responsibility of the Secretary of State for the Southern Department. From 1724, this office was filled by the Duke of Newcastle, who took a lively interest in matters to do with patronage but was hardly concerned with much else. The empire looked rather like the later 'commonwealth of nations' with various quasi-independent polities prospering (for most did, most of the time) in their own different ways.

In England itself, however, and also in Scotland, taxation, seen as oppressive, provoked quite dangerous opposition at times. Looking for ways of relieving the 'landed interest' of as much of the burden as possible, Walpole shamelessly made up his mind to squeeze the poor, taxing virtual necessities - malt, beer and salt. In 1724 he replaced the import duties on tea, coffee, cocoa and chocolate with excise paid inland, aiming in part to check smuggling. He did not succeed in this, but revenue increased and in 1733 he tried to extend the idea to tobacco and wine. He had to back down in face of violent popular outrage and fierce opposition in Parliament.

Ordinary people hated Walpole's excise and thought it no crime to evade it. The eighteenth century really was the heyday of smuggling which romantic history makes it seem, and the smugglers, everywhere in Britain, were much admired and zealously supported by the common people. Most smugglers were themselves manual workers. One could earn five or ten times as much in a night as a labourer won in a day.

There was much smuggling out, of wool, to the Continent. The staples of smuggling in were brandy and tea. Till 1723 there was a customs duty of 14 per cent by value on all tea imported by the EIC, plus a further tax of about 5s. per lb. Walpole replaced these with an excise duty of 4s. per lb. which lowered the price only a little. But the habit was spreading fast and wide. While a rich man might pay 36s. a lb. for the finest 'Hyson' and a middle-class lady perhaps 12s. for her 'Bohea', the poor were beginning to buy small quantities which they drank very weak, or to fall for nasty adulterated products – unless they could get good cheap leaf from the smugglers.

The scale of smuggling was so enormous that all statistics purporting to show imports and exports in the eighteenth century must be used with caution. Adam Smith would dismiss figures such as these as 'those public registers of which the records are sometimes published with so much parade, and from which our merchants and manufacturers would often vainly pretend to announce the prosperity or declension of the great empires.' Between 1723 and 1732, 250 Customs Officers were beaten up or otherwise abused; six were murdered. Of boats engaged in smuggling, 229 were confiscated, and about 2,000 people were prosecuted. Nearly 200,000 gallons of brandy were seized. Yet these impressive totals represent only the government's direct confrontations with the smugglers, and its very limited success. Witnesses before Parliament in 1745 estimated that over 3 million lb. of tea were coming in illegally every year – more than three times the amount 'fairly' imported.

The salaries of rank-and-file customs and excise men were low and irregularly paid. They were easily bribed or intimidated. The jagged coastlines of Scotland made smuggling easy. The Isle of Man was still 'part of the crown but not of the realm of England'; duties were lower there, and the rise of Liverpool and Whitehaven as ports on the nearby mainland had a very great deal to do with the ease with which small boats slipped across to make landfall at dusk. Kent and Sussex, close to France, were estimated to have more than 20,000 professional smugglers. From Lydd, in Romney Marsh, an official reported in 1734 that 'The smugglers pass and repass to and from the seaside, forty and fifty in a gang in the day time loaded with teas, brandy and dry goods; that above two hundred mounted smugglers were seen one night upon the sea beach there waiting for the loading of six boats and above one hundred were seen to go off loaded with goods . . .' Reaching London in the small hours, smugglers could dispose of their goods to the waiting tea dealers and be out of town again before morning. Soldiers sent into the area to cope with its resolute, armed gangs commonly shirked combat and sought collaboration instead. Even after pitched battles between the gangs and the law, no convictions followed. A customs officer wrote to the treasury from Folkestone in 1744 comparing the situation there to that of a 'frontier town in a state of war'.

Next year, the excise on tea was cut to 1s. a lb., though a 25 per cent tax was put on sale at EIC auctions. Thereafter, however, duties rose again and the war between government and smugglers went on with little abatement for decades. In its own way, it represented the growing importance of foreign trade to the whole United Kingdom. The colonies and the East Indies, in particular, counted for more and more. Exports from England and Wales to mainland North America rose from around £250,000 per annum in 1701–5 to £1.8 million by 1766–70. Exports to the British West Indies started higher (£305,000) but rose less fast, to £1.4 million. In the first period, these New World markets took nearly 10 per cent of metropolitan exports – in the latter, nearly 25 per cent. The colonial share of imports entering England rose from 15 per cent in 1700 to 40 per cent in 1760. Exports to the East Indies rose from £100,000 per annum to over £1 million in the first seventy years of the eighteenth century.

Textile materials (linens, calicoes, silk, flax, hemp, cotton wool) made up about 30 per cent of English imports in 1750 as in 1700. But over the same period 'groceries' (tea, coffee, rice, sugar, pepper and other non-European products) rose from about one-sixth to over a quarter; by 1772 they would contribute over a third. Imports of coffee and sugar waxed enormously, imports of tobacco considerably, but tea, taking merely the figures for legal imports, was the most spectacular acrobat: 70,000 lb. a year in 1700–4, 3,550,000 lb. in 1750–4. British exports, meanwhile, were growing far more varied. Woollens in 1700 still made up approaching three-fifths of all exports; by 1750 they were contributing less than half. The captive markets in the colonies were an immense, perhaps a decisive, stimulus to home industry. Fast-growing populations on the North American mainland cried out for nails and pans, ploughshares and buckles, anchors and soap, knives. Meanwhile, West Indian planters required large stocks of identical garments for their slaves, and the East India Company placed orders in bulk, nagging and prodding industry towards mass-production even in years when the armed forces which fought the empire's battles were not in search of great supplies.

Three world-transforming events were in the making; one within Britain itself, in industry, one on the North American mainland, the third in Bengal. All three would burst out during the astonishing upward sweep in British trade fuelled, after 1739, by world-wide war. Meanwhile, under Walpole, the empire, most misleadingly, gave an appearance of solid, even of stolid, stability. Only one new colony was added, Georgia in the 1730s. The slave trade grew and grew in old channels, without flooding, and the Lancashire cotton industry rose quietly in response, as Liverpool, from the 1730s, moved up to dominate the commerce in Africans.

Europeans, from the fifteenth century, had invented a transoceanic pattern of commerce which linked four continents; their own, America, Africa and Asia. With English and other traders nesting at Canton, in China, from 1700, the pattern was nearing completeness.

Africa was the source of cheap labour. America was the continent where it was needed. The northern red man still brought in furs as a prelude to his own liquidation. Amerindians, and blacks, in Latin America, laboured to mine the bullion which European traders needed for commerce in the East. India had no gold of its own, but used a gold and silver currency. The world's bullion drained towards the realm of the Mughal emperor, where it commanded more real goods in exchange than it could do elsewhere – hence the cheapness of Bengal textiles for foreigners. In China, silver was the basic instrument of large-scale exchanges. Chinese production of silver was too low for the Manchu empire's needs. Even a poor Chinaman would carry around with him scissors and a precision scale, as one European reported in the 1730s, so that he could cut and weigh silver, originally put into circulation in loaves, to make the exact sum required for exchange. The ingenious heathen could snip off half a farthing with preternatural exactitude, but his economy, settled in such ways, was now beginning to look old-fashioned compared to that of the realm of George II and Walpole. The world was still the world's world; within a few lifetimes it would become Europe's world.

II

Cathay had been the original goal of European seafaring. But the scholar-officials of the Chinese empire scorned trade and regarded commerce with foreigners not as a normal and obvious activity but as a deviant one, to be permitted as a privilege only under close restriction. In the years which followed the conquest of Ming China by the Manchus in 1644, the isolation of the country became, for a time, still more complete.

But in 1670 the EIC chief at Bantam made a deal with the Ming regime which still held out on Formosa and which momentarily held Amoy, an island harbour off the Fukien coast. An EIC base was established here, and even after the town's conquest by the Manchus ten years later, English trade was still tolerated. In 1684, thinking of China's need for Japanese copper, the great Manchu emperor K'ang-Hsi decreed the South China ports open to foreign commerce. Local officials remained obstructive, but eight English ships did business on the coast between 1690 and 1696, twenty in the next seven-year period, by which time the French were also sending vessels direct to China. And in 1699 a 'New Company' ship, the *Macclesfield*, arrived in Canton and began a trade there. This port soon replaced Amoy as the main focus of English activity. The so-called 'Ostend Company', based on the Austrian Netherlands but largely a screen for British and Dutch interlopers, arrived there in the second decade of the eighteenth century, and after diplomatic pressure, in 1727, persuaded the Austrian Emperor to suspend the Ostenders' charter, the Dutch East India Company moved in and provided the British with their hardest competition.

While the rewards for Europeans were great, so were the difficulties of this trade. What would the Chinese take, apart from silver? The British used their position in Bengal to advantage, sending thence to Canton raw cotton, cotton yarn and then, in spite of prohibitions by emperors from 1729 onwards, opium to fuddle the Manchu's subjects. With the vaulting demand for tea, the China trade in the course of the eighteenth century outstripped the trade with India itself, the proportion of EIC tonnage devoted to it rising to more than half. Yet the conditions imposed in Canton were humiliating. The city stood forty miles up the Pearl river, at the apex of a vast estuary. Europeans dropped anchor at Wampoa, twelve miles below the city, and their movements were more and more restricted to this anchorage and to the waterfront street in Canton itself where their factories stood side by side. Europeans could deal only with a selected group of merchants, which came to be called the 'Co-Hong', and the 'Hoppo', the local imperial functionary, pressed hard on both groups of traders. It was forbidden that foreigners should learn Chinese. No white women might be introduced into the Canton, and even the men were not allowed to reside there except during the season when the ships were in.

The round trip at best took nearly two years. EIC ships carrying textiles, lead and silver coin left England in December or January and arrived, with good luck, on the South China coast in the following August or September. Having collected their tea and coped with the Chinese officials, they would sail around the New Year. One or two might get to London in time for their tea to be offered at the EIC's December, or even its September, sales, but most took longer, and some much longer. The value of the cargoes, which grew steadily richer, supported this huge consumption of time and effort.

The law of 1700 which had forbidden the use in England of Asiatic silks, printed calicoes and dyed calicoes had actually increased the demand for raw silk, cotton yarn and plain cotton pieces. Eventually, protests from woollen and silk manufacturers secured legislation in 1720 forbidding the use even of calicoes dyed and printed in Britain, with certain exceptions. Tea supplanted cotton piece goods as the EIC's most valuable import. The amount of leaf brought home multiplied five times in forty years after 1718.

EIC trade more than doubled in value in the forty years up to the half century. In the last years of Anne's reign the Company had been sending an average of eleven ships East every year; by the mid-1740s, the average was twenty, and their tonnage was much larger. However, the EIC did not fit out monstrous Indiamen like its European competitors. One reason belonged to the Age of Reason, when religion had lost its compulsive hold. A clause in its 1698 charter obliged the Company to provide a chaplain for every ship over 500 tons. Prudently, so as to save the expense of a salary, it never chartered a vessel of more than 499 tons, until the clause was repealed in 1773. Its ships at Wampoa were dwarfed by 1,200-ton Danes and 1,500-ton Frenchmen.

The East, like the West Indies, had its influx of Scots after the Union. Cordially, but with patient discretion, Walpole as early as the 1720s found ways of using East India patronage to gratify his Scottish supporters, while enterprising mariners and professional men inserted themselves by their own efforts. An Ayrshire seaman named Macrae governed Madras with success in the late 1720s, and a list of surgeons in the fort during that decade shows Munro, Ramsay, Lindsay and Douglas following each other in quick succession. The Scots moved into a concern which was now running more or less smoothly. Each presidency went on its own way except in 1714 when all three combined to send an embassy to the emperor Faruksiyar, which after three years won an impressive new *farman* (imperial grant), after a Scottish surgeon had luckily cured that potentate of VD. The emperor confirmed that the EIC in Bengal had the right to trade free of customs in return for an annual payment of 3,000 rupees. An upturn in the fortunes of the French Company was of most moment. Between 1720 and 1740, its trade increased ten times, to become nearly half as great as that of the EIC. This new rivalry coincided, a fateful conjuncture, with a general crisis in the Mughal empire.

Decline was obvious by the 1720s when the Mughal empire was virtually divided in two; Asaf Jah, a frustrated chief minister, returned from Delhi to the Deccan provinces and became in effect independent there. In 1738, the

Marathas burst into the suburbs of Delhi and dictated a peace which divided the northern and southern portions of the empire by the cession to themselves of the province of Malwa. Next year, the Persian King, Nadir Shah, invaded India and plundered Delhi. Wholesale disintegration would soon set in. The Marathas were the chief solvent. By the mid-century they had spread right across central India, occupying Orissa and attacking Bengal, making the entire empire their field for plunder.

All empires come to an end, except China's, and the Mughal power, based on the spread of alien Muslim adventurers, had never founded itself on native loyalty. But it seems clear that trade with Europeans was not, before the 1740s, a cause of the re-division of India. About its effects in West Africa, historians are less certain.

III

Now that it had lost its monopoly and had none the less to maintain its forts, the Royal African Company could not effectively compete with the slavers of Bristol and Liverpool. Its forts decayed and from 1730 it was given a State subsidy of £10,000 a year to help with their upkeep. After 1746, the subsidy was withheld and four years later Parliament replaced the RAC with a 'regulated' company which took over the general management of the African trade and the forts. Any man could join it on payment of a small fee. The booming 'open' trade built on monopoly's thankless achievements.

While London merchants had been ensnared in two monopoly companies – the RAC which acquired slaves, then the South Sea Company which sold them to the Spaniards in the New World – Bristol merchants, followed by those of Liverpool, had moved in to seize most of the African trade. In the second quarter of the eighteenth century, Liverpool began to overhaul Bristol. Closeness to the Isle of Man, as we have seen, made evasion of duty on produce brought home easy. The lean and hungry acumen of the outsider helped to enable the Liverpool men to undercut their rivals by £4 to £5 a head and still show a profit. Smuggling into the Spanish New World brought them coin which increased their capacity to give credit to British planters. While Bristol and London skippers could eat ashore on occasion and drink Madeira, their Liverpool counterparts gnawed salt beef on shipboard and washed it down with rum punch – though after virtual monopoly was secured, the port came to regard slaving captains as a special breed, indulged and even honoured, whereas skippers in other trades were still treated as parsimoniously as before.

Liverpool, with 35,000 people by the 1750s, was something like a frontier town still, graceless and raw. Slaving captains and the merchants who sent them were commonly pillars of the local churches. Practically everyone had some direct stake in the town's characteristic trade. The ships employed were typically 250 to 300 tons, heavily armed, built for speed, and carrying a larger crew than normal.

No one in Liverpool was likely to challenge a trade of such value, when hardheaded thinkers on economic questions concurred on its prime importance. An anonymous pamphlet of 1749 set forth a long settled British view. 'The most approved Judges of the Commercial Interests of these Kingdoms have ever been of the opinion that our West India and African Trades are the most nationally beneficial of any we carry on.' Between 1709 and 1787, while British shipping engaged in foreign trade quadrupled, vessels clearing for Africa multiplied twelve times. And up to 1770, one-third of Manchester's textile exports went to Africa, one half to the New World.

Appropriate attitudes to race hardened. In the sixteenth century there had been little attempt to distinguish between the sorts of mankind on anatomical physiological or cultural grounds. The Book of Genesis still explained everything. All men were descendants of Noah, even if he had cursed Ham. But the 'scientific revolution' of the seventeenth century had fostered a tendency among advanced intellectuals – Sir William Petty, for instance – to play with polygenetic theories which presumed that different species of men had different origins. By the 1720s the idea that savages (that is, Red Indians and Africans) were a link in a chain between apes and men and so were inferior biologically, had gained a great deal of ground. Thus a British doctor wrote of Africans at this time that, 'As for their Customs, they exactly resemble their Fellow Creatures and Natives, the Monkeys.' Another traveller, in 1735, wrote of 'A Colour, Language and Manners, as wide from ours, as we may imagine we should find in the planetary Subjects above, could we get there', going on to suggest that 'the black and white Races have, *ab origine*, sprung from different-coloured first Parents.'

'Racialist' rationalisations emerged in close conjunction with the new scientific thinking which, within two and a half centuries, would indeed take men into space and their hardware on to 'planetary Subjects'. They relate to an intellectual movement from Christian orthodoxy which made Deism intellectually fashionable, and, in effect, ushered God out of a universe which He was still supposed to have created, but which He had left to the operation of comprehensible and consistent natural laws. (Of these 'Gravity' was well established by Newton; 'Evolution was, so to speak, still evolving.)

Loss of faith in miracles and in the possibility of supernatural events meant, in effect, that, from the early eighteenth century, few learned men really 'believed' in God in the old way. Will to believe replaced instinctive belief. The excesses of evangelical Christianity, as these were breaking out, in Horace Walpole's day, in Britain and the American colonies would seem largely to have stemmed from the desperate wish of the intellectuals who promoted them to go on believing. Doubt, creeping always upon the most pious now, like a thief in the night, could be kept at bay by the manic indulgence of emotion. The urge to cultivate rapture and awe and joyful release also helped create, from the mid-century, the Protean 'Romantic' movements with its tempting array of alternative new religions. ('Nature' or 'Homer' or 'Motherland' might do instead of Jehovah.) Like evangelicalism, this current in literature and the arts bore men away from easy acceptance of slavery.

Yet Deism too might encourage kind words for the savage, emphasising his reason or good manners rather than his wildness, because it was one way to undermine Christian superstition. Voltaire extolled the cool Chinese religion. Of course, men must conceive the polished and pale (if haughty) mandarin to be a very different fellow from the naked African. But did not the red prince, the black priest, worship the One God in his own way? Had not the revered poets of Rome extolled the virtues of shepherds? Was not the simple life, amid unspoilt nature, in most agreeable contrast to that of the corrupt cities, some of which were beginning to grow monstrous in size as well as in immorality, or to the luxury of a cynical court? Mrs Aphra Behn's play *Oroonoko*, first published in 1688, held the stage throughout the eighteenth century. It portrayed an African prince of most elevated feelings who died a slave, tortured to death, in Surinam. Esteemed essayists and poets – Addison, Steele, Pope, common reading among the middle and upper classes – had begun in the early eighteenth century to develop a potent rhetoric of (condescending) sympathy for the blackamoor.

In 1733 distinguished intellectual circles in London encountered a literate Africa, Job ben Solomon, son of a Muhammadan priest among the Fula people of Senegambia, who captivated them with his stories of slaying lions with poisoned arrows, and his explanations of how he coped with two wives. The circumstances of his arrival in Britain were equally dramatic. He had been kidnapped into slavery – ironically, on a journey made to sell two boys as slaves. The philanthropic General Oglethorpe had secured his release. After being introduced to the Hanoverian royal family, Job sailed back to the Gambia a free man. In 1747 a veritable African prince appeared in England. His father, King of Anomabu on the Gold Coast, had sent one son to France, with gratifying results, and so tried to despatch another to England. An English sea-captain, however, sold the young man into slavery. When English ships bombarded the King into agreeing to exclude French traders, it was settled that in return the English would find his son. So he was tracked down in the West Indies, redeemed, and much admired in London; he was taken to see a performance of *Oroonoko* and was said to have been deeply moved. As an African of 'noble' birth he himself matched the literary stereotype of 'Guinea's captive kings'.

Francis Moore, who had been an RAC factor in up-country Gambia, published an account of that region in 1738. He portrayed the Fula people as hospitable and generous to neighbouring peoples when famine struck. They were strict Muhammadans who would not touch alcohol; they were rarely angry, yet very brave; they were skilful herdsmen, great huntsmen and good agriculturalists. But Moore also said that rulers near his post used the slave trade to provide themselves with pocket money and to dispose of unwanted subjects. 'Not only Murder, Theft and Adultery, are punished by selling the Criminal for

a Slave, but every trifling Crime is punish'd in the same manner. There was a
Man brought to me in *Tomany*, to be sold for having stolen a Tobacco-Pipe.' But
as Moore showed, most slaves were not bought direct from source. African
merchants were bringing down to the Gambian posts 'in some Years Slaves to
the Amount of 2000, most of which, they say, are Prisoners taken in War.'

It seems that one way or another, virtually every people in West Africa lost
men through the trade. There had been no reservoir of slaves surplus to local
needs before the Europeans arrived. The demands of the white traders
encouraged rulers to set about increasing greatly the numbers of slaves and other
saleable subjects beneath them. Europeans on the coast listened anxiously for
news of wars inland; though they would dislocate trade for a time, prolonged
peace might halt the flow of supplies altogether. It would be hard to say where
normal, as it were 'natural', warfare ended and deliberate raiding for slaves
began. Certainly, much commercial raiding went on. Since both raiding and
trading required much labour and capital, they were generally financed and
directed by a few big men – 'kings, rich men, and prime merchants', as one
observer noted. Oligarchs in such African ports as Whydah and Old Calabar
collaborated with other oligarchs in London, Liverpool and Nantes in the
shipping of thousand upon thousand of African men, women and children.

To some historians it has seemed obvious that the demand for slaves
transformed the interior of West Africa and pulled wealth and power towards
the coast where new states were formed. It has also been held that the exchange
of slaves for firearms meant that the latter became decisive in African political
history. The first proposition is doubtful, the second more so. African
potentates certainly valued muskets, and local soldiers and blacksmiths became
adept in their use and repair. But trade muskets took a long time to reload and
were not always triumphant, as the famous Asante power found.

The Asante ('Ashanti') burst unexpectedly into the view of Europeans in
1701, when they humbled the state of Denkyira, on the Gold Coast, with which
the whites were in touch. The Asante state, based on Kumasi, bound together
various Akan clans and family groups around the symbol of the Golden stool of
its rulers, the Asantehene. Exploiting the major gold-workings of the interior
and expanding their power in all directions, the Asante were greatly respected
by Dutch and English alike, and their successful wars brought many captives to
the coast for shipment.

The slaving kingdom of Dahomey had been created about 1625 and became
a byword in Europe for militarism and despotism. Agaja, who ruled Dahomey
from 1708, started a remarkable military training scheme for young boys. In the
1720s he conquered two coastal kingdoms, Allada and Whydah. All trade in
slaves was concentrated at Whydah. On the African side, the Dahomeyan state
assumed a monopoly. An oligarchy of chiefs profited from it. The slave trade
increasingly became the basis of Dahomey's economy. The creation of the
King's famous army of Amazons, several thousand fighting women, seems to

reflect a shortage of men. By the 1760s trade was in decline – it seems that Dahomey's involvement had exhausted the human resources both of itself and of its neighbours.

The trade shifted eastwards. Planters, perhaps because they were used to slaves from other regions, tended to sneer at 'Angola' slaves (who in fact came from regions both north and south of the Congo river) – in the 1720s they were said to be a 'Proverb for worthlessness'. Opinion about the Ibos who came from the Niger Delta and Cross River trade varied extremely; they were popular in some parts of the New World for their gentleness but distrusted elsewhere for their despondency and proneness to suicide.

The Bight of Biafra, relatively unimportant as a source of supply until the 1730s, became the main slave-shipping region before the mid-century. There were no factories here. Traders stayed as briefly as possible in the steamy, unhomelike delta-world of rivers and mangroves. Reliance on Africans ashore was essential. The Ijo city-states of the Niger Delta – Bonny, Elem Kalabari, Okrika and Nembe – and the rather similar Efik state of Old Calabar on the Cross River developed, quite clearly, in response to European demand for slaves. Fisherfolk turned into middlemen-traders. Large canoes with cannon cruised up the creeks looking for slaves, but most came in through peaceful trade. Iboland was the main source of supply. An Ibo clan, the Aro, formed towards the mid-eighteenth century, used their possession of an oracle, the 'Long Juju' of Arochuku, which was venerated by all of their people, so as to make themselves monopolists in the trade. Litigants came from far away to hear the Juju's judgment, and were made to pay a fee or a fine in slaves, whom the oracle allegedly ate. But, in fact, these passed to the coast down a grapevine of Aro traders (along with other slaves whom the clan had bought). The Aro used mercenary soldiers, against trading rivals and against people who defied their oracle, taking over the war captives for sale as well.

Some African slave traders became Christians; conversely, some Europeans joined African associations. In the interior, Islam expanded fast, especially after 1750. Literacy entered the Asante empire not through contact with Christians but from Islam, and by the end of the eighteenth century the Asantehene would be making use of Muslim scribes.

Meanwhile, the Society for the Propagation of Christian Knowledge gave up Africa as a bad job. There was no general transformation of the African economy or of African views of life. Even in the New World, Africans retained much from their own cultures, mixed with elements borrowed from their masters', or imposed by them. In South and Central America, and on a small scale in Jamaica, runaway slaves had established polities of their own. In the West Indies, most of the population was now black, and African gods and legends found a home.

IV

Over the whole period of the slave trade, Barbados acquired some 350,000 slaves, and its unfree black population in 1809 was only about 70,000; in the mid-eighteenth century this island still required an importation of 3,000 a year, or about 5 per cent, to compensate for excess of deaths over births. In the first three-quarters of the eighteenth century, Jamaica imported close on half a million slaves, but its slave population rose by only a little over 15,000.

So Caribbean slaves had a very high mortality rate, and they did not replace themselves. The relationship between these two facts was both more direct and more complicated than might be supposed. The planter did not 'break even' on a slave born on his land until his third decade of life. On the North American mainland, children were valuable. In the West Indies, people commonly died younger. Planters preferred to buy grown slaves from Africa rather than rear them. They consciously discouraged fertility. Pregnant women were neglected, the workload of nursing mothers was not reduced, and the imbalance between the sexes, with male slaves outnumbering female by about four to three, was deliberately maintained.

In the 1740s, men on Jamaica would cost £50 or £100, women only £20 or so apiece. The great planter with several plantations commonly moved slaves at will from one to the other without any concern for settled family life. The slave women seem to have known techniques of contraception, and frequently, it was said, took 'specifics to cause abortions'. Such babies as survived birth more often than not would die in early childhood. Maltreatment of mothers and children was a far more decisive factor in keeping demand for imports high than that which the planters chose to emphasise themselves, the great death-rate among people fresh from Africa. It was true that perhaps a third perished within three years of arrival, some of disease, but others, it seems, chiefly of sheer bewilderment and demoralisation. But given the chance, those who survived would have multiplied.

The head boiler, head distiller and head cooper, vital craftsmen, would form a black élite, along with the black drivers of field gangs, better fed, better clothed and (not always to their advantage) better supplied with rum than field labourers. The diet of slaves on Jamaica, where land had not run out, was probably better in general than on other islands. Slaves could grow provisions of themselves, saving their masters money, and were given a day and a half to themselves each week for that purpose. But heavy work required a more generous diet than the unripe roasted plantain which became the 'staff of life' even on this favoured island.

Compared to semi-starvation, deliberately sadistic treatment was a minor influence on the death-rate. Atrocious things were done, by some planters. An Act was passed in Antigua in 1724 to 'prevent the inhumane murdering, maiming and castrating of slaves by cruel and barbarous persons (as has been too much practiced) . . .' The viciousness of Jamaican whites became especially notorious. The custom was that if a slave was executed for a crime, his owner would receive compensation, and an investigation in 1739 disclosed that in some parts of the island planters were commonly having sick or lame slaves falsely accused in the hope that they would be put to death.

Planters dealt out 'justice' to planters. Though in theory a Jamaican master who wilfully killed a slave might be gaoled (for three months), in practice he would always get off with the claim that his victim had been caught in the act of stealing or running away. Two magistrates (planters) and three freeholders (planters) could form a court to hear the most grave cases, and there was no appeal against their judgment. Yet the death penalty was dealt out far less often in the Caribbean than in England. The slave was part of his master's capital. To whip him was usually preferable to killing him. Punishment was left to the discretion of the magistrates. In Britain more and more offences against property were liable to severe punishment. But a black slave was property.

Even the hostile plantocrat Edward Long could not but concede slaves some musical talents. He noted the songs of derision improvised against white overseers, the African musical instruments which they had recreated, the 'just time and regular movements' of their dances.

Melodies of songs changed over time, but construction, rhythm and form remained basically African:

> If me want for go in a Congo,
> Me cant go there!
> Since them tief me from my tatta [father],
> Me cant go there!

The cultural shifts adopted by African first-comers commonly influenced later arrivals. Thus, though the English lost Surinam in the 1660s, the creole there, while much influenced by Dutch, remained English in main vocabulary. Dialect words picked up by sailors from Cornwall or Yorkshire or Scotland would be preserved in creole tongues while they became obsolescent in Britain itself. But African words also survived in great numbers. Even now, more words in Jamaican creole are drawn from the Twi language than from any other African tongue, reflecting the preference of Jamaican planters for slaves from the Gold Coast.

'Creoles' – slaves born in the Caribbean – looked down on natives of Africa, but the most feared and respected black on any plantation would be the obeahman, who was usually an African. Religious beliefs were generally similar over the whole area from which slaves were drawn, and 'Obeah' emerged as a form of sorcery which all blacks alike considered effective. The obeahman did harm to people at the request of clients who paid him for his 'bad medicine'. He caught and impaled shadows, used fetishes and charms, and on occasion simply resorted to poison. If slaves rebelled, it was he who administered oaths of secrecy.

Ancestor worship, as used in Guinea, persisted to some extent in the New World. So did belief in spirits; the cottonwood tree, for instance, was venerated on Jamaica down to the present century. The funeral rites of the slaves combined elements from diverse African cultures. Other occasions were found for communal recreation, at nights, at weekends, and during the seasonal holidays granted by the masters. These last – Christmas, Easter, 'Crop-over' – anticipated the later West Indian carnival. On a few days each year, the slaves could release their pent-up aggression and sense of injustice, in ritual forms which left the planters unscathed. They would dress as finely as possible, speak to their masters with impolite familiarity, and assume gala-day names borrowed from those of the leading whites on the island. While creole slaves mimicked white recreations, tribal groups would identify themselves and appoint their own kings and queens.

In one arena, at least on Jamaica, the slaves were dominant all the year round. The Sunday markets were cheerful occasions. Slaves sold the pigs, goats and hens which they had reared and the crops which they had grown. They also purveyed stolen sugar, and their markets, paradoxically, were the main local source of this staple substance, for urban whites as well as for free non-whites. With the proceeds of trading, the slave would probably earn just enough to enable him to purchase necessities – salt and fish and beef, on occasion cloth. Very few could save anything, but markets permitted 'Quashee' to escape for a day from the shadow of 'buckra', his white owner.

'Quashee' was the West Indian's counterpart of the white North American's black 'Sambo' and of the Englishman's Irish Gael 'Teague', later 'Paddy'. He was the stereotype figure evolved so as to relieve the planter from the necessity of questioning who his alien labourer really was, and then, out of defeatism or with cunning, accepted as a model by the victim himself. Quashee, like Paddy, was always evasive, and could not help lying. He was capricious and unpredictable; generally lazy and childlike, happy-go-lucky and cheerful, but also viciously revengeful, and tyrannical when he was placed in authority. He either was, or let himself seem, very stupid; yet he was also a sharp judge of character. This convenient monster was not merely a product of white imagination. Slavery hardly encouraged its victims to show any eagerness to work or any sense of responsibility in their master's business. To be able to turn a good lie might save a man's life, and the alien language of the whites, as the slave used it, offered ample scope for irony, reservation, double-meaning and whimsy. Long noted that the 'better sort' of slaves were 'very fond of improving their language' and caught at any 'hard word' which the whites used in their hearing, to 'alter and misapply it in a strange manner'. Quashee could play Quashee to serve his own ends – for instance, by bungling so as to wreck the arrangements of an obnoxious overseer till the man was exasperated into resignation.

'Anancy the spider man' became Jamaica's folk hero, derived from the *Ananse* of whom the Akan peoples of the Gold Coast told stories. He was voracious, selfish and lazy and callous, but he was a brilliant trickster. To survive at all, the slave needed to show some of the cunning and resourcefulness of the Maroons at large up in the mountains.

There had been Maroons, slaves escaped from the Spaniards, before the English conquest of Jamaica. A second sizeable group was formed in 1690 after an uprising of slaves, which included, perhaps, the Gold Coast 'Coromantee' named Cudjoe who became the most famous Maroon leader. Other fugitives – mainly, it has been said, Coromantees – joined this body later. The outlaws became a serious problem. They stole cattle and carried off slaves from the lands of isolated settlers. In 1720 the Jamaican authorities brought in some fifty Moskito Indians to act against the Maroons, but most of these were either killed or forced into the guerrilla groups. Cudjoe, flanked by his two 'brothers', Accompong and Johnny, commanded a dangerous force, though his group and the 'Windward Maroons' in the east of the island cannot have numbered much more than 1,000 altogether.

By the 1730s whites were acutely worried. Governor Hunter sent three major militia expeditions against the Maroons in that year; all were farcically unsuccessful. Hunter had been clamouring for regular troops, and the home government heeded his request at last and despatched two regiments from Gibraltar. Malaria and yellow fever ran through this force, and left the survivors wholly demoralised – at one funeral, a colonel, a major, two captains and a lieutenant were buried. Within nine months of their arrival, the Duke of Newcastle ordered their return though Hunter was able to persuade over 200 to stay by the promise of special bounties. The crisis grew. Nanny Town, headquarters of the Windward Maroons led by Quao, was three times captured by the militia, three times retaken. A large expedition of 600 men, half of them regular sailors or soldiers, was ambushed by the Maroons and routed. Newcastle soon ordered the despatch of 600 more regulars.

In 1738 a new governor, Edward Trelawny, arrived with a sensible new policy settled in Whitehall. The Maroons could not be defeated, so a treaty must be made. Cudjoe himself was ready to negotiate. The Maroons had been hard pressed. Their provision grounds had been destroyed one by one, and Cudjoe had retreated west into the Cockpit Country, a tract of some 500 square miles sliced by deep depressions between precipitous towers of rock.

A grand military push was prepared, but first the soldiers sought to bring Cudjoe to terms. One Dr Russell was with the advanced party who first clapped eyes on the legendary Coromantee. 'Cudjoe was rather a short man, uncommonly stout, with very strong African features, and a peculiar wildness in his manners.' He was shirtless, and his clothes and skin were coated with the red earth of the Cockpits. His men were 'as ragged and dirty as himself', but like him they had guns and cutlasses.

A treaty was made in March 1739. The leader and his people were confirmed in their liberty and were to hold 2,500 acres of land. They would have redress if injured by whites. Two Europeans nominated by the governor were to reside with the Maroons, though Cudjoe was to be chief for life. The Maroons undertook not only to send back at once any slaves who ran away to join them, but also to help actively in operations against rebels. Not long after, Quao made a similar treaty with the whites.

The Maroon leaders, now 'captains' regularly commissioned, were given silver chains and medals with their names on them and paid regular visits to the governor's mansion. Their followers settled down in their villages and came to terms with the money economy. They hired themselves to planters for wages, grew provisions which they sold to neighbouring settlements, vended their jerked pork and made large profits from trading in tobacco. They remained a distinct people, with no religion which the whites could recognise, practising polygamy and using a dialect which mixed African languages with Spanish and English. But they were now of immense use to the planters. Had they been exterminated, fresh groups of runaways would have sprung up in the woods and would have proved just as dangerous in time. Now they policed the interior themselves, and co-operated with what seemed like zeal in the suppression of slave revolts.

Jamaica, nevertheless, had relatively more of these than any other slave society in the New World except perhaps Brazil. Its insecurity reflected the temptations offered by its mountainous interior, and the high proportion of Africans, men who had known freedom, among its slaves; about half the population were newcomers in the middle of the eighteenth century, more than a quarter even at its end. Furthermore, the proportion of whites in Jamaica was uniquely low and absentee ownership was unusually common. Perhaps the planters' quixotic preference for fierce Coromantees was also important – certainly, Gold Coast slaves were commonly to the fore in risings. It was Coromantees who planned the great rebellion of well over 1,000 slaves which lasted for months in 1760, till its leader Tacky was killed by a Maroon, and which brought death to 60 whites and three or four hundred rebels; afterwards, 600 slaves were executed or transported.

In 1736, a lurid and interesting conspiracy was uncovered on Antigua, where some 3,000 whites and 150 regular soldiers confronted 24,000 blacks. Certain privileged slaves seem to have realised how weak their masters' position was. Court, said to be 'of a considerable family in his own country', was a Coromantee, well treated by his master. 'Tomboy' was a master carpenter who was allowed to take black apprentices and to make all the profit he could from his craft. Another principal, 'Hercules', was 'an Excellent Tradesman and almost the Support of the poor family that own'd him.' Like Tomboy, he was a creole, island-born, and so were other leading insurrectionaries, Jack and Scipio, Ned and Fortune, Toney, Secundi and Jacko. 'A new government was to be established when the whites were extirpated: Court was flattered by all with being king, but the creoles had privately resolved to settle a commonwealth and make slaves of the coromantees.' Court, however, used African rituals to bind his force together, 'the coromantees knowing but the creoles not understanding the engagement entered into.' An oath was taken by 'drinking a health in liquor with grave dirt and sometimes cock's blood infused, and sometimes the person swearing laid his hand on a live cock. The general tenour of the oath was to kill the whites.'

Tomboy was to get the job of carpentering seats for the great ball to be held in the capital, St John's, on October 11, 1736, the anniversary of George II's coronation. All the leading whites would be present. He would lay gunpowder in the house and this could be fired as the dancing went forward. Several hundred slaves were to enter the town and put the whites to the sword. The forts, and the ships in the harbour were to be seized. But the ball was postponed until October 30. In the interim, several slaves gave the plot away. The toll of executions was huge. Five men were broken on the wheel, six were 'gibbeted alive', seventy-seven were 'burnt'. The shock of discovery was for the whites compounded by the fact that skilled and trusted slaves had been to the fore. Many could read and write well and had been baptised. No fewer than twenty-three drivers, twelve carpenters, and seven coopers were amongst those convicted, along with musicians, masons, coachmen, waiting men, a sugar boiler, a drummer.

We can now see that the gravest danger to the whites in all slave societies came not from fresh Africans running into the woods, but from such talented and frustrated men, who could imagine themselves as commanders and magistrates. Yet the Antigua outbreak was exceptional. The black élite was generally quiescent. It would seem that its members commonly found their own condition comfortable enough to reconcile them to white dominance. Eruptions of violence were more inevitable than they were typical. The races lived together, in the colonial towns, without murdering each other so often as to make life intolerable for either. A free non-white middle class began to emerge.

Freedmen were commoner on the French than the British islands; towards the end of the eighteenth century, the ratio of free 'persons of colour' to slaves would be 1:64 on Jamaica, 1:25 on Martinique. But a slave woman who slept with a British planter and produced a child stood a fair chance of freedom. Planter fathers were often ready to acknowledge their mulatto children and even to bring them up under the same roof with their legitimate white ones. Rich coloured inheritors were a disturbing thought. Jamaican law, from 1762, laid down that no white person could leave more than £2,000 to a negro or mulatto (though private Bills could still be brought to get round it).

But on Jamaica, uniquely among British New World colonies, the passage of generations could turn a mulatto white. This was because of a shortage of British women. On Barbados white women outnumbered men now, in the Leewards the sexes were roughly equal, but on Jamaica there were two British males for each white female, and open concubinage with black girls resulted. Under a law of 1733, all who were 'above three degrees removed in lineal Descent from the Negro ancestor' could exercise the rights of whites. The catalogue of colours ran like this: the daughter of a white man and a black woman would be a 'mulatta': if she cohabited in turn with a white man, their offspring would be 'tercerons', and the child of a daughter marrying a third white man would be a 'quateron'. The fourth stage was critical. A fourth white man must bed the quateron to produce a 'quinteron'. Any true quinteron passed as white. With matters arranged like this, black and mulatto freemen would naturally seek brides of the palest shade available, and the atrocious colour snobbery of the Caribbean was under formation. Faithful domestics rewarded by manumission, blacks who saved enough to purchase their liberty, and others who fought well against rebels or informed against slave conspiracies, joined mulattoes in a small class of coloured freemen. There were 'upward of three thousand seven hundred' on Jamaica by the 1770s.

Jamaica alone still imported sizeable numbers of white indentured servants. One Jamaican Act of 1703 ineffectually laid down that each planter must employ one white for every ten blacks; another in 1720 raised the ratio to 1:30. But the total yearly fine of 270s. was much less than the cost of maintaining a servant. Planters paid up, and within a few years the Act was essentially a revenue measure, raising thousands annually. There was, of course, a steady call from the estates for white clerks, slave drivers, and craftsmen. White employees, however, were hardly more charmed by plantation life than the slaves. They were free to go and most quickly went.

There were still Caribbean frontiers to attract whites impatient with life on the sugar islands. The logwood cutters of the Central American coast continued to supply a valuable trade. In 1716, the Spaniards flushed the British out of the Bay of Campeche, but the settlement at Belize, though attacked by Spain and destroyed time and time again, still remained a base for the cutters. The Moskito Coast further south was a safer place. A fertile and healthful territory stretched about 300 miles along the coasts of Honduras and Nicaragua, abundant in game and famous for its turtles, with mountains behind it which helped to keep out the Spaniards. Paradisal anarchy prevailed. The 8,000 or so Moskito Indians, and the tribe of Samboes of mixed Indian and African blood who rather outnumbered them, were not over-deferential to the 'kings' who were recognised in Jamaica. Amongst them lived some 150 whites, some 170 half-castes and 800 slaves; about half of these incomers were concentrated in and around the main settlement on the Black River. There was no real authority until 1749, when a 'Superintendent of the Shore' was appointed, under the governor of Jamaica.

A more violent temperament might have picked the Bahamas. This group of 29 islands, 661 cays and 2,387 rocks totalled in land area just a little more than Jamaica. A Puritan named William Sayle had sought, in 1648, to establish an ideal community on an island named 'Eleuthera' after the Greek word for freedom. The first colonists had eked out a quarrelsome existence on the proceeds of braziletto wood, ambergris and gleanings from wrecks. The group had then been granted to the proprietors of Carolina. Governor Trott in the 1690s laid out Nassau on New Providence and built a fort there. Then he was dismissed for providing sanctuary for Captain Avery, perhaps the most prodigious of all pirates, who had captured the Mughal Emperor's daughter in the Indian Ocean. Sacked by a Franco-Spanish expedition in 1703, Nassau was left almost deserted. The islands had long attracted pirates; now pirates took them over completely. Even before the peace of 1713 released, as usual, a spate of unemployed privateers into outlawry, there were at least 1,000 active pirates on the Bahamas, outnumbering the two hundred or so settler families. Amongst whom Edward Teach, 'Blackbeard', is still well remembered.

There was so much competition that Blackbeard took no great pickings. But in the summer of 1718 he blockaded Charles Town, South Carolina, and terrorised the colony and its shipping for a week, seizing passengers from merchant vessels and holding them to ransom. Further pirates followed him there, and the colony was in fear for months. Governor Spotswood of Virginia sent out two sloops at his own expense. They found Blackbeard's ship, with its crew of twenty-five, lurking in Ocracoke Inlet (Cape Fear). Blackwood took a bowl of liquor, 'drank damnation to anyone that should give or ask quarter' and then proceeded to wreak havoc with his guns. He boarded one of the opposing vessels and fought its commander hand to hand till he himself fell, pierced by twenty sword wounds and five pistol shots.

Meanwhile, Captain Woodes Rogers had arrived at Nassau. He was famous for a privateering voyage around the world in 1708–11, during which he had rescued Alexander Selkirk, the prototype Robinson Crusoe, from an island in the South Pacific. He had come up with a project for developing the Bahamas as a base against the Spaniards. Thomas Pitt was a member of the company which he founded. Duly appointed governor by George I, Rogers arrived in New Providence in July 1718. The notorious Charles Vane, skull and crossbones hoisted, at once sailed off and never came back. Other pirates acknowledged Rogers's reputation by firing muskets into the air and shouting huzzas for the King. Most of them after a time skulked away. Though piracy in the New World persisted intermittently into the nineteenth century, its heartiest days were over.

Rogers was not impressed with the non-pirates under his rule. '. . . For work,' he wrote, 'they mortally hate it, for when they have cleared a patch that will supply them with potatoes and yams and very little else, fish being so plentiful . . . They thus live, poorly and indolently, with a seeming content, and pray for wrecks or pirates . . .' When the Crown bought out the proprietors and the company in 1733, there were still little over a thousand people on the three inhabited islands, but they included a fair number of slaves, and it was in a way of a mark of the arrival of Property and civilisation that there should have been a black conspiracy, next year, to rise and destroy the whites. Though as late as 1788 the islands' assembly would include, besides four planters and five merchants, six 'licensed Wreckers', the Bahamas gradually evolved into a minor but fairly respectable Crown Colony, prospering in wartime partly in the old manner, as a privateering base, and as a mart for illicit trade with the enemy.

Further south, Anguilla in the Leewards, and a couple of the Virgin Islands, had become a refuge for small white planters, debtors and criminals. Pardoned pirates joined them there. The governor of the Leewards reported in 1728 that he had a lieutenant governor on each of the British Virgins, 'but if his cudgell happen to be a whit less strong than a sturdy subject's, Good night, Governour.' However, cotton became a profitable export; in 1743 Tortola, Virgin Gorda and Anguilla between them produced a million lb. of cotton.

Cotton was a crop for small men. The grip of sugar on the main British islands grew more and more absolute. In 1770, sugar, rum and molasses would make up 93 per cent of exports from Barbados, 89 per cent of those from Jamaica. Sugar was more than ever a crop for the rich. A bigger plantation meant lower unit costs, greater ease in procuring credit and more chance of riding over the dangers of hurricanes, floods, glutted markets, and slave rebellions. By 1754, in Jamaica, 467 people, about three in ten of the patentees, owned between 10,000 and 22,000 acres each, some three-quarters of all patented lands. In St Andrew's parish near Kingston at this time, there were 154 estates, ranging from a truck garden of three acres to Philip Pinnock's plantation, the biggest on the island. Of these estates 128 produced no sugar and the owners cultivated provisions, grew the minor staples – coffee, ginger, or cotton – or raised livestock on a moderate scale. The 26 sugar plantations ranged from 257 acres up to Pinnock's monster of 2,872, and in slaves employed from 30 to 280; only 3 of them gave any land to the minor staples, and 8 had no area at all set aside for provisions or pasture.

The growing exhaustion of the soil in Barbados and the Leewards was met by asking for harder labour from still more slaves and by applying more and more manure. The industry grew less efficient. Antigua, though half its worthwhile land was uncultivated as late as 1734, followed the same downhill (or dunghill) course as Barbados, but more rapidly. By 1756, when it was said to be completely cultivated, it was still crying out for slaves.

French Martinique, though larger, was likewise showing signs of exhaustion after mid-century. Not so Jamaica. To keep prices up, three-quarters of the good land on that island was still deliberately left unused in 1752. The island could have produced more sugar, or could have become self-sufficient in food, but neither aim suited its magnates, who were content to exploit the captive British market. In Jamaica, a planter exhausting one tract could move on to another. Here, in the first three-quarters of the century, sugar production went up ninefold while the slave labour force increased only fourfold. Population rose from 7,000 whites and 45,000 blacks in 1703 to 18,420 whites and 205,261 blacks in 1778.

But the attitude of the Jamaican plantocracy was, in effect, handing the lead to France. While the French had acreage on their side – St Domingue was more than twice the size of Jamaica, Martinique was bigger than all the British Leewards put together – this need not have been decisive so early. By 1740, St Domingue was producing well over double Jamaica's output and more than all the British colonies combined. Meanwhile, British re-exports of raw sugar to Europe dropped by two-thirds in the ten years after 1717, and by the mid-century French sugar was selling there at half the price charged for the substance in England.

Two things made this position tolerable. Firstly, the market for sugar in Britain itself was relatively huge. British planters were supported by the high prices paid by more and more consumers at home, where consumption per head was eight times as high as in France. Secondly, since the French trading system was even more porous than the British, people in Britain and in her North American colonies could cream off profits from the booming French islands. These depended on Irish beef and New England provisions. Nor could French merchants supply all the slaves they needed. Though, by the 1740s, the French were creating two-fifths of American sugar production, and the British only a quarter, this did not undermine British supremacy in New World commerce and at sea.

And even on Barbados, it was still worthwhile to grow sugar. Paradoxically, sugar created huge fortunes at a time when even great magnates were chronically in debt. The resident merchant class in the West Indies, except at Kingston and Bridgetown, had withered away, so the planter typically sent his produce home to be sold by a merchant there who disposed of his sugar and bought stores for the plantation on his order, taking commission on both operations. It suited British merchants to have colonists in their debt; they could be sure of commissions on future consignments of sugar, and the sugars which reached them acted as good securities. The merchants became in effect the planters' bankers, loaning them money which in the last resort came from the planters themselves, and charging high rates of interest for doing so.

This meant that division of opinion between merchants and planters was almost ruled out. Their combined 'West India interest' was made still harder to defeat by the fact that the most unlikely people depended for at least part of their income on sugar. Comparatively few great merchants were not trading with the West Indies in one way or another. Numerous gentry families had interests in the Caribbean. The major absentee planting families – Long, Codrington, Lascelles, above all Beckford – were amongst the wealthiest in England. Their interests coalesced in the Planters' Club founded in the third decade of the eighteenth century. Their opulence, and its employment in politics, helped force up the price of parliamentary seats.

The sugar lobby worked against what a later age would consider the 'national interest', making its product needlessly dear to consumers. Yet the trade figures seemed to justify sugar's claim more or less to *be* the 'national interest'. From 1660, imports of sugar always exceeded combined imports of all other colonial produce. Over the sixty years after the Treaty of Utrecht, the tiny islands of Montserrat and Nevis, combined, were a better market for British exports than the giant colony of Pennsylvania. Imports from Montserrat alone were three times higher than those from Pennsylvania. As a consumer of British goods, Jamaica equalled New England, and it exported to Britain six times as much as all the northern and middle colonies on the mainland put together. And these figures take no account of the magnitude of the slave trade.

The West India lobby crushed the attempt of the Jamaica Assembly to subject absentees to extra taxation. This was the one rift in the sugar interest, widened as more and more successful planters left the islands to build Palladian houses and keep graceful horses in some gentler English landscape. This was bad for the white community on the island, bad for the soil, and commonly bad for the absentee himself or for his heirs. Renting to tenants had many dangers. The usual policy was to leave a manager in charge, with perhaps a planter appointed attorney to watch over him. If, as was often the case, he was paid with a percentage of the crop, he would have an overbearing impulse to achieve the largest production possible in the short run, sabotaging his employer's long-term interests as he drove slaves to death and raced the estate through mounting debts towards foreclosure.

However, absenteeism did provide opportunities for industrious persons to build up fortunes from nothing on the islands as agents, attorneys or overseers. For the Scots, at any rate, Jamaica was still a frontier. Edward Long reported in the 1770s that there were reckoned to be a hundred people of the name of Campbell residing on the island, all claiming relationships with the Duke of Argyll. He thought 'very near one third' of the island's whites were Scots by birth or descent. Many Scots had arrived as indentured servants, 'actually kidnapped by some *man-traders*' or sold by their Highland chiefs. The Scots, Long wrote, thinking of Lowlanders, were especially zealous in service, 'sober, frugal and civil; the good education, which the poorest of them receive, having great influence on their morals and behaviour.' It was a strange place for the ideals of John Knox to bear fruit, but so they did. Scots who were skilled craftsmen, coming out under indentures, often acquired 'very handsome' fortunes. Scots also provided some of the ablest surveyors, a rare and necessary skill in an island where ownership of land was so obsessively interesting.

Free coloured people, and creole slaves, who sought to assimilate white culture, are said to have digested Scottish influence as they did so – Scottish fiddle-playing, Scottish dances. But Scottish forms were often hard to distinguish from Irish, and the Hibernian presence in the West Indies had older and wider strata than the Caledonian. In Jamaica during the eighteenth century the preponderance among servants of Irish Catholics posed a serious political problem, since it was feared that they would not stand as militiamen against their French and Spanish co-religionists. Montserrat remained an essentially Irish colony – in 1768 slaves there would sensibly plan a rising on St Patrick's Day, when all the whites would be deep in drink. Here there were some rich Catholic planters, but most of the Irish who entered the Caribbean élites were of course Protestants. On Jamaica, men named Kelly and Concanen figured notably in the factional squabbles which historians dignify with the name 'politics'.

The constitutional struggle begun in the 1670s wrangled on deep into the eighteenth century, over the freedom of the Assembly to pass its own laws and over the question of whether the governor should have a permanent revenue and thus become independent of the planters.

A traveller had remarked in 1711 that 'the Late Governor lived the meanest of any Gentleman in the Island.' Even though commissions and fees in respect of the granting of licences, passes and so forth could bring in over £6,000 a year, the governor would find it hard to make his standing felt among so many rich men. The House of Assembly was his greatest trial. Every freeman with at least £10 a year in income could vote in the elections for its forty-one members, who had themselves to be worth more than £300 a year. So far as the whites went, this was government far more representative than Britain's, and the governor could not hope to buy or suborn a majority of the colonists.

In 1728 the Assembly agreed that the imperial government should have its permanent revenue, at last, in return for its confirmation of all the laws and privileges of the colony. But the £8,000 a year granted was inadequate and over the next twenty years the colony was constantly at war, first with Maroons, then with European enemies. A standing army was required, and the money for this was voted annually, so any measure to which the House of Assembly thought the governor might object was tacked on to the Bill which provided the cash. Time and again, the planters and the governor grimly played chicken against each other. If the governor rejected the Act he would run the risk of mutiny among the troops, slave rebellion, French or Spanish conquest. But then, so would the planters.

Edward Trelawny, governor from 1738 to 1752, was a member of the Cornish mafia which played a large role in the politics of Walpole's England because of the quite disproportionate number of borough seats, guaranteed rotten, which were at the disposal of local gentry. Trelawny was able, though with much difficulty, to triumph over the faction opposing him on the island because of his clan's weight at Westminster, even though Rose Fuller, his chief opponent, came from a family allied with the Duke of Newcastle himself.

But Trelawny, a supple, intelligent operator, succeeded at the cost of compromising himself pretty completely with the planter class, relying heavily on the talents of Charles Price, greatest planter of his day, whose younger brother had had the prudence to settle in Cornwall for his health, so that the absentee branch of this family also carried, as it were, the southpaw punch which was so useful at Westminster. Charles Price was Speaker of the Assembly almost continuously for eighteen years from the mid-1740s. It was not public spirit alone which sustained his concern with the sordid, faction-ridden affairs of the island. Control of the government was a key to cheap land. By an Order in Council of 1735, no grant should exceed 1,000 acres, yet in some thirty years Price patented no less than 8,707 acres. He bought up adjacent land when it came on the market cheaply and at his death, besides about 1,800 slaves, he owned 26,000 acres, quite likely the largest individual holding in the island's history.

Edward Long, the Jamaican historian, wrote admiringly of his cultivated friend Price, of his 'delicacy of humour', of his 'inflexible' love of 'truth'. Sir Charles, as he became, did indeed live graciously. He built himself a mansion 'of wood, but well finished' with a lake in front frequented by wild ducks. The elegant garden had walks shaded with coconut trees, cabbage palms and sandbox trees. From the great triumphal arch at the end of one walk there was a fine view across a vale to the sea, and Price owned a local beauty spot, the White River Cascade, a fall of 300 feet or more. Long, who noted that 'theology seemed his favourite science; and the Great Author of nature, the chief object of his study', praised Sir Charles for recognising the fall's natural beauty and for refraining from making any 'improvement'. The black people of Jamaica found their own way of remembering this pioneer of Romantic taste and worshipper of that deistical whig God who had arranged the world so wisely; a certain species of large rodent, which he is supposed to have imported to wipe out the native breed, is still known as the 'Charles Price rat'.

Though, few, if any, could have matched Price's opulence, every substantial planter had his 'great house' on the edge of his estate, usually in a commanding position equally conducive to fine views and to defence. Built of wood, on stone supports, it stood one storey high. Cool and spacious piazzas ranged along its sides. Hospitality was no hardship when households commonly employed twenty or thirty servants. On Antigua, in the early 1770s, a Scotswoman, Janet Schaw, would share with a fellow countryman who owned five plantations 'a family dinner, which in England might figure away in a newspaper, had it been given by a Lord Mayor, or the first Duke in the Kingdom.'

The planter might have to work very hard during the harvest, but otherwise riding round his estate to look at his gangs at work was more routine or amusement than serious labour. He hunted, he fished, he spent all day in a tavern, he raced horses, he gambled on them, played billiards, cards and backgammon, and gambled on those too. On Jamaica, Long observed, 'Drunken quarrels happened continually between intimate friends; which generally ended in duelling. And there were very few who did not shorten their lives by intemperance, or violence.'

Spanish Town, Jamaica's capital, offered amenities but it was eclipsed by Kingston, where thirty-five wide and regular streets had many houses aspiring to elegance and where, by the 1770s, 11,000 or more people lived. West Indian society was no longer wholly philistine. Long, and a younger Jamaican, Bryan Edwards, emerged in the late eighteenth century as remarkable writers, able students of culture and society, of history and natural science. Barbados acquired a printing press in the 1730s and with it a newspaper, in which gentleman planters could publish their lamely derivative verses. What now most clearly distinguished Bridgetown or Kingston from Boston or Philadelphia was the almost complete lack of educational facilities. Provision existed in Jamaica for schooling fewer than fifty boys. Unlike their North American counterparts, West Indian planters could commonly afford to ship their offspring to England and keep them there.

Long complained that British girls picked up from slaves not only their 'drawling, dissonant gibberish' but also 'no small tincture of their awkward carriage and vulgar manners.' He drew a depressing picture of life on a 'sequestered country plantation' with its stunted Tatiana, 'a very fine young woman aukwardly dangling her arms with the air of a Negroe-servant, lolling almost the whole day upon beds or settees, her head muffled up with two or three handkerchiefs, her dress loose, and without stays. At noon we find her employed in gobbling pepperpot, seated on the floor, with her sable hand-maids around her. In the afternoon she takes her *siesto* as usual . . . When she rouses from slumber, her speech is whining, languid and childish. When arrived at maturer years, the consciousness of her ignorance makes her abscond from the sight or conversation of every rational creature.'

Among the innumerable casualties of empire, we should not forget these idle women, often married very young, for whom the highest fulfilment would be to coquet with HM sailors, while their drunken husbands played with mulatto mistresses. Janet Schaw was impressed with the ladies of Antigua. Society was less opulent here; even the richest women carried the keys and supervised their households closely. But she noted the pallor of their cheeks – from childhood they were 'entirely excluded from proper air and exercise'.

But she liked the Leewards men very much – 'the most agreeable creatures I ever met with, frank, open, generous, and I dare say brave . . . Their address is at once soft and manly . . . their whole intention is to make you happy.' White Caribbean society was more easy-going than Britain's and, perverse though this may seem, more democratical in temper. Only sailors, and maybe some Irish servants, mingled with any black men as equals. Otherwise, all whites stood together, and class divisions between them were felt to be narrowed. Bryan Edwards would remark on the 'independent spirit' they showed and the 'display of conscious equality throughout all ranks and conditions. The poorest White person seems to consider himself nearly on a level with the richest, and, emboldened by this idea, approaches his employer with extended hand . . .' In the character of its social relationships, as in the ideas of its political leaders and in the quality of its best intellectuals, British West Indian society was closer to that of British North America than people now generally suppose.

V

But whereas West Indian planters wanted no new frontiers, in the mainland colonies the idea was gaining ground that the whole continent, as far as the still uncharted coasts of the Pacific, could rightfully be occupied by Englishmen. Colonists had their imaginations drawn to the interior by the growing French threat on their undefined borders.

The French, aware that pre-eminence over all North America might grossly increase British power in Europe, were now committed to struggle for the continent. The Treaty of 1713 was a setback, but far from crippling. The French retained valuable fishing rights on the northern and eastern coasts of Newfoundland. 'Nova Scotia' was absurdly misnamed. There were few if any Scots there, and virtually the only British settlements were Annapolis Royal, a village capital where a small garrison held a neglected fort, and Canso, a fishing station with some dozen permanent residents. About 5,000 French-speaking Acadians either refused to take an oath of allegiance to the British Crown or did so with qualifications, including exemption from military service against the French or their allies. Most of the area was still dominated by Micmac and Abenaki Indians who remained loyal allies of the French.

The French held Cape Breton (Île Royale), commanding the entry to the Gulf of St Lawrence. A few score settlers crossed from Newfoundland and made this bleak spot a dominating competitor in the fishing industry. The waters were ice free, and ships could seek cod as early as February and go on as late as Christmas. Here, at Louisbourg, from 1720, at vast expense, the French Crown erected what was, or seemed to be, the strongest fortress on the continent.

Travelling past Louisbourg, up the St Lawrence, and on, the French reached their vast, vague empire stretching to the Gulf of Mexico. Around 1740, there were only some 50,000 French subjects in North America. But they were far more unified than the British confronting them. In theory, the governor general and intendant in Quebec commanded all. Though in practice Louisbourg and Louisiana had separate governments in direct communication with Paris, there was far less chance of dispute than existed between a dozen or so British regimes. And French motivations were simpler. Furs, and, increasingly, war, were the key to all. The French Crown poured in money and soldiers, yet there was no conflict between its aims and the gratifications of the white native Canadians who got on with their farming without much direct contact with France.

Quebec, with 8,000 people in the mid-eighteenth century, was not eclipsed by the British New World ports. Its churches and public buildings were striking.

Montreal, however, was merely a frontier town, dominated by soldiers and fur traders. While Canada had over 40,000 people by 1740, to the south, via the Great Lakes to the Mississippi basin, there were very few French indeed. At vast expense the Crown maintained half a dozen military posts. Settlement round them was scant; Detroit, where a few hundred colonists farmed, was exceptional. A little group of agricultural villages in the 'Illinois Country' along the Mississippi had 1,536 French settlers, 890 blacks, and 147 Indian slaves in 1752. So much for the vast province of 'Louisiana', except that in the far smaller area which still bears that name, a few thousand whites, whose slaves outnumbered them, sweated, squabbled and perished without much profit amid swarms of mosquitoes, propped up by the French Crown lest the British move in. New Orleans, founded in 1718, became the seat of government four years later.

During Queen Anne's war, the French beaver-hat trade had lost its export markets and the nation's warehouses had filled with surplus furs turning rotten. The greater cheapness of British trade goods, furthermore, was asserting itself strongly among the red men. That the French fur trade recovered was largely, perhaps chiefly, due to the support and persistence of the French State. The French Crown subsidised high prices to draw the Indians from Port Oswego, set up by New York in the 1720s, to its own fortified posts, Frontenac, Niagara and Detroit.

In the early 1730s, the explorations of the Sieur de La Vérendrye greatly strengthened the French in competition with the Hudson's Bay Company. Followed by the erection of several forts, they won the trade of Lake Winnipeg's drainage basin and the Saskatchewan river valley. *Voyageurs* setting off each spring to take trade goods and military supplies to New France's far-western outposts started to father a future nation of half-castes, the Métis, on the plains. The best furs were diverted to Montreal away from the HBC's York factory.

But English fur exports rose from £44,000 in 1700 to over £263,000 by 1750. Beaver hats accounted for more than 85 per cent of this latter figure. The main markets were in the New World itself – the British West Indies and the Spanish and Portuguese colonies. The Hudson's Bay Company prospered, despite the French. Mercantilists gloated that hats, passing through Spain to the Spanish New World, were contributing, like the slave trade, to 'dispersing the wealth of the Indies' into British hands. And this was achieved by a company which in the mid-century had only about 120 officers and servants and brought home only three or four ships a year.

Overheads were high, and French competition pushed them up. The cost of carrying on the trade and maintaining half a dozen factories ran at four or five times that of trade goods sent out. Hence the Company was mean with its employees, expecting them to live as much as possible off the bare lands around them, to cut their own timber, to brew their own beer and even to manufacture and mend trading goods. Prospects, for those who could stand the climate, were not bad; the chief officers in the Bay were still generally promoted servants. In the eighteenth century, Orcadians – they must not simply be called Scots, as the islands had their own special history and still retained much of their Norse heritage – were recruited in preference to Londoners, who drank too much and were hard to discipline. The Orkneys were a port of call on the way to the Bay. Hudson's Bay ships took off peasants and fishermen who were used to inclement weather and short rations, like the local breeds of cows and sheep which were also introduced to the Bay. Compared with the affable French Canadians, the Orkney men were tightfaced and unenterprising, but they gave the forts a most solid backbone.

James Isham, a promoted clerk, was in charge at Churchill from 1741–5, and wrote a vivid account of life on the Bay. HBC orders from London denounced the practice of keeping Indian mistresses – wives, or squaws, in effect – but Isham like many others went on regardless, and eventually left all his property to his half-breed son Charles, who found employ with the Company and became very useful. (Another half-breed, or perhaps full-blooded Indian, was actually put in charge at Churchill in 1759–60.)

Company policy was to restrict most servants from having more than a minimal contact with red men. The aim, commercially shrewd, was to thwart the 'private trade' which was so commonplace in the East Indies. Indians were not to enter the factory itself. Trade was carried on suspiciously, through a window or hole in the wall. Isham reported a typical speech of an Indian chief to a factor: '"You told me Last year to bring many Indians, you See I have not Lyd, here is a great many young men come with me, use them Kindly! use them Kindly I say! . . . we have come a Long way to See you, the french sends for us but we will not here, we Love the English, give us good black tobacco, moist & hard twisted. Let us see itt before op'n'd, – take pity of us, take pity of us I say! – the Guns are bad, Let us trade Light guns small in the hand, and well shap'd, with Locks that will not freeze in the winter . . . – Let the young men have Roll tobacco cheap, Ketles thick high for the shape, and size . . . – Give us Good measure, in cloth . . . Do you mind me!, the young men Loves you by coming to see you, take pity, take pity I say! – and give them good, they Love to Dress and be fine, do you understand me!" – here [added Isham] he Leaves of and they all say ho!'

The Indians truly did depend on trade goods – relying on white men's weapons, they might die in the winter for want of powder and shot, and the failure of a ship from Britain to get through could mean disaster for tribes around the posts. Conversely, the white men depended on Indian hunters to reinforce their monotonous diet of flour and cheese, pease and small beer. So far as fending for themselves went, the British showed little enthusiasm for gardening in this unfecund clime.

Nevertheless, the region was alluring enough to Arthur Dobbs, a prominent Irish Protestant landowner, who around 1730 became interested in the quest for a North West Passage, which the Company had neglected, began a twenty-year assault on its monopoly, and was at last able, in 1748, to obtain a House of Commons inquiry. Though the Royal African Company went down at this time, the Hudson's Bay Company stood up. MPs were swayed above all by the need to maintain a united front against France.

And the HBC was now stirring from what one former employee dubbed its 'Sleep by the Frozen Sea'. From 1754 onwards the Company ordered a stream of inland voyages. In that year, Isham, now at York Fort, sent an outlawed English smuggler, Anthony Henday, with his resourceful native 'bed-fellow' and a band of Crees, to persuade the Indians of the Plains to trade with the Company. He travelled over a thousand miles altogether, probably saw the Rocky Mountains, got on well with the Blackfoot Indians, and established for the first time the hitherto unsuspected extent of French influence in the interior.

And the French remained serious competitors in the fisheries. There was now what historians euphemistically call a 'commercial community' at St John's, Newfoundland. (A contemporary described it as a 'nest of little pedlars'.) A Vice-Admiralty Court was set up in the mid-1730s and actually checked illegal trade somewhat. But government remained careless and sketchy.

In 1726 it was reported that 65 out of 420 families on the island kept public houses. The fishing masters recruited seamen in Ireland and by the mid-century perhaps a quarter of the island's 3,000 or so inhabitants were Irish Catholics. Most people were in the strong grip of merchants. The New Englanders could demand high prices in winter, make profits of up to 400 per cent, entice people into contracting large debts and then sell them as indentured servants, sometimes shipping as many as sixty in a single sloop.

Though salmon fishing and sealing had begun to develop, cod remained the colony's reason for being. An estimated 450,000 quintals (hundredweight) of codfish a year were cured and exported around 1740, six or seven times as many as were caught off New England. The Newfoundland trade in 1753 employed over 15,000 men and some 1,675 ships and boats. The Channel Island of Jersey, a paradise of smuggling, actually had a larger stake in the trade than either Bristol or London. This was a commerce unlike any other except that in South Carolina rice; both commodities went direct to Southern Europe, there being little market for either in Britain itself.

VI

Newfoundland, it will be clear by now, was merely one of the many places where the 'old colonial' system leaked rather copiously. Perhaps it only worked so well because it leaked and desired commodities found their vents somehow. The expansive energies of the British economies, in the New World as in the home islands, were outgrowing the very system set up, successfully, to promote their expansion.

Colonial customs were not at this time expected to produce a significant revenue. The aim, rather, was to regulate trade. The customs ran at a loss; at mid-century, the returns of some one or two thousand pounds per annum would be nowhere near meeting the costs of enforcement, £7,000 or £8,000. In Walpole's day, the increase of population and trade in British North America was not met by a proportionate rise in the numbers of officials appointed to enforce the regulations. These were scattered along the seaboard, in forty-seven different ports, where approaching ninety surveyors, riding surveyors, comptrollers, collectors, searchers, prevention officers, land waiters, tide waiters performed their various tasks, or failed to do so. Breaches of the Acts of trade were tried in Vice-Admiralty Courts, of which there were eventually a dozen. Since these courts had no juries, local prejudice in favour of smugglers was less likely to sway their decisions; but common law courts in the colonies claimed authority over ships seized by the Royal Navy in adjoining waters, and they were prone to discharge convicted traders. Meanwhile, it was impossible to prevent customs officials (and even naval officers) from engaging in trade on their own account. It was common for one official to hold several posts. Salaries were inadequate, and the use of ill-paid deputies by absentee office-holders further weakened enforcement.

The situation was not, after all, very different from that in various ports in Britain. Colonial administration was still conceived at home as no more than part of the normal government of the king's realm. Decisions were taken by the Privy Council sitting as a Committee, usually acting under the advice of some other board or department. The Treasury was now clearly the most powerful department under the Crown, but it had no 'colonial policy'; its interests were financial, and its normal view was that colonial governments should be financially self-sufficient. There was precious little money raised in the New World. Virginian planters since the 1680s had paid an export duty of 2s. a hogshead on their tobacco. Barbados and the Leewards still produced their 4½ per cent duty on exports. Jamaica from the late 1720s paid its £8,000 a year towards its own government. The Crown drew petty sums from various sources – quitrents and treasure trove, fines and mines, waifs and strays and so forth. Whatever revenue the Treasury spotted, it would take away from the New World and apply to non-American purposes. The colonies received as little naval and military protection as could decently be provided. Once troops got to the New World, they were neglected.

Virginia and Maryland tobacco, like Carolina rice, was clear gain to Britain in mercantilist eyes. Another positive virtue of North America was that it promised greater self-sufficiency in naval stores. The New England forests abounded in tall trees suitable for the production of masts and timber for ships. In Massachusetts, from 1691, and eventually in the whole region from Maine to New Jersey, all trees above 24 inches in diameter standing on land not privately owned were reserved to the British Crown. However, many officials took bribes and connived in evasion of the law by favoured colonists, much to the indignation of those not favoured.

Colonial white pine trees were excellent, but the Navy Board in Britain rated American pitch and tar much lower than the products obtained from Sweden. However, the long war between Sweden and Peter the Great's Russia deprived Britain of most of its 'naval stores' from the Baltic. An Act of 1705 offered bounties for the production in the colonies. The response was enthusiastic; to the surprise of theorists, it came not from New England but from the Carolinas, where access to pitch-pine from rivers was still easy and where cheap slave labour was abundant for the lengthy and skilful processes involved. By 1715, America was producing almost half Britain's supplies of tar and pitch; over the next eight years the proportion was four-fifths – more than sixty thousand barrels a year. Then the Board of Trade, convinced that the Swedish product was better, persuaded Parliament to reduce the bounties on naval stores produced by American methods. South Carolina now switched its main attention decisively to rice, and North Carolina, with no such alternative staple, became the main producer of tar and pitch.

New England oak was abundant and excellent. With other necessities easily to hand, the colonial shipbuilding industry was more than competitive; it cost about twice as much to create a merchant ship in Britain as it did in Massachusetts. Boston in 1720 had fourteen yards turning out about 200 ships a year. Other New England ports would quite soon outstrip Boston. By the 1730s, New England and New York had several sugar refineries. But rum was the pride and shame of Yankee enterprise. The rum made in Boston and Newport drove Red Indians mad, enserfed rough fishermen from Cape Cod to Newfoundland, traded for slaves on the coast of Guinea, and found its greatest outside market of all in the southern mainland colonies. William Byrd II, travelling in North Carolina, reported an impromptu roadside meal of half a dozen very fat rashers of bacon fried up in a pint of rum.

A report that 10,000 beaver hats were being made annually in the northern colonies pressed Parliament into the 'Hat Act' of 1732. It was ineffectual, like Acts restricting the production of woollens and, in 1750, colonial iron. Charcoal was still the basis of ironmaking. With wood in Britain itself running short the colonies could exploit a natural advantage. Governor Spotswood of Virginia set the pace for the colonists there. By the early 1720s, his crude, heavy metalware was on sale in Williamsburg, his pig iron was being exported to Britain. The Pennsylvanian Quakers were not behind, and by 1740 Philadelphia had a steel furnace.

As an increasing American population produced more, and in greater variety, from its farms and crafts and industries, it was starting to outgrow the capacity of the British and British colonial markets to absorb its exports. The mounting wealth of the well-to-do in American seaboard towns owed a great, if incalculable, amount to illegal operations. One governor wryly noted, early in the century, that while poor pirates were hanged, 'rich ones appear'd publicly, and were not molested in the least.' Their cash and cargoes were very welcome.

Smugglers, as in Britain, perhaps still more so, were admired rather than deplored. Yankee go-getters showed greater and greater independence of ties with London. Rich colonial merchants, instead of insuring ships through London, began from the 1720s to insure American vessels themselves. Only wealthy Virginia planters still depended on London or Bristol credit; farmers elsewhere were chiefly in the grip of local merchant classes.

Since there was no market yet in Britain for transatlantic foodstuffs – they were too bulky to bear the costs of transport – colonial capitalists had perforce to continue devising schemes, licit and illicit, for triangular or polygonal trades which sent their skippers roaming the Atlantic in search of bills. A Quaker merchant wrote in 1741: 'We make our Remittances a great many different ways sometimes to the West Indies in Bread, Flour, Pork, Indian Corn, and hogshead Staves, sometimes to Carrolina and Newfoundland in Bread and Flour sometimes to Portugall in Wheat, Flour and Pipe Staves sometimes to Ireland in Flax Seed Flour, Oak and Walnut Planks and Barrel Staves and to England in Skinns, Tobacco, Beeswax, staves of all Kinds, Oak and Walnut planks, Boat Boards, Pigg Iron, Tarr, Pitch, Turpentine, Ships, and Bills of Exchange.' In other words, having taken provisions and timber to the Caribbean, Lisbon or the 'Wine Islands', vessels might go on to Britain either in ballast or laden with sugar, molasses, rum or Madeira. The ship itself might then be sold; otherwise it would come home laden with British (or bootleg European) manufactures. A typical homeward cargo might consist of twelve crates of earthenware and twenty casks of nails, six dozen scythes, twenty reams of paper, three gross of ink powder and bolts of various textiles, including Persian and Chinese taffeta.

Rising consumer demand in mainland America for such commodities made the Caribbean more and more vital to the prosperity of colonists further north. So far, in mercantilist terms, so good. The interdependence of the British New World colonies was satisfactorily represented by the large numbers of yellow-visaged Jamaicans, Antiguans and Barbadians to be seen mingling with the ruddy-faced locals in North American seaboard towns. The trouble was that the British West Indies did not increase their demand for provisions and wood at the same pace as mainland production rose; and in any case French or Dutch sugar and molasses were cheap enough to smother any freakish strength of national loyalty among the Bostonians or the Quakers of Newport and Philadelphia. Mainland interests were therefore increasingly tied to those of the foreign islands with which mainlanders more and more traded.

Meanwhile, over the vast and growing area of mainland white settlement, there was more trade than one port could dominate. Boston was losing its pre-eminence. Its population, 16,258 in 1742, had by then started to decline somewhat. Its growth was being checked by the rise of other ports. Its immediate New England hinterland, which included Connecticut and New Hampshire, remained comfortable rather than opulent, but smaller coastal towns even here were flourishing and competing.

Newport was Boston's most formidable New England rival, with over 6,000 people by the 1740s, by when its merchants had started their own direct trade with the Old World, and had intervened on the Guinea coast. New York (11,000) was the liveliest place in British North America. A Scots doctor, Alexander Hamilton, who left a vivid account of his travels through the colonies, observed that one had to be a 'good toaper' to get on well with the inhabitants. 'To talk bawdy, and to have a knack att punning passes among some there for good sterling wit.' New York was also breaking away from Boston's hegemony. But its growth was outstripped by that of Philadelphia, which was now, with some 13,000 inhabitants, clearly becoming the North American capital. The rich farming lands around and behind were now the granary of the southern colonies; the port even shipped flour to Boston. It dominated, besides Pennsylvania, the trade of Maryland, Delaware and West New Jersey, with its own home-built merchant fleet. Its men took the lead in the colonial production of pig and bar iron which was leaving Britain's own behind.

About 800 families of Quakers made up little more than a quarter of the town's population by the mid-century: but they dominated the place. The whole Quaker community had shifted upward socially over the years. Artisans and labourers had fathered merchants and master craftsmen. The jealousy of the Yankee Congregationalists was heartily reciprocated, fed not only by rivalry in trade but by memories of Puritan persecution. The élite of Quaker traders felt less in common with their non-Quaker fellow citizens than with those other prosperous Quakers in Britain and the colonies with whom they corresponded ceaselessly regarding 'prices current and the prosperity of Truth'. And a growing distance was emerging between simple country Friends in Pennsylvania and these Philadelphia grandees whose ways were suspiciously worldly.

Hamilton dined at a Philadelphia tavern where a 'knott of Quakers', characteristically, 'talked only about selling of flower and the low price it bore.' But in this place, a 'great hall well stoked with flys', he also found a 'very mixed company' – Scots and English, Dutch, Germans and Irish, 'Roman Catholicks', Anglicans, Presbyterians, 'Newlightmen, Methodists, Seventh day men, Moravians, Anabaptists, and one Jew.' This represented the range of peoples and sects now settled in the hinterland. There would have been Africans there as well, although Hamilton did not mention them. Pennsylvania's population included several thousand blacks.

The intellectual life of Philadelphia was enormously enhanced by so many diverse influences, as it took over from Boston the cultural leadership of the colonies. The town pioneered in the 1720s a native style of Georgian architecture. Its grandees built themselves impressive country houses. The larger American ports were now ahead of their British counterparts in amenity. Boston and Philadelphia had underground sewers at a time when Bristol still suffered from unpaved gutters running down the centre of its streets. But while the North American towns were absolutely bigger than they had been, the proportion of population now living in them had declined: 5.4 per cent in 1742 compared with 9 per cent fifty years before. This was still mainly a territory of planters and farmers, and as the frontier was extended, so its overall rural character grew more, rather than less, pronounced.

It was, however, a rural ambience modified from its beginnings by commercial capitalism. This was true even in the Chesapeake colonies, which still lacked really substantial towns. Williamsburg, capital of Virginia, was a village with some two hundred houses, a few good shops, a College, a Capitol. The Virginian population was thinly dispersed. But the whole region was concerned with commerce. Tobacco production mounted fast – 20 million lb. in 1700, 80 million in the mid-1730s, 220 million in 1775. With the crop exhausting the soil so rapidly, the tidewater lands of the first comers were worked out. Planters aimed at large holdings, with plenty of land in reserve, to be cleared when slack times came.

However, tobacco remained a crop for the small man as well as the great planter. Even in the longest-settled counties of Virginia, two-thirds of white landholders had farms of 200 acres or less. Settlement now surged past the fall line which limited navigation, into the 'Piedmont', where most of the pioneers were small producers using the labour of themselves, their families, with one or two indentured servants or convict labourers. With tidewater land failing in productivity, the old advantage of nearness to the sea was outweighed by those of virgin soil. The patterns of Chesapeake life began to modify. Real towns – Baltimore, Richmond and so on – emerged on the fall line towards the mid-century. And the character of trade changed. By navigable water the pattern had been for large planters to deal direct with agents in London; small men commonly sold their crops to the great, who received in return goods from Britain which they traded among their neighbours. Now, in the Piedmont, the enterprising tobacco merchants of Glasgow led the way in opening stores which sold British goods to planters on the security of their tobacco and reduced them to a more obvious dependence.

But Carters and Byrds in Virginia, Dulanys and Carrolls in Maryland, could still set the tone of society and dominate politics, owning thousands of acres and hundreds of slaves. Whereas the petty farmers enjoyed, in their neat timber houses, a coarse plenty in cows and pigs, corn and vegetables, growing just enough tobacco to meet their needs for goods from outside for the next year, the rich men, in their fine brick mansions, formed one of the most remarkable ruling classes in history, and aimed at an almost visionary ideal of self-sufficiency which was far more than sufficiency.

It was true that the plantation would be like a small village, with, in an extreme case, its own mill, its wheat silo and ironworks, its forge, turner's shop, wheelwright's shop, carpenter's shop, shoemaker's shop, with tanners and sawyers and weavers, with slave children busy making nails and veteran slave women spinning yarn, with distillers making peach brandy, with excellent home-grown cider, with beer as good as any from England made in the planter's brewery. But Virginia also imported 'vast quantities' of Bristol beer, and this was less esteemed than such foreign potions as wine and arrack, brandy and rum.

Large planters conceived themselves as 'patriarchs'. It was the slave's 'duty' to serve his master well. The master preferred to call his blacks 'servants' and the whippings he gave them 'correction'. He took an obsessive interest in the characters of his 'family' of slaves, doctoring them devotedly when need arose, and, conversely, exercising stern parental authority. This was a more intimate attention than an English landed gentleman commonly accorded to his domestics and labourers. But, it was also sound business, or appeared so.

The planter, however 'opulent' he might seem, was, like his West Indian counterpart, always in debt. As Thomas Jefferson would note wryly, debts had become hereditary from father to son and many Chesapeake estates were 'a species of property annexed to certain mercantile houses in London'. The planter's chosen role of serene, luxurious, generous patriarch was in sharp conflict with the reality of his position. He was, in fact, a trader himself, snared in a most complex business. Robert Carter ('King Carter'), who died with 300,000 acres, wrote once to his London factor, 'I cannot allow myself to come behind any of these gentlemen in the planter's trade.' No Virginian 'gentleman' scorned 'trade'. The real sources of the great planter's power were his roles as middleman slave dealer reselling to petty planters and traders, as retailer of European goods, as contractor to hiring out slave artisans, and as manufacturer bringing on to the market the products of his home industries. And, of course, as an entrepreneur making tobacco, and looking, as King Carter's son put it, 'into every hole and corner' of his plantation, counting seedlings, stores and crops to make sure that slaves and overseers did not cheat him, working, in fact, a long, hard day. The enviable way of life was won by effort no less than that of a Scots factor and, in terms of hours spent, not remote from that of his slaves.

The contrast with such Jamaicans as Charles Price is obvious. What was it, however, that made the Virginian 'gentleman' different from the English ironmaster or clothier? Clearly the paradox that he belonged to a 'bourgeois' class orientated to the land. He was not an 'aristocrat' – one writer familiar with both England and America described George Washington as the son of 'creditable Virginia Tobacco Planter (which I suppose may, in point of rank, be equal to the better sort of Yeomanry in England).' The basis of the Virginian planter élite was sharply different from that of the English gentry. In the years since the Restoration, the latter had developed legal devices designed to ensure that estates passed on intact from eldest son to eldest son; by now half or more of England, probably, was held under 'strict settlement', to the disadvantage of younger offspring. This in part reflected the growing shortage of land. In Virginia, there was no deficiency. Younger sons, even younger daughters, could be granted landed inheritance, receiving tracts outside the home county while the eldest son took the 'home' plantation. But where was 'home'? This class was not rooted. With soil so quickly exhausted, its members would not be tied to a single place. And entail was ruled out by the fact that the slaves without whom land would be worthless had to be moved to fresh land and could only be kept in one place at the cost of economic suicide. Hence, four male Carters in the third generation were sitting together in the Assembly. The great families, expanding amoeba-like, intermarried incessantly with each other and produced a ruling class, compacted into a cousinry, in which every man was the equal, and no more, of every other. This provided an arena for easy give and take of ideas in debate, and for common action in the defence of the ideals of the group, which included the belief, rarely found in the West Indies, that every substantial man should play a responsible part in public affairs and do his duty in the commonwealth. Such was the background of Washington and Jefferson.

However, in a muted, more dignified mode, the Virginia gentleman's pleasures were the same as those of the Irish squireen or Jamaican buckra. Hospitality was free and easy, extended visits were 'almost the only kind of group life the region afforded.' Men hunted, raced the excellent local breed of horses, gambled away their acres, danced until they dropped.

South and North Carolina were separated by the proprietors in 1712, and continued to develop in markedly different directions. North Carolina was perhaps the most rural of all colonies, where the largest 'town' had only 150 buildings. Wealth here was distributed with relative even-ness among many petty but well-fed farmers. The colony preserved for a long time its reputation as a haven for criminals, debtors and runaway blacks. Children remained unbaptised, government feeble.

South Carolina, in extreme contrast, became the closest equivalent on the mainland to Jamaica. This was not inevitable. Though rice cultivation had begun in the 1690s and slave population had overtaken white in the first decade of the eighteenth century, Carolina had remained a frontier society, heavily committed to the trade in deerskins. A bitter war with the Yamasee Indians (1715–17) fed growing resentment of the Colony's proprietors in England. The war cost £116,000 in two years, yet the proprietors by their own admission sent less than £1,000.

In 1729, the Crown at last purchased the colony from the proprietors. Parliament was persuaded to permit direct shipment of rice to Spain and Portugal, the colony's natural markets. A boom followed. Between 1732 and 1738, the market value of rice rose by 75 per cent and exportation from the colony nearly doubled, to 67,000 barrels per year. With deerskins, livestock and timber to export, as well as rice and, later, indigo, South Carolina became the richest of all the mainland colonies, and the one most favoured by legislators in London.

The cypress swamps of its 'Low Country' by the coast were excellently suited to rice. Much capital was needed for irrigation works and, like sugar, this became a crop for grand slave-owners. African labour was more obviously desirable than it had been in the early days of sugar. Much rice was grown in West Africa. Some slaves would be more familiar with its planting, hoeing, processing, cooking than, in the first instance, their masters were. Rice prices fell low in the mid-1740s, but indigo, a recent re-introduction, became extremely profitable after Parliament, in 1748, offered bounties for its cultivation. The crop complemented rice; it grew best on higher and better-drained soils.

Although it possessed other possible harbour sites, the colony depended on Charles Town to take off its produce, and become a kind of city-state. With approaching 7,000 inhabitants, Charles Town rose from the ashes of a fire in 1740, which destroyed many crude old wooden buildings, with an elegant architectural manner of its own, mixing West Indian notions with the classical style now prevailing in Europe. Nowhere else in the New World was urban life more gracious, for the rich. Planters flaunted their new wealth in their elaborate town residences, drinking fine wines in airy high-ceilinged rooms. There were dances twice a week in the Assembly rooms, public concerts from 1732, a theatre from 1735, and, by the mid-1760s, three newspapers.

The Carolina élite, some 2,000 people, was 'full of money' but empty of public spirit. Few people bothered to vote, though suffrage was, among whites, virtually universal. Twice in the late 1740s it proved impossible even to muster a quorum in the Commons House, and assemblies were dissolved without effectually having met at all. Local government was non-existent. Half or more of the parishes had no ministers.

Granted that two-thirds of the population were slaves by 1720, and that blacks came to outnumber whites by as much as eighteen to one in certain parishes, South Carolina might seem to have been no more than a flashier, faster Jamaica. But there were important points of difference. The colony was more than self-sufficient in food. Though schools were far less numerous than in more northern provinces, private tutors were abundant. Absenteeism was rare.

In Virginia, blacks made up 40 per cent or over, in Maryland over 30 per cent, in North Carolina only about a quarter. From Pennsylvania northwards, blacks were concentrated in the port towns. Early in the eighteenth century, they made up approaching a quarter of the people of New York City; in 1720 one Bostonian in six was black. However, in the mid-century, taking New England as a whole, blacks were 3 per cent only of the people. In New Jersey and Pennsylvania the figure was about 8 per cent. Rhode Island and New York, the latter with one black face among seven or eight, were the two northern colonies most concerned with slavery at home – though all, of course, drew benefits from slavery in the West Indies.

Slave labourers, seamen and craftsmen played a role out of proportion to their numbers in Northern economies where white workmen could not be checked from moving on to acquire land. In Queen Anne's day a French Huguenot named Elias Neau, who had himself served seven years as a galley slave, started a school for blacks in New York City, which soon had scores of pupils. Many New England churches had blacks as full members. Interracial marriages occasionally occurred in the Northern colonies, though both Massachusetts and Pennsylvania had laws against miscegenation. In New York free blacks, and in New England even slaves, could testify against whites in court. A few free Northern blacks and mulattoes voted in elections. But even here, many slaves ran away. Slaves were forbidden in New England to wander beyond town limits without a pass, to remain on Boston common after sunset, to build bonfires or drink in taverns. What might be defined as the first known American lynching occurred at Roxbury, Massachusetts, in 1741, and the first serious slave revolt on the mainland occurred in New York City in 1712. Some two dozen slaves erupted, coupling arson with butchery. Several committed suicide rather than submit; seventeen were executed. The town remained edgy. In 1741 a purported plot was unearthed, thirteen blacks were burnt, eighteen were hanged and seventy were shipped out of the colony.

The fear of servile insurrection cannot be dissociated from the precocious beginnings of anti-slavery argument in North America. The first published protest against the institution had been made by a small group of Pennsylvania Quakers as early as 1688. The first true 'abolitionists', men who devoted a great part of their lives to agitation, were Philadelphia Friends. William Sandiford (1693–1733) was ostracised by other Friends and boycotted in his shop. Benjamin Lay, an eccentric hunchback who died in 1759, refused to use slave-grown produce, lived in a cave outside the town in preference to a man-made building, denounced slave-holding Friends at Meetings dressed in sackcloth, and stood barefoot outside in the snow to draw attention to the plight of slaves who had to spend the whole winter thus. His Meeting disowned him in 1738. But by the time of his death, a genuine anti-slavery movement, powered by idealism and fear, was emerging in America, led by Anthony Benezet, a Quaker schoolteacher and powerful scholar.

Yet meanwhile Rhode Island Quakers had played a part in the growing colonial participation in the slave trade. In the mid-eighteenth century, Newport had roughly half its merchant fleet, perhaps 170 ships, engaged in slaving. The American vessels – mostly about 40 or 50 tons – were far smaller than their British rivals and were amongst the most cramped and least seaworthy involved in the commerce. Their share was never great (6,300 out of 97,000 blacks carried from Africa in 1768). However, Southern merchants and planters commonly bought an interest in African voyages undertaken by English slavers. In the first sixty years of the century, British North America seems to have imported altogether some 170,000 slaves.

How did conditions compare with the West Indies? Smaller farmers, in North and South, worked, with their sons and white servants, beside their slaves; this meant both constant social intercourse and constant surveillance. Even large planters of tobacco and rice, worried about problems of supervision in their absence, divided their land into portions with never more than thirty slaves to a 'quarter', creating a different environment from their Caribbean counterparts. But not an idyllic one. At the peak of the harvest season, a fifteen-hour day was demanded in Virginia. Rice was even more exacting than tobacco.

Mainland slave codes, in some particulars, were more repressive than Caribbean ones. In the West Indies, a black culture was developing which was shared by a black majority and which had considerable impact on white habits. The North American slave or freeman was commonly less hard used physically, but psychologically his position was perhaps even more humiliating. Typically he worked in a smaller unit, and had more contact with whites, who were increasingly proud of their own American ways and saw him as a regrettable aberration. He himself was more distanced from African culture, because of a feature which made slavery on the Northern mainland unique in the New World: the rapid increase, by breeding, of numbers of native slaves. By 1720 the annual rate of natural increase in British North America was surpassing the annual rate of importation, and by the 1780s, only one slave in five would be African born. In 1800 there would be a million blacks in America. If the birth- and death-rates had matched those of the West Indies, there would have been only 186,000. Besides relative freedom from lethal diseases, the main reason seems to have been attitudes among planters, at least north of Charles Town, which were not, always, more truly humane, but which made interbreeding among slaves easier. The contrast between Virginia and South Carolina bears this out.

The Virginians, as we have seen, were not men who found wealth easy to come by. Even in 1699, at the peak of a mania for purchasing slaves, the Assembly prudently put a duty of 20s. a head on each import. They were beginning to guess that their speculative euphoria had been not entirely wise. In 1710, the House of Burgesses passed an Act creating a duty of £5 per slave, its members, according to Governor Spotswood, 'urged what is really true . . . that it will be impossible for them in many years to discharge the debts already contracted for the purchase of those negros if fresh supplys be still poured in upon them while their tobacco continues so little valuable . . .' In force till 1718 it effectively stopped importation. In 1723 the Assembly tried to impose a duty again, this time only 40s. But British slave traders now protested so strongly that the colony's legislation was vetoed by the King in Council. An acceptable formula was found in 1723; the duty was to be paid by the buyer, *ad valorem*, and this measure became virtually permanent.

It was not effusive love of black people which made Virginians uneasy about the trade. On the contrary, they showed growing prejudice. Virginians were very worried at this time by the risk of slave uprisings; two hundred slaves had attempted insurrection by 1730, and trepidation flavoured a now famous letter

which William Byrd II sent to the Earl of Egmont six years later. Byrd feared a
revolt which would 'tinge our Rivers as wide as they are with Blood.' He wished
Parliament would stop 'this unchristian Traffick of makeing Merchandize of
Our Fellow Creatures.' If it went on, there would be so many blacks in Virginia
that he feared it would become known as 'New Guinea'.

Such men as Byrd were inwardly divided on the issue of slavery. It did not
suit their exalted image of America as a Utopian land of self-sufficient
gentleman farmers. Indians, by contrast, were romanticised in their minds as
true native Americans; Byrd fulsomely advocated interbreeding with them, and
laws against miscegenation did not apply to them. Feeling this way, the
plantocrats' attitude towards 'creole' slaves was in effect quite generous. They
believed that American natives *should* be baptised, and this view was unique
among British New World planters. Such blacks were suitable for training in
white skills, and this, in Virginian eyes, more or less implied conversion.
Planters had slaves taught to be expert forgemen, blacksmiths, sawyers,
bricklayers and so on. Many were able to read and write, and could hold their
own in every respect except skin colour with white artisans in the same crafts.
Many ran away, a common aim being to pass for free in one of the towns. That
so many escaped recapture for so long shows that Virginian slave society was
uniquely permissive and open. Those whites prepared to accept and employ
runaways violated the slave code, like many blacks, with impunity. Numerous
domestics and skilled slaves were smooth-tongued and spoke excellent English.

South Carolina was very different, with its rush of wealth, its careless rulers,
its spate of fresh imports – 32,233 slaves between 1724 and 1739. In these years,
attitudes prevailed which exactly matched those of Jamaican planters. Planters
came to value fresh imports above the survival of people whom they already
owned. The lot of slaves therefore grew worse. The militia, from 1721, was
transformed from an army into an internal police force; by 1740 all its members
were supposed by law to take part in regular patrols. To check runaways, scout
boats ranged the coasts, and garrisons were set up on the edge of settlement
inland. The aim was to make this mainland colony as difficult to escape from as
any island.

The effort defeated itself. Increasing white control was met with increasing
black resistance. In the late 1730s the Spaniards in Florida shrewdly published
a decree granting liberty to black fugitives reaching them from the English
colonies. Runaways responded in spate. In September 1739, a score of slaves,
many of them newly arrived Angolans, rose near the Stono river in South
Carolina, seized arms, burnt houses and killed more than twenty whites. Rebel
numbers grew, and it was almost a week before the largest party was beaten in
pitched battle thirty miles to the south, clearly heading towards Florida. The
whites remained fearful for months and then, the next summer, some sixty-
seven slaves were brought to trial for a fresh conspiracy. The shock was such
that the government laid down penalties for harsh masters, and, while blacks

were put under more restrictions than ever, a prohibitive duty was temporarily set on fresh imports.

But the black to white ratio did not alter markedly. This was the only part of North America where, as in the Caribbean, Africans were thrown together, from different tribal backgrounds, in areas where they greatly outnumbered whites who took little or no interest in their personalities. A creole language, 'Gullah', evolved as their common tongue, retaining strong African elements. There were quite large numbers of Red Indian slaves in the colony - 1,400 were counted in 1708. Domiciled alongside them and more at home than their white masters in a subtropical environment, Africans played a mediating role vital to South Carolina's development. Besides their skill in rice-planting, they were often adept at fishing with nets. Expert African canoemen became the backbone of the transport system; and blacks, used to crocodiles, coped far better with alligators than Europeans. They became pathfinders, guides and interpreters. Indian and African skills fused in such crafts as the weaving of baskets from palmetto leaves. Blacks created the bases of the colony's material life, and were essential to its expansion.

But this was true, if less obviously so, in most other North American colonies. In 1700 there had been, at most, one black to ten whites in British North America. By 1770, the proportion would be one to five, the highest in the history of the northern mainland, despite a remarkably high white birth-rate in the colonies, and a renewal of heavy white immigration.

VII

Between 1700 and 1760, while the population in England and Wales grew by about 23 per cent, that of the American mainland colonies multiplied six times. 'In 1700,' Richard Hofstadter has observed, 'the colonies were small outposts of Western civilisation, an advance guard on the fringe of the raw continent numbering about 250,000 souls. By 1750 there were 1,170,000 . . .' And those would increase fivefold again in the next half century. The mainland white population passed that of Scotland and would, by 1800, stand at half that of the whole island of Great Britain.

Men of the time did not make or use many statistics, but they were aware of changing balances within the empire, of a vast area already settled and of the far vaster area which might yet be settled. Better diet than in Europe implied lower infant mortality and less disease among children. The ease with which land was acquired encouraged parents to have more offspring, since their labour, before they were ten, would be useful. Patrick Henry, born in Virginia in 1736, was one of nineteen siblings. One Rhode Island woman who lived to be 100 could count 205 descendants surviving before she herself died.

Rising population pushed the frontiers forward. In the 1720s movement began into the Cumberland Valley, an avenue leading from Pennsylvania to the back-country of Virginia. By 1716 rangers from that colony had found a passage

over the Alleghenies. By 1724 there were immigrants, Germans, in the Valley of
Virginia. Within a quarter of a century, the whole Valley was settled, with
movement west from Virginia itself having met there a spate, about double its
volume, of pioneers flooding south from Pennsylvania. Virgin land was
worthless without occupants. Speculators often pulled settlement forward –
offering inducements, providing the capital needed to buy out the Indians,
constructing defensive works, and so on. Competition between them for buyers
helped to keep the price of land low, as did competition between colonies. Trade
with the red men remained valuable. South Carolina alone sent Britain perhaps
a million and a quarter buckskins in twenty years from 1739 – they were in great
demand for riding breeches – and they were so much used as a form of currency
in the back-country that their value became a standard measure in Pennsylvania;
hence one surviving usage of the word 'buck', for dollar.

New Englanders were moving eastward into Maine in quest of lumber, and
reserves of cultivable land in Massachusetts, Connecticut and Rhode Island
were almost exhausted by the mid-century. So pioneering in New York
accelerated as the shortage of acres in New England made the terms of the great
landowners there more acceptable. Thus the Iroquois now felt the pinch.

Even in Pennsylvania, where a tradition of just dealing had been established,
time eroded red-white relations. In the 1720s the Delaware Indians from eastern
Pennsylvania began to trek westward in face of white pressure. The
Pennsylvania authorities now preferred to deal direct with the Iroquois and use
them to keep the local Indians in line. As Delawares moved west, so did the fur
traders who battened on them. Pennsylvania's trade reached as far as the shore
of Lake Erie.

There was, as we have seen, much use of Indian slaves in South Carolina.
Inland tribes in that region came to own black slaves, and provided red ones to
the British for shipment out of Charles Town to the West Indies. But this did
not imply easy relations. The so-called 'Yamasee' war of 1715–17 arose out of
South Carolina's failure to regulate its Indian trade. Practically every Indian
nation which did business with the colony was involved. The Yamasees
themselves were chased into Florida, but ten years of diplomatic struggle
between British and Spaniards followed for the control of the Creek nation.
Meanwhile, the French in Louisiana seemed menacing. By 1730 the Board of
Trade had made up its mind that colonisation must be effected south of the
Carolina settlements.

Enter James Oglethorpe, soldier and philanthropist, shrill and unbearably
garrulous, nevertheless commanding respect as a man of courage, integrity and
idealism: in short, because he was not a Walpolian whig. His father after the
Revolution had been for several years an active Jacobite intriguer, making his
peace with William III only in 1696, the year in which James Oglethorpe was
born. An elder brother was given a Jacobite barony by the Pretender, their three
sisters settled in James's court, and their mother, a friend of Jonathan Swift,

continually intrigued on behalf of the Stuarts. Till his dying day (1785) James Oglethorpe supported the doctrine of the Divine Right of Kings, but he sat in the House of Commons from 1722 as a loyal Hanoverian tory.

In this period, the defence of humane values largely depended on such tories. Oglethorpe spoke up for the oppressed British seaman and published in 1728 a pamphlet attacking the press-gang. A close friend had been sent to gaol for debt and had died of smallpox there. Oglethorpe pressed for a parliamentary inquiry into the state of the prisons, succeeded, and chaired the committee set up. Fearsome extortions and cruelties were exposed, but the several gaolers put on trial were all acquitted; the whig state looked after its own. Oglethorpe now devised a plan for a colony which would give harbour to debtors who would otherwise suffer in prison. Parliament approved the project in 1732. A new kind of charter was granted. Oglethorpe and nineteen associates were made 'Trustees for establishing the colony of Georgia', on territory between the Savannah and Altamaha Rivers, but the composition of the governing Council would be controlled by the Crown, and the colony would revert to the King after twenty-one years. Besides money given to them by charitable individuals, the Trustees were provided with £10,000 by Parliament, the first such grant ever made. Oglethorpe's publicity beckoned to the 'unfortunate', who could now be 'carried gratis into a land of liberty and plenty', and the Trustees hearkened to the plight of Protestants recently expelled by the Archbishop of Salzburg from his lands in Germany. By the end of their term, the Trustees would have sent 2,127 people to Georgia 'on the Charity'.

Oglethorpe himself sailed with the first batch of 130 lucky unfortunates. In February 1733 they began to erect 'Savannah' on the river of that name, ten miles from the sea. Since the Yamasee war, the region had been deserted. The coastal plain stretching south was replete with malarial mosquitoes. The colonists found scalding droughts and drenching rains, with frosts in winter which led to 'Chamber-Pots frozen under the Bed'. Yet under Oglethorpe's guidance, the settlement started well. He had a sincere respect for Indian rights. He got on very well with the Creeks, helped greatly by a remarkable Indian woman, a princess of their nation, named Mary Musgrove, whose white husband kept a store of Savannah.

The philanthropic vision of the Trustees prompted a quixotic and ineffectual ban on rum in the colony. Their prohibition of slavery, however, was not simply due to the growing revulsion felt in certain circles in Britain, and by Oglethorpe himself. Experience had shown that plantation colonies were hard put to defend themselves. This must be a white man's buffer settlement, unworried by dangers of servile rebellion, always ready to take up arms. Plantations, besides, would spread people too widely. A single colonist might hold in Georgia only fifty acres. However, from the outset, men entering at their own expense, with a certain number of servants, could get 500, later 2,000 acres.

At first the settlers were buoyed up by their trust in Oglethorpe and their gratitude for the new chance he offered. Even after Savannah had forty houses, Oglethorpe continued to live in a tent. He accepted hard rations, was last in bed and first out.

He was soon at odds with South Carolina over the Indian trade. He told the Chickasaws that he was himself a red man, 'an Indian, in my heart that is I love them', and his popularity with them struck against the influence of Charles Town traders. On a visit home in 1734, he took several Indian chiefs with him; a dazzled government gave him £25,800 to set up a chain of twenty forts against the French and Spaniards. He recruited Highland Scots and settled them on the Altamaha, where their village gained the nostalgic name of Darien. He set up garrison after garrison, village after village. In 1737 he wheedled £20,000 more out of Parliament, and permission to raise a regiment with himself as Colonel. In military terms, the colony was a success. But the settlers were now turning sour.

Oglethorpe was preoccupied with his role as soldier. While the Highlanders zealously kept to their clearing and planting of land, most of the rest grew lax. The village capital, Savannah, was ridden with quarrels, bootlegging and pilfering. Elsewhere men gave up in disgust and towns were abandoned. New settlers would not come. The colonists who remained grumbled about rum, tail male and, above all, the prohibition of slaves. Even the parson, a young Oxford scholar named John Wesley, embroiled himself in a feud with a great rogue named Causton, the colony's storekeeper, which split Savannah into two parties.

'The first Rise of it was upon young *Williamson's* marrying Mr *Causton's* Niece, whom the Parson had a Liking to for himself . . .' The spurned Wesley refused to administer the Sacrament to the new bride. And he preached against the magistrates, of whom Causton was one, calling out from the pulpit that the colonists should remember they were Englishmen and 'insist upon their Rights, when they found themselves oppressed . . .' Soon, however, the ineffectual firebrand gave out that he was returning to England. The magistrates ordered the constables to apprehend him if he tried to go. But the parson slipped away with three others, all of whom left large debts behind them, and one of whom was deserting his wife and child.

However, the next summer there was a new clergyman in the colony, George Whitefield. This very young man had no trouble at all in 'captivating the People with his moving Discourses'. His manner was open, jovial and easy. The church was soon far too small to hold those who wanted to hear him, and the colony's labour was soon being diverted from its lethargic agricultural pursuits to build the orphanage which he proposed near Savannah.

Oglethorpe's treaties with Indian nations were soon being ignored by the colonists. After 1740 the land laws were relaxed, larger holdings were permitted. Then, from 1750, slaveholding was legalised. When the colony reverted to the Crown in 1753 it still had only 2,381 whites and 1,061 blacks. But rapid growth followed to about 33,000 by 1773, by which time 'Scotch-Irish' settlers had completed the long trail from Philadelphia through the back-country and were invading lands in western Georgia which the Creeks and Cherokees had to cede.

By 1672, an estimate had suggested 100,000 Scots in Ireland; most were Lowlanders, most were concentrated in Ulster. In the fifteen years after James III's defeat at the Boyne, when Lowland Scotland was humiliated by famine and shocked by the Darien disaster, and when land in Ulster left tenantless was going cheap, tens of thousands more went over. In 1715, Ulster had perhaps 600,000 people, a third of them Presbyterians and most of these of Scottish origin. The appellation 'Scotch-Irish' had been used by an American colonist as early as 1695, when there were already a few Ulstermen in the New World. It stuck, despite the chagrin expressed by the inhabitants of Londonderry, New Hampshire, in 1720, at hearing themselves called *Irish* – 'when we so frequently ventured our all for the British Crown and Liberties against the Irish Papist.' It was the badge of one of the most remarkable folk movements in history. Some writers have claimed that between about 1717 and 1775 as many as a quarter of a million Scotch-Irish entered North America, and though this figure must be too high, we can say with some certainty that during their last and greatest surge, in 1771-4, approaching 40,000 people emigrated from Ulster in four years. They brought to North America the militant traditions of Londonderry and Enniskillen from the Jacobite war of 1689. They formed the largest single ethnic group emigrating to North America during the colonial period.

The home government did not encourage emigration from the British Isles. Mercantilist thinking now emphasised the value of labourers and a large population. In the case of Georgia, for strategic reasons, English migration was positively assisted. But with dissenters tolerated and civil strife abating, voluntary colonists from England were relatively rare after 1689. The coming of peace in 1713 brought back the old problem of surplus convicts. An Act four years later established official policy for the rest of the century. Transportation for seven years was introduced for the first time as a punishment for English people convicted of certain lesser offences, while men and women pardoned for greater crimes would be transported for fourteen or twenty-five years. The penalty for premature return would be death. Convicts were handed over to official contractors who were paid £5 a head for taking them but expected to make a good profit from selling them in the New World at £8 to £25, they were kept chained below decks throughout the voyage, and deaths in transit seem to have averaged 15 per cent or more, a rate bad by the standards of slave trade. Altogether some 30,000 felons seem to have been despatched in the eighteenth century. Two-thirds, probably, went to Virginia and Maryland. The assemblies in both colonies tried to block the flow in the 1720s, but the home authorities would not let them.

Meanwhile the trade in indentured servants remained 'the backbone of the whole migratory movement'. White servitude did not end in North America until the nineteenth century. Its continuing importance is obscured by the greater number of black slaves. In Maryland there were 3,003 servants and 4,657 slaves in 1707; by 1755 the respective figures were 6,871 (excluding 1,981 convicts) and 46,356 blacks and mulattoes. The great majority of servants now were non-English. There was a trickle of Welshmen and Scots, but most of the incoming servants in the mid-eighteenth century were 'Irish', of one sort or another. Maryland, from 1699, tried to restrict the entry of people from Ireland by a heavy tax on their import. Pennsylvania, following suit in 1729, also put a tax on Germans.

By now the influx of Germans was alarming colonial English chauvinists. The first large wave, which lent Germans in general the misleading name of 'Palatines', began from the Rhineland in 1708–9. This region had suffered twenty years of war. Various Protestant sects endured persecution. An exceptionally bad winter was the trigger. Some 13,000 Rhinelanders, by invitation, arrived in England. Many went on to the colonies. The German lands, including Switzerland and Austria, now seemed to others, as they had done to Penn, an abundant reservoir of likely settlers. Agents ('newlanders') were sent through the area. A new form of servitude was devised. As people turned up in the ports without enough money to pay their passages, merchants took what they had, put them on board with their families and possessions, and contracted to deliver them. After arrival, the emigrant would have a short period in which to 'redeem' himself by finding the balance of money owing. If he could not, he was sold into servitude for a time depending on the size of his debt. The system was adopted in Britain, especially in Ireland, but it never wholly replaced the old one there, whereas almost all Germans went out as 'redemptioners'.

The Scotch-Irish often fared badly. A height between decks of 4 feet 6 inches was thought worth boasting about in advertisements; the *Sea Flower*, leaving Belfast with 106 passengers in 1741, lost 46 of them at sea from starvation, and when help arrived six of the corpses had been eaten. But of all white immigrants to North America, the Germans probably suffered the worst horrors. Their vessels were so commonly swept with typhus that it became known as 'Palatine fever'. Yet the 'redemptioner' was commonly a more substantial immigrant than the ordinary indentured servant. He had some goods, a wife and family, and very often a valuable skill. Germans kept coming over because they thought they could thrive better in the New World than the Old. They were frequently right, and in any case they enjoyed the religious freedom.

Most Germans were members of a Lutheran or Reformed Church – 'church people'. From 1736 there was a small but highly significant influx of 'Moravians', adherents of a pietistic and pacifistic sect which had broken away from Lutheranism. In North America, as in the West Indies, they had important influence as missionaries. They were the most civilised of frontiersmen, skilful craftsmen and engineers who insisted on education for both sexes and cultivated choral and instrumental music.

By 1775 at least 100,000 Germans had arrived in North America and the

'Pennsylvania Dutch' (*Deutsch*), may have made up a third of that colony's population. As they settled there, or moved south along the frontier, they brought agricultural and other techniques superior to any the British had used. Their inventiveness, and their care in agriculture, put the Scotch-Irish greatly to shame.

The Scotch-Irish were not forced across the Atlantic by persecution. Many Presbyterian fears had been set at rest by the successful Hanoverian Succession of 1714. Under George I their religion enjoyed complete toleration and Irish Presbyterians who wanted political office seem to have got their share of it in spite of the Test Act. Meanwhile Ulster was clearly becoming the most advanced province in Ireland. The growing linen industry gave small farmers extra income from weaving in their homes.

Nevertheless, economic conditions underlay the westward flow. Ulster depended so heavily on linen that any adverse fluctuation in its price meant hardships for whole communities. But when linen prices were high, landlords raised rents. In parts of Ulster, these quintupled in the second and third quarters of the eighteenth century; but the average price of Irish linen cloth advanced by only one-fifth over the longer period from 1710 to 1770. The strong competition of Catholics for land forced rents up to the highest possible level, so even a small shortfall in the harvest would result in destitution. Meanwhile, year after year, fleets came from Philadelphia and New York bringing flax seed to the Irish ports. This was bulky. The linen goods taken back were less so. There was plenty of space for emigrants on the ships bound for America.

During normal times, it was mostly farmers who went, but when food was very dear wage-labourers predominated. There was a good proportion of skilled craftsmen. The price of a passage fell over the years as trade with America increased. But before the 1770s most emigrants did not pay their own way; they went as indentured servants.

In Ulster, by contrast with Germany, the emigration business was usually a sideline for merchants and shipowners meeting spontaneous demand, and relying on newspaper advertisements. At times, the close-knit Presbyterian minority would be seized by an epidemic of wanderlust.

As a series of natural and man-made calamities struck Ulster from 1715 to 1720 – drought, dear food, epidemics, rising rents – a first, smallish spate of something over 2,000 emigrants headed west to try their luck in Boston. A few Scotch-Irish had recently been welcomed as frontier settlers in New England. But they had aroused sharp ethnic and religious prejudice. Over the next couple of decades, Boston successfully shooed off Hibernian aliens. The Irish authorities, also, were starting to worry about this effusion of Protestants. 'No Papists stir . . .', Archbishop King lamented in 1718. 'The papists being already five or six to one, and being a breeding people, you may imagine in what condition we are like to be in.'

But of roughly 15,000 emigrants to North America leaving Ireland in the

1720s, northern Protestants made up the great majority. A fever set in about 1724. The long thirty-one-year leases given after the end of the Williamite war were now expiring, as twenty-one-year leases had done in the previous decade. On one estate near Lisburn, thirty-four farms which had rented for a total of £90 in 1719 were let for £223 in 1728, and this coincided with near-famine. This time the wave toppled on to the ports on the Delaware. As with the Germans, Philadelphia became the main port of entry for the Scotch-Irish, who continued to come in at an average rate of one or two thousand per annum until, by 1769, some fifty or seventy thousand more had settled. Then, another fever set in.

James Logan, Provincial Secretary of Pennsylvania, who was an Ulsterman himself, shared the general local alarm and disgust over the incoming Scotch-Irish hordes. For a time, he refused to grant them land. This merely encouraged them to squat wherever they saw vacant ground. When the authorities burnt down their cabins, the Scotch-Irish simply squatted again. From 1743, the proprietors tried, with some success, to decant them into the Cumberland Valley in western Pennsylvania. This became almost their exclusive preserve.

Scotch-Irish families were ready to move, settle awhile, move on again. During the 1730s, encouraged by land speculators and by the Virginian authorities, they began to stream into the Chesapeake back-country. Part of it became known as the 'Irish tract'. By the 1740s, the Scotch-Irish were fanning into North Carolina; by the 1760s their southward sweep met fresh westward waves of immigration from Ulster through Charles Town, incited by South Carolina's offer of bounties to white incomers.

A novel society was coming into being in the area which has been called 'Greater Pennsylvania' – the hilly southern back-country stretching about 600 miles from the northern boundary of Maryland to the Savannah River. In 1730 the only white men seen there had been occasional traders or hunters. By 1775 it contained about 250,000 people of European, American and African birth. The dominance of the sea over patterns of settlement was broken. The 'Great Philadelphia Wagon Road' followed old Indian tracks from Pennsylvania down to Georgia, linking lands claimed by six colonies. By the 1760s it was the most travelled way in America, with towns springing up along its route, and with large covered wagons pressing down it, sometimes a hundred at a time. Welshmen and Englishmen used it, and Scots traders, as well as the large caravanserais of Germans and Ulstermen.

Many parts of the back-country swiftly became more thickly populated than the Tidewater and Low Country plantation lands. Small and medium-sized farms predominated. The Scotch-Irish pioneered in the making of whisky from rye or barley. Such cash crops as hemp, flax, tobacco and indigo were variously cultivated where the soil was suitable, and after about 1750 the back-country moved beyond subsistence farming and began to send food surpluses to the ports. The lead deposits found in the Valley of Virginia in the 1750s were of immediate value. Lead bullets defended the frontier.

Though the Scotch-Irish from the outset showed no respect for the Indians or their rights, most of the land they moved through was not permanently settled, and serious conflagration was avoided until the 1750s. When it came it was terrible. The score seems to have varied between three and fifty dead whites for every dead Indian. But the red men were outnumbered, and the Ulstermen proved matchlessly savage fighters. Inspired by the discovery that killing of red men freed new lands for whites, Irish traditions of genocide found new expression in a New World.

Women, perhaps outnumbered three to one in the early days, had to be tough under frontier conditions. Though the Germans tended to treat marital bonds with European solicitude, the Scotch-Irish became notorious for cohabitation and wife-swapping. An Anglican clergyman, Charles Woodmason, would leave a vivid if prejudiced picture of life in the South Carolina back-country in the 1760s. His parish was 150 miles broad by 300 long. He rode miles day after day, eating rough food in dirty smoky cabins or alone in the woods. Flies and mosquitoes abounded. The people seemed hardly less pestilential, though curiosity would always muster him a congregation. At a place named Granny Quarter Creek he confronted 'the lowest Pack of Wretches my Eyes ever saw . . . As wild as the very Deer – No making of them sit still during Service . . . How would the Polite People of London stare, to see the Females (many very pretty) come to Service in their Shifts and a short petticoat only, barefooted and Bare legged – Without Caps or Handkerchiefs . . .' (This was, incidentally, the depth of winter.) Wild Presbyterians mustered to harass him, set up drunken whoops and halloos outside the doors of the makeshift buildings he preached in. However, he had a still greater aversion for Baptists. He wryly observed that one thing which united jarring denominations was a common passion for strong liquor. '. . . Married many Rogues and Whores on Beaver Creek,' he noted once in his journal; elsewhere he remarked that the girls he hitched were almost invariably pregnant. Mating took place early. Girls married at fourteen. He would often see ten or fifteen children in a single cabin.

But after a few years, such ill-fed savage-looking persons would be making a modest profit from cash crops and aiming to build comfortable frame houses and imitate the comforts they had seen among classes above them in Europe or on the east coast. They were followed into the back-country by planters with their slaves, merchants and craftsmen, lawyers and ministers, and, of course, land speculators. Though social relations were more fluid on the frontier, communities there were no more, if no less, egalitarian in temper than those in settled areas to the east. Perhaps one man in twelve on the frontier was a slave.

Everywhere in the mainland colonies, both appointive and elective public offices were securely in the hands of wealthier men. Rival factions among the élite appealed to the electorate, seeking to gain control of the very palpable fruits of office. Massachusetts was fairly quiet after 1741 under the fifteen-year rule of Governor Shirley, who used patronage cunningly to exalt a powerful oligarchy and to end half a century of factionalism. Pennsylvanian divisions were stabilised in the same period, as squabbling factions among the Quakers united to form, by 1736, a single well-disciplined party, staunchly supported by the Germans of the rural hinterland. Its main plank was opposition to Penn's heirs, the proprietors. Scotch-Irish frontiersmen worried about Indian attack adhered to the rival 'Proprietory Party'.

The authorities in London refused to recognise the parliamentary status which the assemblies insisted they had, but they would not pump in the money required to free governors from dependence on local complaisance. Most assemblies came to control the appointment of the agents who officially represented their colonies in London, and they regulated colonial courts of common law. So they were, in effect, little parliaments; yet their electoral basis was strikingly, and increasingly, different from that of Walpole's loot-fed assemblage of clients at Westminster.

A political leader in New Jersey told the peripatetic doctor Hamilton that the House of Assembly there was 'chiefly composed of mechanicks and ignorant wretches, obstinate to the last degree . . .' In Virginia, probably well over half, perhaps 85 per cent, of all adult white males had the vote at any one time. The Massachusetts qualification for electors – a 40s. freehold or £40 worth of property – could pretty easily be met by any farmer or artisan. In other colonies also, the vast majority of white men could expect to acquire enough during their lifetimes to meet the requirements for suffrage. With an Anglican clergyman, Alexander Hamilton visited a small log cabin up the Hudson River occupied by man, wife, and seven children. These were poor people by colonial standards, yet their 'very neat and clean' dwelling contained 'a looking glass with a painted frame, half a dozen pewter spoons and as many plates, old and wore out but bright and clean, and' – pregnant detail – 'a set of stone tea dishes, and a tea pot'.

A Rhode Island sea-captain, about this time, remarked that 'A man who has money here, no matter how he came by it, he is everything, and wanting that he's a mere nothing, let his conduct be ever so irreproachable.' The status which money conferred could be earned by hard work. The effective ethos of American society was 'bourgeois', middle class, meritocratic. Wealthy and poor men alike looked towards the middle. While the labourer could see his way open to middle-class prosperity, the rich man, as Richard Hofstadter observes, 'had to exercise his power in the knowledge that his way of doing so must not irritate a numerous, relatively aggressive and largely enfranchised middle class public.'

The towns spawned flourishing newspapers: Boston, which led the way, had its first in 1704, six by 1734. As other colonies followed the lead of New England and Virginia, half a dozen new colleges, all of which later became universities, sprang up along the seaboard between 1746 and the mid-1760s. America shared in the eighteenth-century 'Enlightenment'. Philadelphia became the local centre, and Benjamin Franklin, citizen of that place, one of the movement's leading prophets and ornaments.

Franklin epitomised the land of opportunity which America had become. Born in 1706, the tenth son of a Boston tallow-chandler and soap boiler, he migrated to Philadelphia. By 1730 he was sole proprietor of a press and newspaper. Shopkeeper, paper dealer and book importer as well, he throve together with his chosen city. His writings gave voice to the ethos of middle-class America, above all his *Poor Richard's Almanack* (1733–57), which sold 10,000 copies a year. 'Work hard and count your pennies.' 'Love your neighbour, but don't pull down your hedge.' Franklin expressed a secularised puritanism. As a young man, he made it his business to shun places of idle diversion and seem an 'industrious, thriving young man'. To *seem* such was good for one's credit. The gist of this brilliant, witty, nauseous moralist was: fornicate and cheat by all means, but don't be caught at it. However, his public spirit was perfectly genuine. In 1727 he and some friends – silversmiths, glaziers, printers, shoe-makers, ironmasters – formed a club, the 'Junto', dedicated to civic improvement: which came.

Five years later, thanks to the Junto, Philadelphia acquired the first subscription library in America. Before long the place had several more. Labourers read books. Almost everyone read books. The city had eight printing shops in 1740, twenty-three by the mid-1770s, churning out almanacks, sermons, pamphlets, textbooks and pirated English bestsellers. Over the same period, newspapers increased from two to seven, full of new ideas, of controversy on all subjects, of schemes for civil and philanthropic good works. The town acquired a police force, seventeen fire companies, a hospital, as well as dozens of clubs of all kinds and no fewer than three masonic lodges. Evening schools also flourished, offering practical instruction for working men and apprentices in such skills as book-keeping and surveying. Genteel perusal of ancient authors, as practised at English universities, had no obvious use to such people. The more practical, democratical Scottish view of higher education made better sense to middle-class America. When a college was set up at Philadelphia in the 1750s, its curriculum tended towards utility, and its provost came from Aberdeen University. In 1765, the city founded the first medical school in America, with a professor who had studied in Edinburgh.

Franklin's own interest in electricity was aroused by another Edinburgh-trained scientist. The pioneering experiments which he published in London in 1751 gave Franklin a European reputation as a 'natural philosopher'. He was, in the Philadelphia of his own day, far from alone in intellectual eminence. Benezet's writings on slavery greatly influenced British and European thinking; David Rittenhouse was a renowned astronomer; John Bartram, a versatile naturalist, was much admired by Linnaeus himself and helped Franklin to found, in 1744, the American Philosophical Society, a counterpart to the Royal Society of London.

Yet meanwhile the country estates around Philadelphia, without droves of black slaves in attendance, provided the closest replica anywhere in the colonies of the life-style of the English gentry. When a fox-hunting club was formed in 1766, Philadelphians brought in English red foxes – to no avail, since they swiftly interbred with the local variety. Bostonians who could afford it were equally servile to metropolitan 'standards'; one merchant sent his watch to be cleaned in England. Virginian planters modelled their habits and ideas on those of the area round London, which they considered their 'home', despising Bristol, Scotland, and other provincial parts of Britain. They, and their blacks, spoke extremely 'pure' English, with no trace of a regional accent.

But the Scotch-Irish and German presence was waxing yearly, and slave numbers were running into hundreds of thousands. The colonies were ceasing to be more or less wholly English in speech and in origin, and Franklin disliked this vociferously. At the mid-century he, like his fellow colonials, had no idea of a wholly novel 'American' identity. They had no bards to sing about such a fancy. They produced no distinctive creating writing. Before the 1760s, they found no spokesman to spell out grievances against Britain who was remotely comparable in passion and power to the great Irishman, Jonathan Swift. And Swift's better writings found few colonial readers. Colonists there had no causes for complaint which were as urgent as those of Ireland.

VIII

Ireland was an extremely unhappy country in the second and third decades of the eighteenth century. Others besides Ulstermen were hurt as the long leases of the 1690s fell in, as harvest failures were frequent, and as the short upsurge of agricultural prices aggravated all problems. William III had given vast estates to his favourites. George I and George II both gave pensions to their mistresses drawn from the Irish revenues. The London regime gave an Irish peerage, an Irish estate, an Irish pension, as usual rewards for political and military service.

Since most new, and many old, owners lived all or most of the year in England, capital drained from the poorer island. An estimate of 1729 showed, beside £300,000 a year paid out of Irish taxation to English holders of Irish office or pensions, a further £30,000 going to some fifty-four peers and eighty-three other wealthy absentee owners. Such payments were not taxed.

The effects on agricultural standards were deplorable. An Act of 1695 had eliminated the customary rights of tenants of confiscated lands. The sitting tenant could not expect preference when a farm was re-let; a Catholic would very often be turned out in favour of a Protestant. Hence there was no point in trying to farm well, or to improve the property. Meanwhile, the absentee, to save himself bother, commonly let large tracts of land on long leases to 'middlemen', sometimes themselves absentees, who in turn had recourse to under-agents and stewards. These in turn employed bailiffs, petty despots, to wring profit from helpless papist tenants living on very small parcels of land for which they paid the highest conceivable rents.

The local agents of distant landlords swelled a notorious class of quarrelsome squireens. Like any parasite class in an undeveloped country, they revelled in exceptional freedoms. Servants' wages cost next to nothing. Provisions were very cheap. There were fine local horses to hunt with and race. Swift's friend Lord Orrery, though Anglo-Irish himself, found even the famous hospitality horrible. 'Drunkenness is the touchstone by which they try every man, and he that cannot or will not drink, has a Mark set upon him.'

Great parts of the island looked, and were, ruined. There were many actual ruins – 'broken abbeys, roofless churches, battered castles, burnt houses, deserted villages . . .' The cabins of the poor were famous for their decrepitude. They were commonly made of sods and mud, thatched with bracken or furze or fern, chimneyless, full of choking smoke. Livestock still shared such quarters with man, wife and children.

The roads teemed with beggars, many of them blind. In the seventeenth century, the lives of the Irish poor had not been obviously harder than those of many in England. Now the growing contrast invited sensitive men to compare the condition of the poor Gaels with that of blacks in the West Indies. '. . . The poor people in Ireland,' Lord Chesterfield wrote of the 1740s, 'are used worse than negroes by their lords and masters, and their deputies of deputies of deputies.'

In some parts of the remote and mountainous west, where Gaelic Catholics of old lineage had hung on to some land, bonds between gentry and commons might be traditional, strong and affectionate. The landlord would talk English to visitors, but he could use Gaelic with his own people. The secret economy of the smugglers who naturally favoured the rugged Irish coasts brought wine and brandy from France, and friars and soldiers slipped in from the Continent with news of relatives serving in armies abroad. The exploits of the Irish Brigade were toasted. The work of the Gaelic poet still had its natural setting.

People from settler families, even Protestants, were not always aloof from Gaelic culture. 'English' children learnt Gaelic from their nurses. Gentry needed it to direct their workmen. Arthur Young in the 1770s would find English spoken without admixture of Gaelic only in Dublin and in some parts of Wexford.

Yet he would also emphasise the cruelty of social reforms. 'The landlord of an Irish estate, inhabited by Roman catholics is a sort of despot who yields obedience in whatever concerns the poor, to no law but that of his will.' He could use his cane or his whip on anyone answering back with as little fear of punishment as Sir Charles Price. '. . . A poor man would have his bones broke if he offered to lift his hand in his own defence . . . Landlords of consequence have assured me that many of their cottars would think themselves honoured by having their wives and daughters sent for to the bed of the master . . .'

And the cottier's life at subsistence level was also endured patiently, with the help of the tuber which God had given His island. By this time, the words 'Irish' and 'potato' already fitted together as naturally as 'Virginia' and 'tobacco', while the crop was still almost unknown in Scotland and hardly used in England except in the north. The potato adapted well to poor bog lands. It was easy to cook on the customary cauldron over the traditional peat fire; it could be stored through the hungry winter; it was not hard to cultivate with simple peasant tools. On one Irish acre (equalling 1.6 English) a man could grow enough for a family of six to subsist on.

Ireland was normally more than self-sufficient in oats, its main food cereal. The very poor relied on oatmeal from the spring onwards after the store of potatoes had run out. At this stage in Irish history, famine only came when harvests failed in other countries and grain could not be imported. But strike it did, long after England and even Scotland had ceased to know it. A disastrous harvest in 1728 brought famine to many parts of the island. In 1740–1, deaths may have reached 200,000 or even 400,000.

Such was the Ireland to which, as his native land, Jonathan Swift came reluctantly back in 1713, Dean of St Patrick's Cathedral, Dublin, to be confined there for life by the utter defeat of his English tory patrons. His never-equalled gifts as pamphleteer found scope as economic and other issues, from 1719 to 1725, brought a new phase of constitutional conflict between the Irish and British Parliaments.

The subservience of the Dublin Commons was usually not too difficult to secure. As at Westminster, patrons controlled representation. There was no Act ensuring regular elections, so one sufficed for George I's reign, and one parliament only sat through the 33-year reign of George II. The Irish Commons had no control over the Dublin executive, made and unmade no ministries, had no settled party divisions or coherent 'Country' opposition. Yet the British Parliament managed, for a few years, to unite this caucus of toadies and squires against it. A disputant in an Irish lawsuit appealed, with success, to the Irish House of Lords. His opponent appealed to the House of Lords at Westminster, which decided in his favour. The Irish Lords refused to execute the decision and insisted on their right to final jurisdiction in their own island. The British Parliament, in 1719, retorted with an Act declaring that it could bind the Irish with whatever laws and judgments it pleased. Though this was no more than an emphatic re-statement, the 'Declaratory Act' was enough to incense every Protestant in Ireland. Swift launched himself into Irish politics with an anonymous pamphlet proposing a boycott of English imports.

The ground was prepared for the struggle over 'Wood's halfpence'. Ireland was offered a favour denied to the American colonies, but in such a manner that England received no credit. The island was chronically short of coin of small values. In 1722 the King's mistress, the Duchess of Kendal, was granted a patent to issue copper coin to the total of over £100,000. She sold it to a Midlands ironmaster named William Wood. No one in Ireland had been consulted. As the coins arrived, many refused to accept them. The Dublin Parliament drew up angry protests. The newly appointed primate of the Church of Ireland, Boulter, marvelled that 'people of every religion, country and party here, are alike set against Wood's halfpence . . .'

Swift, inventing a low-born opponent for the plebeian Wood, launched the first of his 'Drapier's Letters', purportedly by a Dublin tradesman, in March 1724. He averred that the Irish were paying £90,000 of good gold and silver for coins so small and of such base metal that they were really worth no more than £9,000. He pictured Conolly, the immensely rich Speaker of the Irish Commons, sending 'Two Hundred and Forty Horses' to bring up his half-year's rental in halfpence. He called, 'Stand to it One and All, refuse this Filthy Trash.' Swift moved on, in his fourth 'Letter', to seditious animadversions on the constitutional ties between Ireland and Britain. A jury refused to find a true bill against his printer. Before long, the government had to capitulate. In September 1725 the Irish Parliament was told that Wood's patent had been ended. But the ironmaster ('Brazier', Swift had called him) privately had the last laugh; Wood was compensated with a pension of £24,000 issued to a fictitious Thomas Uvedale Esq., and drawn from the public funds of Ireland.

Though his birthday was hailed in Dublin with bells and bonfires, Swift despised even Protestant Ireland:

> Remove me from this land of slaves
> Where all are fools, and all are knaves
> Where every knave & fool is bought
> Yet kindly sells himself for nought.

But he spoke out for Protestant Irish grievances in a stream of further tracts. Why did the Navigation Acts prevent Ireland from exporting her produce and wares wherever she pleased? Why were men born in Ireland overlooked for office in Church and State in favour of Englishmen? Why were the Irish revenues decanted to bribe English politicians?

Swift was a favourite and spokesman of the poor weavers in Dublin amongst whose dwellings his own deanery was set. His compassion took the application of his writings beyond the narrow self-interest of the Ascendancy class. His 'Modest Proposal for Preventing the Children of poor People in *Ireland*, from being a Burden to their Parents, or Country, and for making them Beneficial to the Publick' forks with appalling ferocity at the rooting assumptions of Whiggery, Money, Property and Commerce. The Irish economy was so weak that 120,000 children born annually must become beggars or thieves. But why not breed babies for the table? – 'a young healthy Child, well nursed, is, at a Year old, a most delicious nourishing and wholesome Food . . . very *proper for Landlords*, who, as they have already devoured most of the Parents, seem to have the best Title to the children', while England, Swift suggested, would gladly eat up the whole Irish nation – without salt. Swift deftly parodied Petty's 'political arithmetic' and took the logic of the slave trade only a bare step further.

But the prophet was not fully understood in his own country, and Swift's moral victory over Wood's halfpence soon counted for little enough. A resentful Walpole made sure that less patronage went to natives of Ireland. For the time being, however, quiet returned. The Dublin Commons was 'managed' for the London government by a group of local politicians who received coveted posts and dealt out spoonfuls from the jampot of patronage. Henry Boyle, Speaker of the Commons for twenty-three years from 1733, was the most powerful of these 'undertakers'. The Irish Assembly had its conceit, flattered by the erection on College Green of an opulent new Parliament House, started in 1728.

Other imposing buildings came to grace the capital. They reflected an improvement in the general economy which made the grievances of the rich easy to bear and so deprived the poor of spokesmen. With its university, three good theatres, and fine musical life (Handel's *Messiah* had its première here) Dublin was lively enough for its resident upper and middle classes. It had 200,000 people by the end of the century. Britain, of course, was Ireland's main trading partner, and Dublin was the chief port in dealings with Britain.

By the 1730s, Irish exports were surging upwards, and linen led the rise. The chief centres, in Ulster, still relied on Dublin for their working capital, and that city handled most of their products. In 1698, Ireland had exported less than half a million yards of linen; by the 1790s the figure would be over forty million yards annually.

Irish beef gave Cork importance to the entire Atlantic economy. Exports boomed as the French expanded their sugar plantations in St Domingue, and in 1739 the call of the English woollen industry compelled the repeal of import duties on yarn from Ireland, so that for a while spinning supplemented the incomes of landless labourers in the south-west.

So the Irish economy was on the upswing from the 1730s. Dublin government action often aimed directly at stimulating it. The landed men in Parliament had a direct interest in the extension of cottage industries on their estates, and the Linen Board established in 1711 worked usefully to develop weaving. An Act of 1730 appointed four 'Commissioners of Navigation', and a canal from Newry to Lough Neagh was soon put under construction in the vain belief that supplies from deposits in County Tyrone could break the English monopoly in coal. The grand Canal between Dublin and the Shannon followed (1756–1804).

Inevitably, a Catholic middle class grew as fast as industry and trade. Able papists, barred from the professions and from government, and hard-pressed to operate as landowners, gravitated, like Jews and English Dissenters, into commerce. The wealth which was gradually amassed among them made the Penal Code seem more and more archaic and ridiculous, even to intelligent Protestants. There was toleration of papistry, up to a point. Under an Act of 1703, more than 1,000 secular priests had been registered and given legally recognised status, but bishops, along with regular clergy, were banished, so that in theory no new ordinations were possible. In practice, however, unregistered clergy managed to operate, and new recruits were smuggled in from abroad.

The established Church of Ireland was infiltrated, like other denominations, by coolness, tolerance, scepticism and politeness. The Penal Code relaxed as Philadelphia fervour waned. But there were still no papist churches. People worshipped in barns, in houses, and in the open air. Andrew Campbell, illegal Catholic Bishop of Kilmore from 1753, could only travel among his flock in the guise of a bagpiper and hold confirmations for children secretly at fairs. So the Penal Code, indirectly, and paradoxically, reinforced Catholicism in Ireland, creating a special, perhaps unique, closeness between the priests and the folk who protected them.

In 1732 there were, in spite of the laws, 51 friaries, 9 nunneries and at least 594 popish schools, according to an official report. These last were in no way weakened by the foundation, from 1733, of 'Charter Schools' by voluntary subscription, supported also by public funds, and aimed at rescuing children of the 'poor natives' from 'ignorance, superstition and idolatry' by instruction in the 'English tongue and manners, and the Protestant religion'. They spread widely, but their obvious propagandist intent alienated the people from them, and they dwindled on with the most ignominious of reputations. That Irish labourers could strike judicious observers as better educated than their English counterparts must be attributed to the 'hedge schools', meeting in huts or in barns or in ditches, where children of poor parents could acquire literacy, and even Latin.

L. M. Cullen has argued a case which makes the mid-eighteenth century seem, as Irish history goes, a prosperous interlude. 'Under the penal laws the rent of land let to a Catholic was to be not less than two-thirds of the annual value of the property leased. In fact, this was unenforceable. Otherwise the substantial investment by Catholics in livestock in grazing and dairying districts could not have taken place.' The restriction of leases to Catholics to thirty-one years mainly affected the well-to-do. While the old dispossessed proprietors saw any lease at all as a symbol of confiscation, to lesser countrymen it represented a measure of comfort and security. The worst excesses of the middleman classes were not general outside the bitterly poor south-west.

The famine in 1740–1 was not soon repeated. The Irish population rose from something like 2½ million in 1700 to 4 million in 1780. Though the Irish cultivator under George II was generally far worse off than his English counterpart, conditions were not absolutely so bad as they later became. Absenteeism actually diminished. Ireland, moreover, was uncannily peaceful. The 'rapparees', successors to the 'tories', found plenty of scope in the mountains and bogs of the west, but after the 'Houghers' who terrorised Connacht in 1711–13, destroying cattle and sheep in protest against the extension of pasture, there was no violent movement of agrarian defiance for half a century. All countrymen, Protestants as well as papists, large farmers as well as smallholders, grumbled against the tithes paid to the Church of Ireland clergymen. Otherwise, the people seemed lost for a grievance. Exports rose from £992,832 in 1730 to £1,862,834 in 1750. Over the whole century, they multiplied six times in value.

A modern visitor to Dublin sees in its fine buildings signs of an eighteenth-century heyday. Yet what, he asks himself, did this culture produce? Apart from Swift, the most famous native writers – Goldsmith, Burke, Sheridan – flourished not in Dublin but in London. Why was Dublin more provincial, in certain respects, than Philadelphia? Proximity to England is not the only answer. Catholic Ireland, in close touch with Europe, received not the brave new ideas of the Enlightenment but, from its clergy, the counter-arguments to them. Its horizons were narrowed by its cherished priests. Its Gaelic poetry took on during this century an increasingly more democratic character, escaping from a parasitism upon a dying aristocracy. But though some Protestant gentlemen went to the funeral of the famous blind Connacht poet Carolan in 1738, and others began to take a genteel proto-Romantic interest in Irish scenery and in native antiquities, the culture of the Ascendancy stood remote from that of the Catholic masses. Its favourite art-forms were architecture and oratory. Like the style of its grander country houses, rhetoric dressed with classical dignity its ignoble rootless provincialism. Trinity College, Dublin, with its fine new buildings, lagged intellectually far behind the University of Edinburgh for all the barebones scruffiness which the latter's premises shared with the rest of that surprising northern city.

IX

Adam Ferguson (1723–1816), one of Edinburgh's intellectual luminaries, would illustrate the differences in tone between Scottish and Irish culture by his deprecation of Europe's obsession with the 'grammar of dead languages' and with 'beauties of thought and elocution' now remote from the active and vivid life of the Greeks and Romans whence they had sprung. Never, anywhere, have remarkable collective experiences found better match in fresh and radical theory than in the Scotland of Ferguson's long lifetime. A Highlander, he stood on a cultural watershed, regretting the loss of the heroic virtues found among 'primitive' peoples like his own as commercialism surged forward, yet extolling the struggle and energy which now drove man on.

In Lowland and Scotland likewise, the casualties of historical advance had seemed to many immense and insufferable. The aristocracy largely favoured the Episcopalian Church which had gone down in defeat in 1689–90 and which was now deeply involved with Jacobite intrigues. Jacobitism, both hardline and sentimental, had become a focus of patriotic feeling; the cause of the Stuarts was rather perversely equated with Scotland's nationhood lost at the Union. 'Cameronians', ultra-Presbyterians, also regretted that event – Patrick Walker, for instance, who wrote in the 1720s of 'the Scots blood gone out of our veins, honesty out of our hearts, and zeal off our spirits; and the English abominations drunk in as sweet wine with pleasure . . .' But Walker's chapbook lives of his heroes, the Covenanting martyrs and prophets, joined the folk songs and old poems now collected and published by Allan Ramsay amongst the elements making for cultural continuity. Just before the Union, Fletcher of Saltoun had written that 'if a man were permitted to make all the ballads, he need not care who should make the laws of a nation.' Old ballads were still sung; new songs were written, and so traditional stories of feudal violence persisted alongside those of a persecuted Kirk to give Lowland Scottish culture a flavour still unique, as different strains in the country's historical heritage worked with amazing speed towards modernisation.

An intellectual dawning had begun among 'landed' and 'professional' classes in the late seventeenth century. In practice, in Scotland as in Virginia, the two classes were hard to distinguish. Lawyers were drawn overwhelmingly from the landowning class. Because Roman Law was at the basis of Scots Law, and this was to be studied on the Continent, not in England, many young men went for training to France and Holland, where they were exposed to the best Continental thinking. From the study of the law branched interests in moral philosophy and in political science; in 1719 the Faculty of Advocates sponsored the appointment of a lawyer as first Professor of Civil History in the University of Edinburgh. That institution and its Glasgow counterpart hummed with advanced European ideas, and by the 1720s their students were outraging staunch old-time Presbyterians by their freedom of thought.

Fresh thinking among men of high status met and meshed with growing demand from the townsmen and even the country people for education. As in Franklin's Philadelphia, such subjects as navigation, book-keeping, geography, modern languages, medicine, seemed roads to prosperity. The striving of Scottish surgeons in the employ of the Royal African Company and the East India Company anticipated the rise from the 1720s of the Edinburgh Medical School to international pre-eminence. In England the 'modern' curriculum, as distinct from the classics, was left to the Dissenters in their famous Academies, and to private initiative generally; the ancient Universities eschewed it. In Scotland, free enterprise raced with official action by universities and town councils. With medicine, science was welcomed into the highest planes of education. Teachers at all levels competed for pupils; the earnings of professors as well as dominies depended on the classes they could attract. Since Kirk sessions and town councils fixed on the lowest possible fees in the schools they provided, so as to give the able poor the greatest possible chance, and since inflation ate these away as the century progressed, masters were spurred to keep up their incomes by teaching, cheaply, the practical subjects demanded by traders, farmers and even landowners for their sons.

By the mid-century, almost everyone in the Lowlands seems to have been able to read and write. Very few other cultures could then match this achievement, though Calvinist New England was one competitor. Parents were glad to pay for their children's instruction and private 'adventure' schools supplemented those offered by the parishes. The Lowland peasant, it has been observed, 'was not merely able to read, but apparently loved reading'.

His zeal for self-improvement marched with the drive of Lowland landowners to catch up with England. To crave assimilation was an expression of patriotism. Economically, Scotland seemed plainly inferior. The most gifted Scots of the day shared the common inferiority complex. Robert Adam, the architect, who migrated to England, told his sister that he thought it a pity that 'such a genius' as himself 'should be thrown away upon Scotland where scarce will ever happen an opportunity of putting one noble thought in execution.' The great philosopher David Hume shared in the general, abject contempt of the middle and upper classes for their own Scottish accent, and he strove to eliminate Scottish turns of phrase from his writings. Such men ardently wished that the English would accept them as fellow 'Britons'. James Thomson, the major Scottish poet, another migrant to England, wrote 'Rule, Britannia!' But the many displays of English prejudice, ranging from cheap jokes to violence, often spun Scots away rebuffed. Hume, feeling slighted, sneered at 'Barbarians who inhabit the Banks of the Thames'. Scots, unable to consummate the Union as they wished, tried harder than ever to surpass the southrons.

The way in which Scotland was now governed gave them room to do so. N. T. Phillipson characterises its position as being, like that of the American colonies, one of 'semi independence'. Draft legislation about Scottish affairs was generally vetted by Scottish lawyers in Scotland. Though Walpole brought Scottish patronage firmly under the British Treasury, the few Englishmen given posts north of the Border were greatly outnumbered by Scots preferred to positions in England. There was a kind of implicit bargain (sweetened, as we have seen, by colonial and East India patronage) whereby Scottish MPs and peers propped up Walpole and his cronies with their votes, but the Scottish 'managers' controlled their own patch. Two factions of Scottish whigs contended over the spoils, the old 'Squadrone' versus the grouping, largely Campbell, which was led by the Duke of Argyll ('Red John of the Battles') and his brother Archibald, Lord Islay. The 'Shawfield Riots' in Glasgow against Walpole's Malt Tax made Scotland, in 1725, seem close to rebellion. In their wake, the 'Squadrone' Secretary of State for Scotland was deposed, and his post was not filled again. Walpole relied on the Campbell brothers. Islay would earn the nickname 'King of Scotland', though he exercised his strength discreetly. '. . . Slow, steady [and] revengeful', Horace Walpole would call him. 'He loved power too well to hazard it by ostentation, and money so little, that he neither spared it to gain friends or to serve them.' He worried over minute matters of patronage and managed elections by skilful horse trading; the Duke of Newcastle, who could appreciate such skills, saw Islay as 'the absolute Governor of one of His Majesty's Kingdoms'. He was too astute to create an exclusionist 'in' faction. A gifted outsider need not appeal to him in vain. In his dark and devious mode, he can even be styled a Scots patriot. His brother, an impulsive and generous man, certainly stood forth in that role to effect. As Campbell chief, he had the reflexes of an independent potentate, and over the famous 'Porteous Riots' he made himself spokesman for Scotland's honour.

The riot arose from Scotland's extreme addiction to smuggling. In 1736, after the execution of a smuggler, an Edinburgh 'mob' threatened Porteous, the captain of the City Guard, who ordered his men to fire. Several people were killed. Porteous was tried and condemned, but during six weeks' respite given to him, the well-disciplined 'mob' took over the city, forced the prison, and lynched him. Despite Argyll's protests in the House of Lords, Scotland's capital city was fined and its provost deposed.

Yet, as a rule, Lowland Scotland, after the Union, was the section of the empire which gave Westminster and Whitehall least trouble. The myth that the Scots are a naturally radical people is not borne out by the eighteenth-century record. The anti-paternalist strain which had emerged with the Cameronians expressed itself fanglessly in schisms within the Kirk, creating a sizeable body of 'dissenters'. But a quasi-feudal respect for lairds still prevailed, and helped them transform the country's agriculture.

Scottish lairds were distinguished sharply from English gentry by their relative poverty, made worse by the Darien disaster. Grand Tours were out of the question; even London or Bath outpaced their means. They stayed in their bleak homeland and made Edinburgh their social centre. The place was little more than a grotesque procession of huge tenement buildings down the spine of its Castle Hill, and in an age of filthy cities it was notorious for its slovenliness. But the taste for new ideas was becoming as strong as the passion for claret. Lowland landowners, conscious now of a novel unity, which was cemented by jealousy of the English, turned their minds to making Scotland prosperous.

England had no 'agricultural revolution'. The term is misapplied to a country where novel techniques came in gradually from the seventeenth century onwards. But it suits eighteenth-century Scotland. The rallying cry of the revolutionaries was 'improvement'. Their new methods were called 'English husbandry'. Notable early 'improvers' tended to be more idealistic than businesslike. They were patriots with a vision which more and more of their countrymen came to share and which embraced, as well as new crops and tools, manufacturing, schooling and the reform of manners. What they launched was, in effect, a movement for self-colonisation.

As in England, the old communal methods of cultivation must go. Capitalist farmers must emerge with consolidated holdings. So fewer tenants could hold land, yet remodelled farms would produce more food. To meet the twin problems of surplus produce and surplus people, the improving laird conceived the planned village. Scotland, outside the Lothians, lacked villages of the English type. Country people were scattered in hamlets. A movement began to create villages. It is reckoned that in the century after 1745 no fewer than 150 were made. Eventually most parts of Scotland would be affected. The Duke of Perth pioneered in the Highlands, laying out Callander and Crieff in the early 1730s. John Cockburn in the Lothians created, from 1738, a more accessible model at Ormiston. Within a couple of years, a contemporary was writing of the place with excitement, 'His toun is riseing exceedingly . . .' Besides blacksmiths and shoemakers, candlemakers and bakers and maltsters, Cockburn had forty linen looms with weavers to work them, ten spinners providing yarn for each weaver. So much work was offered that there was 'not a boy or a girel of 7 years old' but was busy – 'ye will not see ane in the toun except in ane hour of play.' This was the impression of industrious thriving which later improvers would strive to create. As at Ormiston, new geometrical nicety would rebuke the haphazard character of the old hamlet. The laird would provide attractive stone houses of two or three storeys, with front doors opening directly on to the pavement so as to check the habit of piling midden heaps before dwellings. He would seek to let houses or feus, not only to his own people displaced by enclosure, but also to respectable skilled men from outside. The village was to become a centre of education, to have a refining effect on the vicinity, introducing new habits of consumption, selling tea to rustic wives.

Cockburn was harbinger of changes which would rush to a head later in the century, preached and pushed forward by clergymen, hailed, if sometimes uneasily, by intellectuals. The titles of the master works of the 'Scottish Enlightenment' suggest the struggle of brilliant men to come to terms with the time's divisions as they experienced them in person: Francis Hutcheson's *System of Moral Philosophy* (published posthumously in 1755); Hume's *Treatise of Human Nature* (1739–40) and *History of Great Britain* (1754–63); Ferguson's *Essay on the History of Civil Society* (1767) and Adam Smith's *Wealth of Nations* (1776). 'These thinkers', Duncan Forbes writes, 'were primarily humanists and moralists, but as such they were deeply concerned with the nature of that commercial civilisation which had begun to change the face of Scotland so dramatically, for better and for worse.' Ferguson would regret that in the capitalist world 'man is sometimes found a detached and a solitary being: he has found an object which sets him in competition with his fellow creatures, and he deals with them as he does with his cattle and his soil, for the sake of the profits they bring.' Like that of other Scottish philosophers, his thinking emphasises warm counter-values - sympathy, heroism, love of mankind. It was from these scholars that the movement against slavery in the English-speaking countries would receive most of its intellectual energy – almost all the leading Scottish thinkers deplored it. Yet they sought to balance the claims of humanism with those of economic advance. Hume, before his friend Smith, argued for free trade against the mercantilists.

An equivalent to the Lowland Scottish self-colonisation of the eighteenth century may be found in the Japanese self-westernisation in the late nineteenth, which was still swifter and equally successful – but the Scots helped to pioneer the industrial revolution which the Japanese adapted wholesale. Meanwhile, Scottish thriving in most parts of the empire suggests a different comparison, with the Jews. The English had plenty of anti-Scottish jibes to match their anti-Semitic ones. In Jamaica, 'Scotch Attorney' or 'Scotchman hugging a Creole' became the local name for a species of vine which twined round the trunks of trees and destroyed them. A writer of 1740 reported that the slaves there correctly held that 'England must be a large Place, and Scotland a small one; for Scots Bacceroes (which they call all white Men) all know one another, but *English Bacceroes no known one another.*' As peasants and ministers collaborated with lairds at home, Scots merchants and professional men carried overseas a precious readiness to help each other out. St Andrew's Clubs sprouted in major American towns.

Until the 1760s there was little emigration to the New World by Scots people wishing to become farmers, though Scots judges shipped beggars, gypsies and the like to the colonies under indentures, and at least 639 Jacobite rebels, most of them Scots, were transported in 1716. Some pockets of Highland settlement were established; besides the Gaels at 'Darien' in Georgia, a none-too-scrupulous gentleman named Lachlan Campbell brought over some 500 Highlanders to New York colony in the late 1730s. Lowlanders, by contrast, generally went to the colonies as transients, planning to stay for as long as it took them to grow wealthy. There were clusters of Scots merchants in the cities, and, more famously, the Glasgow tobacco men who invaded the colonies on the Chesapeake.

In 1769, Scotland would actually take more imports from Virginia and Maryland than did England. By then it would be rare to find a storekeeper, agent or factor in Virginia who was not a Scot. Their incursion was gradual until the 1740s, rapid thereafter. Illegal traders from Scottish ports had been roaming the Chesapeake for a quarter of a century before the Union. Those who followed after 1707 found London merchants in control of the business of the Tidewater and pushed, with advancing settlement, into the back-country, where they established chains of stores depending on collecting and distributing points in the towns which grew up along the fall-line. Meanwhile, they ousted the English from much of the tidewater trade. Their lean and hungry enterprise made them hated and affluent and Glasgow a great and wealthy town. Scottish imports of tobacco, 2½ million lb. a year in 1715, rose to 10 million in 1743 – then, by 1771 to 47 million.

Scots had more than their fair share of colonial patronage. Most of the early missionaries of the Anglican Society for the Propagation of the Gospel seem to have been Scots – by a pleasant irony, the first bishop in English-speaking North America would eventually, in 1784, be consecrated by episcopalian clergy at Aberdeen. The three-quarters of a century after the Union saw some thirty governors and lieutenant governors of Scottish birth appointed in North

American colonies, while Jamaica had as many Scots governors as English.

But perhaps the main sphere of distinctive Scottish impact was intellectual and was epitomised by that Dr William Small, Professor of Mathematics and Philosophy in the College of William and Mary, who taught there, around 1760, a young Virginian named Thomas Jefferson. 'It was my great good fortune,' Jefferson wrote later, 'and what probably fixed the destinies of my life . . .' Scottish teachers and professional men put North America in touch with the Enlightenment of their own homeland. And Scotland was still the main centre of that Presbyterian creed which was becoming one of the most widespread religions of the mainland colonies.

Romans and Hardy Races

I

The 1730s and 1740s saw the ebullition, in North America and in Britain, of a movement which conditioned all future events in the Atlantic world. It was led by young men, some very young indeed. It gave the English-speaking countries most of their common hymns, learnt by generation after generation of children. It created modern Wales, bringing religious reformation at last to an inchoate and backward-looking country. Explosive and partly subversive in itself, it pre-empted revolution in Great Britain while it prepared bases for revolt in America. One direct result, over some fifty years, was the creation, in Methodism, of an important nonconformist denomination. But its first character was ecumenical. The movement swept across most of the divisions between Protestants, drawing in Anglicans and Dissenters with others who had known no serious creed. Calvinist and Arminian believers embraced for a while in the vivid dawnlight of evangelicalism.

Evangelical Christians laid drastic emphasis on the 'conversion' of the individual and on his personal faith in Christ. They had no taste for the intricate theological wrangles which had obsessed the seventeenth century. What they demanded was the experience of passion, despair and joy, gushing tears, a vital religion, to counter and oust the empty rituals of whiggish Anglicanism and the tepid restraint of old-fashioned dissent, by the revival of religious awe and the cultivation of 'enthusiasm'.

Prototype evangelicals can be detected in the early eighteenth century wherever zeal still ran high among clergy and laity; for instance, amongst the founders of the Society for the Propagation of the Gospel. The characteristic impetus of the movement was in fact missionary, the urge to reach out to the godless – English or Celtic, red, even black – left to their 'ignorance' and 'depravity' by Property and its hard-drinking, pluralist parsons. Before the end of the century, evangelicalism would be giving English-speaking Protestantism its first enduring successes among tropical pagans. But the flashpoint, the real beginning of the movement, came in the mid-1730s as news reached Britain from Massachusetts which inspired serious Anglican clergy and deeply impressed such Dissenting leaders as the hymn-writers Watts and Doddridge.

The state of religion in North America was complex. In 1740, taking all colonies together, 246 Anglican churches were greatly outnumbered by 'dissenting' places of worship – Congregationalist (423), Presbyterian (160), Quaker (approaching 100), and those of the fast rising sect of Baptists (96) whose anti-intellectualism went well with conditions on the frontier where learned preachers were rare, and whose stress on adult conversion (and immersion) suited places where children grew up with little or no religion. There were in addition something over 200 Dutch and German Protestant churches, apart from the European pietist sects. Catholic places of worship were few, something over a score, mostly in Maryland and Pennsylvania, and the groups of Jews in the seaport towns were as yet less prominent than in Jamaica. So America was overwhelmingly Protestant, and the greatest bulk of its religious people were found in Calvinist denominations. New England Congregationalism had, in Connecticut at least, come close to Presbyterianism in form and the two bodies tended to affiliate in self-defence in colonies further south where Anglicanism was established by law.

Even in New England, it seems, not more than one person in seven was now a church member, in the Middle Colonies this was one in fifteen, and further south participation was lower still. Virginia was plagued with drunken, incompetent parsons. Here was a natural arena for 'revival'. In the 1720s, a smouldering started in the middle colonies. A Scotch-Irish Presbyterian divine, William Tennent, began to train ministers and to demand from them the experience of 'conversion'. His son Gilbert, from 1729, established himself as a great revivalist preacher, a fiery man who scorned polish and gentility. He would soon split the Presbyterian Church with his attacks on 'unconverted' ministers whose dull sermons, he said, proved them worthless.

The Congregational Church in New England, though still established by law, had lost vitality. 'Arminianism' (that is, open-mindedness) had been infecting its intellectuals. The churches had ceased to make rigorous demands of their members. As in England itself, doctrine had superseded heart-felt belief. Once the force of complete conviction which had produced the doctrines had faltered and failed, revival could only take shape from deliberate excitement of emotion to the point of ecstatic delusion.

About 1734, strange things happened in several individual congregations, notably that of Jonathan Edwards at Northampton, Massachusetts. Edwards, the most formidable theologian of his day, was too much an intellectual to be a typical revivalist, but had special stature as a subtle apologist for enthusiasm. A spontaneous mania in his congregation, after a young woman 'of easy ways' had undergone a surprising 'conversion', fed a craze which swept up and down New England's western frontier. The 'Great Awakening' would smoulder and blaze for decades in North America. But after the first great surge of emotion, a bitter aftermath set in, marked by suicides among people desponding over the states of their souls. For a few years, revival abated in New England. Initiative shifted to Englishmen and Welshmen.

Two mighty Welsh preachers, both in their early twenties, were launched in 1735 with the separate conversions of Howel Harris and Daniel Rowland. These men combined forces a couple of years later. Meanwhile, Oxford had formed, and Georgia was transforming, the cardinal English evangelists: John

Wesley, his younger brother Charles, and George Whitefield.

The Wesleys' High Church, tory father, a zealous parson in that wild country, the Lincolnshire Fens, was greatly drawn to missionary work and was naturally an early and eager supporter of the scheme for Georgia colony. John, born in 1703, became a fellow of an Oxford college, and was drawn into the 'Holy Club' formed in 1729 by his brother Charles within that university. So was George Whitefield, son of a tavern-keeper, who supported his studies at Oxford by working as a serving-man. The club, which never had more than twenty-five members, emphasised personal discipline, charity and frugality. John Wesley drew up 'methodical' rules of behaviour, a 'scheme of self-examination' ('Have I prayed with fervour? . . . Have I daily used ejaculations? . . . Have I been zealous to do and active in doing good? . . .'). So the Club's denigrators described it as 'Methodist'. Membership did not imply 'conversion'. Whitefield experienced the joy of 'conversion' in 1735. For the Wesleys, release proved harder. The brothers sailed with Oglethorpe, founder of Georgia, when he returned to his colony late in 1735, eager to minister to debtors and Red Indians. Both were disillusioned. John was unable to start an Indian mission and his prim devotion to Anglican ritual was not much appreciated in Savannah. Charles became Oglethorpe's private secretary, quarrelled strongly with him and left after five months.

Yet Georgia gave the brothers experience and ideas which determined the subsequent character of 'Methodism'. Huge American parishes meant that clergy had to ride almost incessantly from one settlement to another. The idea of the Methodist 'circuit' stems from this. And the colony had attracted a band of Moravians, who influenced the Wesleys profoundly. Moravians stressed the value of hymn-singing; Charles went on to become the most effective hymn-poet in English. John seized on Moravian methods, 'select bands', the 'love feast', and practised them in Savannah, along with such innovations as lay assistants, extempore prayer, extempore preaching.

'Conversion' came in the aftermath of shame. 'I went to America,' John Wesley cried, 'to convert the Indians; but O! who shall convert me?' A Moravian, Peter Böhler, was on hand in London to console both young men. 'Preach faith till you have it,' he said; 'and then because you have it, you will preach faith.' The preacher, once he had tasted the power which came from moving others, could constantly renew his own 'faith' by new experience of the excitement of preaching, which in turn renewed and 'converted' his hearers. The problem was to get started. On May 21, 1738 Charles underwent a dramatic 'conversion'. Three days later, John, hearing something by Luther read aloud, 'felt', as he put it, grace for the first time. '. . . I felt I did trust in Christ, Christ alone for salvation; and an assurance was given me that He had taken away *my* sins, even *mine*, and saved *me* from the law of sin and death.' All sense of strain and effort left him. A slight, morose and neurotic young man became the cheerful, unresting leader on horseback who rode and preached his way to the centre of English history.

Whitefield, an even more prodigious traveller, came back to Britain for a short time and began to evangelise round about Bristol, addressing thousands in the open air. In March 1739, John Wesley went down to hear his old friend. Early next month, he began his own career as mass orator there, preaching to some 3,000 in a brickyard. Whitefield was a self-styled 'Calvinist', but admitted that he had not read Calvin, and in practice believed like Wesley that all who came might be saved. Their missions were equally offensive to most of the establishment. 'It is monstrous,' a Duchess complained, 'to be told that you have a heart so sinful as the common wretches that crawl upon the earth.' In the 1740s, the 'Methodists' were smeared with the bogey-word 'Jacobitism'. Magistrates, in some places, permitted riots against them. But where clergymen were slack, where, as in certain industrial areas, population growth had outmoded old parish boundaries, where the unwashed and unwanted were not catered for by the Church of England, Methodism gathered its converts together. Wesley created a mass movement, the first organisation of its kind. Between his conversion and his death in 1791 he preached no fewer than 52,400 times. He would leave behind him a body of 136,000 'people called Methodists' with some seven times as many 'adherents'.

Though by 1784 he was ordaining clergymen under his own authority and his movement had acquired clearly separate legal status, Wesley thought of himself as an Anglican till his last day. Anglican evangelicalism grew up in free and easy commerce with Methodism. The tours with which George Whitefield shocked North America into its 'Great Awakening' reached members of every denomination.

His voice was magnificently apt for his purpose. The great actor David Garrick remarked that Whitefield could make an audience weep or tremble merely by pronouncing the word 'Mesopotamia'. He said much about hell fire, he could be heard over vast distances, and almost at will, it seemed, he could send people into fits. In 1739–41 he ranged the entire North American seaboard, meeting and encouraging Tennent and Jonathan Edwards, setting other itinerant preachers in motion, spreading hysteria wherever he went, then leaving others to cope with its consequences. Whitefield even dampened the merriment of Charles Town, until, as he noted with pleasure, 'the jewellers and dancing masters' began 'to cry out' that their craft was in danger. Though he soon transferred his energies back to Britain, he returned to America several times to keep 'rebirth' booming, and eventually died there in 1770.

When he first visited Wales, early in 1739, Whitefield was only 24 and the local revivalists who met him, Harris and Rowland, were 25 and 26 respectively. By the time these men were old, the character of the Welsh people would be well set on the way to transformation. In the 1730s the country, still generally Welsh-speaking, was dominated by not very wealthy, mostly tory, gentry and was infested with Jacobitism. The Society for the Propagation of Christian

Knowledge had turned its attention to this near-heathen land, and in the first four decades of the eighteenth century founded almost 100 schools, where instruction was usually in English. One of its teachers was the Reverend Griffith Jones (1683–1761), a shepherd's son who had become a clergyman only with difficulty, and who ran into trouble with the hierarchy for preaching in parishes other than his own, and even in unconsecrated places, as he tried to take Christianity to a people with few parsons. In 1731 Jones launched his own educational campaign, sending out itinerant teachers who would stay for three months in any one place, long enough to teach local children to read. By the time of his death, over 150,000 people had passed through these 'Circulating Schools', besides unregistered adults who came at night; and the movement went on and even grew thereafter. The passion for learning rooted itself.

It was under Jones's ministry that Daniel Rowland experienced 'conversion'. Whitefield himself witnessed Rowland's effect in 1743: 'At seven of the morning have I seen perhaps ten thousand from different parts, in the midst of sermon, crying *Gogunniant – bendyitti* – ready to leap for joy.' While Rowland was an ordained minister, Howel Harris, a Breconshire schoolteacher, never regularised his position. This little man, who has been called 'the greatest Welshman of his age', exemplified the obsessional 'method' of the revivalists; as his diary shows, he would ask God 'about buying a pair of gloves' and even inquire 'His will if I should take tea'. No scholar, he felt that the substance of his preaching 'was all given unto me in an extraordinary manner, without the least premeditation.'

Harris joined with other Welsh evangelists in an association in 1742, but eight years later, after about 400 'Methodist' societies had been founded in South and Central Wales, Harris split away and repudiated the name 'Methodist', but his organisational gifts had helped to ensure that Calvinistic Methodism would become almost the national Church of Wales. Other forms of dissent flourished in the climate of fervour which revival created and canalised – Baptist and Independent churches were soon spreading even faster than Methodist ones. The gentry continued to favour Anglicanism, and their alienation from the Nonconformist masses grew clear and unbridgeable. Between 1716 and 1870, no Welsh-speaking Anglican bishop held any Welsh see, but evangelicalism boosted the Welsh language wherever that was still dominant, in particular by encouraging hymn-writing. The distinctiveness of Wales became more, not less, marked as a result of the revival.

The distinction of Lowland Scotland, by contrast, was that enthusiasm made little mark on its industrious and quiescent people. The Kirk was a very different case from the Church of England. Its organisation remained comprehensive. Its central role in Scottish life was accepted. For geographical reasons – clergy and elders from far away found it hard to attend – its annual Assembly, now Scotland's only national forum for debate, fell under the control of 'moderates' from Edinburgh and the Lothians, cool men, new 'whigs' as opposed to old 'Whiggamores'. The restoration of lay patronage after the Union rankled with many ministers and laymen, and a struggle over this issue, 1732–40, led to the secession of Ebenezer Erskine and three other ministers who founded their own denomination. The 'Seceders' invited Whitefield to Scotland, but finding that he would not swallow Presbyterianism, they denounced his 'wild enthusiasm'. Preaching in Established churches, he made his impact. There was one spectacular outburst, in 1742, in the Clydeside parish of Cambuslang, where the minister had been impressed by news of the New England revival. After several months of daily sermons, tears and conversions, Whitefield himself came in June and characteristically preached three times in one afternoon, finishing after 1 o'clock next morning. In August 30,000 people gathered for an open-air rally. However, excitement died away, and for half a century evangelical influences penetrated Scottish life by degrees, without much further dramatic incident.

Ireland was still less touched. Since the character of Catholicism was so different, it would be misleading to say that its priests conducted a non-stop religious revival. But religion was close to the people as nowhere else. Belief had never been lost or suspended or challenged by the queries of Reason and Enlightenment. 'Enthusiasm' could find few crannies to enter.

Evangelical theology, if it deserves that name, was optimistic and easy to understand. It could be preached like thunder and sung with fervour. It made outcasts feel true men. It devalued the scholarship which the well-to-do had paid to acquire. 'I bear the rich and love the poor . . .' Wesley said. He wrote a tract addressed to smugglers, he founded schools and devised many cheap textbooks, and when, in his respectable old age, at Whitehaven, all the local clergy and most of the gentry turned out to hear him, his comment in his journal was that 'they all behaved with as much decency as if they had been colliers.' In 1774, he published an attack on slavery.

Though Whitefield himself became a slave-owner, his 'Great Awakening' touched many black people. As he left Philadelphia in 1740, he found that 'near fifty negroes came to give me thanks for what God had done to their souls.' In a pamphlet of that year he declared that blacks were no less, but no more, 'conceived and born in Sin' than white men. Other evangelists also preached to mixed crowds. The Baptists in particular had an influx of black members. No one could be turned away or excluded; and anyone slighted and aggrieved by his treatment could set up as a preacher on his own account. Blacks began to preach. Women were known to preach.

The Great Awakening flowed across the borders between colonies and stirred many people into a consciousness of common concern. Yet it was also divisive. Many who disliked 'enthusiasm' drifted towards Anglicanism, which therefore increased its hold among the wealthier. Even New England colonies, like the others, emerged riddled with sects – 'New Lights' versus 'Old Lights', Baptists rampant. America was already precociously tolerant; now with more sects, more dissenters, the pressure to do away with remaining discriminations increased. Popular initiative in social and political life was heightened.

In Wales also the long-term effect would be to inflate the uppishness of the low and to bring snobs into contempt. Scotland remained comfortably under the control of its lairds and ministers. But why did Methodism not shake the English class structure more strongly?

Wesley himself despised gentlefolk, and he was as savage as Marx about the idiocy of farmers and agricultural labourers. Hence he mostly ignored the south-eastern counties, heartland of agriculture and squirearchy. This area was dismissed in Methodist circles as a 'wilderness'. Penetration here, although it came, came slowly. The chief centres of Wesley's own activity were London, with its sprawl of suburban poor, Bristol, and Newcastle. Hence his regular journeys took him from south-west to north-east and back, from the tin-miners of Cornwall, through the seamen and colliers of Bristol, among the industrial workers of Staffordshire, Lancashire and Yorkshire, and up to the classic Northumberland coalfield. These regions, where Methodism grew fastest, would within Wesley's own lifetime begin to receive the impact of novel industrial growth. Before and while the impact was felt, Methodism brought people a new sense of their own worth, and training in leadership and organisation, but also integration into a movement anxious to emphasise its non-subversive character. In the 1740s, Wesley's own toryism had been in opposition to insolent well-heeled whiggery. When he died, 'toryism' itself, mutated, had become the blazon of order and Property.

The revival in early days generated real frenzy. It is hard for us to imagine how exciting it must have been to encounter young Whitefield, or Wesley's piercing eye. The great revivalists sought to induce, in themselves as in others, not merely one experience of self-transcendence, but renewed, and again renewed exultation. Men must weep and cry out in terror and penitence and joy again and again. Tears flowed not only at great open-air gatherings, but indoors, over the sacraments – one was saved, one was saved – the tears proved it.

Such displays were not genteel. They were 'primitive'. They were atavistic. They were meant to be so. Wesley extolled the 'primitive Christianity' of the earliest centuries of the Church. Excited readers were discovering Homer. Winckelmann was about to deify ancient Greek sculpture. Macpherson would soon unveil the spurious beauties of his *Ossian* poems purporting to come from ancient Gaelic tradition. Mountainous scenery, hitherto sensibly shunned as barren and dangerous, was beginning to draw cultivated men with its inexplicable appeal. The cult of the 'sublime' was emerging; it was good to be frightened.

Many factors beside the decline in Christian faith and the call for revival, or for substitutes, must explain the shift in the consciousness of educated Europeans and colonists, about the middle of the eighteenth century. The artificiality of life amid the teacups in towns which grew bigger and bigger, or in country houses with more and more amenities and the growing knowledge of regions outside Europe where men might look uncouth, but still seemed heroic, prodded thinkers to seek out the unspoilt, to masturbate their passions, to cherish tears. So must, in England, the sordid nature of politics dominated by 'interest' and by the quest for safety, by Walpole. In the age of Wesley, many men craved war. They yearned for heroes, Plutarchian, Roman, noble. So they invented the radiance of William Pitt.

II

More powerful, palpable interests demanded war. When it came it would be brazenly, nakedly fought for the sake of trade. British commerce seemed not to be growing fast enough while in thirty years after 1710 French trade between colonies and metropolis rose from 25 million livres to 140 million livres a year. Merchants clamoured for war and forged links with the opposition of 'outs' who sincerely or cynically called themselves 'Patriots'.

The opposition craved war because it seemed that so long as Britain was prosperous and at peace, no crisis could arise drastic enough to unseat Walpole. There seemed to be ample pretext. The hostility of the Florida Spaniards to the new Georgia colony was now added to the longstanding uncertainty of the valuable British logwood trade. The Treaty of Utrecht had not pacified British greed. The British wanted from Spain a freedom of trade which they would not accord foreigners in their own colonies.

Under the Treaty, the South Sea Company had been given the right to send one ship a year of 500 tons (later 650) to Porto Bello, laden with British merchandise. Its goods would be exempt from duties, but the King of Spain would have a quarter share in each vessel and would take 5 per cent of the profits on the rest. The first ship sailed only in 1717, and a mere eight voyages were undertaken altogether. But whenever a South Sea Company vessel was in port, it served as a depot for contraband trade. Carrying neither provisions nor water, it was necessarily accompanied by sloops from Jamaica. These secretly carried merchandise. But the Company, operating its own racket, faced competition from British freelances who picked their own time and place for selling all year round and could offer lower prices to the Spanish colonists. The Spaniards acted against smugglers. The freelances made their own reprisals. These would be punished in turn by confiscation of Company property.

The Spanish authorities claimed the right to stop and search ships anywhere in American waters, and coastguard vessels (*guarda-costas*) were fitted out and manned by shady persons who got their pay from the sale of the prizes they brought in. A ship might be seized and condemned merely because it was carrying logwood or seemed headed towards an unlawful destination. Probably some of the British traders who suffered were actually innocent. Seizures were not very numerous, thirty-eight over seven years. But the *guarda-costas* were commonly violent. In 1738, the opposition rejoiced, and the public shrieked, over the tale of Captain Jenkins's ear.

William Beckford MP, West India merchant and wealthy absentee planter, proudly produced before the House of Commons one Robert Jenkins, who claimed that seven years before a coastguard, ransacking his ship, had cut off his ear with a cutlass. He happened to have it with him, pickled. He was wearing a wig, which he was not asked to remove. Beckford himself later cast doubt on the story. But this ear was what the warmongers needed. Other atrocities were announced, or invented. But Walpole coolly negotiated a new Convention with Spain, signed early in 1739. Spain agreed to pay £95,000 as the estimated excess of Spanish over British depredations.

Enter the hero. William Pitt, aged 30, made his reputation as the greatest orator of his time by denouncing the Convention of Pardo in the House of Commons: '. . . Is this any longer a nation, or what is an English parliament, if with more ships in your harbours than in all the navies of Europe, with above two millions of people in your American colonies, you will bear to hear of the expediency of receiving from Spain an insecure, unsatisfactory, dishonourable convention?' This performance marked the first emergence of blatant imperial boasting as a factor in British public affairs. The empire had been seen as a useful business proposition. Pitt, though a spokesman for merchants, would give it the glamour of heroic myth.

In 1702, Thomas Pitt, governor of Madras, had bought a huge diamond from an Indian merchant for £24,000. He hoped to dispose of it for ten times as much. It was still unsold when he was dismissed from the East India Company's service in 1710 and came home, and its fate obsessed him until, seven years later, the Regent of France took it for a mere £125,000 or so. The nabob's rough temper bore hard on his own children – 'What hellish place is it that influences you all?' – as well as upon their estranged mother. His son Robert reacted by turning tory. William, Robert's second son, was a favourite with his brutal grandfather. He did not in later life display much liking for East India men; his vision of empire centred in the New World, and William Beckford became a close ally. Nevertheless he could not escape his heredity. Gout struck him down in his late thirties. In the eighteenth century gout was a hold-all name for diseases, and while Pitt undoubtedly had gout proper, his contemporaries attributed other illnesses, and his long phases of deep depression, to 'gout in the stomach', 'gout in the bowels' and 'gout in the head'. He shared in the strain of neurotic disorder, even madness, which appeared elsewhere among old Thomas Pitt's descendants. It helped to account for the spell cast by his oratory.

In private life he was charming, a dazzling talker. His tastes reflected the current shift in sensibility. He pressed a young nephew to read the epic poets of antiquity, Homer and Virgil: '. . . They contain the finest lessons for your age to imbibe; lessons of honor, courage, disinterestedness, love of truth . . .' One of his friends was 'Capability' Brown, the celebrated landscape gardener. Pitt's own talents in this field were recognised by his friends. Nothing pleased him better than to be building bosky bowers and Temples of Pan, to design a walk or judiciously place a rotunda. But his public manner was stiff and formal, a mask. The stilted language of his speeches was won by hard labour. Upright and graceful in posture, he transfixed the Commons with an eye 'that would cut a diamond'.

'Had he lived four centuries earlier,' one biographer writes, 'miracles would have taken place at his tomb.' Oratory was in his day a source of real power. MPs had been saturated during their education in the orators of antiquity. They adored a dramatic style allied to language controlled in the interests of aesthetics rather than reason. They did not mind Pitt's artificial manner, and forgave his dishonesty and opportunism as they drank in his 'ornamental eloquence'. It may be compared to what Whitefield did for the vulgar. It helped vinous, self-interested MPs to believe that they sat in an imperial 'senate' as dignified as they thought that of Rome to have been. As Horace Walpole wrote he spoke 'to the passions' rather than 'to the question'. Since most MPs were uncommitted and their votes could be swayed, such performances could help a man to office, if that was the only way to keep him quiet; and word of them reaching outsiders all over Britain could focus public opinion, of which governments had to take account. He symbolised for parts of the public at large their own growing appetite for world power, their wish to emulate and surpass the feats of ancient Rome. He was on excellent terms with a group of poets, attached to the opposition, who were now striking up imperial themes.

One must be careful not to equate too closely the 'patriotism' of Jenkins's Ear days with the 'jingoism' of the 1880s. However, crude prejudice against other people was easily fanned. In 1753 there would be a nasty outburst of anti-Semitism when the government carried a Bill providing for the naturalisation of foreign-born Jews after three years' residence. (British-born Jews were citizens already.) Six months of agitation forced the ministry to repeal their own Bill. The more positive aspects of English patriotism were seen in the vast increase among ordinary people of interest in their own country's past. Shakespeare's history plays were greeted with fresh delight – Garrick made his name in 1741 with a performance as Richard III. Propagandists for war against Spain invoked Oliver Cromwell. Samuel Johnson, still a struggling young writer, turned out short lives of Drake and of Admiral Blake.

Proto-imperialism, like jingoism later, was probably dependent on the existence of literary hacks. With popular publishing and journalism flourishing in a new and regular way, a class of mercenary writers arose, the denizens of London's Grub Street and like squalid suburban purlieus. Under constant danger of pillory, gaol or fine for obscene and seditious libel, this class was likely to revel in bombast and war-whoops against safely distant foreigners.

But respectable writers of large talent had long been turning to imperial themes. While the Muse expressed her disgust at the base days of Walpole in satire, her inveterate bent to ennoble and to praise sought outlet in celebration of commerce. The wool trade and even the sugar plantation were sung through extensive poems. But commerce as an end in itself could not satisfy. James Thomson, in 1749, produced an early intimation of nationalism proper, a new religion, suggesting that the whole community of the 'ever-sacred country'

> ... consists
> Not of coeval citizens alone:
> It knows no bounds; it has a retrospect
> To ages past; it looks on those to come.

The 1740s saw a climax of patriotic self-praise. Arne produced his definitive setting of 'Rule, Britannia!' in 1740, and 'God Save the King' was first printed four years later.

War had finally come in October 1739. Huge crowds cheered the proclamation in London. Enthusiasm ran just as high in Bristol and Glasgow, Liverpool and Edinburgh. One of the noisiest voices baying for war in the Commons had been that of Admiral Edward Vernon. Now he had his chance. By November 20, he was off to Porto Bello with six ships. It was not hard to bring the neglected fort to capitulate. Vernon seized all the vessels in the harbour, blew the fort up, and threw the town's trade open. Both Houses of Parliament voted their thanks. London gave Vernon the freedom of the City. Countless crude medals were manufactured, all showing Vernon's head with the legend, 'He took Porto Bello with six ships.' That head became a favourite decoration for inn signs, and districts in many different parts of England and Scotland were dubbed 'Porto Bello', while far off in Virginia Peter Jefferson, whose son Thomas was not yet born, applied that name to a small tract which he had purchased.

A combined operation was planned against Cartagena. Hacks wrote premature ballads extolling its capture. But the town did not fall. Yellow fever scourged the forces. Vernon quarrelled with the army commander. Another attack launched at Cuba failed, and then an attempt to seize (shades of the Scots) the isthmus of Darien also proved abortive. By the end of these failures, nine-tenths of the force had been laid low by disease.

Meanwhile, undeclared war with France had begun. Then a jangling of dynasties in Europe produced the 'War of the Austrian Succession'. France attacked Austria. Britain supported her. But Walpole was hardly the man to run a war which he had entered so reluctantly. He had recently stripped the Duke of Argyll of his posts. In the election of 1741, Argyll sided with the 'Squadrone', and Walpole lost seats in Scotland, while Cornish borough-mongers swung away from him. He soon found that he could no longer control the Commons securely, and went at last in January 1742. The new ministry drew some of the 'outs', including Argyll, into coalition with a Walpolian core centring on the two Pelhams, Newcastle and his brother Henry. By the end of 1744, Argyll was dead and Henry Pelham had achieved primacy. The war had been going badly, both in Europe and in the New World. Pitt, still 'out', insisted that Britain should not waste money on allies in Europe, but should attack France and Spain on the high seas. When the Commons were asked to sanction the taking of 16,000 of George II's own Hanoverian troops into British pay, Pitt declaimed that 'this great, this powerful, this formidable kingdom, is considered only as a province to a despicable Electorate.' The last phrase, to define Hanover, was a neat one, but George II would be very slow to forgive him.

Meanwhile, those American colonists whose virtues Pitt proclaimed so loudly were given a chance to show their own relish for empire. In 1740 troops from Georgia and South Carolina besieged St Augustine in Florida, which would not fall. Two years later the Spaniards riposted with an attack of their own, but Oglethorpe, with luck on his side, ambushed a large part of their force at 'Bloody Marsh' and catastrophe was averted.

When formal war with France began in 1744, a *petite guerre*, raiding and counter-raiding, broke out again in the northern borderlands. Governor Shirley devised, and the General Court of Massachusetts accepted, a scheme for the capture of the French fort at Louisbourg which threatened all British interests in the region. William Pepperell, a merchant, sailed as leader of 4,000 colonists. The famous fort proved far less formidable than legend had made it. After six weeks' siege, in June 1745, it surrendered. The good news reached England as that country faced its most obvious peril since the Armada. Prince Charles Edward Stuart, son of the Jacobite Pretender, landed in the Hebrides.

III

'The Young Pretender', at 25, was not in fact much younger than his father had been during his sojourn in Scotland in 1715, but his ardent high spirits were in extreme contrast with James III's moroseness. Charles was martial, fond of outdoor sports, not much interested in religion, and able to win men's hearts with his charming familiarity of manner. His father was an Englishman brought up in France, his mother was a Polish princess, but 'Charlie's' own name always evokes Scotland.

'O Charles son of James, son of James, son of Charles, With you I'd go gladly when the call comes for marching', a Gaelic poet, Alexander Macdonald, now wrote, and he, or one of his fellow-clansmen, describing how this 'tall youth of a most agreeable aspect in a plain black coat with a plain shirt not very clean . . .' landed on the Scottish mainland, would add, 'at his first appearance I found my heart swell to my very throat.'

English Jacobitism was virtually dead. Wesley was now taking a different creed to the very regions where it had been strongest. Sir Watkin Williams Wynn MP, greatest landowner in North Wales, had helped revive a Jacobite club. This 'Cycle of the White Rose' and its South Wales counterpart, the 'Sea Serjeants', bringing together local magnates, had great political influence. But Sir Watkin was down to his last £200 in ready money. Few Welsh Jacobites made any move. Of the 'Seven Men of Moidart' who landed with Charles Edward, four were Irish. Yet Ireland, as in 1715, was quiet, under the rule of its cleverest eighteenth-century viceroy, Lord Chesterfield, who gave official permission for the opening of Catholic churches and encouraged the landed classes to wear clothes made of Irish materials at official receptions. Gaelic Scotland was the last support of the Stuarts.

Though there had been no pitched battle between clan armies since the 1680s, the chief was still looked to as a commander in war. Cattle stealing was still endemic, and while chiefs now stood aloof from rustling themselves, many protected raiders. The whole clan was still conceived as an armed force; its officers were the 'tacksmen', close relatives of the chief who lived on the difference between the rents they collected from his followers and those they paid over to him. A good chief represented his people before the civil authorities, taking their cases through the higher courts. He succoured the old and looked after surviving dependants of those who had served him. He chartered grain for his clan when the harvest failed.

In return for his dutifulness, he exercised simple pomp. On a formal visit to an equal, he took with him a 'tail' – his Henchman (a foster brother), his poet, his spokesman, the gillie who carried his sword, another whose job was to carry his own person over fords, another to lead his horse in difficult paths, his baggage man, his piper, the piper's own gillie, besides other hangers-on, and gentlemen-kinsmen to keep him company.

Lowlanders rarely entered the region; an Englishman, Edward Burt, said that if one had to do so he made his will 'as though he were entring upon a long and dangerous Sea Voyage.' Sheep could be seen grazing on top of squalid turfed houses. Women at work on the harvest, girls fulling cloth with their feet, men launching a boat, were incited to effort by the strains of the bagpipe. Wooden ploughs and spades broke such ground as was cultivated, but the way of life was still pastoral. The clansman kept goats and sheep mainly to feed his household, black cattle to pay the rent. Cattle were still driven up to summer shielings. In spring, as stores of food failed, people still bled their beasts and boiled the blood into cakes. The commoner frequently had nothing but his plaid, and used it also as bedding at night, so that it reeked one Englishman's nose most offensively. 'A small Part of the Plaid . . . is set in Folds and girt round the Waste to make of it a short Petticoat that reaches half Way down the Thigh, and the rest is brought over the Shoulders, and then fastened before . . .' This belted plaid or 'kilt' was generally worn 'so very short, that in a windy Day, going up a Hill, or stooping, the Indecency of it is plainly discovered.'

Inverness, the one sizeable place, was a frontier town. The people there, it was remarked, would not call themselves Highlanders 'not so much on account of

their low Situation, as because they speak *English*.' Yet 'within less than a Mile
of the Town', few people spoke 'any English at all'. Trade, as carried on at the
town's four or five fairs every year, was unimpressive. A small roll of linen cloth
or a piece of coarse plaiding was relatively big business, and most Highlanders
brought in no more than two or three small cheeses, a bit of butter, a few
goatskins. Archaic self-sufficiency still seemed dominant.

Yet Highland society was fast changing. The Gaelic script had gone out of
use. The bardic caste had been eclipsed as new forms of verse were used by
gentlemen, even by working people. Education was eroding the traditional clan
solidarities. From Civil War days, the Presbyterian synod of Argyll had striven
to supply Gaelic-speaking ministers, and had given the Western Highlanders
books of devotion in their own language (though the New Testament was not
translated till 1767, nor the whole Bible till the nineteenth century). It had
established numerous schools, and from 1709 onwards the Scottish Society for
the Propagation of Christian Knowledge, set up in imitation of the London
body, had complemented the work going forward in Wales, founding 176
schools in fifty years. All these taught English, and forbade the use of Gaelic.
Meanwhile, the Highlanders had bred a native professional class of clergy and
dominies, and kinsmen of chiefs were practising law in Edinburgh. Thus many
chiefs were uneasy in their position. It was irksome for a man of education, with
aspirations to live like an English gentleman, to find that the reverence of his
followers, while deep, was also conditional. He had to pretend a warm
familiarity with clansmen all of whom claimed to be blood relations.

Glasgow now had a serious trade with the Western Highlands. Even before
the end of the seventeenth century, clansmen had followed the herring south
down the coastline in summer, docking at last at Greenock on the Clyde, where
they acquired in exchange wares from Glasgow. There had long been a regular
traffic in cattle from the islands. Macleod of Dunvegan, on Skye, was sending,
by the early eighteenth century, large droves to market and this trade provided
his tacksmen's main income. The beasts crossed the narrow sea to Kyle of
Lochalsh at low water; a boat with four oars would pull five swimming cows
joined jaw to tail with withes, on their way to the Perthshire town of Crieff
where the great stream of livestock stemming from the isles converged with
another moving down from Caithness in the far north. The yearly fair at Crieff
had started in 1672; fifty years later it was said that 30,000 beasts sold there in a
single autumn, bringing in 30,000 guineas. Some of the Gaelic drovers then took
cattle on to Norfolk, where they would fatten for the London market.

The chief's taste for fine wine and excellent linen depended for satisfaction on
the cattle trade. Traditional rustling was a brake on it. Military attitudes faltered
before commercial ones. Some chiefs came to prefer cash to men. Norman
Macleod, 22nd chief of his name at Dunvegan, would run up vast debts with his
gambling, his tastes for books and mangoes, his mansion near Edinburgh. As
early as the 1720s, he was dabbling in 'improvement', introducing clover to

Skye, growing exotica such as cauliflowers and cherries in his garden, trying to work a lead mine, and adventuring money in a fishery company. In 1739, it emerged that one of his tacksmen had abducted more than a hundred men, women and children from Skye and Harris, some of them plucked from their beds at night, so that they could be sold as servants in America; when the ship was refitted in Ulster, they escaped and told the tale. Macleod of Dunvegan and his neighbour Macdonald of Sleat were implicated in this operation.

Chiefs who sold their clansmen to keep their cellars full violated the old ethos more crudely, but no more decisively, than the great house of Argyll. By the early eighteenth century, this had at least 500 square miles of rent-paying land. The Duke was, on top of this, overlord, or feudal superior, of most of the chiefs and landowners in Argyll itself and in parts of Inverness-shire, whose estates covered about 3,000 square miles. He was the law in the Western Highlands. As hereditary sheriff of Argyll, he administered justice. As hereditary lord-lieutenant, he had legal control of armed forces. From his clan and vassals, he could muster an army of well over 5,000. His territories were an enclave of relative civility and of 'improvement'. The second Duke, Red John, constructed new towns, new villages, new piers and new canals, and established new industries. Though his clansmen still revered him as 'son of Great Colin', he lived in London during most of the year, and needed all he could get from his lands to support a life-style as lavish as that of other whig magnates. Tradition snapped. First in Kintyre about 1710, then in his other estates in 1737, Red John offered tacks – leases – of farms in open auction to the highest bidder; Campbell or non-Campbell, Gael or Lowlander, he would now take as tenant whoever offered most money.

The dominance of Argyll gave the London government what hold it had in the Highlands, yet it was also a source of weakness and danger. Bitter resentments confronted Campbell success. MacLeans, Macdonalds, Camerons, Stewarts nursed their grudges. Argyll was a whig, so these clans were Jacobites, regardless of what Stuart kings themselves had done or attempted to do to the Gaels. Nor could the government buy their leaders over. The pot of patronage was not full enough to feed faceless little men so far from London.

As soon as possible after the 1715 rebellion, the government had disbanded Highland Companies raised officially by clan chiefs and had neglected the region. Various clans still levied blackmail in adjacent Lowland areas. General Wade was sent to investigate the position and then allowed to implement his own report. He began to build military roads, though 250 miles of these by 1740 still barely touched the problem of Highland communications. Six new Highland Companies were created. But by the 1730s, the State's presence in the Highlands was weakening again. Argyll's innovations on his estates made danger greater, as Campbells who lost tacks wavered in their loyalty. By 1740, cattle raiders were attacking Inveraray itself, presumably with the connivance of local Campbells.

The French of course took an interest. The Jacobite intriguer Murray of Broughton arranged for massive support in the Highlands if Charles Edward would cross with 10,000 French troops and adequate arms and money. But when Charles, in February 1744, joined two regiments of cavalry and twenty battalions of foot assembled at Gravelines under Marshall Saxe, the aim was to land in Essex. It was only after yet another Protestant gale had shattered the expedition in harbour, and the French government had lost interest, that the Young Pretender struck out for the Highlands. The ship carrying his soldiers was disabled by a British man-of-war and returned to France. Hence Charles's arrival with so few companions, and hence the news which greeted him that Macleod of Dunvegan and his neighbour Macdonald of Sleat would not give the support which they had promised.

But others were less cautious. Anti-Campbell clans rallied. Sir John Cope, the government's commander in Scotland, went north, dithered, and then let the rebels pass him. At Perth, Charles was joined by the brilliant Lord George Murray, who became joint commander of an army now 2,400 men strong. The dragoons left to guard the Lowlands retreated before them. Charles took Edinburgh without bloodshed. There was no overt opposition when James III was proclaimed from the Market Cross.

Cope took up a strong position near the coastal village of Prestonpans to the east of Edinburgh. His 2,200 men nearly matched Charles's force in numbers and far surpassed it in equipment; some of the Jacobite troops had only scythes mounted on poles. But Charles's Highlanders surprised Cope's force, on the morning of September 21, with a charge on their classic model; men stripped off their plaids, fired their muskets, and raced in headlong, sword in one hand, round shield in the other. It was all over in about ten minutes. While the Jacobites lost some thirty-odd men, Cope fled with only four or five hundred.

Charles was master of Scotland by default. The coalition government of 1742 had revived the office of Secretary of State for Scotland and had given it to a veteran of the Squadrone faction, the Marquis of Tweeddale. His appointment vexed the Campbell faction. Lord Islay, who had inherited the Dukedom of Argyll from Red John in 1743, had acted shrewdly on his own patch, amending his brother's policies over tenancy, but he was not going to help Tweeddale, and the latter in turn had shrunk from precautionary reorganisation in the Highlands for fear of giving power to political enemies. So Charles had been able to march south without serious opposition.

For five weeks, wearing always a Highland plaid waistcoat, he held court at Holyrood Palace. His army grew. But very few Lowlanders joined, and no Presbyterians. His force, it is reckoned, numbered three Catholics to every seven episcopalians. It came mainly from the central and west Highlands and from the episcopalian Lowlands of the north-east, where Jacobite lairds had called in bands of clansmen to bully reluctant tenants into arms. Less than half the Scottish Gaels supported Charles, and the ex-Covenanting south-west was emphatically against him. But if this was not the 'Scotch rebellion' which distant English imagined, neither was it a Scottish civil war. The propertied classes largely sat on the fence. If Charles had wanted no more, he could perhaps have made his father king of an independent Scotland. But that was not his conception at all.

In November, against the judgment of most of his advisers, he marched 5,000 men into England, where three Hanoverian armies awaited him. He reached Lancashire without resistance, but he was drawing no English recruits of note. When Manchester was captured, the pro-Stuart townspeople, who welcomed him, provided only a few score soldiers. But a brilliant feint by Murray outwitted the Duke of Cumberland, George II's second son, who was commanding an army twice as large as the Jacobites'. By early December, Charles's troops were at Derby, only 127 miles from London.

There was a run on the Bank of England. The capital was in some fear. Charles was for pressing on. But Murray saw that any further advance would be opposed by overwhelming force as the three Hanoverian armies united. Though Charles raged at his Council, it overbore him. Retreat began on December 6. General Oglethorpe failed to cut off the Scots as ordered, and people remembered his Jacobite family background; he was court-martialled, and though he was acquitted, the founder of Georgia never saw active service again. Charles got safely across the Border, leaving most of his guns behind.

The Campbells at last had been raised in arms. Eighteen new Highland Companies had been formed, and wavering chiefs had been won over by the offer of commissions. Edinburgh had been reoccupied by the Hanoverians. Another great Highland charge brought Charles victory at Falkirk in January, but then his clansmen, as always, began to flock home with their booty.

Murray favoured a Highland guerrilla campaign. But when Cumberland marched to meet the Pretender in April with troops thoroughly trained in new tactics to quell the terrible Gaelic charge, Charles chose confrontation in pitched battle. He still had approaching 5,000 men, but very little artillery. Cumberland, with 9,000, including many pro-Hanoverian Gaels, reached him on April 16 at Culloden, near Inverness, on Drummossie Moor. He had plenty of guns. For an hour, Charles's Highlanders stood and fell under Cumberland's cannonade. A ragged charge, bloody fighting, were followed by a general rout. No quarter was given, on Cumberland's orders. Dragoons hacked down rebels and bystanders alike on the road to Inverness. With a price of £30,000 on his head, Charles began those wanderings through the Highlands and Isles which fused him with that region in myth forever. He got away on September 19, with 130 other fugitives. France had lost interest in him. The Jacobite cause petered out in a few shadowy plots. When James III died in 1766, even the Pope would not recognise his heir, who lingered in Italy as a pitiful drunkard practising in seclusion upon the bagpipes, till his misery ended in 1788.

Seventy-seven Jacobite rebels were formally executed, 610 were transported to the New World. Meanwhile, 'Butcher' Cumberland's reign of terror in the Highlands affected far more people. The search for fugitives was a pretext for burnings and seizures of cattle. Most of the chiefs of the disaffected clans now went into exile, and the government acted to ensure that the Highlands would never again be a base for rebellion. The Highland dress was banned, kilt and tartan. A new Disarming Act was fiercely enforced. A commission of Lowland gentry was put in to run estates forfeited by rebels. Both the Jacobite generals of the '45 were 'improving' Highland landlords, and one of them, the Duke of Perth, had controlled the Crieff cattle tryst. The old order had been decaying within. Now it was systematically smashed from within. Clan feeling remained strong among the poor, but chiefship in the old style was no longer possible and gave way, at best, to paternalist landlordship.

Perversely, the poorly supported tribal rising in 1745 provided new symbols of lost Scottish nationality. Pathos, yearning and fatalistic defiance, these feelings expressed by the many fine Jacobite songs made them a toothless surrogate for nationalism. They evoked heroism untainted with interest, and feudal values which seemed far more noble than the ethics of Money and Property. Lord George Murray had written to his brother, 'My Life, my Fortune, my expectations, the Happyness of my wife & children are all at stake (& the chances are against me), & yet a principle of (what seems to me) Honour, & my Duty to King & Country, outweighs evry thing.' Old Macdonald of Keppoch had cried out as his followers hung back at Culloden, 'My God, have the clansmen of my name deserted me', and rushed forward, pistol and sword in hand, to be shot down. Such men seemed to redeem the most squalid era of British public life, providing examples more estimable than those of 'Butcher' Cumberland and of Islay-Argyll.

This was the want of uplift and heroes which made Pitt indispensable to the British. He would one day boast that he had been the first English Minister to arm 'the hardy and intrepid race' of the northern mountains and direct the 'valour' and 'fidelity' of Highlanders against the enemies of his own country. Earlier ministers had in fact used Gaels to fight British battles overseas. But people believed Pitt and that was most significant. With the last tribal region of Britain now tamed, Pitt would seem to focus an inchoate sense of united, self-confident British identity in which almost every section of Scottish society soon came to participate with some zeal.

Henry Pelham needed the dangerous Pitt as a colleague; after the Jacobite rising he threatened to resign unless Pitt received office. George II still refused. Pelham resigned. No one else could form a government. So Pitt was given an Irish sinecure position, and then, just after Culloden, he succeeded to the notoriously lucrative post of Paymaster to the Forces. Not for the last time, Pitt seemed to have sold out. His reputation faltered. However, he turned disadvantage to triumph. Ostentatiously, he refused the perquisites of office.

Instead of using the balances passing through his hands for his own profit, he lodged them with the Bank of England for public use. No other eighteenth-century statesman made such a gesture.

Pitt had developed important contacts with merchants. Urged on by William Vaughan, a New Hampshire fish merchant, he now argued unavailingly that the capture of Louisbourg should be followed by an attack on Quebec. His more regular Sancho Panza would later be William Beckford, opulent, vulgar, rather absurd, but well able to enhance Pitt's awareness of the nature and importance of West India trade and so to help him develop his vision of world empire resting on sea-power.

IV

One ocean remained unmastered, the Pacific. The British had attempted little there. But war with Spain prompted a bold incursion. In the autumn of 1740, Commodore George Anson set off with half a dozen ships and a general commission to do what he could where he could against the Spaniards in the Pacific. The tale of this expedition is macabre. As troops, Anson was provided with aged pensioners from the army's hospital at Chelsea. Numbers were made up with raw marines. Struggling round Cape Horn, the squadron suffered terribly from scurvy, that vile disease which brought spots and ulcers all over the body, swollen legs, putrid gums, extreme lassitude. The survivors took some prizes along the Chilean and Peruvian coasts, and captured a galleon from Mexico as it approached the Philippines. Anson returned in June 1744, after nearly four years, with loot valued at £1,250,000. But 1,051 men had perished, over half the total, amongst them all the pensioners who had set out.

It had been impossible to keep Anson's intentions secret, because he had had to stop for refreshments on the Brazilian coast. Hence people began to talk of the value of seizing the Falkland Islands as a stepping-stone to the Pacific. Anson himself was a hero despite his party's misfortunes, and was enabled to make his mark as a reformer within the navy. From 1751 to 1762, with just one short break, he would be in charge at the Admiralty. Improvements in tactics and personnel would stand to his credit. He would resist the prevalent custom of patronage and insist on promoting officers solely on merit.

There was plenty of room for reform. French and Spanish naval vessels were faster and better proportioned. The navy's growth increased problems of manning. It had 302 ships, 43,537 men in 1744. By 1762 there would be 432 ships and 81,929 men.

'No man,' Dr Samuel Johnson remarked, 'will be sailor who has contrivance enough to get himself into a jail, for being in a ship is being in a jail, with the chance of being drowned.' The scale of wages in the navy was not altered between 1653 and 1797. The Able Seaman was supposed to receive 24s. a month, less deductions, the Ordinary Seaman only 19s. This was half or a third of what could be earned on merchant ships, less even than was given to common soldiers. Food was monotonous and often disgusting. The ships were disease-ridden, with typhus killing even more people than scurvy. Discipline may have been less savage than in the army, but in the war of 1739–48, there were twenty occasions when a sailor was 'flogged round the fleet', that is, whipped alongside every ship, with the rigging manned so that everyone could see the lash fall in the boat where the culprit was tied to a scaffold. After more than a hundred strokes, the man was usually maimed for life. The vicious punishment of 'running the gauntlet', where the entire ship's company were given knotted cords to strike at a man's bare back as he ran between their lines, was not abolished until 1806. Not surprisingly, the navy suffered such heavy desertions in the 1740s that clemency had to be offered to lure men back. Because of the risk of desertion, shore leave could rarely be granted in home ports, and boatloads of whores were needed to slake the lust of sailors who were in truth near-prisoners. No pressed man could be trusted to stay in the service, and half of the navy were pressed.

At the outbreak of war, the government issued warrants to local authorities, admirals and captains who then organised 'press-gangs' of hired thugs. Masters and officers of merchant ships were generally invulnerable. Otherwise, no seaman was safe, and the men in charge of pressing could therefore extort plenty of bribes. The gaols were raked for men. Liverpool crimps brought over poor Irish and sold them to the gangs. But most impressment was done on the water. While outward-bound ships were normally exempt, vessels returning home would be accosted. Violent affrays were common. Thus, in 1740, returning East India ships, met by pressmen in the Downs, fired on their boats and wounded several. Most of the merchant seamen aboard escaped.

The freeborn white in the New World colonies was luckier. Acts of 1708 and 1746 gave him virtual immunity. One admiral was arrested for pressing in Antigua and another was exasperated into making the threat that he would bombard Boston unless he got the men he wanted.

But the colonies were a major source of strength at sea. North America provided masts and naval stores. The mainland's abundant produce made it easy to victual British squadrons in the West Indies. The French, by contrast, were cut off in wartime from normal sources of supply in Ireland. French campaigning in the West Indies was sharply limited. In some years there was no French naval presence at all. The British had permanent squadrons; the one based in Jamaica since Queen Anne's reign had ten or fourteen men-of-war in the 1740s, and there was a 'station' in the Leewards established in 1743. There were dockyards in Jamaica and Antigua, and the squadrons were regularly relieved by convoys from home.

The maritime population of France actually declined in the eighteenth century. The French could not maintain their commerce and man their navy at the same time. The British could manage both, largely because from Queen Anne's day the Navigation Acts were amended to permit three-quarters of a merchantman's crew during wartime to be foreign-born. Aliens were swept into the navy also, leading to frequent diplomatic protests.

The French spent far less on their navy, which in the 1740s was at best little more than half the size of their main rival's. Its permanent officers, the 'Navy of the Red', were an exclusive aristocratic élite, despising the bourgeois 'Officers of the Blue' drawn in wartime from the merchant marine. The British navy was somewhat more meritocratic. Chances of promotion from the lower deck were now small. But commissions could not be bought. No one could be commissioned lieutenant until he had served six years as midshipman or mate and had passed an examination. Further promotion might go by merit as well as by influence. The British navy was probably the best-officered in Europe.

Commanders conducted war with a constant eye for pecuniary gain. Once a man had achieved the rank of captain, he received only half pay except when he was actually used. Hence a general avidity for prizes, shared by the ordinary seamen, whose zeal was kept up by the chance of a share in a sacked port or a captured treasure ship. Anson was only one seaman who made a huge fortune from prize money.

Providing convoys for merchantmen was a major duty for the navy. The system was far from perfect. But the weaker French mercantile marine was simply swept from the seas once the chief French naval squadrons were smashed. More than 3,000 British ships were taken in the war of 1739–48, nearly as many as those lost by France and Spain together, but they were a much smaller proportion of the island nation's whole tonnage.

A British force deployed in the Channel could hope to choke enemy commerce. Blockade of Europe severed the French from their colonies. The French convoy system broke down. British power at sea had already doomed the Young Pretender to failure, when Anson, in May 1747, caught a French fleet off Cape Finisterre and chased it till six men-of-war and several Indiamen were forced to surrender. The French forces now engaged against the British in India were denied timely succour.

V

Under the emperor Muhammad Shah (ruling 1719–48) Mughal India had lost coherence. The flow of revenue to Delhi dwindled as provincial governors (*nawabs*) asserted *de facto* independence and founded dynasties of their own. Military adventurers, above all the ranging Marathas, found in the growing anarchy a chance to establish new, ill-defined and predatory realms. The situation in the Carnatic epitomised the whole.

Three European powers held cities in the Carnatic, in each of which a few hundred white men ruled unknown thousands of Indians. These were, in the whole Indian pattern, no more than petty states established, like others, by alien opportunists. South of the British headquarters at Madras, the French held Pondicherry, and further south still, the Dutch possessed Negapatam.

Involvement in native politics and in succession disputes in Java would give the
Dutch by 1772 complete control of the island. But overall, their strength was
clearly waning in the East as it was in Europe.

That left the French to duel with the EIC. The struggle was not for
territories, let alone empire. Though the French company was supported by the
State (which guaranteed its dividends from 1723) its personnel in India aimed
straightforwardly, like the British, at private wealth.

But Dupleix, who had been in India since 1722 and had married a woman
partly of native descent, was transformed from a man preoccupied by his own
private trade into an ambitious military schemer by what seemed to him British
treachery. As governor of Pondicherry, he hoped, when undeclared war
developed in Europe, to arrange a mutual pact of neutrality with the British as
in Queen Anne's war. He thought that he had achieved agreement. Then, at the
end of 1744, a small British squadron arrived in Indian waters where the French
for the moment had no warships, captured the French China fleet, and several
ships in the French 'country' trade.

The French held Île de France (now Mauritius) and under its governor, La
Bourdonnais, Port Louis there had become a well-equipped naval base. An
improvised fleet of armed commercial ships arrived on the Coromandel coast in
June 1746. French sea-power momentarily ruled the coast. Madras swiftly
surrendered, after only six casualties. If the treaty which La Bourdonnais now
concluded with the Madras Council were followed, he would receive a
handsome cash reward, but Dupleix would get nothing. The two Frenchmen
quarrelled. Another hurricane forced La Bourdonnais to return to base, leaving
Dupleix with 1,200 extra soldiers, brought from Île de France, and his chance
to denounce the treaty and plunder the town.

The immediate military sequel had epochal implications. Dupleix had kept
the Nawab of the Carnatic out of the contest by suggesting that he was taking
Madras only in order to hand it over to him. Anwar-ud-din Khan now
demanded the city. Dupleix retorted that since the British had owned the place
by absolute sovereignty, he himself had a perfect right to keep it. The Nawab
sent troops. Twice, with ease, the French repulsed them.

How was it that Paradis, a Swiss engineer officer, with 230 'European'
soldiers, 700 Indian troops, and no artillery, was able to attack and rout the
Nawab's force of over 10,000 men, which had the support of guns? 'National
spirit' was hardly the reason. Robert Orme, who knew India at this time, wrote
that 'The European troops in the service of the colonies established in Indostan,
never consist intirely of natives of that country to which the colony belongs: on
the contrary, one half at least is composed of men of all the nations in Europe.
The christians, who call themselves Portuguese, always form part of a garrison
. . .' These 'pretended Portuguese' were known as 'Topasses' because they wore
hats. 'The Indian natives, and Moors, who are trained in the European manner,
are called Sepoys: in taking our arms and military exercise, they do not quit their

own dress or any other of their customs. The Sepoys are formed into companies and battalions, and commanded by officers of their own nation and religion. These troops of the natives, who bring with them their own arms, and continue in their own manner of using them, retain the names they bear in their several countries. On the coast of Coromandel the Europeans distinguish all the different kinds of undisciplined militia by the general name of Peons . . .'

The key to European success from the 1740s lay in the training which, as Orme stressed, all these troops save the 'Peons' were given. Whether Pathans or South Indian Hindus, 'Topasses' or Germans, Swedes or Irishmen, the men in the cosmopolitan armies gathered by Dupleix and by his British enemies, though prone to desert from either to the other, depended on their current employer for pay, and were prepared to be drilled. All 'Europeans', and Sepoys, had musket and bayonet, while field-pieces could discharge ten or twelve shots a minute. The native-led armies which met them also had muskets, but they were not trained to use them in the disciplined way which now brought momentous results. Native rulers had guns, but set greatest store by unwieldy pieces of vast size. Their traditions of warfare were antiquated and uneconomical.

The Mughals and their viceroys had adopted the classic form of the Indian army, more than two thousand years old, a core of elephants surrounded by a crowd of cavalry. Infantry was despised and its best use not understood. Cavalry, often superb as individual fighters, were unwilling to risk their mounts against guns, and their tremendous surges forward were quite easily smashed by smaller European squadrons riding with discipline stirrup to stirrup. Indian armies were commonly huge – in 1750, one camp exceeded twenty miles in circumference and was thought to contain a million people. But they were correspondingly clumsy in movement. The mighty-seeming hosts would be composed for the most part of loose groups led by vassals and allies, each of whom was quite likely awaiting the chance to sell his defection for a good price. But while loyalty to a common cause was rare, and national feeling in effect unknown, the death or flight of a leader, conspicuous on his elephant, was enough to precipitate rout. Both sides would use, and expect, treachery. Unless a leader commanded overwhelmingly superior forces, he would seek to win by ruse or intrigue. Men who played war as a deadly game in this way were suddenly, in the 1740s shown to be highly vulnerable when faced with Europeans, whose attitudes to fighting were more direct and whose disciplined infantry was a factor hitherto unknown in Indian battle.

The most remarkable of these Europeans, Robert Clive, had arrived in Madras as a 'Writer' in the EIC service in June 1744, just before war broke out. Two years later, he escaped from the city after the French had captured it. Like others, he made his way to Fort St David, the second-ranking British settlement, only a dozen miles from Pondicherry. In just over eighteen months, this place experienced five French attacks. Dupleix was thwarted by the arrival of Admiral Thomas Griffin, who blockaded Pondicherry itself. Anson's action off Finisterre preserved the British command of Coromandel waters. The fifth French attack on Fort St David was beaten off by the garrison there, amongst whom Clive was now commissioned at Ensign, at the age of twenty-one.

St David was relieved of all danger by the arrival in July 1748 of the strongest British squadron yet seen in Indian waters, thirteen ships of the line and a score of smaller craft, under Rear-Admiral Boscawen. The French were now besieged in turn. The British massed 4,000 'Europeans' (half of them genuine articles fresh from Scotland, Ireland, and the English gaols) and about 2,000 native foot. Dupleix had less than 5,000 men to oppose them. Disease more than equalised matters. While the French during six weeks of siege lost only about 250 men of all races, over a quarter of the 'Europeans' on the British side died or were incapacitated, chiefly by sickness. A French sally sent the British troops flying from their trenches. Only one platoon remained, and this was about to run away when 'their officer, ensign Clive, reproached them sternly for their pusillanimity, and represented the honour they would gain by defending the trench . . .' and thirty or so soldiers, 'animated by his exhortation', fired with such deadly aim upon the confident enemy that the French in turn fled. If there was an element of classical embellishment in Robert Orme's account of the incident, it served to encourage the faith, which Clive himself shared, that the British were now finding heroes to emulate the ancient Romans. However, the monsoon approached. The British retired. News came of peace made in Europe.

Within that continent, French arms had triumphed everywhere. But the British navy had redressed the balance. Anson's successor in the Channel, Rear-Admiral Hawke, had caught another outward-bound French convoy off Finisterre in October 1747. The impact of the rout of the navy on France's colonial commerce can be measured; worth 24 million livres in 1743, its value sank to 7 million in 1748. The Nantes slave trade had been almost destroyed. So England was able to gain surprisingly good terms at the Treaty of Aix la Chapelle. Frederick the Great of Prussia kept Silesia. Otherwise, all conquests were handed back. The original cause of war between Britain and Spain was not settled at all. Jenkins's Ear had produced effects as absent as itself. A treaty of 1750 put formal end to the South Sea Company's trading career.

When Britain handed back Louisbourg in return for Madras, there was fury in New England. This was a colonial conquest, after all. What right had London to give it away? Even in England, the concession was disliked. Tobias Smollett would complain that the British government had given up 'the important isle of Cape Breton, in exchange for a petty factory in the East Indies, belonging to a private company, whose existence had been deemed prejudicial to the commonwealth.' But in North America, as in India, British and French alike saw the inconclusive treaty as only a truce.

VI

To Londoners and Parisians, Yankees and Canadians, India and the affairs of its 'petty factories' formed a remote arena of exotic and mysterious sideshows. White men in Pondicherry and Fort St David, hearing about events in Europe and the New World only months after they had occurred, continued to act as local circumstance and personal greed and ambition seemed to dictate. By mere and yet most portentous coincidence, the first climax of Anglo-French imperial rivalry in America deposited small forces of national rather than company troops in India at just the juncture when, as it happened, their deployment could begin to revolutionise the subcontinent and world affairs.

Dupleix, somewhat cocksure after his capture of Madras and successful defence of Pondicherry, resentful of the part played by the Nawab of the Carnatic, Anwar-ud-din Khan, and short of money to support the large force which he now had on his hands, decided on a gamble. He accepted the proposal from Chanda Sahib, representative of the old ruling family, that the French should help him oust Anwar-ud-din in return for reimbursement after the event. Meanwhile, the British executed a smaller project of their own. Boscawen, both admiral and general at Fort St David had the taste for loot, and the sharp eye for it, of successful men of his class. He liked the proposition made by Shahaji, a former raja of Tanjore, who was seeking to regain his throne and promised the fort of Devikottai, some land around it, and payment of expenses, if the EIC would give him mercenaries. The first attempt, by land and sea, was a disastrous failure. To regain prestige, the EIC sent a fresh expedition under Major Stringer Lawrence.

Lawrence, already fifty when he had arrived in India, had fought in Europe and at Culloden. He created an adequate little army. In June 1749 he took Devikottai. The British, finding that Shahaji had no popular support, made terms with the actual ruler of Tanjore, and duly acquired the fort and a lakh of rupees. But Dupleix was after bigger stakes, and his schemes now forced the EIC into a strange, sluggish war at second hand where each European side backed rival native princes and pretenders.

British and French forces remained small. Dupleix began with some 1,200 'Europeans' in his garrison, the British with only some 800. Over the four years 1750–3, 2,500 reinforcements despatched by the French company reached India, while his EIC rivals received over 1,800, of whom 500 were Swiss. It looked as if Dupleix might manage to drive them out of South India. While directors of the two companies in Europe wanted only the profits of peaceful commerce, Dupleix's schemes involved their employees in a life and death struggle.

In August 1749, the French and their allies defeated and slew the Nawab. Chanda Sahib was thus installed, and Dupleix's rewards were large grants of land for the French. The EIC had to secure itself, and supported Muhammad Ali, the dead Nawab's son. The intervention of Nasir Jang, viceroy of the

Deccan, further widened the scope of the contest. Months of manoeuvre followed, in which the British openly sided with Nasir Jang against his French-backed nephew, Muzafar Jang. Then in December 1750 Nasir Jang was defeated and killed by a French army. The French now seemed all-powerful, with Muzafar Jang recognising Dupleix as governor of all India south of the river Krishna and with their most notable soldier, Bussy, installed at Hyderabad as the viceroy's chief support. The British now had to build up their own coalition against Dupleix and his allies and puppets. Saunders, the president at Fort St David, sent, in May 1751, eight or nine hundred troops to support Muhammad Ali at Trichinopoly. Dupleix in turn despatched an army to capture that place, officially in the interests of Chanda Sahib. As a long siege proceeded, Robert Clive marched into fame.

He came from a long-established but now hard-pressed family of country gentry in Shropshire. He was one of eight children, and was packed off to Madras at the age of seventeen. The declassed youth was reserved and aloof during his early days in the East, oppressed, it seems, by his consciousness of the need to economise and thrive for the sake of his family. War came as a relief, but as fighting ceased after the capture of Devikottai, Lieutenant Clive was glad enough of the lucrative position of commissary to the EIC troops, which soon brought him a fortune of £40,000.

In 1750 he suffered what seems to have been his first attack of an illness combining nervous depression with physical symptoms, to counter which he employed opium. His manic-depressive temperament baffles brief description; deeds rather than words expressed his full character, and his deeper motivations elude his biographers. His strengths and his limitations alike reflected the old-fashioned area on the marches of Wales where he had grown up. Stringer Lawrence, who liked and encouraged the young soldier, and who in return awakened his devotion, was also a 'Marcher' by birth. Neither man would have risen high in conventional English society. Both found scope in India. The elements of Clive's personality may have been quite simple. He loved pomp, luxury and pre-eminence, and projected himself robustly into an antique mould of heroism. His manners suited war and command and Sepoys. In the drawing-room he appeared uncouth. By 1752, he owned a gold coat, and a gold turban.

Muhammad Ali, encircled in the great rock fortress at Trichinopoly, wanted his British allies to make a diversion towards Arcot, Chanda Sahib's capital, some three-score miles south of Madras. Clive was selected to lead the expedition. He was given 210 'European' troops and 600 Sepoys. Of the eight officers with him, only two had seen action and four had come straight from merchant life. Ten miles from the city, the expedition marched into a violent thunderstorm. Clive led them on regardless through rain and lightning. This was too much for the garrison at Arcot, which saw such egregious progress as an omen. The fort was abandoned. On September 1, 1751, Clive took possession of the citadel.

Chanda Sahib could not let Clive stay there endangering his own revenue collection. On September 24, his troops took over the town itself. Fifty days of close siege of the fort by them made Clive a hero. His troops were in danger of starvation and under constant fire from a force of 10,000. Four men were shot dead when at Clive's side; such luck in a leader impressed Muslims and Hindus. Climax came on November 14. The besiegers were worried by news that a Maratha chief had agreed to come to Clive's aid. They decided to storm the fort, and attempted to batter down the gates with elephants which had pikes fastened to iron bands around their heads. Clive's men fired at these unlucky creatures, which turned and trampled on the troops behind them. Though Clive had only 240 men of all races fit for duty, fighting went on all day and the enemy was repelled at every point. Besides the Marathas, there was an EIC relief force advancing, and the besiegers now suddenly withdrew.

How Clive would have performed in the set-piece battles of Europe cannot be known or guessed. Under Indian conditions, where reputation might by itself bring victory, he had shown himself fortunate, and an effective leader of men. 'Sabit Jang', men called him: 'Steady in War'. After Arcot, the tide turned against the French. Clive soon won his first victory in the open field, at Arni, expelled the French garrison from Conjevarum and then, early in 1752, at Caveripauk, routed a force, larger than his own, which Dupleix had sent against Madras. In September Clive's capture of two important French forts made Muhammad Ali the ruler of the whole Carnatic. Then Clive *Bahadur*, Clive the Brave, as the Nawab had officially styled him, suffered one of his phases of illness and asked for home leave. He arrived in England again a famous man, in October 1753, rich enough to redeem the mortgages on his family's home, to pay his father's debts, to give his sisters allowances, to buy a Cornish borough seat in Parliament and to set up a genteel establishment in the West End of London. The public acclaimed him. The EIC directors gave him a gold-hilted sword set with diamonds.

Dupleix's diplomacy lured key native allies from the EIC and in December 1752 he resumed the offensive. In August 1754 one Godeheu arrived at Pondicherry, sent to replace Dupleix by authorities at home who had long disapproved of his unofficial war. By the end of the year, Dupleix was on his way home and the two companies had agreed a provisional treaty. It is hard to believe, however, that this could have stabilised matters, even if fresh war had not broken out between England and France on the other side of the world.

Horace Walpole noted in 1754 that people in England were beginning to think 'that an East Indian War and a West Indian war may beget such a thing as a European war.' They had just heard of the defeat of a very young Virginian colonel named Washington in the Ohio country, south of the Great Lakes.

The growth of Britain's seaboard colonies had now shifted the whole balance of empire so as to give ministers in London, on the one hand, somewhat dizzying visions of vast markets opening up as the land beyond the mountains was settled.

Louisbourg, handed back, had been made stronger than before. To match it, the British government took a strikingly novel step. Halifax, Nova Scotia, was to be built up as both military base and naval station. In a year over 3,000 settlers were sent out at public expense.

Meanwhile, the governor of New France, De la Galissionière, was attempting to make good the French claim to the entire Mississippi basin by linking Canada and Louisiana with a line of forts which would shut the British off from the west. In 1749 he despatched 200 people to the Ohio valley, where they claimed the territory for France and expelled British traders found in Indian settlements. Two great consortia in Virginia were now competing for western lands. A coterie of prominent families – Lee, Mason, Fairfax, Washington – had organised the 'Ohio Company' in 1747. This was granted 200,000 acres, providing that within seven years it built a fort near the Ohio River's 'forks' and settled a hundred families. The Loyal Company, which included Thomas Jefferson's father, was granted, without obligation to colonise, 800,000 acres in 1749–52.

Traders from Pennsylvania had penetrated the Ohio Valley and had drawn the red men there into the British trading sphere. The French had to act. In 1752 they sent a party of Ottawa Indians led by a Wisconsin half-breed to chastise the Miamis for their defection. Then an expeditionary force of 2,200 went in the next year to cut and fortify a route from Lake Erie to the upper Ohio and to build forts on that strategic line.

Hence the first fame of George Washington, six years younger than Clive, also a man of action rather than eloquence, but better adapted to neo-classical taste: the noblest Roman, time would reveal, of them all. Slow in thought, marmoreal in his silences, six foot two, with huge feet and hands, immensely dignified in his bearing, he had no talent for oratory to match his taste for pomp and circumstance, but he was a splendidly graceful horseman, incapable of fear, or at least of revealing it. In habits he typified his own planting class. He was rarely seen with a book but obsessively interested in farming technique; an excellent businessman of that special Virginian breed, regretful that he had to own slaves but prepared to work them as hard as might be. He attended church because everyone did so and worried very little about spiritual or moral issues. Manners, however, exercised his attention; in his fourteenth year he had drawn up a hundred or more 'Rules of Civility', which he employed to subdue his raw-boned provincial gaucheness: 'SHAKE not the head, Feet or Legs, rowl not the Eyes, lift not an eyebrow higher than the other, wry not the mouth and bedew no mans face with your Spittle, by approaching too near him when you speak.' But his predisposition to become a statue was not wholly evident in the early 1750s, when his career as warrior began with his colonelcy, in the Virginian militia, acting directly in the interests of his class. Born on a 1,000-acre plantation along the Potomac, protégé of Thomas, Lord Fairfax, who owned almost a quarter of Virginia and had employed him to survey the frontier lands, inheritor of the large estates of his brother, who had helped found the Ohio Company, Washington volunteered to beard the French. The Ohio Company wanted to set up its own fort on the Forks. Members like Washington wanted those foreigners out.

The 21-year-old colonel made a 500-mile journey to warn the French off Company territory. Washington was no diplomat, and never learnt French. The hated rivals were gentlemanly, but frank. 'They told me,' Washington recorded, 'That it was their Absolute Design to take Possession of the Ohio, and by G— they would do it . . .'

The British government gave Governor Dinwiddie permission to repel force by force. With a small sum obtained from the grudging Virginia Assembly, he sent an ill-equipped force of 400 to protect a party which was now building the Company's fort on the Forks. The commander died on the way and Washington, second in command, took charge. He proved himself a resourceful leader of raw troops in frontier conditions and ambushed a party of French soldiers in May 1754, killing the leader and nine other men. This small affray by the Monongahela River can be called the start of the new Anglo-French war. As the French advanced, Washington fell back to an improvised fort where, in July, he was besieged and forced to surrender after nine hours and a hundred casualties.

New York interests feared the effect of war on relations with the Indians. The Iroquois were now restive and were complaining of lack of British protection. The Board of Trade in London had pressed for a conference of colonists with Iroquois to forge a new understanding, and while Washington was engaged with the French, this met at Albany. It was unsuccessful. Only seven colonies were represented. The treaty made with the Indians was harsh and led to trouble later.

An attempt was made at Albany to find a basis for union between the colonies. The common danger from French and Indians made this seem desirable; so, in some minds, did grandiose new ideas of 'empire' in the New World. Benjamin Franklin was the leading imperialist in the colonies. At Albany, he was one of a steering committee which, after four days, unveiled a plan by which there should be a federal union of the colonies from South Carolina to Maine, with an annual 'Grand Council of Delegates' elected by the colonial assemblies and a 'President General' appointed by the Crown. This central government would control Indian affairs, declare war and make peace, raise and equip soldiers, and levy taxes.

The plan, however, was not accepted by even one of the colonial assemblies, and while the British government was sympathetic, it thought that the present crisis was not the time to attempt a novelty like this. Parliament never considered the scheme. Political attention in Britain was absorbed by the lengthy manoeuvres within the whig ruling élite which had followed the death, in March 1754, of Henry Pelham. His brother, Newcastle, more or less took charge.

The government now decided to undertake a limited campaign in North America, to which both British and colonists would contribute. Some petty forts were to be captured in four distinct offensives; that was all. But the decision had great significance. Britain was assuming responsibility for the defence of the colonial frontier. In retrospect, the commitment would seem fateful.

A force of 6,000 colonials failed to flush the French out of Crown Point on Lake Champlain. In Nova Scotia Fort Beauséjour was captured. Meanwhile, in April 1755, General Braddock had arrived in Virginia from Ireland with two regiments, which were to be augmented in the colonies, and then to strike at Fort Duquesne on the Forks.

With Washington as his aide-de-camp, Braddock left Fort Cumberland on the Potomac in June on a 122-mile march through mountains and primeval forests such as his British regulars had never seen before. Besides his two regular regiments, he had recruited several hundred colonial troops. Within nine miles of Fort Duquesne, a couple of hundred French Canadians and some 600 Indians trapped him, firing rapidly from cover behind trees and ridges. Out of 1,460 men on the British side, 863 were killed or wounded by this unseen foe. Their bare bones and battered skulls still littered the field twenty years later. Braddock himself died of his wounds.

Repercussions were manifold. Letters captured in Braddock's baggage warned the French of the fourth prong of attack, a colonial force under Governor Shirley of Massachusetts which was advancing to capture Fort Niagara. That too aborted. Secondly, colonists had their eyes opened to British vulnerability. 'This whole Transaction,' Franklin would write, 'gave us Americans the first Suspicion that our exalted Ideas of the Prowess of British Regulars had not been well founded.' The *Boston Gazette* charged the British troops with cowardice and compared them unfavourably with New Englanders. Thirdly, the danger from Indians, now attacking along the whole frontier, was such that the Quaker pacifists of the Philadelphia Assembly could not defeat a clamour for retaliation. By the spring of 1756 the colony was committed to war for the first time.

Fourthly, the British Cabinet put behind it ideas of limited war. New France, like Carthage, must be destroyed. The way to all-out war with Old France was cleared by the so-called 'diplomatic revolution' in the early months of 1756 when the alliances of the 1740s were reversed; Britain came to terms with Prussia, and the enraged French King reached an understanding with Austria. Formal declaration of war came in May, after the French had attacked British-held Minorca. The 'Seven Years War' followed.

VII

Fifteen thousand French troops had landed in Minorca. Port Mahon, the capital, was blockaded. The British government, concerned about the Channel, could spare insufficient reinforcements for the Mediterranean. Rear-Admiral

John Byng, arriving with only ten vessels off the island, had rather the worse of an engagement. Instead of remaining at hand to interrupt French reinforcements and supplies, he retreated to Gibraltar. At the end of June the small British garrison on Minorca surrendered.

Pitt, a sick man wandering from watering place to watering place in the early 1750s, had recently taken on a new lease of life, making a belated marriage and razoring Newcastle and his Cabinet with oratory as high pitched as ever, enhanced now by the bandagings and strange clothing which he employed to advertise his supposed decrepitude, and to dramatise himself as a prophet battered by fate but still mustering voice on behalf of his country. Towards the end of 1755 he had reminded the House of the 'long-injured, long-neglected long-forgotten people of America', in an oration which finally cost him his post as Paymaster General. Cassandra-like, he had predicted the fall of Minorca and the violence of his recent speeches contributed greatly to the mood of panic and rage which now gripped, it appears, British 'public opinion'. In the latinate words of Tobias Smollett, 'The populace took fire like a train of the most hasty combustibles . . .' Mobs erupted all over the country, burning the admiral in effigy, chanting 'Hang Byng or take care of your King.' The Lord Mayor of London presented an address to George II demanding punishment of 'the authors of our late losses'. Port Mahon had been a useful centre for British traders, and naval weakness in the Mediterranean shocked and frightened merchants dealing with Italy and the Levant. Trade again demanded vigorous war. Trade now hoisted Pitt to power.

Newcastle and his colleagues offered the over-cautious Byng as a scapegoat, employed agents to blacken his name in the ale-houses and hired mobs to whip up fury. Shamefully, Byng was court-martialled and executed for what had been, at most, an error of judgment. But meanwhile bad news from America was confirming the dread Pitt's prophetic status.

In a remarkably drastic measure, in 1755, ten thousand French-speaking Acadians had been rounded up and shipped off from Nova Scotia to various parts of the New and Old Worlds. But attempted British blockade failed to prevent large reinforcements reaching Canada, and in 1756 a new commander, the Marquis de Montcalm, arrived in the St Lawrence.

An 'enlightened' aristocrat, lively, impassioned, generous and rash, he disliked the cynical profiteering and the rude colonial habits which he found in Quebec, as well as the barbarousness of France's Indian allies and the tactics of *petite guerre* which the Canadians had learned from them. The governor, Vaudreuil, a native Canadian, was for his own part resentful of Montcalm, of French neglect and of French condescension. Canadians were as free-spirited as Yankees, and the French army in the New World was weakened, like the British, by quarrels between regular soldiers and Colonial militiamen. Nevertheless, using Vaudreuil's strategy rather than Montcalm's, the French were able to thwart an attempt by Lord Loudoun, the new British commander, to drive them back in the critical Hudson–Montreal corridor.

Such news swelled the clamour for Pitt now heard in England. The King had to give way, and in November a new government emerged with Pitt as Secretary of State. On one main point he swiftly compromised with the King. For years he had been denouncing the subsidising of foreign allies and the hiring of foreign troops, but he was now prepared to apply British funds to the support of a huge army on the Rhine, and to lavish financial assistance on Frederick the Great of Prussia. His idea was that while Frederick tied down the French in Europe Britain would further assist him by diversionary raids on the French coast. Spain should be kept neutral while the traditional blockade of the French navy supported major attacks on French colonies and commerce. An 'expedition of weight' was to go which, by the summer, would give Loudoun 17,000 troops to attack first Louisbourg, then Quebec.

As a safeguard against invasion, Pitt now got the reactivated militia which he had been demanding for some time. A bolder step was the arming of Highlanders who had been 'out' in the 1745 rebellion. Newcastle was seriously alarmed when one of Pitt's first actions was to raise two regiments of Gaels. At the time, Pitt insinuated cynically that it was best to kill such creatures off in Canada; but the prowess of the Highland troops made him proud of what he had done. 'I sought for merit wherever it was to be found . . .' he would brag one day, 'I found it in the mountains of the North. I called it forth . . .'

Despite the vigour which he showed in his first weeks in office, Pitt did not satisfy George II, who found the long speeches which his minister made to him in private both affected and incomprehensible. At the first chance, in April, he thrust Pitt out again. Pitt retorted with an elaborate publicity stunt, in which a dozen cities and towns testified their esteem for him by conferring their freedom upon him, and in some cases making him presents – 'the rain of gold boxes'. Twelve weeks of especially intricate factional intrigue followed his dismissal. The crisis was resolved when Newcastle agreed to combine with his enemy Pitt. Newcastle's job was to find cash and provide secure majorities in the Commons. Pitt was to run the war. He had, in the phrase of the time, 'stormed' the King's closet.

Pitt was Secretary of State at the Southern Department (which dealt with France, Southern Europe, the Far East and all the colonies). He made his 'Northern' counterpart no more than a cypher, and domineered over the titular First Minister, Newcastle. His strategical talents are questionable. In any case, his capacity to affect events was limited. Letters from India took six months or a year to reach London. While orders for America might get to ports there in six weeks, they might then have to make a long journey up country. But Pitt had a simple objective – crush France – and this gave a certain unity and drive to what were in effect almost four different wars in four continents.

France's population was more than double that of Great Britain. The cost of fighting such an enemy put a severe strain on Britain's resources. Supplies voted at home and in the colonies rose from £7 million in 1756 to nearly £19 million in 1761. Houses and windows were taxed. Heavy duties to malt hit everyone. The money was squeezed from a British population of between five and a half and six million, many of them very poor. In 1748 Britain had had 49 regiments of infantry; by 1761, there would be 115, and the strengths of battalions would have been greatly increased. All this did not imply 'total war' as a later century would know it, but a navy of 70,000 men, an army of 140,000, were prodigious by earlier standards.

Britain had striking advantages. Votes of the Irish Parliament paid for over twenty regiments. And the large colonial population of British North America made the task of the French in the New World daunting. The problem was to mobilise it effectively. Pitt's policies made this easier. Colonial assemblies were promised some repayment for the cost of raising armed forces. In the end about two-fifths of the whole military outlay of the colonies was returned to them. Furthermore, the home government would supply free arms and artillery, tents and provisions, if a colony found adequate numbers, clothed and paid them. In 1758 Pitt laid the bogey of precedence; henceforth, he ordained, a colonial captain would rank above a regular lieutenant.

But most colonists did not like the war, which was so patently being fought in the interests of men like Franklin – expansionists, speculators, ambitious politicians – and of fur traders and Yankee merchants. While assemblies in Connecticut and New York were ready to give generous support, and Massachusetts, required to raise 2,300 troops, actually found 7,000 and even offered to send men to help defend Britain against invasion, Virginia and Maryland showed less eagerness. The three colonies – Rhode Island, Maryland and Delaware – which had no foreign frontiers were not interested. New Hampshire and North Carolina pleaded poverty. Assemblies sometimes laid down that their troops must serve only under such-and-such a commander and be used only for such-and-such operations. The troops themselves seemed of poor quality. 'They fall down dead in their own dirt,' a British officer named James Wolfe reported, 'and desert by battalions, officers and all.'

Meanwhile, naval power, not weight of numbers on land, was still the key to success in America. Manning was harder than ever. Over the whole war, 133,708 sailors would be lost through disease or desertion, as compared with 1,512 killed in action. But British command of the seas was soon such that the French government gave up even trying to keep its colonies fully defended. By 1763, France would have lost 109 warships to Britain's 50.

Conquest was not seen as an end in itself. Fisheries, factories, naval bases, were the objectives. The capture of a French colony would give Britain an extra counter in peace negotiations. If Martinique could be exchanged for Minorca, this might save handing over Cape Breton Island again and thus would give Britain control of New World cod. Like the Dutch before them the British aimed to be masters of every sea. They were already reckoned to own a third of all the tonnage of shipping in European hands. It seemed as if Pitt wished to engross all. Neutral ships were searched. British privateers attacked neutral vessels. Dutch and Swedes, Danes, Russians and Spaniards were bitter.

City interests doted on Pitt's war. Wealthy businessmen gathered more wealth by financing the loans on which Pitt depended. Ironmasters throve on the making of cannon. Traders gloated over the capture of fresh markets and the expansion of access to raw materials. In 1759, when a new tax on sugar was proposed in the Commons, Pitt's ally Beckford opposed it with a tedious speech about sugar, sugar, again sugar, which drew 'horse laughs' from the House. When Beckford sat down, Pitt rose. 'Sugar, Mr Speaker,' he began. Another laugh. 'Sugar, Mr Speaker,' Pitt thundered. Hush supervened. Then Pitt whispered in his sweetest tone, 'Sugar, Mr Speaker: who will laugh at sugar now?'

For all this, 1757 went badly for British interests. Frederick the Great lost a third of his army at Kolin in Bohemia. Most of Hanover was overrun by the French. Loudoun, reinforced too late and hearing that there were twenty-two French battleships in harbour at Louisbourg, called off the attack. Blockade of the French ports was not yet effectual. A well-equipped raid on Rochefort failed because of quarrels between the commanders. The new Militia Act provoked dangerous riots in many counties; the poor rightly feared that militiamen might be sent to fight overseas, as had in fact happened in Huntingdonshire. Amid all this word had arrived, in June, that a year before the Nawab of Bengal had crushed the British factory at Calcutta.

VIII

Even after Dupleix's recall, the viceroy at Hyderabad was still in effect a French puppet. Bussy's role as his adviser was a direct threat to the British in both Madras and Bengal. In 1754, for the first time, Royal troops, 900 of them, were sent to India, with a small squadron commanded by Admiral Watson. An attack on Hyderabad through Bombay, with Maratha allies, was projected.

Clive came back for the new round. He now had a royal commission as Lieutenant-Colonel as well as the East India Company rank of governor of Fort St David, second man on the Coromandel Coast. EIC servants in Bombay, a relatively modest and prudish establishment, were not attuned to the new, grandiose, *realpolitik*. The Council there shied away from the attack on Bussy now proposed, and it was not made. To appease the frustrated Marathas, Watson and Clive, in collaboration with them, attacked and seized, with much loot, the west coast pirate stronghold of Gheria some 180 miles south of Bombay. Clive had just taken up office at Fort St David when word came of shameful events at Calcutta.

The British in Bengal enjoyed, under the 1717 *farman*, exceptional privileges in a region relatively much more stable, and hence more propitious for commerce, than the war-torn Carnatic or than Surat and Bombay under the

Maratha shadow. The Bengal *zemindars* (revenue collectors) were in some cases rulers of huge areas, though others were quite small fry. They governed on the whole equitably, under Nawabs who had in the past rarely much annoyed the British.

Though still nominally subject to Delhi, the Nawab ruling the three provinces of Bengal, Bihar and Orissa had for some time been effectively independent. In 1740 the title had been usurped by an able soldier of fortune from Turkestan, Alivardi Khan. Almost at once, he faced heavy Maratha incursions. After years of fighting, he was forced, in 1751, to concede them Orissa and to pay them tribute. His constant need for money to fight wars created resentment and instability. Merchants and landholders were squeezed, while Muslim commanders chafed as Alivardi raised Hindus into positions of power. A dominant force in Bengal was the family of Jagat Seth, 'Banker of the World', the title bestowed in 1715 on a Jain named Manik Chand after he had lent the Emperor ten million rupees. His adopted son had controlled the mint at Alivardi's capital, Murshidabad, and the EIC had been among the Seths' clients.

Bengal, for all the antiquity of its civilisation, had become a kind of frontier. Maraths and Afghans hovered over an arena where Persians and Armenians, Punjabis, French, Dutch and British schemed for wealth and intrigued with well-to-do Bengalis. The soil was generous. Its tillers were quiescent. The prizes were lavish, and EIC men, who had gambled their lives in a deadly climate, were not disposed to resist their temptation.

There were only some 750 white men in the whole province. But Calcutta's population now stood at maybe 120,000. The god Property was respected here as it was everywhere that people spoke English, and its veneration lured more and more of the Nawab's richer subjects, who found British 'justice' to their taste and settled in Calcutta with their dependants. The whites relied on their trading on Asian middlemen, Asian agents and even on Asian capital. While ambitious Indians were commonly attracted to serve EIC men as personal factotums – *banians* – almost every European was deep in debt to wealthy natives.

White merchants kept many servants and were carried about in palanquins. But they longed to reach home again and, if possible, to live in Britain in an equally grand way. The Nawab now seemed to be blocking their ways to wealth. There was friction over customs duties. EIC men claimed that the Emperor's *farman* of 1717 implied that their private trade should be free of them. The ruler's officials did not agree, and strove furthermore to block altogether British participation in the valuable internal trades in salt, betel nut and tobacco from which the Nawab drew much revenue.

British enterprise in Bengal was faltering. Around 1750, Bengal's share in the EIC's total Indian trade had been as high as two-fifths; in 1753–6 it slumped to little over a quarter. Prices of goods in Bengal had once been lower than elsewhere in Asia. But recently this had ceased to be true. In some sixteen years, the price of rice in Calcutta had tripled or quadrupled while that of textiles had risen by nearly a third. Coinciding with disruptive wars and political problems in Western India, in Persia and in Arabia, this inflation had helped produce a slump in the 'country trade' with points west on which EIC men had depended for their private fortunes. Bankruptcies of Company servants had become quite common.

In 1754, higher demands for commission from native brokers prompted the EIC men to replace these independent intermediaries with agents employed full-time by the Company. Discontented ex-brokers joined the voices at Alivardi's court which condemned Europeans for whatever went wrong with the Bengal economy. But Alivardi did not want to tangle with the whites. Calcutta was now Bengal's main port. He told one of his generals, Mir Jafar, that the Europeans were like a hive of bees; their honey was good, but if one disturbed them, they would sting one to death.

Yet they were fragile. There were about eighty covenanted EIC servants at Calcutta and the four subsidiary factories, Kasimbazar, Dacca, Balasore and Jugdea, under a governor, Roger Drake, of sordid reputation. The least mediocre were probably William Watts, in charge at Kasimbazar, and John Zephaniah Holwell, born in 1711 the son of a timber merchant, trained as a surgeon, who held the lucrative post of *zemindar* at Calcutta. Holwell had been in Bengal for nearly a quarter of a century, and his capacity to survive had brought him exceptional opportunities to adjust his temperament to local notions of graft, extortion, corruption and intrigue.

In 1756 Alivardi Khan died at a great age. His chosen successor was Siraj-ud-daula, his grandson, still in his early twenties. Siraj was volatile, lustful, and tactless, and alienated veteran Muslim commanders by his dependence on Hindu ministers. Within his own family, his succession was opposed by his aunt, Ghasita Begum, and by a cousin who was governor at Purnea.

He was marching against the latter in May 1756 when he heard that the man had recognised him as Nawab. At the same time he received an insolent answer from the EIC to an order, issued to all Europeans, that any new fortifications must be demolished. The French and Dutch replied with due courtesy. Having just overawed his native enemies, Siraj did not need to accept British bluster, and he would have lost face if he had done so. He returned to Murshidabad and ordered the seizure of the EIC factory at Kasimbazar.

Siraj, mindful of happenings further south, feared the Europeans. But he did not wish to expel them. Their honey fed courtiers, bankers, merchants, the Nawab himself. He proposed merely to teach the British a lesson. Their trade was prevented from moving up and down river. Watts, encircled at Kasimbazar by a vast army, had less than fifty troops, and swiftly submitted. He was politely treated in captivity. Drake, however, refused to be reasonable. Diplomacy failing, Siraj moved against Calcutta.

The garrison of only 180 fit soldiers, under an incompetent leader, had no cartridges ready, no shells fitted, no fuses prepared. The militia, untrained, numbered about 250, largely half-caste 'Portuguese' and Armenians. Siraj's huge force appeared on June 16. Three days later, Drake, the commandant and several Council members prudently took themselves off to the relative safety of ships on the river. In a panic flight of whites and Eurasians, numerous Portuguese women were drowned with their children. Holwell was left in charge of the fort, but he and all the rest would have been evacuated had not ships summoned on their behalf run aground. With the houses around the fort in flames, scores of soldiers deserted. On June 20, after puny resistance, the fort fell. Through folly, or over-confident scheming, Drake had almost undone the psychological impact of the success of Dupleix and Clive. All Europeans in Bengal felt dishonoured. Contemptuous natives now called them 'sister-fuckers'.

It was thanks to John Zephaniah Holwell that a signal instance of cowardice or worse was eventually alchemised into the classic fable of white heroism and heathen devilishness. Holwell's good would be interred with his bones; almost no one remembers that he was one of the first whites in India, who, however obtusely, made serious efforts to understand Hinduism. But the tale, as he wrote it, of the 'Black Hole of Calcutta' became and perhaps remains the most famous single episode in the whole history of the British Empire. Holwell was something of a pioneer in the evolving genre of 'sentimental' pseudo-documentary which would shortly be raised to eminence by Laurence Sterne. His literary skills were sufficient to create a story later too useful to be discarded. Whatever atrocities the British might justly be charged with, not merely in India, but anywhere in the tropical world, the 'Black Hole' would serve to show that dusky fiends had surpassed them. The bodies of suffering Christian martyrs at its base seemed to transform the edifice of British power in India from counting-house or barracks into cathedral.

When Siraj-ud-daula entered Calcutta on June 20, he ordered that the captive Holwell be released from his irons and that the prisoners should be decently treated. Many simply walked out and escaped. Some drunken soldiers remained and began to be a nuisance. Siraj asked if a dungeon was available. Of course there was one; every British garrison needed a place to confine disorderly men, and until 1868 such a lock-up would always be known, officially, as a 'Black Hole'. Prisons in England were at this time foully insalubrious. Calcutta's 'Hole' must have been a nasty place at the best of times; eighteen feet long by fourteen or fifteen wide with two barred airholes opening into a low veranda. Siraj probably did not realise how small it was when he ordered that all the prisoners, Holwell included, should be confined in this noisome den. Several wounded officers and a sick chaplain were among them, but even Holwell exempted Siraj himself from any charge of deliberate cruelty. The Nawab left the fort in the early evening, and did not return till the following morning.

The stifling tropical night overpowered men drunken, wounded and sick.

The gaolers did not go beyond their orders to relieve their suffering. When the cell was opened, a number of men had perished horribly, leaving 23, or 21, survivors. What is not known is how many had gone in. The maximum number of Europeans left in Calcutta, it can be shown, was no more than 64, but Armenians and Eurasians may also have been present. Recent scholars accept figures of between 18 and 43 deaths, though precision will never be possible, and the real total may have been lower. Accounts which present themselves as first-hand evidence hover about 146 prisoners, which seems to have been the figure decided between Holwell and a couple of others soon after the event. Released from the Hole on Siraj's return to the fort, Holwell had little time to recover from what had happened before he was taken up river to Murshidabad, recalling the shameful loss of Calcutta, and wondering how his own future prospects, within or without the EIC, might be affected by the débâcle.

All sight of Siraj's easy conquest is lost in the horror of his narrative. Holwell himself emerges as a prodigious hero. He urges calm upon his shocked companions as they realise what hell they have been forced into. When the guards respond at last to the call for 'water, water' everyone else in the Hole falls into 'agitation and raving' at the mere sight of it. Holwell foresees that its effects will be 'fatal', yet nevertheless he passes it on to the rest in hats, keeping up this strenuous action for nearly two hours, while his comrades trample each other to death in their lust for it and the guards, 'brutal wretches', laugh at the scene. But when he finally lays his weary form down on a bench and cries out for water himself, the others, crazed though they may be, still have 'the respect and tenderness' for him 'to cry out, "GIVE HIM WATER, GIVE HIM WATER!"' and not one will touch it until he has drunk. However, finding this relief insufficient, he sucks away at the perspiration collected in his shirt. Since almost all the others have stripped (at his own prudent suggestion) his colleague Lushington sucks at the same source, afterwards assuring Holwell that he believes 'he owed his life to the many comfortable draughts he had from my sleeves.' Crushed, as the night proceeds, under three other sufferers, Holwell, sucking away, retains enough presence of mind to keep consulting his watch to note the time for the sake of posterity. But towards two o'clock he can bear it no more and faints. Next morning the survivors cannot persuade the guards to open the door, so one of them prudently thinks of searching for Holwell in the hope that he may have influence enough to gain their release. They find him under a heap of dead, but alive.

With what Olympic skills in gymnastics does Holwell, hemmed in as he describes, contrive to sample and reject the refreshing qualities of his own urine? The absurdities of his tale are such as almost to reinforce its authority. What man in his senses would hope to be believed, unless such improbable episodes were in fact true? But it would seem that the writer invented each detail in turn so as to forestall obvious questions. Why don't they take off their clothes? Holwell says they did. But how does he himself survive? An account in an

English newspaper of the fate of the crew of a British privateer seized by the French, who were confined in the hold of their captors' ship, where twenty-seven out of eighty-three suffocated, clearly spurred Holwell's imagination, supplying one of his more poignant details. But his finest stroke was without doubt to acknowledge that other survivors would not confirm his story, observing that their accounts were 'so excessively absurd and contradictory, as to convince me, very few of them retained their senses . . .'

Tobias Smollett at once paraphrased the tale without question in his own standard *History of England*. Robert Orme in his authoritative *History of . . . The British . . . in Indostan* (1778) likewise repeated. But for its full effect, the legend had to await a writer of genius, Thomas Macaulay, who in his essay of 1840 on Clive related it as a tale surpassed by 'Nothing in history or fiction' which 'awakened neither remorse nor pity in the bosom of the savage Nabob.'

Drake and his fellows had fled down river to Fulta. Holwell eventually joined them there, and signed the Council's letter to the directors in London which gave a summary account of the fall of Calcutta. This letter does not mention the 'Black Hole'. At the time, in Bengal and Madras, the alleged event made no stir. The British did not denounce Siraj for this war crime. No compensation was ever demanded for the victims, real or purported. Much Company property had been lost in Calcutta and the other factories – valued at over three and a half million rupees. But nearly two million rupees' worth would be recovered intact in due course; Siraj looked after what fell into his hands. The Nawab wrote to Madras in conciliatory fashion, blaming the 'wicked and unruly' Drake for what had happened.

However, British prestige in Bengal had to be reasserted. Even before the end of July, a small force from Madras under Major Kilpatrick arrived at Fulta, a most unhealthy spot, where refugees and soldiers wasted away. Kilpatrick felt he could not recapture Calcutta, and awaited further help from the south. When it came, Clive was in command. Clive's ambition was far from slaked with the governorship of Fort St David, and he was fired by the prospect ahead. He set off with eight ships and more than 1,700 troops, most of them natives, in mid-October, but stormy weather caused delay and before he arrived at the mouth of the Hugli early in December, 673 soldiers had been lost on the way, when two vessels had turned back. Even with Kilpatrick's men, and natives recruited locally, this would not be a large force.

But they moved purposefully up river. Their first objective was the fort of Budge Budge. After one of Siraj's armies had been beaten off in a fierce skirmish, the place was captured by the drunken bravado of a lone Gaelic sailor, one Strahan, who scaled the walls and cried 'The place is mine', upon which others rushed forward and the fort fell with only one British casualty. Though Strahan was severely rebuked by Admiral Watson for his anarchic behaviour the swagger of the British sailors, like the great guns on the great ships they manned, struck fear into the Nawab's forces. Calcutta was reoccupied without fighting on

January 2, 1757 and a week later the town of Hugli was captured and plundered. Clive recruited two or three hundred fresh Sepoys, meanwhile quarrelling with his British associates. His right to command was disputed by Captain Coote, a prickly Anglo-Irishman. '. . . They are bad subjects and rotten at heart,' he wrote to Governor Pigot of Madras. '. . . The riches of Peru and Mexico should not induce me to dwell among them.' The flash of exotic ambition is seen for a moment. Clive was thinking of Cortés and Pizarro.

Responsible business-like apprehension made him wish to attempt a treaty with Siraj without further fighting. But Clive's embassies were unavailing. Early in February, the Nawab came to Calcutta with 40,000 troops. Clive had less than 2,000 but a surge of rashness saved him. He mounted a night attack, probably aiming to capture or kill Siraj. Technically, it misfired. About a tenth of the troops were killed or wounded, very heavy losses for so small a force. But the bungled action worked. In skirmishes, Siraj lost over 1,000 men, and Clive had given him a serious fright. He retreated about six miles and swiftly came to terms. A treaty of February 9 gave the British almost all they had hoped for – their privileges confirmed, compensation for the Company, presents for Clive, Kilpatrick and others. Clive thought his business in Bengal was done.

But Siraj was inclining towards the French, and the British position was full of risks still. Admiral Watson had heard in January that Britain and France were officially at war. He wanted to attack the French in Bengal and refused to sign a treaty of neutrality which they offered. This boisterous seaman threatened Siraj horridly: '. . . I will kindle such a flame in your country, as all the water in the Ganges shall not be able to extinguish.' At last Siraj, jolted by rumours of Afghan invasion and anxious to have British help against it, gave what Watson took to be tacit permission for an attack on Chandernagore. In March, Watson's guns overwhelmed the French fort. When the news reached London, East India stock would go up by 12 per cent. Siraj had lost any chance of substantial French support.

The Nawab's court was now wormed with French and British bribes. An EIC man at Murshidabad, Luke Scrafton, could not resist a Roman analogy, writing to Calcutta that Siraj's court might be 'compared to that of Ptolemy's that reigned in Egypt when Pompey fled there after the battle of Pharsalia, that is that the head and members are all as corrupt and treacherous as possible . . .' Clive, he suggested, 'should be the Caesar to act as Caesar then did, take the Kingdom under his protection, depose the old and give them a new King to make his subjects happy.'

By April, the EIC men in Bengal had made it their definite policy to depose Siraj. They hardly required to start from scratch. In one of his tantrums Siraj, most unwisely, had struck Jagat Seth across the face. The central force in the plotting came from the Seth bankers. Two other key figures were Rai Durlabh, Siraj's Bengali treasurer, and a senior general, Mir Jafar. The British now fell in with the Seths' suggestion that Mir Jafar should be installed as Nawab. They demanded a very high price for their soldiers. All the chief EIC men, like the Indian plotters, were to receive lavish rewards. On June 13, Clive began to march on the Nawab's capital.

The British were gambling. Calcutta was left almost undefended. If their fellow-plotters had turned upon them, they might have been swept from Bengal. The EIC had a treaty with Mir Jafar. But Clive could not be sure that the man would keep faith. Mir Jafar was terrified when Siraj, warned by the French of the plot against him, dismissed him from his post of commander-in-chief, though the Nawab himself was too fearful and irresolute to have the conspirators put to death. The plot might have broken down in timidity and confusion.

As the British had prepared to push north, even Watson had advised Clive that he could not be too cautious. Clive had 613 European infantry, about 100 Eurasian Topasses, 171 artillerymen and 2,100 Sepoys. He had no cavalry and could deploy only eight fieldpieces and two howitzers. The monsoon was coming. A crisis must be forced quickly.

On June 19, Clive reached Katwa, a fortified town on the west bank of the Hugli, about eighty miles north of Calcutta and forty from Murshidabad. Word from Mir Jafar was eagerly awaited. Clive sent to tell him that unless he proved his good faith by coming to Plassey, a place fifteen miles to the north-east, the British would not cross the river. The reply came at last at 3 p.m. on the 22nd. Mir Jafar's note urged Clive to proceed. The British began at once to cross the Hugli, which contemporaries would match with Caesar's Rubicon, and marched on towards Plassey.

Clive met more than he expected. His men, having marched through heavy rain, had in some cases bivouacked only at 3 a.m. Daybreak on June 23 revealed an unnerving panorama. On the wide, lush plain, the Nawab had assembled, by Clive's own reckoning, 15,000 horse, 35,000 foot and forty pieces of artillery. Siraj had proved in the past that he could win battles. Fifteen thousand of his troops were his own personal force, whose loyalty was not suspect. His foot were equipped with matchlock muskets. Clive's fieldpieces were small six-pounders; the Nawab's cannon were mostly twenty-four- or thirty-two-pounders, and native artillerymen were directed by a force of French experts. When someone asked him what he thought would happen, Clive replied, 'We must make the best fight we can during the day, and at night sling our musket over our shoulders and march back to Calcutta.'

At 7 a.m. he sent a desperate note to Mir Jafar – 'If you will come to Daudpur I will march from Placis to meet you, but if you won't comply even with this, pardon me, I shall make it up with the Nawab!' But the Nawab's forces took the initiative out of his hands. The heavy guns began to crack at about eight. Thirty men fell in half an hour. Clive could only withdraw his men behind an embankment where they were relatively safe. For hours the cannonade continued, with the lighter British guns retorting. One howitzer shell did signal work, mortally wounding Mir Madan, the main general still faithful to Siraj.

About noon, a heavy monsoon shower stopped the guns. Clive went to change his wet clothes at a hunting lodge which he had made his headquarters. In his absence, the battle was transformed. Siraj had ordered his men to withdraw to their entrenchments. Seeing the enemy gunners beginning to leave their advanced position by a water tank, Major Kilpatrick at once moved up with two guns. Clive reappeared very angry and threatened to arrest Kilpatrick for taking an undue risk. But the initiative had passed to the British. Clive took charge himself, and called up reinforcements.

At this point the Nawab's cavalry and foot made their first move towards active intervention. Some found a strong position near a second water tank. Clive sent Captain Eyre Coote to deal with them. The attack succeeded. Then the British troops charged. Bravado once more brought reward. The enemy fled.

Siraj, long harried by fears and suspicions, had entered the battle in trepidation. Astrologers, possibly bribed by the plotters, had reported bad omens. Mir Madan had been brought back to die in the Nawab's own tent. Siraj pleaded with Mir Jafar to attack. Mir Jafar played canny. His force, a huge body to the east of the British position, did advance during the afternoon, but fell back promptly in the face of British fire. As the British attacked, Siraj's nerve broke. He rushed away from the field. By 5 p.m. Clive was victorious. Only then did he receive a note from Mir Jafar, advising him sagely to do what he had already done.

Perhaps 500 of the Nawab's troops had been killed, amongst whom the death of Mir Madan may have been virtually decisive. The British had lost twenty-two men, and had another fifty or so wounded; these casualties, Clive himself noted, were 'chiefly blacks'.

Siraj found himself friendless. Within ten days of the battle, he was brutally murdered and hacked to pieces by Mir Jafar's son. Mir Jafar reigned in his place at Murshidabad, confirmed the EIC in its privileges, ceded to it twenty-four *parganas* south of Calcutta, provided compensation for past losses and promised support against all enemies.

Many British involved in Mir Jafar's takeover did not survive long to enjoy the profits. Watson died in the sultry heat of August, after a day when birds dropped dead from the sky. Kilpatrick followed him in October, when of 250 men who had come with him from Madras fourteen months before, only five survived, and these were thin and sick. But for numerous others the gamble paid off richly. 'The first fruit of our success,' Scrafton wrote, 'was the receipt of nearly a million sterling, which the Soubah [Mir Jafar] paid us on the 3d July, which was laden on board two hundred boats . . .' The triumphant progress of this treasure past French and Dutch to factories to Calcutta, 'with music playing, drums beating, and colours flying', was an apt symbol of the exorbitant appetite now growing by what it fed on. In the end, Clive personally received £234,000. Members of the Calcutta Council got handsome cuts. The army and navy shared fifty lakhs of rupees (over £500,000). Altogether, at least £1,238,575 was handed out to Europeans. And Rai Durlabh took, as agreed, a commission of 5 per cent on all he had negotiated during the plotting for the British.

This man had misled them. As treasurer he should have known that the Nawab's coffers could not afford all that was promised. Though Clive would later profess himself 'astonished at my own moderation' when he could have ransacked Bengal's gathered riches, he like the others pressed for the full claim. No one saw anything wrong in taking huge presents, which Eastern potentates commonly made. The King's army and navy depended on booty and such-like for the incentive to fight at all. Clive was never furtive about his spoils.

But the sheer scale of the gifts accomplished psychological revolutions. At home, men accustomed to the slow plunder by Walpole and his whigs of Britain itself were nevertheless outraged as well as envious. Perversely, the hauls of Clive and his colleagues helped to stimulate a growing movement in favour of cleaning up British public life.

Scrafton, writing some three years after Plassey, still did not talk of further conquests. He dwelled on the gains for British trade. But neo-Roman boasting was bound to creep in. '. . . What prospect,' Scrafton asked, regarding Plassey, 'was there that such a handful of men should overcome such numerous forces? . . . No longer considered as mere merchants, we were now thought the umpires of Indostan . . .'

So important a happening as this battle calls for a summary verdict. This is hard to give. The actors were complex human beings whose self-contradictions make moralising treacherous. Siraj was not quite the vicious despot of legend, nor the patriot merciful to a fault. Holwell does not make a suitable martyr nor a double-dyed racist villain. Mir Jafar was not a traitor to India but a foreign adventurer taking one more chance. In the long perspective of history, everyone seems to be dwarfed by the crucial factor of British sea-power. Even if the French had given Siraj more help and Plassey had gone the other way, British dominance of sea-lanes to India should have enabled the EIC to reassert itself in Bengal.

Clive's triumphs in the Carnatic had been much like those of a brilliant guerrilla. They had given him natural ascendancy over small forces of British troops, a reputation to impress Sepoys, and an aura to terrify Siraj-ud-daula. The morale of the British soldiers and sailors was high. Clive was swift to exploit the chances they brought him.

When the news reached London, King George spoke warmly of Clive. Pitt in the Commons praised him, not quite backhandedly, as a 'heaven-born general who had never learned the art of war'. Yet Beckford sneered at him in the same House as a 'dirty writer' and Plassey made only a moderate impact at home. War had been bringing more comprehensible triumphs.

IX

In 1758 Fort St Louis in Senegal was seized, with booty worth nearly a quarter of a million pounds. The naval blockade of France tightened, and in April Admiral Hawke drove a relief expedition for Louisbourg ashore after finding it in the Basque roads. Pitt's American programme for 1758 was the by now habitual one – attacks aimed at Louisbourg, Fort Duquesne and Ticonderoga. Colonial legislatures responded to his call that they should furnish, clothe and pay 20,000 troops. The results must have enhanced their confidence in their own prowess while confirming their poor opinion of British regulars. Montcalm at Ticonderoga had only 3,500 French regulars with which to resist General Abercrombie who marched north with 6,000 regulars and 10,000 colonial troops. But he threw up an entrenchment, thickly defended by a log barricade eight feet high and, outside that, an 'almost impenetrable frieze of branches placed in layers with their points sharpened . . .' Abercrombie absurdly hurled his men at the branches for four hours while the French fired from behind cover. Nearly 2,000 British troops were killed and the 42nd Highlanders, for all their hardy race, lost half their men. But a mere colonial named Bradstreet, commanding 3,000 colonial troops, dashed to Lake Ontario and destroyed Fort Frontenac, and Brigadier Forbes with 4,000 colonials and only 1,600 regulars (mostly Highlanders like himself) hewed a new route across the Alleghenies to Fort Duquesne, which was renamed Pittsburgh.

Louisbourg had faced in July the assault of 13,000 soldiers and as many sailors, carried in 180 ships. The British general, Amherst, did not display much flair, but his second-in-command, a young man named James Wolfe, displayed brilliant opportunism, taking a detachment one foggy day to set up a battery in a commanding position, whence the fort was bombarded to ruins and surrender. The news lit bonfires in London and Boston, set off fireworks in Philadelphia, and prompted the residents of Halifax, Nova Scotia, to consume 60,000 gallons of rum.

With Louisbourg bagged at last, Pitt turned his attention to the West Indies. He was an unflinching friend of the West India lobby, yet created problems for his allies by his readiness to grab French sugar islands, despite Beckford's warnings that this would produce a glut.

An assault on Martinique failed in January 1759, but the expedition went on to capture Guadeloupe in the spring. This was joy for the Yankee rum-cobblers, whose ships now poured in to purchase molasses; joy for the Liverpool slavers who over the next four years shipped 12,500 Africans into the island; and joy, not least, for the Guadeloupe planters who began clean slates with new creditors, shipped their sugar away briskly, and enjoyed a uniquely favoured status under generous British rule, which permitted them to retain their old laws, yet gave them the same freedom of trade within the Empire as any of George III's subjects. It was not good news for Beckford and his compeers. The expected glut, and lower prices, resulted. But this pleased customers in Britain, some of whom began to perceive that mercantilism had had its drawbacks, and that general free trade might be a good thing.

The seizure of the so-called 'Neutral' islands in the Windward group soon followed. St Vincent and Dominica had been left to the Caribs. (On St Vincent there were 400 'Yellow' pure-breds and 1,100 'Black Caribs' of part-African parentage.) St Lucia and Tobago were 'neutral' in the sense that neither France nor Britain had established clear title. The French had far more settlers in them, but drove less than half their trade.

In 1759, the 'year of victories', David Garrick wrote 'Heart of Oak', a kind of anthem for sailors:

> Come, cheer up my lads! 'tis to glory we steer,
> To add something more to this wonderful year.

On August 6, Londoners heard of triumph in Europe at last; the British and their allies had beaten a larger French force at Minden. But with 27,000 troops in America, 10,000 in Germany, 5,000 at Gibraltar, 4,000 in Africa, Britain was now short of soldiers for home defence. The militia was called out. Garrick's 'lads' held the wooden-shoed papists off. In August, a fleet under the ubiquitous Admiral Boscawen caught up with a French fleet from Toulon which was trying to slip through the straits of Gibraltar, destroyed several ships in Lagos Bay, and closely blockaded the rest in Cadiz. The French still planned to invade, despite this disaster, and in November, when a westerly gale had blown British ships from their close watch of the Atlantic coast, a fleet locked in. Brest tried to escape south-eastwards. Admiral Hawke, rushing back, chased it into Quiberon Bay, despite a rising hurricane, violent seas, and a lee shore horrid with rocks and shoals. Upon these, two British vessels went down, but as the inspired Hawke savaged it, the French fleet lost five ships, and 2,500 men with them. Its shreds were now trapped in ports from Dunkirk to Marseilles. The coastwise traffic of France was almost paralysed. Pitt was free to send 20,000 more troops to Germany.

Great though such news was, the best had come before it. Besides word of new contests won in India, October had brought the tale, sublime, pathetic and highly neo-classical, of James Wolfe's death as his men won at Quebec. Another three-point attack was mounted in 1759. In the west, Fort Niagara was captured. In the centre, Amherst took Ticonderoga, but was so slow that only at the end of the summer did his threat to Montreal divert troops from Quebec, the target of the main thrust, which was led by James Wolfe, only 32 years old, and specially promoted to major general.

Wolfe was a sickly, odd-looking little man with a turned up-nose, weak chin and receding forehead. The son of a soldier, he had been only 18 when, Brevet-Major at Culloden, he had admired the fierce charge of the Camerons and the resolution with which his own regiment met it. Thereafter, he had worked mainly in Scotland, where he had helped to raise Highland troops. To a friend serving in Nova Scotia, he wrote in 1751 that he thought that 'two or three independent Highland Companies' might be of use in that remote frontier province: 'they are hardy, intrepid, accustomed to a rough country, and no great mischief if they fall . . .' Three years later, to the same correspondent, he sketched ways in which fresh Highland revolt might be stifled before birth; for instance, 'Mr McPherson should have a couple of hundred men in his neighbourhood, with orders to massacre the whole clan if they shew the least symptom of rebellion.' He disliked still more, however, the Lowland Scots of Glasgow – 'they pursue trade with warmth and a necessary mercantile spirit, arising from the baseness of their other qualifications.'

Wolfe, whose father was comparatively poor, was painfully conscious of his own lack of education. ('When a man leaves his studies at fifteen', he once wrote, 'he will never be justly called a man of letters.') But he had an upstart professional disdain, almost Napoleonic in its intensity, for officers without merit except the money which had bought their commissions. His tense temperament might have been at home wielding pike and Bible in Cromwell's army. Now that God had withdrawn, Wolfe's aspiring mind found its expression in a heroic fatalism joined with a lofty and no doubt sincere patriotism. 'What a wretch is he', Wolfe had written, 'who lives for himself alone! his only aim.' England was worth human sacrifice and for all his professionalism, Wolfe believed that risks must be taken. 'In war something must be allowed to chance and fortune,' he had declared. '. . . In particular circumstances and times the loss of 1,000 men is rather an advantage to a nation than otherwise, seeing that gallant attempts raise its reputation, and make it respectable.' When Pitt gave him command, his reaction was characteristically sententious. '. . . I have this day signified to Mr Pitt that he may dispose of my slight carcase as he pleases . . .'

The common problem with combined operations had been jealousy between generals and admirals. Wolfe now showed that he could co-operate well with Admiral Saunders, a fine sailor who was respected for his modesty as well as for the fortune which he had made from prizes. While Hawke and Boscawen penned French fleets in home waters and made reinforcement of Quebec impossible, Saunders performed the astounding feat of conducting twenty-two sail of the line, together with frigates and sloops and about 200 troop transports through 300 miles of uncharted tidal waters without losing a single ship. The generally high standards of British civilian seamanship would before long be epitomised famously by James Cook, former mate of a North Sea collier, who served on the St Lawrence as master of the *Pembroke*. On June 26 the whole fleet anchored safely off the south-east of the island of Orleans, from which they could see, across two miles of water, the citadel of the Upper Town of Quebec, towering over the slate-roofed houses which ranged along the waterfront of the London Town.

No European foe until now had accosted Quebec, and Canada's honour was still not weakly defended. Montcalm had 16,000 men under him. Wolfe had brought only 8,500 soldiers. But a higher proportion of them were regulars – all but 3,500 of Montcalm's troops were militiamen and Indians whom their general (like Wolfe) considered inferior. By mid-July Montcalm's cannon would be short of powder. And the guns and sailors of the British navy meant that the French were effectively outnumbered. However, Quebec on its heights was, as Champlain had recognised long ago, one of the best natural sites for defence in the world.

All the frustrated Wolfe could do was to get his troops ashore and make camp on the south bank of the river, where he found a point from which the Lower Town could be bombarded, with cruel effectiveness. Indian ambushes constantly hit his foraging parties, and his colonial 'Nova Scotia Rangers' had learnt to retort to Indian warfare in kind. Wolfe forbade 'the inhuman practice of scalping', except, he was careful to add, 'when the enemy are Indians, or Canadians dressed like Indians.'

Meanwhile, the thrash of floggings on military backs was heard daily, though Wolfe was not harsh to his men by the standards of his time. Apart from the Rangers, whom he called 'the worst soldiers in the universe', Wolfe's troops were dressed as if for the formal set-piece battle still prevalent in the European arena in an ensemble made, as one sergeant complained, 'so tight and braced so firm that we almost stood like automata of wood . . .' The 'Brown Bess' muskets weighed 50 lb. each and they fired a maximum of about three volleys in a minute. Between each, the soldier had to pull a cartridge from his pouch, bite the top off it, shake powder into his priming pan, put ball and wadding into the barrel, press these down with a ramrod, return the ramrod to a loop on the musket, and fix the bayonet. The discipline required to keep doing such things to order under fire largely explains why battles in Europe were rule-bound, but also why Clive's regulars had made such impact.

On July 31 Wolfe ordered a full-scale attack aimed at seizing a redoubt at the top of a cliff on the extreme end of Montcalm's left flank. It proved abortive, with over 400 casualties. Wolfe lost prestige with his troops who were depressed by outbreaks of fever, scurvy and dysentery. Wolfe himself was confined to bed with a mysterious 'slow fever', and began to seek solace in cruelty. He had not served under 'Butcher' Cumberland for nothing. He offered five guineas for every Indian scalp. He ordered his men to seize the *habitants* and their herds, to lay waste farms and to burn villages. Summer was starting to ebb away. The French might be starved into surrender.

There was news that Amherst was advancing. A final bid must be made before ice froze the river. The sick commander for the first time condescended to discuss matters with his brigadiers. They rejected all Wolfe's ideas and gave him one of their own. British naval command of the river was now such that troops could strike upstream of the city and take its defences in reverse. For ten days, as the attack was prepared, a series of feints and raids kept the defenders dashing to and fro. The French thought the British aimed to land ten or twenty miles above Quebec. On September 10 a still-gloomy Wolfe, staring from the high ground across the river, saw that if the British could climb a precipitous path from a site named Anse de Foulon to the Heights of Abraham West of Quebec, they would find them weakly defended.

The first boatloads of soldiers for the assault began to move with the tide about 2 a.m. on the morning of September 13. The vanguard to scale the Heights first were eight Light Infantry men who had originally volunteered for the army, together with sixteen others whom these had chosen. Of the original eight, six were Highland Gaels, one bore the old Liddesdale reiving surname of Bell, and one the proud Irish title of Fitzgerald. Hence historians write of the valour of 'English troops' at Quebec. A reprieved Jacobite, Donald Macdonald, had picked up excellent French on the Continent. First on top, he spoke to the sentry watching the path, told him that he had been sent to relieve the post, and said that the other guards should be recalled. Most of the French soldiers here were fast asleep, and no match at all for the hardy race. The rest of Wolfe's men scrambled up the 250-foot cliff in the dark. Thousands disembarked before dawn: Light Infantry, Fraser's Highlanders, then Grenadiers.

British soldiery now found themselves on a bare plateau, like a blackboard on which to sketch perfect manoeuvres. There were nearly 5,000 of them making for Quebec when, at 6 a.m., they saw French troops approaching on their left. The British troops formed a line with the Highlanders in its centre. Perhaps 4,500 French drew up opposite. Montcalm rashly attacked before reinforcements could come up. Discipline settled the outcome. Montcalm's colonial troops confirmed his worst fears. Never drilled for formal battle, they pressed forward shouting and firing at random. Wolfe's won the battle with one fearsome unanimous volley at short range. When further British firing stopped after six or ten minutes, the French and Canadians were fleeing in rout before Highlanders hacking them down with broadswords, chasing them without mercy up to the walls of the city. Montcalm had been mortally hurt. The French had some 1,500 casualties in the short, fierce fight. Besides 600 men wounded, the British lost 58 dead, including their general.

Wolfe, wearing a brilliant and distinctive uniform, might seem to have courted that death. He had twice been hit, in waist and groin, while turning the line before the battle began. The third, fatal bullet struck just before he gave the order to advance. Many persons, present or not, were eager to relay his dying words to mankind. Most agreed that, hearing the French were in flight, he said, 'I die contented,' or something similar, and expired with a smile on his wan lips. One heretic was a surgeon, whose job perhaps gives his evidence some authority: he reported Wolfe's final bequest of speech as, 'Lay me down; I am suffocating.'

Never mind. What suited the public would be accepted. Thus it was believed that Wolfe, moving up river to Anse de Foulon, had recited, in the stern of a leading boat, the famous passage from Thomas Gray's recent poem, 'Elegy in a Country Churchyard', about paths of glory which led only to the grave; this despite the fact that the general himself had ordered the rowlocks muffled and strict silence. However, Wolfe had admired Gray and had been attempting verse himself. A sample was found in his pocket after his death:

> Brave let us fall, or honor'd if we live,
> Or let us Glory gain, or glory give –
> Such men [alone] deserve a Sovereign State,
> Envied by those who dare not Imitate.

The rather subversive suggestion that only men like himself deserved to be monarchs could be ignored in delight at this evidence of Wolfe's sense of heroic destiny. He had in fact conspired with that potent new factor in British life, the newspaper-reading middle-class public, in the creation of his own myth.

Smollett admired Wolfe's 'passion for glory' and reckoned that had he lived, 'he would, without doubt, have rivalled in reputation the most celebrated captains of antiquity.' His cult infected even a young Deist named Thomas Paine who wrote, for the social club which he attended in Lewes, Sussex, an elegy on the death of General Wolfe. Horace Walpole would remark that in the late 1750s, 'there were no religious combustibles in the temper of the times. Popery and Protestantism seemed at a stand. The modes of Christianity were exhausted, and could not furnish novelty enough to fix attention.' He did not notice that patriotism had for many usurped the place of religion, perhaps because he was so patriotic himself. Of Pitt's valedictory speech upon Wolfe in the Commons, Walpole said scornfully that all the 'parallels which he drew from Greek and Roman story did but flatten the pathetic of the topic. Mr Pitt himself had done far more for Britain than any orator for Rome. Our three last campaigns had over-run more world than they conquered in a century . . .'

Christ and the classics alike could now be demoted below 'English' heroism. Several painters shortly broke from the theory that martial 'history' themes should be given classical robes, to present Wolfe's death in contemporary dress. A young Pennsylvanian artist, Benjamin West caused a sensation in 1771 with a canvas of the death scene which portrayed various persons as present who had not in fact been there (some had paid him 100 guineas for the compliment), and also an Indian stricken with grief in the foreground, though Wolfe had loathed red warriors and had never commanded any. Despite such anomalies, people swooned with emotion at the first exhibition. West modelled his central figure on a well-known depiction of the dead Jesus by Van Dyck. Engraved for the popular market, his picture was a bestseller in Britain and abroad, and remained a public favourite for many decades.

It had little enough to do with the actual Canada, where the hardy race found much opportunity to display its distinguishing quality. After Quebec had surrendered on September 18, and the French troops had retired to Montreal, the British entered a city, wrecked with their own guns, where people were on the edge of starvation. A miserable winter set in. It was colder than many men there had ever known. Nuns made trews for the kilted Highlanders, '*pauvres gens sans culottes*'. Frostbite and scurvy did their work. Brigadier Murray, now commanding, had over 7,000 men in September; by March more than a thousand had died and only 4,800 were fit for duty. When the French army came back near the end of April, outnumbered two to one now, the British contested a dreadful morning-long battle in the slush of melting snow on the Heights of Abraham till they retreated after suffering 1,100 casualties. But officers had worked with men through the winter to strengthen Quebec's fortifications. The French were kept out.

The great question now was, which nation would get the first vessel up the unfreezing St Lawrence River. On May 9 a British relief ship appeared. Within a week, the French had been driven away, and British naval power had clinched yet another victory. In September 1760, three British armies at last realised the master plan and converged at Montreal, 17,000 strong, against 2,500 French. Canada was surrendered. Britain ruled from Hudson's Bay to the borders of Florida.

X

'The years after Plassey', Philip Mason has written regarding India, 'are in some ways among the most distasteful in English history.' He seems to underestimate Scots rapacity; the East India Company service had long drawn disproportionately from 'North Britain'.

Rumours had located £40 million in Siraj-ud-daula's treasury. It turned out that it held only £1½ million. Sums roughly equivalent to Bengal's revenues of an entire year eventually found their way into British pockets and before long were on their way out to purchase country estates in Britain. The new Nawab was forced to offer instalments from his own revenue. Several districts were handed over to direct British exploitation. Any prospect of independent Asian rule in Bengal was swiftly undermined. Yet noblemen coveting Mir Jafar's position would still be ready to offer fresh baits for British support, until the richest province in India was ruined. EIC men, now entitled to trade free of duty, abused the *dustuck* system without inhibition and further impoverished the provincial revenues, in an exultant and merciless bonanza.

When Mir Jafar was confirmed as Nawab by the Mughal Emperor he asked that Clive should be given imperial rank as a commander, and the Englishman was duly awarded the title of 'Zadat-ul-Mulk, Nasir-ud Daula Colonel Sabit Jang Bahadur.' He was no longer a foreigner, he was 'Flower of the Empire, Defender of the Country, the Brave, Firm in War.'

Room had always been found for foreign entrants into the Emperor's service. Mir Jafar and others believed that they were dealing with a military adventurer of their own kind. They would not easily have understood the thinking which he expressed, in December 1758, to Laurence Sulivan, the new Chairman of the EIC's Court of Directors, that a force of 2,000 Europeans could 'totally' subdue Bengal, and that the 'Great Mogul' would then confirm the EIC's possession if it paid the same rent as former nawabs. The EIC could only maintain its position, or improve it, by 'such a force as leaves nothing to the power of Treachery or Ingratitude'.

But the drive to direct rule which this implied would originate only in India itself; it would not be London policy. Meanwhile, Clive, in effect, proposed and disposed, arbitrating between local notables. The Seth bankers were amongst those elements, dissatisfied with Mir Jafar, which now invited the intervention of the Shahzada (cf. dauphin), the disaffected son of the Emperor, who was cruising as an adventurer, looking for a kingdom, and had picked up the support of the small band of French soldiers driven from Bengal. In February 1759, Clive took the field again in support of Mir Jafar. The Shahzada, besieging Patna, fled at his mere approach. This service won Clive another exorbitant reward. The Emperor had given him rank without the income, in rents from allotted land, which normally went with it. Mir Jafar now assigned him the quitrent due to the Nawab from the twenty-four *parganas* presented to the EIC after Plassey. The Company, gathering revenues on these lands, would now pay nine-tenths of them over to Clive, who thus stood in relation to his employers on a footing somewhere between that of a landlord and that of a feudal superior. On top of his vast capital gain, he now had an annual income of £27,000 or so.

With such prizes in view, it was hardly amazing that the Dutch, at Chinsura on the Hugli, should do their best to take over the British position. Three hundred European troops on the Dutch pay, together with 600 Malays, were despatched from Java. When this force arrived, in November 1759, it was easily crushed both on land and on water, and the Dutch were compelled to pay out about £100,000.

By April 1758 2,000 French soldiers in two regiments had arrived in the Carnatic with a new plenipotentiary, Comte Lally de Tollendal, a man of Irish Gaelic extraction. Fort St David soon fell to him. But by September 1759, when Admiral Pocock, Watson's successor, defeated a French fleet and drove the enemy out of Indian waters for the rest of the war, the initiative in the Carnatic lay with the British. Coote returned next month from England with new troops and the status of commander-in-chief. He captured a place called Wandewash and, though outnumbered, thoroughly whipped Lally's force, in January 1760, when the attempt was made to regain it. In January 1761, after months of blockade, Pondicherry surrendered. The French had no ground in India left.

Clive had come home, in 1760, to a mixed reception. The Duke of Newcastle busied himself to procure a peerage. 'Lord Clive of Plassey' was soon proclaimed, but this was only an Irish title. Real noblemen looked down on this upstart 'nabob'. He and his like would take the role of scapegoats in the phase of political seasickness in Britain which was foreshadowed by the succession, in 1760, of the young George III to the throne.

XI

Tories and independent gentry who had backed Pitt in 1757 now fell away as the Land Tax stayed up at 4s. in the £ and their erstwhile hero completely reneged on his one-time opposition to the Continental involvements. By the end of 1760 there would be 200,000 troops under British government pay, amongst them scores of thousands of Germans.

Pitt's megalomania, arrogance and theatricality had begun to exhaust his colleagues' patience. They had also alienated the young Prince of Wales, George II's grandson, and his tutor Lord Bute, a serious-minded, handsome and priggish Scot of refined taste. George III came to the throne as a raw young man, readily flooded with righteous emotion, not very clever but, for a king, oddly intellectual – a studious patron of arts and sciences. From 1765, a mysterious disease would make him act for long periods as if he were mad.

George II had been seen on three occasions unable to use the most important of the surviving royal prerogatives, his right to choose his own minister; the new King was resolved to have none of that, and to take back royal patronage from the hands of Newcastle and his like. This earnest, uncompromising man would seem to domineer over his ministers and would lend credibility to the charge that he was trying to undermine 'English liberties', to restore a Stuart-style despotism, though this would never be his intention.

At once he insisted that Bute must join the Cabinet, where Pitt was now beginning to face the nemesis of his own vainglory. With almost all France's colonies in British hands, further aggression seemed merely wanton. The Spaniards, neutral till now, were getting very angry over British high-handedness with their shipping and over that tough perennial, logwood cutting; but surely war with Spain was not desirable? The crisis came in October 1761, when Pitt wanted war with Spain and the Cabinet outvoted him. He resigned. Bute took over, the first Scot ever to have such standing at Westminster, which was not lucky for him or his compatriots.

Irony preyed upon Bute from the outset. Spain declared war anyway, early in 1762. Bute, like his royal master, was after peace; negotiations resumed a few weeks later. Yet he found himself presiding over a sudden conquest of prime targets in the Spanish empire. In October 1762 an amphibious force sent from India captured Manila in the Philippines and took a Mexican galleon with some three million dollars on board. Just before this, Havana had been seized. A third of Spain's navy was destroyed there. During the brief British occupation, Cuba's history was transformed. It had been a bucolic island of small plantations, its characteristic crop the world's best tobacco. Now British slavers rushed in 10,700 Africans in nine months. They were to grow sugar. Cuba was launched on its way towards becoming the largest and cruellest of island sugar economies.

Within eight months of Pitt's going, Newcastle had been forced into resignation after forty years of continuous office and constant care over patronage. Now whiggery shattered into a chaos of factions. This made it easy for George III to assert himself, but impossible for him, over the next few years, to find the makings of a stable government.

In November 1762, 'preliminaries' of a treaty were signed at Fontainebleau in France. Britain had such a heap of counters for exchange that the outcome must be excessively in her favour. Only in India was the status quo of 1749 restored, and there the EIC had effectively made that provision nonsensical. In Europe, France returned Minorca and various gains from Britain's German allies. In Africa, Britain handed back Gorée but kept Senegal. When news of Manila's capture came belatedly, that town was restored for a mere ransom, but in return for the restoration of Havana, the embarrassed British had had to demand Florida. The most controversial exchanges involved French America. Canada and Cape Breton Island were ceded to Britain, along with the left bank of the Mississippi. But the French were to retain fishing rights round Newfoundland, with two small islands, St Pierre and Miquelon, as bases. Britain kept Grenada, Dominica, St Vincent and Tobago, but passed back to France the prime sugar islands of Martinique and Guadeloupe, and the fine harbour of St Lucia.

The terms were so good for Britain that they made fresh war sooner or later inevitable. Yet they provoked a well-orchestrated outcry. Bute was hissed, jeered and pelted by a mob in the streets; trying to reach home in a hired sedan chair, he was noticed and its glass windows were shattered. Pitt had in effect timed his resignation well. He could not have won the sweeping peace terms for which he had led his supporters to hope. Now he could gather easy new laurels as prophet. He arrived in the House deathly pale, dressed in black velvet, his legs swathed in rolls of flannel, thick gloves on his hands. His voice was feeble, and he was permitted to sit during parts of a speech which lasted for three and a half hours. He denounced virtually every concession. In exchange for Minorca, Britain was conceding 'the East Indies, the West Indies, and Africa'. Jobs, threats and direct cash bribes of £100, £200, £300 helped win the Ministry 319 votes. Only 65 MPs, including Beckford and Clive, voted with Pitt; but people cheered him in the streets outside. A frightened and jaded Bute resigned office early next year, after the Treaty of Paris had confirmed the 'preliminaries'.

Pitt's prediction that France would become 'formidable' again was of the sort which is bound to be proved true. Any terms which made peace possible must offer a country with such resources the chance to recover. Within eight years of the peace, Bordeaux trade would be running at two and a half times its previous record figure. Recklessly shipping in slaves and developing plantations, the British had actually forwarded the development of several captured islands which they had since returned. By 1775 it could be said that of all imports to Europe from the West Indies, France received nearly half, Britain less than a third.

The 'golden age' of the French islands after 1763 was therefore a somewhat uneasy time for British West Indian interests. The surge forward of British trade in the East and in Africa, let alone the expanding markets of North America, meant that the central importance of the Caribbean was now less self-evident than before. While British grocers, distillers and refiners were calling for cheap sugar, slavers were willing to sell their cargoes wherever prices were highest, inside or outside the empire. The development of the 'ceded islands' also helped push up the cost of Africans; by 1774 a governor of the Leewards would be complaining that the price of slaves had more than doubled in thirty years. Smallholders on the new acquisitions could relish the benefits of growing most of their own food. Sugar gained ground only slowly as coffee, nutmeg and other minor staples prospered. Scots were to the fore in Grenada as it expanded to become a colony second in value only to Jamaica among the British islands, with 300,000 cocoa trees bearing by 1775.

Lands ceded by Spain and France were divided into two provinces, East and West Florida. The Spaniards pulled out almost unanimously, and eleven years after the Treaty of Paris, East Florida still had only 3,000 settlers despite the importation, assisted by government bounties, of some 1,400 Greek, Italian, and Minorcan servants. In West Florida, French settlers stayed on. Governor Johnstone called a representative assembly as early as 1766. Heads of families holding houses were to vote. Here, as in the ceded islands, the empires faced a novel problem. In Britain and Ireland Catholics suffered political disabilities. To what extent did this apply overseas? Canada would be hardest of all to sort out.

The Canadians, native priests as well as farmers, had not wasted much love on metropolitan Frenchmen. After the British conquest, almost no native thought of leaving. General Amherst was conciliatory. The clergy were permitted to free exercise of the Catholic religion, and by 1762 were, in obedience to an order from their bishop, offering prayers for the British royal family. Seventy-five thousand Canadians were now posing as grateful and loyal subjects to George III and were protected by the terms of the Treaty. A British proclamation of 1763 proposed an assembly which would have led to the introduction of English common law and the destruction of Canadian distinctiveness. But the time of its calling was left to the discretion of the governor, James Murray, a Scot full of sympathy for the hardy folk whom he found in Canada, 'perhaps', he remarked, 'the bravest and the best race upon the globe.'

He shared their contempt for the British North American merchants now wending into Quebec and Montreal – 'adventurers', he called them, 'of mean education'. Their aim was to take over the French alliance in trade with the 'Western Indians', at the expense of the Hudson's Bay Company. Murray pointed out that the proposed assembly, in which Catholics would not sit, would make some five hundred Yankees, and the like, masters of many times their own number. The 'old subjects' clamoured for self-government and for Murray's recall. In 1765 law officers in London gave it as their opinion that Canadian

Catholics were not subject to political disabilities, and four years later the Board of Trade recommended that the 'confusion' in the province should be ended by the admission of papists to an assembly.

After most French 'Acadians' had been deported in mass, some hundreds had lingered on in the forests of Nova Scotia, operating, with Indian allies, as small-time pirates and guerrilla raiders. By 1761 they had been rounded up. After they had been used to repair their famous dykes, an attempt was made to deport them in turn, but New England would not have them, and they were brought back. Nor did the French colonies want them; the French authorities said they were now British subjects. Realising at length that they had been abandoned, numerous Acadians settled in Nova Scotia as loyal subjects. There were about 1,500 rooted again within a dozen years of the Treaty of Paris. By this time, however, they were greatly outnumbered by recent English-speaking incomers.

Nova Scotia remained scantily populated. It was virtually an island, attached to the mainland only at its far north-eastern corner and reached from other settled regions by sea; since its own farmed lands were disjoined by rough wooded mountains and there were no roads for wheeled vehicles, its villages also relied on the sea for communication with each other. Governor Lawrence, in 1758, had conducted a busy publicity campaign to attract settlers. For ten years Yankees came in spate, and by 1775 they formed approaching two-thirds of the colony's population of 17,000 or 20,000. There was an orgy of land speculation, in which Benjamin Franklin involved himself. Meanwhile a mainly Scottish consortium acquired most of the island of St John, later known as Prince Edward Island – over 2,000 square miles of fertile ground.

The land boom helped to confirm Nova Scotia as a satellite of New England, with the important reservation that Halifax, isolated from the rest of the colony, was a centre for interests securely tied to Great Britain which sent thousands of pounds every year to the strategically placed little town. Though Halifax had some pretty Georgian houses, most life in Nova Scotia was rudimentary. Despite all the whaling which went on now in the Gulf of St Lawrence, women in this colony could not afford whalebone stays. But like fish oil and furs, walrus ivory and sealskin, whalebone was an esteemed addendum to the comforts of the British middle classes, and Nova Scotia's other staple industries, which were lumber and naval stores, helped to strengthen the wooden walls of the home island, the new maritime Rome.

When the great Scottish architect Robert Adam remodelled Syon House, near London, for Sir Hugh Smithson in 1762, it contained in an anteroom off the entrance hall twelve columns and twelve pilasters of verd-antique dredged up from the bed of Rome's own River Tiber. While foreigners gasped at the private wealth of such British citizens, the pleasure gardens at Vauxhall frequented by comfortably-off Londoners showed the passionate pride of the English in their own history. Besides scenes from the plays of Shakespeare, whose universal pre-eminence was now a national article of faith, paintings displayed there depicted the modern Augustans in action by land and sea. There was Vernon capturing Porto Bello 'with six ships only', Hawke's feat at Quiberon Bay in allegory, Montreal surrendering to Amherst, Britannia handing out laurels to Coote, Clive receiving 'the homage of the Nabob'.

British military success meant that middle-class intellectuals and thoughtful aristocrats on the continent of Europe were drawn towards imitation of British indifference in religion and British representative institutions. British literature was coming into fashion from Lisbon to the Urals. David Hume's writings stirred the great German philosopher Kant from his dogmatic slumbers. Now, from the hardy race, came James Macpherson's alleged translations of the Gaelic epic poet, Ossian. Jefferson, Goethe, Napoleon, would dote on these prose effusions which defied reason and 'enlightenment' in 'the compulsive telling over of defeat, darkness, despair, the eradication of clear outline and all degree, the world torn and scattered.'

For they matched something in the times. Twenty-four years of war between Britain and the Bourbon powers had coincided with an earthquake in European consciousness, or, to change metaphors, with a watershed in social and cultural history. Whatever field one prospects, one finds momentous changes, tending to tear and scatter views of the world still distantly rooted in the Middle Ages. Voltaire detected 'a civil war in every soul'. The period spawned complex novel sorts of men; conservative rebels, classicist proto-romantics, oligarchical democrats, patriot internationalists, despots adjusting their policies to 'enlightened' ideas.

George III was a mild and confused English counterpart of monarchs all over Europe now anxious to assert their authority over excessively powerful nobles. His assault on the whig élite thrust into opposition talented men, who felt that they had a right to rule. They could not, as in the reigns of two previous Georges, legitimise their opposition by flocking around a malcontent heir to the throne, who might soon succeed and hoist them back into office. They had to turn to the middle-class 'public'. They had to play with fire, to run the risk of inflaming a revolutionary conflagration.

The opposition had advantages as they set about inciting paranoia, indignation and panic. Many City of London men were on their side. Industrialists in the Midlands and North were excluded from the franchise and were commonly religious dissenters. The expanding professional and commercial classes bought the newspapers now proliferating everywhere, which found opposition views easy to sell, and spread dangerous notions among clerks and artisans now gathered in larger and larger concentrations by the expansion of London and other cities.

People in Boston and Philadelphia, and wherever prints from those places were read along the entire American seaboard, heard with dismay the howls of the whigs in England. These coincided with increasing strains within Britain's imperial commercial system. It had simply been too successful.

BOOK THREE: 1763–85

The Ruin of Liberty?

I

From the late 1750s, Methodist preachers appeared on the Isle of Man. Wesley himself went there. '. . . A more loving simple-hearted people than this I never saw. And no wonder; for they have but six papists, and no dissenters in the island. It is supposed to contain near thirty thousand people, remarkably courteous and humane.' Yet he was outraged when one of his preachers proposed to publish a hymn book in Manx Gaelic. 'On the contrary,' he wrote, 'we should do everything in our power to abolish it from the earth, and persuade every member of our Society to learn and talk English.' Such a volume was published only after his death.

Though for generations now the gentry and better-off people on Man had used English and had lived very much like their counterparts in Lancashire, the lower classes had clung to Manx. Until the second half of the eighteenth century, there were no wheeled carriages on the island and sleds were employed instead. This peasantry was as archaic as any in Europe. Only the busy smuggling industry had linked Man with the bounding economy of the new Rome across the water.

Lordship over the island had passed in the 1730s, at the death of the childless tenth Earl of Derby, to a distant relative, the Duke of Atholl. The British government was anxious to appoint customs officers for the island. The third Duke of Atholl sold his sovereignty to the Crown in 1765 for £70,000. The Union, consummated by arrogant legislation at Westminster, was most unpopular with the Manx people. The island's own oligarchical little assembly, the 'House of Keys', continued to make laws for its inhabitants, but Britain paid the costs of administration and creamed off surplus revenues for its own treasury. Man woke into the modern world to find itself being cheated. The islanders learnt fast. In 1780, 800 of them signed a petition asking for the House of Keys to be replaced by a popularly elected body. Echoes of Revolution were heard even here.

II

The non-European products generally known as 'groceries', including tea and sugar, coffee, rice, and pepper, had contributed a sixth of English imports in 1700; in 1772 they provided over a third. The East Indies, Africa and the New World were thus critical in the very rapid growth of commerce. The West India islands, which had provided in 1700 approximately a tenth of all foreign trade, now contributed between a sixth and a fifth. The New World colonies combined now sent Britain approaching half her imports, and their call for large quantities of cheap manufactures was having extremely important effects on Britain's western ports and the regions around them.

Nantes, in France, depended heavily on the 'triangular trade' with Africa and the West Indies. But its industrial hinterland was inadequate. Little except for brandy, of all that the slavers sent, was manufactured in France. Since African customers preferred English guns, and the import of these into France was banned, supplies had to be obtained via Holland.

Contrast Glasgow. Imports of tobacco into that trim and pretty town multiplied six times in thirty years to the early 1770s, and Scots came to command more than half Britain's total tobacco trade. Most of the goods they shipped out to the New World originated in Scotland, and about nine-tenths of Scottish linen exports crossed the Atlantic to the colonies. Tobacco merchants were deeply involved in linen manufacture, and promoted and dominated new industries. Visiting Glasgow in 1772, an Englishman saw them at work: '. . . A great porter brewery, which supplies some part of less-industrious *Ireland* . . . manufactures of linnens, cambricks, lawns, fustians, tapes and striped linnens; sugar houses and glass houses; great roperies; vast manufactures of shoes, boots and saddles, and all sorts of horse furniture; also vast tanneries, carried on under a company who have £60,000 capital, chiefly for the use of the colonists, whose bark is found unfit for tanning.' Five hundred men were employed in Bell's Tannery. Five tobacco merchants were partners in it. James Dunlop, scion of a great tobacco dynasty, became probably the most powerful coalmaster in the west of Scotland, investing £10,000 over sixteen years in one field alone. Here trade stimulated industry which helped trade which in turn fostered new industries.

And over 98 per cent of all the tobacco which reached the Clyde was re-exported. France was the main market. The French Farmers General, who had a monopoly in the purchase of tobacco, came to the Scots for cheapness and convenience.

Liverpool was Europe's chief slaving town. In 1771, 107 ships cleared out of Liverpool for Guinea, and drew from that coast 29,250 slaves, not far off the population of their home port. London in the same year sent only 58, Bristol (quite eclipsed now) only 23; the small town of Lancaster chipped in with four. These 190 British ships took from Africa 47,146 people. Around this time, Britain could expect to profit from over half the slaves shipped to the New World. Such dominance has rarely been won by any nation in any branch of commerce.

From the mid-1730s demand for sugar in Europe tended to run ahead of supply. Soil exhaustion limited the advantage which the older British islands could take of growing markets. The idyllic landscape of St Kitts was dominated by huge heaps of ordure, since even that very rich soil was flagging. Jamaicans, however, had plenty of virgin land for expansion, and that island, during its heyday of stench and elegance, brought the Empire, in 1774, a clear profit of over £1½ million, and provided a more attractive outlet for capital than Britain itself could easily offer. The rich who flourished were chiefly absentees. Two-thirds of the annual income and profit of Jamaica went to people residing in the British Isles, with the London West Indies merchants the prime gainers. The wealth of the West Indies was sucked to Europe, like the proceeds of the rape of Bengal. '. . . One country', Richard Sheridan argues, 'had captured a large enough segment of the Atlantic trading area to launch the Industrial Revolution.'

That revolution would involve a momentous shift in the balance of regions within Britain. For centuries London had dominated the island's economy. But compared with Liverpool and Glasgow, London was stagnant. The shipping owned in the City, by 1775, was no greater than at the start of the century; that of the 'outports' had waxed two and a half times. Seen simply by figures of tonnage clearing outwards, Whitehaven in Cumberland, a coal port which had become the main English entrepôt for tobacco, was now a rather close second to London. The turbulence of London politics after 1763 may well have had much to do with the deceleration of the city's growth and the psychological effects of loss of unchallenged supremacy. A similar reflex may help to explain equal, riotous insolence on the far side of the Atlantic, where Boston, once master of a seaboard, had likewise stagnated, and had fallen behind Philadelphia.

In an age of unsanctified prosperity based on slavery and the hard lives of the white poor, men searched with desperation for ideas which would give their lives dignity. The flatulent opulence of Augustan Rome could hardly appeal as a prototype to voteless manufacturers, breadless labourers, debt-laden planters, insecure Yankee smugglers. While some Englishmen revived the subversive levelling attitudes which had flourished in the 1640s, educated American colonists looked back to a different Rome, to that republic established by Junius Brutus who had ousted the Tarquin kings, and defended unavailingly by his descendant Marcus when he assassinated Julius Caesar. Austerity, public spirit, unflinching contempt for tyrants – the cult of such antique virtues had explosive contemporary potential.

III

In 1763, the British North American mainland colonies, excluding Canada, had at least 1,750,000 and perhaps two million inhabitants. Modern estimates suggest that white population grew by over 30 per cent in the 1760s, then by over a quarter again in the following decade, while slave imports, at nearly 6,000 a year, were unprecedentedly high. There was a new spate of voluntary immigration, perhaps 60,000 from Ireland, perhaps 25,000 from Scotland, maybe 15,000 from England and Wales, with untold legions of Germans and others making a total towards or around 150,000 between Bute's peace and 1776.

To a British customs official, Comptroller Weare, present in North America in 1760, it seemed that the colonies were expanding at a rate dangerous to Britain's interests. Settlers would be lured from Europe by the 'property and independency' which they could enjoy in America, having learnt that 'under the forms of a democratical government, all mortifying distinctions of rank' could be 'lost in a common equality'. The colonists would probably think of independence.

But they were not hard done by. They could, save in time of war, export freely to foreign markets most of the foodstuffs which they grew or reared and most of the products of their timber forests. The various Acts against colonial manufactures were scarcely enforced, and evoked little protest. By 1775 the colonies were producing more bar and pig iron than Britain itself. They were beginning to compete in pottery, stoneware, even in glassware. About three-tenths of the ships engaged in the empire's commerce were American built, while three-quarters of all the trade of the mainland colonies was carried in ships belonging to colonists.

The Navigation Acts had in fact encouraged the growth of a large colonial merchant marine – and the extent to which this was devoted to smuggling could be deduced from the fact that in 1760–1, when other colonies, with the war virtually won, expressed their pent-up demand for manufactures in greatly increased imports from Britain, legal importations into New York and New England dropped by approaching half, into Pennsylvania by five-sevenths. British sugar planters could fairly complain that North American trade with the French and Dutch colonies raised the price of provisions to themselves, and that Yankees who could get cheaper molasses from foreigners therefore insisted on cash, always in short supply, rather than produce, from fellow subjects of George III. Yet the islands could not have been fed otherwise. On balance, the system must still seem mutually advantageous. 'The American is apparelled from head to foot in our manufactures . . .', a writer in the *London Magazine* smugly observed in 1766; 'he scarcely drinks, sits, moves, labours or recreates himself, without contributing to the emolument of the mother country.' And the colonists themselves had the good fortune to be tied to a nation whose manufactures were generally declining in price and improving in quality.

They were prosperous. They were dependent. They seemed to be thriving because they were dependent. Credit from Britain provided the main operating capital of American planters and merchants; in 1760, when the value of British exports to the colonists was estimated to total over £2 million per year, British merchants carried over £4 million of American debts on their ledgers. And the late 1760s and early 1770s saw a new peak of colonial prosperity. By 1768, the balance of trade between Massachusetts and Britain was actually in the colony's favour, while the sale of provincial lands provided a fund which obviated the need for taxation.

The British themselves were at this time the most heavily taxed people in Europe, apart from the Dutch. About 1765, they paid an average of 26 shillings per head per year. An excise duty of 4s. on every hogshead of cider (1763) provoked riots in the apple-growing counties. The average tax burden in Ireland was 6s. 7d. per head. For Pennsylvania and Maryland the figure was 1s.; for New York 8d., for Virginia only 5d. South Carolina levied no taxes in 1764 or 1765, and after 1769 made do with no more than port duties. In North Carolina, such small sums as were collected were largely embezzled by the sheriffs. And so on. New World colonists under other powers were also more lightly taxed than their European fellow subjects; but, even omitting customs duties, New Spain, through various impositions, would send about £1,000,000 every year to Old Spain in the 1780s, while Brazil, more populous and far richer than Portugal, quite cheerfully, in the mid-eighteenth century, supported its mother country to the tune of about £900,000 annually.

All European powers acted according to the mercantilist view that colonies must benefit the mother country. All restricted colonial trade – Britain's rules were, in this matter as in others, the most generous. All faced, in the aftermath of the Treaty of Paris, two problems of epochal significance. The rising cost of colonial defence seemed to make it essential to tighten control of New World possessions in the interests of obtaining more revenue – this the Spanish Crown, notably, did with great short-term success. But fresh assertions of power from Europe ran up against growing, distinctive self-consciousness of 'American' or 'creole' identity on the part of important classes in the colonies. From about the 1750s, whites in Spain's vast New World territories started calling themselves '*Americanos*', and people at home began to refer to them as '*criollos*'. As the ideas of Montesquieu and Rousseau began to find hearers in Rio, Port au Prince and Caracas, 'enlightened' men all over the New World envied the freedoms enjoyed by British subjects.

Most British governors depended on salaries voted only for a year at a time. And Whitehall rarely meddled much with colonial legislation; of all the more than 8,500 laws submitted by mainland colonies to the Privy Council before 1775, only one in twenty or so was disallowed. Assemblies had usurped power to appoint various provincial office-holders. They preened themselves on having similar form and status to the Westminster Parliament, and their members showed no enthusiasm for the notion that the colonies might send representatives to that body – such MPs would have no great vote-power, would be expensive to send, and would be out of touch with their electorates. Followers of the whig tradition and students of Enlightenment thought readily argued that the laws of nature prohibited taxation by Parliament of persons not represented within it.

Some colonies, of course, were far more 'democratical' than others. If a 40s. freehold entitled a man to vote in Connecticut, the qualification was £40 in New York. But even the most conservative native Americans shared assumptions about the world which ran counter to those prevalent in the Westminster Parliament elected in 1761, where over half the members were related to baronets and peers, where bought holders of sinecures sat rejoicing in such titles as 'Clerk of the Venison Warrants' and 'Master of the Hanaper' and even able and honourable men, if not aristocratic by birth, depended on aristocratic patronage.

In most parts of Europe at this time, monarchs attacked the privileges of fortunate groups. The colonists whose blessed position George III and his ministers now sought to modify reacted, like French and Swedish noblemen, to defend what they saw as their rights, so their stand was deeply conservative and yet it was also revolutionary. What was conservative or customary in America was radical innovation for Europe.

In Britain, the theory was that all people, even those living in rising towns like Birmingham and Manchester which sent no MPs to Parliament, were 'virtually represented' at Westminster. In Burke's words, Parliament was 'a deliberative assembly of *one* nation, with *one* interest, that of the whole, where, not local purposes, not local prejudices ought to guide, but the general good . . .' But in the colonies, assembly members were generally residents of the localities which they represented and were closely responsible to their constituents. People thought in terms of government 'by' the people as well as 'for' it.

England and Wales had perhaps a hundred and twenty people to the square mile while Virginia had roughly seven. Less cramped, free to cut wood and shoot game, free to move on, men living in that colony, if they were not servants or slaves, had a practical experience of 'liberty', and of 'independence' of limiting ties and bonds. In Britain, deference, sacred social forms, beloved hypocrisies, institutional cosmetics, all masked the processes of politics. In America, Jefferson could plausibly write, 'The whole art of government consists in the art of being honest.'

The colonists themselves expressed their growing self-confidence in a cult of simplicity. To James Otis of Massachusetts, as for many others, in Britain as well as in the New World, it seemed that the Anglo-Saxon ancestors of the English had enjoyed a government 'founded upon principles of the most perfect liberty', with every freeholder entitled to vote, but that the Norman Conquest had brought 'the rage of despotism'. The liberties now possessed by Englishmen had been secured by militant struggle against medieval kings and against the 'execrable race of Stuarts'. For 'King John' and 'Charles I' read 'Tarquin' and 'Caesar', and then the drama is transferred to Rome and the agonies of its republic. It was easy for men of that day to compare George Wythe, who taught Thomas Jefferson law, to the virtuous Cato, and Richard Henry Lee, the Virginian politician, to the great Roman orator Cicero, and such comparisons tugged imaginations towards a republican ideal.

If frugal Romans and rude Anglo-Saxons had held sounder political notions than the courts of eighteenth-century Europe, the same might apply to an unlettered frontiersman. 'State a moral case to a plowman and a professor',

Jefferson would remark to his nephew. 'The former will decide it as well, and often better than the latter, because he has not been led astray by artificial rules.' Such egalitarian theorising might cross over into denunciation of colour prejudice. Philadelphia Quakers, in 1758, gave a practical lead to world opinion when their Yearly Meeting recorded its hope that Friends would free their slaves and ruled that any Friend buying or selling slaves should be excluded from the Society's business affairs.

This was in tune with the vaguely benevolent credo of the lodges of Freemasons. The world's 'mother' Grand Lodge, established in London in 1717, had presided over the very swift and significant spread of Masonry throughout Europe and its colonial settlements. It provided a freely chosen bond between individuals irrespective of class or nationality. While lodges in the English-speaking countries were highly respectable institutions, they were also secure centres for the dissemination of ideas, within and across political frontiers. Washington, Franklin and John Adams were Freemasons; so was their French admirer Lafayette. These men, and scores of thousands of others all over the world, were identified with an optimistic view of human nature, tiptoe on the brink of revolution, alert to notions of 'natural rights' which were as subversive as anything propounded beforehand by Calvinists or in our own time by Marxists.

In America visions of idealised past and ideal future could combine explosively in a chemistry which left natural conservatives heading revolt alongside demagogic or democratical hotheads. Everywhere in the colonies, leading men were likely to venerate an inheritance, the English Common Law, which had been preserved for them by the actions of seventeenth-century revolutionaries; every justice of the peace had to have some knowledge of it.

Jefferson seized, as his personal motto, upon a statement attributed to one of the men who had cut off King Charles I's head – 'Rebellion to tyrants is obedience to God.' Looking backward to the seventeenth century meant recognising the views of such radical thinkers as John Milton. But the writings of the anti-Walpolian opposition in England, which had been read and re-read in the colonies, were a wider and more immediate influence. Their prime ideas were currently being developed by a new generation of British intellectuals – such people as the Welsh savant Richard Price, the great chemist Joseph Priestley, and Major Cartwright, the parliamentary reformer. Propagandists of this school saw government itself as inherently hostile to human liberty, and as properly existing only by sufferance of the people whose needs it served. They commonly shared in the fervent faith in the magical liberty-making properties of the unique British constitution. But opposition writers stirred up the fear that, first Walpole and his 'Robinarchical' corruption, now George III with his Stuart-like lust for despotic rule, threatened liberty throughout the empire. A mercenary army raised by means of taxes wrung from the people might revive the Norman Yoke and reverse the Glorious Revolution of 1689.

Paranoia prevailed on both sides of the Atlantic. Colonists would not have credited that George III himself sincerely believed the British constitution to be 'the most beautiful combination ever framed'. Virtually no evidence exists that any American, except John Adams, thought before 1763 of breaking away, yet agents of Whitehall were reporting back that the Americans craved separation and were only waiting their chance. Some fatalists at home thought like Lord Camden: 'It is impossible that this petty island can continue in dependence that mighty continent, increasing daily in numbers and in strength. To protract the time of separation to a distant day is all that can be hoped.' But how to 'protract' it, save by strong legislation and, if necessary, sheer military force? Meanwhile, colonists were believing the wildest allegations of a 'conspiracy against liberty' in high circles in England.

Of course, British politics really were corrupt. A young Pennsylvanian, John Dickinson, in London as a law student during the election year of 1754, reported in letters home to his father, 'If a man cannot be brought to vote as he is desired, he is made dead drunk and kept in that state, never heard of by his family or friends till all is over and he can do no harm.' Other colonial visitors suffered similar shock.

Benjamin Franklin, it is true, was extremely happy to live in London from 1757 to 1762 as agent for the Pennsylvanian Assembly. His son, aged only 31, was given the governorship of New Jersey. After the pleasures of hobnobbing with the great and the flattering interest of leading intellectuals, Franklin was sorry when he had to go home. The strength of the forces making for irreversible rupture is illustrated by the fact that this Anglophile imperialist, cool and elderly, was moved by the 1770s into support for American independence. He craved high political office in Britain itself. But brilliant plebeians, clear-eyed exponents of middle-class ethics, did not belong in British politics. If the government had been prepared to lavish peerages and other honours upon outstanding colonials at this time, revolution might have been averted. But few Americans were very rich, not many were Anglicans, almost none could shove their way into the queue of aspirants.

Britons commonly saw the colonists as riff-raff, not a patch on your true beef-eating islanders. They were represented as descendants of convicts, as near-Indians tainted with savagery – apart from which many were Irish or German. Yet the colonies were fast maturing a range of institutions to match those of the mother country. Why should men of high local standing and great proficiency meekly accept insolent slights? George Washington, in 1774, broke off relations with an English firm with which he had traded for twenty years when it questioned one of his bills of exchange.

Of course, money was involved there as well as pride. A cynical twentieth-century mind perceives comfortably-off parcels of men in the colonies ridden by fear, greed, ambition and pique, who took leadership upon themselves and worked successfully on the resentments of sections of the masses to provoke an unnecessary breach with the most generous of imperial powers. But the masses were not so easily bemused. From the vantage point of late-eighteenth-century Paris or Warsaw or Amsterdam, events in the New World suggested a new war of faith to young men who found them deeply exciting. Washington, Franklin, Jefferson seemed epic heroes, noble in intellect, fortitude, daring and self-denial, leading a people permeated by the pristine Roman virtues of high moral sense and plain living. And some American leaders believed devoutly in their own virtues, which often has the effect of making men act somewhat less badly than otherwise. They gave themselves ideals worth living up to, and Europe the vision of democratic revolution.

Revolution began in the consciousness of the generation which included John Adams (born in 1735), Patrick Henry (1736), Ethan Allen (1737) and Jefferson (1743). Our knowledge that such men died old and revered should not blind us to the fact that they were, in the 1760s, young and rash. The Great Awakening had set off psychic ferment. Moulds were being broken, or seemed fit to be broken.

The rapidly growing American population was – this is too rarely mentioned – a young population. Young Otis and Henry, with their intoxicating oratory, pointed their coevals vaguely past traditional sources of political power and mystique and mobilised them in the name of 'patriotism'. This generation had grown up with the sense of manifest destiny aroused by the opening of the trans-Appalachian frontier. It could handle, and could be formed by, the periodical press, that relatively new medium which passed controversial ideas and worrying news from colony to colony, making a common response possible. There were thirty-eight newspapers publishing in the mainland provinces by 1775.

The sheer numbers of rising, able young men meant that the imperial authorities could not buy over all the natural local leaders. Thus, Richard Henry Lee, a Virginian anxious to provide for his growing family, repeatedly asked his brother Arthur, who was in England, to secure him a 'place', but Arthur had to reply that 'real merit or virtue' were not justly rewarded within the British Empire. The European middle class, in an age of population explosion, would confront a like shortage of opportunity – but American numbers exploded earlier and ran ahead faster. As they spilled over the mountains westward, the idea that a new land-based, home-made polity would make better sense than adherence to a British system which was in emphasis maritime came to seem natural to young people. 'The Almighty', a South Carolinian would announce in 1776, '. . . has made choice of the present generation to erect the American Empire.'

IV

As Colonel Murray, commanding at Quebec, had observed just after Wolfe's triumph, the flourishing existence of that town had been 'a guarantee for the good behaviour of its neighbouring colonies'. So long as the French enemy prowled to the west, self-interest, even self-preservation, tied the mainland colonies securely to Britain, which bore almost the whole cost of the necessary wars. The victory of 1760 simultaneously withdrew this motive for obedience, gave English-speaking colonials the clear chance of expansion at least as far as the Mississippi and licensed men to react with violence to measures of British ministers which were ill-judged and infirm, and were taken against a background of political turmoil in London which both excited and frightened the colonists.

Much of the rhetoric in their cause, and eventually much of the practical leadership, came from Virginia. This fact was connected with the peculiarities of the Chesapeake region. Whereas most American farmers borrowed from merchants in colonial towns (who themselves depended on credit from people in Britain) the wealthier tobacco planters were directly in debt to British creditors, and grandly so: in the mid-1770s, Virginia and Maryland, with some three-tenths of the mainland colonial population, owned nearly 60 per cent of debts due from the colonies to the mother country. From 1749, the Virginia Assembly shamelessly legislated on several occasions in favour of local debtors as against their British creditors.

By the 1760s, though the Piedmont planters were prospering, large numbers of planters in the traditional Tidewater areas faced bankruptcy. The more sensible plantocrats drove for self-sufficiency in an effort to free themselves from debt and from dependence on British goods. They switched to general farming and to wheat-growing. George Washington was one of the pioneers of advanced methods of husbandry like those used in England. His wife Martha superintended a large establishment, staffed with black labour, which manufactured woollen, linen and cotton cloth. To liberate oneself from tobacco culture was to opt in one's mind for independence.

But the American Revolution belongs to Boston, as the French belongs to Paris, the Russian to St Petersburg. Though the New England provinces were most 'English' in stock of all the colonies, it was here that dislike of the British navigation laws was oldest and most pervasive. John Adams could claim that 'the child Independence was born' in Massachusetts in 1761, with the speech of a young lawyer, James Otis, in a case arising over 'Writs of Assistance'.

A customs office in Salem had asked for such a writ to entitle him to search for goods which he had reason to think had been smuggled. 'Writs of Assistance' had been issued before that to eight customs officers in this colony, and employed without controversy. But Massachusetts had just acquired a new Chief Justice, Thomas Hutchinson, who was also lieutenant-governor. The job had been promised to James Otis's father by two former governors, but Governor Bernard chose instead to insert his own ally. Otis accordingly helped to stir up trouble over the writs. He argued in the Superior Court that Acts of Parliament could not justify them. An Act against the constitution was void, an

Act against natural equity was void. According to John Adams, who was present, Otis 'asserted that every man, merely natural, was an independent sovereign, subject to no law, but the law written on his heart, and revealed to him by his Maker, in the constitution of his nature, and the inspiration of his understanding and his conscience', and he spoke like a 'flame of fire'. The effective use of such writs was thereafter impossible in Massachusetts.

Smuggling was of prime importance to New England. When word came of a new Westminster Act which ordered absentee customs officers to their posts and baited them with an increased share – half instead of a third – of any prizes they seized, the news was said to cause 'greater alarm' in Massachusetts than Montcalm's capture of Fort William Henry had done five years before. The Sugar Act of 1733 had never been seriously enforced in peacetime. The trade in foreign molasses which it taxed was vital to New England's prime industry, rum manufacture. New England fishermen depended on exchanging their lowest-grade fish for molasses. Even 'fair traders' who frowned on the smuggling of European and East Indian goods regarded the twilight molasses trade as respectable. Now tightening up of customs brought visions of ruin.

There were vivid traditions of defiance. The very origins of Massachusetts derived from resistance to royal authority. In 1689, Boston had overthrown Andros, the tool of a would-be despot. 'The town of Boston,' Thomas Hutchinson lamented in 1767, 'is an absolute democracy and I am mistaken if some of the inhabitants don't wish for an independence upon province authority as much as they wish to see the province independent of the authority of Parliament.' The richest man in Northampton, Massachusetts, was a blacksmith. Since workmen could engage in the politics of Boston, and the General Court was dominated by the votes of mere artisans and farmers, the methods of oligarchical rule which prevailed at this time in most other parts of the Empire worked only on sufferance here. A huff and a puff, and the house must come down.

Under Governor Bernard, Thomas Hutchinson had been able to allot most of the choice administrative and legal posts to friends, relatives and political followers, while holding some half-dozen positions himself. To men like that rising young lawyer John Adams, it seemed that liberty was direly imperilled by the concentration of legislative, executive and judicial power in the hands of a small cabal. Great-great-grandson of the exiled heretic Anne, Thomas Hutchinson was to taste, at the end of a long career of public service, equally bitter hatred and rejection.

Born in 1711 into a prosperous Boston mercantile clan, Hutchinson had become the prime representative of his class, jealous on its behalf in defence of the colony's economic interests and of the sacred Massachusetts Charter. Though he sought wealth and power through politics, the shameless flaunting of Robert Walpole or Charles Price was utterly alien to his Yankee spirit. While he despised Puritan fanaticism, he remained a Congregationalist and, in British terms, a Dissenter. Persistent but never rapacious in his quest for profit, he measured himself by the highest standards of public spirit. He embodied many characteristic American traits, virtues, and astigmatisms, but tragically for himself, he could not understand, let alone share in, the heroic idealism which was now coming into fashion. The oratory of a Pitt or a Patrick Henry could not stir him to 'patriotic' fervour. The Great Awakening had, so to speak, found him asleep, and had left him so. He was not and could not be a man of the people. As his family scooped most of the jam and left none for Otis's or Adams's bread, the 'outs' turned to the people to give them their revenge.

Bernard, an inexperienced and undistinguished figure, proved to be no match in political skills for the extremely artful 'patriot' leaders. James Otis was the outstanding demagogue. John Hancock was 'Milch Cow to the Faction', a fashionable, conceited, not very clever young man whose smuggler uncle in 1764 bequeathed him most of his £70,000 fortune. But the most dangerous opposition leader was without doubt Sam Adams, John's older cousin.

A shabbily dressed man who took a pride in his poverty (though it did not prevent him from owning a black slave girl), Sam Adams seemed an old-fashioned Puritan by the standards of his Boston – a scrupulous observer of the Lord's Day whose household was famed for its strictness in religious matters. He was 40 years old in 1762. The son of a prosperous Boston brewer and merchant, he did not partake of his parent's business sense. After he had wasted his inheritance, he had little more than the meagre income brought in by a job as a tax collector in Boston. In politics, however, he was an apt pupil of his father, who had been leader of the popular party in the General Court. Like him, he was a member of the 'Boston Caucus', a club of small shopkeepers, mechanics and shipyard workers which met in the Green Dragon Tavern and controlled appointments to all Boston offices by manipulating the town meeting.

Puritan though, in some senses, he might be, he kept abreast of the times. In his writings, he equated the spirit of old Congregationalist Massachusetts with the republican ethos of Ancient Rome, and he did not object to leaguing with Otis's fellow Freemasons. While his piety gave Adams influence among church people, the 'mob' was his most efficacious instrument. He was popular in the taverns, admired by wharfingers and weavers, bricklayers, shipwrights and tanners. The gulf in income between Boston workers and the likes of Hutchinson was steadily widening, and they responded to Otis's denunciations of wealthy merchants grinding the faces of the poor, eating the bread of oppression without fear and waxing fat upon the spoils of the people.

There was no police force in Britain or America. To create one would have seemed a monstrous threat to 'liberty'. A 'mob' could rule a town for days. The use of troops against it would inflame feeling further ('standing army' . . . 'Turkish despotism'). So when a government decided to employ armed force against English-speakers, it was bound to put itself in the wrong, and was likely to be defeated. The government made the fatal mistake of supposing that it could bully Bostonians though it could not crush John Wilkes.

V

Wilkes had an Irish forerunner, Dr Charles Lucas, an energetic tribune sprung from the Dublin middle classes, who began in 1747 to publish a weekly *Citizen's Journal*. The American colonists paid much attention to Lucas. He revived Molyneux's argument that Ireland was a distinct kingdom whose parliament could acknowledge no superior, he denounced British restrictions on Irish trade, and inveighed against corruption in elections. In 1749 an angry viceroy secured from the Irish House of Commons a series of resolutions declaring Lucas a public enemy and ordering his immediate arrest. The public-spirited (but anti-papist) apothecary was forced into exile for some years.

However, another factor arose towards mid-century to complicate the lives of the Irish ruling class. The Irish treasury, thanks to rising trade, was showing a surplus. The question arose, whose was it? In 1753 the Dublin Commons rejected a money Bill which, sent to England for approval as Poynings' Law required, had been adorned by the Privy Council there with a clause acknowledging the necessity for royal consent to disposal of the surplus. Dublin whoopeed. 'The ladies made balls, the mobs bonfires . . .' The viceroy prorogued Parliament. Speaker Boyle and other defiant office-holders were purged. But government could not go on without their support. Irish politicians discovered how profitable opposition could be as a new viceroy doled out peerages to win back the defectors. Boyle was restored to office and became Earl of Shannon.

'Patriotism' was coming into vogue. Irish MPs outside the golden circle of patronage could draw attention to themselves by talk of national independence. The entire reign of George II had seen only one parliament. His death compelled the first election for thirty-three years. Associations of voters aired popular issues. But the electoral system offered no scope for transformation. Out of a population of some two million, less than a quarter were Protestants, and of these only the 300,000 or so episcopalians were free to take any part in government, though Presbyterians were not wholly impotent, and Catholic landowners could sometimes influence elections by telling Protestant tenants how to vote. However, most of the 109 boroughs, which, with two members each, returned a majority of the 300 MPs, were 'rotten', wholly under their patrons' control; a man wishing to be an MP might have to pay around £2,000 for a borough seat, about the same price as in England. Henry Flood, heir to great estates in Kilkenny, could well afford it. Allied with Lucas, now back from exile, he emerged as the 'patriot' leader in the new parliament.

'Patriots' called for the limitation of the life of parliaments to seven years each, for a habeas corpus Act, and for security of tenure for judges. Men like Lucas or Flood seemed to represent the tide of the age which we can now see was revolutionary – the growth of the middle classes and of the newspaper press with them; their call for wider and truer representation in government. But much of the Irish middle class was Catholic. The aim of well-to-do Catholics now was to prove their loyalty. When, in 1760, a French commander, Thurot, had raided Belfast Lough and briefly captured Carrickfergus, local Catholics had given no sign of sympathy; and when war had broken out with Spain, their bishops had ordered Irish papists to pray for a British victory. The Catholic middle class sought peaceful redress of its grievances, and its spokesmen minimised the claims of the Pope and protested (too much?) their fidelity to the Hanoverian Succession. Their restraint, together with some abatement of Protestant intolerance, meant that religious issues had withdrawn from the forefront of Irish thinking and it was possible for Flood and his allies to focus attention on political questions. Yet ultimately, the orators knew that the very survival of their class depended on the link with Britain. Flood brought dignity to the 'Patriot' cause with his declamation. He had studied with care and effect the orators of ancient Greece and Rome. But he and his fellow 'Patriots' would in the end flinch from the realisation of their rhetoric.

In a sense, Edmund Burke was more 'revolutionary'. The most distinguished Irishman of his day, Burke was emotional to the point of imbalance, 'foaming like Niagra' in the Commons, a prophet of the Romantic era, perhaps the most sincere politician at Westminster, certainly one of the most violent in his language, 'the most eloquent madman I ever knew', according to the great historian, Gibbon. It is amusing that such a man should be hailed as the founder of modern conservatism.

Burke was the son of a Dublin lawyer. His mother was a Roman Catholic. His sisters were brought up as Catholics. In his student days at Trinity College, Dublin, he was a patriotic enthusiast for Irish art, Irish literature, Irish manufactures, much moved by Irish poverty and its injustice. He himself married a Catholic, and throughout his political life his opponents smeared him as a crypto-papist. Yet he became a devoted British imperialist. He went to England aged 21, in 1750, and made his career in that country as writer and politician. By his early thirties, he was beginning to think of himself as English. He entered the Commons in 1765.

With the whig front now in splinters, Burke hitched his career to the faction grouped round the second Marquis of Rockingham, which found it useful to have an orator who could whip himself into strong and noble-sounding feeling even over a case, such as the tax on absentee owners of Irish lands which was proposed in 1773, where his leader's personal interests were sordidly involved. Rockingham, who made Burke his private secretary, was a pre-eminent specimen of the whig aristocracy, pushed into political life neither by fervour nor by aptitude but by 'a sense of what he owed to his position . . .' The British 'outs' shamelessly made capital out of anything which could trouble George III and the men he favoured with office, and their lurid accusations deeply alarmed far-away colonials. King and Parliament hastened ideological crisis forward by the mistake of persecuting John Wilkes.

This squinting satyr, hardly sincere, but a publicist of genius, was the son of a well-to-do Dissenting distiller. He bought the Commons seat of Aylesbury, in 1757, for some £7,000, but lost his hopes of office under the Crown when Pitt left the government four years later. He became co-editor, with the poet Charles Churchill, of an anti-Bute journal, the *North Briton*. The cheap jibe against the Scots made by its title was characteristic of its tone. In April 1763, its 45th and last number appeared, with a hard, sly attack on the King's Speech to Parliament regarding the peace with France. It insinuated that George III was a liar.

The government retorted by issuing a 'general warrant' for the arrest of the author, printers and publishers of the *North Briton*. The charge was 'seditious libel'. Wilkes was sent to the Tower. Opposition leaders flocked to visit him there. Lord Chief Justice Pratt discharged him on the specialised grounds that as an MP his person was 'sacred'. Wilkes played to the gallery, with his speech in court. 'My Lords, the liberty of all peers and gentlemen, and what touches me more sensibly, that of all the middling and inferior set of people, who stand most in need of protection, is in my case this day to be finally decided upon a question of such importance as to determine at once whether English Liberty shall be a reality or a shadow.' As thousands of supporters escorted him home, the slogan 'Wilkes and Liberty' was born.

'General warrants' were soon found to be illegal. But the beaten government struck back. In November 1763 the House of Commons carried, by 273 votes to 111, a motion that No. 45 of the *North Briton* was likely to excite people to treachery. Liable to fresh prosecution, Wilkes slipped across to the Continent and exile, and the House expelled him in his absence.

Wilkes's bravado captivated a very mixed support – among the 20,000 or so 'liverymen' and 'freemen' who dominated the politics of the City of London, among the swelling middle class of professionals, merchants and prosperous craftsmen who lived in the spreading suburbs; and also among the capital's masses of journeymen, apprentices and 'servants', skilled or semi-skilled, drunken or sober – watchmakers, tailors and hatters.

When he returned from exile, Wilkes would show that, although he was no orator, had no political programme, had no original ideas, and had perhaps no principles stronger than self-esteem and a delight in mischief, he could rally besides Londoners, worried country gentry, angry cider producers, rural freeholders threatened by enclosures, merchants in the provincial ports, all manner of 'outs'. Such a vast, diverse constituency could not have been united by any slogan less vague than 'liberty'. Another great binding force was xenophobia. The English reacted to their domestic problems by pouring contempt on alien scapegoats. In 1736, London had seen riots against Irish labourers. Some years later, Jews had been the target. Now the Scots were the great bugbear.

A Scot was identified, presumably, by his accent. There were various Scottish accents; their differences seem to have gone unmarked. Gallovidians and Aberdonians, Gaels and Sassenachs, were all identified as Jacobites at heart. In fact, thanks to English prejudice, some Lowland and whig Scots did forget their hatred of Gaels and Stuarts and acquired fellow feeling for bare-legged Jacobite clansmen. Young James Boswell went to Covent Garden to hear a new opera one night late in 1762 when Bute was Prime Minister and his unpopular peace was being made. Just before the overture, two Highland officers came in: 'The mob in the upper gallery roared out, "No Scots! No Scots! Out with them!", hissed and pelted them with apples. My heart warmed to my countrymen, my Scotch blood boiled with indignation . . . I hated the English; I wished from my soul that the Union was broke and that we might give them another battle of Bannockburn.'

Whig peers were as prejudiced as the 'vulgar'. Lord Shelburne thought that most Scots 'had no regard to truth whatever'. Lord Holland claimed that the Scots inflamed resentment by their own 'excessive' national feeling. Wilkes and Churchill in the *North Briton* crystallised a myth that was to exercise great influence on events over fifteen or twenty years. In the wake of their leader Bute, it was alleged, Scotchmen had swarmed down from their barren homeland, where 'half starved spiders prey'd on half-starved flies', to rob the English of their fruits of their toil, of their trade, of their fat harvests.

The use of Scots soldiers against Wilkesite rioters would produce gleeful furies of indignation. The myth was confirmed! Although Bute had ostensibly resigned from office, he was held to be still behind the throne, exercising what Pitt called 'the secret influence of an invisible power'.

If noble English statesmen believed such nonsense, American colonists can perhaps be excused for their devout faith in the myth. They could see ravenous Scots flocking into their own country. Pitt's army had eventually included a dozen or more 'hardy' Highland regiments. Scots traders following in its wake came to dominate the trade of the conquered area round the Great Lakes. Elsewhere, Virginians nurtured fear, not baseless, that this clannish brood would take over their whole colony. 'A North Briton', William Lee wrote, 'is something like the stinking and troublesome weed we call in Virginia wild onion. Whenever one is permitted to fix the number soon increases so fast, that it is extremely difficult to eradicate them, and they can poison the ground so, that no wholesome plant can thrive.'

VI

From Bute's resignation till mid-1765, George's chosen Prime Minister was George Grenville – aristocratic and unimaginative. He was by prevailing standards hard-working, but the Wilkes affair took up a lot of his time. In any case, his options regarding America were narrow, and a bolder, more independent mind might have hit upon similar measures. Prominent colleagues favoured stronger control of the Empire, but no new credo, no drastic shift in ideas was involved in their attitudes. The government's thinking was in the mercantilist tradition. It had to act, in the early 1760s, because of the pressure of the times.

The Empire was now too large, its problems too diverse and pressing, for Newcastle's style of 'salutory neglect' to be feasible. Its lands, and the interests involved in them, must be defended. But the costs of defence were rising almost intolerably. The British landed classes bewailed their burden of taxes, and loathed as always the very idea of a standing army in peacetime. All considerations pointed one way. An army stationed largely in North America, and paid for by the colonists there, could not only protect the mainland provinces, but could 'stand', well away from Britain itself, at the ready for future wars. The wish to increase central control of what one future proconsul, George Macartney, called in 1773 'this vast empire on which the sun never sets, and whose bounds nature has not yet ascertained', matched all too neatly the growing desire that colonists should pay for the soldiers who guarded them.

The need for extra defences was made plainer by the so-called 'Pontiac Rising' which began in May 1763 and bloodied the frontiers of the Middle Colonies for nearly a year, killing over 2,000 settlers. The destruction of French power had weakened the position of every Indian tribe. Amherst, the commander-in-chief, loathed red men, and toyed with the notion of genocide, even of spreading smallpox among disaffected tribes. He withheld from allies even the customary presents of shot and gunpowder. The revolt threatened Virginia, Maryland and Pennsylvania. As in the case of a Cherokee rising further south, which had been put down in 1761, British regulars proved essential. The provincial legislatures were as reluctant as ever to help. Virginia refused to vote troops for any offensive war. New York, asked for 1,400 troops, provided only 300. Even the frontiersmen themselves held out for bounties on Indian scalps, and would serve only as packhorse and wagon drivers.

Meanwhile, plans for the government of the conquered territories were being completed. Colonists would see some ominous precedents. In Quebec, Governor Murray did not hide his prejudice against 'old subjects' who came in from the British mainland colonies. Papist Canadians were allowed to serve on juries. Murray refused to call an assembly.

The largest problem was that of the western wilderness. The lands between the seaboard colonies and the Mississippi were roamed, or cultivated in pockets, by perhaps 70,000 red men, of whom about 20,000 – Shawnee and Delaware, Wyandot and Miami, Potawatomi, Kickapoo and Cherokee – had claims on the huge area later known as the 'Old North-West' where there were about three red people to thirty-six square miles. Between Louisiana and Canada there were only about 2,000 European people in widely scattered settlements, with a few hundred traders in season around the forts and posts.

Old colonies, under their charters, made competing claims to enormous territories. The colonial love of speculation in land rose to the level of mania after Bute's peace, and British army officers joined in the scramble. A barrage of schemes fell on Whitehall, and ministers there were themselves infected. British manufacturers must welcome the prospect of fresh captive settler markets in the areas later designated Tennessee, Kentucky, Ohio, Indiana, Michigan, Wisconsin and Illinois. But what about the valuable fur trade, ultimately controlled by great merchants in London? This thriving commerce was already in being, whereas new colonies would involve massive outlay by the British treasury, and a succession of costly wars with the Indians.

In its perplexity, the government settled for what seemed the cheapest short-term recourses. British interests currently required that movement of settlers out of the old colonies should flow into Nova Scotia, Quebec and the Floridas, where there was plenty of land to be taken up, papist inhabitants must be outnumbered, and strength would be needed if war began again. The drive over the Appalachians must be slowed to a pace at which it might be possible to sustain peace with the Indians, with firm agreement arrived at over the transfer of each parcel of land.

Hence the 'Proclamation' of 1763. No purchases of kind beyond the Appalachian watershed would be authorised for the time being. The west was to be ruled by the commander-in-chief of the British army. The 'Proclamation' was both ineffectual and resented. Free lands were offered to British soldiers disbanding in North America, and while more than a dozen regiments of colonial and Highland troops were accommodated in Nova Scotia, others were actually moved by the government into the vast new Indian 'reservation'. Yet Virginian speculators in 'Ohio' and 'Loyal' companies met frustration by government veto; not an acre of land was now legally theirs, despite grants approved almost a generation before. Yet the progress of settlement was not really impeded. Anyone willing to risk Indian anger could go ahead. Speculation went on undeterred.

New Hampshire and the area known as Vermont were opened up by squatters and land jobbers, amongst whom Ethan Allen and his three brothers took the lead. Elsewhere, 'long hunters' and traders who found tracks across the 'Proclamation Line', broke down Indian resistance in advance of the frontier. The southern superintendent of the frontier, John Stuart, strove honourably for justice for the Indians but governors and legislatures repudiated or sabotaged his dealings, and Georgia, for instance, contrived to cheat the Creeks and Cherokees of more than two million acres of land.

Stuart's northern counterpart was Sir William Johnson, Irish born, who held a great tract in the Mohawk Valley, and lived in high feudal style there in a stockaded mansion, Johnson Hall. He openly cohabited with the sister of a christianised Mohawk chief, often wore Iroquois dress, and entertained Indians in his house. Johnson never had patience with the 'Proclamation Line'. He controlled the Six Nations of Iroquois and through them, it was reckoned, the

Shawnee and Delaware. Departing from his instructions, he used his power to negotiate a new settlement line, running down the Ohio River to the mouth of the Tennessee, and this was formalised, with Whitehall approval, at the Treaty of Fort Stanwix in 1768, whereby the Iroquois ceded a territory thence known as 'Indiana'. Stuart was then prodded into adjusting the southern 'line' accordingly. The sole inspiration of this change of policy was the pressure from speculators, who sensibly enlisted prominent collaborators in Britain. Ministers, civil servants, MPs, peers, bankers and merchants joined them in the so-called 'Walpole Association' of 1769, which also included Benjamin Franklin, now resident in London again, and extremely active in speculative schemes.

The government now found itself maintaining some twenty-nine remote, exposed and expensive military posts, sixteen of which were directly guarding the frontiers of the old mainland colonies. But what was the point of spreading such a large proportion of the 8,000 British troops now in America out over difficult country in puny parcels?

Edmund Burke would sum up one colonial suspicion; in 1763, so he later alleged, 'the necessity was established of keeping up no less than twenty new regiments, with twenty colonels capable of seats in this house.' Added to the new offices now created in Quebec and the Floridas, it seemed that the colonies were to be loaded with lucrative sinecures for absentees. But the troops were real enough, and some believed that, as one Connecticut man wrote, they were not there to defend the colonists 'but rather designd as a rod and Check over us'.

And Grenville was clear that the colonists must pay for them. The British were about to 'groan' under the hated Cider Tax. Surely their luckier fellow subjects could not fairly object to paying a little?

So two lines were energetically followed. One was administrative. The existing Acts of Trade were to be strictly enforced, as wartime regulations had been. The second line required fresh legislation. For the first time, an Act of Trade was to be introduced with the avowed object of 'applying the produce of such duties . . . towards defraying the expenses of defending, protecting, and securing the said colonies and plantations.' This was the so-called 'Sugar Act' of 1764. While the duty on foreign refined sugar stayed prohibitive, and the entry of foreign rum was simply forbidden, the duty on foreign molasses imported into North America was lowered from 6*d*. to 3*d*. per gallon. This in itself might seem generous; but there were also administrative provisions for the enforcement of this Act and earlier ones. The rum men proclaimed that they would be ruined because, though the duty on molasses was halved, the intention was clearly now to collect every 3*d*. A squadron of warships arrived in American waters. Coastal traffic between the colonies was seriously impeded by zealous naval officers questing for prizes. Merchants required clearance papers merely to cross open sea more than seven miles from the shore in passing between two ports within the same colony.

Men in the seaboard towns were so angry with Grenville that stirrings of a boycott began, with a movement to encourage colonial manufactures. Everything which this government did from now on would be suspect. An Act of 1765 which imposed on colonists, as under English common law, certain obligations to provide troops with accommodation and supplies, ran into furious opposition in New York, where the legislature refused for two years to acknowledge it until extreme pressure was applied by Parliament.

Uncomprehendingly, Grenville went ahead with a new Bill far more obnoxious than the 'Sugar Act'. It commonly took two or three months for a letter to cross the Atlantic. The effects of one decision might not be known before another had to be taken. The Stamp Act was fathered by irreproachable logic out of arrogant ignorance.

VII

Grenville decided that, for the first time, Parliament should directly tax the colonies. He did not act in completely cavalier fashion. He took the trouble to persuade the colonies' London agents of the rightness of his logic and they accepted it, though seven colonial assemblies, hearing of his proposals, petitioned against them.

The Stamp Act taxed many sort of bits and pieces of paper – among them legal documents, pamphlets and newspapers. It meant that a colonist could not acquire land, send a ship out of port, buy playing cards, or sell liquor without purchasing stamped paper. Though British merchants would probably pay out £1 for every £3 disbursed by colonists, the revenue of about £60,000 a year which the measure was expected to yield would be employed solely in America.

Benjamin Franklin, now back in London again as agent for Pennsylvania, sent home a letter full of folksy wisdom urging his fellow countrymen to accept the Act philosophically. 'Idleness and pride tax with a heavier hand than kings and parliaments; if we can get rid of the former, we may easily bear the latter.' He nominated one friend as distributor of stamped paper in Pennsylvania, and advised another to take the post in Connecticut. Meanwhile, Richard Henry Lee, for all his 'patriotic' proclivities, sought unsuccessfully for the Virginian post. He was lucky not to get it.

The sudden explosion of feeling in almost all the mainland seaboard colonies expressed every pent-up fear and resentment of the last five years. Even the Act's moderation intensified suspicion. The smaller the taxes, the worse, argued John Dickinson; they would the more readily be accepted by gullible colonists, and precedents would be set.

The Act bore directly on every leading group. Merchants and gamblers, planters and land speculators, the lawyers and printers who led public opinion, all would be constantly paying out for stamped paper. But money was not the real issue. The Stamp Act was seen as the start of a long process by which the British Parliament, now corrupted by evil men, would shift more and more of the burden of empire from Britain to colonists unrepresented in Parliament, and use illegal taxation in America to pay for judges, admiralty courts, customs collectors, army officers, who between them would destroy liberty. In this revolution of consciousness, all restrictions came to seem irksome and ominous. Opinion swept one way through all the colonies. The somewhat ignoble 'groans' of Virginian debtors and New England smugglers over recent laws were magically dignified by a touch from the threatened goddess, Liberty.

The celestial consort of Liberty was Rhetoric. One patriot urged Rhode Islanders to awaken 'all that is Roman in Providence'. Now Patrick Henry's oratory helped tighten the novel unity of American leaders.

Henry had learnt much from the revivalist preaching of the 'Great Awakening'. His slouching, indolent frame would be transformed as his message seemed to grip him. Ambitious for power in Virginia, he rejected the usual method of fawning upon the successful and chose instead to put himself at the head of popular feeling over the Stamp Act, allied with the disappointed Richard Henry Lee. In May 1765, when only a third of the members of the Virginia House of Burgesses were present, Henry proposed a string of resolutions denouncing the British government. To Thomas Jefferson, still a law student, who stood at the door of the House's lobby to hear the debate, Henry seemed 'to speak as Homer wrote'. Five resolutions were passed by narrow majorities (for example, 22 to 17, 20 to 19). Two days later, the Burgesses withdrew their support for the fifth one and refused to accept two additional motions, one of which argued that colonists need obey no British laws, 'designed to impose any Taxation upon them'. A thin House, bombast rejected – nothing of moment had happened. And yet it had. Because the conservative editor of the *Virginia Gazette* refused to print even the four milder resolutions which had been passed, no correct report was published. Newspapers in other colonies, however, printed every resolution as if the House of Burgesses had accepted them all. Lower Houses in eight other provinces followed Virginia's apparent 'lead', sometimes using the same language. Governor Bernard of Massachusetts, who had been optimistic that 'murmurs' over the Stamp Act would die away, regarded the publication of Henry's resolutions as an 'Alarm Bell'.

Who heard it? Even before the news from Virginia, the Massachusetts House of Representatives had proposed a congress to represent the elected assemblies of the continental colonies. There were sixteen of these, and also nearly that number in the islands – Bermuda, the Bahamas and the Antilles. Out of some thirty separate colonies in the new World, only eight were represented when the 'Stamp Act Congress' assembled at New York in October 1765. Grenville's stricter line with the colonies prompted furious resistance here. After the Board of Trade had disallowed one of its Acts, which tampered with the Acts of Trade, the Jamaica Assembly passed a resolution that they would not bow to 'their Lordships' at home, nor would 'ever at any time suffer them in any Respect to

direct or influence their Proceedings by any Proposition or Decision whatever.'
Otis or Henry could not have gone further. The home government wisely
refrained from comment, but in 1764 Governor Lyttelton could not duck a
conflict with the Assembly over the issue of 'parliamentary' privilege. One of the
members had a coach and horses seized for debt. John Wilkes had been heard of.
The House ordered the plaintiff into gaol, along with the officer who had made
the seizure. Then its members decided, in face of royal disapproval, that their
privileges did not flow from the grace of the King, but were rights inherent in
all assemblies. Lyttelton dissolved no fewer than three assemblies in less than a
year. But this meant he could not get money voted, and could only pay his
soldiers by drawing, with Whitehall consent, on extraordinary funds. Charles
Price and his gang were too many for him, and he shortly retreated from his
post. The home government now conceded that an assemblyman's goods and
chattels, like his person, were free from arrest. Joyful illuminations and
decorations signalled the climb down when word of it reached the island. But
there was another ruling that the Assembly must refund to the British
government the extraordinary money drawn by Lyttelton. This the heroic
planters refused to do. They won complete victory. The matter was dropped.

There was no organised protest on Jamaica against the Stamp Tax, because
there was no assembly sitting. But there were riots against the Act in the
Leewards. Why did the blusterous Caribbean planters henceforward play
almost no part in the colonial struggle against Westminster?

The power of Price, as we have seen, depended on political connections in
Britain. The West Indians were still, in sentiment, wholly 'British'. Success
would carry them back to a plump estate in the home island. Meanwhile, their
need for Britain was overwhelming. Economically, they depended on the
captive British consumers. In a free market, St Domingue competition would
crush them. Local manufactures, besides, were far more exiguous than on the
mainland. These were islands – the British navy could swiftly make them starve.
And they needed the wilting garrisons of the British army. Jamaica in 1760 had
seen its most dangerous insurrection yet. 'Tacky', with a hundred slave
followers, massacred settlers in St Mary's Parish, and inspired revolt in several
other places. About sixty whites (besides hundreds of blacks) were killed. 1766
saw smaller, but still bloody, risings. The postures and declamations of Price
and his gang were flimsier even than those of Flood's Irish 'patriots'.

Nova Scotia is a more puzzling instance. Nearly two-thirds of its settlers had
originally come from New England. But pockets of settlement were dispersed.
The largest, Halifax, was very directly dependent on Britain. Georgia was a
partly similar case, since Parliament still gave it generous grants. It proved to be
the only continental colony south of Maine (and bar the Floridas) where
stamped paper could for a while be distributed. Elsewhere, active resistance had
begun before the paper arrived. Non-payment of debts was effective: as early as
August, a Bristol merchant reported that he and his fellows were at their 'Witts

End for Want of Money . . .' But more violent action began the business of revolution, separating the cautious from the extreme.

Dawn on August 14 1765 in Boston disclosed an effigy of Andrew Oliver, brother-in-law of Thomas Hutchinson, and newly appointed Stamp Distributor, hanged from a tree in the High Street. Later that day a 'mob' attacked and levelled a new building which was reputed to be the intended Stamp Office, beheaded the effigy outside Oliver's house (like Charles I) and finally burnt it on a bonfire (like Guy Fawkes). Then it returned to Oliver's house and broke in. Warned that his life would be in 'Continual Danger' unless he resigned, Oliver quit his Distributor's post.

On the 26th, 'mobs' were out again. One invaded the home of the register of the Vice-Admiralty Court and burnt all the records. Another wrecked the home of the Comptroller of Customs and drank his wine. With the Acts of Trade thus symbolically eschewed, the two groups combined in a fearsome gesture. As Thomas Hutchinson supped there with his family, his town mansion was attacked. He had opposed the Stamp Act. But he had urged caution upon his fellow colonists. He was rich. Now Hutchinson's cash, plate and clothes were stolen, his furniture was splintered, his cellar drunk dry, all his books and papers strewn in the mud, his garden ravaged. Only annihilation could bring satisfaction. The inner walls of the house were smashed. Men worked for three hours to bring down a cupola, and tried to destroy even the outer walls.

Other cautious men, in every colony, were appalled to hear of such an attack on property. The time for choice had arrived. One must decide to resist, at great risk, or to keep quiet, or to side with the passions which had found vent. In Boston, not one rioter could be punished, and even leading merchants and 'men of property' rallied to prevent action against the shoemaker, Ebenezer Mackintosh, who had led the attack on Hutchinson's house. The methods of the Boston 'Sons of Liberty' were copied in other colonies, and every Distributor was soon forced to resign, like Oliver, or to flee.

Yet the tone of the 'Stamp Act Congress' which met in October was relatively moderate. Virginia could send no representatives because Governor Fauquier had refused to convene the Burgesses and so had prevented their accepting the invitation. New Hampshire, North Carolina and Georgia also sent no spokesmen. John Dickinson of Pennsylvania was the chief penman at work in the production of a declaration of 'rights and grievances'. Agreement was easily reached on the main colonial argument, which could be expressed in a slogan: 'NO TAXATION WITHOUT REPRESENTATION'. None the less, the petition sent to Britain was respectful, admitting the colonies' 'due subordination' to Parliament, though it denied that body's right to tax them, and announcing that Americans still 'gloried' in being subjects of 'the best of Kings'.

November 1, when the Act came into force, was generally observed as a day of mourning. The Boston 'Sons of Liberty' hanged Grenville in effigy. In Georgia, where the Distributor arrived only in January 1766, he was able to sell some stamped paper, but soon quit his post for 'parts unknown'. Elsewhere, no such paper was bought at all. Journals bravely appeared without it. Customs officials soon were perforce authorised to permit cargoes to clear the ports without it. Many colonial courts proceeded without it. Gamblers made do with old packs of cards. People married without stamped licences. Life was not too abnormal, except for British merchants, who did not get paid, and royal officials, who were quite helpless.

Grenville had quarrelled with George III and had left office before the effects of his Act were seen. Rockingham had succeeded him. His Ministry had no clear American policy of its own, but at least could abandon Grenville's line without loss of face. The clamour from British merchants made this almost imperative. Orders worth over £700,000 had been countermanded. Debts of £4 million could not be collected. Americans soon heard that the Stamp Act was dead. They had killed it. And the methods, including the violent ones, which they had used, now seemed amply justified by success. The Massachusetts elections of 1766 purged the legislature of cautious elements. The House of Representatives elected Otis as Speaker, Sam Adams as Clerk, and picked a new Council from which supporters of Governor Bernard were excluded.

Members of Parliament were not accustomed to thinking hard about America. But they sensed that the troubles there were somehow related to their own problems with Wilkes and to the foolish behaviour of certain politicians and rustics in Ireland. Methodism and worse were at some dire work. 'Liberty'? For colonial wharfingers? Stands must be taken.

With members feeling this way, a reassertion of parliamentary supremacy must be the price of pushing through repeal of the Stamp Act. A 'Declaratory Act' had been passed in 1719 regarding Ireland, though Parliament had not in fact used since then its clearly proclaimed right to tax that country. The Rockinghams' Declaratory Bill went through the Commons without a division. But it did not explicitly mention the power to tax, and could be misread as excluding it.

This ingenious ministry also revised the laws of trade. The Sugar Act's 3*d*. duty on foreign molasses was replaced with a flat rate of 1*d*. on all molasses. Though the colonists did not object this time, the fact was that the removal of imperial preference made the duty clearly a revenue measure and nothing more; taxation, in fact, without representation. However, the specious Benjamin Franklin, giving evidence to the House of Commons, had spread the wholly erroneous notion that the colonists saw as fundamental the hair-splitting distinction between 'external' and 'internal' taxation. So it was thought that revenue might yet be raised from American trade without protest. The prevailing temper at Westminster combined complacency, apathy, irritation and delusion.

Three months after the Stamp Act was repealed, the fragile Rockingham ministry fell. George III, now wholly weaned from Bute's influence, picked Pitt as his new Prime Minister. The 'great commoner' permitted himself to be translated to the House of Lords as Earl of Chatham, cutting himself off from his Commons base and losing much of his popularity. Then nervous disease laid him low. He pleaded to be permitted to quit, but it was two years before George III released him. The Duke of Grafton meanwhile became the true head of a ministry which bungled over the East India Company, created a new crisis over John Wilkes, and behaved absurdly towards America.

The Chancellor of the Exchequer was now Charles Townshend, much admired for his ability to make a brilliant speech in the Commons when drunk. The land tax kept up the price of wheat, and Townshend was defeated when he proposed to maintain it at the war level of 4s. in the £. He had to seek other sources of revenue. Townshend insisted on the withdrawal of costly posts from the American west, where British control now completely collapsed. He also brought in new proposals to tax the colonies.

His 1767 Revenue Act was a sillier measure than the Stamp Act. At most, it could have produced less than one-tenth of the revenue now lost through reduction of the British land tax. Townshend put duties on glass, paints, lead and paper, which they did not import in large quantities, as well as on tea which they swilled with British fervour. The fund thus raised was to be devoted only secondarily to defence – the first call upon it was 'defraying the Charge of the Administration of Justice, and the Support of Civil Government . . .' Townshend wanted to make colonial governors and officials financially independent of local assemblies. No project was better calculated to inflame North American fears of 'tyranny'.

When the text of the New Revenue Act became known, the Boston town meeting, chaired by Otis, called for a boycott of 'foreign' (that is, British) manufactures, and early next year the Massachusetts House of Representatives addressed to the other colonial assemblies a 'Circular Letter', drafted by Sam Adams, calling for united action. An order came from Whitehall that this must be rescinded. The House refused, and in June 1768 Governor Bernard dissolved it. But Boston was now under the rule of rioters, brought out by the seizure of John Hancock's sloop *Liberty* on a charge of smuggling. The customs commissioners were forced to flee for safety to Castle William on an island in the harbour.

The movement for 'non-consumption' of British goods was resumed. New York and Philadelphia merchants openly imported Dutch tea in great quantities. As colonists found they could ignore the Acts of Trade with impunity, all imperial authority seemed on the verge of collapse.

Sam Adams, for one, was now privately thinking in terms of complete freedom from parliamentary authority. His faction called for, and got, a 'convention' of delegates from ninety Massachusetts towns which was in effect an assembly summoned by colonists without due authority. On September 28, the day before it broke up, about a thousand troops arrived in Boston from

Halifax. Two more regiments shortly followed, from Ireland. To the colonists, it was confirmation that Stuart tyranny had revived. They had heard of the 'massacre' by guardsmen of Wilkesite demonstrators in London in May. The cause of liberty had its martyrs already.

Wilkes returned to England in January 1768 and promptly secured election as MP for the county of Middlesex, where the broad franchise permitted lower-middling men to assert their predilection for 'Liberty'. A joyful mob then roamed the London streets for two days, smashing the windows of many fine houses, including Bute's. Disturbances went on for several weeks, before Wilkes was tried, fined £1,000 and sentenced to twenty-two months' imprisonment on the old charge of 'seditious libel'. When the doors of the King's Bench prison closed upon him at the end of April, continuous riots ensued for a fortnight. In May, watermen, hatters and coal-heavers struck in London, while sawyers attacked and partly destroyed a mechanical sawmill which threatened their livelihoods and the journeymen silk weavers were fighting a cut in wages with acts of industrial sabotage. Reports of food riots and other unrest came in from the provinces.

The situation was growing nightmarish for the rich. Lord Weymouth, Secretary of State, instructed the Middlesex magistrates to employ troops in cases of civil disorder. On May 10, the day when Parliament opened, 15,000 or 20,000 (even as many as 40,000) demonstrators gathered on St George's Fields in Southwark. After they had refused to disperse, troops fired, killing or wounding a score of people.

Colonists shuddered and thrilled when Wilkes published the text of Weymouth's letter with his own comments, alleging a deep-laid government plot against liberty. They were appalled to hear that he had again been expelled from the Commons. Three times the defiant Middlesex voters chose Wilkes again; then after the fourth, his opponent Luttrell was declared the victor, although he had been beaten by nearly four votes to one. Amid all this rioters shouted 'Wilkes and No King' outside St James's Palace itself. Though Wilkes himself never considered crossing the ocean in any lesser capacity than that of governor of Canada, many colonists hoped that their hero would flee Bute's tyranny and settle among them.

In February 1769, a 'Society of the Supporters of the Bill of Rights' was formed in the London Tavern, with MPs and other wealthy persons among its members. Its prime object was to buy off Wilkes's creditors, to whom he owed about £30,000, but it was also the first organisation in Britain to use modern methods of agitation. The Society sent paid agents around the land to make speeches. It used the press cleverly. It organised 'public opinion'. The petitions which rushed towards Parliament after the Commons' recognition of Luttrell as MP for Middlesex were signed by 55,000 people, more than a quarter of England's total voting population. The Society began to look rather like a modern 'political party'. The Wilkesites called for reform of Parliament and appealed to a wide range of other grievances. They sought for a while to build up a nationwide network of 'corresponding societies'.

But Wilkes himself was hardly an ideologist. Released in April 1770, he turned his attention to consolidating a strong position for himself in the City of London, which had elected him an Alderman while he was in prison. In 1774, he became Lord Mayor and, re-elected for Middlesex, was allowed to take his seat in the Commons. But he did little there. Reform was for him a war-cry, not a commitment.

A mass radical movement had come into being; but this, paradoxically, weakened the Westminster opposition. Aristocratic grandees and hangers-on such as Burke were frightened of being too closely identified with this dangerous new sort of thinking 'mob', and in any case disdained the 'democratical' concepts now being voiced. Hence the Rockingham and Chatham groups would be enfeebled by their own caution as drastic events unfolded across the Atlantic. The revision of the Townshend Duties was the last occasion on which politicians and merchants in Britain acted in consort to modify policy in the colonials' favour. Early in 1770, all the duties were abolished except for that on tea, which was retained as a symbol of Parliament's right to tax the colonies.

The Massachusetts lower house voted 109 to 0 for a motion demanding Governor Bernard's recall, and though he had long been anxious to leave his post, his actual departure was hailed as a 'patriot' victory. Thomas Hutchinson was appointed to succeed him, and his weakness was soon exposed. After numerous minor clashes between Bostonians and the hated soldiers, a guard sent to the custom house to protect a sentry there was provoked into firing on a hostile crowd. Five people were killed, others wounded. The 'Boston Massacre' of March 5, 1770 gave Sam Adams what he wanted: an American counterpart to St George's Fields. The patriot leaders demanded that the guards stand trial for murder and that all troops be withdrawn from Boston. Hutchinson and the military commander could only submit to the 'faction's' demands.

But the 'Liberal Party' were soon crestfallen. The soldiers involved in the Massacre, given a fair trial, were all at last acquitted of murder. And the London government's concession over the Townshend Duties seemed to have worked. At first, merchants in the three leading American ports resolved to continue 'non-importation', but in July New Yorkers resumed normal trading, Philadelphia soon followed suit, and Boston itself gave way in October. The 'patriotic' movement fell into apathy and recrimination, just as the Wilkesite turbulence died down in England.

But paranoiac fears persisted, and Chatham, now somewhat recovered, enhanced them by his speeches in the Lords. Was it true that the 'riches of Asia' were subverting the constitution? It was certainly the case that the 1768 election had seen an apparently sinister influx of 'nabobs', buying seats with their spoils, into the Commons, and Massachusetts had been shocked by a rumour that Thomas Hutchinson had received 'a trunk of rich silks, a present from Lord

Clive of £500 value' (though in fact he had merely acquired for sale a consignment of ordinary cloth bandannas). Chatham harped on the 'Secret Influence' of Bute, 'dangerous, base, unconstitutional and wicked' and the colonists believed him. Sam Adams would not have to wait very long before fresh chance was given him to make trouble.

VIII

What another Townshend had been doing in Ireland gave ample fuel to notions of conspiracy.

Ireland had seem 'mobs' as well. A rumour, spread in 1759, of parliamentary union with Britain had brought out a 'mob' which invaded the Dublin House of Commons and compelled MPs to swear that they would vote against it. In the handsome rotunda of their chamber, where Tuscan pillars supported a great gallery in which nearly 700 people could sit to hear an important debate, land-owner members now quaked before the 'public opinion' of the Protestant middling classes, as well as considering angrily and fearfully the dangers they now faced from rural 'mobs'.

In 1759, restrictions upon the import of Irish cattle into England were lifted. Landlords increased the acreage under pasture. Commons were enclosed. Whole villages disappeared. Though graziers paid no tithes for their pasture land, cottiers and small farmers, whether or not they were Anglican, still had to disburse to maintain the 'Church of Ireland'. Half a century of quiet ended. In 1761, the first 'Whiteboys' came out. Wesley, in Ireland soon after, described this beginning. '. . . A few men met by night near Nenagh, in the county of Limerick, and threw down the fences of some commons which had been lately inclosed. Near the same time, others met in the counties of Tipperary, Waterford and Cork. As no one offered to suppress or hinder them, they increased in numbers continually, calling themselves Whiteboys, wearing white cockades and white linen frocks. In February there were five or six parties of them, 200 to 300 men in each, who moved up and down chiefly in the night . . . levelled a few fences, dug up some grounds, and hamstrung some cattle, perhaps fifty or sixty in all. One body of them came into Clogheen, of about 500 foot, and 200 horse. They moved as exactly as regular troops, and appeared to be thoroughly disciplined.'

The movement soon spread over Munster and parts of Leinster and Connacht. Whiteboys tried to settle the rate at which tithes should be levied, as well as attacking the livestock and buildings of unpopular landlords and tenants. On occasions, they moved in great force in the light of day, braving garrisons, releasing imprisoned comrades and overawing whole towns. Exports of grain and flour were sometimes obstructed, blackmail was levied from farmers to pay for the legal defence of Whiteboys on trial. There were few murders, but many displays of outlaw justice and the followers of 'Captain Right', as the Whiteboys called their fictitious, symbolic leader, eschewed highway robbery and took no action except against oppressors and their agents, or people who co-operated with the enemy. Over large areas, no tithes were paid, and evidence against Whiteboys was impossible to procure.

The Irish Parliament retorted brutally. Whiteboy offences were made capital. The power of magistrates was extended. In many areas, landlords armed their more reliable tenants and formed troops of horse to exact revenge. Edmund Burke was aghast at their 'unfeeling Tyranny'. The landed classes invented a 'popish plot' at the bottom of it all, and in 1766 a popular Tipperary priest named Father Sheehy was hanged and quartered after conviction by Protestant magistrates for allegedly 'inciting to riot and rebellion'. Burke inspired an official inquiry which showed that there were Protestant as well as Catholic Whiteboys, that talk of a popish plot was baseless, and that bad agrarian conditions were the cause of the disturbances. But the landed classes persisted in what Burke called 'unmeaning Senseless Malice'.

A similar movement emerged in Ulster, as 'Hearts of Oak' or 'Oakboys' acted against tithes and tyrannous landlords. An unpopular law enabled landlords to force householders to build and repair roads of little use to people at large but of benefit to the great estates. When this was modified, turbulence abated. But in 1770, Lord Donegall, absentee owner of great tracts, demanded heavy fines for renewing the leases on his County Antrim lands, and dispossessed the many who could not pay, then brought in as tenants two or three wealthy Belfast merchants. Rents in some other parts of Ulster were trebled. The 'Hearts of Steel' or 'Steelboys' rose up. In this area, the effect of rackrents, high food prices, and of a slump in the linen trade, was to spur on the existing movement of emigration. In four years some 37,000 people quit Ulster for America, and the Hearts of Steel, losing both leaders and followers, were extinct by 1773.

However, from now on agrarian unrest, in 'Whiteboy' and other forms, would be a perennial feature of Irish life. The labourer's condition was commonly deteriorating. In some parts, everyone could still obtain land and, as population soared, subdivision into smaller and smaller plots brought more and more cottiers and their families into dependence on a diet of milk and potatoes. In others, where commercial farming was well developed, a farmer would be reluctant to grant plots except to such men as he required as labourers, so that landlessness was a goad to class hatred and constant unrest.

British policy towards Ireland took a turn closely related to Grenville's decisions over America. With imperial defence so much of a problem, Ireland offered the delectable prospect of raising troops with money voted by the Dublin Parliament. The 'Irish' army (which was exclusively Protestant) already stood at 12,000 men. In 1767, Lord Townshend, elder brother of clever Charles, was sent over to get it raised to about 15,200.

Townshend at first tried to make a deal with the leading 'undertakers' – the second Lord Shannon, Speaker Ponsonby and John Hely Hutchinson, an able careerist whose avarice was so inordinate that it was said, 'If you gave him Great

Britain and Ireland for a demesne, he would ask for the Isle of Man as a potato garden.' But Whitehall would not accept their terms, and they went into opposition. The British government nevertheless insisted that Townshend must quickly get them more troops from Ireland. The proposal was put to the Dublin Commons in April 1768. They rejected it.

Poynings' Law, so much resented by Irish Protestants, had promoted a regular pantomime of defiance. Bills which the Parliament wanted to pass were sent across to England to be doctored. When they came back, Irish politicians looked them over to see what alterations had been made, and if these were considered excessive or insulting, the Bill was rejected. But commonly the Irish Parliament itself, having satisfied its honour, would then present the rejected Bill as one of its own and, after all, would calmly pass it. Such antics were harmless enough, but in 1769 a novel, more serious, drama was staged. The Commons rejected a government finance Bill on the grounds that it had not taken its rise in their House, then went ahead to pass a money Bill of their own. Faced with this impudence, Townshend prorogued Parliament. Then he shocked the borough-mongers horribly.

They must have expected that, as in the past, the Viceroy would buy back their necessary support. But now they, with their tails of followers, were swept out of all lucrative offices. The nightmare of the American patriots was really enacted in Dublin, with Townshend creating new places and pensions as bribes for those prepared to support his line. When Parliament reassembled early in 1771, he was firmly in control of the Commons. His chief secretary now manipulated the House, buying votes as required from men who were never slow to sell themselves. Townshend resigned in 1772, but his system ticked over smoothly under his successor, and in 1775 the exalted Flood himself deserted the 'patriot' ranks and accepted the Cabinet post of Vice-Treasurer. Parliament, childish in its pride and its sulks, seemed for a blink of five years to be happy sucking its candy.

But these men, whose selfishness was so blatant, whose business was so irregularly conducted, still trembled before 'public opinion'. The effect of dispensing with the 'undertakers' was that, when discontent mounted high, the Viceroy at Dublin Castle would have no buffer, there must be direct confrontation between the public and the British government. British control now depended on visible corruption. Thirty-four Irish politicians were given peerages between 1767 and 1785. The Commons seemed more manageable than Britain's; whereas it was reckoned that 5,723 people controlled half the seats in the Westminster House, a mere hundred or so disposed of two-thirds in the Dublin one. But while most of the House were pensioners and placemen, many of whom had no other profession and depended wholly on the pickings of politics, even these could not always be safely relied upon. As in Britain, there were 'independent' gentlemen representing county constituencies where they were under direct pressure from quite a wide electorate, and as at Westminster such men could be swayed by oratory. Though each had his price, the Castle could not control all of them.

How inconvenient that the rotunda existed! Edinburgh, where the 'Parliament House' was now given merely to routine legal business, was, unlike Dublin, a city of model docility.

IX

A rising Scottish politician named Wedderburn observed smugly in 1768 that while the south of England was 'a great Bedlam under the dominion of a beggarly, idle and intoxicated mob without keepers, actuated solely by the word *Wilkes*', the north was frugal, sober and loyal. The old picture was now stood on its head. London and the Home Counties could hardly be governed; Scotland gave no serious trouble at all.

This was true even of the Highlands. Culloden had swept away the last chiefs who had tried to preserve the old ways. Not only arms, but also the Highland dress, were forbidden for a generation. Within a dozen years rustling had been suppressed with amazing completeness. Over nine-tenths of the people, still, spoke only Gaelic. Smuggling continued to employ an even larger proportion of Highlanders than of people in Galloway or Ayrshire. Gaels still farmed on the run-rig, 'open', system, using primitive ploughs and the 'cascrome', a sort of crooked wooden spade with an iron tip. Localised famines were commonplace. But the Highlands were at last safe for travellers, and had come within the grasp of 'civilisation'.

The chiefs were now anxious to prove their loyalty, and happy, also, to make cash out of purveying their faithful 'children' to the government. Between 1740 and 1815, some fifty or so Scottish battalions were raised, mostly in the Highlands. The army provided scope for Gaelic military traditions. Soldiers could wear the tartan while that was still barred to civilians. Young men could always find employment. Emigration helped to keep the peace as well, and though industry in the Lowlands was not quite ready yet to absorb hordes of dark Gaelic-speaking people, America was taking many off.

In the late 1760s and 1770s, a fervour for emigration emerged both in the Lowlands and in the Highlands, but especially in the latter. Over 20,000 people left Scotland in eight years. The Lowlanders were commonly skilled men seeking to better their lot, especially after an economic crisis in 1772 which threw thousands of artisans out of work.

In the Highlands the initiative came from the higher levels of society. The growing invasion of the area by the values and practices of an up-to-date money economy bereft the tacksmen of their traditional role. Too proud to be mere commercial farmers, some of these minor gentry struck out west, taking bodies of their clan followers with them, and hoping to recreate a life-style where, as one observer reported, 'a tacksman of fifty pounds a year often keeps twenty servants . . .' Other substantial Gaels and Lowlanders, seeing a chance of profit, urged on the movement. Crop failures and cattle blights and overpopulation gave ample spur.

Highland emigrants tended to cluster together in certain districts, clinging to their characteristic dress and to their Gaelic language (which was still spoken in North Carolina in the nineteenth century, in Nova Scotia even in the twentieth). The Highland tradition of rearing cattle flourished on virgin American acres.

In spite of all this, Highland population rose by nearly one-third between 1755 and 1801. The spread of the potato through Scotland was critical. It reached Uist and Benbecula in 1743, Lewis and Sutherland in the 1750s. By 1770 it was on its way to becoming the staple food of the Highlands. It helped to balance the diet and check scurvy in a country traditionally short of vegetables, it provided a safeguard against the failure of the oat crop, which still happened quite frequently, and, as in Ireland, it proved the means whereby an expanding population could be fed from the same, or even reduced, acreage of ground.

In 1747, no fewer than forty-one estates, most of them in the Highlands, were declared forfeited by Jacobite 'traitors'. Five years later, thirteen of these were annexed inalienably to the Crown by an Act providing that their rents and profits were to go towards civilising the Gaels. The Commissioners put in charge came to manage about one Highland parish in seven. They built schools where all instruction was given in English. They enforced new agricultural habits upon their tenants, encouraged them to plant trees, and to build better houses. The making of linen cloth was promoted. New roads and bridges were built.

The Gospel of Work was preached by Lowland incomers, energising but joyless and utterly alien to the traditions of Gaelic society. Scots who had made fortunes by diligence in Jamaica, by commerce or hard soldiering in Bengal, now bought up estates in the Highlands. Their competition raised the price of lands. Rents increased as they tried to recoup their outlay. More 'efficient' use of the soil was essential. Those who could not pay or adapt must now go to the wall, or to America.

For the moment, the prospects seemed good. The terms of trade were moving strongly in the region's favour; between the 1740s and 1790s the price of cattle, the Highlands' main export to the Lowlands, rose 300 per cent, while that of oats, which the Highlands imported, did not quite double. New villages sprang into existence and some – Ullapool, Grantown and Oban amongst them – became important centres of population, industry and 'civility'. Kelp was a godsend to landlords on the remote and sterile western coasts. This was the ash of burnt seaweed, sold to serve as a low-grade alkali in the manufacture of soap, alum, glass and other goods. It was the easiest thing in the world to make it. Your people need do no more than cut the weed from the rocks at low tide, dry it, then roast it to ashes in simple kilns. But it implied the disruption of old ways. Hands and legs, as many as could be found, must be concentrated on the coast, where the traditional cattle economy lapsed and potatoes from small plots became the staff of life.

Another departure from tradition evident by the 1770s was the widespread distillation of whisky. The common drink of the Highlands had been strong ale. But now the landlord was asking such rents, in cash, whisky might seem the best way to pay him. The pattern of taxes in force encouraged illegal production. Over 6,000 illegal stills were seized in the Highlands in the 1780s, though at the end of that decade there were only about 350 legal ones. The delicious peaty flavours of Highland malts commonly reached Lowland palates by bootlegging.

None of this meant that Highlanders were essentially better off. The old customs of the region had been well adapted to its geography. Lowlanders misread what they saw. The Gaelic character seemed to them to be the cause of the region's crude living standards. Hence the Englishman Thomas Pennant's self-contradictory verdict on Sutherland in the 1770s. The people, he wrote, were 'content with little at present, and are thoughtless of futurity . . .' If they were thoughtless, why did they emigrate, voluntarily, as he claimed they did, in response to the pressure of population on grain supplies? If they were 'content' with their own way of life, what was the point of vainly striving to make Sutherland as prosperous as the Lothians?

The truth would only enforce itself slowly against the obstinate optimism of government and 'improvers' that geography, in the Highlands, made high prosperity impossible. It was true that the potato would flourish in soil which had previously been heathery moorland; Lachlan MacIntosh brought home his fortune from India, purchased hundreds of acres of waste near Inverness in 1776, and proceeded to make fertile fields of them. But even at maximum there was scant arable land, while a remote glen, however adept its people, could not compete in textile manufacture with towns and villages close to the great ports. Weavers in Yorkshire and elsewhere cried out for wool. The price was rising. Some men were already glimpsing that sheep might be the best source of profit in the Highlands.

This would be the sharpest break with tradition of all. 'Here are no sheep,' Thomas Pennant reported from Skye, 'but what are kept for home consumption, or for the wool for the cloathing of the inhabitants.' The animals were thin and dark, coarse of fleece. But by the 1760s, new breeds were invading the glens, as Border country men leased lands and introduced large flocks, first in the southern Highlands, then up the west coast, and into the Spey Valley and the Great Glen. The discovery that fine-woolled sheep could live, all year round out in the open, north of the Highland line had, over several decades, famous effects. Eagles were slaughtered in their interests. Vast sheep-walks, employing few men, ousted people.

Sheep symbolised the delight in the values of capitalism now taken by Lowlanders who were themselves far from sheep-like. Scottish Lowland society was better educated, and more disputatious than that of southern England. Everyone knew a good deal, or thought he did. The *Encyclopaedia Britannica* was first published in Edinburgh in 1771 thanks to the energy of obscure young

men, and at once sold widely at home and in the colonies. It represented the
versatile intellect now almost commonplace in Scotland. The middling and
lower ranks of society seemed an inexhaustible reservoir of inventive talent. A
tenant farmer's son, Robert Burns, would become the most famous poet of his
day. Thomas Telford, from a shepherd's cottage, would rise as 'The Colussus
of Roads', the greatest civil engineer of his time. Opportunity seemed open to
all.

A constellation of pioneering Scottish scientists found an eager audience
among practical engineers and industrialists. Dr Joseph Black, who discovered
both carbon dioxide and latent heat, attracted crowds of non-students to his
lectures at Edinburgh University, opening minds to the excitement of science,
while Dr William Cullen of the Edinburgh medical faculty broke radically with
the past in his 1776 catalogue of *Materia Medica* which swept out such
loathsome and useless simples as ants' eggs, millipedes, frogspawn, peacock
dung, dog dung, and powder of Egyptian mummy.

Yet a young English radical, Sylas Neville, who went in the 1770s to become
Cullen's student, was shocked by the political conservatism of otherwise daring
and open-minded men like these. A great geologist, Dr James Hutton, remarked
one day to Neville over dinner that he was 'for having all laws against bribery &
corruption abolished' so that every man could sell his vote as he did anything
else. Joseph Black, who was present, concurred with Hutton in thinking that the
British enjoyed 'perfect liberty' and had 'no political evils to complain of'.

Principal William Robertson of Edinburgh University, a historian matched in
fame only by Gibbon (whom he greatly influenced), led the party of so-called
'Moderates' which now dominated the General Assembly of the Kirk, men who
cordoned the *status quo* in politics, disdained the old theocratic ideals, and
accepted lay patronage over the ministry, which gave Anglicized lairds the
chance to put in polite clergymen. Dissenting religion obsessed many lively
minds in the artisan class which might otherwise have been drawn towards
'democratical' notions. Instead of crying out for 'Liberty', weavers jawed over
theological niceties and purchased books in church history.

This was an easy country to govern. The fifteen MPs who sat for the
Scottish burghs would be elected in 1790 by a total of 1,301 town councillors,
most of them under the thumbs of powerful patrons. In Glasgow, thirty-two
people had the vote. The thirty-three electors of Edinburgh were entitled to
choose their own successors. Since the county franchise depended not exactly
upon a 'property' qualification but on immediate vassalage to the King, or its
equivalent, great magnates could increase their control by creating 'faggot'
voters – men given title deeds or superiorities of nominal portions of land,
whose electoral choices were then controlled absolutely. By 1788, 1,370 out of
2,662 county electors in Scotland would be 'parchment barons' of this species.
A few score people only had any effective say over Scotland's representation at
Westminster.

Scotland was the dreamland of eighteenth-century political 'management'. The 3rd Duke of Argyll who had controlled things so well died in 1761. For a time, no strong personality took his place, but in 1766, Henry Dundas, a man in his early twenties from a not very lofty landed family which had sought fortune through the law, was given the ministerial post of Solicitor-General for Scotland. In 1775, he reached the grander office of Lord Advocate. 'King Harry the Ninth' would soon be more widely known.

Thanks to the complexities of the Scottish legal system, even the wealthiest Englishmen could not in practice buy up Scottish county seats, though Scots of the landed classes were often elected in England. Englishmen did not practise Scottish law, but Scots rose to the highest legal positions in England. The disparity worried James Boswell, a Scottish lawyer, who wished that Englishmen might become Scottish judges. 'Such interchange,' he wrote, 'would make a beneficial mixture of manners, and render our union more complete.'

Boswell's self-division was typical of his class and time. Men with deep feeling for Scotland, true pride in their country, wanted to make themselves more like the English. 'Elocution' was all the rage. Gentility was craved. To be genteel was to be Anglicized. Hence the 'New Town' of Edinburgh was rising. In the 'Old Town', rich and poor had, literally, lived on top of each other. No wonder that few people of rank had resided there. In 1767, James Craig's plan was accepted for the first stage of the 'New Town' to the north of the city. Elegant, regular streets, circuses and crescents, handsome new bridges and public buildings, followed continuously, matching the growth of the well-to-do population, the city's success in attracting men of rank, and its due pride in its own pre-eminence as a centre of literature, science and scholarship.

X

'Moderate' though he was, William Robertson denounced slavery in his historical works. But this was hardly daring. No important philosopher of the day would have defended it. Dr Johnson, 'tory' at a time when the word was coming to mean 'foe of democracy', nevertheless shocked Boswell by proposing, 'in company with some very grave men at Oxford', a toast to the next slave rebellion in the West Indies.

Anti-slavery opinion had been crystallised in a famous ironical attack by Montesquieu in 1748. It appeared in the same work, *The Spirits of the Laws*, in which he extolled the British constitution. 'It is impossible for us to suppose these creatures to be men, because allowing them to be men, a suspicion would follow that we ourselves are not Christians.' Writer after subsequent writer quoted such passages. But Scottish philosophers made the intellectual pikes wielded by those who followed through the breach. Francis Hutcheson's *System of Moral Philosophy* (1755) spoke out for 'benevolence' and denied absolute authority in every sphere. A man must not tyrannise over his wife or children.

His rights over a servant were limited. Slavery was not 'natural', though men since Aristotle's day had argued as if it were.

The first volume of George Wallace's *System of the Principles of Law of Scotland*, appearing in 1760, contained a systematic attack on the legal basis of slavery. The human right to liberty was, he argued, inalienable, since only a madman or someone coerced would give it up. Plagiarised by the famous French *Encyclopédie*, Wallace's view attained comprehensive influence. In the social and debating clubs which proliferated in the Scottish university towns at this time, the subject of slavery was discussed time and again. But there was as yet no interest in practical reform. 'Enlightened' Scots studied the question, not quite in the abstract only, but chiefly for the light which it might throw on their own society. How much subjection could the Scots themselves take without being harmed?

The first efforts to bring bold new ideas into conformity with reality came from the Quakers, in England and America. They were deeply upset by the Seven Years War. Their opposition to it ensured that weaker brethren fell away, and its impotence meant that those who remained were anxious to prove that Friends could achieve something. No fewer than eighty-eight Quakers, probably slave traders, had been members in 1756 of the London 'Company of Merchants trading to Africa'. But in 1758 the London Yearly Meeting, the most influential Quaker body in the world, came out with a strong injunction that Friends must avoid the 'iniquitous practice' of slaving, and three years later it threatened with disownment all Friends who continued to participate. Quakers had moved with the times. Though their prime case was, of course, that slavery violated Christian truth and Christian love, talk of 'liberty' and 'natural rights' figured more and more in Quaker campaigning. The fact that many Friends were now drawn into sympathy with the new evangelical effervescence which was at work in other Churches meant that they could co-operate cordially with Christians of other denominations, as they began to lobby against the slave trade, though without Quaker energy, and Quaker wealth, it is hard to see how an effective movement could have come into being.

Slavery had been justified as a natural concomitant of the slave's sin, while sin had been seen as itself a sort of enslavement. But now a mental somersault brought growing numbers of Christians into assent with a contrary argument. Slaveholding was a sin. The planter, with bloody whip in one hand, glass of rum in the other, was agent of Antichrist or of the devil. Slavery was the root of all corruption. To root it out would realise, through secular politics, millenarian goals. Sin would be defeated.

And if Britons achieved this, it would validate their rule over so much of the world's surface and seas. At times saving the slave would seem almost incidental to the task of saving the British Empire from God's wrath. The first, and greatest, of British pamphleteers in this cause was also the most insistent upon this theme. Granville Sharp wrote in 1776 that the encouragement of the slave trade by Parliament, the toleration of slavery by the colonial assemblies, meant that the 'horrible Guilt' incurred was 'no longer confined to the few hardened *Individuals*, that are immediately concerned in these baneful Practices, but alas! the WHOLE BRITISH EMPIRE is involved . . . and *National* GUILT must inevitably draw down from GOD some tremendous *National* Punishment . . .'

Sharp, as his capitalisations suggest, was fervent to the point of eccentricity. He was lucky in his background. The grandson of an archbishop, the son of an archdeacon, he had wealthy and philanthropic elder brothers who loved and supported him despite the perversity which made him content to work first as a linen-draper's apprentice, then as a petty clerk in the civil service. He shared his family's devotion to music. 'Singing and playing at sight were his favourite recreations.'

Though the Sharp brothers entertained ambassadors, ministers, even the King and Queen, to concerts on a barge which they kept on the Thames, Granville's vision was unclouded with any considerations of interest, cash or political expediency. He was a genuine political radical. He took up the cause of seamen seized by press-gangs. He grew very angry indeed over the plight of the 'black Caribs' on St Vincent, whose land had been stolen from them and whose extirpation was now talked of in high government circles in Britain. He sympathised warmly with the American colonists in their conflict with the British ministry. He backed the demand for annual parliaments in England. When the plight of black people in Britain came to his notice in the 1760s, he began to think the destruction of slavery essential to the redemption of the honour of the Church of England.

In London, Bristol and Liverpool seamen openly sold blacks, now a regular bonus-in-kind for those who served on slaving vessels. Other slaves came in as the property of colonial planters or 'nabobs' returning home to enjoy their spoils. Aristocratic ladies liked to have black boys for servants. When young they resembled pets or exotic ornaments. When older, their famed sexual prowess would provide welcome experimental relief from the embraces of wine-sodden English noblemen. The Duchess of Queensberry's infatuation with a slave named Soubise was only one of many similar scandals. Blacks found other careers within the scope of their supposed innate attributes. Many black seamen clustered in the ports. Black musicians were commonly used in army regiments. Blacks were quite frequently seen on the stage or exhibited as curiosities at fairs. Black heavyweight boxers were champions of England. There may have been 15,000 or 20,000 black people in Britain in the 1760s.

Some found esteem. Dr Johnson employed a black servant for over thirty years, and eventually left him a generous annuity. But one of the two blacks brought by Benjamin Franklin to London ran away from him after a year. Such fugitive slaves and servants were the basis of the free black community which grew up in London. A few blacks prospered as small businessmen. A handful attracted upper-class patronage. Ignacius Sancho rose from the status of servant to that of small grocer through the interest of the Duchess of Montagu. He was befriended by literary men, acquired fame from his writing (after his death), and used his prominent contacts to help other blacks. Most blacks needed help. They mixed in the London underworld with equally poor whites, who by custom gave shelter to runaway slaves and, at this time, displayed little prejudice. Most blacks in Britain were male, but poor white women would marry them. White servants and sailors accepted their black co-workers. But life was hard, at this level, for both colours, and many blacks became thieves or beggars.

In 1765 a black boy who had been savagely beaten by his master went to Dr William Sharp's surgery. Granville, the doctor's brother, saw him there. After four months' treatment, the boy was found work as a chemist's messenger. But his former master noticed him, had him imprisoned, and sold him to a Jamaican planter. Sharp, learning of this, had found what would be his main cause for the rest of his life. He now studied law books as well as the Bible. The English Common Law, he concluded, left no place for slavery. Inferior law must give way to superior. Man's law must bow to God's law. He amassed such weight of legal opinion and scholarly citation that the Jamaican planter dropped the case and relinquished his purchase. Other black people brought their problems to Sharp and he soon succeeded in freeing two more slaves. Meanwhile, as Sharp was well aware, in Scotland colliers and salters were commonly called slaves.

'Serfdom' more exactly fitted their position. Coal-owners, during the seventeenth century, had found it necessary to compel people to such dirty and arduous toil. Now most colliers' children were regarded as serfs from birth. In 1701, colliers and salters, alone in the population, had been excluded from the Scottish equivalent of habeas corpus; in 1708 it had been established that runaways might be brought back even after eight years; in 1762 it transpired that an owner could freely shift his ascripted colliers to any mine where he wanted them. Colliers could not be sold as chattels. They might own property. They were paid wages – and since their servile position deterred new recruits, they were actually paid higher rates than miners in England or farm servants in Scotland. Even so, some wanted freedom. In 1770 a black slave was brought to Fife by a returning planter. Local colliers, salters and farm workers raised funds so that he could apply to the Court of Session for his liberty, but his master died before a decision was reached.

Sharp now also sought a test case. The legal position in England was thoroughly confused. The law was strong in defence of property. Slaves were property. Nevertheless, under the Habeas Corpus Act of 1679, used by John Wilkes, coveted by Irish 'patriots', the shipping of human beings to the colonies against their wish was clearly illegal. Were slaves human beings? This was the fundamental issue which Sharp raised before, or rather against, Mansfield.

Mansfield, a conservative Scot from Perthshire, Lord Chief Justice from 1756–88, was anxious to sit on the fence as long as possible. He was guardian over English commercial law, and to decide that slavery was not legal would deprive owners resident in England of property worth hundreds of thousands of pounds.

James Somerset seemed to provide a cause which would settle the matter. He was a black slave whose Scottish master, Charles Stewart, had been a Crown official in Boston. He had been brought to England, had escaped, had been recaptured and put aboard ship for sale in Jamaica, but then released on a writ of habeas corpus. His case came before Mansfield in eight separate hearings between December 1771 and June 1772. Sharp organised Somerset's side. Three counsel were found to appear for Somerset, all of whom refused to accept any payment. Mansfield showed his bias against Somerset plainly and spun the case out as long as he could, hoping that the two sides would arrive at a private compromise. But as last he gave his judgment, enforced upon him, that the claim of a master to exercise power over a slave was 'not known to the laws of England'.

This was soon followed by clarifications in Scotland. The more enterprising coal-owners there were now irked by serfdom, which deterred fresh labour from entering their fast-expanding industry. They themselves put a Bill through Parliament in 1774 making new recruits to the mines automatically free, though current serfs would have to institute legal proceedings to emancipate themselves and even then might have to wait ten years for liberty. In practice, serfdom continued till a new Act in 1799 at last swept it completely away. Regarding black slavery, however, the Scottish courts were swiftly decisive. In 1778 the case of a black runaway, Knight v. Wedderburn, came up to the Court of Session which ruled that slavery, 'being unjust, could not be supported in this country . . .'

In reactionary Scotland all black slaves were now free in law, though in practice selling of blacks continued. But though humane persons in liberty-loving England had rejoiced over Mansfield's judgment for Somerset, and though Sharp, using the press, had won an important propaganda victory – dazzling enough to blind historians down to very recent times – the truth was that the case had turned on a legal technicality. Mansfield had not said that all abroad; even so, within a year there were fresh instances of forcible removal. In a ruling of 1758, Mansfield himself confirmed that a slave was still a slave on English soil. Slave-owners in the colonies settled matters by making slaves before they left for Britain sign an indenture promising to work for their masters under certain conditions. This was valid under English law, and a court would decide in 1799 that no master was obliged to pay wages to such an 'indentured' black unless a clause specifically exacted them. For sixty years after the Somerset case, there were slaves in England, people were sold, runaways were captured.

Racialism, long latent, was beginning to focus its arguments in opposition to those of Sharp and the Quakers. Each side was abetted in its zeal by the fact that there was still very little up-to-date information to be had concerning the

African cultures from which the slaves came. The few first-hand accounts in print were mainly written by traders who had little prejudice against Africans in mass, but were unenthusiastic about life on the Guinea Coast, knew little or nothing of the interior, tended to see all African cultures as much the same, and, so as to titillate their readers, emphasised the more picturesque and outlandish festivals and customs.

Such details were bad on the whole for the mental images formed of Africa. So, in some of their implications, were certain characteristic currents of new thought, in this age of the revolutionary middle class. Thus the Glasgow philosopher John Millar, in 1771, proposed a four-stage model of human development which would have wide and long-enduring influence. From hunting and gathering, mankind had moved on to pastoralism, then to farming, and then to commerce. Africa, which seemed to lack much commerce, would seem from this model to be more 'backward' than Europe. Why, then, were its people less advanced? Montesquieu had produced another enduring theory, of the effect of the climate upon the human psyche. Northerners were more active in mind and body, southerners more sensitive in soul and spirit. Crudely applied, this produced the stereotypes of the fierce Sicilian and the sexy Levantine – and the concept that Africans were and must be lazy and over-sexed. Meanwhile, reaction had set in against the elegant, but austere and disappointingly rational Newtonian model of the universe. Poets and dilettantes now found chemistry more exciting than physics; its elements were more colourful and diverse than the unvarying laws of gravity and thermodynamics. 'Polygenetic' theories of human origins increased their appeal as against 'monogenetic' ones. The great Linnaeus in 1735 had identified four races, white, yellow, red and black (not at all the obvious division which it now appears to be), and then, in 1758, had divided the genus *Homo* into two species to make room for the orang-utans and for supposed wild men who could not speak. In 1775 a German, J. F. Blumenbach, created a fivefold system by naming three primary races, 'Caucasian', 'Ethiopian' and 'Mongolian', and making Amerindians a mixture of Caucasian and Mongolian and Malays a mixture of Mongolian and Ethiopian.

Blumenbach himself spoke out nobly for the equality of blacks and whites. But even he described 'Ethiopian' physiognomy in unattractive terms. All biologists using any sort of classification felt compelled to decide which order the races stood in, and all, unhesitatingly, put Europeans on top of their scales. As Africans were at the other extreme of colour, they would naturally gravitate to the bottom. Blacks seemed immune to certain diseases affecting whites, and vice versa. Here was a basis seized on by polygeneticists to found a 'scientific' racism.

The spokesmen for the West Indian planters were thus well armed to counter the cock-a-hoop cries of humanitarians over the Somerset case. Samuel Estwick weighed in at once with a pamphlet, cleverly arguing that the whippings slaves suffered were merely comparable to the 'hundreds of stripes' commonly given to British soldiers. He proposed that Negroes were a separate species, utterly lacking that innate 'moral sense' which Hutcheson attributed to human nature.

Edward Long's *History of Jamaica*, published two years after Mansfield's judgment, is the first classic of modern racialist thought. After all, many readers concluded, Long was a brilliant man who knew blacks well at first hand. What he said must be true; even though he asserted that mulattoes were infertile hybrids who could only breed successfully through intercourse with one or other of the 'pure' races; even though he alleged that, when not eating human flesh, Africans consumed by choice meat 'almost raw', putrid and full of maggots; even though he averred that not one black could draw a straight line. These wretches were far better off in Jamaica than in their homeland – domestic slaves in the West Indies lived better than the 'poorer class' in England itself, though not one black ever did half so much work. As for the white Jamaican, he was a model of 'disinterested charity, philanthropy, and clemency.'

His praise for the planters was easily countered by direct observation; a young visitor to Barbados fresh out of England, in the very year when Long's book was published, watched with horror as men were flogged to insensibility 'for the most trifling faults, sometimes for mere whims . . .' Long's more absurd remarks on black intelligence were abashed, if not silenced, as abolitionists brought forward such literate, polished and talented blacks as the author Olaudah Equiano. However, well-meaning Christians, as Christians, were inevitably prejudiced themselves. Their counter-stereotype married Hutcheson's theory of innate moral sense with notions derived from the cult of the noble savage, to produce a view of the African as a charming, perhaps rather childlike creature who would make an apt and easy Christian convert if only the devilish planter would assent to his conversion. John Wesley wrote a tract against the slave trade in 1774 which swung his Methodist followers quite swiftly into the Sharp camp, and painted a most attractive picture of life in the West African interior, about which he knew as little as anyone else.

The strongest force in the abolitionists' favour was not that of their arguments, good though they sometimes were. It was the shift of feeling which made each successive generation of young people in Britain on the whole more sensitive to cruelty. This surely had much to do with growing standards of comfort and hygiene among the middle classes, who were growingly screened from the sordor and brutality which mere survival might entail for the less comfortable. Literary fashion continued its work. One of the more important well-springs of cliché in an epoch well served by such sources was the fiction of Henry Mackenzie, follower of Sterne in the school of 'sentiment'. The young Scot, in this characteristic of his countrymen, somehow found himself able to write pro-slavery pamphlets while loading his lachrymose novels with emotion against the trade. And also against what the British were doing in India.

Mackenzie's *Man of Feeling* swept all before it in 1771. The novel's fainting hero talks to a soldier back from that far land and deplores the rapacity of the East India Company. A neo-classical disdain for riches allies with the new humanitarianism. '. . . What title have the subjects of another kingdom to establish an empire in India?'

XI

From India in the 1760s had come news of revolution upon revolution, each engineered in turn by East India Company servants who pocketed large presents and then, it seemed, set about scheming for the next. The rush for wealth largely destroyed, for a generation of Company personnel, the balance between their private interests and those of the shareholders at home. Finding themselves rulers, they ceased to think like 'servants'. A prime case was John Zephaniah Holwell.

Temporarily in charge in Calcutta after the departure of Clive and of other senior servants hastening home to spend their fortunes, Holwell sought to depose Mir Jafar in favour of Mir Qasim, who was a relative of the Nawab by marriage. Clive's successor as governor, Henry Vansittart, arrived to take over from Holwell in July 1760, but three months later the coup was executed. The price which Mir Qasim had to pay was the cession of three districts for the maintenance of EIC troops and donations worth over £200,000 to the obliging 'English gentlemen', amongst whom Holwell was promised over £20,000 personally. Relations were soon uneasy. Mir Qasim refused to be a puppet. He reorganised his army on European lines. But he had relinquished to the Company about a third of all his revenue from land. He was short of money to support his own power. His attempts to collect his legitimate duties from commerce ran him slap against the private interests of the Company's employees, who claimed the right to trade everywhere duty free.

London policy was to strengthen the Nawab's authority in Bengal as an alternative to direct involvement in government. Vansittart, aware of this, and conciliatory, made a treaty with Mir Qasim. This was grossly advantageous to the Company – in future English merchants were to pay 9 per cent on all goods in transit, Indian merchants 30 to 40 per cent – and, in honour of his diplomacy, Vansittart accepted from the Nawab a present of £70,000. He and his one supporter in 'moderate' policies, a young man named Warren Hastings, were denounced as the Nawab's 'hired solicitors' by other members of the Calcutta Council, which refused to accept the deal. EIC men, it declared, would henceforward pay only 2½ per cent on one commodity only, salt.

Mir Qasim retorted by freeing all trade from duty, depriving the EIC of special advantage. The Council, in July 1763, decided on war. It found that victories now cost more than in Clive's day. The Nawab fled to the province of Oudh and allied himself with the ruler there, and with the new titular Emperor Shah Alam. The EIC now reinstalled Mir Jaffar, who agreed to all their bullying demands, including a limitation of his army.

After months of inconclusive campaigning, a fresh commander, Major Hector Munro, found the Sepoys mutinous, and restored order by having twenty-four ringleaders blown from the mouths of guns – a spectacular punishment, copied from the Mughals, which scattered blood, bone and brains over a wide radius. Then he moved against Mir Qasim and defeated him at Baksar, in Oudh, on October 23, 1764. This victory was far more costly than Plassey. The EIC suffered 847 casualties out of about 7,000 men. But their ablest opponent, well backed, had been decisively defeated. Mir Qasim vanished into obscurity. The Emperor came to terms with the EIC.

Mir Jafar's restoration cost his treasury (and ultimately the people of Bengal) £375,000 due to the EIC's armed forces, £300,000 in compensation for the Company's losses, or supposed losses, in the war with Mir Qasim, and up to £530,000 for 'losses' by individuals, including Vansittart and his councillors. The directors in London now got round at last to banning acceptance of presents from native rulers. But when Mir Jafar died early in 1765, the opportunity was irresistible. In full knowledge of the new ruling, the Council recognised Mir Jafar's son Najm-ud-daula as Nawab, insisted on his appointing Muhammad Reza Khan as his chief minister, and creamed off over £100,000 in donations from both these parties and from others involved. It was the last grand haul of its sort. From now on the nawabship mattered less and less. It would pass, through deaths, from Najm to a second son of Mir Jafar's, then, in 1769, to a third son aged only 12. The resources granted to the incumbent by the EIC would be halved, and then soon halved again. That rupee tree could bear no more shaking. Meanwhile Lord Clive was sent as plenipotentiary to Bengal with instructions to check EIC rapacity.

Clive had returned to England in 1760 to find the EIC in the throes of transformation. Since the reorganisation of Queen Anne's day, there had been very little drama in its internal politics. Every year the outgoing directors had submitted their own list of nominees to the General Court, which, thanks to the mechanics of patronage, had obligingly voted for it.

The virtual acquisition of Bengal transformed the scene from calm to tempest. Directorships now seemed worth hard struggle to get, since their holders shared between themselves the appointments of new Writers and factors, and more and more people wanted to send their sons East. Under pressure from people whose support they sought in Company politics, the directors raised the total of covenanted 'civil' servants in Bengal from 70-odd to 250 in some sixteen years after 1760, while the increase in officers in the Company's army was even more rapid and sudden. In 1772, it would cost a young Scot named Charles Grant no less than £5,000 to acquire a Writership on the black market which was opened by certain directors, though £2,000 or £3,000 would be a commoner figure. Other directors preferred to save their own families, or their political supporters. Each lucky young sprig sent out needed further help from home once he reached India, so that he could leapfrog swiftly into the senior posts where most money was to be made. Control of the Court was therefore sharply contested. And the government could not stand aloof; it wanted its own share of the spoils.

In the spring of 1758, a fiercely contested election produced a new Court of Directors which elected Laurence Sulivan Chairman. He held this post for the next six years. He was an Irishman who had served in Bombay and had risen in the EIC through sheer competence. Though he had brought back a modest fortune he would boast that he had never accepted a present worth more than £20. Bombay had not been a lush pasture. By prevailing standards he was not corrupt. A contemporary said that his 'ruling passion' was the 'vanity of being supposed the head of the India Company and the power of giving protection to his friends in the Company's service.' Towards that end, he was coldly unscrupulous.

Clive had begun to build up his own small family party in the Commons, seeking political power at home. But the need to defend Mir Jafar's great gift of the *jaghir* diverted him into sordid EIC feuding. Many Company men envied him. The source of his huge annual income from the *jaghir* was revenues which the Nawab might otherwise have used to make good his debts to the Company. Clive could thus be accused of virtually pilfering from his own employers. Sulivan seems to have blackmailed Clive with threats of confiscation. Clive threw in his lot with other 'nabobs' who now formed a clear party, the 'Bengal Squad', in Company politics. In 1763 the contest with Sulivan for control was joined. The price of shares soared. Sulivan triumphed in the elections. The Bengal Council was ordered to stop the payment to Clive of his *jaghir*.

What saved Clive was news of the war against Mir Qasim. At the General Court, worried proprietors clamoured that the heaven-born general should be sent back to Bengal. He told them that he would return only if the directors shared their enthusiasm, and this influenced the elections next month. Though there was a dead heat, Sulivan could not secure re-election as chairman, and backed out defeated, leaving Clive's party in command. A ballot followed in which, by nearly three to two, the shareholders agreed that Clive should enjoy his *jaghir* for ten more years.

Clive arrived in Madras, after a voyage of nearly a year, to find that the military work had been done for him by Munro's victory at Baksar. The position in North India was now such that the EIC might have taken control of all Hindustan. In 1761, the Afghans had decisively beaten the Marathas at Panipat to the north of Delhi. Then they had gone home with their plunder. Delhi and the Punjab were left without government. Only three powers had survived; the Rohilla Afghans to the north-east of Delhi, Shuja-ud-daula of Oudh, and the Emperor Shah Alam. At Baksar, two of these had been defeated. Clive might have led the Company's troops to Lahore. What the shareholders who had acclaimed him had wanted was peaceful commerce only. More fighting might bankrupt the EIC.

Clive came swiftly to terms with the beaten powers. Though the EIC troops had overrun all Oudh, Shuja was given back his dominions. Shah Alam accepted the districts of Kora and Allahabad, and an offer of tribute from the EIC. In return, he gave, in August 1765, the *diwani* of Bengal, without limit in time – complete control of all the province's finances.

Neither in the short nor the long run did this arrangement work as Clive had intended. Though Shah Alam and Shuja did form a buffer of allied states against the menace from Afghans and Marathas, the EIC would soon be at war again. To defend a frontier, it transpired, meant conquest, defence of a new frontier, then fresh conquest. Clive underrated the expense, civil as well as military, which the *diwani* would entail, and grossly overestimated the likely revenue. It swiftly transpired that rule in Bengal could only be paid for by pitiless extortion and the ruination of the rich province.

Outwardly this was a new Clive. He had promised to cleanse the 'Augoean [*sic*] Stables'. Almost his first action in Bengal was to make Company servants sign covenants binding them not to take presents. But he saw that rapacity could only be checked if the EIC paid its servants more; while a councillor's official salary was only £300 a year, one could hardly keep up appearances here for less than £3,000. Clive clarified the principle which would make British rule in the East exorbitantly expensive to the natives; men must be paid so that they could live not only in comfort but in splendour.

Clive's reform of the Bengal army provoked another mutiny. Though a Maratha advance was expected, officers in all the three main garrisons tried to resist by simultaneous resignation. Clive worsted them by characteristically swift and courageous action. Loyal Sepoys were used to frighten white officers into submission with their muskets. Seven officers were cashiered, but the rest, chastened, returned to their duties.

Having charged so hard and so fast at so many problems, Clive suffered one of his nervous and physical collapses. Though the Court of Directors implored him to stay, he sailed home from Calcutta early in 1767. His brusque moves in Bengal had made many enemies for him there, and the aftermath of his second governorship gave their abuse much scope. News of the *diwani*, which he imagined would be so profitable, had sparked off a boom in EIC stock, which rose in a year or so from 164 to 273. Speculators sought to manipulate Company affairs in their own interests and this coincided with chaos and suffering in Bengal itself; both raised acutely the question of whether a private trading company should be allowed to control a distant alien province.

The looters of Bengal, like the smugglers of Massachusetts, must be brought under sovereign power. Something had to be done to regulate the internal affairs of a company which, twice in eight months, raised its dividends to satisfy speculators. So in 1767 five separate reforming Acts were passed. Dividends were regulated. The EIC was obliged to pay £400,000 a year to the national exchequer for the privilege of retaining its territorial acquisitions.

In the 1769 election of directors, Laurence Sulivan clawed his way back to the top after a furore of vote creation which had more than doubled the number of electors in a year. Then a sudden fall in the price of stock brought many investors to the brink of ruin. The cause of this disaster was the victory of Hydar Ali over the EIC in the Carnatic.

This region was naturally less rich than Bengal and offered less temptation to unscrupulous traders. EIC personnel therefore enriched themselves by usury. At the fall of Pondicherry in 1761, their puppet Nawab, Muhammad Ali, had owed the EIC vast sums for the help of their soldiers. Over the years, some was paid back, but the Nawab's position worsened continually, as virtually every Company man in Madras obligingly lent him money at very high local rates of interest, ranging up to 45 per cent, till his debt to them exceeded his original obligation to their employers. The manager of all, king spider, was Paul Benfield, an engineer, whose money-lending made him personal paymaster to the Nawab and put him beyond the control of any Company governor.

Since the Nawab met his creditors' claims by assigning to them revenues from his land, the seizure of fresh territories for him – eyes fell again on the Kingdom of Tanjore – became a prime aim for EIC personnel. They met their match in Hydar Ali, a brave, able, ambitious and unscrupulous adventurer who had usurped power in Mysore, westward of the Carnatic, and now menaced every neighbouring state. His bribes winkled native allies away and left the EIC facing alone Hydar's powerful army joined with that of the Nizam of Hyderabad. He ravaged the Carnatic up to the very outskirts of Madras.

So, in 1769, peace was made on Hydar Ali's terms, which included a defensive alliance, but could not stabilise the situation. Hydar remained a natural rival of the Nizam and of the Marathas. Prudence, and its shareholders' interests, should have kept the EIC aloof from entanglements. But the interests of the Nawab's creditors overrode sagacity in Madras. In 1773, the Benfield gang had its way. The Madras Council helped the Nawab annex Tanjore, and his creditors gratefully guzzled that kingdom's revenues.

The situation in Bengal had been even more scandalous. Clive's *diwani* had meant that the EIC had to act as revenue collector over the whole province. It had insufficient European personnel, and in any case its men were ignorant of the customs of Indian rural society. Hence the so-called 'dual system' was adopted, whereby Muhammad Reza Khan acted as deputy (*naib diwan*). This man was himself an outsider, Persian by birth, but deeply devoted to Mughal traditions of government and to the interests, as he saw them, of the Nawab, to whom he was chief minister.

Since Plassey, British involvement in Bengal's internal trade had vastly increased. Whites had set up trading posts everywhere whence their *gumashtas* (native agents) used armed terror, if need be, to exercise independent authority over the natives, to drive out rivals, to regulate prices. Hitherto remote frontier districts had been invaded by ruthless adventurers, and from 1765 such men also moved into Oudh. Some Indians, collaborating with the British, were able to thrive handsomely, but other formerly prosperous merchants and bankers were hard hit, and the cultivators and artisans were helping before the crudest British exploitation. Salt prices soared while the rewards of those who made salt remained stationary. Bihar poppy-growers received lower prices than before Plassey. Weavers' incomes, it seems, were driven down. The rewards for Britons were commonly enormous. Altogether, at least £15 million seem to have been sent home from Bengal by British individuals between Plassey and 1784 – compared with only about £3 million over the previous half century.

A very serious trade recession set in by early 1768. Reza Khan was soon announcing that every branch of Bengal's foreign commerce had been wrecked and that business was 'almost to a total stand'. Harry Verelst, Clive's successor as governor, had enough sense to point out to his masters at home that they could not 'act on the level of mere merchants' now that they ruled Bengal directly. If labouring taxpayers were ruined, the goose which laid the golden eggs would be killed. No protection, no profit. Verelst decided to put British 'supervisors' into the rural districts. Naturally, Company servants scrambled to get these posts, seeing yet further chances for graft and extortionate trade.

Nemesis came. Two sparse crops of rice were followed by the failure of grain and pulse crops. An epidemic ensued. Estimates of mortality range up to half of the rural population. Ten million people may have perished in 1769 and 1770. The EIC had not caused the drought and did not itself spread germs, but its conduct had helped to ensure low morale and low resistance – and its employees, not implausibly, were accused of heartless profiteering in rice.

Remorseless squeezing meant that the value of goods shipped home from the EIC to Britain, which had stood at £437,000 in 1765–6, was up to £633,000 during the famine year, and to £904,000 in 1770–1. One contemporary calculated that Bengal was losing £1½ million annually through her trade with Europe and that specie was draining out at the rate of £500,000 a year. Yet the Company at home was soon in a desperate situation.

Administration in the East was costing more, partly thanks to fear of French resurgence and consequent mounting military expenses, but also because of escalating EIC payrolls. The number of Company servants in the East tripled, as we have seen, in some sixteen years. And pay and allowances had been increased, so that the average given per man was three times as high in 1774 as in 1757; £455 as compared with under £150. Yet between 1767 and 1771, collections of revenue fell by £400,000. Books and pamphlets broadcast indignation through Britain at the horrors heard of from Bengal. Sulivan had been trying to get through the Company's own Bill for reorganising its affairs. The Commons would not have it. Instead, General Burgoyne, denouncing 'the most atrocious abuses that ever stained the name of civil government', carried a motion for a select committee to investigate matters. Though the EIC had kept its dividends up at 12½ per cent, it found itself compelled, in August 1772, to ask the government for a loan of £1 million. Now something simply had to be done.

In 1770, George III had at last acquired a prime minister whom he liked. Chatham's resignation in 1768 had left power in the hands of the Duke of Grafton, who was pushed to resign in turn by a brief unification of the opposition. Lord North replaced him. He suited the King because he was pliable, and remained in office for twelve years because, whenever he wished to resign, George would not permit it. A lazy man with no strong views of his own, let alone any original ones, North, generous, affable and amusing, was very popular and effective in the Commons (where he sat despite his courtesy title).

By March 1773, the Company was again petitioning for support, this time for £1½ million. The Commons resolved that all territorial acquisitions abroad did 'of right belong to the State.' In June, two Acts were passed. One gave the EIC a loan, on certain conditions. The other, 'North's Regulating Act', remodelled government in India. Military rationalisation was a prime consideration. A governor-general in Calcutta, assisted by a council of four, was to have power to superintend all three presidencies in the making of war and peace, though in civilian matters he would rule only in Bengal. Salaries were to be generous beyond precedent – £25,000 to the governor-general, £10,000 to each of his councillors, £8,000 to the chief justice in a new Supreme Court. The Bill passed the Commons with only twenty-one dissentients, the Lords with only seventeen. It remained in force for eleven critical years. The government now had disposal of a fixed proportion of the posts in the Company's service.

But fresh storms were inevitable. One reason was the unsatisfactory nature of the provisions laid down in 1773 for government under the EIC in India. Another was the strong feeling in Britain against 'nabobs'.

Clive, the chief scapegoat, emerged from several bitter attacks in the Commons free from the threat of prosecution but politically thwarted; public odium blocked his way to high office. Plagued by bad health, late in 1774, the victor of Plassey obliged his execrators by cutting his throat with a penknife during one of his fits of depression. Of course the rumour went round that a guilty conscience had killed him, and even the sage Dr Johnson was glad to believe it.

On the question of India, men otherwise opposed might find themselves in perverse agreement. While the great slave-owner William Beckford bellowed in the Commons against 'rapine and oppression', humanitarian feeling shuddered over Bengal as it did over the capture and sale of Africans. The Clives, for all their wealth, were snubbed in polite society and had to fall back on the company of other 'nabobs'.

The word, a corruption of 'nawab', carried with it, besides connotations of ill-gotten wealth and social climbing, the reek of 'Asiatic' despotism and cruelty. People in Britain beheld with disgust a spate of such upstarts buying their way into fine country estates and Commons seats. William Sumner, who received about £25,000 after Mir Qasim's succession to the nawabship, eventually became sheriff of Surrey. William Watts's daughter by a Eurasian woman married Charles Jenkinson, a leading 'King's Friend', who later made her Countess of Liverpool and the mother of a future prime minister. Just as gentlefolk were horrified to hear that some nine families out of ten were now drinking tea twice a day and so aping their betters, they flinched from the 'nabobs' as from agents of social upheaval, insurrectionists. They could rationalise their reaction as pious horror at unchristian habits – these men of vulgar birth slept in the East with Muslim mistresses and returned with livers diseased by excessive drinking. More to the point, the 'nabobs' had grown used to inordinate opulence and pomp such as great noblemen scarce afforded at home. A wealthy squire in the Home Counties might have a dozen or so servants. In Bengal, a mere advocate would maintain more than three score.

But the nabobs inserted themselves into the British social structure with much friction yet no violence. A nineteenth-century author would neatly call the East India Company's service a 'great Monarchy of the Middle Classes.' Writers for the commercial side, cadets for the army, were drawn overwhelmingly from the very strata which elsewhere in Europe made revolution. Merchants, traders and professional people found opportunities there for sons who might otherwise in frustration have shouted 'Wilkes and Liberty' or, later, more dangerous slogans. Warren Hastings, named as governor-general in the text of North's Regulating Act, was in no doubt that India could be a useful vent. Proposing, in 1777, a grand scheme for consolidating British power there, he argued, 'It will afford employment and support to the middle class of the subjects of Great Britain, whose services are less required at home than those of the lower rank of life.'

While other EIC servants mimicked in turn the Mughal rulers of the East and the aristocratic grandees of Britain, Hastings went in for negative ostentation. He flaunted his middle-classness. His secretary, returning home with Hasting's portrait, remarked that he feared that people would not believe that the great governor of whom they had heard so much was 'but a plain looking man like any of us, with a brown coat'. He drank wine only if necessary, and then mixed it with water, ate no supper and went to bed at ten. In his eighties he would take great (if perhaps amused) interest in the ideas of Robert Owen. Politically, he was always a man of the new age, though touched with a somewhat romantic feeling for 'ancient nobility'. He had something in common with Jefferson, John Adams, and other American revolutionaries.

But India gave him a very different direction. He gained immense power without having to force his way up through the compact indignant ranks of the governing classes, though at last he fell foul of the rage which the 'democratical' raree-show of a man in a plain brown coat sending armies hither and thither, commanding in war against the French, making treaties, exerting power without majesty, must evoke in the bosoms of whig aristocrats.

He came from a ruined West Country landowning family. As a boy, Hastings resolved that one day he would buy back the family manor, Daylesford, which had been sold in 1715. An uncle's charity sent him to Westminster School. When Hastings was fifteen, this uncle died, and the more distant relative to whose care he now fell, having some influence in the EIC, found him the Writership which took him to Calcutta in 1750. Organising a sub-factory in a rural district, Hastings developed an unusual gift for understanding and getting on with Indians. He became fluent in Bengali, learnt some Persian, and acquired a good knowledge of Urdu. He was still only 25 when he succeeded Luke Scrafton as representative at the Nawab's court and made himself very unpopular by his support for Mir Qasim. In 1764, he went home with a fortune modest by 'nabob' standards. Whereas the rapacious John Johnstone returned to Scotland next year worth £300,000, Hastings had £30,000, and of this only £5,000 came with him to Britain. In 1767, he heard that the rest, unwisely invested, had all been lost. The EIC sent Hastings to Fort St George as Second in the Council, with the prospect of succeeding to the presidency.

Hastings alone, among EIC men in Madras, took no part in the custom of profiteering from the Nawab of the Carnatic's debts. But his motivations were not of unmixed purity. The wish to keep his adored wife in appropriate style joined his old desire to buy back Daylesford. The East had taught him to judge his fellow men, not by the exalted standards of a Jefferson, but in terms of subtle shades of distinction. He had never lamented, he once remarked drily, 'that all men were not as virtuous and disinterested as myself.' He helped allies who had made vast pickings to send them home, then to cover their tracks. He wished to serve Britain as well. He was loyal to the EIC and to its interests as he conceived them. Such spurs were fiercer with him than with most men. So was an interest in administration. The arts of government delighted him. 'I have catched the desire of applause in public life', he once informed the EIC directors. An enemy's verdict perhaps gets close to his centre – 'fond of power but despises wealth.'

In other historical contexts, such men have striven to reshape whole societies. This the East of his day would not permit. Hastings' inconsistencies, his elusiveness, reflect the enormity of India, where the EIC, now the strongest single power, could not, however, control the situation. Shifting and unpredictable realities encouraged him to make opportunistic responses. His genuine liking for some Indians, and his respect for native institutions, could be overridden by real political pressures. His favourite maxims from the Hindu *Gita* – 'Let the Motive be in the Deed, and not in the Event. Be not one whose motive for Action is the Hope of Reward. Perform thy Duty. Abandon all thought of the consequence' – provided, in practice, a recipe for antinomianism. Whatever he thought he must do was right. Whoever stood in his way – European, Muslim, Hindu – was wrong and might be attacked and pursued vindictively.

His task was to maintain British power in India. He did not believe that this could be liked by the natives. He did not think that it could endure for long: 'All that the wisest institutions can effect in such a system can only be to improve the advantages of a temporary possession, and to protract that decay, which sooner or later must end it.' Yet the work of 'dominion' must go firmly on. '. . . The sword which gave us the dominion of Bengal must be the instrument of its preservation.' India was not America, not a New World fit for first principles to act in. It was very old, and its ruling goddess was decay. Hastings' brilliant mind lavished itself upon shifts, manoeuvres and expediencies.

At the end of 1771, the EIC transferred him from Madras to Calcutta as governor. It was trying to put its own house in order, and Hastings was told to enact certain reforms. The actual administration of all territories was in the hands of two *naib diwans*, Muhammad Reza Khan in Bengal, Shitab Rai in Bihar. The aim now was to make government pay its own way.

Executing orders from home, Hastings abolished the use of 'dustucks' (free passes), suppressed all but five of the custom houses as impediments to the free circulation of merchandise, and lowered the duty on almost all goods to 2½ per cent, payable by Europeans as well as Asians. The purpose of these liberal reforms was to revive the trade of the province. Hastings was also charged with sweeping away the 'dual system' so that the EIC itself took full responsibility for the whole civil administration. Sacrificial victims were necessary. Though Hastings believed Shitab Rai to be innocent, he had both *naib diwans* arrested and tried for peculation, and employed a notorious forger and intriguer named Nandakumar to find evidence and witnesses against Reza Khan. Both men were eventually acquitted by the Council on all charges.

The cultivators of Bengal and Bihar, over all of whom the EIC stood as *diwan*, paid over £2 million every year. Such rapacious men as Johnstone had obtained tax-farms under the native *zemindars* and had creamed off enormous sums at the expense both of peasants and EIC. Then the white Collectors sent in by Verelst had commonly seized with glee opportunities for straightforward embezzlement, for the levying of extra cesses for their own personal profit, and for the receipt of *nazrs* (cf. protection money) from *zemindars*, from tax-farmers, and from their own native subordinates. Hastings believed that Collectorships had become 'more lucrative than any posts in the service.'

The game was not quite over, though Hastings replaced Verelst's district 'Supervisors' with Provincial Revenue Councils and though, under the Regulating Act, all EIC servants concerned in revenue collection were prohibited from all trade. Profiteering from tax-gathering went on, as did gross and blatant frauds in the 'Commercial Department', to which Hastings turned a blind eye. His principle, like Clive's, was that servants should be given official emoluments so large that the temptation to cheat would weaken. After the Regulating Act, he himself was much higher paid than any British public official save the Lord Lieutenant of Ireland, and when, in 1781, he remodelled tax collecting, setting up a Committee of Revenue, its members, rewarded by commission, would legitimately take about £10,000 a year. Under his rule, average earnings in the Bengal 'civil' service would more than triple in seven years, to £2,261 in 1783 – far higher than salaries in the British Treasury, where a Chief Clerk took home £800. Steady income from work done for the Company would begin to replace, for men coming to India, the gambling impulse which had done so much damage. Various lucrative traffics – in salt, betel nuts, rice, tobacco, opium – were now barred to all Europeans or became EIC monopolies. And the flow of presents had dried up.

The boy Nawab's allowance was halved yet again. But neither public opinion at home nor Hastings' own understanding of India permitted him to destroy all show of native rule. He would claim that he had preserved the 'spirit' of the Bengal 'Constitution'. Courts of Justice had to be set up. The Collectorships were soon abolished on orders from home, so that native *diwans* took charge of local justice. The governor and two members of the Council sat as judges in the Civil Court of Appeal at Calcutta, but an Indian presided in the Criminal Court of Appeal, assisted by Muhammadan law officers. The basic principle, as Hastings saw it, was that existing laws should prevail. Muhammadan law was already codified. Hastings now invited ten of the most learned pundits in Bengal to prepare a digest of Hindu law for use in the civil courts.

In external relations, Hastings' great problem was the position in Oudh. Shuja-ud-daula, the ruler, had prohibited commerce with Bengal for fear that his own province might go the same way, overrun by grasping whites. Hastings' aim was a 'free trade' with Oudh. Events seemed to help him to open the country up. In 1771 the Marathas had reoccupied Delhi and Shah Alam let them install him as Emperor there. They forced him to make over Kora and Allahabad, given to him by Clive in 1765. The EIC promptly discontinued its tribute to him and granted these places to Oudh for fifty lakhs of rupees. Hastings noted with gratification that this deal would make the Vizier of Oudh 'more dependent upon us, as he is more exposed to the hostilities of the Marathas . . .' Since the latter claimed Kora and Allahabad, Shuja could not ally with them, and thus should provide Bengal with a permanent buffer. But such hopes of peace did not allow for the machinations of the British military who still squatted in Shuja's domain. The commander-in-chief in Bengal, Sir Robert Barker, intervened, against Hastings' wishes, in the matter of Rohilkand. This small state, governed by a loose confederacy of Rohilla Afghan chiefs, was invaded by the Marathas in 1772. Prompted by Barker, Shuja agreed to help the Rohillas in return for forty lakhs of rupees. (More cash for British commanders.) As Oudh and EIC forces came in, the Marathas fled. Then the Rohillas refused to pay up on the grounds that there had been no fighting. The EIC, in return for forty lakhs, gave Shuja a brigade to help conquer Rohilkand. In April 1774, this was done.

The proprietors in London were shocked by Hastings' involvement in the

Rohilla War. The directors condemned him, but mildly, and they were still pleased that this paragon of (relative) virtue had been named governor-general in India. Hastings would be, as it turned out, the only man to serve as governor-general during the span of North's Act.

XII

In his first year as governor of Bengal, Warren Hastings shipped fifty chests of opium, on his private account, to China. Critical and dramatic though events in India had been, their effect, by making the EIC there primarily a political institution, receiving produce in return for government, was to emphasise the fact that the subcontinent was only a link in the system of trade between Britain and China. The chief value of India was that it produced commodities useful for barter in China and in the Eastern seas. By the end of the Seven Years War Britain had brought home more from Canton than all other European nations combined. Now competition had stiffened again.

There were serious problems over payment. Bengal opium, like Bombay cotton and Cornish tin, was invaluable. But the main recourse must still be silver, and this must come chiefly from Spanish America. Mexican silver could be had in Manila in exchange for British goods brought by merchants trading under the colours of some Eastern prince. Taken back to Madras, it could then be sent to Canton. The British conquest of Manila in 1762 had upset this. Though the place was soon handed back, the flow of silver was dammed. In 1768, the government of Madras was complaining, 'our intercourse with the Spaniards no longer subsists', and was crying out for silver from London. Silver was found somehow; an average of £700,000 a year was sent to China by the EIC in the 1780s.

The bullion problem emphasised the importance of opening up trade in Malaya, the East Indies and Indo-China, where British manufactures and Indian piece goods, opium and saltpetre could be exchanged for gold, sago and drugs, for spices, for sugar and for tin, which in turn would command good prices in China.

In 1760, the governor and council of Madras approved an idea worked out by a Scot named Alexander Dalrymple. Why not set up a mart off Borneo, in the area claimed by the Sultanate of Sulu? In 1763, having made a deal with the Sultan, Dalrymple took possession of the island of Balembangan, and started to introduce Indian and Chinese colonists. Meanwhile, through his diplomatic skill, he was able to gain for the EIC full sovereignty over the whole of the northern tip of Borneo and the adjacent islands, some 20,000 square miles, with the Sultan's son installed to rule as its vassal. But Dalrymple went home to propose even grander schemes. The colony was wiped out by a Suluan nobleman, probably anxious to liquidate creditors who were growing too powerful. The whole Borneo venture had lost the EIC £170,000. A similar scheme (1766–1772) failed in the Strait of Malacca.

Meanwhile, the idea of trade across the Pacific, dormant since Elizabeth's day, was resumed. Besides giving scope to the greatest of all British navigators, it yielded rich farce over the Falkland Islands. These lay east of the Straits of Magellan, two largish pieces of land which, together with islets and rocks, totalled some 4,600 square miles, remote and sun-starved. But they offered large and secure harbours for first-rate ships of war. Though Spain claimed both 'Malvinas', Bougainville, for the French, put a settlement on the eastern 'Malouine' in 1764. In the same year the British government sent out Captain Byron to discover unknown lands in southern latitudes, and to search for a North West Passage up the Pacific Coast. He failed to carry out his orders, but he did claim a harbour, which he named Port Egmont, on 'West Falkland'.

At first, no government was quite sure that the islands claimed were the same. Were Malvinas, Malouines and Falklands not perhaps different groups? It emerged that they were identical. In 1766 Captain McBride arrived to found a colony at Port Egmont and warned off the French next door for trespassing. The French went next year but out of politeness to Spain. The Spaniards now took over East Falkland and, in 1770, expelled the British colony. The opposition in Britain, in fact delighted, hypocritically shrieked that they were appalled. Chatham, on his most high-fantastical form, revived the old Bourbon bogey, and called for war with Spain, no doubt expecting that if it came the public would hubbub him back into office. For a moment war seemed certain. But France urged concessions on the Spaniards, and Lord North's ministry settled all with a curious deal whereby the Spaniards restored Port Egmont on the understanding that the British would shortly withdraw. In 1771 the British reoccupied the place, in 1774 they quit again, but they left behind them an inscription in lead as a token of British possession.

The Pacific Ocean covers more than a third of the earth's entire surface. Since Magellan, voyager after voyager from Europe had crossed it, yet people were sure that somewhere, in temperate latitudes, there must be a great undiscovered southern continent, *Terra Australis*, a new New World. Ancient geographers had insisted that such a landmass was essential to the equilibrium of a spherical earth, and when Marco Polo had written of the riches of the Malayan Peninsula, the text of his *Travels* had wrongly placed it 1,200 miles between south and west of Java.

While the Danish explorer Bering, serving the Russian Tsar, had made sense of the ocean's far north and Russian trappers and seal hunters were already at work in Alaska, such land as had been found in the central and southern Pacific had almost all been lost again. Small specks in a vast ocean could not be accurately charted until secure measurement of longitude at sea was possible. In 1714, the British government had set up a Board of Longitude to adjudicate proposals, and to award, if satisfied, a prize of £20,000. There were now two workable British solutions. One used astronomy, the 'lunar distance' method propounded by Neville Maskelyne in 1763. Another involved a more accurate measure of time on shipboard; in 1764 John Harrison's chronometer passed its first test, a voyage to Barbados.

Some 10,000 islands, very few glimpsed even once by Europeans, lay scattered across some 750,000 square miles of sea. Three different groups of peoples had evolved here, virtually all speaking languages of the 'Austronesian' type. 'Micronesians' lived on west-central Pacific islands. Darker 'Melanesians', some of them almost black, with frizzy hair and broad noses, were ranged in the south-west centre from New Guinea to Fiji. 'Polynesians' inhabited a triangle with its peak in Hawaii, its base on a line between Easter Island and New Zealand, and its western side running between Fiji and Samoa, and of all peoples in the world, they were the greatest masters of basic seafaring. These fair-skinned people were comely by European standards. Those Europeans who cherished advanced and 'Enlightened' concepts, when they encountered or read about Polynesians, thought at first that their visions of the ideal had been realised.

Captain Samuel Wallis was sent out by the British government to look again for *Terra Australis*. In 1767 he reached Tahiti, which he named after King George III and where he and his crew made an idyllic recovery from their hardships. Here were 'noble savages' in the flesh – untouched by the rage for possession, unspoilt by class divisions. Theorisers, enraptured, completely misread Polynesian society. Polynesians fought cruel inter-tribal wars and had chiefs whose punishments involved ritual sacrifice and cannibalism. On some Polynesian islands, if a commoner touched a chief's shadow he would be killed, and elaborate codes of *tapu* (taboo) were often thus protected by capital punishment. However, this was veiled from intellectuals, in Europe and America, whose idealism was touched by what seemed proof of man's inherent goodness – the charm and friendliness of these 'natural' people.

Alexander Dalrymple, quitting his beach-head in Borneo, had returned to Britain in 1765, and stood forth as an enthusiast for the theory of a 'Great Southern Continent' in the most extreme form then possible. New Zealand he averred, was its west coast. Its eastern coast had been sighted many times. It probably had more than fifty million people and covered a greater area than all civilised Asia. His notion was that he would discover the Continent himself, and match the achievements of Christopher Columbus.

The transit of the planet Venus across the sun, a rare event, was expected in 1769. It would not recur for a century. If it were accurately observed at widely different points, astronomers might be able to establish the distance of the earth from the sun. The Royal Society of London appealed to George III for help in sending a team to the central Pacific, one of the best posts for observation, and the King, early in 1768, promised £4,000 and a naval ship. Dalrymple, a member of the Royal Society, also a sailor, also a geographer, also an astronomer, saw his chance. But the Admiralty could not stomach a civilian, let alone such an opinionated one. Captain James Cook was met by destiny.

Before Cook was appointed, the Admiralty had chosen a Whitby collier as the expedition's ship. This was precisely the kind of vessel on which the captain had learnt the arts of seamanship. His father had migrated from Scotland to Yorkshire, where he had risen from labourer to farm-manager, and where Cook was born in 1728. He had gone to sea later than most sailors, apprenticed in the coal trade at eighteen. But the ships which plied between the North and London gave an exceptionally good training. They were big (300 to 500 tons), and very strong in construction. Their moderate draught enabled them to make the best use of the shallow harbours and shallow waters along the coast. Cook studied mathematics and navigation in his spare time, developed a self-taught mastery of coastal surveying and in 1755 decided to 'take his future', as he put it, in the Navy. He joined as mere able seaman, but soon won promotion, and his outstanding work in the charting of the St Lawrence for Wolfe's expedition of 1759 led to fruitful employment over the next eight years. After completing a survey of the St Lawrence, he was sent to work off Newfoundland where, in 1766, he made observations of an eclipse of the sun, which greatly impressed the Royal Society.

Cook's limitations were obvious enough. He seems to have had no religion, and no politics. Like his skill in navigation, his stubbornness and coolness in adversity at sea belonged to the North Sea coal trade, in which disasters and drownings were common enough. Sloppy work by sailors could bring out the heat of his temper. It was not original scientific theories but a devotion to exactitude which would bring him a Fellowship of the Royal Society. He could use the best instruments of his day, and exploit to the full the recent work bearing on longitude. The internationalist idealism of the mid-eighteenth-century intellect touched him and gave him added nobility; he would tell an admirer, a French naval officer, that he worked not for Britain alone but for Europe, and would give him excellent advice on where future discoveries might be made. He was scrupulous and, until his last days, humane in his dealings with coloured natives.

His ship, the *Endeavour*, had the virtues of her own type, and was ideal for work near uncharted coasts. Otherwise, she was much adapted. She was equipped as a floating laboratory, with a library containing every available text on the Pacific. Cook was one of two astronomers appointed to observe the transit. The other was Joseph Banks, FRS, a wealthy young landowner with a passion for botany, who brought on board a personal suite consisting of two artists, a secretary, and four servants, two of them black. Cook's first instruction was to sail to Tahiti. Observation completed, he was to go south in search of *Terra Australis*. The great aim was to find a vent for British trade.

The ship sailed, in August 1768, with seventy-one seamen on board, twelve marines and eleven landsmen. Cook's patient common sense at first bore hard on his sailors. He had no novel ideas about diet or hygiene. The virtues of lemon juice against scurvy had been repeatedly glimpsed and forgotten since

Elizabethan days. The value of hygiene against disease was almost self-evident. But Cook, unlike other commanders, took Admiralty instructions on food and cleanliness seriously, and applied them with rigorous method. He insisted on fresh food at every possible opportunity. 'Scarcly any thing Came wrong to him that was Green.' Cook, navigating by 'lunar distance', arrived in Tahiti with not a single sick man aboard.

The party stayed three months on the island. Scientifically, they failed; both here and at other posts of observation at the North Cape and in Hudson's Bay, there was optical distortion of the readings. But both Cook and Banks observed the Tahitians with objective honesty and humane feeling. This was not quite a paradise. 'Yaws' (a contagious skin disease) was endemic, producing symptoms similar to those of syphilis, besides which Bougainville's sailors (if not Wallis's) had introduced gonorrhoea, which affected about a third of Cook's crew. Cook displayed that prodigious catholicity of appetite which not only permitted him to claim that Tahitian dog, baked for four hours in an earth oven, was the sweetest meat ever tasted, but later to swallow good-humouredly shags, kangaroos, and walrus. Cook established essentially good relations with the Tahitians, before he sailed onward in mid-July 1769 to explore the 'Society' group of islands to the north-west, and then to strike south for Terra Australis.

He proceeded, as his instructions enjoined, as far as 40°S. There was no sign of a continent. The huge swell rolling from southward showed there was no land at all close in that direction. So, on to New Zealand, discovered by Tasman thirteen decades before. He sighted the unknown east coast in October, just in time, as a Frenchman, de Surville, reached North Island only a couple of months later. The Maoris would prove a disappointment to panegyrists of the Southern Continent. No other Polynesian people erected, as they did, large fortified villages. Four or five Maoris were shot within a couple of days in three separate quarrels. Cook was deeply upset and found it hard to justify his own conduct to himself in his Journal. But he learnt to get on with the Maoris, and even to admire them as a 'brave warlike people with sentiments voide of treachery . . .' Having sailed round North Island anti-clockwise, he steered clockwise about South Island, charting 2,400 miles of coastline in less than three months, largely in difficult weather.

Had he now felt able to pass eastwards back to Cape Horn, he could have disposed of the Southern Continent finally. But there were only four months' provisions left and the ship would not stand it. He headed for Java. On the way, he encountered Australia and followed its unknown south-eastern coastline up to a deep indentation, reached in April 1770, first called 'Stingray Harbour' but later, in tribute to so many new plants found there, renamed 'Botany Bay'. The British landing was opposed by two brave aborigines; three discharges of small shot were needed to budge them. Cook admired these people also; straight-bodied, slender-limbed, soft in voice. Nevertheless, without their permission, he took possession of the whole coastline for George III. He found himself, off

Queensland, between coastal shoals and the Great Barrier Reef. On June 11, passing over steep submerged hills of coral, the *Endeavour* struck a ledge and stuck fast. The shallow draught of his ship enabled Cook to attain the safety of a river mouth, where things were patched up as well as possible. Through the Torres Strait, he at last reached Batavia in October. At this point just eight sailors had died, mostly through accidents, an astonishing rate; but now tropical diseases took their toll, and only fifty-six out of ninety-four men reached Britain again, after nearly three years' absence.

Banks was awarded an honorary doctorate by Oxford University. The great Linnaeus suggested that New South Wales should be named 'Banksia'. Cook, who had been to neither Eton nor Oxford, was merely promoted to commander and told that he was to work on correcting existing charts of the English coast. But the crisis over the Falklands had helped ensure the continued interest of Britain, France and Spain in southern latitudes and in the Pacific. Various specifics against disease were to be tested, including Dr James's 'Fever Powders' and a marmalade of yellow carrots invented by Baron Storsch of Berlin. And John Harrison's chronometer was to be pitted against another device made by John Arnold. It won.

Cook was instructed to settle the question of the Southern Continent by sailing at high latitudes right round the globe. Starting from Plymouth in July, Cook crossed the Antarctic circle the following January, the first known commander ever to do so. As he sailed east into the Indian Ocean, conditions were so extreme that even Cook found them 'curious and romantick'. Scores of icebergs might be seen in one day. The ropes were like wires, the sails like boards, the sheaves were frozen fast in the blocks. Sailing at an average latitude of about 60°, Cook sighted not so much as one island, all the way from the meridian of Greenwich to that of New South Wales. With the southern winter coming, he sought the milder clime of New Zealand. He sailed east from there between 41° and 46° till near the meridian of Pitcairn's Island. Again, the ocean proved empty. He turned to Tahiti to stamp out an outbreak of scurvy, with the concept of a great Southern Continent almost destroyed.

Late in November 1773 he pressed again from New Zealand eastward, through empty seas and great ocean swells, determined to go as far south as it was possible for a man to go. The ship was soon directly opposite to London, with an astronomer on board wryly noting that people there, contrary to Dalrymple and other theorists, had 'no Antipodes besides Pengwins and Peteralls [petrels], unless Seals can be admitted as such . . .' In January 1774, Cook reached latitude 71° 10' and found a solid and limitless ice barrier.

Rather than go home at once, he explored northward once more. The Marquesan Islands enraptured him. In a great sweep round the Pacific back to New Zealand, he called at the New Hebrides and New Caledonia. Meeting hostility at the first group, he wrote of the Melanesians calmly, 'One cannot blame them . . . in what other light can they at first look upon us but as invaders of their Country . . .'

In November 1774, he sailed east again through the mid-50°s, surveyed Tierra del Fuego, and crossed the South Atlantic, calling on South Georgia, where the message of his whole voyage was confirmed. Though the latitude was no higher than that of York, on this bleak island not a tree or shrub could be seen, 'no not even big enough to make a tooth-pick'; there was snow and ice at the height of summer, and glaciers could be seen spawning icebergs. He reached home again in July 1775.

Though Cook had explored the east coast of the island of continental size which was later named 'Australia', the old concept of *Terra Australis* was as dead as that huge flightless pigeon, the dodo, latterly extinct on Île de France. By losing only four men from 112, only one of these through disease, and that not scurvy, Cook had shown what care and science could do. However, he had carried so many real or reputed anti-scorbutics that it was not yet clear to him or others that citrus fruits, though simple, were best of all. The Royal Navy did not make its first regular issue of lemon juice until 1795, but after that scurvy was almost wiped out in five years.

For all his great work, the Navy did no more than promote Cook to post captain, but the Royal Society decently made him a Fellow. The epic tale of his voyages gave British readers some pride and relief in these sad new times of war with America.

Revolutions

I

From 1770, for a couple of years, 'patriot' opposition in America lost its momentum. Correspondence between leaders in various colonies almost ceased. British merchandise poured in and local trades throve; New Yorkers had owned 477 vessels in 1762; the city had 709 ten years later. The colonies seemed for a blink less interested in arguments with Whitehall than with quarrels between themselves over frontier lands.

Governor Benning Wentworth of New Hampshire profited exceedingly from fees in respect of grants which he made in lands claimed by New York. The New York authorities fought back. In the 'New Hampshire Grants', later Vermont, they met fierce resistance from the 'Green Mountain Boys', an irregular corps with Ethan Allen as its colonel; one of the archetypal Americans of his age, who could throttle a bear with his naked hands, but who also wrote and published an earnest expression of frontier Enlightenment, *Reason the Only Oracle of Man*. As 'reason', presumably, insisted, the Green Mountain Boys waged a thuggish campaign of terror against settlers submitting to New York jurisdiction. Virtual civil war broke out also further south. The Susquehanna Company based on Connecticut shovelled settlers into land claimed by Pennsylvania and both sides recruited bands of violent men. Virginian speculators struggled with Philadelphia merchants for control of the area round Pittsburgh.

The 'Wild West' celebrated in our own time was here prefigured. Already, along the frontier of the southern colonies, cowboys, both black and white, rounded up every year thousands of branded cattle which ran on open ranges, and drove them down to the coast for shipment to Europe or to the Caribbean. After Daniel Boone and others had explored the Kentucky country, 1769–71 had seen the famous incursion there of James Knox's 'long hunters'. At the site of the future Nashville, moving down the Cumberland River, they came upon such vast numbers of buffalo that they hesitated to disembark for fear of being trampled to death. Another species was following the beaver towards extermination, as Judge Richard Henderson of North Carolina sent Daniel Boone, with a band of axemen, to blaze a trail through the Cumberland Gap. By 1775, Boonesborough, in Kentucky, had been established, despite a bitter war with the Shawnees which had been deliberately provoked by Lord Dunmore, the Scottish governor of Virginia.

There were still British troops in Massachusetts. The redcoats were called 'bloodybacks' by Yankees in bitter allusion to the horrific floggings practised upon these agents of 'Turkish' despotism. Sam Adams still had his knife out for Governor Hutchinson and his clan. Turkishly, it was decided that Hutchinson and other Crown officials were to be paid from England, out of the Royal Exchequer. The news arriving in 1772, that there would be judges supported by imperial funds sent shivers of dread down the spine of every liberty-loving slave-owner, and every self-respecting smuggler.

In June 1773, a closed session of the Massachusetts Assembly had read to it 'letters of an extraordinary nature . . .' which had been forwarded by Benjamin Franklin. Two weeks later, thirteen samples of the correspondence of Hutchinson and others of his clique with a British civil servant named Thomas Whately were broadcast to the world in a pamphlet published by Sam Adams's Boston Committee of Correspondence. Whately was now dead. Franklin's motive was still to preserve the Empire. Out of touch with colonial opinion, he thought that if his fellow Americans saw proof that Hutchinson had instigated the objectionable trend of British government policy, they would become peaceable subjects once the detested governor and his cronies had been driven 'like the scapegoats of old . . . into the wilderness'. Carefully edited by Sam Adams, the letters appeared to establish beyond doubt that the 'conspiracy' against liberty had existed on both sides of the Atlantic. Hutchinson was damned. But the British government was not, as Franklin had foolishly hoped, exonerated.

The Massachusetts Assembly petitioned for Hutchinson's removal from his post. The official hearing by the Privy Council in January 1774 turned into a public tongue-whipping of Franklin before thirty-six of the great men of Britain and a crowd of other eminent persons. Wedderburn, the Solicitor-General, Scot, compatriot of the arch-'conspirator' Bute, declaimed that Franklin had 'forfeited all the respect of societies and of men'. Franklin was shortly dismissed from his post of deputy Postmaster-General of the American colonies. Wedderburn's arrogance helped turn a would-be friend of Britain into a very dangerous enemy.

Just before this, word had reached London of a shocking event which marked the intersection of the crisis in Massachusetts with that in the affairs of the East India Company. With the Company's warehouses choked with 17 million lb. of surplus leaf, an Act had gone through, in May 1773, by which all duties charged on re-exported tea were to be remitted and the EIC was authorised to set up its own retail agencies in the colonies. The main aim was to help it offload its stock. But Americans would now get cheaper tea. All the propaganda of 'patriots' since the Townshend duty had come into force had failed to wean colonists from that delicious beverage. The government hoped that the smugglers would now be beaten out of the market and that colonists, sipping their cheap Bohea, would be reconciled to the one tax still imposed on them. This was naïve. Smugglers had wide support, and to drive them out of business would mean trouble. And legitimate merchants in the American ports would not be pleased by the new EIC monopoly.

Merchants allied themselves again with 'Sons of Liberty'. Intimidation forced the resignations of the men appointed EIC agents, in every port except in Boston, where, as it unsurprisingly happened, two sons of Hutchinson and certain relatives of his were the principal consignees. (The governor himself, though he kept this secret, had nearly £4,000, most of his liquid capital, invested in East India stock.)

In late November, the first consignments arrived in three vessels, each with over a hundred chests. Other goods were unloaded. The tea stayed aboard. British naval vessels blocked the harbour. Under the law, customs officers could have seized the tea to collect the duty upon it after twenty days. On the nineteenth day, Sam Adams produced his most brilliant stroke – a gigantic act of purposeful vandalism. Some two hundred men – artisans, shipyard workers, sailors – mustered in the evening. They were 'cloathed in blankets with the heads muffled, and copper-colored countenances, being each armed with a hatchet or axe, and pair pistols.' These 'Indians' boarded the three vessels. In three hours of sweaty effort, every chest was 'knocked to pieces and flung over the sides.' Choice leaf from Canton worth about £9,000 was shoved into the dark, chill waters of the harbour, where the morning light showed it islanded in windrows, so that boats had to be sent out to carve a passage for larger vessels through it.

Nine days later a ship reached the Delaware with nearly 700 chests of tea. Faced with a huge crowd, the captain was easily persuaded to take it back to England at once. In April next year, the 'Boston Tea Party' was repeated in New York, and the bells of the town's churches pealed for joy. Tea was permitted to land in Charles Town alone – and there it remained unsold for three years.

A new word, 'revolutionary', was first used in 1774. 'Revolution' now cracked what Franklin called 'that fine and noble China Vase, the British Empire.'

The British government decided that Boston must be punished. Four Bills were presented to the Commons. The port of Boston was to be closed to commerce until the inhabitants compensated the EIC. The custom house and the seat of provincial government were to be moved to Salem. A second Bill remodelled the constitution of Massachusetts. A nominated Council replaced the elective one. The Assembly was deprived of its powers to appoint and direct local officials, the freeholders of their right to elect jurymen. Town meetings were to be limited to one per year and restricted to purely local matters. A third Bill, prompted by the 'Boston massacre', provided that people accused of capital offences for carrying out their duties might be sent for trial to Britain or some other colony. A fourth increased the governor's power to quarter troops in private homes.

The parliamentary opposition was weak, and divided. Rockingham, whose loose confederation of supporters numbered probably less than forty MPs, believed in Britain's absolute supremacy over the colonies; Chatham, with at most a dozen followers, believed that supremacy was qualified by natural rights.

Several followers of both groups supported the Boston Port Bill, and apart from Burke almost no one spoke against it. British merchants were far less inclined than before to side with the Americans. They had survived the previous non-importation agreement, and the threat no longer worried them so much.

The 'Coercive Acts' went through by huge majorities. General Gage, commander-in-chief in America, was now given the extra commission of governor in Massachusetts. More troops were sent to Boston. The limited British electorate thought all this well done.

The 'Quebec Act' also went through at this time – most likely precipitated by the crisis, but not directly connected with the Coercive Acts. It stabbed at problems long overdue for solution. Now jurisdiction over the land north and west of a line running along Pennsylvania's western edge to the Ohio, and then along the Ohio to the Mississippi, was given to the governor of Quebec. Regarding Quebec itself the Act regularised, in great part, *ad hoc* arrangements already worked out on the spot. Rule was to be by governor and nominated council – the alternatives, both unacceptable, would have been to give Roman Catholics a full political role, or to set up a farcical system for English-speakers only. Now Catholics would at least be admitted to public office. Full recognition was given to the Catholic Church establishment.

Horrific though the 'Coercive Acts' against Massachusetts seemed to people in all the colonies, the Quebec Act was perhaps a still greater force in unifying a large sector of American opinion against Britain. In the debates preceding it, that detested Scot, Wedderburn, declared flatly: 'I would not say, "cross the Ohio, you will find the Utopia of some great and mighty empire." I would say, "This is the border, beyond which, for the advantage of your whole empire, You shall not extend Yourselves."' Every land speculator in the colonies would find these words, and the Act's provisions, disturbing. Furthermore, the creation of a nominated legislature in Quebec seemed clear evidence that Bute's 'conspiracy' was proceeding. The Canadians, furthermore, were hereditary enemies; could not the government use its papist 'slaves', in standing armies, to 'enslave' Britons and Americans in their turn? Above all, the toleration extended to papistry shocked zealous Protestants of all shades and species.

Gage, arriving in Boston to take up his duties in May 1774, found that he had no control outwith the range of the guns of his warships, which closed the port so effectively that its wharves were deserted, but were of no use in extracting compensation for the drowned tea. The General Court defiantly voted, before Gage closed it, a call for a 'continental' congress to defend American rights. In October, the townships sent representatives to an unauthorised provincial congress. This body effectively governed Massachusetts.

Support had burgeoned in other colonies. Illegal meetings everywhere took up Boston's call for a Continental Congress. It met in Philadelphia in September. The emergent Yankee twang and the prototype Southern drawl were heard together; of the seaboard colonies, only Georgia and Nova Scotia were unrepresented. It might have aborted in internecine quarrels. The sea, which was the main means of communication between colonies jealous of each others' trade and embattled over control of frontier lands, linked each at least as directly with London. But Sam Adams plotted and planned; and the alchemy of shared grievance, and shared risk, worked a miracle.

John Adams, representing Massachusetts, wrote home to his wife that the delegates debated from nine to three, then adjourned, feasted 'upon ten thousand delicacies' and sat drinking madeira, claret and burgundy till six or seven. Conviviality cemented common purpose. Patrick Henry was soon on his feet proclaiming, 'Government is dissolved. Where are your landmarks, your boundaries of Colonies? We are in a state of Nature, sir . . . The distinctions between Virginians, Pennsylvanians, New Yorkers and New Englanders are no more. I am not a Virginian, but an American.' His oratory was admired; so was the military bearing of that magnificent horseman George Washington, who sat mostly silent through the debates wearing his British uniform, and his sword.

No delegate could imagine that things could ever again be as they had been. British rule died as these men discovered that they were all splendid fellows, and all Americans. On October 14 they unanimously agreed on a statement of 'Declarations and Resolves' which referred to the British government as a 'foreign power'. On the 20th, Congress voted to boycott trade with Britain, and from now on rule in America passed into the hands of extralegal 'Committees of Association' erected to enforce non-importation, non-exportation and non-consumption. They encouraged drilling, seized government military stores, set up gunpowder factories, bought arms abroad.

A young Englishman from Derbyshire, Nicholas Cresswell, who had just come to the Chesapeake to seek his fortune, noted in February 1775, 'The Committees act as Justices. If any person is found to be inimical to the liberties of America, they give them over to the mobility to punish as they think proper . . . The people are arming and training in every place. They are all liberty mad.'

The term 'Lynch Law' is said to have derived from the eagerness with which one Captain Lynch of Virginia pursued anyone who was friendly to the British government or disrespectful to Congress. Such persons were now branded 'tories'. Tarring and feathering was the classic punishment. Another favourite was 'riding on a rail', where the victim was jogged roughly along on a sharp rail between his legs. Drenching in dung and simple assault and battery were also efficacious supports of 'whig' rule.

Very few people in America had supported the Stamp Act. But the once solid front against the British government was now fractured. Many men who had led the opposition to Grenville, who had written eloquent pamphlets against Townshend, who had helped to organise boycotts and extralegal congresses, were not prepared to move into revolt, and were denounced by the 'patriots' and subjected to treatment which embittered them permanently. The final sorting of sheep from goats had not yet been done; Congress had not yet deposed the

King in America. But George III himself was in no mood to make life easy for waverers. He was as clear on the value of *force majeure* as any revolutionary in the colonies. On November 19, 1774, he told Lord North, '. . . We must either master them, or totally leave them to themselves and treat them as Aliens.' He was not prepared to recommend the second course.

In February 1775, Parliament declared Massachusetts to be in a state of rebellion. In March it barred all the New England colonies from trade outside the Empire and from the Newfoundland fisheries. The ban was extended to most of the other colonies as each in turn made its sympathy for the Yankees known. Huge majorities backed these actions.

Burke produced a Commons resolution urging, on purely practical grounds, the concession of virtually everything which Congress had demanded. But not many well-to-do people in Britain thought that their empire faced dissolution. A Glasgow 'tobacco lord', William Cunninghame, summed up the complacency of most of his class: '. . . What madmen the Virginians are. How can they live or keep their negroes alive without coarse linens and cloth?'

Like certain modern economic historians, he failed to understand that man does not live by coarse linens, or bread, alone. For revolution to happen, principles, hopes, had to sweep men past calculation into actions which might have ruined them utterly. Patrick Henry might seem at a distance only a vainglorious rhetorician, but his fellow-countrymen found his eloquence uplifting, his voice musical. The extralegal Virginian Convention, in March 1775, heard him call on them to set up and to arm a rebel militia. '. . . Give me liberty or give me death!' By sixty-five votes to sixty they settled for liberty, perhaps, or death. 'Freeborn Englishmen' had become, in their own minds, 'Freeborn Americans'.

Gage received orders to arrest the leaders of the Massachusetts provincial congress. Promptly, on the night of April 18, he sent a force of around 700 light infantry, grenadiers and marines up towards Concord, some sixteen miles from Boston, where the rebels had a dump of arms. The movement was not kept secret. The Massachusetts militia had agreed to turn out at a minute's warning.

The British troops had to pass through Lexington on their way to Concord. Arriving at daybreak, the advance party, hungry and tired after a bad march in the dark, found some seventy 'minute men' lined up on the green to confront them.

Major Pitcairn, commanding, shouted, 'ye rebels, disperse!' What happened then is disputed. In any case, pistol or musket, redcoat or minute man, somebody fired. Suddenly, martyrs and heroes were made. Eight Americans were killed, ten were wounded. One British soldier was slightly injured.

Joined by the main British body, the royal troops proceeded to Concord and destroyed what military supplies were still there. But the countryside had risen, every village. The march back to Boston became a near rout. A British soldier wrote, with due respect, 'We were fired on from houses and behind trees, and before we had gone ½ mile we were fired on from all sides, but mostly from the rear, where people had hid themselves in houses till we had passed, and then fired. The country was an amazing strong one, full of hills, woods, stone walls, etc., which the Rebels did not fail to take advantage of . . . In this way we marched between 9 and 10 miles, their numbers increasing from all parts, while ours was reduced by deaths, wounds and fatigue . . .'

Gage had to send up a relieving force of 1,200 men to get his troops back to Boston. The total British casualties were 273; the rebels lost some 95. The moral effect was enormous. Yankee guerrillas had bested British regulars – who knew very well that they had been bested. The Massachusetts rebels hastened to print and circulate their own account of the affair: the British had fired at Lexington without provocation, and had then burned and raped their way through the countryside, spitting infants and women in childbed with their bayonets.

Word of Lexington took over a month to reach London. But it raced up and down the American coast at the speed of the fastest horseman. As Massachusetts militiamen swarmed around Boston, a contingent from New Hampshire came in to join them by dawn on April 21, having marched fifty-five miles in eighteen hours. Rhode Islanders and Connecticut men followed. Gage was besieged in Boston.

On May 10, the Captain commanding the British garrison at Ticonderoga on Lake Champlain, was startled from sleep in the gray of the morning by a command that he must come forth at once or his men would be slaughtered. Holding his trousers in his hand, he opened the door to confront Ethan Allen, who demanded that the fort must be surrendered, 'in the name of the great Jehovah, and the Continental Congress.' Allen's 'Green Mountain Boys' took about a hundred cannon and moved on to acquire a similar number again by capturing Crown Point, then seized the British sloop of war which cruised on the lake. Rebels commanded the crucial New York–Montreal corridor.

The Second Continental Congress, now meeting in Philadelphia, found Allen's success a momentary embarrassment. This was clearly aggression by their own supporters, and to sustain the role of injured loyal subjects, the delegates came up with the accusation that the Ministry had been planning a 'cruel invasion' from Quebec. After despatching one last loyal petition, begging the King to protect their rights against Parliament, they boldly declared their 'Causes of Taking up Arms'. Congress took on the burden of a sovereign power. It voted to issue several million dollars of its own paper currency, and it adopted the army besieging Boston. Individual colonies would choose officers of ranks up to colonel, but Congress itself would appoint the higher commanders. Washington was the unanimous choice as chief. With other 'Continental' officers, he shortly left for Boston.

He found there not an army, but a revolutionary movement in arms. This 'people's army' had no tents. Men slept on straw under shelters improvised from sailcloth, sacking and boards. There was no notion of sanitation, and no supply system. There were few horses, almost no carts or wagons, and not enough balls for the rare cannon. Men dressed in their usual clothes. Several 'majors' were tavern-keepers in private life. Blacksmiths, even, were captains. These men would not order their friends and neighbours distastefully, let alone flog their backs to a mass of raw flesh.

'I dare say,' Washington wrote, with the values of his class shaping his sentence, 'the men would fight very well (if properly Officered) although they are an exceeding dirty and nasty people . . .' He started a spate of court martials. Three colonels were cashiered. Floggings began.

Let us pause to inspect certain ironies and complexities. As the preachers with Washington's army called down the curses of heaven on Bute and Mansfield, Gage's soldiers in Boston were on the verge of mutiny against their Scots officers, and had to be threatened with exemplary punishment 'for swearing they ought to be commanded by Englishmen, and that they would not sacrifice their lives in an attempt to butcher their friends and fellow-subjects for any interested North Briton upon earth.'

The Glasgow factors, awake at last to the danger, were buying up every leaf of tobacco which they could find in the Chesapeake colonies, so that their seniors made spectacular windfall profits as, with war, the price in some eighteen months soared from below 2d. a lb. towards 2s. The Scots traders in Virginia were, almost to a man, against the political views of their planter clients.

But authorities in Britain still mistrusted all Scots. They reckoned that those who were not still Jacobite rebels at heart were, as Presbyterians, much like New Englanders, surely? Since Charles I's day no attempt had been made to prevent emigration from any British port. In September 1775, emigration from Scotland would be blocked, lest it should swell the ranks of rebellion.

While the American commander before Boston despised the democratical views of New Englanders and imposed on some of the latter such degrading 'Turkish' floggings as, given to redcoats, had seemed to these same Yankees unmistakable tokens of despotism, the British troops confronting them shared their excessive dislike of Scots and, out of the army, at home, might well have joined 'mobs' in the streets for Wilkes.

Do we say then that the confused relationships between Lowland Scotland and Highland Gaeldom, and between England and Scotland since 1707, were in some complicated way a major cause in the breakdown of mutual understanding between the American colonists and Britain? Perhaps historians should think hard about this. But they will not demonstrate that this one factor 'caused' revolution, any more than devoted mythologists can show that George Washington's leadership won independence.

Washington, as it proved, would never beat a British army in pitched battle, but the New Englanders whom he thought so 'dirty' had virtually managed that very difficult feat, a few days before his appointment as commander. Gage had been joined in May by three new generals from Britain: Howe, Clinton and that

'Gentleman Johnny' Burgoyne who had hectored against the nabobs in the Commons. They urged Gage to take the offensive. He aimed to strengthen the British position by occupying the heights on the Dorchester and Charlestown peninsulas flanking Boston. The rebels got wind of this. Their amateur general Artemas Ward and his council decided that the hills overlooking Charlestown must be pre-emptively occupied. For some reason, the force they sent entrenched itself not on Bunker Hill, but on the lower Breed's Hill. Gage accepted a typically slow and orthodox plan for straightforward frontal assault proposed by Howe, who therefore, with his redcoats, marched, on June 17, 1775, slowly uphill in melting summer heat, stopping every few yards to dress ranks. The Yankees watched them shimmering closer and then, when time was ripe, released three shattering volleys in ninety seconds. The redcoats went downhill again. They came up a second time. Again they were hurled into retreat. Howe called for reinforcements. At last, a third assault succeeded.

Over 1,000 redcoats – four out of ten – had been killed or wounded. American casualties had been lighter. Technically, 'Bunker Hill' was a British 'victory', but in fact it was a mortifying setback. Gage wrote, 'The loss we have sustained is greater than we can bear.'

In November, Lord North brought in a Bill which tried to establish a complete naval blockade of America. Meanwhile recruitment went ahead. The government had already planned to gather new regiments of Highlanders and to enlist more marines in Ireland, but these would not be enough. Agreements were entered into with rulers of six petty German states, who eventually provided almost 30,000 soldiers for Britain. The Landgrave of Hesse Kassel was the chief supplier, and so they would be known across the Atlantic as 'Hessians'. News of their purchase shocked Americans. Their use seemed to close all hope of reconciliation.

An Englishman, Thomas Paine, was on hand to help Americans make the decisive break from their former loyalty. The son of a Quaker master-staymaker, he had worked in his father's trade himself, but had failed, and had entered the Crown's service as an exciseman. His first writing had been a pamphlet urging higher salaries for revenue officers. In 1774 disaster pushed him into emigration. His tobacconist's business collapsed. His marriage broke up. The Excise dismissed him. He met Benjamin Franklin, who encouraged him to go to America. Arriving in Philadelphia in November 1774, he soon became editor of the *Pennsylvania Magazine*.

On January 10, 1776, Paine published, at Philadelphia, a fifty-page pamphlet called *Common Sense*. Its clear and forceful prose made seem perfectly obvious certain ideas which men had shrunk from expressing. Paine sharply denied the vaunted perfection of the 'constitution of England', and hurled sarcasm at the hitherto sacred institutions of kingship and hereditary succession. 'Of more worth is one honest man to society, and in the sight of God, than all the crowned ruffians that ever lived.'

The time for debate was over, Paine said. 'Arms as the last resource decide the contest . . . There is something absurd, in supposing a Continent to be perpetually governed by an island.' Paine called for an 'open and determined DECLARATION FOR INDEPENDENCE'.

In three months, 120,000 copies of his pamphlet were printed. By January 19, Nicholas Creswell was noting in Virginia, 'A pamphlet called "Commonsense" makes a great noise.' On the 26th, 'Nothing but Independence will go down. The Devil is in the people.' Governor Dunmore, who had retreated to the safety of a Royal Naval vessel, abetted Paine's propaganda mightily with his raids on the colony's coast, his attempts to bring Indians down on the western frontier, and, most shocking of all, his promise of freedom to slaves who would join the British.

North Carolina, in February 1776, saw the first, poignant, loyalist counter-rising. From the 1730s, Scottish Gaels had settled on the upper reaches of the Cape Fear River. By this time there were perhaps as many as 12,000 Highlanders in the area, rather outnumbered, it seems, by their slaves. They spoke Gaelic and so did their blacks. Many were from Argyllshire, a Campbell stronghold, Presbyterians with traditional Hanoverian loyalties, but among the wealthiest people in the region were Flora Macdonald, once Bonnie Prince Charlie's saviour during his wanderings after Culloden, and her husband Allan, who owned a plantation of 475 acres. Gage sent Brigadier General Donald Macdonald and Colonel Donald MacLeod to create a Highland army. Some 1,300 tartan-clad men mustered to the sound of the pibroch. They marched to join other units at the river mouth. Eighteen miles from the coast, they were opposed by patriot militia. About 50 were killed and 880 captured. The patriots lost only two of their men.

At Boston, Howe had succeeded Gage in command. Over the winter, Washington had brought up fifty-nine guns captured at Ticonderoga. Then he moved on to the commanding Dorchester Heights which Howe had unaccountably failed to occupy. Facing bombardment, Howe evacuated on March 17, taking his troops and 1,100 loyalist refugees off to Halifax, Nova Scotia.

Colonies from Massachusetts to Georgia were now setting up elected 'state' assemblies outwith British law. Men who had usurped power, and had begun to treat with French agents, risked as much if they went back on their 'treason' as if they moved forward to independence. Only victory could safeguard them from reprisals. To break from England was painful. But England, it seemed, had been taken over by liberty-hating Scots. Ezra Stiles of Connecticut wrote in his diary, 'Let us boldly say, for History will say it, that the whole of this War is so far chargeable to the Scotch councils, & to the Scotch as a Nation . . .'

On June 7, 1776, Richard Henry Lee proposed to Congress a resolution calling for a declaration of independence and an American confederation. By July 2, twelve out of thirteen delegations, with that of New York abstaining but approving, declared the bond between the new 'states' and Britain to be 'totally dissolved'. Two days later the great Declaration was adopted.

The committee of five appointed to produce it had included such choice penmen as Franklin and John Adams, but Thomas Jefferson was in effect the author.He epitomised most of what was best in the thought and temper of eighteenth-century 'enlightenment', as well as many common self-contradictions. Six foot two and a half inches tall, lounging, gangling, large-boned, with freckles and red hair, he was not a very good speaker and his manner was shy and scholarly. He had been born in frontier country, thickly forested, where wolves still howled but had grown up in touch with the latest currents of Scottish and European thought. His versatility now seems astounding, though there were others in his time who could match it. His interest in scientific and technological matters was deep and fruitful. Had he never meddled in politics, we would still remember him as a great self-taught architect, designer of his own beautiful house at Monticello.

He was very much a Virginian of his class. He had hardly travelled outside his colony. Virginia was still predominantly 'Anglo-Saxon' in stock, and Jefferson was opposed to mass immigration from European countries where people had been indoctrinated in the perverse ways of absolute monarchy. He disliked manufacturing industry, and wanted to keep it out. Traditional theology did not impress him. Original sin was not for him a reality. He believed that 'goodness lay at the heart of things.' In 1826, near the end of his long life, he would reaffirm his belief in the 'palpable truth, that the mass of mankind has not been born with saddles on their backs, nor a favoured few booted and spurred, ready to ride them legitimately, by the grace of God.'

Yet hc was a devoted holder of individual property rights. As much as Adam Smith's great *Wealth of Nations*, published in this same remarkable year, the Declaration which Jefferson drafted was a refinement of middle-class individualism. 'Liberty' was the twin of 'Property'.

Congress tidied his draft somewhat. It put in some remarks about God, whom Jefferson had almost ignored. It struck out one passage which referred to the slave trade as 'cruel war against human nature itself'. It also removed an abusive remark about the use of 'Scotch & foreign mercenaries'. But the resounding prose was still mostly his. 'We hold these truths to be self-evident: that all men are created equal; that they are endowed by their creator with certain inalienable Rights; that among these are life, liberty & the pursuit of happiness: that to secure these rights, governments are instituted among men, deriving their just powers from the consent of the governed; that whenever any form of government becomes destructive of these ends, it is the right of the people to alter or to abolish it . . .'

'Tories' or 'loyalists' had been declared traitors. All states eventually amerced, taxed or confiscated loyalist property. Some royalists were gaoled, many, most harshly, in cells forty yards below the surface in copper mines at

Simsbury, Connecticut. Others arrived as refugees in Nova Scotia.

This seaboard colony might have seemed an obvious candidate for a fourteenth state. Its Yankee settlers were deeply resentful of the clique of Halifax merchants which ran the colony's government. However, there was very little indigenous revolutionary activity. Congress showed almost no interest in liberating the province, and Washington calculated, probably rightly, that British naval strength made it impossible. Bewildered as to which side they should support, the Nova Scotians consoled and uplifted themselves through a belated 'Great Awakening'. Henry Alline, a young revivalist preacher, went everywhere telling them that old England was corrupt, New England had missed its way, and that they, simple, high-minded men and women, were now God's chosen people.

Congress paid far more attention to Quebec, and had made a sustained effort to bring that colony into the fold. The Quebec Act came partially into force from May 1775. On the new Council, seven members were French-speaking Catholics. For the next dozen years a 'French Party', so-called, although its leaders were British, dominated Quebec's government. English-speaking merchants and traders remained 'out'. But their class was small and as yet hardly rooted. The great mass of Canadian peasants, however fearful they were that the British would tax them hard and that their landlords would raise rents, did not speak Jefferson's mother tongue and were wholly unused to discussing constitutional questions.

An Ulsterman, Guy Carleton, hesitant, plodding and unimaginative, was commander-in-chief as well as governor. It was vital, until reinforcements arrived from Britain, that he should create a Canadian militia. It was equally important to Congress that the Canadians should not arm against them. An energetic propaganda campaign took American agents through the Canadian villages. People wavered and havered. When Ethan Allen tried to seize Montreal with a small force in September 1775, he was swiftly forced to surrender by Canadian townspeople who rallied with a few British merchants. Richard Montgomery, Irish born, made more progress later that month. Despite pressure from priests and seigneurs, the militia did not much help Carleton. The British were able to hold Fort St John on the Richelieu against Montgomery for eight critical weeks. Yet after they withdrew from there in November, the Montreal people, contemptuous of British weakness, opened the gates of their town to Montgomery.

During his flight, Carleton passed an American force led by Benedict Arnold, on its way up river to join Montgomery, after an epic march from the Maine coast through 320 miles of virgin forest to receive at last, after five wasting weeks, a cordial welcome from the Canadians. But Arnold had reached Quebec just too late. Lieutenant-Colonel Allan Maclean had had time to rally a motley force – fellow-Highlanders, Canadians, British seamen, British civilians – which was sufficient to make Arnold head away.

The Canadians now tasted American military occupation, and did not like it. Montgomery found only a few score natives willing to serve with his force. Besieging Quebec, he decided to risk an attack before the engagements of his American troops expired at the end of the year. On the night of December 30, in darkness and driving snow, he was killed as he led his advance party into the Lower Town. The rash assault then ended, though Arnold kept up the siege.

With the help of the priests, offering no reward, Carleton raised 2,000 Canadian volunteers. Arnold, who paid, could attract only 500. In May, British reinforcements arrived at last. They sortied immediately, and the Americans fled. The Americans looted as they fell back, and they left unpaid debts and bitter memories. The *habitants*, still reluctant to serve the British, now recalled that history gave them little reason to like Americans. Two days before Congress declared independence, Carleton shooed the last American soldier out of Canada.

II

In 1776, the first regular coach service was instituted between Chester and Holyhead, in Anglesey, bringing the depths of Welsh-speaking North Wales into rapid communication with England. The 'picturesque' and remote Welsh landscapes were beginning to draw sophisticated tourists. In tune with movements in Scotland and Ireland a literary revival in the Welsh language went on. Three brothers called Morris from Anglesey, all civil servants, had gathered around them a circle of poets and scholars who wrote verse in traditional metres and rescued old texts from oblivion's dust. But not all Welshmen were obsessed with the past. Methodism had brought many of them into a movement belonging to the new age. The American War now added political awareness. The first publication in Welsh purely concerned with politics was also launched in 1776, a translation of a pamphlet on the American quarrel.

The same year brought to print *On Civil Liberty* by the leading Welsh Dissenter, Richard Price, which sold 60,000 copies immediately, then double that number in a cheap edition. Price was a whole-hearted supporter of the American revolutionaries. A campaign for parliamentary reform was gathering momentum – Major Cartwright's *Take Your Choice*, demanding universal male suffrage, also came out in 1776 – and its supporters naturally identified with the democratical persons now causing trouble in Massachusetts.

Granville Sharp, though no Dissenter, resigned his post in the Ordnance Board on the outbreak of war with America – 'that unnatural business'. As well as kindly philanthropists, advanced economic thinkers were questioning the point of the conflict, and the greatest of all British works in economics was yet another new publication this year: Adam Smith's *Wealth of Nations*, a bestseller, attacked both 'mercantilism' and war.

Chatham appealed in the Lords for an end to the war, saying over and over again in his last speeches, 'You CANNOT conquer America'. His rhetoric was madder than ever. He could not bear the thought of his empire's dissolution. In April 1778 he vehemently denied that American independence should ever be admitted. Then he collapsed in the chamber, to die a month later.

To the rather less crazy voice of Burke was added in opposition in the Commons the eloquence of a rising star, Charles James Fox, son of the most corrupt politician of all, himself a rake, gambler and womaniser, but an ardent supporter of the Americans, whom he saw as proponents of true whig principles. However, the regular opposition could never muster more than a fifth of the House. And recognised 'interests' outside Parliament were not applying much pressure against the war. Bristol merchants ceased to oppose it as valuable government contracts offered themselves, and by the end of 1776, the town's leadership was firmly committed to support of the Ministry. Liverpool might have been expected to show truculence. A general embargo on the export of arms, lest these might reach the rebels, had hit the slave trade hard, since guns were still an essential item of barter in Guinea. The war hurt poor Liverpool people – by its end 10,000 were depending on public relief or private charity. However, rich shipowners turned with gusto to privateering, launching, in 1778–9, some 120 private men-of-war in nine months. And from 1780 their slave trade revived.

Glasgow merchants would never again lead Europe in dispensing tobacco, but the war brought no drastic disruption of their prosperity, and trade with the thirteen colonies continued, not only directly through ports still in British hands, but deviously through Quebec, Nova Scotia, and the Dutch and Danish West Indian islands. Upper- and middle-class opinion in Scotland was overwhelmingly pro-government over the war. As in England, it is hard to know what the poor thought or felt, though it is clear that the Edinburgh townsfolk encouraged mutinous Highland regiments.

Eleven new Highland regiments were raised during the war. There were four mutinies in and around Edinburgh in thirteen months, during 1778–9. In one brutal case, some sixty soldiers of Fraser's Regiment and the Black Watch fought a bloody battle at Leith Harbour with Border troops sent in to tame them, and half the Highlanders were killed or wounded. Their grievance had been that they were being drafted into a Lowland regiment. So far from being in tune with democratical Yankees, these Gaels were more feudalist than their own chiefs, who enticed them into uniform with pledges that they would serve only under officers of their own name or race and in the clothing they liked best to wear. Highland self-respect was outraged by army floggings and punishment in the Black Hole.

Amongst poor people in England, as war began, John Wesley found bitterness everywhere. He reported that 'the bulk of the people in every city, town and village' were alienated from George III. 'They heartily despise his Majesty and hate him with a perfect hatred. They wish to imbrue their hands in his blood; they are full of the spirit of murder and rebellion.' This reaction was prompted by a slump in commerce bringing temporary high unemployment. But even as the economy picked itself up, we must suppose that few ordinary Englishmen had much heart for the conflict.

III

If most British people were not eager supporters of North and the King, only a minority of Americans were ardent, committed 'patriots'. The thirteen colonies were an arena of bitter civil war, in which both sides enlisted Red Indian auxiliaries and went in for summary execution of their opponents.

With Britain's world-conquering power behind them, few loyalists can have dreamt at the outset that they might lose. Nowhere did they take the initiative. Patriots acted; loyalists reacted. Patriots found inspiration in hope – they aimed to create the best nation in the world – and where families divided, the younger generation generally tended to be whig. Patriots, full of passionate intensity, made more effective polemicists and speakers. They wanted an independent republic. Anyone could understand what they meant. Loyalists were rarely so sure what they wanted. Most loyalist leaders had been sharply critical of the British government. Few would have liked a simple return to the situation of 1763. Hence their voices were diverse and blurred. Their staple scorn for the patriot leaders took on the sneering accents of aristocratic hauteur. They could not easily appeal to these whom they dismissed as the 'mob', the 'populace' and the 'frenzied multitude'.

Even so, loyalists were very numerous. Perhaps 30,000, perhaps more, actually fought for George III. In 1780, when Washington's army numbered only about 9,000, 8,000 American loyalists were aiding the British. During and after the war, maybe 60,000, perhaps 100,000 loyalists left the colonies as exiles. Perhaps a tenth even of New Englanders, a third or a quarter of southerners, and a half of the people of the middle colonies, could have been described as loyalists.

They came in all shapes and sizes. Even among the Virginian ruling class, where loyalists were exceptionally scanty, men with such great plantocrat names as Byrd and Randolph were found among them. Most Scotch-Irish were patriots, but not all. Natives of Scotland, Gael and Lowlander, rich and poor alike, were generally on George III's side (though two Scots signed the Declaration of Independence, and of thirteen known Scottish parsons in Virginia, eight sided with the patriots). Germans were commonly passive in the south, but those in New York State were largely patriots. While smugglers, of course, were patriots, merchants depending on licit trade with Britain tended, despite all the Acts of Trade, to be loyalist.

Many loyalists lay low. 'We are at present all Whigs', one wrote in 1775, 'until the arrival of the King's troops.' When they did raise their heads, loyalists proved, as soldiers, no whit inferior to their patriot enemies. Some led Indian allies against frontier settlements. Thus, the Cherokees attacked in the south with the help of a few back-country loyalists (though patriot militia beat them so thoroughly that they were never a military threat again). Later, the British made some use of the Creeks, while Iroquois assisted them in the north.

Pro-British Indian raids, however, might kill or alienate potential friends as well as convinced foes. And while every loyalist success strengthened whig determination by the hatred which it evoked, each British failure disillusioned colonials not deeply hostile to the 'mother country'. That section, perhaps the largest of the three, who prudently backed whichever side was currently winning in the locality, selling produce to either army impartially, gradually shifted towards the patriot side as the British showed how vincible they were. George III's forces could never control more than a few scattered strips of land on the coast.

Tight blockade might have brought the rebels to terms. The British fleet, in 1776, captured numerous American vessels, but could not lock the Americans in. The success of rebel privateers rubbed home the truth of Chatham's assertion that America had been 'the nerve of our strength, the nursery and basis of our naval power.' American craftsmen, yards, masts, and timber, had been essential to Britain's naval pre-eminence.

An oak tree took a hundred years to mature. Nearly 2,000 trees must be felled to produce a 74-gun third-rater. Former wars had stripped England's southern counties almost bare, and only increased use of oak and softwoods from America had kept Britain ahead of her rivals. And American seamen had been very useful. In their absence, the pressing service in Britain itself had to work on a larger and more unpopular scale than ever before. By 1779 it employed over 1,000 men. In the whole course of the war, no fewer than 171,000 sailors were found. 18,500 men died of sickness. A quarter, 42,000, deserted. By contrast, only 1,240 perished in action.

The Navy, in any case, could not be used to great, offensive effect when so many troops had to be shipped across, then supplied once they reached America. The British never controlled enough territory to feed their army. Apart from hay and some fresh provisions, everything had to come by sea. There simply could not be enough ships, enough sailors.

The British now put far more men into America than had beaten the French out of Canada. Then, they had had help from the thirteen colonies. Now, British losses had to be replaced by shipping new men across the Atlantic. Washington's men were of course, home-grown; hence, each British casualty cost more. Their home terrain gave the patriots huge advantages. The land was vast. The British army was always short of transport. Its communications were always vulnerable. It could not pursue the rebels far from the navigable rivers. Its men, in any case, were enfeebled by a climate to which their foes were contentedly adjusted. The winters were much colder than in Britain, and the summers were hotter.

Regulars were at a loss against the guerrilla spirit first encountered on the march back from Concord. Anywhere in the colonies, some guerrilla body might come from nowhere to hit the British hard on the nose. The British learnt from their enemies. Before long, they too were using special units of fast mounted infantry. British foot soldiers were superb at close order drill. They were extremely brave under fire. But they fought for their pay, not out of love for their cause. Their virtue was that they obeyed orders. The virtue of the American soldier was that he questioned them. British generals were not inept by European standards. But the very fact that they were professionals was against them. If they followed the 'rules' safely, they would be paid. Patriot commanders were fighting for their lives, and their property. Though they wrangled with each other, fumbled and bungled, the better patriot commanders, technically beaten, were not going to accept defeat tamely. They would come back, and back again.

Internally, the American revolution was drastic in its immediate effects. Perhaps twenty-four people in a thousand were driven into exile, as compared with only five in a thousand expelled in the French revolution a few years later. Great quantities of loyalist-owned land passed into others' hands. Sometimes the effect was to spread property more widely; in New York State, James de Lancey's acres came under the ownership of 275 different people. But more commonly, unto those who had it was given, with merchants, army contractors and revolutionary leaders acquiring large properties.

Until 1781, the Second Continental Congress continued to govern, or rather misgovern, the 'United States'. Articles of confederation, completed four years before, were not ratified until then because of disputes between states over western lands. The country was desperately short of the manufactured goods formerly acquired from Britain, and as English and Scots found ways of getting them in, control returned to British merchant firms. Inflation raged upwards, worsened by the spate of paper currency put out by Congress and the states, and by gleeful profiteering on the part of merchants, contractors and commissaries.

Connecticut, Rhode Island, and, at first, Massachusetts, simply proceeded under their charters, slightly amended to exclude the Crown. Ten other states swiftly produced new constitutions. Pennsylvania's was the most dramatic. Existing leaders were loyalist or timid. In the summer of 1776, Paine and his radical friends supplanted the Assembly with their own provincial conference of delegates, which in turn arranged an elected Constitutional Convention to settle a new form of government for the colony. The new constitution for which this voted, and which operated till 1789, provided for a unicameral legislature, to be elected by all free male taxpayers; for the local election of JPs and sheriffs; and for an enlightened penal code. But a reaction against Paineite ideas was setting in among propertied men. John Adams had led it with a riposte to *Common Sense* in which he argued the case for elected upper houses. His views had great weight with those making constitutions in other states, who mostly found Pennsylvanian 'mobocracy' deeply distasteful. The dominance of existing élites was confirmed. Jefferson could not persuade his fellow Virginians to widen the franchise beyond its colonial limits. However, in all thirteen colonies, governors were now elected. In Europe, this spectacle seemed either outrageous or inspiring. The new states confirmed in law the peculiarities of American life as they already existed in practice. The new nation's leaders all accepted the principle of 'popular government', though they saw 'democracy' as an unworkable or detestable form of it.

Amidst all this, black slaves could hardly be forgotten. When the Declaration of Independence was voted, talking of natural rights for 'all men', colonial anti-slavery campaigners were swift to point out that if Africans were men, they must be included.

Rhode Island had prohibited slave importation in 1774, and proceeded to raise a (separate) battalion of black troops during the war. The shortage of men willing to fight for Washington meant that slaves and free blacks were drawn in elsewhere, though South Carolina and Georgia held out against enlisting them to the end. During or immediately after the war, all states except these same two passed laws against fresh imports. A Pennsylvania law of 1780 provided for gradual emancipation in that state. Massachusetts had outlawed slavery by 1783. Rhode Island and Connecticut followed in 1784. In the north, slavery thus withered away, and even in the south, few at this time actually endorsed it in public. A Virginian law of 1782 made manumission easier.

The 'right' wing in American politics, once loyalists had been extruded, would have seemed 'centre' or 'left' wing anywhere else in the Atlantic world. Americans had displayed the power of the 'people' to seize their own destiny from the hands of anointed rulers and their hirelings. For another hundred years, élitists in Britain would view the new nation with deep disdain and dismay, as a bad example to their own poor. Anti-slavery agitation by otherwise conservative British people would be heated at least in part by a wish to recapture the moral leadership of the English-speaking world from the likes of Thomas Jefferson.

Independency, in 1776, was already a fact. However, the war lasted five more years. Neither side won 'great victories' like Blenheim, though several generals on both sides, including Washington, showed unprecedented talent for handing their own men over into captivity in thousands. Washington, by surviving in command, secured his status as the most overrated soldier of all time and eventual translation into presidency and long-nosed marble. Carleton, by doing virtually nothing, acquired for later historians the aura of having been the best royal general in America, if only he had got round to doing something. Redcoats died. Their comrades sang sadly of lasses at home. American soldiers died. Their comrades sang the same songs. Slaves were still whipped here and there. American farmers prospered, offering produce to either side.

Shortly before the Declaration of Independence, General Howe landed near New York with a powerful force from Halifax. Soon after, Admiral Lord Howe (his brother) arrived with the battle fleet from Britain. Washington needlessly

left behind nearly 3,000 soldiers to fall into British hands. He passed through
New Jersey with a dispirited, dwindling band. But Howe was sluggish in
pursuit. While the British were in winter quarters, Washington scored an
important point. At dawn on December 26, he attacked Trenton, garrisoned by
3,000 Hessians, somnolent after their Christmas celebrations. A third of them
had to surrender. The place was recaptured by the British soon after, but the
Americas' guerrilla dash had had vital psychological effect. Washington shortly
achieved another little victory at Princeton. Frederick the Great himself hailed
his prowess, and a cautious, moderate slave-owner became the hero of a
revolutionary people.

In 1777, Congress was able to raise 34,000 troops, and thanks to secret help
from France and Spain these were well armed and quite well clothed. Benjamin
Franklin had gone to Paris as ambassador from Congress. His reputation as
scientist and *philosophe* preceded him, as did the cult, in French intellectual
circles, of the 'good Quaker'. Dissident young Frenchmen already identified his
country with principles of civil and religious liberty which were eschewed by
their own royal government. New England and Pennsylvania were in fashion;
South Carolina had to be forgotten. Franklin found that the fur cap which he
wore to hide his eczema was hailed as the badge of the honest frontiersman. He
dressed in Quaker fashion, in public, lived in private luxury, and flirted, despite
his advanced age, with pretty noblewomen.

While the French government saw a chance of revenge against Pitt's
conquests, young officers rushed to volunteer for Washington's army. They
were commonly disillusioned by their reception across the Atlantic. The
Americans, who had too few commissions available for all of them, were,
furthermore, still very 'English'. Sam Adams was heartily surprised to hear a
young Frenchman talk of republican principles. 'Where did you learn all that?'
'In France.' 'In France! That's impossible.' Then, after thinking a moment,
'Well,' said Adams, 'because a man was born in a stable, it is no reason why he
should be a horse.' However, French gunpowder came in very handy during the
campaigns of 1777.

In that year the British commanders came up with two good ideas. One was
General Howe's, that he should strike at Philadelphia via the Chesapeake. The
other was Burgoyne's, a push southward from Carolina towards New York,
isolating rebarbative New England. The trouble was that these notions were not
co-ordinated. Howe sailed off in July, beat Washington thoroughly at
Brandywine Creek, and occupied Philadelphia. Meanwhile, Burgoyne had led
nearly ten thousand troops southwards from Canada. Two companies of
Canadian militia went with him; their members deserted in mass on the way,
refusing to serve outside their homeland. Nevertheless, full of bounce, he
recaptured Ticonderoga. After that he made slow, painful progress. The
Americans felled trees in his path. By September, General Gates, opposing him,
actually had more men. Burgoyne rashly attacked a strong American position at

Bemis Heights. British casualties outweighed the value of the ground he took; then a reconnaissance in force was badly mauled. On October 17, at Saratoga, Burgoyne surrendered. His 5,000 remaining men passed into captivity.

North and Parliament now made enormous concessions. The Tea Act and the Massachusetts Charter Act were repealed. Parliament renounced its power to tax the colonies. Five peace commissioners, led by the Earl of Carlisle, were empowered to offer the rebels even more than the first Continental Congress had demanded, though not the independence which the second had actually seized.

It was too late. News of Saratoga prompted immediate French recognition of the new republic. Treaties between the two countries were ratified by Congress in May next year. Carlisle's commission, arriving soon after, could do nothing. There was no French army in the United States until 1780, but the naval effects of the alliance were felt at once.

Spain shortly entered the war against Britain, aiming to get back Gibraltar at last. Britain itself declared war, pre-emptively, on the Dutch, after the Netherlands had entered a 'League of Armed Neutrality' launched by Russia and joined, over two years, by half a dozen other European powers. Even Portugal joined. The dog bit its master. Every navy of consequence, by 1782, was resisting Britain's. This time, there was no land war in Europe to give Britain allies and distract France.

France and Spain between them had half as many ships again as the Royal Navy. Inevitably, the Britain lost control, from time to time, of American waters, where patriot privateers swarmed in hundreds. Before the end, Britain lost about 2,000 ships, and 12,000 captured sailors, to these marauders. To launch another effort in America as large as that which had failed in 1777 would mean almost certain loss of the British West Indies to France. The islands must have priority. Most prominent persons, including George III, believed that Britain would be ruined without them. In March 1778, the Cabinet decided that Admiral Lord Howe must not only send home twenty ships to make good the shortage of cruisers in British waters, but also despatch a strong naval force to the Leewards. General Howe had resigned after Saratoga. Clinton, his successor, was to send 3,000 troops to reinforce the Floridas and 5,000 to the West Indies. The rest of his army was to quit Philadelphia. This left only two points in the thirteen colonies, New York and Rhode Island, in British hands.

The West Indian colonies were indeed in a serious plight. They had utterly depended on North American provisions. Slaves starved. About 3,000 deaths from malnutrition were reported from the Leewards alone by March 1778. Credit collapsed. Insurance and freight rates soared. For the first time, the British islands felt commercial strangulation such as had formerly been the lot of the French.

In the autumn of 1778, the French seized Dominica. To balance this, Clinton's reinforcements captured St Lucia in December. The French regained control of the sea. St Vincent and Grenada fell to them in 1779. Three years later they would add St Kitts, Nevis and Montserrat.

Britain itself was in danger. The exploits of one sea-guerrilla in home waters shook government supporters. He was a Scot, the son of a gardener, born John Paul, to which he added, on his own account, 'Jones'. The first lieutenant commissioned in the infant 'Continental Navy', he went to raid commerce off Ireland, then suddenly hit Whitehaven in Cumbria one night in the spring of 1778. He did little damage, but this was the first time an English seaport had been so raided for over a hundred years. Jones sailed across to his homeland, Galloway, and stole the Countess of Selkirk's silver from her mansion, before her eyes. He was shortly given command of a converted French East Indiaman which he renamed the *Bonhomme Richard*. In it, he cruised right round Britain with a small squadron, capturing prizes and causing consternation. As British ships scoured the seas in vain for him, Jones became a folk-hero in England and Scotland. Ballads were printed in his honour.

One aim of the *Bonhomme Richard*'s cruise had been to divert British vessels from opposing a planned Franco-Spanish Armada. Thirty thousand troops were due to invade from France. Britain could muster only 21,000 regulars on home soil, though 30,000 militiamen also stood ready. The winds were Protestant once again. The attack failed.

For the British, America was now a sideshow, where impotence confronted impotence. The Continental army dwindled in numbers – service was hard, food and clothing were still bad, pay was worth little more than the paper on which it was printed. There were dangerous mutinies, and in the autumn of 1780, the best American general, Benedict Arnold, unmasked as a traitor, went over to the British.

But the British were now too weak to attack Washington's weak army. They could do much damage with raids on the coastline and on the frontier. Some major New York landowners, John and Walter Butler and Guy Johnson (son of Sir William, who was now dead), had retreated into Canada, where they organised loyalists into military corps. Many Iroquois joined them. Loyalist raids along the northern frontier sent panic-stricken settlers fleeing east for their lives. General John Sullivan led a successful American counter-attack. More than forty Iroquois towns and 160,000 bushels of corn were destroyed, and in the severe winter of 1779–80, while many Indians died of starvation, thousands flocked to Niagara to the food and protection of the British. The Six Nations were never a force again, though the Americans soon stood on the defensive once more. Even the northern frontier, then, saw stalemate.

The new British strategy was to attempt the piecemeal reduction of the separate states with the help of loyalist militia. The belief that most of the former colonists were still loyalists was encouraged by leading exiles in London.

'Tories' washed up in Britain, in straitened financial circumstances, had had enforced upon them a dismal recognition of what it meant to be 'colonial' and

'American' in an arrogant, wealthy society. Thomas Hutchinson, the most distinguished of them, died, heartbroken, in 1780, having missed his native land painfully. '. . . I should prefer even my humble cottage upon Milton Hill to the lofty palaces upon Richmond Hill, so that upon the whole I am more of a New England man than ever . . .' Lesser loyalists mostly reacted likewise, mingling as much as possible with people from their own colonies, and gradually migrating from expensive London to Bristol and other provincial towns. But after Saratoga, the influence of their spokesmen grew markedly. They presented the government with an argument which was most reassuring, and perfectly circular. The colonies had been enjoying a virtual Golden Age of prosperity under benevolent rule. Somehow, as one prominent exile put it, they had 'run Mad with too mush Happiness'. A small clique, setting their sights on independence, had 'deluded' the ignorant 'populace'. Their puny minority could be disarmed by the loyal and grateful majority. This notion lured North's ministry as a rope appeals to a drowning man.

The southern states seemed the best bet. The first strokes there had worked well. A British force of 3,000 easily recaptured Savannah at the end of 1778, and within a month Georgia was under control. A royal governor ruled there for three years. Charles Town fell next May, and General Benjamin Lincoln, with over 5,000 men, made another massive surrender. General Lord Cornwallis was left in charge. The position in South Carolina seemed excellent. Cornwallis had 8,000 men. Hundreds of repentant patriots were taking oaths of allegiance to the King. Washington sent General Gates with a sizeable army, but Cornwallis beat this decisively at Camden.

Next year Cornwallis despatched an army under Benedict Arnold to conquer Virginia. It captured Richmond. The legislature fled. Cornwallis defeated another American army in North Carolina and moved off to join Arnold at Yorktown, on the Chesapeake. American armies had been beaten in four states in quick succession. This run of victories would have meant triumph in any European theatre of war. It meant nothing of the kind in this steamy near-wilderness. Cornwallis left behind him about 8,000 troops, most of them loyalists, to defend South Carolina and Georgia. Now General Nathanael Greene, defeated in the open field, could rally enough guerrillas in the creeks and on the hills and in the woods to inflict losses which forced the royal force on to the defensive. Southern back-countrymen changed sides with the tide of war, and as British troops gave way, loyalist militiamen prudently slipped over to join the whigs.

Cornwallis fancied Yorktown as a base, and set about establishing himself there. A French army which had wintered at Newport, well disciplined and well supplied with money, was now ready for offensive operations. Its commander persuaded Washington that the British must be caught in Virginia. A French fleet was in American waters, and Admiral de Grasse agreed to come to the Chesapeake in August, bringing 3,000 French regular troops with him.

Washington brought down 12,000 men. Facing superior forces on the land side, Cornwallis found that de Grasse had cut his seaward communications. He surrendered, with 7,000 troops, on October 19. Lord North, hearing of this in late November, flung his arms wide and cried, 'Oh God! it is all over.' The British still had 30,000 effectives in America. But Yorktown was final because of the juncture at which the news struck. There had been defeats in India, West Florida had been lost, Minorca had been invaded, French and Spanish fleets were menacing in the Channel again, and that squad of independent country gentleman MPs who figure in histories of this period rather like a confused and timorous chorus in some tragedy by Euripides, were 'groaning' under the weight of taxation. The British government gave America up.

IV

Many country gentlemen, however, seemed to have caught bad habits from the rebels. Calls for cheaper government mingled with protests against corruption and aims to make Parliament more representative, in a spontaneous movement which welled up among the electors after Saratoga.

The freeholders of Yorkshire, led by the Reverend Christopher Wyvill, agreed, at a mass meeting of electors, on a petition against waste of public money and set up a committee to carry on correspondence. In 1780, the 'petitioning movement' spread quite widely through the country, infecting even the Isle of Man. Wyvill planned an association on a national basis. One aim was to add to the House of Commons a hundred more representatives of the counties, elected on the broad freeholder franchise. It was decided to hold a meeting in London of deputies elected by local committees. The proponents of this assembly had the virtually revolutionary hope that it might take over effective control of the country from North's corrupt Parliament. Only twelve counties and eight boroughs were represented when it convened in March 1780, but the parliamentary opposition was stirred into action. Next month, the Commons passed a resolution moved by one Dunning which stated: '. . . The influence of the Crown has increased, is increasing, and ought to be diminished.'

It seemed for a moment that North must fall. But the passage of Dunning's resolution paradoxically helped to head off crisis, since it showed that the Commons were not wholly subservient and did something to restore their prestige. The opposition, inside and outside Parliament, was anyway deeply divided over prescriptions. The Rockingham faction, including Burke, favoured aristocratic domination, and accordingly wished to curtail royal influence. But Charles James Fox had become chairman of the Westminster Committee of Correspondence which agreed on proposals which went as far as universal suffrage.

Dr Johnson had remarked a couple of years before: 'Subordination is sadly broken down in this age. No man, now, has the same authority which his father had, – except a gaoler . . . There is a general relaxation of reverence.' Dunning's resolution epitomised the trend, which must have owed much to the inspiration of America, since even those who did not support the rebels could see that their methods had succeeded. More profoundly, it had to do with the vaulting rise of British population and British trade, preceding a change in the character of the whole economy. There was now a big, prosperous, largely Dissenting, largely voteless middle class. Manufacturers in particular had a new self-confidence which jarred against the political system. Growing population increased the sense amongst middle and lower orders of the potential power of sheer numbers. A generation of anti-radical thinkers, including Burke, Henry Dundas and such rising men as the younger Pitt and Wilberforce, had to find new and plausible arguments to justify upper-class rule, the hereditary principle. They would win. But it would be a close-run race. It was not, or did not seem, preordained that Burke and Wilberforce would be held up as heroes for twentieth-century schoolchildren, while a deprecating sneer ('idealist, extremist') still put the dreaded Tom Paine down.

Would angry middle-class persons join with their workmen in a revolutionary movement embracing, before it destroyed them, the 'groaning' squires, and led by such rebel aristocrats as Fox and such ideologues as Price, Paine and Priestley? Or would the division of interest between all propertied men and the unpropertied act to secure the existing élite? 1780, in retrospect, seems to have been a critical year.

Two years before, both Houses of Parliament had comfortably passed legislation, inspired by Edmund Burke, which restored civil, though not political, rights to Roman Catholics in England. Men in governing circles had now grown impatient, as the Quebec Act had shown, with religious intolerance. However, precisely such bitter, hereditary prejudice as had loaded the muskets of New England farmers still flourished in Presbyterian Scotland. The suggestion of similar changes in Scottish law provoked riots in Glasgow and Edinburgh and the formation of a 'Protestant Association'. Lord George Gordon MP appeared at its head. This charming, ambitious young man somehow had equal appeal for Gaelic highlanders and for Lowland heirs of the Covenanting tradition. He wore tartan trews in the House of Commons, spoke in favour of the American rebels, and kept open house for Scots of all ranks and both races. His movement prevented relief for Scottish Catholics. A similar Protestant Association arose in England, and Gordon was asked to become its president.

On June 2, 1780, sixty thousand people marched on Westminster where Gordon presented a petition for the repeal of the Act in favour of English Catholics. A week of astonishing violence, matched in few revolutions, now followed. Gordon's supporters attacked the chapels, homes and businesses of Catholics. They sacked Newgate Prison and freed all the inmates, assailed the Fleet Prison and the Bank of England, and burnt Lord Mansfield's fine house down. Troops regained control of the metropolis. Gordon was gaoled in the

Tower. But religious unreason had saved the existing order. Every propertied man in the country could see what fate might await him if rash political challenge handed initiative over to the 'populace'. The election later that year gave North another House which he could control.

Though Yorktown broke North, it did not break the system. George III had to turn again to Rockingham and his supporters, who were very happy to end the war for him, but had no intention of drastic reform at home. They made a token attack on royal patronage. Burke's 'Economical Reform' Bills pruned the king's household of some of its sinecures. Revenue officers were disfranchised, government contractors were excluded from the House of Commons. But great changes occurred only in Ireland.

V

One Protestant gentlemen claimed, in 1782, 'it was on the plains of America that Ireland obtained her freedom.' American patriots had set the world a portentous example. They were creating a new 'nation'. Their success was not lost on Irish patriots, though as Protestants they flinched from the full realisation of 'nationhood'.

Their favourite orator was now a little hatchet-faced barrister named Grattan. A contemporary described his delivery as 'thin, sharp and far from powerful.' He lacked the fine voice of Patrick Henry, the masterly elocution of Chatham. His style belonged with the dawning Romantic period. He was warm. He was lively. He seemed sincere. He was sincere. The strange mowing action of his arms as he spoke, the very difficulty of hearing him, as another observer reported, 'only excited a more anxious attention to his language.' What fine language that was, too, 'now a wide spreading conflagration, and anon a concentred fire . . .' The man was unbribeable. He seemed to live only for Ireland. Under the impulse of his orations, the influence of 'place, pension, and peerage' had for a moment 'but an enfeebled hold.'

However, his views were well to the 'right' of Thomas Jefferson's. He was an aristocratical whig, who approved of the 'people' – the 'property of the nation' – but distinguished them sharply from the 'populace' – the 'poverty of the kingdom'. In practice, such views had cruel, repressive results. Grattan avoided the taint of consequences. He never held office. He made it a virtue not to hold office. So what went well and inspiringly, what bathed all feeling men in warm emotion, could be attributed to the fire of his speeches. Whatever was bungled, sordid, cruel and self-interested, had nothing to do with him. His oratory was a brilliant fencing weapon. Middle-class Protestantism carried real guns.

During the American war, the Irish middle class discovered its own power. Ireland had new leverage. North needed all the troops the country could give him. Throughout the war his ministry recruited new soldiers heavily from Ireland, including Roman Catholics whose enlistment outraged local Protestant opinion. In October 1775 large majorities in the Irish Parliament denounced the rebellion in America. But the Irish middle class was not so complaisant and gave strength to the pro-American 'patriots', led by Grattan.

Protestant opinion was overwhelmingly on the rebels' side. Besides blood-ties created by emigration, there were obvious parallels between the States and Ireland. If North's gang bullied America into submission, would they not freely tax Ireland in turn? The citizens of Dublin, Belfast and Cork made their sympathy clear from the outset, while in the small town of Tandragee, for instance, a society of Protestant gentlemen toasted 'the memory of the saints and martyrs that fell at Lexington . . .'

In February 1776, fearing that the French would join in the war and that Irish provisions might reach them through neutral shippers, the government imposed an embargo on trade in food except to Britain and colonies still loyal. The patriots called it unconstitutional. One, Hussey Burgh, raved in the Commons that this kind of exercise of the royal prerogative had 'struck the Crown off one king, and Head off another'. The reaction was rhetorically excessive. The British army and navy were willing to pay soaring prices for Irish provisions. But merchants could not unload the low-grade beef which they had been supplying to the French colonies. The war hampered Ireland in her illegal commerce with France, and in that valuable smuggling trade with North America which had consoled merchants for the commercial restrictions imposed by Britain. Wartime depression in England made 1778 a disastrous year for the linen industry. For generations, the answer in hard times had been to emigrate to America. Now that was blocked. Angry men stayed at home.

The attitude of Irish Catholics was the greatest source of relief to the authorities. No one knew, or knows, what the majority thought. But the community's leaders, as war broke out, expressed their 'abhorrence of the unnatural rebellion' and offered 'two millions of loyal, faithful, and affectionate hearts and hands' to the British government. Prominent Catholic individuals gave bounties in support of recruiting drives. Without elementary civil rights themselves, such men were unlikely to be much impressed with Yankee grievances. Government propaganda cleverly stressed certain parallels. Americans owned slaves. They wanted a freer hand against Red Indians. Were they not rather like the Ascendancy blatherers who ground down the Catholic poor of Ireland?

The Duke of Buckinghamshire, Viceroy from 1776, found the Irish administration on the verge of bankruptcy. He pleaded with Whitehall to lift the obnoxious export embargo, and it did so at last during 1778. Patriots now had a new slogan, 'free trade'. Lord North, after Saratoga, was offering the Americans virtual independence within the Empire, with restraints upon commerce abated. Why not Ireland? Let all restrictions be lifted. Let the Dublin Parliament regulate Irish trade.

The army in Ireland, weakened by withdrawals for service overseas, was now inadequate to defend the country against French invasion, or to protect landlords against Whiteboys, manufacturers against their workmen. Government credit had collapsed. Buckinghamshire had to suspend payment of all salaries and pensions. Only loans from the Bank of England shored up his rule. In July 1778 an Act went through authorising, for the first time, the mustering of an Irish militia. But this would cost approaching £40,000 a year. It could not be afforded.

How were rents to be gathered? How were strikes to be broken? In Dublin, Cork and Belfast, spontaneous moves had been made towards creating a Protestant vigilante force. In the autumn of 1778, the 'Dublin Volunteers' were organised under the command of the Duke of Leinster. Similar corps sprang up elsewhere, some raised by great aristocrats, others, later, by county meetings. With the invasion scare continuing, Dublin Castle could not refuse them the arms allocated for the militia.

It looks like a classic revolutionary situation. The regime was hard pressed on the defensive. Most of the ruling class were partially disaffected. And now the people armed. There was just one factor askew. Protestants armed. The Catholic masses were armed, if at all, as soldiers in royal regiments.

Volunteering was great fun. The uniforms, patriotically fashioned from Irish cloth, were brightly coloured and gorgeously faced. After their drilling, performed with great pleasure and pride, the Volunteers drank bumper upon bumper, toasting the Glorious Revolution, the siege of Derry, the battles of the Boyne, Aughrim and Culloden. Since invasion did not occur, their only function was to act as a police force, conducting prisoners to gaol, helping collect tithes, quelling disturbances among the Catholic masses. Yet, to show they were loyally anti-French, some Catholics subscribed to Volunteer funds. A few Catholics were allowed to join the force, despite the laws prohibiting papists from bearing arms.

Grattan proclaimed that 'the Irish protestant could never be free until the Irish Catholic had ceased to be a slave.' Some Dublin MPs had been finding reasons to change their minds about the Penal Code. Ascendancy landowners were less notable, on the whole, for business capacity than for their stomach for liquor. Their relatives in Britain were building fine houses. To match such splendour, they threw up mansions beyond their means, and commonly found they had (as Maria Edgeworth would put it) to 'sell an estate to pay for a house'. Those who were not falling into the powers of Catholic moneylenders were commonly looking for rich Catholic tenants.

From 1762 there had been a movement in Parliament to enable landowners to mortgage estates to Catholics. Seven Bills failed in a dozen years, as did others designed to permit longer leases for papists. However, in 1778 the influence of rich Catholic merchants combined with pressure from Westminster to force 'relief' upon the Irish Parliament, even though Grattan himself still opposed it, along with most of the other patriots. An act was passed under which Catholics might take leases up to 999 years; the reason for denying them outright ownership was that possession of certain lands involved the right to elect MPs.

Opposition politicians at Westminster were pointing to the analogies between Ireland and America. North's ministry itself saw the need for concessions. The Irish might now export most goods to the colonies. They were given equality in the Newfoundland fisheries. But despite North's support, and a plea from Edmund Burke, the most valuable trophy of all was denied; the Commons refused to permit Ireland to import goods direct from the plantations. The Bristol electors threw Burke out at the next opportunity. They did not mind his support for America, but favouritism to Ireland was insupportable.

Irish traders retorted by adopting the Yankee notion of 'non-importation'. In April 1779, an 'Aggregate Body of the Citizens' of Dublin passed a vehement motion and soon began to incite 'mob' action against importers of goods from Britain.

When the Irish Parliament met in mid-October 1779, the streets were full of armed men. On November 4, Volunteers demonstrated around William III's statue. Inscriptions were hung round the pedestal calling for 'A Free Trade – Or Else' and indicating that Volunteers were prepared to die for their country. Twenty counties and many cities and towns saw meetings of electors which instructed or more politely 'desired' their Members of Parliament to vote supplies only for six months, rather than the usual two years, until a free trade was granted. Unlike Wyvill's movement, this gained immediate success. MPs were frightened. On November 15, a 'mob' of 3,000 or 4,000 in Dublin intimidated MPs trying to enter the Commons, while Volunteers stood aloof, permitting, for once, the lower orders to get out of hand. Lord North rushed to announce, on November 25, that Ireland would be freed from unequal commercial restriction.

This went through the English Parliament almost without opposition and received the royal assent before Christmas. Within six weeks, the Dublin 'mob' and its instigators had won a handsome victory. Their triumph was completed by a second Act in February which conceded Ireland's right to import direct from the colonies.

Buckinghamshire bought support in the Dublin Commons by lavish promises and a notable step was made to placate the Presbyterians, through the repeal of the clause in the 1704 Test Act which barred them from full political participation. But the patriots, having tasted the power of public opinion, now determined to use it to free the Irish Parliament from British control. Many corps of Volunteers passed resolutions against 'enslaving statutes'. Meetings in most counties called for the repeal of Poynings' Law. Grattan, in April 1780, moved in the Commons that only the Irish Parliament was competent to make laws for Ireland. Now was the time to claim independence. Britain stood alone in the world, Ireland was 'the only nation in Europe' which was not her foe. But he failed, by ninety-seven votes to a hundred and thirty-seven.

Even many of the professed 'patriot' MPs were as frightened of a head-on clash with Britain as they were of public opinion in Ireland. It soon became clear that the Viceroy had regained control of Parliament. Radicals of the Volunteer Movement now called louder and louder for the reform of Parliament. The two principal boroughmongers were the Duke of Leinster and the Earl of Shannon, controlling ten and eighteen seats respectively. Both were leaders in the Volunteer movement. Both were strongly criticised in the ranks, and though Napper Tandy, a Dublin lawyer who served under Leinster, failed in a move to have the Duke expelled, the various Dublin corps voted seven to three that not Leinster, but Lord Charlemont should review their November 4 parade.

Charlemont, the most consistent aristocratic patriot, now became the effective leader of the Volunteers. Hypersensitive, cultured, and humourless, he disliked speaking in public and suffered from chronic ill health. He claimed that toleration was for him a 'predominant principle', and though he opposed giving political rights to papists, he was anxious to conciliate the majority. Catholics were now being admitted in increasing numbers as Volunteers. It seemed that, among the middle classes, real 'national' unity might be emerging. As the Volunteer movement grew, so did its earnestness. One-day reviews gave way to manoeuvres and parades over two or three. A display given in Belfast in the summer of 1781 was hailed as a 'scene of military grandeur beyond all powers of description.'

On February 15, 1782 delegates from the Volunteers of Ulster met in a Convention at Dungannon which passed a resolution calling for legislative independence for Ireland. It also, momentously, agreed that it held 'the right of private judgement in matters of Religion to be equally sacred in others as in ourselves', and rejoiced 'in the relaxation of the Penal Laws against our Roman Catholic fellow-subjects . . .' The implication of this motion seconded by a Presbyterian minister, passed with only two dissentient voices, was that the British government could no longer rely on religious disunity to maintain its grip on Ireland. The Convention openly threatened revolution. 'We know our duty to ourselves, and are resolved to be free.'

In the two months following the Dungannon Convention, countless Volunteer corps, counties, towns and grand juries held meetings in support of some or all of its resolutions. After North's fall the Rockingham faction, old friends of the Irish patriots, sent over the Duke of Portland as viceroy. By April, Grattan was on his feet proposing independence for the third time and on this occasion, as he knew, no one would dare vote against it. 'I am now to address a free people . . . I found Ireland on her knees. I watched over her with an eternal solicitude; I have traced her progress from injuries to arms, and from arms to liberty. Spirit of Swift! Spirit of Molyneux! your genius has prevailed! Ireland is now a nation!'

Portland saw no alternative to immediate independence. The British Parliament swiftly repealed its Declaratory Act of 1719, its formal assertion of its right to legislate for Ireland.

Grattan was presented with £50,000 by the madly enthusiastic Dublin Commons, but his blink of supreme popularity was soon over. Henry Flood, dismissed from office towards the end of 1781 and now fully returned to the patriot camp, was busy outflanking him on the left. His more muscular oratory suited rank and file Volunteers rather better than Grattan's high-flying cadences. Flood loudly averred that repeal of the Declaratory Act meant nothing – had Britain not legislated for Ireland before 1719? – and he won the leadership of public opinion. Much against its will, the British government bowed, and in January 1783 the Westminster Parliament passed a 'Renunciation Act' establishing Ireland's complete legislative and judicial independence 'for ever'.

Division between Flood and Grattan was soon open. Grattan had made his view clear at his hour of triumph; the Volunteers, having 'given a parliament to the people', should now 'leave the people to Parliament'. That is, pressure on Parliament should cease. Only Parliament should reform Parliament.

In March 1783, delegates of the Munster Volunteers called for the reform of rotten boroughs. Ulster Volunteers followed this up with another fiery session at Dungannon, which summoned a National Convention of Volunteer delegates, to meet in Dublin in November and to deliberate how Ireland might be saved from 'an absolute monarchy, or, that still more odious government, a tyrannical aristocracy.' This Convention seemed a revolutionary challenge. Grattan, though nominated, refused to sit in it, and was duly expelled by his own corps of Volunteers. The delegates, who wore arms, agreed on demands for triennial elections, and for the enfranchisement of Protestant freeholders and leaseholders, but decided against the enfranchisement of Catholics. Flood, in uniform, carried their plan down to the House of Commons and moved there for leave to bring in a Bill for the 'more equal representation of the People in Parliament.' The House voted two to one against receiving it and then passed a resolution expressing 'perfect satisfaction' with Ireland's 'present happy constitution'.

The Convention received this news quietly. Charlemont had packed it with moderate friends of his own. Peace, returning prosperity, independence, defused the issue. Flood's Bill was voted down when he introduced it again in the spring of 1784. Dublin reformers, later that year, called a 'Congress' – fateful, American term. Numerous counties and towns responded. But again, the weight of cautious gentility was felt. It had three sessions, amid decreasing interest, then quietly put itself to sleep. Flood, now a Westminster MP, had turned his attention elsewhere. More sincere reformers still in Ireland began to think in terms of plots and insurrections. The question of votes for Catholics was divisive, and Dublin Castle hoped that it would stay so. Whereas Grattan was almost romantic now on the subject of Catholics, Flood was implacably opposed to giving them any share in the choice of MPs. Charlemont agreed with him. An Act of 1782 which allowed papists to buy estates as freely as Protestants had specifically excluded land situated in parliamentary boroughs.

The results of all the commotion were deeply ironic. Now that Catholics could spend like gentlemen, they proceeded to make gentlemen of their sons, sending them into professions instead of business, and so draining money and talent from commerce and industry. Meanwhile, members of the glorious Irish Parliament enjoyed immense privilege and took little responsibility. In the 1783 elections, 72 owners of rotten boroughs, half of them peers, returned 178 MPs between them. The Protestant landowning class was fulsomely loyal now that 'independence' had been granted. Administration remained in the hands of a viceroy who was a member of the British government. 'Representing' a small privileged group within a minority, the Dublin House of Commons was still dependent on Britain. Its most prominent MP had far less authority than Warren Hastings, the servant of a trading company.

VI

Hastings, however, depended on the support of shareholders at home. Since the Board of Trade, from 1774, controlled promotion and preferment in the commercial branch, and since promotion by seniority was the rule in other branches, Hastings was hard put to find lucrative positions for the failures, incompetents and ruined men sent out to him by the Sulivan party. The British position in Oudh was of great consequence to him, since the Nawab-Vizier there could be surrounded by parasitical British aides and advisers. Elsewhere, official contracts also gave Hastings scope.

The opium monopoly which he established, while it brought the East India Company £1,277,000 profit in its first seventeen years, provided enormous pickings for those who contracted to find the drug. Its main source was in Bihar. It was also made in Oudh, in Benares and in some of the northern parts of Bengal. The fuddling of the Chinese emperor's subjects provided bohea for ladies in England's home counties. In 1781, Hastings awarded the contract to Laurence Sulivan's son, for four years. Stephen Sulivan and his associates arranged that the EIC contracted for too little opium at too high a price, so sold surplus chests at a premium to the Company, and also traded on their own account against the EIC monopoly. Hastings knew what was going on, but ignored it.

He could not have retained authority without using such methods to gratify friends and buy allies. His powers under the 1773 Act were limited. He could not override his council.

His new councillors arrived in October 1774. The nominal second to himself was General Sir John Clavering, the commander-in-chief. Colonel Monson was rash and greedy. Richard Barwell was a prime instance of the 'nabob', who would be loathed for his arrogance in rural Sussex when he bought an estate there on his retirement. According to Philip Francis, he was 'rapacious without industry, and ambitious without an exertion of his faculties or steady application to affairs.'

Francis, the remaining member of the Council, had 'enlightened' views close to those of Hastings. His capacity was perhaps no less. Like Hastings, he had risen by merit, without parliamentary influence or obvious patrons. Francis prided himself upon having 'one or two qualities at least to which this infamous climate cannot reach.' He wanted only enough profit from India to enable him to live at home in comfort, and meanwhile found himself forced, as he saw it, to pass his life 'in one eternal combat with villainy, folly, and prostitution of every species.' He believed that Company rule in Bengal was in principle a bad thing. Hastings was now committed to the reality of EIC rule. The British could not, he said, 'redescend to the humble and undreaded character of trading adventurers.' The governor-general, in Hastings's view, 'should possess a power absolute and complete within himself, and independent of actual control', even though this might seem to contravene the British constitution. In a land of despots one must be a despot. If he could have done so, Hastings would have gaoled Francis for opposing him.

For two years, however, Hastings was steadily outvoted and overruled. Only Barwell allied with him. The sordid issue of patronage was dominant. Hastings's people were pushed out of their places. But the climate helped him defeat his enemies. 'My two colleagues,' Francis wrote wryly, 'are in a woeful condition – Colonel Monson obliged to go to sea to save his life, and General Clavering on his back covered with boils . . . As for Hastings, I promise you he is much more tough than any of us, and will never die a natural death.' With Monson giving up the ghost in September 1776 and Clavering dying a year later, Hastings could sweep his adversaries' support out of office in their turn, and could 'reform' the revenue service so as to gratify his own people.

In Calcutta, a tiny parcel of quarrelsome Europeans lived in a style well adapted to smother human fellow-feeling. Calcutta was a 'City of Palaces'. Its fine houses, in classical style, were literally dazzling, since they were finished in a brilliant white plaster, made out of sea-shells and lime, which blinded the eye. Despite the humidity, ladies followed European fashion and heaped their hair up in fantastic extravaganzas of gauze, powder, feathers and pomade. They wore great hooped petticoats under fine gowns imported from Europe, and drenched themselves in the diamonds and pearls of India. The winter 'season' was lavish with its diversions. Whenever ladies arrived from Britain, they were socially displayed at once for two, three or four nights in succession, during which 'sittings up' even plain spinsters could hope to find husbands. Public suppers on festival days were accompanied by balls where the female minority were danced till they nearly melted. There were also subscription balls once a fortnight from November through to February, and such exotic occasions as the *nautch* given by a rich Hindu for the reigning belle, Miss Emma Wrangham, the 'Chinsura Beauty'.

Work, for Europeans, finished with the early afternoon dinner. This meal reflected the cheapness of food locally. Even pretty girls were described as wolfing some two pounds of mutton chops each at a sitting. A housewife in Calcutta in Hastings's day gave as an ordinary day's bill of fare for dinner: soup, a roast fowl, curry and rice, a mutton pie, a forequarter of lamb, a rice pudding, tarts, cheese, bread and butter, Madeira. Supper, taken late in the evening, might present itself as 'great joints of roasted goat, with endless dishes of cold fish.' Over this collation, the custom in Bengal was for ladies and gentlemen to hurl pellets of bread at each other. Perhaps this mild exercise helped to mitigate the disastrous effects of so much eating and drinking: while a lady would drink a bottle of wine every day, a gentleman was expected to put away three or four. The Calcutta British may have been learning to restrain themselves at table just a little more than in former days – certainly, the death-rate had dropped markedly, and only 44 per cent of the Writers appointed to Bengal between 1767 and 1775 would eventually leave their bones in India. But the context of the incessant quarrelling, over cards, over matters of etiquette, and at Hastings's Council table, was that almost everyone suffered from stomach trouble almost all the time.

From the ordinary EIC servant relying on the business sense of his banyan, to the great men on the governor-general's Council, every EIC person was deeply involved with Asian intermediaries – with such people as the unsavoury Nandakumar, whom Hastings had used to gather information against Muhammad Reza Khan. Snubbed later by Hastings, Nandakumar allied with an Englishman named Fowke who also nurtured a grievance. They brought the charge against Hastings that he had received a large bribe from the Munni Begam whom he had appointed guardian to the young Nawab-Vizier of Oudh.

Shuja-ud-daula had died in 1775. The succession of the young prince Asaf-ud-daula, high-spirited, incompetent and spendthrift, had given the British the chance to screw Oudh harder. They forced the new Nawab-Vizier to pay a heavier subsidy for the use of British troops, and to cede to the EIC sovereignty over the region of Benares. Hastings had certainly taken the 150,000 rupees 'entertainment allowance' offered him by the Munni Begam, Asaf's aunt. (Though Hastings was covenanted with the EIC not to pocket such tempting items, this was far from being the only gift which he quietly held on to.) The Council insisted that he must give the money back. Hastings was not prepared to lose face. Nandakumar was committed for trial on charges of forgery brought against him by an Indian, whom Hastings, or at least his friends, had encouraged to come forward. He was found guilty in the court presided over by Hastings's old school-friend Impey, and, in August 1775, was executed.

His death shocked Hindu opinion. Nandakumar, however unpleasant, had been an important figure. He was executed under English law for a crime regarded by Indians as only a misdemeanour. People in England saw the anomaly. If the Supreme Court in Calcutta applied the whole of English criminal law, would polygamists be hanged? Hastings himself had encouraged the view that it was unjust to make men liable for punishments not sanctioned by their own custom. But Hastings, it would seem, had decided to show that no one could monkey with the governor-general and get away with it.

Hatred at last reached the point, in August 1780, where Hastings precipitated a duel with Francis. He was not an experienced marksman, but Francis had never fired a pistol before. Hastings wounded his adversary quite severely. Francis had had enough. Before the new year, he was gone, predicting that 'desolation' would strike Bengal after his departure. Hastings exulted: 'I shall have no competitor to oppose my designs; to encourage disobedience to my authority . . . to excite and foment popular odium against me . . . In a word, I have power . . .'

Calcutta, from 1780, had its first newspaper. The editor was a 'Wild Irishman' named J. A. Hicky who fancied himself as Bengal's Wilkes. Now that Hastings was omnipotent, the *Gazette* dubbed him 'the Grand Turk' and raked up the scandal over Nandakumar. Hicky was arrested, tried before Impey and a packed jury for libel, and gaoled. The *Bengal Gazette* bravely continued to satirise the governor-general until Hicky's types were seized. His temerity cost him two years in prison.

The middle-class despot used no guillotine. After Nandakumar, his enemies were not murdered. Apologists for British rule in India, anxious to dignify its earliest stages, would later argue that Hastings's ability to act as an autocrat saved the British position in the new war with France. It is hard to evaluate this view. The British in Bengal were no longer directly threatened. Hastings, hard-working, highly intelligent, acted as a successful opportunist, helping to rescue the Bombay and Madras presidencies from the trouble into which they had pitched themselves.

Bombay was the poorest and unhealthiest of the main British settlements in India. In 1736, a Parsi shipbuilder had been persuaded to take charge of the infant Bombay dockyard, which thereafter turned out many excellent vessels, and reconciled the directors at home to the presidency's disappointing returns. The wealthy Parsi community came to dominate the city. They ate pork and beef and drank wine without inhibition. They had no caste distinctions. They took readily to European clothes and manners. While Calcutta and Madras made middle-class Europeans insolent towards natives and poor whites alike, Bombay had retained an antique middle-class character.

But now this settlement too was drawn into military adventures. In 1775, the Bombay Council made a deal with Raghunath Rao, an ambitious intriguer within the Maratha ruling class. The Bombay navy destroyed the Maratha fleet, and its army advanced successfully against Raghunath's enemies. Hastings and the Council in Calcutta were shocked to hear of all this. They ordered immediate withdrawal, and sent their own embassy to the Marathas.

A French agent arriving in Poona, the Maratha capital, was given a good reception there. In 1778 Hastings sent six battalions under Colonel Leslie off on an unprecedented march across India from Kalpi to Surat, and when news of the

French declaration of war reached Bengal the governor gave full backing to the Bombay Council, which despatched a force of nearly 4,000, to put Raghunath Rao on the throne. But confronted by a large Maratha force, this army broke and had to surrender.

Leslie died as his force dawdled across the subcontinent. The abler Colonel Goddard succeeded him, and brought his men into Surat soon after the Bombay army's reverse. His remarkable march restored British prestige. In 1782, the Marathas agreed to the Treaty of Salbai. This procured, as it turned out, twenty years of peace. The Bombay government had to hand back various conquests. The British needed Maratha support, or at least neutrality, in their renewed struggle with Hydar Ali, now made doubly dangerous by French intervention.

Madras had pursued its course of epic corruption. Hastings and his Council accepted, de facto, the coup by which Governor Pigot, in 1776, attempting to clean up the mess created by the Nawab's debts, was imprisoned by Paul Benfield and his gang of profiteers, and died, still in confinement, the next year. Pigot's successor, Sir Thomas Rumbold, picked a quarrel with the Nizam of Hyderabad over a district called the Sarkar of Guntoor.

Grateful to see the British at odds with the Nizam, Hydar Ali, in July 1780, launched a new attack on Madras, and again mastered the whole Carnatic. A French squadron appeared off the Coromandel Coast in 1782. Only nine British ships were at hand to oppose the twelve under Admiral Suffren, and they were worsted in four actions. But, with the Marathas at peace, troops from all the three presidencies under Hastings could now be deployed against Hydar Ali. A force from Bombay seized Mysore, Hydar's capital. Hydar himself had died. His son, Tipu, succeeding him, had to take most of his troops back home, and a large body of French troops, arriving at the Coromandel coast in April 1783, found their expected allies elsewhere. Even so, the British were immensely relieved when word came in June that peace had been made in Europe. War with Tipu continued for some months more, before the Madras government came to terms. These infuriated Hastings, chiefly because it was Lord Macartney who had negotiated them.

Whitehall was taking India seriously. Macartney, who had recently come out as governor of Madras, had been a member of both Irish and British Houses of Commons, chief secretary in Ireland, a diplomat in Russia, a governor in the Caribbean. He could not get on with the upstart Hastings, whom he clearly hoped to succeed. A new breed – the lordly and virtuous outsider – had now appeared in India, ardent to confront the squalid profiteering 'nabobs' of whom Hastings, not quite fairly, could be represented as the ringleader.

In 1781, before Macartney's arrival, the Nawab of the Carnatic had agreed with Hastings to assign his revenues to the EIC for the duration of the war, so long as appointments of collectors were approved by him. Macartney would not wear this. He put in collectors over the Nawab's head. Hastings ordered him to restore administration to the Nawab. Macartney refused to obey until the EIC itself overruled him, and he went home.

Though Hastings had little control over the other presidencies, he had effectively orchestrated campaigns over a vast area against three dangerous enemies, and had shown great prowess as a diplomat. It had all cost a great deal of money. So far as he could, he made the Bengali cultivators pay for it. He increased the assessments of revenue payable by the large *zemindars*, and had screwed further cash out by dubious, furtive means. But not enough. He turned to strong-arm methods. He went up river in July 1781 with a bodyguard of some five hundred troops.

Hastings did not want to see British rule in India extended beyond its present bounds. Excessive expansion, he thought, must dilute and weaken British civil and military power. He could clearly see the evils which had befallen Oudh through its ruler's attachment to the British. The alliance with Oudh, he wrote, 'was in the beginning an unprofitable charge to the Company. It was placed on a footing of mutual advantage to both. It is now become an oppressive burthen on that province, which must soon fall with increased weight on the Company.'

However, the *Gita* said, 'Abandon all thought of the consequence.' The Company must show a profit. Hastings' first target was the Raja of Benares, Chait Singh, installed by the EIC as its *zemindar*. Pressed for troops to defend Bengal, he had called on him to provide the EIC with at least 1,000 cavalry. Chait Singh had offered only 500 and 500 infantry. Hastings now proposed to fine him £500,000 for this impertinence.

He refused to hear Chait Singh's own explanations, and ordered his arrest. The Raja's armed retainers rose up and massacred the British-hired Sepoys who were guarding him. Ghait Singh escaped. For a while, Hastings himself was in great danger. But he kept his nerve and repressed the rebellion. Since his troops had partitioned Chait Singh's treasury among themselves Hastings had incurred the cost of another campaign without getting any loot for the Company. So he decided to suck Benares dry. The area was given to Chait Singh's nephew. Its rent was raised from twenty-two lakhs of rupees a year to forty. This was extortionate, and could only be paid by extortion. The region was swiftly reduced to ruin.

Amongst the native princes who had rallied to Hastings' support, the Nawab of Oudh himself had been pleasantly forward. Asaf-ud-daula was in effect a puppet. His capital, Lucknow, seemed to Hastings himself a 'Sink of Iniquity'. The governor-general maintained a fastidious distaste for the behaviour of the very white men whom he had sent in to batten on Oudh – 'beardless Boys rejecting with indignation the offer of monthly Gratuities of 3000 and 5000 Rupees . . . Men receiving the Wages of Service from the nabob, and disclaiming his Right to command it'.

Asaf's finances recalled those of the Nawab of the Carnatic. British soldiers had lent him money at huge rates of interest, creaming off pensions and *jaghirs* in return. Meanwhile he owed the EIC large sums. Hastings now persuaded him to reduce his army, and to put his public expenditures in the hands of ministers who would co-operate with the British Resident. He encouraged Asaf to get his hands on the *jaghirs* and treasure held by his mother and grandmother, the Begams of Oudh. The EIC's shortage of cash drove Hastings to endorse naked bullying. It was clear that otherwise Asaf could not repay the forty-four lakhs of rupees which he owed the Company.

Accompanied by the British Resident and by EIC troops, Asaf captured the Begam's fortress. But by the Machiavellian test, Hastings' strong-arm methods failed, as they had done with Chait Singh. Asaf's debts were too large. Fifty-five lakhs stolen from the Begams disappeared almost without trace. In 1784, Hastings returned to Lucknow, trying again to sort out Asaf's affairs. The Nawab-Vizier's debts to the EIC now stood at seventy-three lakhs. Hastings recovered about half of this, and arranged a retrenchment in Asaf's expenses. He appeased Asaf by removing the EIC Resident, but left an agent of the governor-general in his place, at a salary of £22,000, who cost the people of Oudh nearly twice as much. Whatever Hastings had wished, and partly because of his own actions, Oudh was now in effect British territory. Hastings' successor would find Oudh 'desolated' by years of British despoliation.

Hastings' term of office had expired in 1779, but Lord North, pressed upon by so many problems, had been happy enough to let him stay in Calcutta. However, Philip Francis had returned to England – 'pale yellow, and a look of diabolic purpose.' He sold his own EIC stock at a loss, allied himself with the parliamentary opposition, and made as much trouble as he could. News of Hastings' fiasco at Benares came opportunely. After Lord North fell, in May 1782, Dundas proposed, and the House of Commons carried, a motion censuring Hastings for having 'acted in a manner repugnant to the honour and policy of this nation . . .' Hastings early in 1783 announced his own intention to resign. The bitterness, though, with which EIC affairs were again debated in Britain meant that no successor was swiftly appointed, and he lingered on for two more years. He finally quit India in February 1785. His first reception at home was flattering. But a week after his arrival Edmund Burke gave notice to the Commons that he would make a motion against him.

Political and moral reformers in England had begun to see India as a sphere where virtuous 'trusteeship' over native peoples could be accompanied by experiments in disinterested administration. While the wealth of India, properly exploited, would compensate for lost New World colonies, the honour recently forfeited at Yorktown could be regained by enlightened rule in Calcutta. Whereas Hastings had reacted on the defensive, his more aggressive successors would seize province after province, but would talk about God and the interests of native peoples as they did so.

Hastings himself had thought, and written, that attempts to convert Hindus to Christianity would be presumptuous. He aimed at 'reconciling the people of England to the natives of Hindostan.' He patronised Charles Wilkins, the first

European ever to translate at length from Sanskrit, who published in 1785 a translation of the *Bhagavadgita*, and in his own introduction to this work implied that *Mahabharata* was as fine an epic as Milton's. The great Hindu writings, Hastings said, would 'survive when the British dominion in India shall have long ceased to exist . . .'

He welcomed the famous scholar Sir William Jones when he arrived as a High Court Judge in Calcutta in 1783, and with him founded the Asiatic Society of Bengal. Jones's pioneering researches displayed the similarities between Sanskrit, Latin and Greek and publicised the existence of an 'Indo-European' family of languages. He studied Indian law, history, religion, literature, music, philosophy and science, and his work had considerable impact on the Romantic poets and philosophers of Europe.

Hinduism appealed greatly to many British thinkers. Burke always 'spoke of the piety of the Hindoos with admiration, and of their holy religion and sacred functions with an awe bordering on devotion', and thought them the most benevolent of all people. Holwell extolled Hindu vegetarianism, and abstention from alcohol, as relics of a 'primitive age' of innocence. Of course, there were beef-eating Englishman a-plenty who saw Hindu eating and drinking habits as signs of ingrained effeteness. The Hindu, Robert Orme said, had 'no chance of opposing with success the onset of an inhabitant of more northern regions.' But he excepted the gallant Rajputs from these generalisations. The cult of the 'martial races' was beginning, whereby coloured peoples would be divided, usefully, into idle weaklings fit only to be ruled, and handsome bullies well suited to keeping the first sort in order.

Lieut.-Col. Alexander Dow, in his *History of Hindostan* (1768–72), praised the Marathas very highly, as a 'great and rising people'. Dow admired Hindu literature as warmly as Hastings. But his generalisation was that the 'Hindoos' were 'of all nations on earth the most easily conquered and governed.' They had no public spirit, no loyalty. 'The people permit themselves to be transferred from one tyrant to another, without murmuring . . .'

But could the bullying of Hindu labour be justified when these were such inoffensive and good-natured people? Christianity offered the necessary argument. The Hindu, like the African, must be found to be in need of tutelage. The fact that his penal code was much less savage than Britain's must be ignored, and attention focused upon such customs as that of *sati*, whereby widows consigned themselves to their husbands' funeral pyres. Holwell excused the custom warmly. He had seen it many times. The action of the women seemed to him both voluntary and heroic. A Scottish footman, who also had seen *sati*, observed more drily and with forceful irony, '. . . They are as glad to burn as two women in England would be to get an estate.' Relative to the world of Fanny Burney and Jane Austen, where heiresses were bought and sold on the British marriage market, the horror expressed at the custom must seem excessive. So, in view of the conduct of EIC personnel, must the odium frequently heaped on the 'trickery', cunning, 'treachery' of the Indians. But the Hindu must be made to seem a ripe subject for conversion. Then extracting the fruits of his labour would be a bounden duty for all good people.

The switch from 'enlightened' appreciation of the Hindu's virtues was beginning by the 1780s under Evangelical direction. Evangelicalism had attracted more and more respectable, well-to-do members of the Church of England. The days when Methodism had seemed subversive were now greatly distant. Evangelicals in India wrote harshly about Hinduism. Charles Grant, on the spot, wrote to inform Thomas Coke, a pioneering Methodist missionary, 'It is hardly possible to conceive any people more completely enchained than they are by their superstition.' He and certain others drafted, in 1787, a proposal for launching missions which stated that the people of India were 'universally and wholly corrupt, as they are depraved as they are blind, and as wretched as they are depraved.' Such Evangelicals were turning the coloured races of the world into the basis of a moral bank, from which Britain would draw more and more heavily. Every Hindu widow saved from the flames, every dark convert lisping his Saviour's name, swelled the funds of righteousness at the disposal of God's chosen Protestant nation for investment in further profitable 'trusteeship' overseas. As Burke prepared his attack on Warren Hastings, the British anti-slavery movement gathered itself formidably together. Its young hero, Wilberforce, showed equal if not more fervour for the cause of intruding missionaries into India, where the natives were sunk, as he put it, 'into the most abject ignorance and vice'.

VII

In 1773, Humphrey Marten, Hudson's Bay Company chief at York Fort, put one of his men in irons and gave him eighteen strokes of the cat for trading, privately, one skin. In the same year, the brig *Nancy* left Dornoch, in northern Scotland, with two hundred emigrants. Of fifty children aboard below the age of four, only one survived the voyage. Altogether, only one hundred people reached New York. The captain of the vessel, in violation of his contract, had issued foul and inadequate food.

Neither episode made a great stir. Floggings of soldiers continued in the British army. Men, women and children were still hanged in Britain for petty offences against property. Why was it, then, that the first national campaign on a humanitarian issue was directed against the slave trade with Africa?

Partly, of course, because that trade was consistently cruel, systematically iniquitous. But partly also because of the American war, which coincided with the publication of two enormously influential books. English translations of the Abbé Raynal's *History of the Two Indies* and Adam Smith's *Wealth of Nations* were both published in 1776. Each went through fifteen editions by 1804. Raynal summed up the objections to slavery of advanced European thinkers, and proposed a scheme for gradual emancipation. Smith seemed to show that slavery was not only offensive to man's innate sense of fellow feeling, but was also economically stupid. It seemed 'from the experience of all ages and nations' that work done by freemen came 'cheaper in the end than that performed by slaves.' The cost of 'repairing' the 'wear and tear of the slave' fell upon the neglectful master or careless overseer. The free man repaired himself.

Smith was a prophet for class-conscious persons in the middle ranks of society who were likely to identify idle, 'negligent' West Indian planters with the 'landed interest' which monopolised British politics. Every year, such elements grew stronger, and anti-slavery opinion with them, while the interests arrayed against it were weakened. American independence removed most English-speaking slave-owners from the Empire. With slavery now outlawed in the northern states of the USA, British Quakers, in constant touch still with Friends across the Atlantic, had to act to save their self-esteem. Such bankers as Samuel Hoare and John Lloyd, amongst the richest men in Britain, were leaders in the Quaker campaign which petitioned Parliament, in 1783, for total abolition of the slave trade. Thousands of copies of a pamphlet by Benezet were distributed through Britain. To do this a network of scores of correspondents was established in the provinces.

VIII

Perversely, much middle-class revulsion against slavery may have drawn strength from middle-class guilt over the epochal transformations which, in the 1780s, were obviously occurring in British industry. Britain's exports quadrupled in volume between 1780 and 1800. Industrial output boomed. The most spectacular climb was in the production of cotton textiles. In the first half of the eighteenth century Britain's consumption of raw cotton wool had risen slowly to about 2 million lb. per year. In the 1760s it had been over 3½ million, in the 1770s over 5 million. Then, apocalyptically, it soared to 22 million in 1787. The chief centre of cotton textile production was Lancashire. By 1801, Manchester–Salford (84,000 people) and Liverpool (78,000) were the largest English provincial cities.

But far more than increases of scale were involved. Since the origins of human industry, the main material used in making machines had been wood. 1784 saw the world's first large-scale all-iron plant, the Albion Flour Mill at Southwark, in London. The motive power here was steam. The implications of steam power were world-changing. For the first time industry itself was set to become a giant consumer of the products of industry. Flowing water remained the chief source of motive power until well into the nineteenth century, but the tendency swiftly emerged for areas where coal was cheaply available to attract manufacturing. Coal drove steam engines. Coal made iron. Iron made engines. A complex of mining, engineering and mass-production of consumer goods began to establish itself on the coalfields. And the astonishing success of the steam engine suggested that further inventions could and should be made. Invention itself, as it were, had been invented.

'Industrialists', a new species of mankind, had invested in large and expensive machinery, thus incurring high overheads. They had a rising incentive to keep plant running as close to full capacity as might be. So they poured out goods in unprecedented quantities. Markets had to be found for them. Prices, cut for the home consumer, increased demand, and again prompted increased production. But where the home market was insufficient, consumers must be found overseas. As overseas markets grew, this likewise triggered increased production at home. As profit margins dwindled, new inventions were sought and found as a way to cut costs. The engineering industry was called on to provide more and more new machines. Coal was ripped at a faster and faster rate from the seams.

At the time of the 1707 Treaty of Union, Britain, for all its commercial prowess, had been what we would now call an 'underdeveloped country'. Perhaps half its arable land had still been cultivated under the system where the strips owned by individuals were mixed together and communal thinking prevailed. With a few exceptions – shipbuilding and textiles were the most important – the country's industries had either produced primary products or had made goods for sale in local markets.

The shortage of wood had begun to press. Britain had abundant coal. In 1709, Abraham Darby, a Quaker ironmaster, began to smelt with coke at Coalbrookdale in Shropshire, so releasing himself from the need for charcoal. Three years later, a steam engine, designed by a gentleman named Savery and a blacksmith named Newcomen, was put to work on a coalfield in the Midlands. It met the practical problem that as demand for coal and tin sent minors deeper and deeper, some way must be found, cheaper than horse power, of pumping water out of the workings. 'Newcomen' engines were slow, unimpressive creations, but they did their job, and spread: by 1775, there were about forty at work in Cornwall, about sixty on the Northumberland coalfield.

Meanwhile, the potential of factory organisation had begun to catch the eyes of some Englishmen. The Royal Arsenal at Chatham, racing out armaments for the wars of William III and Marlborough, had shown how large-scale demand might impel large-scale organisation. And the West Indian slave plantation had revealed the practical efficacity of holding large numbers of workers together under strict discipline. There was an abundance of helpless poor people in England. From the late seventeenth century, the idea of the 'workhouse' evolved as a way of relieving the well-to-do of the need to provide for them through the parish rates. Parishes combined to maintain workhouses where wool was spun, hosiery made, and so forth. The death-rate amongst those employed was horrific. Administered as ineptly and corruptly as other public institutions of the period, these places did not pay. But individual entrepreneurs saw the potential of pauper children. By the 1750s, in cotton-processing Lancashire, such men were in effect buying 'parish apprentices' on a grand scale. 'The poor Children,' one spokesman for Manchester weavers exclaimed, had been 'sold into worse Slavery, and harder Bondage, than the Negroes in our

English plantations in *America*.' The analogy with plantation slavery also struck an economist, Josiah Tucker, observing about the same time the woollen industry in the hinterland of slave-trading Bristol. He saw south-western clothiers bringing adult weavers together in great numbers in the 'same shop', and remarked that the new social distance created, with 'the master . . . placed so high above the condition of the journeyman', was more like that between planter and black 'than might be expected in such a country as England.'

The dependence of hundreds, even thousands, of workers on a single capitalist clothier was an old fact in the textile industries. The bringing together of many machines in one place, where before spinners and weavers had worked at home, was a straightforward logical development. In 1765 Matthew Boulton built his Soho factory outside Birmingham. Josiah Wedgwood, the great potter, established 'Etruria' in Staffordshire four years later. In 1771 Richard Arkwright created a cotton-spinning mill, at Cromford, where he was soon employed about 600 workers, most of them children.

For some two generations, men concerned with the cotton industry had been devising new machines. The ideas involved had been familiar enough to anyone expert with machines in the Middle Ages. The new inventions could have been perfected at any time in the intervening centuries. What had been missing was incentive, and this was given by a sudden doubling of the rate of growth of the British cotton industry in the 1740s.

In 1768 Arkwright, a Lancashire barber and wig-maker, took up someone else's 30-year-old idea for the use of rollers in spinning, in his own 'water frame'. Eleven years later Samuel Crompton, a Bolton weaver, combined features from 'jenny' and 'water frame' in a machine therefore called the 'mule', which produced at last a yarn with which Lancashire could match the fine muslins of India.

The 'frame' and the 'mule' demanded power greater than that of human muscles. Water power had long been used to mill flour and to full cloth. So the early cotton mills sprang up by streams in the countryside, till James Watt's invention made revolution possible.

Watt was a man of the lower middle classes, a mathematical instrument maker with a shop within the precincts of Glasgow University, where the great scientist Joseph Black was lecturing on his own discovery, latent heat. Another professor used a model Newcomen steam engine in his classes. Watt was asked to repair it, and saw that it was wasteful of energy. He discussed its defects with Black and other scientists. Then, in 1765, in his thirtieth year, this sober Lowland Scot, walking on Glasgow Green, hit upon 'conceptually much the most difficult invention of the century.' His separate condenser quadrupled the steam engine's efficiency. John Roebuck, an Englishman who controlled the great Carron ironworks near Falkirk, financed Watt's experiments. But it was the drive and imagination of another Englishman, Matthew Boulton, which eventually proved crucial. Watt was introduced, in 1767–8, first to the famous

Soho works, then to the great manufacturer himself, by the latter's close friend and adviser, Dr William Small, who had not long before been Thomas Jefferson's teacher, had been introduced to Boulton by Benjamin Franklin, and thus provides an intimate personal link between two world-transforming revolutions. For Watt found in Birmingham, where he became Boulton's partner, the engineering skills, still lacking in Scotland, which would make his invention commercially viable. A Midlands ironmaster, John Wilkinson, had recently patented a way of boring cannon which could be used to bore cylinders with hitherto impossible accuracy. In the last quarter of the eighteenth century, Watt and Boulton sold nearly five hundred steam engines.

The early 1780s were the years of 'industrial revolution' (though the term itself would not be coined for half a century). In 1783, another Scot, Thomas Bell, came up with a method of printing calico by power. In 1783–4, Henry Cort devised a superior new 'puddling' process for coke smelting, and finally released the iron industry from bondage to water power by his invention of the rolling mill, which meant that a steam engine could be applied to making bar iron and rolled iron. The next year Arkwright bought a machine from Boulton and Watt and the marriage of steam and cotton was consummated. Mills now sprang up in coalfield towns. In 1782 there had been only two cotton mills in and around Manchester. Within twenty years there were fifty more.

Except for Watt and the scientists, mostly Scottish, who were revolutionising bleaching and thus pioneering the modern chemical industry, the famous inventors were men who, like Captain James Cook, 'discovered' what was there waiting for them, and did not concern themselves with theory. England was not badly off for craftsmen who could read and write and manage arithmetic. The Midlands, home of many small masters in the metal industries, were especially prolific in invention. Even rudimentary education was not always necessary for a technological pioneer – the great canal engineer James Brindley never learnt to spell and was nearly illiterate. Invention bred itself bacterially under the sun of opportunity, which shone for people in Britain hot and high.

Lord Shelburne, most thoughtful nobleman of his day, was struck, in 1766, by the portent of Boulton's Birmingham button. '. . . Instead of employing the same hand to finish a button or any other thing, they subdivide it into as many different hands as possible . . . Thus a button passes through fifty hands, and each hand perhaps passes a thousand in a day . . . By this means, the work becomes so simple that, five times in six, children of six or eight years old do it as well as men, and earn from ten pence to eight shillings a week.' The craftsman who cared for the quality of a product which he finished himself, which reflected his personal prowess, gave way to the child, brain detached from handiwork, limbs moving in alien regular rhythm.

Like other revolutions, this one had its ideologists, limping after reality. Scotland, unsurprisingly, fathered most of them. Adam Smith is regarded as founder of the 'science' of economics. Extending and partially humanising the insights of such bleak thinkers as William Petty, he systematised the subject magisterially. Many readers responded avidly to his defence of 'self-love'. 'It is not from the benevolence of the butcher, the brewer, or the baker that we expect our dinner, but from their regard to their own interest.' Each man was the best judge of his 'own interest'. He should be free to pursue it as he saw fit. If he did so, everyone would benefit. This assertion, detached from Smith's own refinements, cheered (as it still cheers) self-making businessmen. They did not so easily digest Smith's view that amongst the motives from which human behaviour sprung could be found not only self-love, a desire to be free, a habit of labour and a propensity to trade, but also sympathy and a sense of propriety.

Commerce, as Smith saw it, should be the 'bond of union and friendship' between men. Why then was Europe torn by wars? 'Mercantilism' was the culprit. Governments presumed to interfere with the naturally beneficent system, in the interests of their own power. Attempts to do down competitors with protective tariffs were iniquitous. If foreign goods were cheaper, they could be imported. Plenty should be the aim, not power.

Thrift and hard work, the middle-class virtues, were those on which plenty depended. 'The expense of a great lord feeds generally more idle than industrious people . . . Every prodigal appears to be a public enemy, and every frugal man a public benefactor.' Smith developed importantly the theory that labour was the source of all value. Work was 'natural' and therefore good. Labour and 'civilisation' were virtually the same thing.

His view of human nature made much sense in terms of Scotland itself, where thrift had become ingrained by relative poverty and hard work was transforming a barren country. The gospel of work, as Scots proclaimed it, gave bumptious personages a new test for establishing that they were more virtuous than those whom they wished to exploit. People who did not wear trousers, kilted Gaels included, were clearly lazy. People who were poor, British poor included, were evidently the victims of their own indolence. To bully them to work for one's own profit was therefore to do them a good turn.

Smith himself was a moralist, incapable of the crassness of many of his followers. He saw that great cities could be dehumanising and that 'mental mutilation' might result from excessive division of labour. But what he witnessed around him in Scotland gave his study an effervescence of optimism. Smith saw cheaper grain, cheaper potatoes, cheaper 'turnips, carrots, cabbages; things which were never formerly raised but by the spade, but which are now commonly raised by the plough.' Clothes were cheaper. Tools were cheaper. He was glad to see that real wages in Scotland were rising, and with them the expectations of the labouring classes.

His optimism delighted contemporaries who took from his work what it suited them to take and ignored his qualms, his warnings, his reservations. Not all his views were adopted. Not all his views matched the facts which others saw.

Thus he foolishly denounced 'great fleets and armies, who in time of peace produce nothing, and in time of war acquire nothing which can compensate the expense of maintaining them, even while the war lasts.' To decry the long series of conflicts with France was naïve, as most contemporaries realised. The only defence against mercantilist France was, as they correctly reckoned, attack. War favoured many industries greatly. While some British products were relieved of hot foreign competition in the home market, the iron industry progressed under the stimulus of military demand. Wilkinson's amazing career was advanced, as was that of a Manxman named Anthony Bacon who reaped great rewards from victualling troops in the West Indies and in Africa, founded an important ironworks in South Wales, and was one of the largest suppliers of munitions during the War of American Independence.

It was equally misguided for Smith to suggest that protective tariffs and bounties were deleterious. The Welsh tin–plate industry grew behind the shelter of Acts of 1703 and 1704 increasing duty on foreign plate. Paper-making was a similar story. The Scottish and Irish linen industries benefited greatly from public money. Most critically, the cotton industry was protected, after the relevant Act of 1721, against East Indian competition.

Above all, it was naïve of Smith to decry the economic value of slavery. It seems that if all the profits from the slave trade itself, without exception, had been invested in British industry, they would have made little more than one-seventieth of total national investment. If only an average proportion had been reinvested, this would have been no more than one-ninehundredth. But such calculations do little to weaken the argument that slavery was crucial to the take-off of British industrial capitalism. Factories, ironworks and steam engines were expensive to set up. The entrepreneur must find banks ready to lend him money till his firm's profits themselves floated him forward. Here the wealth of merchants trading with slave economies, was, beyond doubt, vitally important. The business of West India merchants with planters had always involved lending, holding and reinvestment of money. Many veered into full-time banking and such famous banks as Barclays and William Deacons began in this way. At one stage, the whole future of Boulton and Watt depended on the arrival of a West Indian fleet in which their London bankers were deeply committed.

Anthony Bacon developed his South Wales ironworks with a West Indian planter as partner. Bacon himself had been a slave trader. So had Samuel Touchet, of Manchester, who in 1747 personally bought over one-fifth of the total import of raw cotton into England, and who financed Lewis Paul's experimental spinning machine. When innovating men required quantities of capital large by the standards of their time, they looked for wealthy partners. In south-west Scotland, merchants trading with the New World were the obvious candidates. Around Glasgow, 'entire industries were dominated by the capital of tobacco lords and West India merchant princes.' Bristol merchants largely financed the Coalbrookdale ironworks, and slave traders from that port were active by the late 1730s in promoting the Welsh copper industry, to which the commerce in people was very important; there was demand on the Guinea Coast for wrought copper 'manillas', rods and copper wire.

Trade with other continents grew faster than trade with Europe. In 1700, Europe took over 75 per cent of British exports; in 1800 only 45 per cent. During the eighteenth century, while industries looking almost entirely to home markets increased production by some 50 per cent, those to which exports were important waxed five and a half times. Cloth was still the most important export industry, but by the end of the century cottons were clearly overtaking woollens, accounting already for a quarter of all textiles exported.

And the rise of cotton depended on the tropics. In the mid-1760s, more than a quarter of all ships owned in the port of Liverpool were 'Guineamen'. Black slaves were sometimes sold in the auction rooms of the Exchange, which was decorated with reliefs of blackamoors and elephants. Raw cotton was brought home by the slavers, along with other West Indian produce. As demand soared, in the 1780s, beyond the potential of the British and French islands, Brazil became essential to Manchester.

Cotton textiles were still increasing their popularity at home. But the British market alone could not have fuelled cotton textiles' exceptional growth. Their natural market was in warmer climes. Of British exports, in 1739, over three-quarters went to tropical and American markets, in 1769 a similar proportion (£165,412 out of £211,606). They competed with linens for the orders of New World planters, but the African coast came to provide their biggest vent. By 1769 nearly half the money earned by British cotton piece goods came from sales in Africa.

Birmingham manufacturers during wars supplied guns to the British army. But in peacetime, they were kept going by the demands of the North American fur trade, by the needs of the East India Company, and by the Guinea slave trade, to which the town supplied 100,000 to 150,000 flint muskets annually. The Midlands nail trade also leant heavily on colonial markets. The growth of both industries stimulated the revolutionary iron industry.

It was colonial trades, calling for large quantities of identical, cheap items, which directed manufacturers in Birmingham, Manchester and Glasgow to the transforming reorganisation of industry. It was foreign, above all colonial, trade which provided the chance of expanding production far beyond the growth of the home market. Without the Bight of Biafra, no Cottonopolis. Without war for trade, no breakthrough in ironmaking, no Watt steam engine. Without Plassey, smaller markets in India.

Had Bengal not come into British hands. when it did, France might have achieved superiority in India during the American War, when her rival was momentarily weakened everywhere. But Britain's industrial revolution by then was beginning anyway. Granted that the tropics had made this possible, why was it Britain which had achieved such pre-eminence in the tropics? Why, to ask the same question another way, did France not have a prior, or simultaneous revolution in industry?

In 1789, France's total industrial production was greater than Britain's, French foreign trade was as large, and had been growing faster. French production of pig iron was greater. France had had its own cotton industry since the sixteenth century. Rouen, Manchester's French rival, had kept up with the latest technical developments in Britain, and had forged ahead in techniques of dyeing. Such factors as had helped Britain fight and win three great wars for trade earlier in the century must also explain why Britain could now enter a new industrial league of its own. A medium-sized island had great advantages. Transport of goods was intrinsically easier. No point in Britain was very far from the sea. Cook's home port of Whitby at one time had five shipyards, and, with upwards of 10,000 inhabitants, owned, in the mid-eighteenth century, over 200 ships. Its coastal coal trade reflected Britain's greatest luck, the natural abundance of this mineral. While France still mined and used very little, British production had tripled during the century down to the 1780s. Coal was available in the hinterland of all three great western ports.

Arising from geographical conditions, there were all-important cultural ones. French industry largely concerned itself with the production of luxuries, fine things for élite markets. The French class structure was more rigid, the middle class was less powerful, the agriculturalists were poorer. Compared with the United States, Britain was thoroughly 'European' in its emphatic social hierarchy and the arrogance of its aristocratic élite. Compared with France, Britain was almost 'American', a land of quite widely diffused wealth and quite flexible social relationships. In the absence of legal barriers between classes, Britain differed from other European countries. Most noblemen married outside the peerage. The younger son of a baron was plain 'Mr'. A vulgarian absentee planter like Beckford, an overweening 'nabob' like Barwell, might encounter sharp snobbish prejudice, but the very sensitivity of the English over matters of class reflected fluidity and uncertainty.

Bankers, for instance, were highly regarded men, socially indistinguishable from their customers. The British banking system was better than that of France. By 1784 there were a hundred and twenty banks in England outside London. 'Country banks' mobilised the wealth of landowners for possible use in industrial development. The landowning classes themselves threw up men who adventured in industry, while manufacturers such as Arkwright ended their lives as 'improving' landlords. Set beside hard-working Virginian planters, British landowners might seem idle and wasteful. Contrasted with their European counterparts, they were besottedly practical commercialists. The English gentleman's passion for foxhunting and horse racing gave the island pre-eminence in the breeding of showy bloodstock. But this hobby related to, even encouraged, a craze for 'improving' strains of useful livestock. 'Improvement' was the fashion. George III led it, establishing model farms on the royal estate at Windsor and writing for agricultural journals under the pseudonym of 'Mr Robinson'.

As cities grew, their call for food brought opportunity. A new profile of English country life had emerged; a relatively small number of landlords, a middling number of tenant farmers, and a mass of labourers working for money. The tenant farmer was the beneficiary of enclosures of common lands, which were the great mainsprings of 'improvement'. In Tudor days, enclosures had been for pasture. Now the aim was commercial production of cereals, profiting from rising prices as the growth of population accelerated and manufacturing industry increased its sway.

Enclosure enabled landlords to raise rents. After 1760, the new device of the private Enclosure Act meant that it was no longer necessary for a great landlord to secure the agreement of small landowners in the area. He could now force them to comply, and the whole weight of sovereign king-in-parliament was behind him. Perhaps half of England had been enclosed already, while over large areas of the south-west, west, north and south-east open fields had either never existed or had been outmoded for centuries; but change in the Midland heartland of English agriculture was drastic. Before 1760, there had been only 130 parliamentary enclosure awards. In the next fifty-five years over 1,800 more went through, concerning 7 million acres.

Thanks to expanding acreage and 'improving' agriculture, Britain could industrialise swiftly without needing to import much food. Corn output nearly doubled between 1700 and 1820. Technical change did not yet produce rural depopulation. Numbers employed on the land continued to rise. But it was no longer the case that everyone born in the countryside had automatic access to the land. As more and more children were born, young people had to look for work elsewhere. In this way, change in agriculture provided one necessary condition for industrial revolution – a mobile labour force willing to gravitate to the new centres of innovating industry.

Population of England and Wales seems to have risen from about 6½ million in 1750 to 9 million at the end of the century. Over the same period, Scotland's increased from about 1¼ million to 1,608,000. There is no reason to suppose that this sharp rise had much to do with increasing prosperity. Growth was swift in the most backward regions – the Highlands, rural Wales, Ireland. There were comparable increases elsewhere in Europe – the Continent's population rose from 120 to 210 million in the century after 1750. The upsurge was world-wide. Chinese population also increased enormously. It may be that for reasons not yet known epidemic and pandemic diseases abated in virulence during the eighteenth century. A shift in weather, altering climates, is another possible factor.

Population explosion occurred at just the right time for British industry. In Britain guild regulations and other medieval restrictions on the mobility of labour were moribund. New workers could move wherever pay was available. In other European countries, rulers interfered, on 'mercantilist' grounds, with economic organisation. The British State let revolution in industry happen, hardly intervening at all. Such State action as there was tended to favour take-off. Protective tariffs aided industry. The tax system helped rich individuals grow richer, transferring money to them from the poor. The money needed to fight war after war was chiefly raised by indirect taxes on commodities used by everyone – alcoholic drinks, bricks, salt, glass, tea and sugar and tobacco. It was handed over to holders of government bonds, to contractors, to shipbuilders and to ironmasters. The profits and capital of business were virtually untaxed.

The innovations in transport which opened up Britain's little local markets and fused them in a single great one were eased by landowners through an assembly of landowners. From the first decade of the eighteenth century, private Turnpike Acts gave powers to self-appointed boards of local trustees to borrow money with which to improve and keep up certain stretches of road, and then to recoup by levying tolls on passing vehicles and animals. Two thousand road Acts passed through Parliament in the eighteenth century, three-quarters of these in the last fifty years.

Canals were the most captivating harbingers of revolution. In 1757, the first industrial canal was fashioned, joining the river Mersey with St Helens to bring Cheshire salt to Lancashire coal. By 1790, London was linked by inland waterway with Hull and Liverpool, Bristol and Birmingham. Sleepy villages became thriving landports. Josiah Wedgwood's fine pottery slipped safely down still waters to its markets. Coal moved in bulk from mine to distant town.

Rural England was studded with wonders. To Arthur Young, the view of the Bridgewater Canal crossing the river Irwell at Barton Aqueduct seemed 'somewhat like enchantment'. Over one river, another river 'hung in the air, with barges sailing upon it'. The Romans long ago had built mighty aqueducts, but never anything like the great iron bridges, the first of which, in 1779, crossed the Severn at Coalbrookdale with a span of 100 feet. Yet even as new awareness of man's inventive potential grasped delighted imaginations, the maiming and twisting effects of this revolution were plain.

Common lands were enclosed which had given grazing, firewood, berries, nuts and play room to the meanest, and many villagers were forced into greater dependence on the poor law, with its dismal workhouses. Isolated new farmhouses rose, where portly wives of port-drinking tenants pestered their consorts to buy pianofortes, and to despatch the girls to boarding schools so that they might be worthy of more genteel husbands. The old villages grew more squalid. Some became towns within a generation. Oldham in Lancashire, in the 1750s, was a 'handful of scattered hamlets set in unimproved moorland'. By 1800 it was one of the largest towns in England.

St Helens already portended urban horrors to come, with its glass works and copper works fouling every stream and blighting every plant and tree. Water power was intrinsically clean. But as the use of steam spread, so did soot and filth. The moral environment created by the industrialists was alien and shocking. Under the old conditions of domestic industry, the worker had had some control over his own rate of labour. He could take a free day for sport or sleep. The rites of 'St Monday' were religiously followed. The new-style entrepreneur would have none of that. He had lavished money on building and plant. Every machine was geared to the regular beat of the engine. The owner himself was enserfed psychologically by the genie he had released to work for him. The problem of disciplining men unused to regularity obsessed him. The public clock in the medieval town had given Western man his sense of 'time'. Now the clock set up prominently in the factory made Time tyrannise the natural rhythms of dawn, noon and sundown.

The entrepreneur built houses for his imported workers. He also erected churches, where parsons or ministers preached the virtues of obedience, regular habits, sobriety. Evangelical Christianity found a new role. Having wakened men, it was used to put them to sleep. 'I have left most of my works in Lancashire under the management of Methodists,' the first Robert Peel wrote in 1787, 'and they serve me exceedingly well.' With its rows of mean identical houses, with its shops where workers exchanged credit slips given them by their employer for goods which he sold them himself, with its blackening monitory chapel, 'The industrial unit,' T. S. Ashton observes, 'was often not a single establishment but something approaching a colonial settlement.'

Adults, in this generation, reacted much like slaves new fetched from Africa. So industrialists preferred child labour, which could be trained to factory ways, from infancy. At Arkwright's three mills in Derbyshire in 1789, about two-thirds of the 1,150 workers were children. Children commonly laboured at this time up to fifteen hours a day, six days a week. If not children, women at least were more malleable than men. ('Wholesale' it was. 'TO LETT', an advertisement called in a Manchester newspaper, 1784, 'THE LABOUR OF 260 CHILDREN. With Rooms and every Convenience for carrying on the Cotton Business.')

The factory owner usurped the place of the father, reminding his children meanwhile of a still greater Father in Heaven whose practice, concerning rewards and punishments, was far more drastic than mere fines for drunkenness, sloth and gambling, bonuses for subservient behaviour. The surest defence of his rule, in these early days, was the wages he managed to pay. Mechanisation gave the chance of higher wages with lower prices. The new industry not only paid its workers more money but also drove up the wages of agricultural labour in the vicinity. However, it brought periods of high cyclical unemployment. Cash was then an overweening tyrant. Things which people had grown, reared or made for themselves in the older life-style now had to be paid, paid, paid for.

The manufacturer might be genuinely kind and well meaning, in so far as his business would let him. Or he might, mouthing slogans from Adam Smith, excuse hard behaviour by saying that what suited his interest must, however obscurely, be for the good of the victims of *laissez faire*. These new masters came from diverse backgrounds. Some were aristocrats, like Lord Dundonald in Fife, who gladly freed his collier serfs, but forced on one of his chemical workers a contract for twenty-five years. Some were former helots themselves, like David Dale, a herd boy, then weaver, then small pedlar, who began to import cotton yarn and started in 1786 the famous model paternalist mill at New Lanark. Most, however, came from the middling ranks, sons of landowners, sons of merchants or traders. The antinomian arrogation of nabobs had its counterpart in the amazing John Wilkinson, accused of smuggling arms to the enemy during the American war, who came to be mine-owner and coal merchant as well as smelter and founder, and who paid his workmen in his own personal coinage, where his own head stood in place of the king's, with one of his own tilt forges featured on the reverse. Richard Arkwright, a less engaging upstart, rode into Derby in 1787 in a style which would have impressed Calcutta, with a tail of gentlemen, thirty javelin men in rich liveries, and trumpeters dressed in scarlet and gold.

Yet a very large proportion of manufacturers were sober-sided persons. Nonconformist Protestantism came into its own. Ironmasters were commonly Quakers, cotton spinners commonly Unitarians. Dissenters were blocked from civil and military office. They ganged closely, and lent each other money readily. Denied upper-class status, they spurned upper-class prodigality. Clustering in business, they saved, invested, and helped each other forward, the Panzer division of the middle class.

Aggressive middle-class consciousness emerged. Adam Smith, as a Scot of his time and station, had respect for aristocracy, but even his writings took on a somewhat Paineite flavour as, drawing his distinction between productive and unproductive labour, he coolly listed churchmen and members of the armed forces together with 'menial servants' and 'buffoons', and added the King himself for good measure. The 'princely Boulton', as Watt called him, was ready to express contempt for the landed gentry. Middle-class consciousness was commonly just as bitter against the labouring classes. As early as 1755, we find a spokesman for the Manchester employers attributing to the character of the poor the existence of poverty in this thriving town. 'The Poor refuse or neglect to help themselves, and thereby disable their Betters from effectually helping them . . . They are so familiarised to Filth and Rags, as renders them in a manner, natural . . .' Only low wages and harsh poor laws could goad such undermen to work hard. If they got too much money, they would labour only four days a week, then flock to alehouses and cockfights. A magistrate near Bolton, Lancashire, noticed with horror in the summer of 1783 that 'there was so little appearance of want . . . that one evening I met a very large procession of young men and women with fiddles, garlands and other ostentation of rural finery, dancing morris dances in the highway merely to celebrate an idle anniversary, or, what they had been pleased to call for a year or two, a fair at a

paltry thatched alehouse upon the neighbouring common.' Finery . . . dancing
. . . fair . . . alehouse . . . common – all the preferred resorts and amusements of
the poor could be summed up and dismissed with that one word 'idle'.

Nostalgia for a past of fresher air, idealised in receding retrospect, would
persist among industrial workers for generations, and would be a main force
propelling immigrants to other continents, where a man might stand tall and
free on his own land.

IX

The balance of regions within Britain was shifting. The growth of Birmingham
and Manchester would create what were almost rival capitals, dominated by the
middle classes, where men in plain dress with broad provincial accents would
sneer at the fopperies of London high society. The industrial revolution reached
Scotland and Wales as quickly as it happened in England. Lairds and Welsh
squirelings had been different sorts of men from the dominant English landed
gentry. But industrialists behaved much the same anywhere.

Rosalind Mitchison observes that 'Scotland packed into about thirty years of
crowded development between 1750 and 1780 the economic growth that in
England had spread itself over two centuries.' It could not have done so without
direct help from English experts, or without the opportunities which the
Empire had given to Scots themselves. Men came back from the East and West
Indies laden with money, and set about running their estates so as to make more.
Those lairds who had never left had to keep up with the nabobs. In the 1760s
and 1770s 'improvement' began to sweep forward with Cossack velocity. By the
end of the century, tenant farmers in south-east Scotland who had imitated
English methods were teaching the English new tricks in their turn, and
'Lothian husbandry' was becoming the cynosure of progressive eyes everywhere
in Europe. Innovation in industry was likewise seeded from England. Two
Englishmen, John Roebuck and his partner, established the first Scottish
chemical works, at Prestonpans in 1749, and the first great ironworks, Carron,
ten years later. New ideas of colliery engineering and management came in from
the south, and English workmen were brought north as supervisors. The new
cotton technology rushed in when Lancashire yarn manufacturers found that
they had a surplus and disposed of it to the west of Scotland linen industry,
which had run into hard times and underemployment. South-west Scotland had
plenty of water power and wages were low. Lancashire spinners saw they could
profit from both. As Glasgow and Paisley became great cotton towns, local men
learnt fast. By the 1790s they were introducing their own innovations.

Scotland was well prepared to seize its hour of national glory. The labour
force was adaptable and inventive. The system of poor relief through the
churches was far more flexible than the English poor law, and made labour even
more mobile than in England. Besides this, traditions of thrift had produced an
exceptionally strong banking system, the assets of which, it is estimated,

increased six times between 1750 and 1770, largely thanks to the proceeds of empire overseas.

Linen output had risen thrice in volume and four times in value between 1736 and the slump in 1772. Textile working, therefore, was well known. While linen continued to grow, more than doubling its output in the next fifty years, cotton now outstripped it. Imports of raw cotton wool into the Clyde rose in value from £150,000 per year in the early 1770s to £2,000,000 by 1789, then to £7,500,000 in 1801. Textile production spread up remote braes and Highland glens. Cotton chiefly accounted for an increase of 270 per cent in shipments of British manufactures from Scottish ports between 1770 and the end of the century.

Every middle-class group in Scotland, even authors, benefited from their bonanza. (William Robertson received £4,500 for his second work of history.) There was little or no tension here between 'aristocrats' and middle classes. Landowners, professional people, merchants, manufacturers shared a common enthusiasm and rose alike in wealth. Scottish artisans, Watt in the lead, had an education which helped them see and seize the opportunities of the new age. Everyone in the Lowlands seemed to be climbing socially at the same time, uniquely combining clannish deference with American appetite for adventure. The conquest by man of his own innate sin was somehow proved possible in this bare, windy country, where mind and hard work had triumphed over matter, and Covenanting arrogance was reborn as practical, hard-driving, censorious Scots took their new economic and technological gospels to the English and other unregenerate races.

Yet certain losses were irreparable, and would seem tragic. Glasgow would be transformed from a notably clean and stately town to a smoky sprawl with the worst housing conditions in Europe. Social apartheid would divide Edinburgh. The Georgian New Town now going up would survive as a dignified symbol and product of success, but the Old Town, where as late as 1773 a dowager duchess was still found living sandwiched 'between a fishmonger and a crowd of tailors and milliners', was beginning its decay into a dangerous slum. While Burns was publishing his poetry, the almost miraculous culture from which he sprang, of peasants with barefooted wives and children who lived in low two-roomed houses ('but and ben') yet shared with servants and cottars a passion for reading, was being seen off by the march of enclosure. That closeness of Scots well-to-do and poor to each other, which had made revolution possible, was fractured as industrialism advanced.

Wales could not make its own revolution. Towards the second half of the eighteenth century, Carmarthen, with some 5,000 people, was its largest town. Grass grew in the main streets of Swansea, the chief Welsh harbour. Coracles were still used on the River Taff at Cardiff. Bristol's September Fair was the pivot of economic life in South Wales. Wool from South Wales went to the clothiers of south-west England. The Drapers Company of Shrewsbury dominated and exploited from England the cottage woollen weavers of

Denbigh, Merioneth and Montgomery, as they had done in Tudor days, and profited from the ready market which cheap Welsh cloth found in the slave-owning colonies. The main support of Wales was the trade in cattle and sheep which were driven across the border in thousands every year for fattening in the Home Counties. Without the returning drovers, rural Wales would have had little currency and no news. The gentry, some of whom still employed harpers, mostly lived in dwellings which hardly exceeded the size of a good farmhouse. Yet there was very little pauperism. Meagre self-sufficiency prevailed. Labourers and small farmers teetered always on the edge of poverty, but strong family feeling and fellow feeling ensured that very few toppled over. Nucleated villages of the English type were rarely found outside the richest lowlands, and these were the only areas which were much affected by enclosures. Welshmen with a head for business went to England. Their own country still looked economically much as it had done in the reign of Elizabeth.

But then large parts of Wales were shaken suddenly from a quasi-feudal, near-tribal way of life to suffer under the dominance of alien entrepreneurs. Big monopolistically integrated concerns ruled where previously there had been few enough little ones. In these early stages, very few Welsh people profited much from their country's natural wealth.

The temptation of Wales to capital was its profusion of minerals. Merchants from London and Bristol laid the basis of iron and coal industries. Progress was slow till the American war. The demand which that brought set a new pace. It gave John Wilkinson his chance to make great the iron furnace at Bersham, in North Wales, which he had inherited from his Lancashire father, and which he married with the coal mines he owned. It spurred the development of the vast acreage which Anthony Bacon had acquired in South Wales. And then Cort's invention of the 'puddling' process made coal and iron a still more attractive combination.

From 1761, British warships were sheathed with copper bottoms to protect them in tropical waters. The discovery of copper in Anglesey shortly preceded the American war. Thomas Williams (a Welshman, for once) built furnaces, wire mills, rolling mills. He sold sheathing and nails to the navies of Europe, and cheap brass ornaments to the British slave traders. The Parys Mine Company minted its own coinage. The Anglesey mines faltered and died in the nineteenth century, but at their peak of breakneck exploitation, Parys Mountain had dominated the world market for copper.

In the 1780s cotton mills came to Flintshire, as they did to many country districts in Britain so long as water power was commonly used and steam engines were still rare. As Watt's invention and its successors ramped wider, proximity to coal would be decisive. This would be the misfortune of Ireland.

There was no human reason why Ireland should not have shared to the full in the integrating experience of simultaneous revolution shared by the three neighbour countries. It was less 'backward' than Wales. The Newry Canal and the Grand Canal had actually preceded the famous artificial navigations of England. The small coalfield in Leinster had had its first steam engine as early as 1740. After the Seven Years War, Ireland too saw the arrival of large-scale flour mills, breweries, grain mills, sugar refineries, glass factories. The climate was ideal for textile production. The cotton industry naturally spread from England, and very large mills sprang up – using water power.

So much water, so little coal, meant a tragic distance opening up between Ireland's experience and that of Britain. In the 1780s, Ireland and Devon between them produced less than one-fourhundredth of the coal mined in the British Isles. And large-scale emigration had started from Ireland to industrial Lancashire. By the early years of the next century, perhaps one person in ten in Manchester would be Irish.

X

After Rockingham's sudden death in July 1782 William Petty, Lord Shelburne, became Prime Minister. He too owned vast estates in Ireland, where he had been brought up. A haughty grandee, whose affected manners and obvious contempt for most other people made him extremely unpopular in Parliament, he nevertheless numbered among his friends many of the most brilliant plebeians of the day, Price, Priestley, and Benjamin Franklin among them.

Shelburne was a proponent of Smithite ideas, of 'burning all Tariffs and opening every Port Duty free . . .' He saw close connection between American and Irish problems, and hoped unavailingly that both countries might be sister states of Britain within an empire based on equality and reciprocal concession. In negotiations to end the war with America, his attitude was as conciliatory as possible.

After Yorktown, all notions of further offensive against the United States were abandoned. The great aim was to save the West Indies. Good luck permitted this. Rodney found himself the first admiral during the war able to fight a major French fleet with a superior British one. In the 'Battle of the Saints' in April 1782, his thirty-six ships overmatched de Grasse's thirty-three and a planned French attack on Jamaica was thwarted. Britain's position in the negotiations was thus less disastrously weak than it might have been.

Hostilities were suspended early in 1783. The terms of the proposed treaties evoked a hypocritical chorus of horror from the followers of Fox and North, now strange bedfellows in opposition, and Shelburne was forced to resign. But basically everyone wanted peace. Shelburne's deal went through. France handed back six of the West Indian islands captured during the war, but Britain returned St Lucia, the French forts in Senegal and Gorée, and the French factories in India. Spain did well. The Floridas and Minorca were confirmed in Spanish possession, but Britain kept Gibraltar, and Spain guaranteed the British right to cut logwood in Honduras Bay.

The terms agreed with the United States were perhaps, thanks to Shelburne, unnecessarily generous. American fishermen were given great privileges in imperial waters. A geographically meaningless northern boundary for the USA was drawn through the drainage basin of the Great Lakes. The western limit of the new nation was set at the Mississippi. Beyond that, the Spanish claim still held. Shelburne aimed at free trade with the US, giving their subjects a right to participate equally in the trade of the Empire. This would have been greatly to the benefit of the British West Indies. But mercantilism still ruled most thinking in Britain. The Commons defeated Shelburne's proposal. It was hoped that those northern parts of America which Britain still held would replace the States as suppliers of fish, lumber and flour to the West Indies.

Shelburne was replaced by a coalition between Fox and North. This was deeply obnoxious to George III, and he soon seized the chance to bring this ministry down which was afforded by its problems over India.

It was clear that something had to be done. The failure of the British government to secure the recall of Hastings, in the face of the support given him by the East India Company's shareholders, showed that in practice the Company was not under effective State restraint. Yet it owed the State, in 1780, more than £4 million. Two parliamentary Committees of Enquiry were set up in 1781, one 'select', on the administration of justice in India, one 'secret', on the causes of the war in the Carnatic. An immediate outcome was a Bengal Judicature Act (1781) which meant that the British Crown clearly assumed responsibility for creating a new judicial system in India. But the chief importance of the Committees lay in the expertise acquired through them by the chairmen, Edmund Burke and Henry Dundas respectively.

Dundas's interest was opportunistic. It was a way of advancing his career, and incidentally, as it would turn out, the careers of countless fellow Scots. He was a very able man who argued hard for the changes which his judgment told him were necessary. Burke, by contrast, developed sincere passion. His committee was briefed to consider 'how the British possessions in the East Indies may be held and governed with the greatest security and advantage to this country, and by what means the happiness of the native inhabitants may be best promoted.' Report after report passed censure on Hastings's administration. What Philip Francis now told him persuaded Burke that Hastings was 'the greatest delinquent that India ever saw'. Meanwhile Dundas presented the Commons with a string of resolutions condemning Hastings' foreign policy as one of aggrandisement damaging to British honour and interests. The Rockingham whigs had long defended the EIC on the grounds that private property was sacred. Now Burke, with a consensus of leading politicians, agreed that the Company must be thoroughly regulated. The younger Pitt spoke for others when he observed that if Britain hoped to draw commercial profit from India, she must prevent extortion there by her own subjects, and bring the inhabitants happiness and tranquillity.

In March 1783 the EIC once again had to petition for financial assistance.

Three Bills in succession now aimed to settle the problem. Dundas had decided that Lord Cornwallis, despite his surrender at Yorktown, was the man to restore propriety to British rule in India. The subcontinent had been plagued by grasping commoners. A nobleman must clear up the mess. But Dundas's Bill was blocked and the Fox–North ministry then had a try itself. Burke, now having a brief taste of office, was largely responsible for its proposals. Men such as Dundas and Pitt had broken with old whiggery in their readiness for a strong executive, but Fox and Burke shuddered at the idea of giving the Crown more power.

In November 1783, Fox introduced a Bill to remodel the EIC's constitution. The Court of Directors and the Court of Proprietors were to be swept away and replaced by seven commissioners. Young Pitt denounced this as 'one of the boldest, most unprecedented, most desperate and alarming attempts at the exercise of tyranny, that ever disgraced the annals of this or any other country.' Burke, defending the Bill, advanced his famous concept of trusteeship. The EIC's servants must be baulked from exploitation. '. . . Animated with all the avarice of age, and all the impetuosity of youth, they roll in one after another; wave after waves; and there is nothing before the eyes of the natives but an endless, hopeless, prospect of new flights of birds of prey and passage, with appetites continually renewing for a food that is continually wasting.' Rolling or flying, this Bill was not going to stop them. The King saw to that. It passed the Commons by a two-to-one majority, but was defeated in the Lords after George III had made it known that he would regard any peer who voted for it as 'not only not his friend, but his enemy.' Fox and North were dismissed. Pitt, only 24, became Prime Minister. Dundas was his most powerful colleague. The Indian issue had served them well.

Widespread indignation over Fox's apparent attempt to supplant King and Parliament in favour of an aristocratic oligarchy helped to ensure that over a hundred of his supporters were swept out in the general election that followed. Though no one could have guessed it at the time, Pitt would be Prime Minister for almost a generation. Behind and around his slender figure most of the wealthy rallied themselves. One might almost speak of a new, one must certainly speak of a restyled, ruling class. Except for his relatives the Grenvilles, Pitt lacked support among the great landed families who had dominated politics so long. Besides the backing of George III, he could look for support to reformers, now disillusioned with Fox, to merchants, shocked by the India Bill and affectionate to the memory of Pitt's father, and to such men as John Robinson and Charles Jenkinson, eager administrators, 'King's Friends'. Peerages and knighthoods were lavished on such persons, and on new rich upstarts, swamping the old whig aristocracy.

Pitt was tough, almost transparent, plastic. So young that he had no existence in politics predating the new élite which he fronted, he was the ideal chairman for an industrialising country which might have been torn apart by the contention of rival wealthy classes. This cool, calculating man, a disciple of

Adam Smith, was at home in the new world of steam. Personally incorruptible, he was a 'reformer', but one without warmth of passion, quick to bow principle to exigency. He was what the times made him – priggish, shifty and competent. His only obvious failing, not endearing, was the drunkenness in which bluff Dundas instructed him.

In this new consolidated ruling class – moderately reforming and avid for expanded trade at first, reactionary, but still expansionist, as the years lined boy Pitt's face – Scots were included, perfectly at home. Ironically, Dundas did possess almost the influence once falsely attributed to Bute. His arrival epitomised social change. He was middle class, from the legal profession. Even more than Pitt, he was indifferent to high-sounding ideas. He was the great 'manager', the great fixer. He fixed in turn for North, Shelburne and Pitt. His talents were obvious. His price was high. Pitt gladly paid it. Dundas went on from strength to strength. By 1790 he had firm control of thirty-two of the Scottish MPs. Even this did not satisfy him, and in 1796 he ensured that only one opponent sat among the Scots in the Commons.

He was a genial man who never tried to lose his Scottish accent. His blunt, sensible speeches sounded candid. He was good at telling funny stories to children and talked charmingly to old ladies. He found jobs for young Scots who were not connected with important families and otherwise went out of his way to help quite humble fellow countrymen. Unlike the icy Pitt, he was popular wherever he went.

India gave him the patronage which he needed to rule Scotland. It was characteristic of his cheerful disdain for principle that he should actually seize much of the power which Pitt had accused Fox of aiming at. This was through the India Act of 1784.

It established six commissioners in a body commonly known as the 'Board of Control', comprising the Chancellor of the Exchequer (Pitt), a Secretary of State for India (Dundas) and four Privy Councillors appointed by the King. This had power to send secret orders to India through the EIC directors. The Court of Proprietors was deprived of any right to annul or suspend what the Board of Control had approved. Government in India itself was given to a governor-general, Cornwallis, with a council of three. The lesser presidencies were now definitely subjected to Calcutta. The Board did not appoint or dismiss EIC servants in India. But Dundas made sure that any new directors were friends of his. Since no one whom he did not support could get elected director, he could send Scot upon Scot rolling or flying into India. However, the boys were well educated, and Dundas did not knowingly give jobs to incompetents.

General Oglethorpe, born at the time of the Darien débâcle, died in 1785 soon after he had called to congratulate John Adams, the first US Ambassador to London. During his long lifetime he had seen other extraordinary changes besides American independence and the thriving union between Scotland and England. In his childhood, few people had taken tea. Now labourers drank it.

The sugar and tobacco colonies westwards had been Britain's overseas empire, which he had founded a colony to defend. Now the East Indies dominated the minds of statesmen, Georgia was part of a new and separate empire, and the West Indies, though still greatly valued, were starting to matter less than the coalfields of Wales.

The planter class of Jamaica was more dependent than ever on Britain, and knew it. It now faced a long and bitter defensive battle against the advancing anti-slavers. The island could have done without fresh slaves. It could have been self-sufficient in food. But its whites refused to adjust themselves to a new age. Though even Wales was covered with improving Agricultural Societies, Jamaican planters remained indifferent to experiment. The British government, alarmed by the problem of feeding the West Indies, sent warships to the Pacific to collect plants. Hence the famous story of Captain Bligh, sent to bring breadfruit from Tahiti, whose crew mutinied and founded, with Polynesian concubines, a macabre society on little Pitcairn Island. Bligh eventually reached the West Indies with breadfruit in 1793, but the slaves refused to eat it and it was fed to pigs.

Jamaican white society had some reinforcement as rising 1,700 mainland loyalists, with more than 7,500 slaves, sought refuge after the evacuation of Savannah and Charles Town. In the Treaty of Versailles, the undertaking was given that Congress would recommend the individual states to consider reparation to loyalists. The failure after that to make good loyalist losses became a pretext for Britain to retain its frontier posts in the ceded portion of Quebec. Despite the treaty, tories returning to the United States were tarred and feathered, harassed and abused, until some US citizens gradually realised they and their money could be useful. Before long, active and even prominent loyalists, if they accepted republican citizenship, were tolerated well enough. Some served on state legislatures and in Congress. Some became Jeffersonian Democrats.

However, the vast majority did not go back. The British government gave over £3 million in compensation to its unlucky subjects. About half of the émigrés settled in parts of North America still British. Nova Scotia took perhaps 35,000, an influx outnumbering the previous population. They were given free land, arms, spades, and clothing and so on. The region offered little scope to professional men, and the clamour for jobs helped inspire the British government to divide the colony in 1784, creating New Brunswick and with it a second administration.

Some 6,000 to 10,000 loyalists went to 'Canada' proper. New York tories, mostly modest farmers, knowing of good lands beyond Montreal, settled along the St Lawrence and the Niagara rivers, chiefly to the west of the old French area, and gave what became known as 'Upper Canada' an English-American character distinct from that of French-speaking 'Lower Canada'.

The new political division between British and US empires was natural and yet artificial. For all France's military support for the States, French merchants lost heavily trading with America after the war. They were not willing (or able?) to give the long terms of credit to which the Americans were accustomed; they would not modify their products to suit American taste. Preferring to stick with their old suppliers, the Americans, by 1790, were importing as much from Britain as ever, and nine-twentieths of American exports still went there. British merchants soon resumed control of the Chesapeake tobacco crop. Since the leaf now mostly went directly to Europe, Glasgow lost its pre-eminent entrepôt status, but dozens of Scottish stores soon flourished again on the Piedmont. And British slavers found markets on the mainland; in thirty years after the war, despite laws against it, the US imported as many Africans as had come in during the previous one hundred and sixty.

For a while, Southern states continued to relax their codes and make manumission of slaves easier, but this trend was reversed as a new crop tied them almost as tightly to Britain as in colonial days. A young New Englander named Eli Whitney, staying on the Georgia estate of the widow of the revolutionary General Greene, heard that upland cotton would be a suitable crop if the laborious process of picking out the seeds could be circumvented. In a few months, by April 1793, he had perfected a machine so efficient that one black could grind out 50 lb. of fibre in a day. Manchester soon reaped the benefit.

With the British exporting freely to America but denying Americans access to the West Indies, self-interest might have brought the rebels back into the British political sphere. Instead, they agreed on a Federal Constitution in 1787, opting for nationhood and for the creation of a strong state, aiming at domination of a continent. As Washington, the first President, put it, the new republic was 'an infant empire'.

Congress firmly decided, in 1788, against the British government's suggestion that the USA might care to buy convicts, as in colonial days. So Whitehall turned its mind to the Pacific and what Captain Cook had discovered there.

XI

The Hudson's Bay Company faced strong competition, by the early 1770s, from British fur traders, based on Montreal, who had backing from London commercial interests and had allied themselves with the French Canadian experts in the trade. Both parties to the struggle pushed exploration westwards, so that while Cook sailed the Pacific, others were moving towards it overland.

In 1773, an ex-sailor named Hearne, in HBC employ, guided by a Chipewyan Indian, struck the Coppermine River and followed it to its mouth in the Northern Sea. Next year, he founded a new post in the interior, Cumberland House, at a point which gave his company the key to a whole system of waterways. But the Montreal 'pedlars' fought back, and by 1779 had coalesced into a formal 'North West Company', which with annual trade worth £100,000 a year, compared with the HBC's £30,000, was able to dictate prices on the London market. The small Montreal concerns who had stayed outside it were digested in 1787, and under the leadership of a Scot named Simon McTavish, its brave and brilliant explorers continued to rout the Hudson's Bay men. Through it, the sons of Scottish lairds and ministers found, as Samuel Vetch had once prophesied, scope for success in the prairies.

Hearne's discovery rated, for a while, as the largest new contribution to geographical understanding. He had shown, at last, that there simply could not be a North West Passage out of Hudson's Bay. The spread of tea drinking had revived interest in the Passage – tea was a bulky commodity which reached Britain on the longest of all trade routes. Hearne's findings left just one chance Alaska might be an island, and it was thought that there might be an open sea Passage south of it, then round the north of Canada – there was a theory that sea water did not freeze.

So Cook was sent out by the government on a third voyage. He was to reach Francis Drake's 'New Albion', then coast north. If he failed to find a North West Passage, he might look for a North Eastern one around Siberia. He left in July 1776, before word of the US Declaration of Independence had reached London, and before it could be fully appreciated that one effect of discoveries made by him might be to establish British claims to North America's west coast in opposition to those of a new American empire.

On his way, he discovered Hawaii and the Sandwich Islands. Reaching the North American mainland in March 1778 he visited Nootka Sound and traded with the Indians there. Sailing along the barren rugged shores of Alaska, behind which great white peaks towered inland, Cook established that the Bering Strait was the only approach on this side to the Northern Sea. At last in $70\frac{1}{2}°$ N he ran into an impenetrable wall of ice, and turned back. In the Aleutians he found Russian traders bullying a peaceful native people and exchanging tobacco, now a local addiction, for the very valuable skins of the sea otter. Then he returned for another look at Hawaii.

The Hawaiians, at first, were very willing to feed the strangers. But they chafed as this costly visitation protracted itself. As Cook tried to leave, the *Resolution* was damaged in a gale. When it came back with its companion, the pilfering which Cook had encountered widely in the Pacific started up here as well. Cook's temper had worsened with age. When Hawaiians stole a cutter from the *Discovery*, he reacted with fatal fury.

He went ashore to take a hostage towards regaining the boat, loading his own double-barrelled shotgun and telling the nine marines who escorted him to put ball in their muskets. Nemesis came very quickly. A huge crowd pressed him back down the beach. When a native rushed at him Cook fired. In the sudden affray, seventeen Hawaiians were killed, four of Cook's marines, and the captain himself, struck down with a club from behind as he waved for more men to come ashore. Captain John Gore eventually brought the two ships home in October 1780.

The death of Cook was a blow to the myth of Pacific paradise, as were the pictures of human sacrifice witnessed on Tahiti which this expedition brought back. But his voyages had helped ensure that Polynesian societies would grow less rather than more happy. Cook's third visit to Tahiti was followed by an epidemic. The island's population, perhaps 40,000 before its discovery, was halved by the end of the century.

Europeans could not be blamed in respect of germs whose existence they did not yet recognise. But the traders who swarmed in Cook's wake, seeking sandalwood, sea-otter skins and the dried sea-slugs and birds' nests which the Chinese loved to eat, brought with them the casual rapacity for their class and age, and the whalers who came again and again did not scruple to pay for supplies with cheap firearms and crude spirits. To complete the rape of Paradise, missionaries appeared; there were British ones on Tahiti by 1797, telling the people about original sin.

After Cook, it seemed that the British would go everywhere. Even in defeat the British government had conducted the War of American Independence with a strategic boldness such as the elder Pitt had never matched. In 1781 it had sent an expedition to conquer the Cape of Good Hope, an essential staging post on the way to the East – Cook had compared it to 'one great Inn fited up for the reception of all comers and goers.' St Helena was no longer adequate to the East India Company's requirements. Declaration of war on Holland gave Britain a chance to strike at the Dutch empire. A French expedition got to the Cape first, but from now on its conquest would be a prime British consideration. In the same year, the British had tried, but failed, to establish a base in Celebes from which to seize control of the East Indies. And the Cabinet had previously approved an idea, not, however, put into execution, for an invasion of South America from India.

The products of revolutionary industry, pouring out faster and faster, must be sold. The younger Pitt and his colleagues, like the classes whose support they mobilised, believed that markets must be captured, and could be captured, all over the globe. Despite the loss of the North American colonies, Britain was stronger than ever before. Not far behind brave explorers and honest if foolish missionaries, Manchester cotton would follow Birmingham guns.

Bibliographical Note

The bibliography of the first edition of *Revolutionary Empire* included hundreds of titles. Since 1981 these have been supplemented, and in some cases may be held to have been superseded, by many more titles. Nothing dates so fast, oddly enough, as most synoptic works of historiography. Several of the more recent histories of Scotland available to me in the 1960s when I first took an interest in the subject now seem unbelievably thin and obtuse after the spate of studies preceded and often inspired by T.C. Smout's path-breaking *History of the Scottish People 1560–1830* (1969). But fine, original, imaginative work like Smout's does not, I think, date, as I concluded when I finally got round to looking at P. Hume Brown's splendidly detailed *History of Scotland* (1898–1909). As with other good writing one uses bifocals, as it were, on Hume Brown, to filter out unusable old ideology while commanding the vision provided by strong argument and well-constructed narrative.

In the 1970s, working on this book, I found that to grasp, in chronological sequence, 'what happened' I often had to go to the spacious narratives of writers before 1939. Post-war historiography was strangely averse to narrative. For instance, I was influenced, like so many others, by the mighty labours of Christopher Hill on the English Revolutions and their origins, but frequently baffled by his apparent assumption that his readers knew the story already. I owed more than I cared to admit to such old-fashioned chaps, weighted though they were with inane old assumptions or offensive imperialist ideas, as the authors of the first volume of the *Cambridge History of the British Empire* (1929), Richard Bagwell's *Ireland Under the Tudors* (1885–1890), J.A. Williamson's *Age of Drake* (second edition, 1946) and Basil Williams's *Life of William Pitt, Earl of Chatham* (1913). The historiography of British India offered choices between the hard old imperialism of H.H. Dodwell (*Dupleix and Clive*, 1920) and the unconvincing post-1947 liberalism of 'Philip Woodruff' (Philip Mason, *The Men Who Ruled India*, vol. 1, 1953). It was a relief to turn to such antiquarian works as H.E. Busteed's *Echoes from Old Calcutta* (1908) and H.D. Love's *Vestiges of Old Madras* (1913). (Fortunately P.J. Marshall published in 1976 *East India Fortunes: The British in Bengal in the Eighteenth Century*, a fountain-head of nitty-gritty.)

Most of the best writing I came across was in printed primary sources, from Hakluyt's wondrous Elizabethan collection of 'Voyages' to the brilliant Calcutta diaries of William Hickey. But I read some splendid works of what must be termed 'academic historiography', books which embody profound and fundamental research, inordinate erudition, strenuous and triumphant imagination, mastery of prose, and sometimes all four together. I would like here to draw others' attention to certain 'history books' which changed the way I understood the modern world.

For the title of the book and its general perspective, I am indebted to R.R. Palmer's *The Age of the Democratic Revolution 1760–1800* (1959–1964) and E.J. Hobsbawm's *Industry and Empire: An Economic History of Britain Since 1750* (1968). Vincent T. Harlow's monumental *The Founding of the Second British Empire 1763–1793* (1952–1964) might be seen as the last and greatest product of British 'imperialist' historiography. Still thinking of the later chapters of my book, J.C. Beaglehole's *Life of Captain James Cook* (1974) is surely an enduring masterpiece. Eric Williams's *Capitalism and Slavery* (1944) will endure for different reasons. Borrowing ideas from L.J. Ragatz, *The Fall of the Planter Class in the British Caribbean 1763–1833* (1928), and C.L.R. James, *The Black Jacobins* (1938), and applying evidence with a broad and sometimes slapdash brush, Trinidad's future black Prime Minister enforced attention to the thesis, which now seems to me utterly incontrovertible, that the 'take-off' of 'industrial revolution' in Britain was fuelled by profits from slavery and slave-grown products.

Williams's book might be classed as an enduring polemic. But so, in its very different mode, is R.H. Tawney's *Religion and the Rise of Capitalism* (1926), informed by the ethical passion of a great egalitarian Socialist, like E.P. Thompson's so-widely-seminal *Making of the English Working Class* (1963), which influenced me deeply like many in my generation. Tawney's book takes us back to the period of 'European expansion'. Exploring this subject I encountered Joseph Needham's colossal series of volumes on *Science and Civilisation in China*, published with various collaborators from 1954 onwards. Also Fernand Braudel's *Capitalism and Material Life 1400–1800* (translated, 1973), a 'taster' for the great trilogy *Civilisation and Capitalism 15th-18th Century*, not translated until 1981–1984. I feel deeply indebted to J.H. Elliott's brief and brilliant *The Old World and the New 1492–1650* (1970), to the wonderful erudition of C.R. Boxer in *The Dutch Seaborne Empire 1600–1800* (1966) and *The Portuguese Seaborne Empire 1415–1825* (1969), and to J.H. Parry for his companion volume on *The Spanish Seaborne Empire* (1966) and his *Trade and Dominion: The European Empires in the Eighteenth Century* (1971). I think Samuel Eliot Morison's 'old salt' account of *The European Discovery of America: The Northern Voyages 500–1600* (1971) will always be a pleasure to read.

European contacts with non-European peoples had been extensively and incisively explored years before Edward Said's *Orientalism* (1979) began to make the subject intensely fashionable: see Philip Curtin, *The Image of Africa* (1964); Margaret T. Hodgen, *Early Anthropology in the Sixteenth and Seventeenth Centuries* (1964); Winthrop D. Jordan, *White Over Black* (1968) and V.G. Kiernan, *The Lords of Humankind* (1969). Also of fundamental importance in relation to 'race' and 'racism' are David Brion Davis's surveys of *The Problem of*

Slavery in European Culture (1966) and . . . *in the Age of Revolution 1770–1823* (1975), and D.B. Quinn's numerous studies of *The Elizabethans and the Irish* (the title of his book of 1966).

Looking at Britain's New World colonies I encountered that master historian, and superb writer, Richard Pares – *War and Trade in the West Indies 1739–1763* (1936); *A West India Fortune* (1950); *George III and the Politicians* (1953). And how can one express one's awe at the scholarship of Perry Miller, vivifying *The New England Mind: The Seventeenth Century (1939)*, a seminal book followed by further detailed analyses as in *Roger Williams* (1953). For detail I always enjoyed using Wesley Frank Craven's *The Southern Colonies in the Seventeenth Century* (1949), Richard S. Dunn's *Puritans and Yankees: The Winthrop Dynasty of New England 1630–1717* (1962) and the same writer's *Sugar and Slaves: The Rise of the Planter Class in the English West Indies 1624–1713*. Edmund S. Morgan's *American Slavery, American Freedom: The Ordeal of Colonial Virginia* (1975) is a powerful book. Bernard Bailyn's *The New England Merchants in the Seventeenth Century* (1955) is as masterly as his vividly realised *Ordeal of Thomas Hutchinson* (1975). And I have a special affection for Richard Hofstadter's beautifully written *America at 1750* (1972).

I realise that I have ungratefully failed to mention numerous books which I admired, enjoyed and was instructed by. Of making many books there is no end, but much study is not always a weariness of the flesh.

Index